Global Markets, Domestic Institutions

Global Markets, Domestic Institutions

Corporate Law and Governance in a New Era of Cross-Border Deals

Edited by
Curtis J. Milhaupt

COLUMBIA UNIVERSITY PRESS   NEW YORK

COLUMBIA UNIVERSITY PRESS
Publishers Since 1893
New York, Chichester, West Sussex
Copyright © 2003 Columbia University Press

Library of Congress Cataloging-in-Publication Data

Global markets, domestic institutions : corporate law and governance in a new era
    of cross-border deals / edited by Curtis J. Milhaupt.
        p. cm.
    Includes index.
    ISBN 0–231–12712–X (cl. : alk. paper)—ISBN 0–231–12713–8 (pa. : alk. paper)
    1. Corporate governance—Law and legislation.   2. Corporate law.   3. Corpo-
rate governance.   I. Milhaupt, Curtis J., 1962—

K1327.G583 2003
346'.0664—dc21   2003046058

Columbia University Press books
are printed on permanent and durable acid-free paper
Printed in the United States of America

♾

All the citations to information derived from the World Wide Web (URLs) were
accurate at the time of writing. Neither the volume editor, the contributors, nor
Columbia University Press is responsible for Web sites that have changed or expired
since the time of publication.

c 10 9 8 7 6 5 4 3 2 1
p 10 9 8 7 6 5 4 3 2 1

For Conrad
C.J.M.

Contents

Contributors

Brian R. Cheffins is the S. J. Berwin Professor of Corporate Law at the Faculty of Law, University of Cambridge. He has held visiting appointments at Duke, Harvard, Oxford and Stanford Universities. Professor Cheffins is author of *Company Law: Theory, Structure and Operation* (Oxford, 1997) and various articles on corporate law and corporate governance.

John C. Coffee, Jr. is the Adolf A. Berle Professor of Law at Columbia Law School. His principal interests are corporations, securities regulation, class actions, criminal law, and "white-collar" crime. Professor Coffee served as a Reporter for the American Law Institute's Principles of Corporate Governance, is the author of leading texts on corporate and securities laws, and has been a member of advisory committees or boards for numerous organizations, including the SEC, the New York Stock Exchange, and Nasdaq. He is a Fellow of the American Academy of Arts and Sciences.

Luca Enriques is Associate Professor of Business Law, University of Bologna. He joined the Faculty of Law in 1999, after working for the Bank of Italy in Rome. He has published two books and numerous articles on topics relating to corporate law, corporate governance, takeovers, institutional investors, and corporate groups.

Ronald J. Gilson is the Marc and Eva Stern Professor of Law and Business at Columbia Law School, and the Charles Meyers Professor of Law and

Business at Stanford Law School. Professor Gilson has written extensively in the areas of corporate governance, corporate acquisitions, and venture capital and private equity, including *The Law and Finance of Corporate Acquisitions* (Foundation Press, 1995, with B. Black). His articles have appeared in leading law journals as well as the *Journal of Financial Economics*.

Jeffrey N. Gordon is Alfred W. Bressler Professor of Law and Co-Director of the Center for Law and Economic Studies at Columbia Law School. He has written extensively about corporate governance, mergers and acquisitions, and the political economy of corporate law, especially problems arising from the adjustment costs of economic change.

Zohar Goshen is Professor of Law, the Hebrew University of Jerusalem. He has held visiting appointments at a number of U.S. law schools, including Yale and Columbia, and has served as a director of the Israeli Securities Authority (Israel's SEC). Professor Goshen writes in the areas of corporate and securities law.

Michel Goyer is Assistant Professor of Management, BirkBeck College, University of London. Formerly affiliated with the Center for European Studies at Harvard University, Professor Goyer's interests focus on the political economy of West European nations with a particular focus on corporate governance in France and Germany. He holds a doctorate in political science from MIT.

Joongi Kim is Professor of Law at the Graduate School of International Studies, Yonsei University in Seoul, Korea. His research interests focus on corporate governance, financial regulation, corruption, and international trade.

Kon-Sik Kim is Professor of Law and Director of the Center for Financial Law, Seoul National University. He teaches in the fields of corporate, securities and financial law, and has published several books, including a textbook on securities regulation.

Lawrence S. Liu is a partner in the law firm Lee and Li and a professor at National Taiwan University and Soochow University, in Taipei. He practices and writes in the areas of corporate, securities, and competition law. He is an adviser to many Taiwan government agencies and engages in legislative drafting and applied policy research in the areas of economic law reform and corporate governance.

Curtis J. Milhaupt is the Fuyo Professor of Japanese Law and Legal Institutions and Director of the Center for Japanese Legal Studies at Columbia Law School. He has written widely, most often in comparative perspective, on topics ranging from corporate governance and financial regulation to organized crime and the market for legal talent. Professor Milhaupt has been affiliated with a number of think tanks, governmental organizations, and universities in Asia, and was a member of an international advisory team on Korean unification.

Yoshiro Miwa is Professor of Economics at the University of Tokyo. Miwa has written widely on economic issues—most recently on corporate finance, corporate governance, and government regulation. Professor Miwa is currently collaborating with Mark Ramseyer on a series of books and articles exploring the ties between corporate governance and corporate finance in Japan.

Katharina Pistor is Associate Professor of Law, Columbia Law School. Her principal research interest is the comparative analysis of law and legal change, with special emphasis on corporate governance in transition economies and emerging markets. Professor Pistor has consulted with the World Bank, the EBRD, and the G-24 on the process of legal change in transition economies and emerging markets.

J. Mark Ramseyer is Mitsubishi Professor of Japanese Legal Studies at Harvard University. He has written widely on the intersection of law and economics in Japan—most recently in litigation, judicial structure, and corporate governance. Professor Ramseyer is currently collaborating with Yoshiro Miwa on a series of books and articles exploring the ties between corporate governance and corporate finance in Japan.

Edward B. Rock is the Saul A. Fox Distinguished Professor of Business Law and Co-Director of the Institute for Law and Economics at the University of Pennsylvania Law School. He has written widely on corporate law, corporate governance, and securities regulation. While a Fulbright Senior Scholar at the Law Faculty of the Hebrew University of Jerusalem, he became interested in the intersection of law and cross-border venture finance.

Mark J. Roe is the Berg Professor of Corporate Law at Harvard Law School, where he teaches corporate law and bankruptcy law. He is the author of *Strong Managers, Weak Owners* (Princeton, 1994) and *Political Determinants of Corporate Governance* (Oxford, 2003).

Lynn A. Stout is Professor of Law at the UCLA School of Law. She lectures widely and is the author of numerous articles on the stock market, finance theory, corporate governance, and the economic analysis of social norms. She has also taught at the Georgetown University Law Center (where she was Director of the Georgetown-Sloan Project on Business Institutions), Harvard Law School, NYU Law School, and the George Washington University National Law Center, and has been a Guest Scholar at the Brookings Institution in Washington, D.C.

Randall S. Thomas is Professor of Law and the Director of the Law and Business Program at Vanderbilt University Law School. His recent publications are concentrated in several areas at the intersection of law and finance, including theoretical and empirical studies of shareholder voting, executive compensation, and the theory of the firm. He has also applied economic analysis in numerous studies covering a broad variety of legal issues in the fields of corporations, securities law, bankruptcy, environmental law, and civil procedure.

Mark D. West is the Nippon Life Professor of Law and Director of the Center for Japanese Legal Studies at the University of Michigan. He has served as an Abe Fellow at the University of Tokyo and as a Fulbright Senior Research Scholar at Kyoto University. His research focuses on the interrelation of law and social and economic change in Japan.

Chenggang Xu is Lecturer in Economics at the London School of Economics. His research interests include economics of organization, economics of transition, contract theory, and the Chinese economy. He served as an advisor to the State Council of China on corporate governance and financial sector reform.

Preface

Today, corporate governance reform is at the top of the public policy agenda from Washington to Seoul. The urgency and scope of the international corporate governance debate is the product of many factors, including the difficult and still incomplete transition from socialist to capitalist institutions in Eastern Europe, the Asian financial crisis, the corporate and accounting scandals epitomized by the Enron debacle in the United States, persistent economic malaise in Japan, and the vast economic and political fallout from each of the foregoing phenomena. But perhaps above all, the corporate governance debate is given momentum by that myriad of inchoate forces known as "globalization," which pit the indigenous rules, practices, and norms of national economic systems against the corrosive impact of transnational markets for capital, products, information, and talent.

The importance and timeliness of this topic prompted the Center for International Political Economy (CIPE), a nonprofit organization devoted to research on emerging trends in the global economy, to commission a comparative corporate governance study by a group of the world's leading corporate law scholars. This volume is the culmination of that study.

The ideas presented in this volume were developed at two Columbia Law School forums. The first, an authors' workshop attended by a small group of experts in October 2001, provided an informal forum for the vetting of preliminary drafts. The second, a public conference held in April 2002, was attended by a large number of scholars, policymakers, and practitioners from many parts of the world. At this conference, an extraordinarily talented cast of corporate and finance scholars provided valuable commentary on each of the chapters, significantly improving the final product. I speak for all the authors in thanking William Allen, John Core, Merritt Fox, Henry Hansmann, Reinier Kraakman, Jonathan Macey, Peter Muelbert, Hugh Patrick, Roberta Romano, Andrei Schleifer, and David Weinstein for their contributions. Bernard Black and Michael Klausner contributed valuable insights at both the authors' workshop and the public conference.

Focusing the attention of some thirty distinguished scholars from around the world on a single (if broad) theme and bringing them together for several days of discussions—in many cases not once, but twice—is a complex and expensive undertaking. The two Columbia conferences, like the larger research project of which they were an integral part, were made possible through a substantial grant from the Center for International Political Economy. In my capacity as project director, I thank John D. Langlois, President and Executive Director of CIPE, for the generous financial support of his organization. As editor of this volume, I thank him for his intellectual contributions throughout this endeavor. I am also grateful to David Leebron, Dean of Columbia Law School, for his encouragement and financial support. Finally, thanks are due to Christopher Gulinello, an Associate-in-Law at Columbia Law School, who provided excellent assistance in preparing the manuscript for publication.

Curtis J. Milhaupt
July 2003

Global Markets, Domestic Institutions

Introduction

The Dynamic Tension in Corporate Governance

Curtis J. Milhaupt

A dynamic tension has emerged in the field of corporate governance. Markets for capital, products, and managerial talent are expanding rapidly across national borders, yet domestic laws and practices have never had greater impact on corporate structures and cross-border deals. This dynamic tension between global markets and domestic institutions fuels the debate on corporate governance reform now raging in virtually every region of the world.[1] It also frames the intellectual agenda of the distinguished contributors to this volume.

Indisputably, the pace and effects of globalization, particularly in the realm of corporate activity, have intensified dramatically at the turn of the century. Institutional investors seeking higher returns and greater diversification, firms outsourcing critical factors of production, entrepreneurs seeking capital, and managers restructuring troubled enterprises now routinely face counter-parties who do not operate within their own legal systems or political environments, and who do not necessarily share the same social priorities. Consider just a few examples and statistics. Daimler Benz merges with Chrysler, foreign firms bid for Daewoo Motors and Hynix, as Korean *chaebol* restructure under pressure from the government and the IMF, foreign investors acquire one of Japan's largest and most troubled banks. In 2000, the combined global market capitalization of the non-U.S. companies whose stocks were traded on the New York Stock Exchange would have constituted the second-largest stock market in the world, and non-U.S. companies accounted for about half of all new listings on that exchange (NYSE 2000: 3, 5). Foreign direct investment (FDI) has expanded rapidly around the world, fueled by a boom in cross-border merger and acquisition activity[2] and by the existence of more than 60,000 transnational companies with over 800,000 affiliates abroad (UNCTAD 2001: 1).[3] As one official study reports,

> [G]eographical patterns of FDI reflect efficiency considerations of [transnational corporations] in light of increasingly competitive pressures, coupled with technological advances that enable real-time links across long distances and the liberalization of trade and FDI policies. . . . Even such critical corporate functions as design, R&D and financial management are today becoming increasingly internationalized to optimize cost, efficiency and flexibility (ibid: 5).

Yet despite all this global corporate activity, the impact of *domestic* institutions on corporate governance and cross-border deals has never been more acutely felt or more widely discussed. The Asian financial crisis, among many other recent events, vividly demonstrated that local laws and corporate governance practices can have dramatic consequences for international capital flows, stock market performance, and the economic stability of entire regions of the world (see, e.g., Johnson et al. 2000). Not coincidentally, active scholarly debates in comparative corporate governance today are swirling around questions deeply rooted in the political, social, and particularly legal institutions of separate countries. One influential line of empirical research, which is explored and questioned in some of the essays in this volume, indicates that the origin of a given country's legal system and the quality of its corporate law affect patterns of share ownership and the size of its capital markets (La Porta et al. 1997; 1998). Perhaps most strikingly, this work finds that common law systems provide better investor protections than civil law regimes. Thus, according to this line of research, more robust capital markets and more dispersed ownership are found in countries adhering to the common law tradition.

While this legal approach to corporate governance is intuitively plausible—surely law "matters" to economic organizations—the precise relationship between corporate law and corporate governance remains highly controversial. Other research suggests, for example, that corporate governance practices are linked to a wide range of country-specific, *non*-legal institutions in ways that are still not completely understood. An apt example can be drawn from fiduciary duties, the very core of U.S. corporate law and the subject of many of the contributions to this volume. Despite the prominent role of fiduciary concepts in U.S. corporate law doctrine, the prospect of directorial liability for violation of these principles is actually very remote. This is due in part to the emergence, subsequent to the development of fiduciary doctrine, of legal technology such as indemnification and insurance, which is designed to allow firms to calibrate the level of liability to which their directors are exposed. As Rock (1997) and Stout (chapter 2 of this volume) suggest, fiduciary duties might therefore best be understood as authoritative instructions that managers "behave themselves," even where errant conduct is unlikely to be legally punished. Thus, for some scholars, the legal principle at the center of U.S. corporate law functions chiefly in service of social and behavioral constraints, bounds on managerial misconduct that may be highly contingent on historical and social context. Moreover, in recent decades corporate characteristics in different countries seem to have moved in tandem with the competitiveness of product markets, labor market patterns, the left-right character of government, and the degree to which the state retains control rights over firms through discretionary interventions in the economy (see, e.g., Roe, chapter 4 of this volume; Pagano and Volpin 2001; Milhaupt 1998).

In grappling with important questions arising out of the tension between global markets and domestic institutions, the contributors to this volume advance several debates at the heart of the current academic and policy debates in corporate governance: What *is* "good" corporate law and what are its limitations? Precisely *how* does the quality of corporate law affect corporate governance? Is a well-developed fiduciary "culture"—one of the most distinctive features of U.S. corporate law—a key to the relative success of U.S. corporate governance? If so, can the substantive content of fiduciary duties and the mechanisms for their enforcement be transplanted to improve corporate governance elsewhere? Is the quality of corporate law linked principally to statutory protections, or to the training and attitude of judges deciding corporate cases? Or does the quality of corporate law and governance vary according to something else entirely, such as general social norms, or self-regulation via stock exchanges or codes of conduct?

A second ongoing debate advanced here is the question whether different corporate governance systems are converging. Moving beyond the dichotomous views that have dominated the literature to date,[4] contributors to this volume pursue the question from a variety of fresh perspectives. What features of "high quality" governance systems merit widespread adoption, and what tools are available to policymakers seeking to adopt or avoid features of the U.S. model? Is there an important, but heretofore overlooked, "international relations" component to corporate governance convergence motivated by broad concerns for political and economic integration rather than commercial competition? This volume represents a step toward answering these and other important questions.

The book is divided into three parts: Part I provides novel perspectives on the role of fiduciary duties in corporate governance, and the "transplantability" of Anglo-American fiduciary duty law as a means of reforming corporate governance elsewhere. As noted above, fiduciary duties lie at the center of U.S. corporate law. They are one of the principal means of combating a serious agency problem in corporate governance—self-dealing by managers and controlling shareholders. Yet despite the centrality of fiduciary duties to the U.S. approach, they remain highly controversial as an organizing principle of corporate governance.[5]

Zohar Goshen (chapter 1) finds that corporate self-dealing is addressed around the world either through "property rules" (voting to approve a conflict-of-interest transaction by a majority of the minority shareholders) or "liability rules" (a fairness test applied ex post by courts). On the basis of an empirical analysis of several countries, Goshen argues that the choice between the two types of rules is a function of the total transaction costs in a particular legal system. Thus, any solution chosen to cope with the self-dealing problem must conform to local conditions. Goshen's conclusion contradicts the view, prevalent among convergence optimists, that there is a single solution to the agency problem—"one efficient corporate law"—suitable for every country. Rather, his perspective suggests that there are multiple mechanisms available to deal with the central corporate governance problem of interested party transactions.

Lynn Stout (chapter 2) suggests that fiduciary duty rules are best understood as open-ended standards of behavior that are difficult to enforce through external sanctions. As a result, fiduciary duty rules work best when they are "internalized" by corporate officers, directors, and controlling shareholders. She argues that while this sort of altruistic or "other-regarding" behavior is in fact common, it is also socially contingent—that is, largely determined by perceptions of others' needs, expectations, and behavior. This implies that there may be significant obstacles to a meaningful transplantation of U.S.-style fiduciary duties into the corporate laws of other countries, even if that constitutes good public policy. At the same time, however, Stout surveys evidence indicating that altruistic behavior can be encouraged by authority figures (such as judges), holding out the potential for fiduciary duties to play a larger role in corporate governance, at least in some countries. Stout's study suggests that corporate law's primary role could lie in facilitating a fiduciary culture.

Parallel to Stout's inquiry, Katharina Pistor and Chenggang Xu (chapter 3) ask whether courts or legislators should be the primary lawmakers and enforcers of fiduciary duty, an amorphous principle. Pistor and Xu apply incompleteness of law theory, a new approach drawn from incomplete contracting theory, to analyze the proper allocation of lawmaking and law enforcement rights. They apply this theory to emerging case law in transition economies, arguing for a "structural transplant" of residual lawmaking power to courts in the corporate setting. That is, emphasis should be placed on designing procedural rules to permit shareholders to bring, and courts to decide, corporate cases, rather than attempting to codify fiduciary duties in detail.

At this point in the debate, Mark Roe (chapter 4) contributes a straight-forward, but powerful insight: Even high-quality corporate law has its limits. As he notes, "corporate law does little, or nothing, to directly reduce shirking, mistakes, and bad business decisions that squander shareholder value." Institutions apart from corporate law make managers loyal to shareholders, and the nature of these institutions varies from country to country. While, as noted above, the recent empirical line of research finds that "high-quality" corporate law (i.e., law with robust protections for minority investors) is associated with dispersed share ownership, Roe points out that ownership may fail to separate from control *either* where risk of expropriation *or* managerial mistake is high. Since corporate law addresses only the former problem, concentrated ownership may persist even in countries with "perfect" corporate law. Moreover, there are sound theoretical reasons to believe that strong investor protections may actually work to entrench concentrated ownership under certain conditions. Thus, Roe concludes that the quality of corporate law cannot be the only explanation for the existence of concentrated firm ownership in some of the world's wealthy countries and dispersed ownership in others.

Part II examines the intersection of globalization and corporate governance reform in specific substantive areas and countries in Europe and Asia. While most of the essays in this part focus on specific countries, the questions pursued by the authors have more universal import. This part begins with several novel approaches to the question whether global market forces

are causing national systems of corporate governance to converge. Brian
Cheffins and Randall Thomas (chapter 5) examine the extent to which
executive pay in major industrial countries is converging toward U.S. practices, in which chief executive officers are highly paid and compensation is
linked to corporate performance. They assess factors that are likely to influence a shift in pay practices around the world, including cross-border investment by Anglo-American institutional shareholders, the emergence of a
global market for executive talent, disclosure regulation, accounting rules,
tax policy, and "cultural" values. While the authors demur on the question
whether the U.S. model is normatively superior to alternative pay practices,
they provide a road map for policymakers seeking to replicate or avoid that
model.

Michel Goyer (chapter 6) examines the different responses of German
and French conglomerates to the demands of Anglo-American investors. He
finds that while large German and French companies have changed their
corporate strategy in response to increased foreign institutional ownership
(which seeks to minimize the "conglomerate discount" stock markets impose on the shares of highly diversified firms), they have done so in different
ways and without any strategic process of convergence. French firms have
been aggressive in reducing diversification by selling off assets outside core
business lines. German firms have not gone as far in dismantling conglomerates, but they have done more than their French counterparts to enhance
financial transparency. Goyer argues that the institutional arrangements
affecting workplace organization—specifically the very different position of
employees in the production processes and overall firm strategies in the two
countries—explain why French and German firms have responded quite
differently to the demands of Anglo-American investors. Change might not
yield convergence.

Jeffrey Gordon (chapter 7) introduces a provocative new insight into the
convergence debate by turning attention toward what he terms the international relations perspective: the idea that the pace of convergence in corporate governance depends crucially on a country's commitment to international economic and political integration. To illustrate this insight, Gordon
argues that Germany has undergone a significant shift in public and political sentiment toward shareholder-oriented capitalism over the past decade,
a shift that was catalyzed in significant part by the German desire to promote integration of the European Community. A major exception to this
trend was Germany's pivotal role in scuttling the proposed 13th Company

Law Directive on Takeovers, which would have introduced a decidedly shareholder-oriented approach to takeovers in Europe. Yet even this episode can be seen as an attempt to ensure that European integration occurs on a "level playing field" in which German firms (and national interests) are not placed at a comparative disadvantage to those of its neighbors. Thus, Germany's movement toward and away from shareholder capitalism in the past decade needs to be understood as part of that country's larger international aspirations. Gordon's analysis suggests that public policymakers, not simply investors and managers, may have reasons to favor (or disfavor) certain forms of capitalism; their goals can at times override local frictions to bring about convergence, and at other times insert barriers to convergence that would otherwise have taken place. Some departures from the convergence path may even be strategic moves by the policymakers of one country designed to prompt other governments to dismantle barriers to greater integration.

In the final essay with a European focus, Luca Enriques (chapter 8) asks perhaps the most basic question of any in this volume: What makes corporate law "good" anyway? Enriques starts from the premise that the quality of corporate law is largely a function of *judicial* approaches to conflicting interest transactions, not of "law on the books." On the basis of an extensive survey of Italian case law, Enriques finds that the Milan court (widely regarded as Italy's best forum for the resolution of corporate law disputes) does not perform well, because its judges are overly deferential to insiders, too formalistic in their reasoning, and pay little attention to the incentive effects of their decisions. Like many other chapters in this volume, Enriques' contribution highlights the complexities inherent in corporate governance reform—complexities related directly, if unquantifiably, to the domestic moorings of universal statutory corporate law principles.

The essays in the latter half of part II focus geographically on Asia, analyzing important recent developments in Japan, South Korea, and Taiwan, while continuing the analytical inquiry into the impact of law on corporate governance. In all three jurisdictions, policymakers, courts, and corporate managers are struggling to adapt to the changed political economies of a region still coming to grips with life after high growth, the Asian financial crisis, and recurrent turmoil in the banking sector. Milhaupt and West (chapter 9) argue that Japanese firms are hindered by a one-size-fits-all approach to corporate governance practices, which they link to an institutional environment left over from the heyday of a main bank–oriented economic system. That same environment stifled takeovers with low-quality financial information and an approach to minority shareholder protection based on rigid corporate and securities rules. They argue that a recent trend toward increased M&A in Japan, partially the product of a more deal-friendly legal environment, is spawning a broader range of governance practices, managerial innovations, and structural shifts in the corporate lawmaking processes. Their empirical account of M&A in Japan challenges several prevailing theories in comparative corporate governance, including the role of functional substitutes and the equation of "high quality" corporate law exclusively with legal protections for minority shareholders.

Yoshiro Miwa and Mark Ramseyer (chapter 10) reach quite different conclusions about the situation in Japan. They assert that the protracted recession has little to do with deficiencies in Japanese corporate governance. Examining data from the regional banking industry—one of the worst performing sectors in the stagnant economy—Miwa and Ramseyer find nothing to suggest that governance structures explain the poor performance of the banks. They argue that, on the contrary, the proclivity of policymakers and academics to link corporate governance and economic performance has resulted in misguided corporate law reforms in Japan. In advancing this argument, Miwa and Ramseyer remind us that while the corporate governance reform debate is ubiquitous, researchers have yet to establish clear linkages between corporate governance practices and economic performance in many countries.

Korea presents an interesting contrast with Japan. In many ways, corporate and banking reform has proceeded more rapidly and extensively in Korea, due in part to IMF and World Bank pressure during the Asian financial crisis. Yet much remains to be done, and the path forward is complex. Kon-Sik Kim and Joongi Kim (chapter 11) analyze the successes achieved and obstacles encountered by the courts as policymakers have attempted to increase the relevance of corporate law—particularly fiduciary duty principles—in reshaping Korean corporate governance. A series of legal reforms has been enacted to untangle ties among the subsidiaries of the *chaebol* conglomerates, reduce excessive leverage, and eliminate opportunities for expropriation by controlling shareholders. Yet, in the absence of flexible legal standards and broad remedies applied actively by the courts, most of the new rules designed to import fiduciary principles into Korean corporate governance can be circumvented, and the depth and longevity of reform in Korea remain in question.

Lawrence Liu (chapter 12) uses the framework of "political ecology" to analyze the corporate finance and governance system in Taiwan. He explains how economic development policy and corporate law have been closely intertwined with Taiwan's uniquely precarious geopolitical situation. Despite tangible corporate and financial reform coinciding with greater democratization, Liu asserts that the existing legal and policy paradigms are inadequate to address the challenges brought on by globalization, which for Taiwan means principally integration with mainland Chinese markets and entry into the World Trade Organization. Liu leaves the impression that, as with Korea and perhaps Japan, recent legal reforms have yet to be completely internalized by all relevant actors, creating a gap between the formal law and actual practices.

Part III focuses on the crucial issue of capital formation in a world of global markets. Because the United States offers the deepest, most liquid, and arguably best regulated capital markets in the world (the last assertion being perhaps more controversial today than at any other time in recent history), "globalization" in this context typically signifies either the desire of non-U.S. firms to tap U.S. markets or the hope of foreign policymakers to replicate U.S. success in creating a vibrant market for entrepreneurial finance. John Coffee (chapter 13) examines the increased level of competition for corporate listings that is developing among securities markets. Coffee argues that this competition, which is fueled by cross-listing of shares on foreign markets, will not produce conformity, but rather specialization and a likely dual equilibrium under which "high" and "low" disclosure exchanges persist side by side, reflecting differences in the clientele served by these exchanges. That is, some exchanges will impose high disclosure and transparency standards and seek to protect minority shareholder rights. Firms that wish to credibly promise that they will protect shareholder-rights expectations will list on those exchanges. Under Coffee's "bonding hypothesis," these firms will disproportionately be those with high earnings prospects that require equity finance. In contrast, other firms will persist in listing on lower cost, relatively opaque exchanges that service firms with concentrated ownership, in which the controlling shareholders will continue to extract high private benefits of control. In Coffee's model, law matters, but the firm chooses its listing based on whether it is seeking to maximize shareholder value or the private benefits of control. Coffee's analysis, which proposes a limited form of "exitless" regulatory competition, challenges those securities-law scholars who favor a policy of "issuer choice"—namely, the ability of firms issuing securities on public markets to select the regulatory regime that will govern them. Strong markets require strong laws, he argues, and issuer choice undercuts that possibility.

Complementary to Coffee's analysis of international stock market competition motivated by cross listings, Edward Rock (chapter 14) explores the relationship between corporate identity and the raising of capital by start-up firms. Rock shows how little-noticed features of U.S. securities law provide a ready mechanism for firms to "pass" as American, even though their center of activity is off shore. He examines the phenomenon of Israeli firms passing as American corporations for purposes of raising capital on the NASDAQ, and contrasts the case of Taiwan, where a highly successful indigenous venture capital industry has traditionally relied much more extensively on domestic exit strategies centered on the Taiwan Stock Exchange. Since the availability of exit (often in the form of an initial public offering, or IPO) is crucial to the success of a venture capital market, an important implication of the Israeli experience is that cross-border barriers to IPO exits can be surmounted where domestic stock markets are weak, perhaps even with the help of U.S. securities law.

Building on the question of institutional supports for successful private equity markets raised in the preceding chapter, Ronald Gilson (chapter 15), provides guidance to policymakers seeking to emulate one of the key U.S. economic success stories over the past decade—a vibrant venture capital market. As Gilson points out, the government played little role in this success story; private ordering is the essence of the U.S. venture capital market. Yet because other countries have little hope of replicating the idiosyncratic U.S. environment for this type of private ordering, Gilson discerns a role for governments in engineering private equity markets. He identifies three central inputs necessary to the engineering process: capital, specialized financial intermediaries, and entrepreneurs. "The problem," as Gilson notes, "is that each of these inputs will emerge if the other two are present, but none will emerge in isolation of the others." To overcome this simultaneity problem, he recommends that governments in effect play the role of limited partners—providing capital to a highly incentivized financial intermediary, but avoiding direct participation in the capital allocation process.

As readers will no doubt have gathered by this point, there are far too many valuable insights contained in this volume to summarize comprehensively in an introduction, and the foregoing sketch is not intended as a substitute for the chapters themselves. I close, therefore, by highlighting two striking and related insights emerging from this study.

First, "globalization" and "global markets" are misleading terms, because they mask the local nature of much of the activity occurring within those rubrics.[6] Many of the contributions to this volume suggest the extraordinary complexity of meaningful corporate governance reform—complexities linked to the deep roots of corporate activity in domestic political economies. Virtually all firms, including the most internationally active, are still heavily influenced by the local institutions from which they emerged. Moreover, domestic institutions still serve as the principal interface between local firms and foreign investors. Thus, paradoxically, global markets have *enhanced* the importance of "getting the institutions right" on the domestic level.

As to the question what "getting the institutions right" means, academics are generally wary of providing explicit policy recommendations in a research project such as this, and for the most part, readers of this volume are left to draw their own conclusions about how corporate governance reform should best proceed in their own jurisdictions. Indeed, some readers might plausibly infer from this volume that corporate law as conventionally understood is not the foundational institution on which healthy economic performance is based, so reformers would do well to expand their focus. To the extent that corporate law is important, however, this volume sheds light on what really counts. Several chapters point to the crucial role of the judiciary in contributing to a healthy corporate governance environment.[7]

Commentators, in this volume and elsewhere, lament the lack of training, experience or interest in corporate finance and governance among judges in their home countries. This is simultaneously cause for alarm and a bit of optimism. Courts will never contribute meaningfully to good corporate governance if judges remain ignorant of such basics as the valuation of assets and enterprises, a concept central to the sound resolution of virtually every dispute between corporate insiders and minority shareholders. Yet a degree of optimism may be warranted, because quantifying (and maximizing) the value of the corporate enterprise is a concept that can transcend national and cultural boundaries. If judges can be taught to detect self-dealing and other forms of expropriation and to import universal notions of valuation into their decisions, one important corporate governance tool would be enhanced. The prospect of judicial improvements along these lines does not seem farfetched.

The second major insight emerging from this study relates to the uncertain nature of corporate law development. We have only fragmentary knowledge of the conditions under which a given country's corporate law, often borrowed piecemeal from other systems, comes to engage productively with other economic institutions.[8] Alan Watson is justifiably famous for pointing out that borrowing is the main way that law develops everywhere. Yet as Watson himself noted, the validity of his claim that "transplanting legal rules is socially easy" (Watson 1993: 95) rests on several major assumptions. First, legal transplants may operate quite differently in the host than in the home society without great difficulty. Second, law often has little impact on individual conduct. Third, creating law for a particular society is often far less important than having *a* set of rules in place. These assumptions may hold in some countries, for certain types of legal transplants, some of the time. But they apparently do not hold for corporate law in a new era of cross-border deals. As the recent experience of countries as diverse as Italy, South Korea, Russia, and Taiwan indicate, enacting new, "high quality" legal rules is indeed relatively simple. But making them work, and understanding their true significance for corporate organization and behavior, are tasks big enough to occupy many good minds for a long time.

Endnotes

1. A recent report of the Council on Foreign Relations (2002: 5, 30) captures both the importance and complexity of the issue: "[C]orporate governance reforms are on the policy agenda in the United States and many countries around the world, and they remain a central point of contention within regional organizations such as the EU. . . . [T]hese reforms are embedded in a broad set of institutions—including property rights, law enforcement, regulatory compliance, reputational intermediaries, official transparency, and reasonably efficient capital markets—without which improved corporate governance cannot achieve the desired ends."

2. Cross-border M&A increased at an *annual* growth rate of 50 percent from 1996–1999 (UNCTAD 2001: 1–2).

3. On average, 60 percent of the assets, employment, and sales of the world's twenty-five largest transnational corporations are now located outside their respective "home" countries. Even for the ten largest transnational corporations from developing economies, the average is 31 percent.

4. Convergence optimists focus on the power of markets to induce universal adoption of the shareholder primacy norm and related enforcement mechanisms. Skeptics assert that path dependence and entrenched political interests can, and sometimes do, prevent universal adoption of shareholder wealth maximiz-

ing corporate law and practices. Compare Hansmann and Kraakman (2001) with Bebchuk and Roe (1999).

5. See Romano (1991), Easterbrook and Fischel (1991), Cioffi (2000: 524): "Fiduciary duties provide an inherently flawed foundation for corporate governance. . . . "

6. For a similar point in the context of international political economy, see Gilpin (2001).

7. At the very least, one can point to a good judiciary in some nations with well-developed capital markets and a weak judiciary in some nations with poorly developed capital markets.

8. Indeed, the same can be said of legal development generally: debates about central issues such as the meaning of "the rule of law," the viability of legal transplants, and the nature of legal change remain at relatively crude stages.

References

Bebchuk, Lucian and Mark Roe. 1999. A Theory of Path Dependency in Corporate Ownership and Governance. *Stanford Law Review* 52: 127–170.

Cioffi, John. 2000. A Review Essay on Comparative Corporate Governance: The State of the Art and Emerging Research. *American Journal of Comparative Law* 48: 501–534.

Council on Foreign Relations. 2002. *Reputations at Risk: Corporate Governance and American Foreign Policy*. Report of the Roundtable on Corporate Governance.

Easterbrook, Frank and Daniel Fischel. 1991. *The Economic Structure of Corporate Law*. Cambridge: Harvard University Press.

Gilpin, Robert. 2001. *The Global Political Economy: Understanding the International Economic Order* (Princeton: Princeton University Press).

Hansmann, Henry and Reinier Kraakman. 2001. The End of History for Corporate Law. *Georgetown Law Journal* 89: 439–468.

Johnson, Simon, Peter Boone, Alasdair Breach and Eric Friedman. 2000. Corporate Governance and the Asian Financial Crisis, 1997–98. *Journal of Financial Economics*. 58: 141–186.

La Porta, Rafael, Florencio Lopez-de-Salinas and Andrei Shleifer. 1997. Legal Determinants of External Finance. *Journal of Finance* 52: 1131–1150.

——. 1998. Law and Finance. *Journal of Political Economy* 106: 1113–1155.

Milhaupt, Curtis J. 1998. Property Rights in Firms. *University of Virginia Law Review* 84: 1145–1194.

New York Stock Exchange (NYSE). 2000. *Fact Book*. Available at www.nyse.com/pdfs/07_INTERNATIONAL.pdf.

Pagano, Marco and Paulo Volpin. 2001. The Political Economy of Corporate Governance. CSEF Working Paper No. 29.

Rock, Edward. 1997. Saints and Sinners: How Does Delaware Corporate Law Work? *UCLA Law Review* 44: 1009–1083.

Romano, Roberta. 1991. The Shareholder Suit: Litigation without Foundation? *Journal of Law, Economics and Organization* 7: 55–87.

United National Conference on Trade and Development (UNCTAD). 2001. *World Investment Report.* New York: United Nations.

Watson, Alan. 1993. *Legal Transplants: An Approach to Comparative Law.* Athens, GA: University of Georgia Press, 2nd Edition.

Part I

Fiduciary Duties and
Corporate Governance

1 Controlling Corporate Self-Dealing

Convergence or Path-Dependency?

Zohar Goshen

The problem of corporate self-dealing is a manifestation of the fundamental "agency problem" pervading corporate law (Jensen and Meckling 1976). The self-dealing problem may be found in a wide variety of corporate transactions such as those between a corporation and the party that controls it, a subsidiary, or a director or officer of the corporation.[1] Legal systems in different countries address the self-dealing problem in different ways. For instance, in Delaware, transactions involving a conflict of interest are subject to the "entire fairness" test,[2] while in the United Kingdom transactions involving conflict of interest require the approval of the disinterested shareholders ("a majority of the minority").[3]

Which approach is preferable? Convergence theories imply that there exists "one efficient corporate law," while path-dependency theories suggest that the efficient law might vary depending on the specific characteristics of a given country. Is there, indeed, "one efficient solution" to self-dealing? Answering this question requires an analysis of the economic effects of the diverging solutions provided in different countries. The primary aim of this essay is to provide such an analysis through the application of the liability rule/property rule distinction (Calabresi and Melamed 1972) to the different solutions provided for corporate self-dealing.

A property rule validates consensual transactions. A transaction can be performed only with the consent of the parties, at a price that is a function of their subjective evaluation. This category includes systems that require the approval of the disinterested "majority of the minority" to validate self-dealing. A liability rule, on the other hand, validates nonconsensual transactions. A transaction can be imposed on an unwilling party subject to objectively determined adequate compensation. This category includes systems that use the "fairness test" as a measure to validate self-dealing.

Characterizing the solutions to the self-dealing problem as either property-rule or liability-rule protections provides a powerful framework to examine the parameters influencing the choice between them. The choice between a liability rule and a property rule is affected by adjudication and negotiation costs. The level of these costs, in turn, is influenced by factors such as the effectiveness of the judicial system and the efficiency of market mechanisms. Consequently, the efficiency of a given rule is dependent on the economic, legal and social conditions in a given country, ruling out the possibility of "one efficient solution." Indeed, the efficient solution to corporate self-dealing is path-dependent.

Section I describes the voting process as a means of extracting group consensus and presents the problem of conflicts of interest in voting. Section II analyzes the possible solutions to the problem. In Section III, the liability/property rule distinction is applied to the fairness test and the majority of the minority rule. Section IV describes the different factors affecting the choice of an optimal solution. Section V examines the relative weight of each factor empirically, as these come into play in Delaware and the United Kingdom.

I. On Voting and Self-Dealing

Voting is most commonly accepted as the best method for extracting group consensus from among the disparate subjective assessments of individuals within a group. The voting mechanism is based on the assumption that the majority opinion expresses the "group preference," that is, the optimal choice for the group as a whole (Nitzan and Procaccia 1986). In voting for or against a transaction, each member of the group subjectively assesses the merits of the proposed deal and expresses her particular informational perspective. The voting process aggregates the subjective assessments of individual group members into a single coherent stance that expresses the group's consent. The majority view is presumed to be the best indicator of an efficient transaction (Nitzan and Paroush 1982; Bebchuk 1988).

Voting, however, is by no means foolproof.[4] It does provide an effective means of formulating the group's stance from among the various individual positions of its members, but only if each member's vote is based on an honest appraisal of her best interests as a member of the group ("sincere voting") (Sen 1973). Whenever voters take into account how other members of the group will vote ("strategic voting") (Goshen 1997) or vote according to a personal interest conflicting with the interest of the group ("conflict-of-interest voting") (Goshen 2003), the voting procedure ceases to function as an indicator of efficient transactions. Here I focus on solutions to the problem of conflicts of interest.

The conflict-of-interest problem manifests itself in circumstances where some voters in the group have interests as members of the group which conflict with their interests external to the group, resulting in balloting which does not necessarily express the "group preference." The problem is common where a transaction is proposed between the group and one of its members. Then, the basis for the voter's decision will no doubt focus on self-interest and her personal stake in the outcome, and not on the transaction's value for the group as a whole. A conflict-of-interest situation may therefore neutralize the voting mechanism's ability to determine group preference (Arrow 1963).

Nonetheless, it does not necessarily follow that all transactions bearing an element of conflicting interests are bad (inefficient) transactions. In certain situations, a transaction with an interested shareholder may be the best option available to the group. Indeed, a self-dealer may have a competitive edge in the market, or even an advantage stemming from her proximity to the group, which ensures that a deal with her is in the group's best interests.

The fact that self-dealing may be either good (efficient) or bad (inefficient) is at the root of the conflict-of-interest problem. It requires a system that can screen self-dealing and provide a mechanism that maximizes the execution of efficient deals and minimizes the execution of inefficient ones. The main corporate law mechanisms designed to accomplish these goals are reviewed below.

II. Possible Solutions to Self-Dealing

A. Prohibition on Self-Dealing

One extreme solution is the outright prohibition of self-dealing. This solution endorses a fundamentally negative view of any transaction tainted by a conflict of interest. Historically, courts adopted a solution consistent with this view: any deal born of conflict-of-interest voting was voidable and could be repudiated by the corporation, regardless of its terms or its desirability to the corporation (see Marsh 1966). Indeed, this approach "solves" the problem; self-dealing will rarely occur under a regime prohibiting it. If self-dealing is considered pernicious, an outright prohibition is a simple solution: such a rule is easy to apply, obviates the need to grapple with evaluations, and prevents most bad (inefficient) deals. If, however, the initial position is that a significant number of transactions are efficient despite the presence of a conflict of interest, an outright prohibition will exact too heavy a price: the loss of too many efficient transactions. An outright prohibition is irreconcilable with the goal of increasing the performance of efficient transactions, and is therefore too extreme to serve as a general solution to the problem.

B. The Fairness Test

Another approach allows the self-dealer to vote but requires that the minority receive fair compensation. When a minority claims the compensation is unfair, a court's scrutiny will be needed to objectively determine the fairness of the deal. Suppose, for example, that a controlling shareholder has sold the company an asset for $100. A claim that the transaction violates the fairness test will obligate the court to determine whether the asset is indeed worth $100.

A solution based on the fairness standard, in effect, allows the person with a conflict of interest to effect a "taking"—to impose the transaction on the minority, subject to the right to challenge the transaction as unfair. The minority, however, is not assured the best attainable deal. The fairness protection is no more than a guarantee that the transaction will be fair, and that the minority will gain some portion of the profit reaped by the transaction on terms similar to those that might be expected of a transaction between willing buyers and sellers.

This solution requires routine recourse to the courts for an objective assessment of the transaction. When called upon to do so, the court must base its decision on value assessments made by professionals. However, a determination of the "objective" value of an asset is not an exact science: evaluations are influenced by subjective assumptions. Moreover, evaluations are subject to tendentiousness; specifically, a rendered opinion is liable to be slanted to meet the demands of the party who has commissioned it. This will often mean favoring the party interested in seeing the transaction performed (Bebchuk and Kahan 1989). The court will be compelled to decide between the inevitably differing opinions tendered by the opposing parties in order to determine the "correct" fair value. Yet, despite the drawbacks of a reliance on courts and professional evaluations, there is no other means of determining the objective value of an asset.

C. The Majority of the Minority Rule

Another solution to the problem is to use the voting mechanism as a means of determining the group's consent. Those with a conflict of interest are excluded from the vote, resulting in the decision being made by "a majority of the minority." The vote of a self-dealer contributes no pertinent information as to the benefits of the transaction to the group as a whole. Indeed, only those members of the group with no ulterior interests are relevant if the vote is to express the "group preference."

The ban on conflict-of-interest voting will prevent a self-dealer from imposing a transaction on an unwilling minority. That is, the minority's consent is required. Since such an approach is based upon the subjective assessments of the participants in the ballot, it is not necessary to bring the transaction before the courts for an objective evaluation. If the remaining participants in the ballot (the minority) form a large group, it will be reasonable to assume that the vote does, in fact, reflect the group preference. Placing decisionmaking in the hands of the minority, however, is liable to prevent the attainment of efficient transactions in certain situations. When the minority is composed of a small group, the threat of strategic voting will arise. Since the interested majority obviously will support the transaction, the minority, or some of its members, can attempt to hold out for a larger share of the transaction's expected profit. So long as the extorted sum leaves the majority with some amount of profit, the transaction may still be performed. But if the minority, or some of its members, hold out for too great a share, an efficient transaction may be lost. Likewise, even a "reasonable" hold-out will preclude a transaction if the majority refuses, for strategic reasons of guarding its reputation, to accede to the minority's demands.

D. *Nonintervention*

An approach at the other extreme of possible solutions is to avoid any intervention and leave the issue to market forces. It might be argued that nonintervention will provide corporations with the opportunity to generate appropriate tailor-made protections against self-dealing. Investors, for their part, will pay an appropriate price for a security with a defense against self-dealing, and little or nothing for one without such protection (see Easterbrook and Fischel 1982). In an efficient market, and absent transaction costs, the prices of securities will reflect the value of the different defenses they carry. In such a market, each corporation can accord its securities with the protection most appropriate for its needs, and each investor can choose the type of protection she requires. Nonintervention, therefore, would prove to be an effective solution in a perfect market (Fischel 1982).

However, where transaction costs are present and the market is not efficient enough to accurately price the different securities, nonintervention will fail. Different protections or their absence will not be priced accurately due to free riding and asymmetric information. Consequently, a dynamic leading to diminishing standards known as "the market for lemons" (see Akerlof 1970; Leland 1979) will lead firms to arrive at a common and inefficient point: no defense. The conclusion that nonintervention is inefficient in imperfect markets is supported by empirical findings.[5] For this reason, imposing a mandatory protection will be more efficient, leading to information cost savings and reduced transaction costs (see Gordon 1989; Romano 1989; Klausner 1995).

III. Characteristics of the Solutions

The preferable solutions that emerge out of the foregoing discussion are the "fairness test" and the majority of the minority rule. The ensuing discussion, accordingly, will concentrate on these solutions and their basic tenets.

A. *Property Rules Versus Liability Rules*

The protections against self-dealing can be classified according to the well-known distinction between liability rules and property rules. A liability rule allows a transaction to be forced upon a party, provided that "fair" compensation is paid. Of course, the fairness of the compensation (the price of the deal) is determined based on objective market-value terms. A property rule, on the other hand, allows only consensual transactions. In this case, the price of the transaction will be determined by the parties according to their respective subjective valuations. According to this classification, the fairness test is a liability rule protection, while the majority of the minority is a property rule. As shown below, this classification is based on the type of valuation that characterizes each rule, and the ramifications of their respective distributive effects.

However, the ultimate characterization of a rule as either a liability or property rule is dependent on the remedies provided by the courts when the rule is violated. In this respect, two issues are critical: access to courts and the type of enforcement.

1. Access to Courts. Once a rule is violated there should be a remedy. The first step in obtaining a remedy is gaining access to the court. Mechanisms such as derivative suits or class actions with appropriate incentives to use them must exist in order to facilitate access to courts (see Coffee 1985). A rule "on the books" without any possibility of accessing the court in order to enforce the rule is useless, and thus, such a regime should be regarded as a system of nonintervention.[6] However, access can be provided in different degrees. One legal system may allow any shareholder to bring a derivative suit, while other systems may restrict this right to shareholders holding 5 percent of the shares, or 10 percent of the shares, or restricting this right altogether. Similarly, access to courts may be denied indirectly by curtailing incentives and imposing high risks and costs on those attempting to bring suit.

2. Type of Enforcement. Once a rule is "on the books" and access to the court is obtained, the crucial element is the type of enforcement provided. A system could have a property rule protection on the books but a liability rule protection in practice, and *vice versa.* A brief example will illustrate this point. Assume that the law of a particular country requires majority of the minority approval for a conflict-of-interest transaction. This suggests that this country has adopted a property rule protection. Now assume that the interested majority shareholder does not refrain from voting and accordingly causes the corporation to approve the conflict-of-interest transaction. If a court facing a claim based on this transaction does not invalidate the deal but looks only to its fairness, then it becomes evident that the law of that country is better characterized as a liability rule rather than a property rule.[7]

Whether the law as stated "on the books" is in effect the real approach of the law in any given country depends on the quality of the courts and judges in interpreting and effectively implementing the law as it is stated on the books. If courts and judges refuse or are unable to enforce the law as it is stated in the statutes, then it is obvious that the law will be different from that envisioned by the legislators.[8] In sum, the crucial factors in determining whether a particular rule is a property rule or liability rule are access to courts and the type of enforcement available. While access to court is primarily controlled by the quality of the law, the type of enforcement is primarily controlled by the quality of the judiciary. In the following analysis, I assume a proper characterization of the rules.

B. Subjective Versus Objective Valuations

The two types of rules can be distinguished according to the valuation method each rule employs. The "fairness rule" assumes that, once self-dealing is permitted, the majority can force a transaction upon the minority. The protection afforded to the minority ensures that a fair price is obtained. A fair price need not be the best price. The fairness rule establishes a regime of involuntary transactions, and thus replaces subjective valuations of the contending groups of shareholders with an objective measure by the court.

The majority of the minority rule negates the ability of the majority to force a deal upon the minority. A transaction will only transpire if the majority of the minority has consented to it. This rule empowers the minority to strive to obtain the maximum price it can achieve. Placing the decision in the minority's hands maintains a regime of voluntary transactions and preserves the role of subjective valuations.

C. Division of the Surplus

The two types of rules can, as well, be distinguished according to their respective effect on the division of the surplus arising out of the self-dealing transaction. A voluntary transaction between individuals generates a surplus, as a result of the difference in subjective values the parties attach to the deal. The difference between the valuations of the buyer and seller represents the surplus from the transaction. That is, if A values an asset at $100, while the same asset is worth $200 to B, the $100 difference in their valuations would constitute surplus. Any price that the parties strike between $100 and $200 would thus be an efficient transaction.

If the asset has a market price that is located within the range of possible prices, the parties will effect the transaction at the market value. The forces of supply and demand will determine the division of the surplus between the parties. On the other hand, when an asset has no market price, the division of the surplus will be subject to negotiation, and the outcome will depend upon external factors, such as the negotiating skills and bargaining power of each party (see, e.g., Cooter 1982). If the price is set at $101, A receives $1 and B $99 of the surplus, whereas if the price is $199, the division of the $100 of surplus will be reversed. In either instance, the transaction will be efficient and "fair" in the sense that it will be effected with mutual consent and, as such, will be upheld by the courts.

When the asset is protected by a property rule, the buyer has no means of compelling its purchase. The seller can negotiate freely in an attempt to secure a larger share of the surplus. The buyer's success in closing the deal will depend on her negotiating skill and whether substitutes for the asset are available. Conversely, where the asset is protected by a liability rule, the buyer need not enter negotiations at all; she can simply take the asset by offering a price that is objectively fair. What is a "fair" price? If the court's test is based on the price set between a willing seller and a willing buyer, then a fair price will mean any efficient transaction, that is, any price between $101 and $199 (Eisenberg 1988). Accordingly, it may be assumed that the buyer will offer a price closer to $101 than to $199 because under a liability rule, the buyer will endeavor to set a price by which most of the surplus will vest with him.

The two solutions to the conflict-of-interest problem will have different effects on the division of surplus between the parties in the corporate context. The liability rule approach will give an advantage to the majority, while the property rule approach gives the minority more bargaining power (Ackerman 1986; Haddock et al. 1987). Suppose that a group of voting shareholders has an asset which it values at $100, and the majority group is interested in purchasing the asset, since it values the asset at $200. With a liability rule the majority can force the transaction upon the minority, contingent upon its obligation to ensure a fair price. The majority can offer a price in the lower range of possible surplus values, such as $101, and still live up to the fairness standard. As long as the actual price falls between $100 and $200, the minority will have sustained no actionable wrong. Since the same transaction could potentially take place even under a regime of strictly voluntary transactions, it cannot be deemed unfair.[9] The mere fact that the surplus has been divided inequitably does not demonstrate per se that the transaction is unfair.[10]

A property rule, which requires the minority's approval for a transaction in which a conflict of interests arises, empowers the minority to demand a larger portion of the surplus (for example a price of $199) than it would receive under the liability rule. Yet abusive holdout by the minority may also lead to the loss of worthwhile transactions. Thus, in the above example, let us assume that the majority offers a price of $180 and the minority demands $201. Although seemingly an irrational demand, this is possible since, in actuality, the minority has no way of knowing precisely what value the asset has to the majority, and may mistakenly demand too much. The majority would not proceed with the transaction and the minority will remain with an asset worth $100 (by its own assessment) instead of the $180 which it might have received. An efficient transaction will thus be foiled.

Furthermore, the majority will know beforehand that the minority can extort a higher price, and that in any transaction it will propose, the minority will be unwilling to relinquish a sizeable portion of the surplus (Hermalin and Schwartz 1996). Therefore, the majority will refrain from initiating transactions with the minority and will seek out less problematic alternatives. Only when the minority possesses a unique asset will the majority be forced to address the minority's excessive demands, and even in such circumstances, some such transactions will fail to take place because of holdout attempts. The transfer of the power to approve the deal to the minority enhances the minority's ability to demand a larger share of the surplus in those transactions that are performed, but reduces the total number of transactions involving the minority that will in fact be performed.

The fairness doctrine, on the other hand, does not guarantee the minority a large portion of the surplus, but it does guarantee that efficient transactions will be carried out. The majority will not be deterred by hold-out problems and can push through any transaction it wishes, provided always that the minority will receive a fair price. The fairness protection reduces the profit on each transaction, but ensures the maximum number of transactions. However, just as the transfer of the decisionmaking power to the minority carries an inherent risk that extortionate demands will doom efficient transactions, the fairness rule approach transfers power to the courts, which may erroneously ratify inefficient transactions or ban efficient ones. To illustrate, in the above example, an inefficient transaction would occur if the majority proposed a price of $95, and the courts approved the deal, overriding the minority's objections, based on a (faulty) objective assessment of the price.

IV. Factors Determining the Right Solution

Which of the different alternatives is the optimal rule? Indeed, the classification of the "fairness test" as a liability rule and the majority of the minority as a property rule presents the problem of choosing the appropriate solution as a choice between a liability rule and a property rule. According to Coase (1960), absent transaction costs, the rule adopted is irrelevant: in either case efficient transactions will be performed. Where transaction costs are incurred, however, the choice between the rules depends upon which legal rule better ensures the realization of efficient transactions and the avoidance of inefficient ones. The transaction costs include adjudication costs and negotiation costs. Indeed, negotiation costs are primarily responsible for the failure to bring about efficient transactions. However, this alone cannot allow an abstract determination of efficiency. It is the *relative* magnitude of the different costs that is important, and a relative measurement can only be done in a specific context of the specific economy.[11]

The first element of importance in measuring the relative costs is the *scale of the problem* as it is reflected in the *frequency* (the number of occurrences) and *quality* (the division between harmful and beneficial) of transactions involving self-dealing. The initial size of the problem is determined by the overall frequency of transactions involving self-dealing, as this number will determine the population of cases that should be screened by the legal regime. In markets where concentrated ownership and cross-holdings of corporations are widespread the frequency of self-dealing is expected to be higher. Since the majority of the minority rule applies to *all screened* transactions,[12] while the "fairness test" only applies to *challenged* transactions,[13] different frequencies will result in different transaction costs.

Similarly, the quality of the transactions will affect the *expected damage* of each screening device, as neither rule is perfect. Indeed, in a market in which 90 percent of the conflict-of-interest transactions are beneficial while only 10 percent are harmful, the effect of the two alternative rules will be different than if the situation were reversed. The majority of the miinority rule is likely to prevent most of the harmful transactions, but it will also lead to the rejection of some beneficial transactions as a result of strategic behavior. The fairness test is likely to facilitate most of the beneficial transactions, but it will also lead to the approval of some harmful transactions as a result of the inefficiencies and errors endemic to the legal system. Thus, different qualities of self-dealing will result in different transaction costs.

However, the rule itself, in turn, will affect the initial frequency and quality of conflict-of-interest transactions, as each rule has different effects on the incentive to engage in a self-dealing. For instance, a majority of the minority rule entails the costs of securing minority support with low probability of success when expropriation is contemplated. This should deter some transactions, harmful and beneficial, and thus will decrease the frequency of conflict-of-interest transactions. Similarly, if under a "fairness test" the probability of securing court approval for expropriation is high, the frequency of conflict-of-interest transactions will increase while the quality will decrease.

Beyond the rule itself, other factors influence the scale of the problem and consequently the relative costs of the different rules. One such factor is the market for corporate control. The market for corporate control challenges inefficiency both by imposing a potential threat of a takeover as a deterrent to poor management, and by the steps taken once a takeover has actually been executed (Manne 1965; Easterbrook and Fischel 1981). The most important factor determining the existence of a market for corporate control is whether shareholding is dispersed or concentrated. While dispersed ownership allows hostile takeovers to take place, concentrated ownership can render the company immune to takeovers. It makes no difference how inefficient the controlling party is; so long as it holds an absolute majority, the controlling interest cannot be usurped other than through a consensual private transaction.

The effectiveness of the market for corporate control will affect the relative costs of the rules. Under a liability rule regime, an effective market for corporate control will result in fewer cases of exploitation and the scale of the problem will decrease. An ineffective market for corporate control, however, will not prevent exploitation, leaving the minority to rely mainly on the legal system. Consequently, the efficiency and effectiveness of the judicial system will determine the ultimate scale of the problem.

Similarly, under a property rule regime, an effective market for corporate control will reduce the scale of the problem. Theoretically, under a property rule the minority can protect its own interest more effectively than will the indirect threat of a takeover. In practice, however, the ability of the minority to protect itself depends on the sophistication of the investors constituting the minority and the effectiveness of the court in enforcing the property rule. With effective enforcement of the property rule and the presence of dominant sophisticated investors exploitation of the minority is difficult. Consequently, control will have little value to an entity interested in profiting at the minority's expense, as well as to a potential acquirer aiming to remove a party acting to the minority's detriment. In the absence of both effective enforcement and sophisticated investors, however, an effective market for corporate control will decrease the scale of the problem.

Indeed, the presence of sophisticated investors is another factor affecting the relative costs of the different rules. As will be explained below, these investors affect negotiation costs under a property rule and negotiations "in the shadow" of a liability rule. However, the presence of sophisticated investors might, as well, affect transaction costs in another indirect way. Being long-term repeat players, sophisticated investors are more likely to provide the appropriate ground for breeding positive social norms. Although social norms do not carry legal or economic sanctions, they are able to restrict minority expropriation and unfair dealing. Consequently, a business community that follows social norms that respect minority rights will decrease the scale of the problem. With this background, we can now turn to an analysis of the relative costs of the two rules.

A. Transaction Costs of the Majority of the Minority Rule

The majority of the minority rule predicates the performance of a transaction on the ability to secure the consent of the disinterested members of the group. This consent, of course, will reflect a range of subjective assessments on the part of the voters. Generally speaking, court intervention to evaluate the fairness of the transaction will be unnecessary, since the transaction will take place under market conditions. The voting process itself, however, is susceptible to many possible distortions. For example, voters may be provided with misleading or insufficient information; managers or controlling owners may hold proxies from disinterested voters; certain voters may be promised benefits and thus are no longer "disinterested;" intimidation of voters with threats of retaliatory behavior may take place; or there may be hidden or unknown business or personal ties between voters and management, or between voters and the controlling owner.[14]

The risk of a flawed ballot obligates the court to evaluate whether proper procedure has been maintained and that those voting were, in fact, disinterested. As compared to evaluating the transaction's merits, the court's role is relatively uncomplicated. The court should have no difficulty in checking the procedures followed and the information that was supplied to the voters. While it is difficult to determine whether a given voter is indeed disinterested, the determination will not entail high costs, since the courts are practiced in contending with issues of deceit. In addition, the probability of a large number of irregularities taking place in the voting process is small. Since large numbers of shareholders will participate in the vote, the chances of irregularities being discovered are high. Indeed, a property rule should involve low adjudication costs. It should be emphasized, however, that the ability of courts to enforce a property rule in some predictable and consistent manner is the *minimum* level of efficiency and effectiveness required of any judicial system (Pistor et al. 2000). Otherwise, high adjudication costs in enforcing a property rule (due to inefficient or corrupt courts) are tantamount to a system of nonintervention, with an inability to contract around the absence of a minority protection.[15]

A property rule that transfers the decision into the hands of the minority represents a "negotiation" between the majority and the minority.[16] Negotiations involve several types of costs. The first is administrative costs: dispatching notices that inform of an impending ballot and provide appropriate background information on the transaction to all voting shareholders, with each voter returning a proxy form indicating her vote. These costs certainly do not prevent negotiations from taking place, and, indeed, for shareholders they are part of a routine practice.[17]

Second, the voting process requires that the voters study the material, develop a position, and vote. This can be expensive for the voters, and often many will refrain from voting or blindly support management's position. The absence of part of the voting public will detract from the quality of the decisionmaking process. Moreover, a minority's blind support of management—generally the interested party—will thwart the purpose of having the matter put to the disinterested minority.

Third, the voting process will also be susceptible to strategic voting. Some of the voters can adopt a hold-out strategy and turn down an efficient transaction in order to raise the price of their consent. The proponent of the deal himself can adopt a strategy of "signaling," by refusing to bow to extortion, striving to earn the reputation of a staunch negotiator, and prevent future hold-out attempts. If the minority consists of a very large group of voters among whom coordination is impractical, then a hold-out strategy will not be pursued. However, if the minority is made up of a few individuals or institutions who might easily join together, then hold-out will again be a significant risk.

The amount of these costs will be affected, in turn, by the prevalence of self-dealing that will trigger the need for shareholder votes. Negotiation costs will rise with the frequency of self-dealing transactions. Markets that are characterized by cross-ownership, concentrated ownership, and a centralized economy can be expected to have more self-dealing transactions. Consequently, higher negotiation costs should be expected.

Indeed, negotiation costs are not determined in the abstract. An additional important feature affecting the total amount of negotiation costs is the presence of sophisticated investors in the minority group. Where sophisticated investors are involved in the management of a corporation, the participation of informed and able investors in the decisionmaking process can improve the quality of decisionmaking (see, e.g., Black 1992). Unfortunately, at times these investors themselves act in collusion with management or the controlling owner against the remaining shareholders, directly or indirectly (see, e.g., Rock 1994; Eisenberg 1989). Similarly, institutional investors will, at times, exacerbate the hold-out problem. Such investors can communicate among themselves with relative ease to form a coalition. Since these investors are sophisticated professionals, however, they will not demand an extortionist price that will cause the transaction to fall through, since they are able to correctly assess the profit to be gained by closing the deal.

Additionally, when the minority is dominated by sophisticated investors, the market will operate efficiently. Sophisticated investors invest in the collection and evaluation of information, and act in accordance with their findings on a consistent and professional level. Such investors are capable of pricing securities so as to incorporate the risk of self-dealing. In an efficient market, corporations seeking to raise capital to finance their business activities will have to pass the scrutiny of underwriters, investment banks, and other professionals who broker between corporations and potential investors. Efficient corporations will manage to raise capital on favorable terms, whereas inefficient corporations will find capital available to them only on expensive terms, if at all (Stout 1988). Corporations in which the majority exploits the minority will have difficulty raising additional capital; under such circumstances, it is obvious that investors will be unwilling to provide capital to the corporation as part of the minority. By contrast, corporations structured so as to protect the minority will raise capital more easily and cheaply. Indeed, efficient capital markets provide some protection to the minority,[18] thereby reducing the prevalence of self-dealing and negotiation costs.

Furthermore, sophisticated investors are active in the market on a long-term basis, behave consistently, and can thus properly appreciate a good reputation and punish a bad one. Indeed, sometimes social sanctions play a role in preventing abuse of the minority (Fama 1980; Rock 1997). The role of reputation in the business community is a nonlegal factor that serves to reduce the risk to minority shareholders. A controlling owner who is interested in receiving public approval and maintaining a positive image as an honest dealer will refrain from abusing the rights of the minority even when no economic or legal sanction is threatened. The presence of sophisticated investors is an important ingredient supporting the breeding of positive social norms. Consequently, in a business community in which reputation plays a significant role, self-dealing transactions might be avoided and negotiation costs will be lower.

Finally, sophisticated investors contributing to an efficient market and the development of social norms might justify even a nonintervention approach, since the parties involved—the corporations and the investors—can devise proper defenses. When, on the contrary, minority investors are generally unsophisticated, protections imposed by law will have greater importance.

B. Transaction Costs of the Fairness Test

A liability rule validates a self-dealing transaction on an objective, non-consensual basis, and as such does not require negotiation. However, the parties can negotiate "in the shadow" of the liability rule to avoid legal intervention (Ayres and Talley 1995). Negotiations in the shadow of the rule enjoy the benefits and costs of being informal. The costs of these negotiations will depend on the presence of sophisticated investors and the effectiveness of the judicial system. The more effective and precise the courts, the easier it is for sophisticated investors to anticipate judicial rulings and avoid the need for actual recourse to courts. The cost of these negotiations and the degree to which litigation can be avoided will depend on the specific characteristics of a given jurisdiction.

On the other hand, a liability rule rests upon a protection that requires routine intervention by the courts. The courts will be called upon as a matter of course to rule whether a given self-dealing is (objectively) fair. This does not mean that all transactions where a conflict of interest arises will entail litigation, since in many cases the minority will consider the proposed transaction to be fair while in other cases negotiation will yield a settlement. But those cases that do reach the courts will necessitate an examination of the merits of the deal, in a process for which adjudication costs will be considerable. It will be necessary to elicit professional opinions as to the value of the transaction, and the court will be compelled to decide between the inevitably differing opinions that will be tendered in order to determine the "correct" value of the transaction.[19]

Determining the objective value of a transaction is a complicated process requiring a high degree of competence from the courts, since such valuations involve future projections of different variables (interest rates, etc.), and the use of complex financial models.[20] A liability rule based on judicial rulings, therefore, relies on the existence of professional institutions capable of providing worthy assessments, as well as competent courts possessing the necessary level of expertise to rule effectively in such areas. The professional standards of these institutions and the courts will obviously determine the direct adjudication costs.

However, the efficiency of the adjudication process will also influence the indirect adjudication costs. Indirect adjudication costs will depend on the frequency of wrong decisions in a given system. Any deviation from economic efficiency—the approval of an unfair transaction or the rejection of a fair one—means increased costs. The use of objective standards simplifies the task of evaluations; however, where no market price exists, an "objective" value will be the product of subjective assessments, so that the risk of mistakes is not eliminated. Every mistaken decision harms the welfare of society as a whole. The number of faulty decisions will be reduced if professional institutions are more trustworthy and impartial, and the courts more competent. When, on the other hand, the professional institutions cannot be relied upon or slant their opinions to the benefit of those soliciting them or when the courts are incompetent, overburdened, or corrupt, the number of wrong decisions will be much larger and their attendant costs much more significant.

High indirect adjudication costs may inflict a severe blow to economic efficiency. First, it will affect the willingness of investors to invest in corporations as minority shareholders. Second, it will frustrate effective negotiations "in the shadow" of the rule. Third, it will place unnecessary costs on the majority to create reliable and cost-effective alternative defenses to secure potential investors. The savings in information costs gained by the existence of legislatively imposed protections will be lost, as the market will in any case be forced to provide its own solutions.

V. An Empirical Overview

A brief empirical survey[21] of the protections provided to minority shareholders in a number of countries confirms the above analysis. It also reveals information on how the factors outlined above affect the choice of rule to be applied in each system.

A. The United States (Delaware)

Delaware, widely recognized as the most significant jurisdiction for corporate law purposes, has adopted a liability rule to govern self-dealing. In particular, Delaware imposes the "entire fairness" test on the party interested in seeing the transaction approved, and such party must demonstrate both fair dealing and a fair price.[22] The situation is different in those cases in which a majority of disinterested shareholders has endorsed the transaction: Where a controlling shareholder engages in self-dealing, the "entire fairness" test remains the standard by which the transaction is judged, yet the burden of proof to show that the transaction is unfair passes to the party attempting to block its performance.[23] When, however, the interested party is a director or manager without a controlling interest in the corporation, the transaction is measured against the business judgment rule, an entirely different standard.[24] As demonstrated below, what is believed to be a complicated, incoherent, and unexplainable system of rules, is, in fact, a coherent and very efficient solution to the self-dealing problem.

An evaluation of the various characteristics of the American market supports the adoption of a liability rule. To begin with, the Delaware courts are unique in their expertise in appraising values and in their mastery of corporate law in general. Additionally, in handing down decisions, the Delaware courts function with the efficiency, reliability, and speed crucial to a dynamic business world. Next, shareholding is widely spread among diverse investors, so that a market for corporate control is possible and active (Roe 1993). In addition, the capital market is fairly efficient, a large segment of minority shares are held by sophisticated institutional investors, and the business community in America is very sensitive to business reputation with regard to the management of corporations (Rock 1997; Black 1990).

The consequence of these features is that adjudication costs are low, both because of an efficient legal system and because of the parallel activity of market and social mechanisms. Negotiation costs are similarly low due to the presence of institutional investors and the efficiency of the capital markets. As noted above, in such circumstances, market conditions resemble an environment without transaction costs and any solution would provide efficient results. Therefore, a minimal and flexible protection that the parties may use as a baseline will be most favorable. A liability rule will avoid the need to vote on every self-dealing transaction, requiring courts' ruling only on a minority of litigated cases, while leaving the parties free to shift to property rule protection. In practice, the courts have rendered support to arrangements whereby the parties have contracted around the fairness rule and have conditioned the deal upon approval of the majority of the disinterested minority.

Ostensibly, under a property rule regime, no need arises to determine whether the transaction is fair, since the minority can fend for itself. Therefore, when the parties choose to make self-dealing contingent upon the approval of a disinterested minority, such a transaction should be judged not against the fairness rule, but by the business judgment rule. As described above, however, a change in the requisite judicial standard will be acceptable only for those transactions involving directors or managers who do not possess a controlling share, whereas those transactions to which a controlling shareholder is a party will still be subject to the fairness standard, though the burden of proof will shift to the opponents of the transaction.

Why would the controlling person condition the deal upon receiving the majority of the minority support, even though "entire fairness" remains the test, and only the burden of proof shifts? The answer lies in the partition of the surplus. The controlling person faces two choices: to make the deal and bear the burden of proof that the deal is fair; or to make the deal with the majority of the minority support and shift the burden of proof to the party opposing the deal. In the first case, the controlling person could approve a deal on the lower side of the surplus. To obtain the approval of the minority, the controlling person will have to offer a higher price. The price, however, will not be as high as it would have been under a property-rule regime. Here, the negotiating power of the minority is limited by the knowledge that even if their support is not given the controlling person can still conclude the deal and bear the burden of proof. Nevertheless, the price offered to the minority must be higher than it would have been had their support not been sought. The effect of the rule shifting the burden of proof is to provide the minority with some negotiating power: the minority has "something" to sell to the majority.

In fact, this is an insurance transaction: the controlling person pays a premium (increased price) to the minority in order to increase the chances that the deal will not be stalled, by reducing the risk that the deal will be struck down by the courts. That is, in cases in which there is a risk that the court will err in determining the value of the deal, the controlling person can buy insurance (minority support), shift the burden of proof to the plaintiff, and increase the chance of maintaining the deal's validity.

The rationale behind the courts' refusal to deviate from the fairness test in controlling owner's self-dealing, even when the approval of a disinterested minority is secured, is the concern for procedural flaws in the voting process. A controlling shareholder may exploit its position to distort the voting, whether by threatening the minority with future reprisals or by abuse of the wide discretion afforded by proxies.[25] Rather than tackling the problem of faulty procedure by insisting on free and fully informed voting by the disinterested shareholders, the courts have preferred to cling to the fairness test.

There is, however, another way to understand the court's position. Courts are reluctant to pass judgment on valuation and thus focus on procedural flaws in the process of approving the deal. Shifting the burden of proof provides the market with the incentive to seek the support of the majority of the minority, thereby reducing the need for judicial judgment on the value of the deal. In fact, in terms of my analysis, courts prefer a shift from a liability rule—which would require the courts' ruling over valuation issues—to a property rule—in which the courts' role is to evaluate the appropriateness of the voting procedure.

An alternative approach would distinguish between an *ad hoc* decision to supplant the liability rule with a property rule, versus a *consistent* commitment to do so. When conditioning the self-dealing upon the approval of the majority of the minority is limited to a *specific* transaction, the controlling shareholder maintains the right to base other transactions (or even the present one) on the fairness standard. In these circumstances, there is a legitimate basis for the courts' concern over distortions in the voting process and intimidation of the minority. In the future, the controlling shareholder can use the liability rule to initiate transactions that are injurious to the minority (for example, a freeze-out merger).

When, however, the parties determine that *all* self-dealing will be subject to the approval of the disinterested minority — for example, as a condition set forth in the articles of incorporation — this concern is reduced. The controlling shareholder is unable to force the current transaction upon the minority, nor harm the minority by future reprisals, since a majority of the minority will again be called upon to endorse the deal. Once the threat of intimidation of the minority has been removed, the potential for irregularities in the voting process can be addressed directly. Therefore, in such conditions, the fairness rule can be replaced with the business judgment rule, even when a controlling shareholder is a party to the transaction.

In sum, the application of the theory provided in this essay shows that what many scholars believed to be a confused and incoherent system of rules of Delaware courts is, in effect, an efficient and coherent system. A lack of theory caused observers to see "indeterminacy" in these rules. Once a complete theory is provided, they evince clarity.

B. The United Kingdom

The United Kingdom shares many characteristics with the United States in terms of its capital markets and economic and social environments. The capital markets of the United Kingdom are very liquid and are comprised of mostly public corporations (Black and Coffee 1994). Institutional investors have an extremely strong presence in the capital markets, controlling 70 percent of the shares of publicly traded companies (Cheffins 1997; Black and Coffee 1994). Furthermore, institutional investors have become much more active in monitoring and participating in the affairs of their portfolio companies over the last decade. Indeed, the "British capital markets match those of the United States in being extremely active and well developed" (Coffee 1991: 1309).

Given these characteristics, it can be expected that, like the United States, the United Kingdom would adopt a "fairness" approach to dealing with conflict-of-interest transactions. Indeed, the general rule followed in the United Kingdom is that a majority shareholder is free to vote his shares at a shareholders meeting called to approve a transaction in which he has a personal interest (Davies 1997). Even a director who is also a shareholder may vote on a transaction in which he is interested when the law requires that such transaction receive the prior approval of the shareholders.[26] Against this freedom to vote with conflicts of interest, Section 459 of the Company Act provides that minority shareholders can present a petition of *"unfairly prejudicial"* transaction,[27] and the court has wide discretion in deciding upon the appropriate remedy.[28] While the cases are few, the courts have held that Section 459 provides protections to minority shareholders in conflict-of-interest transactions (Davies 1997: 735).

However, while Section 459 theoretically seems to provide adequate protection for minority shareholders in conflict-of-interest transactions, in practice it has not. The primary reason for this is the general nature of the judiciary in the United Kingdom. The vast majority of judges lack any particular expertise in the realities of the corporate world (Davies 1997: 309). In comparison with judges in the United States, especially those in Delaware, these judges do not "have the same experience with the mechanics of corporate deal-making" and do "not bring to the bench the same level of expertise as [their] Delaware counterparts" (Cheffins 1997: 312). In addition, more than their counterparts in the United States, judges in the United Kingdom strictly adhere to the principle of stare decisis and follow the rule of law as stated in previous cases. Indeed, Section 459 was enacted with the express intent of changing the conservative approach of judges with respect to actions brought by minority shareholders (Davies 1997: 735–40). Despite the intent of Parliament in enacting Section 459, however, the lack of judicial activism has resulted in Section 459 not being utilized effectively (Cheffins 1997: 335). Furthermore, even when the courts have ruled for minority shareholder petitions under Section 459, they provided little guidance in these decisions for future claimants. In short, given relatively inefficient and ineffective courts in corporate law issues, the choice of liability-rule protection for minority shareholders resulted in inadequate protection due to high adjudication costs.

However, given the strong presence of institutional investors, the lack of adequate protection has led to private regulation avoiding the need to rely on courts' rulings (Cheffins 1997: 364–420). The London Stock Exchange has stepped in and filled the void with its own rules for conflict-of-interest transactions.[29] According to Section 11 of the listing rules, commonly called the "Yellow Book," in order to maintain a listing on the London Stock Exchange, corporations must submit all transactions involving a 10 percent shareholder to a general vote of the shareholders, with the interested shareholder not being allowed to vote.[30] The listing requirements in effect provide a property rule protection for minority shareholders, thereby minimizing the need to rely on courts' rulings in determining fairness. Indeed, the strong presence of institutional investors within the United Kingdom's commercial and social norms leads to lower negotiation costs under the property-rule protection. Thus, the case of the United Kingdom is one in which private contracting has shifted from the default liability rule to a property rule, thereby shifting from high adjudication costs to low negotiation costs.

The Delaware and United Kingdom examples demonstrate that the relative weight of the different characteristics in a given system will affect the choice of the appropriate rule for the protection of minority shareholders from the problem of conflict-of-interest voting. Indeed, there is not "one efficient solution" suitable to all. This conclusion is confirmed by examination of a larger sample of countries (Goshen 2003). For example, while Canada has overcome the ineffectiveness of its courts by shifting from a liability-rule to a property-rule through private ordering (on a path similar to that of the United Kingdom), Italy has shifted from a property-rule to a liability-rule, thereby exposing corporations to the ineffectiveness of Italian courts.

Conclusion

The notion of "one efficient corporate law" underlies many of the convergence and path-dependency theories. Through the case of regulating corporate self-dealing, this essay illustrated that such a notion is unfounded. Indeed, corporate self-dealing can be addressed by a number of means. Determining which of these rules is preferable is, in fact, a choice between liability-rule and property-rule protection, depending on the total transaction costs incurred in a given system. These costs include both the negotiation costs attendant upon a property rule, as well as the adjudication costs associated with a liability rule. The sum of these costs is influenced by the efficacy of the judicial system and of market mechanisms, such as the market for corporate control, the capital market, and the types of investors active in the market. In the end, the solution adopted must conform to the local conditions in each country. Regulating self-dealing is path-dependent.

Endnotes

The essay is based on an article published by the author in the California Law Review as "The Efficiency of Controlling Corporate Self-Dealing: Theory Meets Reality."

1. See e.g., Kahn v. Lynch Communication Systems, Del. Supr., 638 A.2d 1110 (1994); Cookies Food Products v. Lakes Warehouse, Iowa Supr., 430 N.W.2d 447 (1988); Ripley v. International Railways of Central America, 8 N.Y.2d 430, 209 N.Y.S.2d 289 (1960).
2. Weinberger v. UOP, Inc., Del. Supr., 457 A.2d 701 (1983).
3. London Stock Exchange Listing Rules §11. Available at http://www.fsa. gov.uk/pubs/ukla/chapt11–2.pdf.
4. Most securities holders adopt a strategy of "rational apathy," because of the problem of free riding, the public-good quality of information, and the lack of incentives for an individual to gather, process, and use information (the expected return from making a good decision is lower than the cost of investing in information).
5. A study of 49 countries has shown that countries with poorer investor protections, measured in terms of both the character of legal rules and the quality of law enforcement, have smaller and narrower capital markets (La Porta et al. 1997). Moreover, this study supports the proposition that in legal systems which provide ineffective enforcement of contracts it is difficult to contract around inefficient legal arrangements and impossible to signal commitments for fair dealings to the market.
6. Indeed, there are countries in which the legal rights are not coupled with effective access to courts (La Porta et al. 1997).
7. This is the case in Italy (see Enriques this volume).
8. See ibid.
9. See, e.g., Revised Model Business Corp. Act § 8.61, note on Fair Transactions (1989) ("It has long been settled that a 'fair' price is any price in that broad range which an unrelated party might have been willing to pay or willing to accept, as the case may be, for the property, following a normal arm's-length business negotiation, in the light of knowledge that would have been reasonably acquired in the course of such negotiations, any result within that range being 'fair' . . . ").
10. See, e.g., Case v. New York Central Railroad, 204 N.E.2d 643 (N.Y. 1965) (Consolidation of taxes between the parent company, which suffered losses,

and its subsidiary, which registered profits, created a tax saving of which the vast part was enjoyed by the parent).

11. Indeed, sometimes it will be preferable to bear the hazards of holdouts (negotiation costs) than to rely on a corrupt court system (adjudication costs). This was the case at a certain time in Russia (Black and Kraakman 1996).

12. Different systems limit the number of screened cases by the size of the transaction or the size of the shareholdings of the person having conflicts of interest.

13. Some systems limit the number of challenged cases by requiring a certain minimum shareholding to bring a derivative suit.

14. See, e.g., Citron v. E.I. du Pont de Nemours & Co., Del.Ch., 584 A.2d 490, at 520 (citing Kahn v. Lynch, note 1 above, with approval).

15. Indeed, there are countries in which the system of legal enforcement is so weak that the mere existence of minority shareholders' right to vote does not provide the shareholders with any meaningful protection due to the inability to enforce their rights (La Porta et al. 1997). Thus, this kind of "protection" should be regarded more like a nonintervention regime than a property rule.

16. Indeed, the application of the liability rule/property rule distinction to cases of individual rights and to group rights differs greatly. An important distinction should be noted: while a property rule concerning individual's rights allows for direct and normal negotiations, negotiations with the minority do not take a similar form. Voting is a more complicated form of negotiations. Sometimes it involves voting on a "take-it-or-leave-it" offer. Sometimes it involves informal discussions between some institutional shareholders and the company before an offer is put to a vote. And sometimes, preliminary negotiations take place through a committee of the board of directors appointed for this purpose. In any case, the important feature is that in the end nothing compels a voter to accept an offer she deems inappropriate.

17. This description is not true in every country. There are countries in which the corporate law substantially increases administrative costs (La Porta et al. 1998) ("In some countries, shareholders must show up in person, or send an authorized representative, to shareholders' meeting to be able to vote. . . . In Japan, for example, about 80 percent of companies hold their annual meeting on the same week, and voting by mail is not allowed. . . . In some countries, law requires that shareholders deposit their shares with the company or financial intermediary several days prior to a shareholder meeting. . . . This practice prevents shareholders from selling their shares for several days around the time of the meeting . . . ").

18. Yet the effectiveness of the capital market protection—efficient as it may be—is limited. In practice, public corporations in the United States often fund their activities through undistributed profits, rather than by raising capital from the public, thereby avoiding the disciplining effect of the market. In any case, when corporations subject themselves to the constraints of the capital market, they

are, in fact, signaling their commitment to protect minority shareholders (Goshen 1995).

19. See, e.g., Kahn v. Household acquisition Corp., 591 A.2d 166, 175 (Del. 1991). In re Shell Oil Co., 607 A.2d 1213, 1222 (Del. 1992), the Delaware Supreme Court recognized the difficulties raised by the battle of experts in appraisal proceedings, and recommended that the Chancellor appoint its own expert witness.

20. See Weinberger v. UOP Inc., note 2 above (all commonly accepted valuation methods must be taken into account).

21. For additional empirical assessments, see Goshen (2003).

22. See Weinberger v. UOP, Inc., note 2 above.

23. See Kahn v. Lynch, note 1 above.

24. See Michelson v. Duncan, 407 A.2d 211 (1979); In Re Wheelabrator Tech. Shareholders Lit., 663 A.2d 1194 (1995). This rule, in fact, treats the transaction as if it involved a third party.

25. See Citron v. du Pont, note 14 above.

26. Davies (1997: 708) citing Northwest Transportation Co. v. Beatty (1887) 12 App.Cas. 589 and Northern Countries Securities Ltd. v. Jackson & Steeple Ltd. (1974) 1 W.L.R. 1133 (Davies describes the surprising ruling in this case: "[I]t was held that although, to comply with an undertaking given by the company to the court, the directors were bound to recommend the shareholders to vote for a resolution they, as shareholders, could vote against it, if so minded."). See also Cheffins (1997: 324) referring to Gower's discussion of the seminal case of Regal (Hastings) Ltd v. Gulliver: "The case involved directors who had, by virtue of their position, made a personal profit by buying and selling shares in another company. On the facts of the case these individuals were liable to account. Still, Lord Russell said: 'They could, had they wished, have protected themselves by a resolution (either antecedent or subsequent) of the Regal shareholders in general meeting. In default of such approval liability to account must remain.'"

27. Indeed, Section 459 of the 1985 Company Act, provides: "A member of a company may apply to the court by petition for an order under this Part on the grounds that the company's affairs are being or have been conducted in a manner which is unfairly prejudicial to the interest of its members generally or some part of the members (including at least himself) or that any actual or proposed act or omission of the company (including an act or omission on its behalf) is or would be so prejudicial."

28. See §461(2) of the 1985 Company Act.

29. The London Stock Exchange is designated the competent authority for enforcing statutory guidelines, and its own listing requirements are given just a slightly lower status than statutory ones (Cheffins 1997: 368).

30. See London Stock Exchange Listing Rules §11. Available at http://www.fsa. gov.uk/pubs/ukla/chapt11–2.pdf. §11.4(c) and (d) provide that in a transaction with a "related party", defined in §11.1(c) to include a greater than 10% shareholder, the company must, "(c) obtain the approval of its shareholders either prior to the transaction being entered into or, if it is expressed to be conditional on such approval, prior to completion of the transaction; and (d) where applicable, ensure that the related party itself abstains, and takes all reasonable steps to ensure that its associates abstain, from voting on the relevant resolution."

References

Ackerman, Susan Rose. 1986. I'd rather Be Liable Than You: A Note on Property Rules and Liability Rules. *International Review of Law & Economics* 6: 255–63.

Akerlof, George A. 1970. The Market for "Lemons": Quality, Uncertainty and the Market Mechanism. *Quarterly Journal of Economics.* 84: 488–500.

Arrow, Kenneth J. 1963. *Social Choice and Individual Values.* New York: Wiley.

Ayres, Ian and Eric Talley. 1995. Solomonic Bargaining: Dividing a Legal Entitlement to Facilitate Coasean Trade. *Yale Law Journal* 104: 1027-1104.

Bebchuk, Lucian A. 1988. The Sole Owner Standard for Takeover Policy. *Journal of Legal* Studies 17: 197–229.

——— and Marcel Kahan. 1989. Fairness Opinions: How Fair Are They and What Can Be Done About It?. *Duke Law Journal* 1989: 27–53.

Black, Bernard. 1990. Is Corporate Law Trivial?: A Political and Economic Analysis. *Northwestern University Law Review* 84: 542–97.

———. 1992. Agents Watching Agents: The Promise of Institutional Investor Voice. *UCLA Law Review* 39: 811-93.

——— and Coffee, John C., Jr. 1994. Hail Britannia?: Institutional Investor Behavior Under Limited Regulation. *Michigan Law Review.* 92: 1997–2087.

——— and Reinier Kraakman. 1996. A Self Enforcing Model of Corporate Law. *Harvard Law Review* 109: 1911–81.

Calabresi, Guido and A. Douglas Melamed. 1972. Property Rules, Liability Rules, and Inalienability: One View of the Cathedral. *Harvard Law Review* 85: 1089–1128.

Cheffins, Brian R. 1997. *Company Law: Theory, Structure, and Operation.* Oxford: Clarendon Press; New York: Oxford University Press.

Coase, Ronald. 1960. The Problem of Social Cost. *Journal of Law and Economics* 3: 1–44.

Coffee, John C., Jr. 1985. The Unfaithful Champion: The Plaintiff as Monitor in Shareholder Litigation. *Law & Contemporary Problems* 48: 5-72.

———. 1991. Liquidity v. Control: The Institutional Investor as Corporate Monitor. *Columbia Law Review* 91: 1277–1368.

Cooter, Robert. 1982. The Cost of Coase. *Journal of Legal Studies* 11: 1–33.

Davies, Paul L. 1997. *Gower's Principles of Modern Company Law*. London: Sweet & Maxwell.

Easterbrook, Frank H. and Daniel R. Fischel. 1981. The Proper Role of a Target's Management in Responding to a Tender Offer. *Harvard Law Review* 94: 1161–1204.

——. Corporate Control Transactions. *Yale Law Journal* 91: 698–737.

Eisenberg, Melvin A. 1988. Self-Interested Transactions in Corporate Law. *Journal of Corporate Law* 13: 997–1009.

——. 1989. The Structure of Corporation Law. *Columbia Law Review* 89: 1461–1525.

Fama, Eugene E. 1980. Agency Problems and the Theory of the Firm. *Journal of Political Economy* 2: 288–307.

Fischel, Daniel R. 1982. The Corporate Governance Movement. *Vanderbilt Law Review* 35: 1259–92.

Gordon, Jeffrey N. 1989. The Mandatory Structure of Corporate Law. *Columbia Law Review* 89: 1549–98.

Goshen, Zohar. 1995. Shareholder Dividend Options. *Yale Law Journal* 104: 881–932.

——. 1997. Controlling Strategic Voting: Property Rule or Liability Rule? *University of Southern California Law Review* 70: 741–804.

——. 2003. The Efficiency of Controlling Corporate Self-Dealing: Theory Meets Reality. *California Law Review* 91: 393–438.

Haddock, David R., Jonathan R. Macey and Fred S. McChesney. 1987. Property Rights in Assets and Resistance to Tender Offers. *Virginia Law Review* 73: 701–45.

Hermalin, Benjamin E. and Alan Schwartz. 1996. Buyouts in Large Companies. *Journal of Legal Studies* 25: 351–71.

Jensen, Michael C. and William H. Meckling. 1976. Theory of the Firm: Managerial Behavior, Agency Costs and Ownership Structure. *Journal of Financial Economics* 3: 305–60.

Klausner, Michael. 1995. Corporations, Corporate Law, and Networks of Contracts. *Virginia Law Review* 81: 757–852.

La Porta, Rafael, Florencio Lopez-de-Silanes, Andrei Shleifer and Robert W. Vishny. 1997. Legal Determinants of External Finance. *Journal of Finance* 52: 1131–50.

——. 1998. Law and Finance. *Journal of Political Economy* 106: 1113–55.

Leland, Hayne Ellis. 1979. Quacks, Lemons and Licensing: A Theory of Minimum Quality Standards. *Journal of Political Economy*. 87: 1328–46.

Manne, Henry. 1965. Mergers and the Market for Corporate Control. *Journal of Political Economy* 73: 110–20.

Marsh, Harold. 1966. Are Directors Trustees?—Conflicts of Interest and Corporate Morality. *Business Lawyer* 22: 35–76.

Nitzan, Shemuel and Jacob Paroush. 1982. Optimal Decision Rules in Uncertain Dichotomous Choice Situations. *International Economics Review* 23: 289–97.

—— and Uriel Procaccia. 1986. Optimal Voting Procedures for Profit Maximizing Firms. *Public Choice* 51: 191–208.

Pistor, Katharina, Martin Raiser, and Stanislav Gelfer. 2000. Law and Finance in Transition Economies. *EBRD Working Paper No. 49.*

Rock, Edward B. 1994. Controlling the Dark Side of Relational Investing. *Cardozo Law Review* 15: 987–1031.

——. 1997. Saints and Sinners: How Does Delaware Corporate Law Work?. *UCLA Law Review* 44: 1009–83.

Roe, Mark 1993. Some Differences in Corporate Structure: Germany, Japan, and the United States. *Yale Law Journal* 102: 1927–97.

Romano, Roberta 1989. Answering the Wrong Question: The Tenuous Case for Mandatory Corporate Laws. *Columbia Law Review* 89: 1599–1617.

Sen, Amartya. 1973. Behavior and the Concept of Preference. *Economica* 40: 241–59.

Stout, Lynn A. 1988. The Unimportance of Being Efficient: An Economic Analysis of Stock Market Pricing and Securities Regulation. *Michigan Law Review* 87: 613–709.

2 On the Export of U.S.- Style Corporate Fiduciary Duties to Other Cultures

Can a Transplant Take?

Lynn A. Stout

The U.S. system of corporate governance is one of the most highly regarded in the world. In the typical large U.S. firm, equity ownership is separated from control of the corporate enterprise. Instead of being run by shareholders, the firm is governed by a board of directors that hires executives to manage the business on a day-to-day basis. This structure allows millions of passive investors to share in the profits that flow from large-scale enterprise, permits entrepreneurs to raise hundreds of billions of dollars in a thriving public securities market, and efficiently delegates control over trillions of dollars of corporate assets to a cadre of professional managers. The result is an engine of wealth creation that has played a central role in the development of the American economy.

How has passive, dispersed shareownership managed to evolve in the United States? This pattern stands in marked contrast to much of the rest of the world, where public securities markets are relatively undeveloped and where large corporations tend to have a core shareholder or shareholder group (e.g., a family, a bank, or the government) that owns a controlling block of shares and exercises significant influence over the firm's management. A recent series of influential articles by Raphael LaPorta, Florencio Lopez-de-Silanes, Andrei Shleifer and Robert Vishny suggest that the answer may be found in U.S. corporate law (LaPorta et al. 1997; 1998; 1999). In particular, La Porta et al. argue that countries with legal systems rooted in the common law, such as the U.S. and the U.K., offer minority shareholders meaningful protection from opportunistic exploitation by corporate managers and controlling shareholders. As a result, investors in common-law countries are willing to adopt passive investment roles. In contrast, corporations organized under civil codes provide minority shareholders with far less protection, leaving investors relatively distrustful and unwilling to accept noncontrolling positions in such firms. The result, they conclude, is that dispersed shareownership is less likely in civil-code nations. They support their thesis with statistical analyses that find that a large and well-developed public securities market is correlated with a common law legal system.

The possibility that the success of the American public corporation stems from the superiority of U.S. corporate law naturally raises the question whether the adoption of similar legal rules in other countries might produce similar economic benefits.[1] This issue is of special interest to transitional and developing states: it is a tempting prospect to think that, by modifying their rules to more closely approximate U.S.-style corporate law, such nations might spur the process of economic development. At the same time, there seems reason to question how easily one can export the formal legal rules of one nation to another. Commentators have raised concerns about "transplant shock"—the possibility that legal rules that work well in one nation may not work well, and ultimately may be rejected, in a nation with a different historical, political, or cultural background (Berkowitz et al. 2003; Milhaupt 2001: 2097–2102).

This essay explores the problem of transplant shock by focusing on an element of domestic context that has attracted little formal scholarly attention, but that may play an important role in determining the likely success of some types of legal transplants. This element might be labeled *local inclinations toward other-regarding behavior*. Although the meaning of this awkward phrase is explored in greater detail later, as an introductory matter it might be described as a tendency toward *cooperativeness, trustworthiness, concern for others*, or, more broadly, *altruism*.

This essay argues that altruistic behavior may play an essential, if poorly understood, role in the success of the American corporate governance system and the American public corporation.[2] In particular, altruistic behavior helps explain the otherwise-puzzling success of one of the most basic constructs of U.S. corporate law—the concept of fiduciary duty. Although the rules of fiduciary duty *in theory* require corporate officers, directors, and controlling shareholders to refrain from using their power over the firm to benefit themselves at other corporate participants' expense, *in practice* these rules are open-ended standards that are only imperfectly and incompletely enforced by legal sanctions. Nevertheless, we observe a relatively high degree of compliance with fiduciary duty rules by U.S. corporate insiders.[3] This compliance can be understood as a form of altruistic behavior—insiders often opt to "do the right thing," even in the absence of effective external rewards and punishments.

If this hypothesis is correct, a successful transplant of formal U.S. corporate law may depend, to a significant degree, on the extent to which we can expect the local population to exhibit a similar degree of altruistic compliance with fiduciary standards. To shed light on this complex problem, this essay explores some of the experimental evidence that has been compiled on the general phenomenon of altruistic cooperation with others. This evidence indicates that altruism is common, and that some degree of other-regarding behavior can be observed in a wide range of societies and cultures. It also suggests, however, that cultures differ significantly in their overall inclinations toward altruistic behavior.

This possibility hints at some potential obstacles that may be faced in exporting U.S.-style corporate law to different societies. Although there are likely many causes of transplant shock, cross-cultural differences in the incidence and determinants of other-regarding behavior may play an important role, especially in the case of open-ended legal rules, like fiduciary duty rules, that are difficult to enforce through external sanctions. Recognizing this reality can help us avoid some of the pitfalls to be encountered in exporting U.S.-style corporate law to other nations, and perhaps identify ways to increase the odds that a corporate law "transplant" will take.

Focusing on the phenomenon of altruistic behavior may also offer insights into the meaning and influence of the phenomenon that scholars often refer to, perhaps for lack of a more precise word, as "culture." As Licht et al. (2001:1) have recently observed, "the need to take culture into account in comparative corporate governance analysis is now widely acknowledged." But what do we mean by "culture"? And how does it influence behavior, including the behavior of corporate participants? Recent studies exploring these questions have focused on such factors as language and religion (Stulz and Williamson 2002), national crime rates and ethnic homogeneity (Coffee 2001b), or how local populations rank the importance of values like "autonomy" or "equality" in surveys (Licht 2001). Perhaps such variables are important causal factors in their own right. But they also may be proxies for a deeper phenomenon—local tendencies toward other-regarding behavior.

I. On Fiduciary Duties

As noted earlier, U.S.-style corporate law has been praised for offering superior protection to outside investors against insider opportunism. One of
these supposed protections is the concept of fiduciary duty. It is a basic
canon of American corporate law that the directors of the firm, its officers,
and its controlling shareholders all owe the firm fiduciary duties of care and
loyalty. The first sort of duty is said to require directors, officers, and controlling shareholders to act with the care of the "reasonably prudent person." In
other words, the duty of care discourages corporate insiders from behaving
foolishly or negligently.[4] The duty of loyalty supposedly provides further protection for minority investors by punishing managers and controlling shareholders who behave dishonestly. In particular, the duty of loyalty prohibits
insiders from using their influence over the firm to line their own pockets
through "looting" and other types of unfair self-dealing.[5]

At least, that is what fiduciary duties do in theory. In practice, both the
duty of care and the duty of loyalty are rarely enforced through external
sanctions. This is particularly obvious in the case of the duty of care, where
the business judgement rule protects corporate managers from liability for
breach of the duty of care for even the most foolish decisions, provided they
have met the modest procedural requirement of having "informed" themselves before making a decision.[6] In the unlikely event that the business
judgement rule fails to provide complete protection from charges of negligence, U.S. corporate law permits (and corporations generally employ) a
variety of other common arrangements—including D&O liability insurance, indemnification agreements, and charter amendments of the sort
authorized by Delaware Code Section 102(b)(7)—to further reduce the
already negligible risk that corporate directors or officers might ever actually
pay damages for breach of the duty of care.[7]

The case for the toothlessness of the duty of loyalty is more subtle. When
a manager or controlling shareholder steals from the firm by entering an
interested transaction or taking a corporate opportunity, there is some positive probability that a court might someday hold the transgressor liable for
breach of the duty of loyalty (although this probability is significantly
reduced when the transaction is approved by the firm's disinterested directors, who are themselves subject only to a duty of care analysis).[8] What's
more, the sorts of corporate arrangements commonly used to insulate corpo-

rate insiders from liability for breach of the duty of care—indemnification agreements, exculpatory charter provisions, and so forth—are often unavailable in loyalty cases.

Nevertheless, there remains a rather obvious problem, from a rational choice perspective, with relying on the duty of loyalty to deter insider opportunism. This problem is revealed when we consider the nature of the *remedy* imposed in loyalty cases. As a general rule the remedy for a breach of the duty of loyalty is to require the erring insider to return whatever it is of value that she has taken from the firm, either by paying a "fair price" in an unfair self-dealing transaction, or by turning over to the corporation any profits earned by stealing a corporate opportunity.[9] In other words, the remedy for a breach of the duty of loyalty is to *make the insider return what she has stolen.* Given any realistic chance that a loyalty violation might not be detected or punished (and given the cost of monitoring, the squishiness of concepts like "fair," the vagaries of the civil justice system, and availability of offshore banking accounts, there is always such a chance), there are innumerable circumstances where rational and purely self-interested corporate insiders might calculate they can profit from self-dealing.

Common-law rules of fiduciary duty, which on first inspection seem to protect minority shareholders from insider opportunism, look more like legal fig leaves to the informed observer. In theory, corporate insiders who shirk and steal are liable for damages. In practice, damages are rarely imposed, and are usually inadequate in amount when they are.

Of course, corporate officers, directors, and controlling shareholders may sometimes be deterred from behaving opportunistically not only by legal sanctions but also by what might be called "market sanctions"—if a breach of fiduciary duty is detected, they may lose their present positions, and future business and employment opportunities as well. Similarly, legal scholars in recent years have suggested that corporate insiders may also tend to follow fiduciary duty rules out of fear of "social sanctions" that might be imposed by third parties (public expressions of disapproval, social shunning, and so forth) (Rock 1997; Skeel 2001). Perhaps when the possibility of market and social sanctions is added to the rather dim prospect of legal sanctions, breach of fiduciary duty is punished sufficiently in the U.S. to discourage even a rational and purely selfish insider from behaving carelessly or disloyally.

This hypothesis cannot be rejected *a priori.* Yet certain realities of the business world suggest that, in many situations, market sanctions and social sanctions, alone or together, may not have enough deterrent value to keep purely selfish corporate insiders from breaching their duties of loyalty and care. For example, the fear of a tarnished business reputation might well discourage a relatively junior corporate executive in her thirties or forties from shirking, or from trying to reap a personal profit from interested transactions with her firm. However, the typical board Chair or Chief Executive Officer (CEO) is an individual in her late fifties, sixties, or even seventies. As a result, she enjoys control over millions of dollars in corporate assets in an "endgame" situation where the profits that can be reaped from opportunistic behavior may substantially outweigh the value of spending a few more years in her present position.[10]

Similarly, before one assumes that the fear of social sanctions plays an important role in motivating corporate insiders to behave loyally and carefully, one might ask why a purely self-interested person would care about others' opinions so much they would pass up the opportunity to expropriate vast amounts of wealth.[11] One might also ask for evidence that social sanctions actually are applied to individuals who breach their fiduciary duties. Corporate insiders accused of actual crimes, like securities fraud, sometimes suffer notoriety. But a charge of breach of fiduciary duty through negligence or self-dealing seems far less likely to trigger social disapproval, or even much attention. And even in criminal cases, corporate wrongdoers often seem to keep their friends, families, and country club memberships.[12]

A careful analysis consequently gives rise to a suspicion that, in the U.S., external sanctions alone—including not only legal sanctions, but also market and social sanctions—may be inadequate to explain why corporate insiders largely refrain from exploiting minority shareholders. From the perspective of the cold and calculating individual, breach of fiduciary duty often pays.[13] If this hypothesis is correct (and I ask the reader to assume it is, if only for purpose of discussion) an interesting puzzle emerges. If the American corporate governance system encourages corporate insiders to act like careful and loyal fiduciaries, it somehow does so while giving those insiders rather little external incentive to behave carefully and loyally.

How has this system managed to work well enough that it is viewed as a paragon of protection for minority shareholders? The answer may be that U.S. corporate insiders often behave like fiduciaries not because of external constraints, but because of *internal* ones. Elsewhere, Margaret Blair and I have argued at length that in successful firms, corporate participants (including directors, officers, and controlling shareholders) tend to adopt norms of cooperation and legal compliance and follow them, to at least some extent, even when a failure to do so would be unlikely to be punished adequately (Blair and Stout 2001). In lay terms, corporate insiders act like fiduciaries not only because they fear external sanctions, but also because they have internalized a sense of obligation or responsibility toward others, including that abstract other, "the firm and its shareholders."

Space constraints preclude a full review of that argument here. Suffice it to say that if this hypothesis is true, perhaps the American corporation can trace its success not only to American corporate law, but also to the Americans themselves.

II. On Other-Regarding Behavior

More than a century ago, Alexis de Tocqueville offered the following insight into American social life:

> The Americans . . . are fond of explaining almost all the actions of their lives by the principle of self-interest rightly understood; they show with complacency how an enlightened regard for themselves constantly prompts them to assist one another and inclines them willingly to sacrifice a portion of their time and property to the welfare of the state. In this respect I think they frequently fail to do themselves justice . . . (de Tocqueville 1834: Book II, Chapter 8).

Whether or not de Tocqueville's observations were accurate in the nineteenth century, there is much evidence that they are accurate today.[14] Americans frequently behave in a cooperative, altruistic fashion toward each other, and frequently sacrifice their own interests to serve broader social goals. Although they may believe their other-regarding behavior is driven by self-interest, an external observer could conclude otherwise. Americans frequently incur costs themselves in order to help others. In the language of rational choice, Americans display *other-regarding revealed preferences*.

To the reader who has studied economics, my use of the adjective "revealed" to modify the noun "preferences" is an immediate clue that I am not discussing people's subjective motivations, desires, or yearnings. Rather, I am discussing how they actually behave. The fact that people often *act* as if they want to help others does not prove that they experience *feelings* of altruism. One can hypothesize any number of motivations that might lead a rational individual to conclude that she will feel better off, subjectively, if she sacrifices to benefit someone else. People may sacrifice for others to avoid the pangs of guilt, to experience the pleasure of feeling good about themselves, or because they hold a religious belief that they will receive a reward in the sweet hereafter. The point is that such motivations and incentives for apparent altruism are internal. From an external perspective, self-sacrifice makes the sacrificing party worse off. Hence self-sacrificing behavior "reveals a preference" for helping others, instead of a preference for helping only oneself.

Extensive empirical evidence documents that most Americans do, in fact, reveal other-regarding preferences, and on a regular and predictable basis. The literature on altruistic behavior is vast (see, e.g., Fukayama 1995; Sober and Wilson 1998; Tyler 1990; Mansbridge 1990), and I will not attempt a general survey here. Rather, I will focus on an especially compelling, persuasive, and useful subset of that evidence. This is the empirical evidence that can be found in over four decades of published studies on human behavior in a type of experimental game known as a "social dilemma."[15]

Social dilemmas are experiments intentionally designed to ensure that each experimental subject's self-interest conflicts with the interests of the other subjects. A typical example is the "Give Something Game."[16] In the Give Something Game, a group of n subjects is provided with an initial monetary stake. Subjects are then told that they can choose one of two strategies for playing the game. The first strategy is simply to keep their stake for themselves. In the parlance of experimental gaming, this is called "defecting." The second strategy is to donate some or all of their stake to a common investment pool. This is called "cooperating." Subjects are instructed that any money donated into the pool will be multiplied by some factor of $(n-1)$ or less, and redistributed among the players. But—here's the catch—the money in the pool will be distributed among the players *pro rata* whether they chose to contribute or not.

As an example, consider a Give Something Game with four players who are each given $10 and told that any money donated into the common pool will be doubled and distributed *pro rata*. Consider for a moment how a purely selfish actor like *Homo economicus* would play this game. The answer is obvious—a purely selfish player would always choose to defect and keep her $10, hoping to benefit as well from any money other players might be foolish enough to donate to the common pool. If all the players do this, each leaves with only $10. If all cooperate, each leaves with $20. If three out of four cooperate and the fourth defects, the three cooperators leave with $15 and the defector leaves with $25.

A social dilemma game like the Give Something Game thus creates a payoff structure similar to the familiar Prisoners' Dilemma of game theory. The best group outcome requires all the players to cooperate. Unfortunately, no matter what the other players do, each individual player always maximizes her own payoffs by choosing to defect. Thus cooperation is an altruistic act that benefits others, while simultaneously imposing a cost on the cooperating player.

What do real people do in social dilemmas? At this point, social scientists have published the results of hundreds of studies, run over a period of nearly half a century, in which U.S. subjects have been asked to play social dilemma games (Dawes 1980; Dawes and Thaler 1988; Dawes et al. 1990; Sally 1995). The behavior described in these studies is remarkably consistent. On average, U.S. *subjects contribute approximately 50 percent of their initial stake in a social dilemma game* (Dawes and Thaler 1988: 89; Sally 1995: 62).

It is important to emphasize that this result is observed even when experimenters go to great lengths to ensure that the subjects in the game understand that they will receive no extrinsic reward or recognition for cooperating. For example, many social dilemma experiments involve games played by strangers who are told that they will play only once, and who are assured that their choice of strategy will not be revealed to either the experimenter or their fellow players. (This structure eliminates any possibility of social disapproval or vengeful "tit for tat") (Sally 1995: 65, 67). Moreover, experimenters in a number of studies have "debriefed" their subjects after play to determine whether they understood the payoff function in the game. They have found that subjects do, in fact, understand that cooperation reduces their own payoffs (i.e., cooperation is an altruistic act) (Sally 1995: 70). Again, this finding does not amount to proof of *psychological* altruism, meaning that people truly care about others' welfare. But it does provide persuasive evidence of *behavioral* altruism—whether or not people care about others, they often *behave as if they do*.

III. On Other-Regarding Revealed Preferences and Fiduciary Duties

What does this have to do with U.S. corporate law? To understand the strength of the connection between corporate governance and other-regarding behavior, let us return again to the concept of fiduciary duty, and particularly the example of the fiduciary duty of loyalty. The keystone of the duty of loyalty is the legal obligation that the fiduciary use her powers not for her own benefit but for the exclusive benefit of her beneficiary. It is highly improper—indeed proscribed—for a fiduciary to extract a personal benefit from her fiduciary position without her beneficiary's consent, even when she can do this without harming the beneficiary (Blair and Stout 2001: 1782–83).

The duty of loyalty thus can be described *as a legal exhortation that a fiduciary reveal an other-regarding preference function* (ibid.: 1783). Regardless of their own subjective motivations and desires, fiduciary law commands fiduciaries to act *as if* they want to improve their beneficiaries' welfare, and are indifferent to their own. This insight sheds light on the rhetoric courts often apply in duty of loyalty case. Consider the oft-cited chestnut from Judge Cardozo's opinion in *Meinhard v. Salmon*:

> Many forms of conduct permissible in a work a day world for those acting at arms length, are forbidden to those bound by fiduciary ties. A trustee is held to something stricter than the morals of the marketplace. Not honestly alone, but the punctilio of an honor the most sensitive, is then the standard of behavior. . . . *Salmon had put himself in a position in which thought of self was to be renounced, however hard the abnegation.*[17]

From a rational choice perspective, Cardozo's claim that Salmon as a fiduciary ought to have "renounced" all "thought of self" makes no sense. *Homo economicus* cannot do so. Self is all that interests her, all that motivates her.[18] The rational choice model consequently implies that if we want someone to behave like a fiduciary, the best we can do is to try to harness her self-interest by designing compensation and liability rules (carrots and sticks) that will lead her to conclude that any decision that benefits her beneficiary necessarily benefits herself, and any decision that harms her beneficiary necessarily harms herself. Without such external incentives, there is no reason for a purely self-interested actor to behave like a loyal and careful fiduciary.

Yet as we have already seen, there is reason to suspect that U.S. corporate law does not (and perhaps cannot) provide the fine-tuned incentives that would motivate purely selfish corporate insiders to do a good job of serving the interests of the firm and its outside shareholders.[19] Market sanctions and social sanctions may only begin to fill the gap. Despite this worrisome possibility, we nevertheless expect corporate officers, directors, and controlling shareholders to behave like other-regarding fiduciaries. What's more, corporate insiders for the most part seem to behave this way, at least often enough that U.S. corporate law is regarded as providing superior minority shareholder protection. Somehow, insiders have managed—at least to some extent—to internalize "norms" of cooperation and trustworthiness that prompt them to behave in an other-regarding fashion (that is, to confer benefits on or refrain from imposing costs on others, even when this requires some degree of self-sacrifice). This is not to say that corporate insiders in the U.S. never shirk or steal. The point is that they do not seem to shirk or steal nearly as much as they might.

This kind of cooperative effort and self-restraint can be described as a form of altruistic behavior. Corporate insiders who work harder than they must, and refrain from stealing when they might, are behaving in an other-regarding fashion, even though the "other" in this case may be an abstract group like "the shareholders," or even an abstract ideal like "do the right thing." The result of such seemingly irrational self-restraint and cooperation is a thriving corporate sector that generates wealth for directors, officers, and shareholders alike. In other words, American business life may resemble a social dilemma experiment, and the behavior we observe in business may often resemble the behavior we observe in social dilemmas. At the level of the individual, altruism is irrational. At the level of the group, it is highly advantageous.

If this thesis is true, it immediately raises the question of whether the patterns of self-sacrificing, cooperative behavior observed in American public corporations (and American social dilemma games) can be expected to be found outside our borders. A recently published study hints at some interesting possible answers.

IV. On Other-Regarding Behavior Abroad

As noted above, an extensive body of literature documents how subjects behave in social dilemma games. This literature, however, is limited in that it is composed almost entirely of studies of U.S. subjects, usually university students. As a result it remains something of an open question whether the other-regarding behavior observed in U.S. social dilemma experiments is representative of human behavior generally, or whether it departs significantly from what we would find elsewhere. Would cross-cultural study find significant differences in other-regarding behavior?

Until recently, very little direct evidence could be brought to bear on this question. In May of 2001, however, a study was published in the *American Economic Review* by a collaboration of prominent business, economics, and anthropology scholars (Henrich et al. 2001). These researchers conducted a cross-cultural study in which they arranged for subjects from fifteen small societies scattered across the globe to participate in a variety of experimental games. The cultures tested ranged from foraging groups, to nomadic herders, to agricultural communities.[20] Most experiments were structured so that the subjects played anonymously, for stakes that approximated a day or two's wages in the local economy. Experienced field researchers recruited the subjects, tested them to ensure that they understood the nature of the game they were playing, and eliminated players who did not appear to grasp the game (ibid.: 74).

Social dilemma games were among the games studied. In particular, Henrich et al. arranged for social dilemma games to be played by subjects drawn from seven of the fifteen cultures studied. They reported two very interesting general results.

First, altruism appears to be a widespread, and indeed possibly universal, behavioral phenomenon. In each of the seven societies in which social dilemma games were administered, cooperation rates were significantly above the null hypothesis of zero. The researchers also administered another game designed to test for other-regarding behavior, known as the "ultimatum game," in each of the fifteen societies studied, and observed other-regarding behavior in each. In their own words, the authors concluded that "the canonical model (of self-interested behavior) is not supported in any society studied" (ibid.: 73).

A second important general finding of the study, however, was that while none of the cultures conformed to the neoclassical model of rational selfishness, they nonetheless showed significant differences in the incidence of altruistic behavior. For example, cooperation rates in social dilemma games ranged from a low of 22 percent among the Machiguenga of the Peruvian rainforest, to a high of 58 percent among the cattle-herding Orma of Kenya (ibid.: 75–76). In ultimatum games, the researchers observed similar and parallel differences between cultures in the incidence of other-regarding behavior.[21]

It is of course risky to reach conclusions about cross cultural differences based on a single study, no matter how carefully done. It is to be hoped that social scientists will undertake more studies of this sort. In the meantime, however, these results strongly suggest (1) that other-regarding behavior can be observed in other cultures, and (2) that the incidence of such behavior varies from culture to culture.

Such findings undermine the prospect that we can transplant U.S. corporate law rules to other nations and, without more, produce the relatively cooperative and other-regarding behavior we see among corporate participants in the U.S. This is not to say that a low incidence of cooperation in social dilemma games among a particular population necessarily implies a low incidence of compliance with fiduciary duty rules. Perhaps the Machiguena, who are relatively ruthless in social dilemma and ultimatum games, would behave like model citizens in the corporate context. Similarly, if the Orma of Kenya were installed in corporate headquarters, they might act in such a shamelessly self-interested fashion as to make Gordon Gekko blush. But evidence of cross-cultural differences in altruistic behavior in experimental games suggests just that—cross-cultural differences do exist.

Which leads to the question, what is their source? Why do some populations tend to cooperate more in social dilemma games while other populations cooperate less? If we can understand why some populations cooperate more than others in social dilemma games, we may be able to gain a better understanding of the sorts of societies in which corporate participants might comply voluntarily with open-ended fiduciary duty rules even when these cannot be well enforced. Put differently, we may be able to better distinguish cultures which are likely to accept a transplant of U.S. corporate law, from cultures which are likely to reject it. This might allow would-be reformers to avoid some costly mistakes.

In addition, if we can identify the determinants of altruistic behavior, these may prove to be variables policymakers can influence or change. This raises the hopeful prospect that a society that otherwise might be prone to reject a transplant of other-regarding fiduciary duty rules might be transformed into a society in which cooperative compliance with such rules becomes more likely.

V. On Some Causes of Other-Regarding Behavior

Thus there is much to be gained from identifying the causes of other-regarding behavior. The balance of this essay is devoted to considering this question, as well as some of the policy implications that flow from different theories of causation. My remarks are necessarily speculative and preliminary, as no predominant theory of the cause of altruism has emerged in the literature, and one is unlikely to emerge until after much further study. Nevertheless, the limited evidence available suggests at least three possible sources of the behavioral variations experimenters observe in social dilemma experiments: (1) genetic differences ("nature"); (2) past environment ("nurture"); and (3) present social environment (or, perhaps, "culture").

A. *Nature*

Let us first consider the possibility that cross cultural differences in altruistic behavior have a biological basis. In particular, let us consider the possibility that cooperative behavior has its origins in an important subcategory of biological causes—genetics.[22]

A significant body of evidence supports the claim that altruism is "genetic" in the sense that evolutionary pressures have caused *Homo sapiens*, like many other social species, to develop a capacity for behavior that decreases evolutionary fitness at the individual level while increasing the evolutionary fitness of the group.[23] The more interesting question, however, is whether this capacity for altruism is uniform in the population (almost everyone has a genetic capacity for other-regarding behavior, just as almost everyone has two legs), or whether we can expect to see significant differences among individuals in genetic predisposition to cooperate (some people are predisposed to cooperate while others are predisposed to defect, just as some people have light eyes and others have dark eyes).

As an empirical matter, it should be noted that there is considerable formal (not to mention informal) evidence to suggest that individuals vary considerably in their predispositions to cooperate. As an example, consider the finding that U.S. subjects who play social dilemma games with strangers contribute, on average, about half their initial stake. This average turns out to be a blend of two modes of behavior: many subjects contribute their entire stakes, while many others contribute nothing.[24] Thus U.S. subjects tend to divide into two camps, those who contribute everything and those who freeride on the contributors' efforts.

Could such choices have a genetic origin? One can easily imagine a "cooperator" gene that causes individuals who carry the gene to be predisposed to altruistic cooperation, while individuals who lack this gene are pre-disposed to selfishly defect. Although this hypothetical example of genetic influence is so grossly oversimplified it would make a geneticist wince,[25] I nevertheless offer it (with due apologies to the field of genetics) to illustrate a simple point: some of the differences we observe in other-regarding behavior among individuals may be inherited.

What are the implications of this hypothesis for comparative corporate law? Pessimistic, one can argue, because it raises the possibility that cross-cultural behavioral differences in altruistic behavior reflect differences in gene pools (e.g., the proportion of genetic "cooperators" found in the local population).[26] If this is true, and if the success of the U.S. corporate governance system depends on altruistic compliance with underenforced rules, it seems plausible that U.S. law will not work well in societies where the population has little or no genetic predisposition toward altruism.[27] Moreover, because population genetics change slowly over periods of generations, this is likely to remain true for the foreseeable future.

B. Nurture

Given the pessimistic implications of a genetic explanation for other-regarding behavior, it is perhaps good news that, while a genetic cause cannot be excluded, considerable empirical evidence suggests that nature is not the only or even the most significant factor in determining the incidence of altruistic behavior. Nurture may matter more.

Consider an interesting result that has been frequently observed in social dilemma games played among university students in the U.S.: economics majors cooperate, on average, far less than non-majors (Sally 1995: 62–63). A famous example can be found in an early study by Marwell and Ames (1981: 306–7), reporting the results of a series of social dilemma games in which cooperation rates averaged between 40 and 60 percent. There was, however, a notable exception to this pattern. In a series of games played by economics graduate students, the cooperation rate averaged only 20 percent. Put differently, economics graduate students seem even less coopera-tive than the Machiguenga.

Why do economics majors cooperate so much less than other students? At least two explanations come to mind. First, something about the study of economics may attract individuals who are predisposed to behave self-interestedly. (One can see how the study of *Homo economicus* might especially appeal to *Homo economicus* himself). Thus the low rates of cooperation observed among economics majors playing social dilemmas stems from selection bias: defectors are more likely to study economics than cooperators.

The second possibility is that economics majors begin their studies just as cooperative as the next person. However, something about the process of studying economics changes their behavior compared to their peers', decreasing their relative willingness to behave altruistically. Put differently, economics courses somehow turn cooperators into defectors.[28] Although there are a number of mechanisms by which environment can influence behavior, in the case of an intelligent and speaking species like *Homo sapiens*, one of the more significant influences may be one's own past experiences and the experiences described by others. In lay terms, cooperation and defection may be learned behavior.

A decade after Marwell and Ames published their results, Frank et al. (1993) set out to shed further light on the question of why economics majors cooperate less than nonmajors. They administered a series of social dilemma games to university students at varying stages in their educational careers. They found that while both economics majors and nonmajors began their undergraduate studies equally willing to cooperate, over time economics majors' cooperation rates stayed stable. Meanwhile, the cooperation rates of other students *increased*. This result suggests both that cooperation may be learned (undergraduates become more altruistic with each year of study), and that studying economics somehow interferes with this learning process.[29] The bottom line, Frank et al. concluded, was that the differences in cooperativeness they observed between economics majors and nonmajors "are caused in part by training in economics" (ibid.: 170).

If a predisposition to cooperate with strangers is indeed caused largely by environmental factors, and particularly if it is a learned behavior, it will be acquired only under favorable conditions. Those conditions may include explicit lessons about the value of altruistic cooperation that are taught by authorities such as parents, teachers, and religious leaders. (Conversely, behavior may also be influenced by explicit lessons concerning the virtues of self-interest. Almost every introductory economics course at some point recites Adam Smith's parable of the invisible hand, and one wonders if economic students are taking such sermons too much to heart.) They may also include the implicit lessons of one's own experience in past social interactions. As the social dilemma game illustrates, "irrational" cooperation often produces a better outcome for a group and its members than "rational" defection does. Individuals who frequently participate in cooperative group activities may learn habits of cooperation that make them more likely to cooperate with strangers in novel situations as well.

This hypothesis was indirectly tested by Henrich et al. (2001: 75–76) in their comparative study of cooperative behavior in fifteen small societies. To help identify the determinants of other-regarding behavior, the authors regressed the cooperation rates they observed in experimental games on a variety of individual subject characteristics, including age, sex, and relative wealth. But they also regressed their findings on two group variables. The first group variable was a rank-order measure of the importance of cooperation to daily economic production in the society studied. For example, Lamelara whale-hunters rank high on this scale,[30] while the Machiguenga, who are economically independent at the family level, rank low. The second group variable was a rank order of market integration, meaning how frequently people participated in market exchanges with strangers. The more frequently subjects participated in markets, the higher the ranking.

The results of the regression revealed that these two group variables predicted *nearly 70 percent* of the variance observed in the subjects' cooperative behavior. In contrast, the individual variables of age, sex, and relative wealth were not statistically significant (ibid.: 76). This finding indicates that altruistic cooperation in experimental games is highly correlated with past social patterns. People who have often cooperated with others in their daily economic lives are more likely to cooperate with strangers in an experimental game as well.

What are the implications for comparative corporate governance? They are at least a bit more optimistic than the implications of a genetic explanation for differences in altruism. How much more optimistic depends, in large part, on how easily and how quickly a predisposition for cooperation or defection can be acquired. If the learning process is quick, it seems possible that a society in which altruistic cooperation with strangers is uncommon might be shifted relatively easily toward cooperation (the emphasis here is on "relatively") simply by exposing the populace to new situations in which cooperation proves beneficial.[31] If, on the other hand, the learning process is slow and incremental—if cooperation and defection are habits that tend to last a lifetime—we again are likely to be faced with situations where a transplant of open-ended fiduciary duty rules to a society where other-regarding behavior toward strangers is uncommon is unlikely to significantly change behavior. The best we can hope for is to avoid such mistakes.

C. Culture

So far, the discussion has been cast in terms of a tension between nature (genetics) and nurture (learning) as potential explanations for differences in cooperative behavior among individuals and societies. This is well-known terrain, and many intellectual battles have been fought over it, including battles over the source of differences in intelligence, criminality, and so forth.[32] But to understand the causes of altruistic behavior we may need to explore less familiar territory as well. In addition to nature and nurture, there is a third and more subtle possible source of differences in altruistic behavior that merits consideration. This third source might be described generally as *present environment* (to distinguish it from past environment, which influences learning). More particularly, it might be called *present social context*. As will be seen, this concept may come as close as any to capturing what most people mean when they refer to "culture."

To understand how present social context (as opposed to basic personality, whether innate or acquired) may influence cooperative behavior, let us return to the finding that U.S. subjects exhibit an average 40 percent to 60 percent cooperation rate in social dilemma games. This average obscures the fact that subjects' behavior in social dilemmas can easily be changed. In particular, experimenters can increase or decrease cooperation rates dramatically by manipulating certain variables. This effect is so strong that studies have reported cooperation rates among U.S. subjects as low as 5 percent and as high as 95 percent (Sally 1995: 62, 71). It is important to bear in mind that in *all* of these studies, payoffs were structured so that a rationally selfish player would choose to defect. Nevertheless, in some cases virtually all the subjects chose cooperation, while in others almost all defected.

Such results cut against the notion that individuals tend, whether by nature or nurture, to divide into permanently fixed personality types (e.g., "cooperators" and "defectors"). True, different individuals seem more or less predisposed to cooperate in a social dilemma situation.[33] But at least in the U.S., almost everyone—even economics majors!—seems capable of other-regarding behavior, in the right circumstances. Similarly, almost everyone seems capable of behaving selfishly, in the right circumstances.

What are "the right circumstances"? Why would the same person cooperate in one social dilemma game, and defect in another? At this point, the evidence strongly indicates that cooperation rates in social dilemmas are largely determined by *social context*.[34] Put differently, cooperation rates are largely determined by experimental subjects' perceptions of *other people*, including such matters as: the subjects' beliefs about what other people expect; the subjects' beliefs about what other people want; the subjects' beliefs about what other people's payoffs will be; and the subjects' beliefs about how other people are likely to behave.[35] *Homo economicus* would be utterly indifferent to such matters unless they changed his own payoffs. *Homo sapiens* seems keenly interested in them.

As an example, let us consider a social variable that has proven highly significant, in a statistical sense, in determining cooperation rates. This variable is the experimenter's requests. Put simply, subjects in social dilemma games tend to do what an experimenter asks them to do. If the experimenter asks them to cooperate, they cooperate; if the experimenter suggests they defect, they defect (Sally 1995: 78). A purely selfish person would ignore such requests, because they do not change the fact that defecting offers superior payoffs. Nevertheless, we see large changes in behavior in response to mere intimations about the experimenter's desires. In one experiment, for example, researchers presented subjects with a social dilemma game they called the "Community Game," and observed a cooperation rate of approximately 70 percent. They then presented similar subjects with the same game, but called it the "Wall Street Game." The cooperation rate dropped to 33 percent (Ross and Ward 1996: 106–7).

A variety of other social variables have proven similarly important in determining cooperation rates among U.S. subjects in social dilemmas. Examples include a subject's perception of how much her cooperation will benefit others (the greater the benefit to others, the greater the likelihood of altruistic cooperation) (Sally 1995: 79); whether the subject feels a sense of common social identity with the other players (subjects randomly divided into subgroups cooperate more with members of their own "in-group" than with members of their "out-group") (ibid.: 78–79); and whether a subject expects her fellow players to cooperate or defect (if a player believes her fellow players will "play nice," she is far more likely to "play nice" herself) (Dawes 1980: 187). Again, none of these matters would interest a purely selfish person. Nevertheless, each significantly influences the incidence of cooperative behavior.

Such findings paint something of a Jekyll-and-Hyde portrait of human nature. Most people appear to have at least two distinct personalities. One is cooperative and other-regarding; the other purely selfish. Which personality emerges in a particular situation is heavily influenced not only by predisposition (whether a product of nature or nurture) but also by social context—

our perceptions of the needs, expectations, identities, and likely behavior of those around us.

V. On Fiduciary Duties, Again

These observations offer some useful lessons about how we might best go about exporting the notion of fiduciary duty to other nations. One of these lessons is that, even in a society where other-regarding behavior is common, corporate insiders will be unlikely to behave like fiduciaries if the local social context does not support such altruistic behavior.

As an example, let us return to the finding that U.S. subjects are highly responsive to experimenters' requests in social dilemma games. This finding suggests that, if we want to encourage individuals to follow imperfectly enforced corporate law fiduciary duty rules, it might be extremely useful to find some person or organization that has the sort of authority enjoyed by the experimenter in a social dilemma game, both to "instruct" them that they ought to behave in an other-regarding fashion, and to explain exactly which "other" they ought to be serving.[36] Interestingly, a number of corporate theorists have suggested that this is the role played by the Delaware Chancery and Delaware Supreme Court, whose judicial opinions encourage corporate insiders to serve the interests of the firm and its shareholders not primarily by threatening them with the prospect of personal liability, but by offering "sermons" on the proper deportment of corporate officers, directors, and controlling shareholders.[37] Similarly, a legal transplant of U.S.-style fiduciary duty rules to another culture may be more likely to "take" if we can enlist the help of a respected local authority—which might, or might not, be a court—to perform a similar sermonizing function.

The possibility that social context is an important determinant of altruistic behavior also sheds a more optimistic light on the question of whether one can successfully transplant open-ended fiduciary duty rules to cultures in which altruistic behavior is relatively rare. This is because, so long as other-regarding behavior is not completely lacking in a particular society (and even the Machiguenga have a positive cooperation rate in social dilemmas), we can hold out hope that altruistic compliance with fiduciary duty rules can be encouraged by identifying and providing the right sorts of social signals. If we can identify the social conditions that trigger cooperative behavior in a particular culture—even a culture where cooperation is rare—

and replicate those conditions in the corporate arena, we may be able to increase the odds of a successful transplant.

Heinrich et al. offered a similar speculation:

> A plausible interpretation of our subjects' behaviors is that, when faced with a novel situation (the experiment), they look for analogues in their daily experience, asking "What familiar situation is this game like?" and then act in a way appropriate for the analogous situation. . . .
>
> The Machiguenga show the lowest cooperation rates in public-good games, reflecting ethnographic descriptions of Machiguenga life, which report little cooperation, exchange, or sharing beyond the family unit. By contrast, Orma experimental subjects quickly dubbed the public-goods experiment a *harambee* game, referring to the widespread institution of village-level voluntary contributions for public-goods projects such as schools or roads. Not surprisingly, they contributed generously (58 percent of the stake), somewhat higher than most U.S. subjects contribute in similar experiments (Henrich et al. 2001: 76).

It should be noted, however, that this analysis suggests there are at least two components to what we call "culture." The first is the objective signals that the members of a particular society receive about what others expect, how others are likely to benefit, and how others are likely to behave in a particular situation. The second component is how members of a particular society *subjectively interpret* those signals in light of their past experience. Henrich et al. followed identical protocols with their experimental subjects. Nevertheless, the Machiguenga, accustomed to competing with strangers, viewed the social dilemma game as a competitive game, while the Orma interpreted an identical situation as a cooperative *harambee* game. Nurture enters the picture again, not a source of differences in basic personality (we all have at least two, a cooperative personality and a competitive personality), but as a source of differences in whether a particular social situation is perceived as calling for our altruistic personality.[38]

This hypothesis—that social context can trigger cooperative behavior, and that perceptions of social context are influenced both by the objective signals we receive and the way in which we subjectively interpret those signals—carries both positive and negative implications for our ability to successfully transplant open-ended, U.S.-style fiduciary duty rules to other cultures. The good news is that, in theory, it may be possible in a very broad range of societies to structure local social context in a way that supports altruistic behavior, including altruistic compliance with underenforced fiduciary duty rules. The key is to find the local equivalent of the *harambee* game, and to persuade the populace that corporate relationships are analogous.

The bad news is that, in practice, it often may be extremely difficult to figure out exactly how to go about this. As Henrich et al. suggest, in some societies there may be only a very few cooperative social institutions we can analogize to, none of which looks much like a modern corporation. What's more, it may be very difficult for an outside observer to recognize truly cooperative institutions.[39] Thus one of the most important lessons to be learned from social dilemma studies may be that the answer to the question whether a legal transplant will "take" is something that must often lie beyond the provenance of the armchair theorist. This category includes, sadly, the armchair legal theorist, the armchair rational choice theorist, and the armchair development theorist.[40] Lawyers, economists, and World Bank analysts, whether working alone or working together, may rarely be able to determine reliably whether and under what circumstances a transplant of U.S. legal rules to another culture is likely to be rejected. If we want to gauge the odds of a successful transplant—or better yet, increase those odds—we must enlist the aid of anthropologists, sociologists, historians, and political scientists as well.

Conclusion

The success of the U.S. business firm has sparked great interest in the question of whether and to what extent we can transplant U.S.-style corporate law to other nations. This essay argues that to understand the difficulties involved, we must first understand that a key component of U.S. corporate law—the concept of fiduciary duty—is an open-ended standard of behavior that cannot be perfectly enforced or even well enforced. Nevertheless, U.S. corporate law seems to mostly work in the United States. The essay posits that one of the reasons this is true is that American corporate insiders tend to "internalize" fiduciary duty rules, and altruistically comply with them even when noncompliance would produce greater extrinsic rewards.

If this hypothesis is true, it suggests that an export of formal U.S. legal rules beyond our shores is unlikely to succeed unless the citizens of the importing nation adopt a similar pattern of altruistic compliance. Unfortunately, the available evidence suggests that there may be significant cross-cultural differences in the incidence of such altruistic behavior. Although we do not yet fully understand the sources of such differences, some of the more obvious possibilities include nature, nurture, and social context (culture). Which source is most significant matters, because depending on the source and determinants of altruism, the task of successfully exporting U.S. corporate law may range from merely difficult, to impossible.

Much work remains to be done before we will know which adjective applies. In the meantime, however, there is much we can take of value from the preliminary evidence available. Perhaps the most basic lesson is that the adoption of formal rules of law that resemble U.S. corporate law may not, alone, be sufficient to produce results similar to those observed in U.S. corporations.[41] Human behavior can, of course, be influenced by government-imposed sanctions: most of us are willing to slow down to avoid a speeding ticket. Thus the fact that U.S. courts do sometimes impose liability on corporate insiders for breach of fiduciary may play an important role in explaining the relative success of the U.S. corporate governance system. But law is not the only means of regulating behavior. Behavior is also influenced by market prices, by technological developments that make new things possible and, as argued here, by social conditions that promote cooperative vis-à-vis self-regarding patterns of behavior. Thus corporate insiders may refrain from exploiting minority shareholders because they fear they will be held liable in a derivative suit, because they fear a hostile tender offer, because improved accounting standards make their exploitation too observable, or because they simply feel "it would be wrong." To understand why good corporate governance systems work and why bad ones fail, each of these mechanisms must be taken into account.

Endnotes

Earlier versions of this essay were presented in October of 2001 and April of 2002 at conferences sponsored by the Columbia Law School and the Center for International Political Economy, and I would like to thank the participants for their helpful comments and questions. I am also indebted to Stephen Bainbridge, Stuart Banner, Margaret Blair, Ronald Gilson, Jeff Gordon, Bill Klein, Reinier Kraakman, John Langlois, Lynn Lopucki, Curtis Milhaupt, and Mark Roe for their insights and suggestions.

1. This possibility also lies at the heart of a heated debate among modern corporate scholars over whether different nations' corporate laws can be expected to converge over time toward a single, uniform model. According to one group of prominent scholars—the "convergence school"—dispersed share ownership and delegation to professional managers offers such efficiency advantages that, in an increasingly competitive global economy, U.S.-style corporations and corporate law eventually must triumph over other corporate forms, such as majority shareholder-dominated firms or state-run enterprises, in the Darwinian struggle for corporate survival. Perhaps the strongest contemporary statement of this thesis can be found in a recent article by Hansmann and Kraakman (2001). They argue that "as equity markets evolve in Europe and throughout the developed world . . . convergence in most aspects of the law and practice of corporate governance is sure to follow" (ibid.: 468).

    The convergence thesis has been challenged by an opposing school of scholars who argue that because corporations are institutions deeply rooted in their local political and social contexts, corporate governance is "path-dependent"—starting from different points, different nations have evolved different corporate laws and corporate governance patterns (Bebchuk and Roe 1999; Milhaupt 1996; Licht 2001; Roe 2000).

    It should be noted that the argument that corporate law is path-dependent does not necessarily imply that different nations cannot achieve good results, or even functionally similar results, through different institutions. For example, Coffee has suggested that "wholesale transplantation of common-law rules is not necessary" for dispersed shareownership to develop in other nations as other institutions, especially stock exchanges, "can potentially provide functional substitutes" (Coffee 2001a:11).

2. The possibility of altruistic behavior is notably missing from most contemporary analyses of corporate governance, which generally assume that corporations are peopled by *homo economicus*—purely selfish actors unburdened by moral constraints or concern for others. Nevertheless, there is reason to believe that other-regarding behavior may play a central role in successful corporate governance (Blair and Stout 2001).

3. See Black and Kraakman (1996: 1928–29): "Few American corporate managers doubt that they work for the shareholders" and "most managers in developed countries routinely follow laws of all kinds and think of themselves as law-abiding." See also Tyler and Blader (2002: 4), reporting results of empirical study concluding that "social motivations," including concerns for ethics and justice, were important determinants of rule-following behavior in two large U.S. financial firms.

4. See generally Clark (1986: 123–40) for a description of the duty of care.

5. See generally ibid.: 41–157 for a description of the duty of loyalty.

6. See generally Stout (2002) for a discussion of the insulating effect of the business judgment rule.

7. Del. Code Ann., tit. 8, § 102(b)(7); see Clark (1986: 664–74) for a discussion of indemnity and insurance.

8. Del. Code Ann., tit. 8, §144(a)(1).

9. Clark (1986: 175, 224).

10. For example, although Kenneth L. Lay was pressured to resign at age 59 from his position as Chairman and CEO of Enron in the wake of allegations of fraud and mismanagement, he made more than $100 million from the sale of Enron shares the year before he resigned (Norris and Barboza 2002).

11. For a further discussion and critique of the social sanctions argument, see Blair and Stout (2001:1795–96) and Stout (2002: 682).

12. For example, perhaps the highest-profile securities fraud case of the late twentieth century was the case against Michael Milken, who eventually served 22 months in jail. Today Michael Milken has a personal fortune of nearly one billion dollars and is a sought-after speaker, author, and philanthropist (Cohn 2000).

13. See Byrne et al. (2002: 70), observing a sense that "no matter how serious their failure or how imperiled the corporation, those in charge seem always to walk away vastly enriched, while employees and shareholders are left to suffer the consequences of the top managers' ineptitude or malfeasance," and France (2002: 33), noting that "[e]xecutives almost never go to jail for cheating shareholders . . . [and they] rarely . . . face financial penalties."

14. There is an extensive literature on altruistic behavior and its role in social organization. For some useful introductions, see Fukayama (1995) for a discussion of the role of cooperative behavior in economic development; Sober and Wilson (1998) on evolutionary and cognitive theories of altruism; Tyler (1990) on the importance of willing compliance with and internalization of legal rules; and Mansbridge (1990) on the general nature and importance of altruism.

15. Much of the literature on altruism is theoretical or anecdotal in nature, or presents the results of idiosyncratic studies that have not been replicated. However, the social dilemma literature is both extremely well-developed and empirically grounded, and so I have focused on that literature here. It should be noted that the social dilemma results are consistent with the broader literature.

16. As a hint of the relevance of this type of experiment to business behavior, it is perhaps worth noting that the Give Something Game is also sometimes called the "Investment Game."

17. 163 N.E. 545, 546–48 (N.Y. 1928) (Emphasis added).

18. In theory, one can modify rational choice theory to take account of the possibility that people have altruistic preferences (get pleasure from helping others). In practice, most rational choice analysis and most corporate governance dis-

cussions implicitly assume that corporate insiders and other individuals care only about their own welfare, narrowly defined.

19. In addition to using fiduciary duty rules to threaten corporate insiders with legal punishments, one can use contract rules to try to design compensation systems that offer rewards. However, it turns out to be almost as difficult to design good "carrots" as effective "sticks." Although corporate directors and officers are often paid handsomely, there is at best only an indirect connection between their pay and how well they actually perform their roles. As an example, consider the case where the connection between pay and performance is probably tightest—the CEO. In the U.S., CEOs receive the lion's share of their compensation in the form of stock and stock options (Cheffins and Thomas, this volume). Yet the value of such packages depends on a host of variables outside the CEO's control (most obviously, general stock market trends, as determined by interest rates and the larger economy). Moreover, there are ways a CEO can manipulate stock prices to benefit herself while simultaneously harming the firm and its shareholders—in the extreme, by cooking the books.

    The connection between pay and performance is weaker still for lower-level executives and directors, who can free-ride on their peers' efforts. And while majority shareholders might benefit from a rise in stock price (which also benefits minority shareholders), they can also benefit from simply appropriating the firm's wealth (which hurts other stockholders). Thus, in the complex and uncertain world of business, it is impossible to draft complete contracts that perfectly "bond" corporate insiders' interests to those of the firm and its minority shareholders.

20. It can be argued that such societies differ far more from U.S. culture than the cultures of developed nations do. Interestingly, a cross-cultural study of behavior in ultimatum games played by university students in Israel, Japan, the U.S., and the former Yugoslavia provides some support for this hypothesis, because it found evidence of cross-cultural differences in other-regarding behavior in ultimatum games, but on a smaller scale than was found by Henrich and his colleagues (Roth 1992; see also Henrich et al. 2001: 74–75). Transplant shock due to differences in the incidence and determinants of other-regarding behavior accordingly may be more of a concern in the case of developing nations such as Korea or Brazil, than in the developed world.

21. For example, the Machiguenga of Peru on average offered to share only 26 percent of their stakes with their partner in an ultimatum game, while the average Orma shared 44 percent (Henrich et al. 2001: 74).

22. Differences in behavior can have a biological cause without being genetic in origin. For example, someone may become aphasic (unable to speak) as a result of head trauma even though he has the genetic potential for speech and could speak prior to the injury.

23. For a comprehensive review, see Sober and Wilson (1998).
24. "Typical distributions of public goods games contributions with students have a U-shape, with the mode at contributing nothing, a secondary mode at full cooperation, and mean contribution between 40 and 60 percent" Henrich et al. (2001: 75).
25. For a friendly introduction to the complexities of genetics and heritability and how these interact with environmental influences, see Dennett (1995).
26. To return to the oversimplified example offered earlier, the idea here is that if the cooperator gene is present in different proportions in different populations, populations with a large proportion of genetic "cooperators" would display more altruism in social dilemma games (and possibly in firms) than populations with a higher proportion of genetic "defectors."
27. Conversely, populations with a greater genetic predisposition toward altruism may do even better with the U.S. corporate law than U.S. citizens do; perhaps we should install the Orma in corporate headquarters, after all.
28. This possibility has implications for those who value the altruistic qualities of their friends and companions: the slogan "friends don't let friends study economics" comes to mind.
29. Ultimatum game studies also suggest that other-regarding behavior increases with age. An example can be found in an experiment reported by Camerer and Thaler (1995). In this experiment, kindergarten students were asked to play an ultimatum game with M&Ms. They behaved much more like *Homo economicus* than adult subjects do, leading Camerer and Thaler to speculate that "the tendency [to behave in an other-regarding fashion] is learned. . . . " (ibid.: 217).
30. Just try hunting a whale by yourself.
31. This observation conjures up the image of development agencies funding an army of field researchers to recruit entire populations to play social dilemma games.
32. For a recent example, see Dickens and Flynn (2001).
33. As noted earlier, even when faced with the same social context, some U.S. subjects cooperate more than others. Thus, by selecting "cooperative" personalities, researchers can get higher cooperation rates (Alcock and Mansell 1977).
34. A statistical analysis of more than 100 reported studies found that while cooperation rates in social dilemmas were somewhat negatively correlated with the magnitude of the subjects' personal benefits from defecting, "all the other variables that should affect a selfish decider are either not meaningful or have the opposite sign," and a variety of social variables that should be irrelevant to selfish subjects were quite important (Sally 1995: 77).
35. Although social context is highly important in determining cooperation rates among U.S. subjects, it should be noted that cooperation rates can be changed by manipulating two other factors as well. The first is the subjects' predisposi-

tions or "personalities" (see note 33 above). The second factor or variable is the personal cost of cooperation to the player. Studies have found that as the personal cost associated with adopting a cooperating strategy in a social dilemma increases, cooperation rates decline (Sally 1995: 75–76). Put differently, people seem more inclined toward other-regarding, "nice" behavior when it doesn't cost them too much.

What does this tell us about the circumstances under which we might expect U.S.-style fiduciary duties to work? Most obviously, there is value to legal enforcement of fiduciary duties, especially the duty of loyalty. If corporate directors and shareholders are free to steal from the firm without fear of sanction, then the opportunity cost of other-regarding behavior increases, and the incidence of other-regarding behavior will likely decrease.

36. The idea that corporate insiders ought to behave in an other-regarding fashion does not address the issue of exactly which "others" they ought to serve. In the United States, courts generally describe insiders' fiduciary duties as running to "the firm and its shareholders" (see Mills Acquisition Co. v. Macmillan, Inc., 559 A.2d 1261, 1280 (Del. 1988)). The meaning of this phrase is debatable, as it remains unclear whether the interests of the firm include only the interests of the shareholders, or might be read to include other groups as well (Allen 1992). However, at a minimum it implies that insiders ought not to direct their altruism toward, for example, an incompetent manager, or a controlling shareholder involved in a self-dealing transaction.

37. See Blair and Stout (2001); Eisenberg (1999); Rock (1997); and Skeel (2001).

38. This possibility offers hope to the poor, disdained economics graduate student. Perhaps he cooperates less in social dilemmas not because he is more selfish, but simply because his training leads him to recognize a social dilemma as just that, and to mentally categorize it as a competitive rather than cooperative situation. Indirect evidence of this can be found in an experiment that found that students in economics classes were more likely than students in other classes to seal and mail a "lost" letter enclosing currency apparently intended to repay a personal loan (Yezer et al. 1996), suggesting that while economics students may cooperate less in formal social dilemma games, they may be more willing to cooperate in "real world" situations.

39. For example, cooperative behavior in a particular culture that appears altruistic on first inspection may in fact be driven by non-legal "social" sanctions that are not readily apparent to someone outside the society. For a discussion of social sanctions, see text accompanying notes 11–12 above.

40. The author concedes immediately that she falls into the first category.

41. It also may not be necessary. There is reason to suspect that business institutions within a particular society are likely to evolve toward the most efficient form possible, given local conditions and constraints. Thus nations with differ-

ent legal regimes may be able to evolve corporate governance patterns that resemble those observed in the U.S. (including well-developed securities markets and dispersed share ownership) through the development of institutions that look different from ours, but perform similar functions.

References

Alcock, James E. and Diana Mansell. 1977. Predisposition and Behavior in a Collective Dilemma, *Journal of Conflict Resolution* 21: 443–56.

Allen, William T. 1992. Our Schizophrenic Conception of the Business Corporation. *Cardozo Law Review* 14: 261–81.

Bebchuk, Lucian Arye and Mark J. Roe. 1999. A Theory of Path Dependence in Corporate Ownership and Governance. *Stanford Law Review* 52: 127–70.

Berkowitz, Daniel, Katharina Pistor, and Jean-Francois Richard. 2003. Economic Development, Legality, and the Transplant Effect. *European Economic Review* 47: 165–95.

Black, Bernard and Reinier Kraakman. 1996. A Self-Enforcing Model of Corporate Law. *Harvard Law Review* 109: 1911–82.

Blair, Margaret M. and Lynn A. Stout, 2001. Trust, Trustworthiness, and the Behavioral Foundations of Corporate Law. *University of Pennsylvania Law Review* 149: 1735–1810.

Byrne, John A., Louis Lavelle, Nanette Byrnes, Marcia Vickers, and Amy Borrus. 2002. How To Fix Corporate Governance. *Business Week*, pp. 69–78 (May 6, 2002).

Camerer, Colin and Richard H. Thaler. 1995. Anomalies: Ultimatums, Dictators, and Manners. *Journal of Economic Perspectives* 9: 209–19.

Clark, Robert C. 1986. *Corporate Law.* Boston: Little, Brown & Co.

Coffee, John C., Jr. 2001a. The Rise of Dispersed Ownership: The Roles of Law and the State in the Separation of Ownership and Control. *Yale Law Journal* 111: 1–82.

———. 2001b. Do Norms Matter? A Cross-Country Evaluation. *University of Pennsylvania Law Review* 149: 2151–77.

Cohn, Edward, 2000. The Resurrection of Michael Milken. *The American Prospect* 27 (March 13, 2000)

Dawes, Robyn M. 1980. Social Dilemmas. *Annual Review of Psychology* 31: 163–93.

——— and Richard H. Thaler. 1988. Cooperation. *Journal of Economic Perspectives* 2: 187–97.

———, Alphons J.C. van de Kragt, and John M. Orbell. 1990. Cooperation for the Benefit of Us—Not Me, or My Conscience. In *Beyond Self-Interest*. Jane J. Mansbridge ed. Chicago: University of Chicago Press.

Dennett, Daniel C. 1995. *Darwin's Dangerous Idea: Evolution and the Meanings of Life*. New York: Simon & Schuster.

De Tocqueville, Alexis. 1834. *Democracy in America.*

Dickens, William T. and James R. Flynn. 2001. Heritability Estimates Versus Large Environmental Effects: The IQ Paradox Resolved. *Psychological Review* 108: 346–69.

Eisenberg, Melvin Aron. 1999. Corporate Law and Social Norms. *Columbia Law Review* 99: 1253–92.

France, Mike. 2002. Punishment for Corporate Fraud? How Radical. *Business Week,* p. 33 (March 11, 2002).

Frank, Robert H., Thomas Gilovich, and Dennis T. Regan. 1993. Does Studying Economics Inhibit Cooperation? *Journal of Economic Perspectives* 7: 159–71.

Fukayama, Frances. 1995. *Trust: The Social Virtues and the Creation of Prosperity.* New York: Free Press.

Hansmann, Henry and Reinier Kraakman. 2001. The End of History for Corporate Law. *Georgetown Law Journal* 89: 439–68.

Henrich, Joseph, Robert Boyd, Samuel Bowles, Colin Camerer, Ernst Fehr, Herbert Gintis, and Richard McElreath. 2001. In Search of Homo Economicus: Behavioral Experiments in 15 Small-Scale Societies. *American Economic Review* 91: 73–78.

La Porta, Rafael, Florencio Lopez-de-Silanes, and Andrei Shleifer. 1999. Corporate Ownership Around the World. *Journal of Finance.* 54: 471–517.

——— and Robert Vishny. 1997. Legal Determinants of External Finance. *Journal of Finance* 52: 1131–55.

———. 1998. Law and Finance. *Journal of Political Economy* 106: 1113–50.

Licht, Amir N. 2001. The Mother of All Path Dependencies: Toward a Cross-Cultural Theory of Corporate Governance Systems. *Delaware Journal of Corporate Law* 26: 147–205.

———, Chanan Goldschmidt, and Shalom H. Schwartz. 2001. Culture, Law, and Finance: Cultural Dimensions of Corporate Governance Laws. Available at http://papers.ssrn.com/sol3/papers.cfm?abstract_id = 267190.

Marwell, Gerald and Ruth E. Ames. 1981. Economists Free Ride, Does Anyone Else? *Journal of Public Economics* 15: 295–310.

Milhaupt, Curtis J. 1996. A Relational Theory of Japanese Corporate Governance: Contract, Culture, and the Rule of Law. *Harvard International Law Journal* 37: 3–64.

———. 2001. Creative Norm Destruction: The Evolution of Nonlegal Rules in Japanese Corporate Governance. *University of Pennsylvania Law Review* 149: 2083–2129.

Norris, Floyd and David Barboza. 2002. Enron's Many Strands: Ex-Chairman's Finances: Lay Sold Shares for $100 Million. *New York Times,* p. A1 (February 16, 2002).

Rock, Edward. 1997. Saints and Sinners: How Does Delaware Corporate Law Work? *UCLA Law Review* 44: 1004–1107.

Roe, Mark J. 2000. Political Preconditions to Separating Ownership from Control. *Stanford Law Review* 53: 539–606.

Ross, Lee and Andrew Ward. 1996. Naive Realism in Everyday Life: Implications for Social Conflict and Misunderstanding. In *Values and Knowledge*. Edward S. Reed et al. eds. Mahwah, N.J.: L. Erlbaum Associates.

Roth, Alvin E., Vesna Prasnikar, Masahiro Okuno-Fujiwara, and Shmuel Zamir. 1992. Bargaining and Market Behavior in Jerusalem, Ljubljana, Pittsburgh, and Tokyo: An Experimental Study. *American Economic Review* 81: 1068–95.

Sally, David. 1995. Conversation and Cooperation in Social Dilemmas: A Meta-Analysis of Experiments from 1958 to 1992. *Rationality and Society* 7: 58–92.

Skeel, David A. Jr., 2001. Shaming in Corporate Law. *University of Pennsylvania Law Review* 149: 1811–68.

Sober, Elliott and David Sloan Wilson. 1998. *Unto Others: The Evolution and Psychology of Unselfish Behavior*. Cambridge: Harvard University Press.

Stout, Lynn A. 2002. In Praise of Procedure: An Economic and Behavioral Defense of Smith v. Van Gorkom and the Business Judgment Rule. *Northwestern Law Review* 96: 675–93.

Stulz, Rene and Robin Williamson. 2002. Culture, Openness, and Finance (manuscript on file with the author).

Tyler, Tom R. 1990. *Why People Obey The Law*. New Haven: Yale University Press.

—— and Steven L. Blader, 2002. The Psychology of the Corporate Actor: Ethical Values, Procedural Justice, and Rule Following in Work Organizations (manuscript on file with author).

Yezer, Anthony M., Robert S. Goldfarb, and Paul J. Poppen. 1996. Does Studying Economics Inhibit Cooperation? Watch What We Do, Not What We Say. *Journal of Economic Perspectives* 10: 177–86.

3 Fiduciary Duty in Transitional Civil Law Jurisdictions

Lessons from the Incomplete Law Theory

Katharina Pistor and Chenggang Xu

Fiduciary duty is a core concept in Anglo-American corporate law for delineating the rights and responsibilities of directors and managers, as well as dominant shareholders vis-à-vis minority shareholders. Yet its precise meaning is difficult to discern without reference to a large body of case law. Judge-made law has over time carved out a subset of specific obligations and standards of conduct derived from this principle. Most widely accepted are the duty of care and the duty of loyalty, where the duty of loyalty refers to situations in which conflict of interest is present. The meaning of each of these obligations is explained by referring to a subset of more specific obligations. Some of these obligations have been codified.[1] This is true in the U.S., for example, for the duty to disclose material information to investors and shareholders. Those that have not, or where codification still leaves sufficient room for ambiguity as to the scope and meaning of the law, are derived by courts in the process of adjudication.

Thus, in Anglo-Saxon countries, courts are in charge of determining the boundaries of managers' obligations to shareholders—boundaries which are inherently difficult to circumscribe exhaustively. As Clark puts it, "this general duty of loyalty is a residual concept that can include factual situations that no one has foreseen and categorized" (Clark 1986: 141). The broad and encompassing nature of fiduciary duties appears to be a crucial factor in explaining the importance it has acquired in Anglo-American jurisdictions (Clark 1986; Coffee 1989; Eisenberg 2000; Johnson et al. 2000). It has allowed courts to take account of the changing nature of the business

enterprise while maintaining at least the semblance of undisputed principles for determining what is right and what is wrong in corporate conduct.

As many have pointed out, the corporate law in the U.S., especially in
Delaware, has developed from a (fairly) prohibitive, or mandatory law into
an enabling corporate law, which allows shareholders to opt out of many
legal provisions and substitute their own contractually determined arrangements (Coffee 1989; Black and Kraakman 1996). Nevertheless, shareholders
(or rather those controlling the process of charter and bylaw making) have
not been able to opt out of the principle of fiduciary duty, which has gained
in importance as the law has become more enabling (Coffee 1989). The
contrast with corporate law in many civil law jurisdictions is stark. German
law, for example, explicitly states that all provisions of the corporate law are
mandatory, except where otherwise stated,[2] and courts have not played an
important role in determining the rights and wrongs of corporate conduct, at
least not for publicly held corporations.[3]

The same qualities that make the concept of fiduciary duties so resilient
over time make it extremely difficult to transplant to other legal systems. The
meaning of fiduciary duty cannot easily be specified in a detailed legal document. Attempts to do so will either leave out many actions or factual situations "no one has foreseen or categorized" (Clark 1986), or will be phrased
so broadly that the meaning can be understood only in the context of specific cases. Thus, transplants of substantive rules can at best be partial. In
this essay, we investigate alternative strategies for countries wishing to
develop the institutional framework for effective enforcement of fiduciary
duties. We suggest that it might be advisable to shift attention from *substantive* to *structural* transplants, or put differently, to focus more on the allocation of lawmaking and law enforcement powers (LMLEP) than on the contents of specific legal rules.

The process of legal reform in transition economies to date has entailed
primarily the transplantation of statutory law from Western European or
U.S. legal sources (Pistor 2000). These transplants have focused on the contents of legal rules and principles of corporate law known in the West—that
is, on *substantive* transplants. Even when U.S. law was taken as a model, the
role of courts was kept at bay, because the local court systems were deemed
untrustworthy (Black and Kraakman 1996). In this paper, we ask whether a
superior mode of transplantation might be a *structural transplant*, defined as
the imitation not of substantive rules, but of the allocation of LMLEP. We
address this question drawing on our earlier work on the incompleteness of

law (Pistor and Xu 2002; Xu and Pistor 2002). The thrust of our argument is that every legal system must allocate the right to deal with future contingencies that were unforeseen when the law was announced. The reason is that law is intrinsically incomplete, meaning that it is impossible to design a law that would specify all future contingencies, and thus could act as an effective deterrent device.[4]

When law is incomplete, the effectiveness of law and law enforcement is contingent on how a legal system deals with the right to determine the content and meaning of law when future contingencies arise—how it allocates LMLEP to deal with future scenarios. A legal system may allocate these powers to courts or to regulators, or a combination of the two. It may also decide that private parties should resolve these issues by denying (easy) access to the formal legal system. In our other work, we identify three factors that determine the optimal allocation of LMLEP: the degree of incompleteness of the law, the ability to standardize actions that may result in harm ex ante, and the level of expected harm (Pistor and Xu 2002; Xu and Pistor 2002). Applying this framework to the problem of fiduciary duty, we argue that courts are the optimal holders of LMLEP for this area of the law. Law is highly incomplete, but actions cannot be easily standardized, thus making it infeasible to allocate LMLEP to regulators. Moreover, because the level of expected harm is relatively contained, reactive law enforcement is sufficient for remedying harmful actions.

The effectiveness of the courts' residual lawmaking powers depends on the willingness of victims to bring cases to court, which in turn depends on the actual or perceived quality of the courts. If courts are weak, they may not be effective residual lawmakers and law enforcers, even if they are vested with extensive residual lawmaking powers. Courts in transition economies are widely perceived to be weak, inexperienced, or even corrupt (Black and Kraakman 1996; Glaeser et al. 2001), although a number of empirical studies paint a somewhat different picture (Hendley 2001; Hendley et al. 1997). Vesting courts with LMLEP will therefore require extensive institutional reform in many transition economies. Governments wishing to credibly commit to a structural transplant would need not only to change statutory law in order to explicitly allocate lawmaking powers to courts, they would also need to strengthen courts as independent institutions and ensure that they have sufficient resources to fulfill this task. Even this may not be sufficient, as ultimately it will depend on the courts to use the opportunity the law gives to them to engage in lawmaking activities. Our main point is that while this is a difficult task and will take time to accomplish, it cannot be easily circumvented by writing law that limits the role of courts in this crucial area of the law.

In the second part of the essay, we analyze the statutory and case law in three jurisdictions (Poland, Russia, and Germany) on matters that would fall within the scope of fiduciary duty in Anglo-Saxon countries. The focus of our analysis is the allocation of LMLEP in these jurisdictions and how courts have made use of their empowerments. A hallmark of all three jurisdictions is that case law is scarce, even in Germany, a highly developed market economy with extensive experience with corporations and corporate law. We suggest that case law evolved in these jurisdictions whenever procedural rules gave access to judicial review and substantive rules were sufficiently specified to serve as guidance. Analyzing available case law, we argue that even in civil law countries or countries with a socialist legal past, it is not impossible to vest courts with more expansive LMLEP. Yet, in light of their legal heritage it might be advisable to specify some typical applications of legal principles in statutory law as guidance for potential litigants and judges alike. At the same time, the law should be clear that judicial review will not be limited to these typified cases.

I: Incompleteness of Law and the Allocation of LMLEP

In this part of the essay we explain the core elements of the incomplete law theory we use as a framework to determine the optimal allocation of LMLEP for handling cases related to the proper governance of corporations.[5]

A. Incompleteness of Law

If law were complete—if a law could stipulate unambiguously all future contingencies—it could fully deter harmful actions, including actions that may result in the violation of fiduciary duties. The key task for such a law would be to stipulate the appropriate level of punishment and to ensure that the probability of detection would be sufficiently high. Indeed, much of the traditional literature on law enforcement (Becker 1968; Polinsky and Shavell 2000; Stigler 1964) focuses on these variables and treats law implicitly as complete. By contrast, if law is incomplete, law cannot effectively deter. In this second-best world, legal systems need to allocate LMLEP to deal with future contingencies that were unanticipated at the time law was made, in order to enhance (not to perfect) the effectiveness of law enforcement. Absent the allocation of LMLEP, many actions will not be sanctioned, even if they result in substantial harm. Legislative change may make law more complete after assembling sufficient experience, but this will have only prospective effect. Moreover, new actions or factual situations the revised law did not contemplate will undoubtedly arise, leaving it once more incomplete.

A similar argument has been made in the economics literature with regards to contracts: parties to a contract cannot foresee all future contingencies and therefore cannot write a complete contract (Hart 1995). However, parties can renegotiate the contract in the future once new uncertainties have been resolved and thus make the contract highly complete. Law can be regarded as a grand social contract in that it attempts to offer legal guidance for outcomes to future generations of citizens. In countries governed by the rule of law, law is purposefully designed to address a large number of cases and to last for long periods of time. The use of abstract language in statutory law is a means to ensure its generality. Even case law is made not only for the specific case at hand; the court's ruling applies equally to other cases with a similar (not necessarily identical) factual basis (Ginsburg 1996). If contractual parties cannot write complete contracts, lawmakers should be even less able to write complete statutory law. In fact, to write a complete law, lawmakers would need not only unlimited foresight, but also unbounded rationality. They would need to be able to anticipate the impact of the rules they make on all potential parties concerned and write rules that can achieve the first–best results from a social welfare perspective.

An important reason why it is difficult to write even fairly complete law is that the meaning and scope of law is continuously challenged by socioeconomic and technological change. In a static world, law can achieve high levels of completeness. Take, for example, the development of criminal and tort law until the mid-nineteenth century. Statutory and case law by that time had well specified the meaning of theft of assets and the conditions for holding someone liable for deceit. Increasingly, however, objects such as electricity, ideas, and telephone lines became subjects of appropriation that differed from cases for which the law had been designed. Similarly, the legal principles governing fraud and deceit were developed for cases where asymmetry of information between the parties was limited and the truth of the matter was easy to verify. With the growth of markets for financial instruments, the asymmetry of information between seller and buyer increased, as did the value of information. Someone with the power to change and adapt law had to decide whether existing legal principles that had been developed with different cases in mind should be used to resolve these cases, or whether different principles were needed, and if so, how to stipulate such principles.

Given the incompleteness of law, a crucial question is who should hold the power to interpret or make new law in the future and to resolve questions about the application of existing law to new cases. Unlike contracts, where the parties to the original contract or their assignees have the power to renegotiate, for law the question who holds residual lawmaking power is less obvious. Thus, legal systems must allocate these rights. In doing so, legal systems must address two questions: who should hold these rights in order to ensure effective law enforcement, and what factors should be considered in allocating these rights to different agents.

The notion that law is ambiguous or indeterminate—concepts that are close to our term "incompleteness"—has long been recognized in the legal literature (Hart 1961; Solum 1999). In addition, a substantial literature has analyzed the optimal choice between standards and rules (Kaplow 1992; 1995; 1997). Thus, the claim that law is incomplete is not a novelty to most lawyers. What our theory seeks to add is that incompleteness of law is not merely a matter of choice, but at a fundamental level law is intrinsically incomplete; that is, lawmakers *cannot* write a complete law. To enhance the efficacy of law, legal systems must therefore allocate LMLEP. The key contribution of the incompleteness of law theory is its emphasis on properly designing enforcement institutions as a response to incompleteness of law.

The concept of fiduciary duty discussed in this essay is an example of a highly incomplete law. This broad principle encompasses all actions that might violate the rights of principals by fiduciaries. To avoid imposing the risk of excessive law enforcement on fiduciaries, however, the law must be able to exclude actions from its applicability that do not warrant liability, and must be able to do so with sufficient certainty ex ante. Specific applications of fiduciary duty can, and indeed have been, carved out and codified. Examples include the duty to disclose information to shareholders and to notify them in advance of shareholder meetings, and conflict of interest provisions in corporate statutes that specify circumstances when directors may not act on their own, but must seek independent directors' or shareholders' approval or abstain from voting. Indeed, closer inspection might reveal that there are more cases where codification might be possible and desirable. Where rules can be sufficiently specified, codification can save costs for individual actors, as well as law enforcers. The codified parts of fiduciary duty would not form part of the residual anymore. Yet, they would still share the same value judgment and should carry comparable sanctions.

B. *Allocating Residual Lawmaking and Law Enforcement Powers*

Once the notion that law is intrinsically incomplete is accepted, the question arises who should hold residual lawmaking and law enforcement powers. We argue that this should be determined by the lawmaking and law enforcement functions different agents perform. Legislatures are agents that make law ex ante, but typically do not exercise any law enforcement powers. Courts usually make law ex post, that is, after the critical facts of a case have been revealed. However, once made, case law also has ex ante implications for actions taken in the future. In addition, courts exercise law enforcement powers. An important feature of courts is that they enforce law only after some other party brings an action. This party may be the victim, or it may be a state agent, such as a prosecutor or administrative agency. The reason that courts do not act on their own initiative follows from the rule of law notion that courts should act as neutral arbiters.

Similar to courts but unlike legislatures, regulators combine lawmaking and law enforcement functions. Like legislatures, they make law ex ante. Regulators, however, are typically vested only with limited lawmaking powers defined by certain activities or sectors; yet within the scope of their lawmaking powers they can change the law more flexibly and with fewer procedural requirements. This allows them to be more responsive to socioeconomic or technological change than legislatures. However, a similar function could be achieved by setting up a special parliamentary committee to deal with a specialized area of the law. The distinctive feature of regulators thus lies not in greater flexibility and greater expertise than legislatures, but in combining lawmaking and a particular type of law enforcement power that is different from the courts' law enforcement powers. What distinguishes regulators from courts is that they can enforce law proactively. In contrast to courts, regulators can launch an investigation, enjoin actions, or impose fines on their own initiative. These particular features make regulators potentially very powerful law enforcers. These very same features raise concerns, as regulators may use these powers excessively and thus suppress potentially beneficial actions or engage in rent-seeking activities.[6] To optimize law enforcement it is therefore important to identify the conditions under which the benefits of LMLEP allocation to regulators outweighs its potential costs.

C. Allocating LMLEP for Resolving Fiduciary Duty Cases

According to our theory, the choice between regulators and courts depends on the degree of incompleteness of law, the possibility of standardizing, at reasonable cost, actions that may result in harm, and the degree of harm that may result from harmful actions (Pistor and Xu 2002; Xu and Pistor 2002).

When law is highly complete, it can determine appropriate sanctions ex ante, and reactive enforcement by courts is sufficient to enforce the law effectively. When law is highly incomplete, the optimal allocation of LMLEP is determined by the degree of expected harm and the costs of standardizing actions that might result in harm.

An example where high levels of expected harm are matched with reasonable costs of standardizing actions are disclosure requirements for firms issuing shares to the public, or safety standards imposed on producers of pharmaceuticals, automobiles, or aircraft. Disclosure rules capture only one particular aspect of the relation between firms (and their agents) and investors. This is, however, an area where past experience suggests that lack of disclosure may result in substantial harm not only to current shareholders or future investors in a particular firm, but also to investors more broadly and ultimately the functioning of the financial market as a public good. When firms come to the market, investors face a lemons problem (Akerlof 1970). Incidences of misrepresentation of information may seriously discourage investments in shares, as is evidenced by market crashes in response to the revelation of stock fraud schemes (Milgrom and Stokey 1982). Thus, the expected degree of harm is high. Fortunately, however, disclosure rules can be standardized at reasonable cost. Lawmakers can define the type of information that must be disclosed, and adapt these rules over time as market behavior changes or as it becomes apparent that investors require different information.[7] They can also use this information to determine whether fur-

ther action is needed, such as the initiation of proactive enforcement activities in the form of investigations.

By contrast, when individual actions are not expected to generate much
harm, or if standardization of such actions entails high costs, allocating lawmaking and law enforcement powers to the courts is superior even when law
is highly incomplete. Law enforcement related to fiduciary duties is an example where the level of incompleteness is high, standardization is possible only
for some areas—leaving a large undefined residual—and the expected harm
is relatively contained. Fiduciary duties govern the relationship among stakeholders in a particular undertaking (management versus shareholders, block
holders versus minority shareholders). The harm done when these duties are
violated is typically confined to a subset of these same stakeholders. While
investors may be wary of investing in that particular firm in the future, their
confidence in investing in shares in general will be shaken only when fiduciary duty violations are systemic. Reactive law enforcement can compensate
those shareholders that have actually incurred damages. In fact, empirical
studies suggest that law suits brought in response to alleged violations of fiduciary duty have not had a significant impact on share value of the company
involved, much less on other companies' shares (Romano 1991). Law
enforcement by regulators may not only be unnecessary, but even harmful,
because it is extremely difficult to stipulate ex ante the type of actions that
may result in harm. Allowing regulators to proactively enforce the law in
these cases would likely result in excessive intervention in the operation of
private businesses. Thus, the direct cost of regulating all possible actions that
might result in violations of fiduciary duty principles would be excessive.
Moreover, such regulation would likely err in discouraging or preventing
actions that could be economically beneficial. In these cases allocating residual lawmaking powers to regulators does not appear to be a viable solution.
Instead, vesting courts with ex post LM and reactive LE powers is superior.

Since it is impossible to write a fairly complete law that would comprehensively deal with actions that may be considered violations of fiduciary
duty principles, failure to allocate LMLEP to courts implies that these
actions cannot be resolved within the formal legal system. One may argue
that this is desirable, as the stakeholders' concerned best deal with these matters informally and litigation may only disrupt, rather than improve, relations
among these stakeholders. Indeed, German law has quite consciously limited
the justiciability of corporate affairs precisely for these reasons, and any
attempt to extend the right of shareholders to bring litigation confronts the

argument that this is better left to negotiations at the company level.[8] However, empirical evidence suggests that this strategy might not be conducive to capital market development. Available empirical studies have shown that among countries with developed financial markets, those with better minority shareholder protection, including "anti-directors' rights" that allow shareholders to take management to court, have less concentrated ownership and more developed capital markets than countries that do not offer similar protections (La Porta et al. 1997; 1998). While the relevance of the individual legal indicators used to assess the quality of minority shareholder protection in these studies may be subject to dispute (Pistor 2001), an important structural feature that distinguishes countries with better shareholder protection is that they tend to vest shareholders with litigation rights against directors and management. In other words, they provide a framework for solving these disputes within the formal legal system. This seems particularly important for transition economies, where the extensive process of reallocating property rights in firms is recent, the contents of shareholder rights is still uncertain, and minority shareholders have been systematically disenfranchised by company insiders (Black et al. 2000; Frydman et al. 1996; Pistor 1998).

The importance of adjudication of shareholder rights as a means of controlling management also seems consistent with the "Delaware puzzle." The puzzle is that companies incorporated there have higher market value than companies incorporated elsewhere in the U.S. (Daines 2001), although the Delaware statutory law is rather weak in protecting shareholder rights (Arsht 1976; Cary 1974; Larcom 1937). In fact, Delaware statutory law is not a stellar performer on the scale of shareholder rights identified by La Porta et al.[9] Several authors have suggested that the solution to this puzzle lies in the function of the Delaware courts (Fisch 2000; Coffee 1989; Daines 2001). This is consistent with our theory. The fact that Delaware courts exercise LMLEP and that—perhaps because of the enabling nature of the corporate law—they were increasingly called upon to resolve disputes, resulted in courts developing a large volume of case law. In doing so they have specified the meaning of the principle of fiduciary duty over time, or made the principle more complete. Given the higher level of completeness of the case law (but not the statutory law), shareholders are better protected in Delaware than in other states that do not have an equally comprehensive body of law.

To summarize, our basic argument is that the principle of fiduciary is a highly incomplete legal principle. To ensure effective law enforcement, residual lawmaking and law enforcement powers must be allocated. Since the actions that may violate fiduciary duty principles do not lend themselves well to standardization, and the expected harm affects primarily the company's shareholders, not investors or society more broadly, residual lawmaking and reactive law enforcement by courts is optimal.

II: Case Law From Civil Law Jurisdictions

In this part, we analyze relevant case law using the theory summarized in the previous section. We focus on cases which, in the Anglo-Saxon context, would be analyzed under the rubric of fiduciary duty in order to identify the allocation of LMLEP in these jurisdictions and to assess how that allocation has affected the resolution of conflicts between managers and shareholders. Our analysis reveals that the allocation of LMLEP, as reflected in substantive and procedural law in all three jurisdictions, is suboptimal. Russia seems closer than the other jurisdictions to allocating LMLEP to courts, but has limited this allocation to only a subset of rules. Poland's very broad substantive principle of fiduciary duty has not given rise to much litigation, and in Germany procedural rules have limited the scope of judicial lawmaking with respect to the duties management owes to shareholders.

An important caveat to these conclusions is that in transition economies case law is only emerging. In fact, in many countries not a single case concerning the violation of fiduciary duty has been reported in the higher courts.[10] It is therefore difficult to predict whether the few cases we have reviewed are indicative of future trends. But at least they allow us to take a glance at the evolving law.

Germany is the only nontransition country included here. German law has long influenced the development of statutory civil and commercial law in Central and Eastern Europe (Pistor 2000). It is therefore reasonable to assume that German case law may also gain influence in countries that borrowed German statutory law. In this sense, the analysis of German case law on fiduciary duty may hold important clues for the evolving case law in transition economies. But there is another, potentially more important, reason for including German case law in this analysis. German corporate law has consciously limited the scope of LMLEP for conflicts between managers and shareholders, but has allowed litigation for conflicts among shareholders. Thus, Germany offers a good opportunity to analyze the impact of alternative procedural rules on litigation outcomes.

A. Poland

Poland recently enacted a new Companies Act.[11] Currently available case law however, is based on the Commercial Code (CC), which was originally enacted in 1933 and formed the basis of the evolving postsocialist corporate law. The analysis that follows thus relates to the CC. The code included almost identical provisions on the liability of managers and directors in close and publicly traded corporations. Article 474 of the CC on publicly traded corporations read:

1. A member of the company's governing bodies and the liquidator are liable to the company for damage caused by their actions which are contrary to the law or the provisions in the Company Statute.
2. A member of the company's governing bodies and the liquidator are liable to the company for any damage caused as a result of their failure to exercise the care of a diligent trader.

The key issue in this provision is what is meant by "diligent trader," a highly incomplete legal term. No further specifications can be found in the law, leaving it to holders of LMLEP to decide this issue. Absent reference to regulators, this issue could be decided informally by the parties concerned or by the courts, provided, of course, that procedural rules exist to ensure that management can be sued for violating its duties of a "diligent trader." Article 474 explicitly states that directors are liable to the corporation, not to shareholders directly. In principle, the corporation and not its shareholders shall take action against members of the governing bodies. The CC did, however, allow shareholders to bring an action on behalf of the corporation, if the corporation had itself failed to act for more than a year after having discovered the facts giving rise to liability claims (Art. 477 CC). Given these procedural constraints and the highly incomplete principle embodied in statutory law, it is perhaps not surprising that case law is scarce. In fact, for publicly traded corporations, there has not been a single ruling by the Polish Supreme Court. We therefore report a 1998 decision of the Katowice Court of Appeal.[12] The decision deals with the duty of care of members of the board of directors. No claim of conflict of interests was made in the case.

The plaintiff was a shareholder of the Bank Ślaski SA (the Bank). Defendants were members of the board of directors (management board) of the

Bank.[13] The Bank was privatized in 1994 and a special unit inside the Bank, a brokerage house with substantial organizational and financial independence, was charged with organizing the issuance of shares. The task of supervising the activities of the brokerage house was delegated to one member of the board. When shares were offered in the privatization process, they were heavily oversubscribed, and the Bank was unprepared to deal with the situation. In particular, the Bank had failed to set up appropriate internal procedures to ensure that the relevant rules and regulations on privatizing the Bank were fully complied with. This failure constituted a violation of securities regulations, for which the Polish Securities and Exchange Commission (KPWiG) fined the Bank. Moreover, the member of the board that had been in charge of supervising the issuance of shares was fired. In the case brought before the court, the plaintiff demanded that other members of the board reimburse the Bank for the fine it paid to the KPWiG. The defendants argued that they had fulfilled their obligations under the law by delegating the task of supervising the share issuance to one of their members and therefore were not liable. The court of first instance denied a cause of action. Upon the plaintiff's appeal, the Katowice Court of Appeal reversed the decision. The official summary of the court ruling states:

> The care of a diligent trader should include: foreseeing the results of planned actions, undertaking all possible factual or legal measures in order to fulfill the obligation undertaken, showing foresight, conscientiousness, carefulness and care in order to achieve the results in accordance with the company's interests. A large degree of independence of a brokerage house and its financial and organizational separation, which allowed it to make decisions by itself, did not exclude it from the supervision of the bank, and the manager of the office was appointed and dismissed by the bank's management board. To designate one of the members of the bank's management board to supervise the activities of the brokerage house should normally not release the remaining management board members' from their responsibility in this respect.[14]

Essentially, the court replaced one highly incomplete term—the care of a diligent trader—with a set of others. These terms remain sufficiently broad to be used to hold members of the governing bodies of the corporation liable for virtually any conduct that ultimately results in harm. After all, the wording of the court's ruling suggests that they are required to undertake *all* possible factual or legal measures to further the interests of the corporation. This ruling will therefore be of little guidance to managers and lower courts in determining in future cases the actions—or failures to take action—which should result in legal liability. In fact, as stated, the ruling may deter risk taking on the one hand and the delegation of responsibility to certain directors on the other, if such measures fail to shield the remaining board members from liability.

The decision evidences a lack of experience with corporate decisionmaking processes and a reluctance by the court to develop criteria to delineate actions that should result in personal liability from those that should not. Given that common law courts have taken many decades to develop a body of case law in this area, this may not be surprising. The point is that transition economies need to catch up quickly in addressing the subtler problems of corporate governance, and courts need to live up to this task by developing better guidelines on permissible and impermissible corporate conduct. Procedural rules that make it difficult to bring court actions do not facilitate this learning process. A possible solution could be to carve out aspects of fiduciary duty that lend themselves to greater specification in the law. This approach has been attempted in Russia, as will be discussed in the following section.

B. Russia

Russia enacted its law on joint stock companies in 1996. The law is based on a draft developed with the help of American legal experts Bernard Black and Reinier Kraakman (Black and Kraakman 1996; Black et al. 1996). While the law has many traces of American corporate law, it is not simply a copy. Instead, the authors sought to create a new type of corporate law, one that would rest primarily on procedural rather than substantive provisions to ensure that shareholders could self-enforce the law and would not have to rely on courts viewed as slow, incompetent, and corrupt. The law avoids broad concepts and instead attempts to spell out the rights and obligations of shareholders and directors in great detail. As in Poland, case law is only emerging. Until 1998, cases that reached the Supreme Arbitrazh Court (SAC) in Moscow were still based on the old corporate law. In the majority of cases concerning violations of shareholder rights, corporations brought actions seeking to void contracts that had been entered into in violation of provisions that required approval by all members of the board or the shareholder meeting. It appears that litigation was thus used strategically by the company to escape contractual liability, not by shareholders to enforce their rights (Kursynsky-Singer 1999).

The new corporate law carved out certain aspects of the fiduciary duty principle, namely transactions in which a director or a director's affiliate has an interest. The law defines factors that suggest an "interest," establishes procedures for approving transactions where a conflict exists, and stipulates that violations of these rules result in liability vis-à-vis the company or voidance of the transactions.

Article 71 of the 1996 Russian Law on Joint Stock Companies (JSCL) states in Section 1:

> The members of a company's board of directors (supervisory board), the company's individual executive organ (director, general director) and (or) members of the company's collegial executive organ (managing board, directorate) and equally the managing organization or manager when exercising their rights and fulfilling their duties must act in the interest of the company, exercising their rights and fulfilling their duties with regard to the company in good faith and reasonableness.[15]

The SAC has not had the opportunity to determine the meaning of good faith and reasonableness. However, it has dealt with a number of cases concerning violations of statutory provisions on conflict of interest situations, Articles 81–84 of the JSCL.[16] Thus, legal provisions that stipulate in substantial detail the actions that may give rise to liability have resulted in litigation, while provisions that establish management obligations in broad, ambiguous terms have not. Given the limited LMLEP courts in civil law jurisdictions exercise in general, and in the highly positivist postsocialist countries in particular, this is not surprising. Potential litigants will carefully weigh the costs of litigation against the benefits, which are highly dependent on the court's willingness to exercise LMLEP in a reasonable manner when given the opportunity.

Article 81 defines an "interest" in a company's completion of a transaction. The persons who might have an interest include the members of the board(s), or shareholder(s) holding together with affiliated person(s) 20 or more percent of the company's voting shares. An interest exists if these persons, their spouses, parents, children, brothers, sisters, and all their affiliated persons participate directly in the transaction, hold a significant stake (20 percent of voting shares) in the other party to the transaction, or occupy an official position in that party.

The effort to write a highly complete law notwithstanding, the conditions that indicate an interest all contain terms and concepts that require further interpretation. To put it differently, the law remains incomplete. The provisions require, for example, that someone must act "in the capacity of representative or intermediary." The law does not simply stipulate that "the general director" or "a member of the board," has an interest, anticipating that others may be acting as agents of the corporation and thus could find themselves in a conflict of interest situation.

An interested person must disclose that interest to the supervisory board, inspection commission, and auditors. Transactions that are affected by an interest must be approved by a majority vote of the company's disinterested directors. If the company has more than 1,000 shareholders, the directors making the decision must be both disinterested and independent.[17] Moreover, it must be established that the value the company will receive for property alienated or services delivered does not exceed market value, or conversely, that the value of the property acquired or services accepted is not below market value.[18]

Violations of conflict of interest provisions have two legal consequences. First, the transaction may be deemed void (Art. 84, Sec. 1). Second, the interested person is liable *to the company* for the amount of losses caused to the company (Art. 84, Sec. 2).[19]

An action for the invalidation of contracts can be filed by shareholders as well as by the parties to the transaction, namely, the corporation and the counter–party. The SAC had to clarify that organizations that were not a party to the transaction, including the company's creditors, had no right to file for invalidation of such transactions. In a recent survey of judicial practice concerning the conflict of interest provisions of the JSCL, the SAC summarized the legal issues that arose in case law.[20] In all cases the plaintiff sought to void the contract rather than to pursue liability of the interested persons. In contrast to the cases brought under the previous law, however, several cases were brought by disgruntled shareholders. A possible explanation for the scarcity of shareholder action is that the law clearly stipulates that violations of the conflict–of–interest provisions result in liability vis-à-vis the corporation, not the shareholders, and Russian law does not provide for derivative actions. Thus, it is unclear whether shareholders would indeed have standing if they sued for damages (Black et al. 1998).

Several decisions addressed the issue whether an interested person was in fact a party to a transaction, or a representative of that party. Thus, courts had to deal with the ambiguities the law could not fully resolve ex ante. For example, a director who bought shares of his company from an underwriter argued that he had no "interest." The court rejected the argument on the grounds that the underwriter acted on behalf of the company, not as an independent agent, and voided the contract.[21] In another case,[22] Informenergo and Gala-Inform entered into a contract over parts of a building, the value of which exceeded 2 percent of Informenergo's assets. Thus, approval by the shareholder meeting was required.[23] The general director of Informenergo had an interest in the transaction by virtue of the fact that he—together with other affiliates—held more than 20 percent of the stock in Gala-Inform.[24] The lower court denied an action brought by Informenergo to void the contract. It held that because the general director had authorized a third person to sign the contract on behalf of Informenergo, the director himself was neither a party to the contract nor acted as a representative, and thus a conflict-of-interest situation did not exist. The SAC reversed, explaining that the delegation of power to execute the contract on behalf of the company did not eliminate the conflict-of-interest situation.

Other cases addressed the question whether the conflict-of-interest provisions apply to a transaction concluded *after* the conflict-of-interest situation had been eliminated or *before* it came about. In one case, the plaintiff, a close corporation, had acquired shares in a joint stock company. The general director of the joint stock company was a cofounder of the plaintiff, holding 20 percent of its stock. He sold that stake prior to the transaction in question. The court ruled that because the conflict-of-interest situation must exist at the time the transaction is concluded, there was no violation. The SAC explicitly stated, "by virtue of Article 81 of the Law on Joint Stock Companies an interest in the transaction has to be ascertained at the time it is entered into."[25]

In a separate case, a joint stock company concluded a contract to acquire goods from another corporation. The value of the transaction exceeded 2 percent of the corporation's assets. Within a month after entering into the agreement, the general director of the plaintiff corporation acquired a 20 percent stake in the seller. The court held that in these circumstances approval by the shareholder meeting was not necessary. The transaction was within the realm of ordinary business transactions and the conflict-of-interest situation arose only after the transaction had already been concluded.

Existing case law from Russia reveals that courts are still struggling with recognizing conflict-of-interest situations.[26] Take, for example, the following case, in which a company demanded that its bank carry out a transaction in foreign currency. The bank refused to follow the order on the grounds that it violated conflict-of-interest provisions, because the customer was also a major shareholder of the bank. A lower court ruled that the bank's refusal to execute the order was improper. The SAC, however, reversed, arguing that the transaction was in compliance with banking and currency regulations and that the bank had no right to refuse to execute the order. The ownership relations were regarded as immaterial for this decision.[27]

In part, deficient legislation can be blamed for these results. In fact, commentators have pointed out even before case law emerged that the law would give rise to ambiguities (Black et al. 1998). But even the best law cannot stipulate all future contingencies unambiguously, and legislating against actions that by their very nature are hard to capture in clear cut statutory provisions inevitably results in incomplete law.

C. Germany

As noted above, German corporate law is largely mandatory law, leaving less scope for opt out than corporate law in Anglo-Saxon countries. Contrary to what one might expect from a civil law jurisdiction, the law does not spell out in great detail the obligations of various stakeholders. Instead, the corporate law subjects managers to a general standard of a diligent entrepreneur.[28] Several provisions further prohibit members of the board from competing directly or indirectly with the corporation,[29] and subject credit contracts between board members and the corporation to the approval of the supervisory board.[30]

These provisions have been interpreted as statutory specifications of the general duty of loyalty (Hopt and Wiedemann 1992; Hueffer 1995). In theory, they could have served as a focal point for courts to develop principles of corporate conduct similar to the case law that evolved in common law jurisdictions on the basis of fiduciary duties. However, a substantial body of case law has not yet developed, because the law does not give shareholders easy access to the courts for violations of fiduciary duties by management. The law does not provide for derivative actions, and shareholder suits against management are available only after attempts have been made to persuade the supervisory board to bring a case, and only if the legal threshold for bringing a case has been met.[31] Thus, the law clearly expresses a preference for resolving conflicts over the scope of managers' and directors' fiduciary duties internally rather than in the court room.

By contrast, shareholders have a right to judicial recourse against decisions taken at the shareholder meeting, if such decisions violate their rights.[32] The difference in access to judicial recourse for conflicts between managers and shareholders on the one hand and among shareholders on the other is clearly reflected in the volume of case law that has developed for the two types of conflicts.[33] Only rarely have courts had occasion to clarify the meaning of fiduciary duties owed by management or members of the supervisory board in publicly held companies.[34] But they have been very active, particularly over the past two decades, in developing case law on the duties shareholders owe to each other.

Still, it took many years for courts to acknowledge a fiduciary relationship among shareholders of a corporation. Fiduciary duties (*Treuepflichten*) had previously been recognized only in highly personal relations, such as partnerships or employee relationships (Wellenhofer-Klein 2000). In 1975, however, the German Supreme Court (BGH) recognized such a duty among shareholders for close corporations.[35] In 1988, it extended this ruling to joint stock companies in the *Linotype* case.[36] In this case, a minority shareholder challenged a decision to liquidate the company that had been approved at the shareholders meeting solely by the vote of the majority shareholder. The undisputed purpose of this decision was that the majority shareholder wished to integrate certain operations of the company into its own company, but could not achieve this by way of merger, because under the law this required the consent of all shareholders.[37] Prior to the shareholders meeting, the majority shareholder had already met with the management board and discussed the details of the transaction, including the value of the assets that were to be transferred. The court held that the majority shareholder violated his duty of loyalty vis-à-vis the minority shareholders by discussing these issues without giving the minority shareholders a chance to participate in the deal or to acquire the company or its assets.

In 1995 the duty of loyalty was extended to minority shareholders who could exercise a veto over a decision that determined the future existence of the corporation. In the *Girmes* case, the court ruled that the exercise of veto power by minority shareholders at a shareholders meeting which blocked a decision that might have saved the company from liquidation, constituted a breach of their fiduciary duty vis-à-vis other shareholders.[38]

An important feature of these cases is not only that courts used the duty of loyalty to limit the powers of controlling stakeholders vis-à-vis other stakeholders (Wellenhofer-Klein 2000), but that they employed a broad legal principle to balance the mandatory statutory law. In *Linotype*, the duty of loyalty was used to assess strategies designed to circumvent a unanimous vote on the winding up of the corporation. In *Girmes*, it was applied to mitigate the powers that arose from the supermajority requirements the law mandates for changes in corporate capital. Note that German courts have used fiduciary duty quite differently than courts in Delaware. While in Delaware the concept has been used as the ultimate bastion of shareholders rights against the backdrop of a highly permissive corporate law, German courts have used the same principle to balance the rigid mandatory law. The lesson seems to be that a mandatory statutory law designed ex ante is ill equipped to regulate the complex relations among key stakeholders in the corporation. This requires a careful balancing act, which even in the eyes of civil law scholars, is best performed by the courts (Hüffer 1990; Lutter 1998).

Our analysis of the German case law is consistent with a study by Johnson et al. (2000) who examine how courts in French civil law countries have dealt with cases in which corporate insiders used their position to transfer corporate assets either directly to themselves or to another company they control (tunneling). They point out that clear, rigid statutory rules may invite strategies that conform to the letter of the law, but dilute corporate assets in favor of the insiders. By contrast, the broad notion of fairness embedded in fiduciary duty allows courts in common law countries to assess the substantive terms of the entire transaction. Using our framework of the incompleteness of law, we similarly argue that when it is not possible to identify ex ante the type of actions that will amount to a violation of the law, residual lawmaking powers should be allocated to courts, not left with legislatures.

III: Transplanting Fiduciary Duty

The incompleteness of law has important implications for transplanting law from one system to another. Given that neither statutory nor case law will specify all relevant contingencies, the effectiveness of transplanted law depends on how the law will be understood, interpreted, and ultimately applied by domestic institutions in the transplant country. This depends largely on how agents holding LMLEP understand and interpret the law. If law were complete, the task would be much easier. Law could give clear guidance to social and economic actors as well as to law enforcers, and thus should deter in transplant countries as effectively as in origin countries. The incompleteness of law is therefore an important element in explaining the transplant effect (Berkowitz et al. 2003), which refers to the phenomenon that recipients of legal transplants tend to have much less effective laws and legal institutions than countries that indigenously developed their own formal legal order. The intuition behind these empirical results is that the latter (origin) countries are in a better position to make the law relatively more complete over time through adaptation, and are more effective in developing complementary law enforcement institutions than are recipients of foreign law. The incompleteness of law theory predicts that the more incomplete the law, the less effective the transplant will be. The transplantation of open-ended concepts, such as fiduciary duty, therefore seems particularly difficult, because it cannot provide clear guidance for actual behavior or as an effective deterrent against violations. A response to this problem has been to favor "bright-line" rules over broad legal concepts in legal reform projects (Hay et al. 1996).

However, bright-line rules do not eliminate the incompleteness problem. They are relatively easy to draft, but are likely to overdeter, since many actions that are flatly prohibited may potentially be welfare enhancing. Another caveat is that they can be easily circumvented, implying that they may underdeter as well (see Kim and Kim, this volume). Bright-line rules may limit the role courts play in applying and interpreting the law; in fact they are designed to limit the courts' power. This may be sensible in areas where other institutions, such as regulators, could effectively enforce the law. In areas where this is not the case, as for violations of fiduciary duty principles, disempowering the courts may in effect disenfranchise shareholders.

Giving courts residual lawmaking powers implies taking the risk that courts will arrive at solutions that may not be desirable from either an economic efficiency or social welfare standpoint. Lack of independence and impartiality of courts is an important explanation for why some legal systems have opted to restrict the courts' lawmaking powers, or why policymakers have advised Russia to limit the role of courts in corporate law (Black and Kraakman 1996). But this argument is only partly convincing. Courts are reactive, not proactive, law enforcers, meaning that courts get involved as arbiters only when a dispute is brought before them. A likely response to courts that are corrupt or politicized is therefore less litigation, not excessive litigation.[39]

The reactive nature of court actions limits the scope for misuse, but does not rule out the possibility that some parties may use courts strategically. Some of the Russian case law discussed above could be interpreted as a strategic use of courts by companies wishing to escape contractual liability. Courts may be more vulnerable to such pressures when dealing with open-ended standards than when dealing with clearly specified rules.[40] But this danger has to be weighed against the potential benefits of making a broader range of actions justiciable. If courts do not handle these issues, who is better placed to delineate the rights and obligations of corporate actors?

If there is no good alternative to courts, then the question becomes, if and how courts in countries that typically do not vest courts with much residual law-making powers could be induced to play a more active role in enforcing fiduciary principles. Simply incorporating fiduciary duty principles in statutory law is unlikely to be effective. In addition, procedural rules should be designed to give minority shareholders standing in court. Still, our survey of the emerging case law in transition economies suggests that even procedural rules may not be sufficient, at least if the law incorporates only the broad outlines of fiduciary duty principles. Instead, the law should enumerate typical actions that might be considered a violation of fiduciary duty principles, but explicitly add that other, similar actions, should be treated by courts in the same manner.[41] Such an approach would prevent courts from hiding behind formalistically interpreted statutory law and force them to assess the merits of different cases.

None of the forgoing suggests that courts thus empowered will arrive at the same solutions as common law judges in the U.K. or the U.S. In fact, allocating lawmaking powers to courts is likely to result in greater divergence rather than convergence of the law, as judges will respond to cases brought before them which are bound to differ from cases litigated elsewhere.

Conclusion

The major proposition of this essay is that courts should hold residual lawmaking powers over conduct that may violate the principle of fiduciary duty. The principle of fiduciary duty exemplifies a highly incomplete law. Its very nature as a residual makes it impossible to write a fairly complete law. Where lawmakers have attempted to do so, they have usually carved out only a subset of issues for which sufficient experience existed, and which therefore allowed a good approximation of issues warranting regulation. However, they have not been able to replicate the reach of the fiduciary duty principle as enforced by courts in common law jurisdictions.

In transition economies, courts may not yet be in a position to play an effective role in developing norms for corporate conduct. The scarcity of cases that have made it to the courts so far can be taken as an indication that there is little demand for their actions. However, the lack of litigation may well lie in the uncertainty about the courts' residual lawmaking powers and the lack of clear procedural rules to support litigation. Remarkably, Russia, a country where litigation rates have been comparably low, has seen the largest number of cases among the transition economies we investigated on conflict-of-interest problems. Perhaps it has also experienced the most extensive violation of shareholder rights. An alternative explanation is that by explicitly regulating conflict-of-interest matters in statutory law and referring the solution of these matters to courts, the legislature confirmed that these issues were justiciable. The main function of these provisions was thus to encourage litigation by allocating residual lawmaking powers to courts. This does not mean that the law has effectively resolved all relevant issues. But the fact that private parties have responded to an explicit allocation of residual lawmaking powers is encouraging. At the same time, it is worth noting that where the scope of the courts' residual lawmaking powers was too broad, i.e., where the law was too ambiguous, litigation has not occurred.

In sum, the Anglo-American concept of fiduciary duty may not be easily transplantable either to civil law systems or to transition economies. However, an important insight to be gained from the history of this concept in Anglo-American law is that a core feature of this concept is the allocation of lawmaking powers to courts, which exercise law enforcement powers reactively and make law ex post. A normative implication of this analysis is that reform efforts should focus on improving the courts, not on circumventing them. In addition, procedural rights should be strengthened and substantive rules should be designed to encourage, rather than discourage, litigation in the corporate realm.

Endnotes

We are indebted to Dimitri Gavriline, Moscow, and Professor Stanislaw Soltysinski, Warsaw, for locating relevant case law. We would also like to thank participants at the authors' workshop and the conference on "Global Markets, Domestic Institutions: Corporate Law and Governance in a New

Era of Cross-Border Deals" held at Columbia Law School in October 2001 and April 2002 respectively. Special thanks to our commentator at the conference, Reinier Kraakman, and to the participants at the seminar on Politics, Law and Development and NYU Law School, in particular to the chair of that seminar, Lewis Kornhauser. All remaining errors are those of the authors.

1. The Securities and Exchange Act includes numerous provisions that could be regarded as a specification of directors' duties vis-à-vis their investors. Similarly, state takeover rules specify the standards of behavior of directors in a takeover situation. Yet, most of these provisions remain rather ambiguous and require further specification by courts.

2. Compare § 23 of the German Law on Joint Stock Companies (AktG).

3. This is different in limited liability companies (GmbH), where courts have played a much more active role. We suggest that this is related to procedural rules that make it easier for shareholders in closed corporations to bring judicial action than in publicly held ones.

4. We recognize that lawmakers have some discretion to determine the relative completeness of law as suggested in the rules versus standards literature. See Kaplow (1992; 1995). However, even the most ambitious lawmaker would not be able to write a fully complete law.

5. In this essay we focus on publicly held corporations. However, similar conflicts arise in close corporations. In fact, some jurisdictions, including Delaware, hardly distinguish among these two types of companies when it comes to the application of fiduciary duty principles.

6. This is the classic objection raised against regulators. See G. Stigler (1964); J. Stigler (1971); and Posner (1974).

7. Of course, one may dispute whether changes in disclosure rules in fact respond to investor interests. For a critical assessment of disclosure rules in the U.S., see, e.g., Benston (1976).

8. For a discussion of German law, see Part II, Section C below.

9. The one-share-one-vote rule is only optional; shares *can* be blocked before the meeting; cumulative voting is only optional; preemptive rights require explicit recognition in the corporate charter. Delaware does, however, offer proxy by mail, the right of 10% shareholders to call an extraordinary shareholder meeting, and—in our view most importantly—the right of shareholders to sue management.

10. Unfortunately, given lack of access to the relevant cases, we could not extend the analysis to cases resolved at the trial court level (courts of first instance).

11. The new Companies Act was adopted September 15, 2000 and entered into force January 1, 2001. A German translation of the Act can be found in Breidenbach (2001).

12. I Aca 322/98, November 5, 1998.

13. Under Polish law, a corporation may have a two-tier management structure, consisting of a management board and a supervisory board. See Art. 377 CC. A corporation with share capital of less than PLN 500,000 may choose between a supervisory board and an audit committee. Corporations that exceed the stipulated share capital must have a supervisory board.

14. Prof. Stanislaw Soltysynski provided the translation of the summary.

15. Translations are from Black et al. (1998).

16. Several U.S. jurisdictions have also codified conflict of interest situations. See Delaware General Corporate Law § 144. Note, however, that the Delaware law precludes the voidance or voidability of transactions concluded by interested directors, if their interest was disclosed and the transaction was "fair"—introducing another broad concept that requires fine-tuning by case law. For a much more detailed elaboration on conditions that lead to a conflict of interest, see § 8.60–8.63 of the Revised Model Business Corporation Act.

17. An independent director is defined as "a member of the company's board of directors (supervisory board) who is not the company's individual executive organ (director, general director) or a member of the company's collegial executive organ (managing board, directorate);" or a person "whose spouse, parents, children brothers, and sisters are persons occupying official positions in the company's management organs." Art. 83, Section 2 para 2 JSCL.

18. See Art. 83, Section 2 para 3. The provision makes explicit reference to Art. 77 of the JSCL, which explains how to determine market value in an economy that is still in transition from a centrally planned economy: "The market value of property, including the value of a company's shares or other securities, is the price at which a seller having full information about the value of the property and not obliged to sell, would agree to sell it, and a buyer having full information about the value of the property and not obliged to acquire the property would agree to acquire it" (Art. 77 JSCL). The law provides that market value is determined by the company's board of directors (supervisory board).

19. In other words, Russia combines the liability rule with the property rule. See Goshen, this volume.

20. Obsor praktiki pazrescheniia sporov, sviazannykh s zakliucheniem khoziaistvennymi obshchestvami krupnykh sdelok i sdelok, v soverschenii kotorykh ime'etsia zainteresovannost' (Survey of practical decisions of disputes related to the conclusion of major transactions and transactions affected by conflict of interest). Information Letter of March 13, 2001, No. 62, published in Vestnik Vyshevo Arbitrazhnovo Suda Rossiiskoi Federatsii No. 7 (2001): 72, 79 (hereinafter Information Letter No. 62).

21. Ibid.: 79.

22. Presidium Supreme Arbitrazh Court, 27 July 2000 (No. 8342/99).

23. See Art. 83 JSCL.

24. The general director held 40% in AOZT Flesch-Invest, which in turn held 50% in OOO Flesch and 50% in Flesch-Market. Flesch Market held 50% in OOO Tovarischestvo Flesch, which was the sole founder of Gala-Inform.

25. Information Letter No. 62, p. 80.

26. An alternative interpretation would be that courts are simply corrupt and use formalistic excuses to serve one party's interest.

27. Information Letter No. 62, p. 82.

28. § 93 Aktienggesetz (AktG).

29. § 88 AktG.

30. § 89 AktG.

31. Until 1998, the threshold was 10 percent. It is now 5 percent.

32. Arguably this treatment reflects the problems that arise from the ownership structure of German firms. Even large firms have a tradition of highly concentrated ownership. This allows block holders to monitor and control management (Roe 1993), but it also places minority shareholders at risk of blockholder dominance.

33. This proposition is further supported by the fact that for limited liability companies, where judicial recourse is available, courts have developed extensive case law on the duties managers owe to shareholders.

34. In a case decided in 1954, the German Supreme Court had to decide whether the supervisory board could dismiss the chairman of the management board on the grounds that he refused to produce a false statement on the ownership of shares in a third company. The chairman had been asked to certify that the sole shareholder of the parent company owned the shares personally, rather than through the parent company itself. Since the law allows dismissal only for cause, the question arose as to whether his behavior amounted to a breach of trust, which the court denied. For details, see BGHZ 13, 188, 189. Two years later the court acknowledged the right of the supervisory board to dismiss the chairman of the management board on the grounds that his behavior had violated the trust relationship between management and the supervisory board. See BGHZ 20, 246.

35. ITT-Decision, BGHZ 65, 15 (1975).

36. Linotype decision, BGHZ 103, 184 (1988).

37. The transfer of assets has been a common strategy to circumvent the rigid requirement of unanimous approval of a merger. § 65 Umwandlungsgesetz (Transformation Law) passed in 1995 requires a qualified vote of three-fourths of the shareholders. Corporate statutes may stipulate higher majority requirements.

38. Girmes Decision, BGHZ 129, 136 (1995). When the Girmes Corporation became insolvent, a shareholders meeting was convened to decide on a 5:2 decrease in corporate capital. The editor of a shareholder rights journal obtained proxies from minority shareholders to block this decision, arguing

that a ratio of 5:3 would still save the company without as much dilution of minority shareholders. Because an agreement could not be reached, the refinancing arrangement failed and the company soon entered into bankruptcy proceedings. Shareholders voting with the majority sought damages for the loss of their stake in the corporation, arguing that if the change in corporate capital had been implemented, the company would not have been bankrupted.

39.   Russian litigation data for commercial disputes in the first half of the 1990s suggests that this was indeed a widespread response to a court system whose trustworthiness was in doubt, not least because of its roots in the socialist system (Pistor 1995, 1996). In contrast to other transition economies, where litigation rates boomed after the onset of radical economic reforms, litigation rates in Russia declined by 30 percent annually in 1993 and 1994. Since 1995 the trend has been slowly reversed.

40.   In this sense, the narrow wording of the conflict of interest rules might be regarded as effective limits on discretionary judicial power.

41.   Bernard Black has indicated to the authors that this approach was attempted for the Russian corporate law, but was rejected by Russian legislators. This suggests that Russian lawmakers consciously chose to reject a structural transplant.

References

Akerlof, George A. 1970. The Market for "Lemons": Quality Uncertainty and the Market Mechanism. *Quarterly Journal of Economics* 84: 488–500.

Arsht, Samuel S. 1976. A History of Delaware Corporation Law. *Delaware Journal of Corporate Law* 1: 1–22.

Becker, Gary S. 1968. Crime and Punishment: An Economic Approach. *Journal of Political Economy* 76: 169–217.

Benston, George J. 1976. *Corporate Financial Disclosure in the UK and the USA.* Lexington, MA: Lexington Books.

Berkowitz, Daniel, Katharina Pistor, and Jean-Francois Richard. 2003. Economic Development, Legality, and the Transplant Effect. *European Economic Review* 47: 165–95.

Black, Bernard, and Reinier Kraakman. 1996. A Self-Enforcing Model of Corporate Law. *Harvard Law Review* 109: 1911–82.

Black, Bernard, Reinier Kraakman, and Jonathan Hay. 1996. Corporate Law from Scratch. In *Corporate Governance in Eastern Europe and Russia.* R. Frydman, C. W. Gray and A. Rapaczynski, eds. Budapest, London, New York: Central European University Press.

Black, Bernard, Reinier Kraakman, and Anna Tarassova. 1998. *Guide to the Russian Law on Joint Stock Companies.* The Hague, London, Boston: Kluwer Law International.

——. 2000. Russian Privatization and Corporate Governance: What Went Wrong? *Stanford Law Review* 52: 1731–1803.

Breidenbach, Stephan, ed. 2001. *Handbuch Wirtschaft und Recht in Osteuropa*. Munich: C.H. Beck.

Cary, William L. 1974. Federalism and Corporate Law: Reflections upon Delaware. *Yale Law Journal* 83: 663.

Clark, Robert Charles. 1986. *Corporate Law*. Boston, Toronto: Little, Brown & Company.

Coffee, John C., Jr. 1989. The Mandatory/Enabling Balance in Corporate Law: An Essay on the Judicial Role. *Columbia Law Review* 89: 1618–91.

Daines, Robert. 2001. Does Delaware Law Improve Firm Value? *Journal of Financial Economics* 62 (3): 525–58.

Eisenberg, Melvin Aron. 2000. *Corporations and Other Business Organizations*. 8 ed. New York: Foundation Press.

Fisch, Jill. 2000. The Peculiar Role of the Delaware Courts in the Competition for Corporate Charters. *University of Cincinnati Law Review* 68: 1061–1100.

Frydman, Roman, Katharina Pistor, and Andrzej Rapaczynski. 1996. Investing in Insider-Dominated Firms: A Study of Russian Voucher Privatization Funds. In *Corporate Governance in Central Europe and Russia*. R. Frydman, C. W. Gray and A. Rapaczynski, eds. Budapest, London, New York: CEU Press.

Ginsburg, Jane C. 1996. *Legal Methods — Cases and Materials*. Westbury, New York: The Foundation Press.

Glaeser, Edward, Simon Johnson, and Andrei Shleifer. 2001. Coase vs. Coasians. *Quarterly Journal of Econmics* 116 (3): 853–99.

Hart, H.L.A. 1961. *The Concept of Law*. Oxford: Oxford University Press.

Hart, Oliver. 1995. *Firms, Contracts, and Financial Structure*. Oxford: Clarendon Press.

Hay, Jonathan R., Andrei Shleifer, and Robert W. Vishny. 1996. Toward a Theory of Legal Reform. *European Economic Review* 40 (3–5): 559–67.

Hendley, Kathryn. 2001. Beyond the Tip of the Iceberg: Business Disputes in Russia. In *The Value of Law in Transition Economies*. P. Murell, ed. Ann Arbor: University of Michigan Press.

Hendley, Kathryn, Barry W. Ickes, Peter Murrell, and Randi Ryterman. 1997. Observations on the Use of Law by Russian Enterprises. *Post-Soviet Affairs* 13 (1): 19–41.

Hopt, Klaus J., and Herbert Wiedemann, eds. 1992. *Aktiengesetz: Großkommentar*. 4 ed, *Großkommentare der Praxis*. Berlin, New York: Walter de Gruyter.

Hueffer, Uwe. 1995. *Aktiengesetz*. 2 ed. Munich: C.H. Beck'sche Verlagsbuchhandlung.

Hüffer, Uwe. 1990. Zur gesellschaftsrechtlichen Treupflicht als richterrechtliche Generalklausel. In *Festschrift für Ernst Steindorff zum 70. Geburtstag*. J. F.

Baur, K. J. Hopt and K. P. Mailänder. Berlin, eds. New York: Walter de Gruyter.

Johnson, Simon, Rafael La Porta, Florencio Lopez-de-Silanes, and Andrei Shleifer. 2000. Tunneling. *American Economic Review* 90: 22–27.

Kaplow, Louis. 1992. Rules versus Standards: An Economic Analysis. *Duke Law Journal* 42: 557–629.

——. 1995. Model of the Optimal Complexity of Legal Rules. *Journal of Law, Economics & Organization* 11: 150–63.

——. 1997. General Characteristics of Rules. In http://encyclo.findlaw.com/lit /9000art.html.

Kursynsky-Singer, Eugenia. 1999. Das Aktienrecht in der Rechtsprechung des rußländischen Obersten Arbitragegerichts. *WGO Monatshefte für Osteuropäeisches Recht* 41: 423–38.

La Porta, Rafael, Florencio Lopez-de-Silanes, Andrei Shleifer, and Robert W. Vishny. 1997. Legal Determinants of External Finance. *Journal of Finance* 52: 1131–50.

——. 1998. Law and Finance. *Journal of Political Economy* 106: 1113–55.

Larcom, Russel Carpenter. 1937. *The Delaware Corporation.* Baltimore: John Hopkins Press.

Lutter, Marcus. 1998. Treupflichten und ihre Anwendungsprobleme. *Zeitschrift für das gesamte Handelsrecht (ZHR)* 162: 164–85.

Milgrom, Paul, and Nancy Stokey. 1982. Information, Trade, and Common Knowledge. *Journal of Economic Theory* 26: 17–27.

Pistor, Katharina. 1995. Law Meets the Market: Matches and Mismatches in Transition Economies. Washington, D.C.: The World Bank. (Unpublished background report.)

——. 1996. Supply and Demand for Contract Enforcement in Russia: Courts, Arbitration, and Private Enforcement. *Review of Central and East European Law* 22 (1): 55–87.

——. 1998. Transfer of Property Rights in Eastern Europe. In *The New Palgrave on Economics and the Law.* P. Newman, ed. London, New York: MacMillan.

——. 2000. Patterns of Legal Change: Shareholder and Creditor Rights in Transition Economies. *European Business Organization Law Review* 1: 59–110.

——. 2001. Law as a Determinant for Stockmarket Development in Eastern Europe. In *Assessing the Value of Law in Transition Economies.* P. Murrell, ed. Ann Arbor: University of Michigan Press.

Pistor, Katharina and Chenggang Xu. 2002. Incomplete Law: A Conceptual and Analytical Framework—its Application to Financial Market Regulation. Unpublished paper.

Polinsky, Mitchell and Steven Shavell. 2000. The Economic Theory of Public Enforcement of Law. *Journal of Economic Literature* 38: 45–76.

Posner, Richard. 1974. Theories of Economic Regulation. *Bell Journal of Economic Management* 5: 335–58.

Roe, Mark J. 1993. Some Differences in Corporate Structure in Germany, Japan, and the United States. *Yale Law Journal* 102: 1927–2003.

Romano, Roberta. 1991. The Shareholder Suit: Litigation Without Foundation? *Journal of Law, Economics, & Organization* 7: 55–87.

Solum, Lawrence B. 1999. Indeterminacy. In A *Companion to Philosophy of Law and Legal Theory*. D. Patterson, ed. Malden, MA: Blackwell Publishers Ltd.

Stigler, George J. 1964. Public Regulation of the Securities Markets. *Journal of Business* 27: 117–42.

Stigler, Joseph. 1971. The Theory of Economic Regulation. *Bell Journal of Economics* 2: 3–21.

Wellenhofer-Klein, Marina. 2000. Treupflichten im Handels-, Gesellschafts- und Arbeitsrecht. *Rabelszeitschrift* 64: 564–94.

Xu, Chenggang and Katharina Pistor. 2002. Law Enforcement Under Incomplete Law: Evidence from Financial Market Regulation. Unpublished paper. Available at http://papers.ssrn.com/sol3/papers.cfm?/abstract_id=396141.

4 What Corporate Law Cannot Do

Mark J. Roe

How important is corporate law—and its capacity to protect minority stockholders from insider machinations—in building securities markets and separating ownership from corporate control? Quite important, according to most recent analyses; maybe central. Without such corporate law protections, securities markets, it is said, will not arise. And if corporate law is good enough in technologically advanced nations, ownership will diffuse away from concentrated ownership into dispersed stock markets.

This new perspective greatly contributes to understanding the fragility of capital markets in transition and third-world economies. But it has been used, and I'll argue here overused, to primarily explain the persistence of dominant stockholders and fragile securities markets in many of the world's richest nations in Europe and Asia. I say overused, because there is too much that is critical to ownership separation that corporate law does not reach, *and does not even seek to reach*, in the world's richest, most advanced nations.

The conceptual problem is that current academic thinking in finance lumps together costly opportunism due to a controller's self-dealing and costly decisionmaking that inflicts losses on the owners. The first, self-dealing, corporate law seeks to control directly. The second, bad decisionmaking that damages shareholders, it does not.

Other institutions control the latter, and their strength varies from nation to nation. Owners tend to stay as blockholders—and ownership does not diffuse, and securities markets remain weak—if stockholders expect managerial agency costs to shareholders would be very high if ownership fully separated.

Lost in the current academic debate (and perhaps even lost to policymakers at some international development agencies) is that corporate law does not even try to directly control the costs of straightforward mismanagement. Other institutions do. For these other institutions (product market competition, incentive compensation, takeovers, shareholder primacy norms, etc.), corporate law (other than for takeovers, which given the typical 50 percent premium set only an outer limit to managerial agency costs—more about that below) is usually just a supporting prop, not the central institution.

Even if one thinks law has an equal role to play in both—in motivating managers as well as in deterring insider machinations—the two, motivation and deterrence, depend on *differing* laws. Countries can, and do, deal better with one—motivation—than the other—deterrence. And when they do better with one than the other, they affect which organization—close or diffuse ownership—is favored. One could get all of the corporate law institutions "right," but if *other* institutions are missing that keep managerial agency costs to shareholders low enough (or if other institutions in a society *raise* managerial agency costs), then ownership will not sharply separate.

Data support the view that corporate law is secondary here: among the world's richer nations, several by measurement have *good* minority stockholder protection. But despite protective results that suggest the potential overreaching from majority stockholders is kept in check, ownership has *not* yet neatly separated from control. Our task is to assess the theoretical implications of why ownership did not separate, since these counter-examples tell us that corporate law did not impede it.

If ownership did not separate from control in a nation, we cannot know whether separation failed because blockholder rampages are uncontrolled *or* because *managerial agency costs* would be far too high if ownership separated. *Each* could have prevented separation. Or one alone could have, with the other not standing in the way.

Managerial agency costs come in two "flavors." One, machinations that transfer value to the managers—"stealing," corporate law seeks to control. But the other—"shirking" or pursuing goals other than shareholder value— corporate law largely leaves alone. If underlying economic, social, or political conditions make managerial agency costs very high, and if those costs are best contained by a controlling shareholder, *then concentrated ownership persists whatever the state of corporate law in checking blockholder misdeeds.*

I speculate on what underlying economic, political, and social conditions could make managerial agency costs persistently high. I also speculate on how a shrinking of these agency costs, one plausibly now going on in continental Europe, could raise the demand to build legal institutions that facilitate separation.

Many business features could keep agency costs higher in one nation than another: a weak product market is one; an inability to use incentive compensation effectively because it would, say, disrupt employment relationships within the firm, is a second; a high level of social mistrust that impedes professionalization of management is a third.

Corporate law, when it's effective, impedes insider machinations: it stops, or reduces, controlling shareholders from diverting value to themselves, and bars managers from putting the firm into their own pockets. When, for example, controllers obtain very high private benefits from control, because they divert firm value into their own pockets, then distant shareholders mistrust the insiders, and are unwilling to buy. Ownership concentration should, all else equal, persist. Good corporate law (or substitutes like stock exchange rules, contract, media glare, or reputational intermediaries) can, by reducing this potential for thievery, facilitate separating ownership from control.

But there is more to running a firm than controlling insider machinations. And, to repeat, it is the machinations that are corporate law's primary and direct focus. Managerial agency costs to distant shareholders come in *two* basic flavors: machinations and mismanagement. Law can reduce the first, but does little directly to minimize the second. Not yet fully recognized in the current literature is that the core of American corporate law *avoids* dealing with the second. This is basic to the study of the corporation in American law schools, and basic to its operation of corporate law in American courts: The business judgment rule has courts *refusing* to intervene when shareholders attack managerial mistakes.

Today's corporate theory cannot explain why several wealthy European nations protect minority shareholders well, but nevertheless *still* have concentrated ownership. The most plausible theory is that close ownership persists not because of weak corporate law, but because a) managerial agency costs from dissipating shareholder value would be very high after full separation, and b) concentrated ownership reduces those costs to shareholders enough. I suggest why these costs to shareholders vary from nation-to-nation and firm-to-firm.

Moreover, by shifting our focus from legally malleable private benefits to managerial agency costs we can see why substandard corporate law persists in several of the other richer, well-developed nations. Low-quality law can be a symptom of weak separation, not its base-line cause. *If managerial agency costs from dissipating shareholder value would be too high anyway* (because, say, nonlegal institutions keep them high, or fail to bring them down), then there's little reason for the players (public policymakers, investors, founders and block-owners) to build good corporate law, because it wouldn't be much used.

A roadmap for this essay: I outline in Part I the quality of corporate law argument and why it is important. In Part II, I show why when potential dissipatory managerial agency costs are perniciously high in a society, but containable by dominant stockholders, corporate law quality is irrelevant or tertiary: *even if* it is good, ownership will *not* separate from control. In Part III, I show why the data indicate that the quality of corporate law argument, although it explains transition economies nicely, is overstated for several of the world's richest nations: in too many of them basic shareholder protections seem adequate, stock can be and is sold, but ownership nevertheless does not separate from control. Something else has made concentrated control persist.

Lastly, I conclude. High-quality, protective corporate law is a good institution for a society to have. It lowers the costs of building strong, large business enterprises. It can prevent, or minimize, controlling stockholder diversions, a necessary condition for separation. But among the world's wealthier nations, it does not primarily determine whether it is worthwhile to build those enterprises. It is only a tool, not the foundation.

I. The Argument: Corporate Law as Propelling Diffuse Ownership

Today's dominant academic and policy explanation for why continental Europe lacks deep and rich securities markets is the purportedly weak role of corporate and securities law in protecting minority stockholders, a weakness that is said to contrast with America's strong protections of minority stockholders. A major Europe-wide research network, leading financial economists, and increasingly legal commentators have stated so (La Porta et al. 1998: 1136–37; 1999; Bebchuk 1999; Coffee 1999; Becht and Röell 1999).

One imagines the Nobel Prize winning Franco Modigliani shaking his head in disappointment when writing that nations with deficient legal regimes cannot get good stock markets and, hence, "the provision of funding shifts from dispersed risk capital [via the stock market] . . . to debt, and from [stock and bond] markets to institutions, i.e., towards intermediated credit" (Modigliani and Perotti 1998; see also Modigliani and Perotti 1997).

Leading economists showed that deep securities markets correlate with an index of basic shareholder legal protections. These protections are impor- tant: "[P]rotection of shareholders . . . by the legal system *is central* to understanding the patterns of corporate finance in different countries. Investor protection [is] *crucial* because, in many countries, expropriation of minority shareholders . . . by the controlling shareholders is extensive" (La Porta et al. 2000, emphasis supplied). Leading legal commentators have signed on to the law-driven theory (see Coffee 2001; compare Bebchuk 1999).

At the same time, international agencies such as the IMF and the World Bank have admirably promoted corporate law reform, especially that which would protect minority stockholders (Iskander et al. 1999). The OECD and the World Bank have had major initiatives to improve corporate governance, both in the developing and the developed world (OECD 1999; Nestor 2000; Witherell 2000).

These are valuable initiatives. They could well contribute to reaching their goals of more stable enterprises and better economic performance, especially in transition nations. But corporate law, and the reach of govern- ment policymakers through corporate law reform, has limits. And those lim- its are much closer in than the policymakers and academic theory now dis- cern. Here I demarcate those limits in the world's richest nations beyond which corporate law ceases to be a primary institution.

A. *Protecting Minority Stockholders*

The basic law-driven story is straightforward: Imagine a nation whose law badly protects minority stockholders against a blockholder extracting value from small minority stockholders. A potential buyer fears that the majority stockholder would later shift value to itself, away from the buyer. So fearing, the prospective minority stockholder does not pay pro rata value for the stock. If the discount is deep enough, the majority stockholder decides not to sell, concentrated ownership persists, and stock markets do not develop.

Or, approach the problem from the owner's perspective. Posit large private benefits of control. The most obvious that law can affect are benefits that the controller can derive from diverting value from the firm to himself. The owner might own 51 percent of the firm's stock, but retain 75 percent of the firm's value if the owner can overpay himself in salary, pad the company's payroll with no-show relatives, use the firm's funds to pay private expenses, or divert value by having the 51 percent-controlled firm overpay for goods and services obtained from a company 100 percent-owned by the controller. Strong fiduciary duties, strong doctrines attacking unfair interested-party transactions, effective disclosure laws that unveil these transactions, and a capable judiciary or other enforcement institution can reduce these kinds of private benefits of control.[1] The owner considers whether to sell to diffuse stockholders. With no controller to divert value, the stock price could reflect the firm's underlying value. But the rational buyers believe, so the theory runs, that the diffuse ownership structure would be unstable, that an outside raider would buy up 51 percent of the firm and divert value, and that the remaining minority stockholders would be hurt. Hence, they would not pay full pro rata value to the owner wishing to sell; and the owner wishing to sell would find the sales price to be less than the value of the block if retained (or if sold intact) (La Porta et al. series; Bebchuk 1999); Modigliani and Perotti 1997; 1998).

Hence, the block persists. The controller refuses to leave control "up for grabs" because if it dips below 51 percent control, an outsider could grab control and reap the private benefits.

B. The Attractions of a Technical Corporate Law Theory

The quality of corporate law argument is appealing. Technical institutions are to blame, for example, for Russia's and the transition nations' economic problems. The fixes, if technical, are within our grasp. Humans can shape the results. Progress is possible if we just can get the technical institutions right. If we don't see ownership separation in Germany, France, and Scandinavia, it must be because a technical-fix is missing, one we can provide as easily as downloading a computer program across the Atlantic Ocean. But if it turns out that deeper features of society—industrial organization and competition, politics, conditions of social regularity, or norms that support shareholder value—are more fundamental, we would feel ill at-ease because these institutions are much harder for policymakers to build.[2] These institutions might change over time (and seem to have changed), but they are not in the hands of a technocrat drafting up corporate law reform.

As self-contained academic theory, there is little to quarrel with in the quality-of-corporate law argument. It is sparse and appealing. Good corporate law lowers the costs of operating a large firm; it is good for a nation to have it. But we need *more* to understand why ownership does not separate from control *even where core corporate law is good enough.* Where managerial agency costs due to potential dissipation are substantial, concentrated ownership persists *even if conventional corporate law quality is high.*

Given the facts that we shall develop in Part III—there are too many wealthy, high-quality corporate law countries *without* much separation—the quality-of-corporate-law theory needs to be further refined, or replaced. This we do next.

II. Its Limits: Theory

A. *Where Law Does Not Reach: How Managerial Agency Costs Impede Separation*

Managers would run some firms badly if ownership separated from control. Effective corporate laws constrain managers' overreaching, but do much less to directly induce them to operate their firms well. A related-party transaction can be attacked or prevented where corporate law is good, but an unprofitable transaction law leaves untouched, with managers able to invoke corporate law's business judgment rule to deflect direct legal scrutiny.

Consider a society (or a firm) where managerial agency costs from dissipating shareholder value would be high if ownership separates, but low if it does not, because a controlling shareholder can contain those costs. When high but containable by concentration, concentrated shareholding ought to persist *even if corporate law fully protects minority stockholders from insider's over-reaching.* Blockholders would weigh their costs in maintaining control (in lost liquidity and diversification) versus what they'd lose if managerial agency costs were high. Control would persist even if corporate law were good.

This is a basic but important point, and it is needed to explain the data that we look at in the next part, after we more precisely delineate the two basic institutions needed to stabilize ownership separation.

B. Improving Corporate Law without Increasing Separation

The basic but often missed argument in the prior section—that variance in managerial agency costs can drive ownership structure *even if conventional corporate law is quite good*—can be stated formally in a simple model. High managerial agency costs preclude separation *irrespective of the quality of conventional corporate law.*

Let:

A_M = The managerial agency costs to shareholders from managers' dissipating shareholder value, to the extent avoidable via concentrated ownership.

C_{CS} = The costs to the concentrated shareholder in holding a block and monitoring (that is, the costs in lost liquidity, lost diversification, expended energy, and, perhaps, error).

When A_M is high, ownership concentration persists whether or not law successfully controls the private benefits that a controlling shareholder can siphon off from the firm.

V = Value of the firm when ownership is concentrated.

B_{CS} = The private benefits of control, containable by corporate law.

A few words on the definitions: While no simple framework can account for every variation, this one is quite flexible. For example, one might think about founders who lose touch and who would be best replaced by professional managers open to new ideas. This possibility would not be outside the model: the sign on A_M, managerial agency costs, would change; instead of managers being a cost, they'd be a gain. And C_{CS}, the costs of concentration could also have its sign change from the normal expectation (that carrying a big illiquid, undiversified block of stock is costly): if taxes, say, would be imposed on a dominant blockholder who sold off his or her stock, then concentration could be cheaper to the dominant stockholder than diffusion. C_{CS} would turn negative.

But let us put these aside to focus on the central tendencies here of private benefits of control and managerial agency costs: Consider the firm worth V when ownership is concentrated. Posit first that managerial agency costs are trivial even if the firm is fully public. As such, the private benefits of control, a characteristic legally malleable and reducible with protective corporate law, can determine whether ownership separates from control. Consider the controller who owns 50 percent of the firm's stock. As such she obtains one-half of V, plus her net benefits of control. (In this simple first model, the value of the firm remains unchanged whether it has a controlling stockholder or is fully public.) She retains control when the following inequality is true:

(1) $$V/2 + B_{CS} - C_{CS} > V/2.$$

The left side is the value to the controlling stockholder of the control block: half the firm's cash flow plus the private benefits diverted from minority stockholders, minus the costs of maintaining the block (in lost diversification and liquidity).[3] The right side is the value she obtains from selling the block to the public. Equation (1) states that as long as the private benefits of control exceed the costs of control, then concentrated ownership persists. Because corporate law can dramatically shrink the private benefits, B_{CS}, corporate law matters quite a bit in equation (1). This is the conventional theory[4] that we next amend.

We amend by introducing A_{M}, managerial agency costs from dissipating shareholder value. If those managerial agency costs are nontrivial, then the controller's proceeds from selling into the stock market would be $(V - A_{M})/2$. Concentration persists if and only if

(2) $$V/2 + B_{CS} - C_{CS} > (V - A_{M})/2.$$

Rearranging: concentration persists if the net benefits of control $(B_{CS} - C_{CS})$ are more than the controller's costs of diffusion $(A_{M}/2)$:

(3) $$B_{CS} - C_{CS} > -A_{M}/2.$$

Or, further re-arranging, concentration persists if:

(4) $$B_{CS} + A_{M}/2 > C_{CS}.$$

Quality-of-corporate-law theory predicts diffusion fails to occur when $B_{CS} > C_{CS}$, with corporate law the means of containing B_{CS}. That is correct, but incomplete. Where A_{M} is high, diffusion does not occur *even if B_{CS} is zero and corporate law perfect, because A_{M} could take-over and drive the sepa-*

ration decision. B_{CS}, the controlling shareholder's private benefits, are relatively unimportant if A_M is very high. Only when $A_M \rightarrow 0$ do legally malleable private benefits alone determine diffusion.[5]

C.   Corporate Law's Limited Capacity to Reduce Agency Costs

One might reply that core corporate law when improved reduces *both* the controlling stockholder's private benefits (B_{CS}, by reducing the controller's capacity to siphon off value) *and* managerial agency costs (A_M, by reducing the managers' capacity to siphon off benefits for themselves). And it does so, one might mistakenly then argue, about equally.

1. *The business judgment rule.* This criticism is both right and wrong, but mostly wrong. The reason it is mostly wrong is simple. Managerial agency costs are the sum of managers' overreaching (unjustifiably high salaries, self-dealing transactions, etc.) *and* their mismanagement. Economic analyses typically lump these together and call them "agency costs." But agency costs come from stealing *and* from shirking. It is correct to lump them together in economic analyses *as a cost to shareholders*, because both costs are visited upon shareholders. For example, Fama (1980) notes that agency costs come from "shirking, perquisites or incompetence." But it is *incorrect* to think that *law* (especially American corporate law) minimizes each cost to shareholders equally well (cf. Dooley and Veasey 1989: 521 (Veasey is now the Delaware Supreme Court chief judge); Bishop 1968: 1095 (managers without a conflict of interest always win); Rock and Wachter 2001: 1664–68).

The standard that corporate law applies to managerial decisions is, realistically, *no* liability at all for mistakes, absent fraud or conflict of interest. *But this is where the big costs to shareholders of having managerial agents lie, exactly where law falls silent.*

Conventional corporate law does little, or nothing, to directly reduce shirking, mistakes, and bad business decisions that squander shareholder value. The business judgment rule is, absent fraud or conflict of interest, nearly insurmountable in America, *insulating* directors and managers from the judge, and *not* subjecting them to legal scrutiny.

Consider this statement from a well-respected Delaware chancellor:

There is a *theoretical* exception to [the business judgment rule, protecting directors and managers from liability] that holds that some decisions may be so "egregious" that liability . . . may follow even in the absence of proof of conflict of interest or improper motivation. *The exception, however, has resulted in no awards of money judgments against corporate officers or directors in [Delaware].* . . . Thus, to allege that a corporation has suffered a loss . . . does not state a claim for relief against that fiduciary *no matter how foolish the investment.* . . . [6]

One does not exaggerate much by saying that American corporate law has produced only one major instance in which non-conflicted managers were held liable to pay for their mismanagement: *Smith v. Van Gorkom,*[7] a decision excoriated by managers and their lawyers, and one promptly overturned by statute.[8]

Nor should we think that this is a gap in American law, one that law would fill in if other institutions failed to control managerial agency costs. One *would not* want the judges regularly second-guessing managers. Most American analysts would assume that it would be costly for firms if judges regularly second-guessed managers' non-conflicted business decisions.[9]

2. Controlling shareholders. One might refine this analysis by accounting for a dominant shareholder's errors. But the costs of these errors are usually thought to be smaller than legally uncontrollable managerial error. True, similar legal doctrines (the business judgment rule) shield the controlling shareholder from lawsuits for a non-conflicted mistake. But because the controlling stockholder owns a big block of the company's stock, it internalizes much of the cost of any mistake (unlike the unconstrained managers). A controller has some incentive to turn the firm over to professional managers if he realizes they would make the firm more profitable.

D. *Law's Indirect Capacity to Affect Agency Costs*

We have thus far considered the effects on separation of conventional corporate law, the law of fiduciary duties, of derivative suits, and of corporate waste. Conventional corporate law can reduce over-reaching and, where it or a substitute fails to reduce it, separation should not be wide. But even if it succeeds, managerial agency costs to shareholders could be high and, when high, ownership cannot readily separate. Institutions other than conventional corporate law raise, lower, and control managerial agency costs, reducing them via competitive markets, shareholder wealth maximization norms, incentive compensation, hostile takeovers, and corporate transparency.

For these institutions, law is also relevant. But its relevance is indirect. True, law can potentially encompass everything in a society. Law *could* ban the institutions that indirectly reduce agency costs. *Anything* can be taxed, destroyed, and prohibited.

1. *Through takeover law.* The relevant law here closest to the core of corporate law is takeover law. Takeovers are (properly) seen as heavily law-influenced (see, e.g., Milhaupt and West, this volume). True, private actors must commence the takeover, but then the judge and takeover law make it harder or easier for them to succeed. But takeover law only goes so far. First, there's that persistent and substantial premium. For quite some time an offeror has had to offer a 50 percent premium over the pre-offer trading price in the Untied States. Even if takeovers flatly barred managers from mismanaging the firm anywhere beyond that premium, then—although takeovers keep managers within a 50 percent boundary—other institutions (like product market competition, incentive compensation, professionalism, etc.) would be the institutions that kept most managers from straying so far. Takeovers would provide an outer boundary, but other institutions must be doing the rest of the work. And since 50 percent of firm value is quite a lot, those other, non-corporate law institutions are not trivial.

One might reply by saying that American takeover law is lax, and gives managers too much discretion. Better takeover law—such as that embodied in the British takeover code—would do the job better, keep managerial agency costs low, and facilitate separation.

This kind of rebuttal has two deep problems though: American takeover law might well fail to measure up, but America has now and has long had one of the strongest ranges of ownership separation: even if takeover law in the United States was, and is, imperfect for shareholders, it's in the United States where separation is strongest among the world's richest nations. This combination would, again, suggest that corporate law (here, in the guise of strong takeover law) isn't always the essential ingredient.

Moreover, comparing the United States with Britain is instructive. Critics of American corporate law often point to the British City takeover code as about as good as we can get (e.g., Bebchuk and Ferrell 1999: 1193; DeMott 1983). But how much does that improved takeover law get Britain? I know of no deep measurement, so I undertook one of my own, measuring the premium in hostile offers. The Thomson Financial data yielded the typical premium for the United States—50 percent. And for Britain over the same time period, the premium turned out to be less—40 percent.[10]

That 10 percent differential should not be belittled. Ten percent better management—if that's what better British law would yield—is huge. But 40 percent, the residual, is more (four times more!). And for that big residual, *other* institutions—institutions that get even farther afield from core corporate law—must do the job, institutions such as product market competition and the like.

2. Through antitrust law, tax law, and other institutions. So, although ordinary but mistaken managerial business decisions and corporate transactions are immune from direct judicial attack, other institutions in society affect these business decisions and transactions; and law can facilitate or ban these other institutions. But the other institution (the competitive product market, the incentive compensation, the pro-shareholder norm) is the primary control, with law just assisting or impeding that institution. But for insider overreaching, basic corporate law is a primary and direct deterrent. It is the judge who bars the transfers, orders recovery of the diverted value, and punishes the wrong-doer. The judge intervenes directly.

Consider product market competition, shareholder primacy norms, professionalism, incentive compensation, and transparency. Strongly competitive markets, for example, can be prodded along by good antitrust law, or lost by bad antitrust law. But the primary constraint on managers is the product market, not law.

And shareholder primacy norms, for example, can be facilitated or demeaned by legal pronouncements. But the norm, not the pronouncement, is what directly affects managerial performance. Or incentive compensation can be spurred, or taxed. But once again, it is not the tax rule that spurs managers directly, but the incentive compensation that pushes them.

Although law affects these institutions, law's effects here differ from the effects of conventional corporate law. First, they do not directly invoke the core explanation for good corporate law, namely that it grows out of common law and the judge's capacity to control interested-party, conflict-of-interest transactions that divert corporate value into the controller's bank account. One might now reply that antitrust law and tax law are "part of" corporate law, but most would say that this is a stretch, and a big one. Moreover, other institutions and economic features affect, say, competition. If the economy is small or the technology is not conducive to standard competitive markets, then even perfect antitrust law will leave many industrial segments uncompetitive.

Importantly, law here does not attack the cost to shareholders directly (as law does when the judge punishes a controlling shareholder who diverts value to herself). Law's role is to enhance or impede the private institution that would reduce the dissipation. And these institutions have the potential to be politically charged, and in other nations one or the other or all four *are* politically charged.

E. Even if Law Critically Affects Both

Still, one might reject the proposition that law is secondary in inducing good management for shareholders. Law affects these other institutions that control managerial agency costs (competition, compensation, and so on), and one might believe *these* laws to be central to whether public firms can arise and whether ownership can separate from control.

But even so, the structure of my argument—of *corporate* law's limits— persists: The laws and institutions that affect managerial and agency costs are different from those that affect insider machinations. The two sets are *not* identical. They barely overlap. If one society does better with one set than with the other, the degree of diffusion is deeply affected. Corporate law might minimize insider transactions, but the other laws might fail to reduce managerial agency costs.

Assume arguendo that corporate law, broadly defined, can if "unleashed" affect both private benefits and managerial agency costs. But if other institutions *also* affect managerial agency costs, then corporate law could be perfect but these *other* institutions would affect the strength of ownership separation, via their affect on managerial agency costs.

F. Ambiguity in Recent Legal Theory: Improving It Can Reduce Separation

The recent wisdom—that strengthening corporate law facilitates separation in the world's richer nations—can be challenged. Thus far I have accepted it, but argued that variation in managerial agency costs can trump corporate law's effect. Even if corporate law is good enough, I've argued, variation could depend on the level of managerial agency costs.

But conventional theory is softer here than the dominant literature has it: improving a nation's corporate law can *increase blockholding*. Minorities would feel *more* comfortable in "protective" nations than in non-protective nations. As such, a nation might make corporate law "better," and thereby induce *more blockholders* and not the dispersed ownership that conventional wisdom posits would be the effect. Dispersed stockholders would not fear that blockholders would rip them off, because better law would constrain blockholders.

Consider the three categories of large-firm ownership:

1. Diffuse
2. Public, but with a dominant stockholder, and
3. Privately held.

The quality-of-corporate law thesis assumes that law reform would, monotonically, increase diffusion, moving firms from category 2 (or category 3) into category 1. But that is not the only logical effect of improving corporate law.

Consider firms in categories 1 and 3. Of the firms already public, devices such as pills, caps, and mandatory bids impede a raider from grabbing control to siphon off private benefits. But with private benefits less available, some firms could drop their voting caps, poison pills, and other barriers to blockholder entry, as the siphoning is less important when corporate law improves.[11]

And consider the privately held firms in Category 3. With corporate law improved, an owner could sell a minority stake to the public, and investors could buy, confident that future over-reaching would be minimal.

To illustrate: Posit a nation with 30 large firms, 10 of which are diffusely held, 10 public but with blockholders, and 10 fully private. In the commonly used indices of diffusion, this nation would have a .5 index of diffusion. (Of the twenty largest public firms, 10 lack blockholders.) Then corporate law improves. Ownership of five category 2 block-controlled firms fully separates. The index of diffusion jumps to .75 (because 15 of the 20 public firms would be diffuse).

But five of the 10 original fully public firms now can afford blockholders because infighting would decline when law gets better. If the blockholder would add value by, say, monitoring managers, improving information flow, or making soft deals with corporate inputs (deals that a liquid stock market cannot firm up), then the index of diffusion could *end up where it began, at .5.*

And of the 10 fully private firms (category 3), five owners decide that they can take the firm public and, under the newly improved corporate law regime, investors readily buy up the stock. The index of diffusion would *drop* from .5 to .4.

And a few fully public firms might go private, because managers know that improved law has removed one barrier to cashing in on any improvement in the firm value—the difficulty of taking the firm public later.

Concentrated blockholders have two major roles inside the firm: they steal from fellow stockholders and they monitor managers. If law limits the negative possibility, then that improved law should make minority stockholders *more, not less, comfortable*, with blockholders. Improving corporate law should, in such settings, all else equal, *increase*, as well as decrease, the incidence of blockholding. Which effect dominates is uncertain (see table 4.1).

Getting more public firms for a nation and separating ownership from control is not inherently good. Ownership choice and shareholder welfare expand by improving corporate law. So improving it is worthwhile. But one could not measure the increased quality of corporate law by measuring the change in the number of public firms and the density of separation over time. Corporate law might improve, *and its very improvement might diminish the density of separation.* This ambiguity is a theoretical issue, probably a very important one, but one that we must turn away from, returning now to the basic theory.

G. The Tight Limits to the Purely Legal Theory

Thus, the basic theory here is, if blocks persist, one cannot *a priori* know whether they persist because minority stockholders fear the controller, or because they fear the *managers*, who might dissipate shareholder value if the controlling stockholder disappears. Even if better corporate law usually increases diffusion in rich nations with adequate but not outstanding corporate law (a proposition open to theoretical challenge), concentration might be due to high managerial agency costs and have little to do with core corporate law's constraints on insider machinations.

TABLE 4.1 Indeterminate effect of better corporate law in rich nation.

	Type of firm ownership			
	Diffuse Public	Blockholder but public	Fully private	Index of concentration of public firms
Time 1. Country begins with serviceable but not excellent corporate law				
1. Initial ownership distribution	10	10	10	.5 (10/20)
Time 2. Corporate law improves				
2a. 5 blockholders sell out	15 ◄——	5	10	.75 (15/20)
2b. Caps, pills removed; 5 public firms get blocks	10 ——►	10	10	.5 (10/20)
2c. 5 fully private go public but blockholder remains	10	15 ◄——	5	.4 (10/25)
2d. 5 fully public go fully private in LBO's	5	15	10	.25 (5/20)

If distant shareholders fear unrestrained managers, the controller cannot sell stock at a high enough price and thus she keeps control to monitor managers or to run the firm.

III.   Its Limits: Data

If we could measure the quality of corporate law, then we could see whether ownership is concentrated where corporate law protects shareholders and diffuse where it does not. True, if diffusion correlated with high-quality law, the primacy of the law-as-cause thesis would not be proven: when ownership is made diffuse for some other reason (due to technology, say, or politics) then the diffuse owners may demand legal protections. Corporate law might follow, not lead, market development. But if, among nations with satisfactory corporate law, ownership is still concentrated in several, we would need more than just the legal theory to explain the result.

A. Measuring Quality

1. Corporate law: what counts? Judging how well corporate law protects minority stockholders across nations by examining their corporate law is hard. One must determine which laws are critical. (How did Britain succeed without a derivative suit, the very institution that plaintiff-oriented counsel in the U.S. say is a sine qua non and one that France, seen as a weak corporate law nation by American analysts, allows?) One protection might be missing, but an even stronger substitute might be present. Moreover, the rules-on-the-books could be identical in two nations but if the quality of enforcement (because of a corrupt or inefficient judiciary or regulatory system, or because of differing levels of resources allocated to enforcement) might make the bottom line protections differ greatly. Or *practices* not required by a nation's corporate law could protect shareholders: a legal index might look bad, but the reality could be the opposite if contract, corporate charter terms, or business practices counteract a deficient corporate law.

Undaunted by lawyers' skepticism that one can qualitatively assess corporate law directly, finance-oriented students of corporate governance have built legal indices for many nations. They have accomplished a major undertaking, one that should embarrass many (of us) corporate law professors who have not even attempted what the financial economists have completed. They have argued convincingly that corporate law institutions are weak in many third world and transition nations, that these weaknesses cripple securities markets.[12] These studies have also been interpreted, less convincingly, as showing weak corporate law to be the primary culprit for the weak securities markets on the European continent. Not only do many corporate players in France, Germany, and Scandinavia think their corporate law is fine, but they also sometimes proclaim its superiority in some dimensions over the American variety (Tunc 1982 (French law bans dangerous transactions that American judges weigh, balance, and sometimes approve); cf. Agnblad et al. 2001: 229 (one cannot even find anecdotes of insider machinations in Sweden)).

The indexers consciously do not seek to measure the bottom-line quality of each nation's corporate law but use a few proxies: Possibly the index focuses on rules that are not core shareholder protections, but rather proxy for a total set of institutions that protect shareholders, a set for which there might be more direct measures. Refinement is possible.[13]

One can list differing rules, but it is hard to know a) which rules are substitutes and, hence, which countries truly have gaps in protection, b) which rules really count, c) the extent to which players follow announced rules, and d) whether the rules in focus are the kind that securities market players demand up front as necessary to build securities markets, or whether the rules are just the polish on financial markets that comes once deep securities markets exist for other reasons. Some rules are window-dressing, some really bind. Which is which?

2. *Corporate law: The bottom line.* Can we measure the bottom-line, over-all quality of corporate law? If we knew the nation-by-nation average premium for control, we could. In nations where the premium is high, we would surmise corporate law or its enforcement is inferior; in nations where that premium over the price available to diffuse stockholders is low, we would surmise it to be superior.

Consider a firm worth $100 million, with a 51 percent blockholder who values that block at $60 million and minority stock that trades for an aggregate value of $40 million. If we can observe those numbers, we have roughly measured the value of control: the controller plausibly pays the 10 percent premium (measured as a percentage of total firm value) because he or she can divert 10 percent of the firm's value from minority stockholders into his or her own pocket. If the quality of corporate law principally determined separation, then nations with high gaps between the value of control and that of the minority stock would have more concentrated ownership than nations with smaller gaps (Barclay and Holderness 1989).

B. Data: Nations with Good Corporate Law but Without Separation

1. *Market measures of the value of control.* We have data on the value of a control block. Researchers have looked at the premium paid for a voting block over the pre-trading price. In the United States, it was found to be 4 percent of the firm's value (Barclay and Holderness 1989). For Italy the premium might be 25 to 30 percent or more (Nicodano and Sembenelli 2000; see also Zingales 1994),[14] a difference consistent with the quality-of-corporate-law theory—since ownership is concentrated there and corporate law, as measured, poor (see Enriques, this volume).

But in Germany, the control block premium was recently, and surprisingly, found by Franks and Mayer (2001)[15] to be only about 4 percent of the firm's value, a result in tension with the pure, unrefined corporate law theory, because German ownership is concentrated and it is a rich nation with the world's third largest economy.[16] To be sure, the data could understate the private benefits: benefits might have already been taken before the sale and, hence, the sales price would not reflect them. And firms for which blocks are sold could be those with low private benefits, while those where diversion is high do not trade. But even the reduced fact remains that for those blocks sold, the future private benefits are expected to be about equal to those expected in American block trades.

So, the block premium in Germany is about that of the premium in the United States, 4 percent. We should pause at this finding for Germany. That number suggests we'd need to refine the pure form of the law-driven theory. If control blocks trade at such a low premium in the world's third largest economy, one that is a paradigm of concentrated ownership, *perhaps something else induces concentration to persist.*

An explanation for Germany is that German codetermination—by which labor gets half of the seats in boardrooms of large firms—fits snugly with concentrated shareholding as a counterbalance in large, especially large smoke-stack, industries. That 4 percent premium is *less* than the decline in share-holder value measured when Germany enhanced its codetermination statute in 1976 and increased employee representation in the boardroom from one-third to one-half (FitzRoy and Kraft 1993; Gorton and Schmid 2000; Schmid and Seger 1998; but see Baums and Frick 1999: 206; Frick et al. 1999).

The low German 4 percent control premium also shows why construct-ing an index for corporate law quality is so hard. To divert big value, the controlling shareholder typically needs a big transaction—a buyout, a merger, a related party sale of good or services. And to get a big transaction through a firm, one needs a compliant board. Because the majority stockholder in the United States typically appoints the entire board, it typically controls the full board. But in Germany the blockholder can *never* control the full board, because German law mandates that labor get half of it, and the practice is that banks holding their brokerage customers' proxies get some board seats. Other German corporate law features might be weak, thereby generating an appearance of weak corporate law protections in a cross-country index. But even so, the German blockholder may be stymied in pushing a related-party transaction through because he or she *cannot* control the full German board. Interaction effects impede our identifying one or two key corporate law features that count.

Two other researchers use a differing methodology, but come up with similar data. They investigate the effects of ownership concentration in 100 of Germany's public firms. They conclude that moving a German firm from diffuse to concentrated ownership would double the value of the firm's shares (Edwards and Weichenrieder 1999).[17] Increases in ownership concentration typically *benefit* the diffuse stockholders. That story fits poorly with a pure poor-corporate-law theory,[18] but nicely with noncorporate, managerial agency cost theory.

The new German data on control block premium present a very big counter-example to an unrefined law-driven theory. Counter-examples are important, but perhaps there is some German-specific factor, not replicated elsewhere, that could make the theory generally true, but just inapplicable in Germany. To check, we turn to other data.

2. *Dual class common stock.* Corporate law's effectiveness can be roughly measured via the voting premium when the firm issues stock that votes and stock that does not vote. So, class A stock votes, class B stock does not, but both have the same dividend rights. (Variations abound.) A controller cannot reap benefits by controlling the class B stock, but can by controlling class A stock. Both are formally entitled to the same cash coming out from the company. If the value of class A stock is higher than that of B's, we have a measure of the value that the controller can surreptitiously divert from outside shareholders to herself. Good law should keep that value—and the differential—low. If we could measure the differences across nations, we would have an indicator of the quality of corporate law.

Unpublished voting premium data have recently become available. Table 4.2 shows the voting premium in the world's richer nations. Italy's and France's voting premium is high, America's low—a difference consistent with the legal theory, as Italy is usually said, as is France in the American literature, to have poor protections. Each has concentrated ownership. But the new data increase the tension for the pure legal theory; Germany is a weak corporate law nation in the finance economists' indices, but the dual class numbers here *again* show it protects nonvoting stockholders rather well, vindicating defenders of the quality of German corporate law.[19] And not just Germany: Four Scandinavian nations also protect minority stockholders but have concentrated ownership.

This dual class premium data cast doubt on whether a uni-variable model is enough to explain the richer nations' degree of ownership separation. True, further confirmation, with data collected by other researchers, should be added. And the number of observations—a dozen or so of the richer nations—is low.

TABLE 4.2 Voting premium and ownership separation

Country	Voting premium	Portion of large firms that are widely-held
Australia	0.23	0.65
Canada	0.03	0.60
Denmark	0.01	0.40
Finland	0.00	0.35
France	0.28	0.60
Germany	0.10	0.50
Italy	0.29	0.20
Norway	0.06	0.25
Sweden	0.01	0.25
Switzerland	0.05	0.60
United Kingdom	0.10	1.00
United States	0.02	0.80

Source: Voting premium data comes from Nenova (2000); ownership concentration data comes from La Porta et al. (1999: 492). The percentage of widely held firms for a nation is the percentage of the nation's twenty largest firms that lack a 20 percent or larger blockholder.

Moreover, dual class data are a soft measure of the value of control. If the controller has a majority of the class A voting stock, then the researchers are observing the trading value of the minority stockholders on the class A level, and comparing that data to the trading value of the nonvoting class B stock. But the minority class A stockholder is not a controller, it just has a chance of sometime joining a control block.[20]

Thus while this is the best dual-class data set available, it is inherently imperfect. We can take comfort in that ancillary and qualitative information comports with the numbers. The American premium is low, and U.S. corporate and securities law is usually seen as highly protective. The German premium is low, as is the new parallel German control block data. And the Swedish premium is low as well, and Swedish researchers assert that there are not even anecdotal instances of controllers shifting value to themselves. Two Scandinavian researchers tell us that "the value of control does not derive from the possibility to expropriate the fringe of minority shareholders . . . [but] has to be motivated by some other economic motive" (Bergström and Rydqvist 1990) (emphasis supplied). Other Swedish researchers report that:

Outside shareholders do not refrain [from] investing on the Stock-holm Stock Exchange since 55% of the Swedish population own shares . . . and 33% of outstanding shares are owned by foreign investors. . . . [T]he ratio of the stock market capitalization held by minority shareholders in relation to GDP . . . is 0.51 for Sweden compared to 0.58 for the U.S. . . . *[I]t is not likely that weak investor protection has hampered financial market development in Sweden*. . . . (Holmén and Högfeldt 1999: 39).

The other Scandinavian nations have similar reputations, and they also have low premiums. Moreover, the leading blockholding Swedish investor typically uses dual class stock, but not in a way that locks up control: the Wallenberg family holding company does not take majority control but more typically ends up with 5 percent of the cash flow and 25 percent (not a majority) of the votes (Leser and Rocco 2000: 23), leaving influence in the other 75 percent of the votes.[21] The voting premiums in the world's poorer nations (not noted in table 4.2), which are still in the process of developing securities markets, are high.

* * *

To repeat a proviso: I hardly mean that the data tell us that high-quality corporate law is irrelevant. Rather, some rich nations have high-quality corporate law *but ownership still does not separate*. The point is *not* that good corporate law is irrelevant in the world's richer nations—it keeps the costs of running a big enterprise low—*but when it already is good enough, subtle gradations in its quality do not determine whether ownership diffuses*. Something else is more important, with the leading alternative being that high managerial potential to dissipate precludes strong separation.

3. *Control block premium*. Other new data on corporate law quality are also suggestive, and unhelpful to an unrefined form of the corporate law thesis. The premium in a block sale could reveal the quality of the governing corporate law. Consider a controller who owns 50 percent of a $7,500 company with 100 shares, and sells her 50 shares as a block not at $75 each, but at $100 each, when the dispersed stock trades at $50 per share. The $50 per share premium could measure the private benefits of control, benefits that better corporate law would force the controller to share ratably with the firm's other stockholders. The controller could plausibly siphon off $50/share × 50 shares in value, or $2,500 of the firm's total value of $7,500. The premium is 33 percent of the company's value.

If instead the controller's 50 shares sold for $80 per share while dispersed stock sold for $70 per share, then we could calculate that the market was expecting that the controller could siphon off $250 (from 50 shares × $10/share), or 3.3 percent of the firm's value. We would surmise that the first scenario is one of weak corporate law, the second of stronger corporate law.[22]

Economists have just accumulated such data, in an important undertaking. The last two columns of table 4.3 show the data for the world's richer nations.

A cursory examination shows *no* persistent pattern. If the sample only had, say, Austria, Italy, the U.S., and the U.K., we would get a nice pattern for the corporate law thesis: Austria and Italy have concentrated ownership and high sale-of-control premiums; the U.S. and the U.K. have low premiums and low ownership concentration. For these four nations, there's an excellent fit for a quality-of-corporate-law thesis, suggesting it has some importance.[23]

But most other wealthy nations *also* have low sale-of-control premiums, *despite* their *concentrated* ownership. Note the Scandinavian nations: low premium for control, high concentration. Note Germany and Switzerland: fairly low premia, but concentrated ownership for Germany and middling-concentration for Switzerland. And in this sample, both the Netherlands and France, countries with concentrated ownership, do not look bad in protecting minority stockholders. Overall, the "sign" of the relationship is as corporate law theory would predict, but the significance is low, and the portion of the variation explained (12 percent) is quite low.

Graph 4.1 shows the relationships graphically and the statistical result: satisfactory, but "driven" by Italy and Austria. Graph 4.2 shows those same relationships, but without Italy and Austria.

To be precise, the data tell us that there is a group of rich nations that seem to control insider machinations in the dominant stockholder structures that now exist. If ownership separated further, it is possible that *new* means to divert value would arise and, in the changed circumstances, be uncontrollable. For example, the current controllers might, say, face social constraints that wouldn't bind the controllers if new structures emerged. This type of problem plagues these kinds of observations. We can say for the current measured diversions, controls are in place. That's a lot to say, but it's not everything.

If control premia were our only measure of the quality of corporate law, we would be driven to conclude that that corporate law only weakly explains variation in ownership dispersion in the world's richest nations.

TABLE 4.3. Control premia and ownership separation.

Country	(1) Widely-held at 20% for Medium-sized Corporations	(2) Mean premium as a fraction of total equity[1]	(3) Mean premium from col. 2, "corrected" for industry effects
Australia	0.30	0.02	0.04
Austria	0.00	0.38	0.34
Canada	0.60	0.01	–0.04
Denmark	0.30	0.08	0.03
Finland	0.20	0.10	–0.01
France	0.00	0.02	0.04
Germany	0.10	0.10	0.02
Italy	0.00	0.37	0.30
Japan	0.30	–0.04	–0.04
Netherlands	0.10	0.02	0.02
Norway	0.20	0.01	0.04
Sweden	0.10	0.06	0.03
Switzerland	0.50	0.06	–0.06
United Kingdom	0.60	0.02	0.04
United States	0.90	0.02	0.04
	med20	Block premium/ equity value	

[1]Source: Dyck and Zingales (2001).
Technical data: med20 v. employment
protection

Regression	y = –0.04x + 0.65
Adj R-Sq	0.64
t-stat	–5.24***

4. *And the not-so-rich nations?* One might observe that many poorer nations have decrepit corporate law institutions. This is true, and possibly weak corporate law is keeping them back, but the coincidence of bad law and a bad economy does not tell us enough. To learn that, say, Afghanistan, has poor corporate law does not tell us whether its weak economy is primarily due to its weak corporate law or to its *other* weak institutions. If the other

GRAPH 4.1. Block premium vs. ownership dispersion

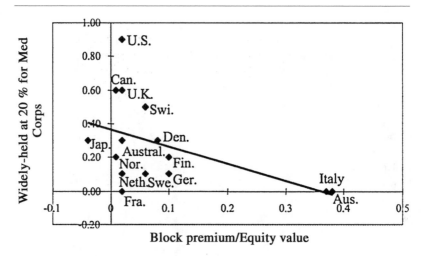

Technical data: med20 v. control premium

Regression $y = -1.02x + .36$
Adj R-Sq $-.12$
t-stat -1.71^*
*Not significant   P value = .11

institutions, particularly the other property rights institutions, are decrepit, *these* may be the critical debilities preventing Afghanistan from developing wealth and complex private institutions that get it ready for public firms and ownership diffusion. Only *then*, when it gets that far, will we be able to tell whether weak corporate law holds it back. The omitted variable might be weak property rights institutions generally, with weak corporate law institutions just a visible, and perhaps minor, surface manifestation of the deeper weakness.

In any case, we are here focusing on the world's richer nations, not its poorer nations. Even if corporate law is the institution holding back the transition and developing nations, the data indicate that it is not holding back every one of the richer nations from getting stronger securities markets and sharper ownership separation. Something else is.

5. *Enforcing contracts.* Bad law sufficiently explains weak securities markets where law is *so* weak that *basic contracts* cannot be enforced—as they

GRAPH 4.2. Block premium vs. ownership dispersion (without Italy or Austria)

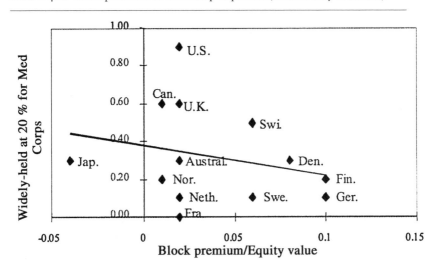

Technical data: med20 v. control premium (without Italy or Austria)

Regression y = −1.58x + .38
Adj R-Sq   −.02
t-stat   −0.84*
*Not significant   P value = .42

cannot be in contemporary Russia, many transition economies, and significant parts of the less developed world—thereby rendering complex corporate institutions impossible (Black and Kraakman 1996; Sachs and Pistor
1997: 3). This is important because a) the quality of contract and corporate
law ought to correlate and b) much that is useful in corporate law can be
built out of good contract law, either directly by public authorities or indirectly by private parties.

Many of the same nations that by measurement have good corporate law
also have good contract law. All the Scandinavian nations, Germany, France
and several other continental European countries enforce commercial contracts as well as the United States does (O'Driscoll et al. 2001: 18 [Denmark,
Finland, Germany, Norway, Sweden, and the United States protect private
property and contract strongly and have largely efficient legal systems]).[24]
This casts more doubt on whether the quality of corporate law thesis

explains enough of why ownership does or does not separate in the world's richer nations. Contract law seems good, and corporate law, which also seems good, is in many dimensions a special form of contract law. Nations that can build one should be able to build the other.

Studies of business climate are consistent: basic *business* institutions in continental Europe and the Anglo-Saxon countries are generally seen as equally business-friendly, but the continental European *labor* markets have been seen as much less business friendly (Sachs and Warner 1998: 24). That unfriendliness could have raised managerial agency costs, as we shall see in the next section.

Nor is it logically correct to assume that where corporate rules are weakly enforced, that weakness is the *primary* cause for weak stock markets in nations that have already built satisfactory contract and property institutions. Were the demand for diffuse ownership sufficiently strong in such nations, investors and firms could try to build the institutions needed for good securities markets. If societies that successfully built other complex business and legal institutions, especially those that effectively enforce commercial contracts, did not try to build these corporate law institutions, then a deeper reason might explain why they did not try.

Thus, one could synthesize the legal and managerial agency costs theories into a two-step argument: When corporate law and court systems are decrepit, public firms will not emerge, because the system fails to protect minority stockholders. This describes many third-world and transition nations. But when either contract or basic corporate law becomes satisfactory, as it is in several western European nations and the United States, then whether a nation builds on what it has (by writing complex contracts, by further improving corporate law, or by developing the ancillary institutions such as stock exchanges or effective intermediaries), becomes a question of whether the underlying potential for low managerial agency costs to shareholders makes it profitable for the players to do so.

C. What Beyond Law is Needed for Separation in the Wealthy West?

I have argued here that corporate law could be fine and ownership might *still* not separate from control. In firms for which managerial agency costs to shareholders would be high if ownership separated, ownership does not readily separate from control. For nations where these costs are systematically high, separation is more rare than where these costs are low. It is more rare *even* in nations where corporate law quality, as measured, is high. Corporate law is insufficient to induce separation. Other conditions have to be met. Here for the sake of completeness, I briefly outline other conditions.

1. *Economic preconditions.* Economic and technological conditions must yield a demand for public firms with lots of capital. If the economy is too poor to have such a demand (many nations still are in this category) *or* if the reigning technologies do not demand large economies of scale, then public firms would not be sought. Moreover, the distribution of wealth and income must be flat *relative to the demand for large firms*.[25] Strongly competitive product markets keep managerial agency costs lower than weakly competitive product markets.

2. *Political preconditions.* Some modern societies are rich, have technological demands for large firms, but their politics stymies separating ownership from control. In strong social democracies, politics drives a wedge between shareholders on the one side, and managers and employees on the other side. Politics there presses firms to expand, to avoid downsizing, and to avoid disrupting employment conditions. These are just the kind of goals that unconstrained managers were said to have in the United States, just the kind of things that the arsenal of agency-cost-reducing tools is designed to handle. And the tools that make managers tolerably loyal to shareholders in the United States—transparent accounting, incentive compensation, hostile takeovers, and strong shareholder primacy norms—are denigrated in the strong social democracies. Social policies there may raise the well-being of most people, but they would do so without much ownership separation in large firms.

In contrast, a more conservative nation typically would not drive a wedge between shareholders on the one side, and employees and managers on the other side. It would facilitate, or at least allow, shareholders and managers to ally themselves. When they are loosely allied, ownership and control can separate. In technical terms, managerial agency costs if unremittingly high can induce concentration to persist, rendering corporate law quality secondary. Graph 4.3 shows a suggestive relationship, that between employment protection and ownership separation.

In societies of the first type, concentrated shareholding is capital's next best means to control managers, and it persisted even after the other economic conditions for separation were met. *Moreover, it has persisted even in such nations that have good quality corporate law.* It budged in recent years

GRAPH 4.3.   Employment protection vs. ownership dispersion (percentage of 20 medium-sized firms without a dominant, 20%+ stockholder, against OECD index of employment protection)

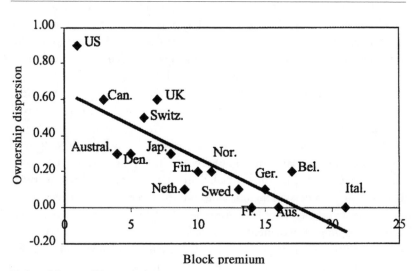

Block premium

Technical data: med20 v. control premium

Regression y = −0.04x + 0.65
Adj R-Sq   0.64
t-stat   −5.24***
***Significant at the .0005 level

Sources: OECD (1994) (employment protection): La Porta et al. (1999) (ownership dispersal of mid-sized firms).

but only as these nations' social democratic political parties shifted right-ward.[26]

3. *Social preconditions.* Some societies are so in turmoil that complex pri-vate institutions cannot be built. Reputations are not worth developing, because no one is sure to be able to use the reputation once built. Private-ordering via, say, a stock exchange would not work, because investors lack confidence in the exchange and fear who might capture it. But once a soci-ety has sufficient regularity so that reputations, private institutions, and, if need be, corporate law can be built, then, if political and economic condi-

tions are otherwise ripe, large enterprises can arise and ownership can separate.[27]

D. Data on Explanations Beyond Law

We have seen agency-cost-based theoretical limits to the legal theory. Can we measure these limits, however crudely? And, in the world's richer nations, can we measure, however crudely, whether corporate law or these other institutions seem to be primary drivers of separation?

Two institutions affect managerial agency costs and vary from nation to nation. One is conventional, one not. Competitive product markets are conventionally said to reduce managerial agency costs (see, e.g., Roe 2001). And, less conventionally, politics affects managerial agency costs, in that strongly social democratic nations historically pressed managers to side with employees when managers made operating decisions that would either favor employees or shareholders but could not favor both. Roe (2000; 2002). (The idea here is not that, say, business schools and leadership skills in these countries are technically weak, but that managers in such countries are pressed to run the firm other than purely in shareholder interests. Hence, the costs to shareholders of having managers run their firms are higher in nations where such political pressures are higher. That society and its citizens may in some ways be better off, but shareholders would find uncontrolled managers more costly to themselves, the shareholders.)

The quality of corporate law helps to predict the degree of ownership separation, as table 4.4 shows. But the other social and political variables—measures of the political pressure on managers—*also* predict separation well, or better.

Table 4.4 correlates a set of political, ownership, legal, and competitive variables. All three political variables predict ownership separation and the depth of a nation's securities market. The two legal variables also predict separation and stock market depth, as does the measure of monopoly strength.

The correlation matrix shows politics persistently correlating with dispersion: the more conservative the nation, the more dispersed is ownership. The matrix also shows that good quality corporate law correlates with dispersion: the higher the quality of corporate law, the more dispersed is ownership.

We can do more with the statistics than say that each one predicts ownership separation. True, it's plausible that the three—corporate law quality,

TABLE 4.4. Correlation matrix[1]

	Political indicators			Legal indicators			Competitive indicator	Dispersion and strength of stock market indicators	
	Political place	Employ-ment pro-tection	Gini	La Porta law	Voting premium	Control premium	Monopoly mark-up	Stock/mkt cap/GDP	Widely-held at 20%
Political place	1.00								
Employment protection	-0.41	1.00							
Gini after-tax	0.49	-0.53	1.00						
La Porta Law	0.39	-0.95	0.65	1.00					
Voting premium	-0.26	0.50	0.28	-0.39	1.00				
Control Premium	-0.20	0.70	-0.34	-0.76	0.42	1.00			
Monopoly mark-up	-0.57*	0.35	-0.42	-0.41	0.39	0.31	1.00		
Stock mkt. capitalization/GDP	0.55*	-0.56*	0.64*	0.70*	-0.23	-0.48*	-0.80**	1.00	
Widely-held at 20% for Medium Firms	0.67*	0.84**	0.67*	0.87**	-0.46	-0.46	-0.57*	0.73	1.00

*Significant at .10 level.

**At .01 level. (Not all significant correlations are highlighted.)

[1] *Sources for data*: Political place comes from Cusack (1997); employment protection from OECD (1994); GINI from Deininger and Squire (1996); La Porta law and widely-held at 20% from La Porta et al. (1999); voting premium from Nenova, supra Table 4.2; control premium from Dyck and Zingales (2001); monopoly markup from Martins et al. (1996); and stock-market capitalization from OECD (1998).

strength of product markets, and intensity of political pressure on managerial loyalty to shareholders—move together. Then we would have to analyze
whether a) one induces the other, or b) some underlying feature induces the
three simultaneously. But we can try other tests, tests that might tell us the
relative strength in explaining ownership separation in the world's richest
nations: We could begin with, say, a law-driven model and see if adding politics does much in explaining the degree of ownership separation. *When we
add political variables to the corporate-law-driven "model," we get much
stronger predictive power than we do with law alone.* In several instances, politics dominates the legal explanation, as table 4.5 shows.

The point, again, is not that corporate law is irrelevant, but that at the
level and quality we see in the world's richest nations, variation in corporate
law ceases sometimes to be a primary explanation. Variation in other institutions—particularly institutions that affect managerial agency costs—take
over to determine how much ownership separates from control.

The first number in each cell is the R^2, the percentage of variation
explained by the variable or variables in play. The numbers beneath the R^2
number in the one-variable model are, first, the coefficient and, next, its t-
statistic, with the asterisks denoting statistical significance. The numbers
underneath the R^2 in the two-independent variable lines are, first, the coefficients for each variable, and, second, in parenthesis, the t-statistic for each
coefficient. The first is the t-statistic of the corporate law variable, the second
that of the political variable. Politics always significantly increases explanatory power. For four of our six cells left-right politics is a much stronger
determinant than the corporate law measure. For the two-variable R^2, significance means that adding the political measure significantly increases
explanatory power.

Let's briefly discuss these results. Take the legal theory: a qualitative index
of corporate law quality, one used frequently now in the finance literature,
predicts ownership separation plausibly, although weakly.[28] We see in table
4.5 that the commonly used qualitative corporate law index predicts the
depth of separation. The measured quality—via the control premium—predicts separation, although more weakly.

But when we add political variables, we get much more explanatory
power than with law alone, often significantly so. Even if law is important,
politics is independently quite important too—maybe more important. And,
if we viewed the world as more likely to start with basic left-right politics first,
with legal institutions being partly derivative of the political equilibrium,

TABLE 4.5. Law and politics (as predicting ownership separation)[1]

Corporate law alone (via LaPorta legal quality index)	.52 .14 (3.69***)			Corporate law alone (via measured legal quality from control premium)	.18 −1.07 (−1.94*)	
LaPorta law + Politics (via GINI)	.71** Law .10 (2.92***	Politics .03 2.60**)		Measured legal quality + Politics (via GINI)	.54** Law −.49 (−.96	Politics .04 2.57**)
LaPorta law + Politics (via political scientists' rankings)	.76*** Law .11 (3.60***	Politics .23 3.30***)		Measured legal quality + Politics (via political scientists' rankings)	.55** Law −.59 (−1.24	Politics .27 2.76**)
LaPorta law + Politics (via employment protection)	.71** Law .03 (.57	Politics −.03 −2.62**)		Measured legal quality + Politics (via employment protection)	.72*** Law .43 (.87	Politics −.05 −4.39****)

*	Significant at the .10 level.
**	Significant at the .05 level.
***	Significant at the .01 level.
****	Significant at the .001 level.

[1]Sources: The qualitative corporate law index is from La Porta et al. (1999). The measured quality of corporate law comes from Dyck and Zingales (2001). The GINI measure for left-right politics came from the Deininger-Squire OECD on-line compilation, described in Deininger and Squire (1996). The data measure income inequality after taxes, for each individual (as opposed to each household). A GINI number depends on assumptions and methodology. From the compilation I used, if possible, the 1991 Luxembourg Income Study data. For Austria, Australia, France, Switzerland, and the U.K., 1991 data wasn't available, so I used the latest Luxembourg 1980's data. For Japan no comparable data were available. The political scientists' left-right rankings came from Cusack (1997: 383–84), which arrays a survey from Castles and Mair (1984). The left-right measure via employment protection came from OECD (1994: 74), which ranked the relative ease of firing an employee in the OECD nations.

then we'd see whether politics predicts separation (it does), and whether legal measures strengthen the prediction (sometimes). This I do in table 4.6.

As table 4.6 shows, politics consistently predicts ownership separation; and, of the six combinations of law and politics, legal quality strongly buttresses the prediction two times, but fails to significantly buttress it the other four times.

Overall: If one blindly followed the regressions in tables 4.5 and 4.6, one could never here reject politics as significantly determining ownership separation. For four of the twelve cells one could not reject corporate law as a significant determinant; for eight of the cells one could reject it.

Roughly these results suggest that controlling insider overreaching—the type of costs of public firms that law can reach—gets us (only) half-way to making public firms viable. If the political environment impedes managerial-shareholder alliances, the second type of agency costs to shareholders would rise, and ownership could not easily separate from control, *even if controller machinations are contained*. In fact, in four of the six cells, law doesn't significantly increase the predictive power of left-right politics alone.

TABLE 4.6. Politics and Law[1]

Politics alone: GINI as predicting separation		Political place as predicting separation		Employment protection as predicting separation	
	.48***		.49***		.70***
GINI + LaPorta law	.71***	Political place + LaPorta law	.76***	Employment protection + LaPorta law	.76
GINI + Measured legal quality	.52	Political place + Measured legal quality	.55	Employment protection + Measured legal quality	.72

[1]Significance and data sources are as from Table 4.5. Coefficients and t-statistics are omitted for brevity.

Conclusion: Corporate Law's Limits

I have here neither denied the value of strong corporate law that protects distant stockholders, nor denigrated its usefulness in building efficacious business enterprises, nor sought to refute its academic utility in explaining some key aspects of corporate differences around the world, especially in transition and developing nations. It is valuable in protecting distant shareholders, as it is often the lowest cost means to protect them. It is useful in thereby building big firms. If it is not present in a society, the society needs substitute institutions. And it is helpful in explaining corporate structures in the world's developing and transition economies, many of which cannot establish good corporate rules of the game.

I have instead sought to map out the limits to the quality-of-corporate-law argument. And these limits are probably much closer than is commonly thought: High-quality corporate law is insufficient to induce ownership to separate from control in the world's richest, most economically advanced nations. Technologically advanced nations in the wealthy West can have the potential for fine corporate law in theory, and several have it in practice, but ownership would *not* separate from control wherever managerial agency costs are high. And managerial agency costs, unlike insider self-dealing, are *not* closely connected with corporate law. Indeed American corporate law's business judgment rule has corporate law *avoid* dealing with managerial agency costs.

Today's reigning academic theory—and the policy program of the international agencies—leaves too many unanswered questions. Why doesn't strong, pro-minority shareholder corporate law lead to *more* blockholders, not fewer, because distant minority stockholders would have *less* to fear of controllers' trampling as law improved? Why do some rich nations lack even *a single anecdote* of overreaching behavior from controllers, yet nevertheless lack strong separation? Why are there so many rich nations with, by measurement and anecdote, low private benefits of control, high-quality corporate institutions, and much minority stock, yet without ownership separation?

By examining a restricted sample of the world's richest nations we can move toward two conclusions, one strong and the other weak. The strong one focuses on the richer nations in the wealthy West: studies that examine corporate law the world over tend to overpredict the importance of corporate law in the world's richest nations. It seems almost intuitive that these nations—where contract can usually be nicely enforced—shouldn't have much trouble developing satisfactory corporate law or good substitutes. Some, by measurement, already have. If ownership still hasn't separated widely, then other institutional explanations are probably in play. The weak conclusion focuses on the world's transition and developing nations: We cannot conclude that improving corporate law is irrelevant there (because we've only examined here the restricted set of the world's richest nations). But we can offer the weak conclusion of the possibility that the development agencies may do everything right in getting the corporate law institutions of these nations ready for ownership separation, and it's at least possible that no one comes to the party.

The quality of conventional corporate law does not fully explain why and when ownership concentration persists in the wealthy West, because core *corporate law does not even try to directly control managerial agency costs from dissipating a firm's value.* The American business judgment rule keeps courts and law out of basic business decisions and that is where managers can lose, or make, the really big money for shareholders. Nonlegal institutions control these costs. In nations where those *other* institutions, such as product competition or incentive compensation, fail or do less well, managerial dissipation would be higher and ownership cannot as easily separate from control as it can where dissipation is lower. Corporate law quality can be high, private benefits of control low, but if managerial agency costs from dissipation are high, separation will not proceed. Even if we believed law to be critical to building these *other* institutions, the analysis would persist because *different* laws support the agency cost controlling institutions (antitrust and product market competition; tax law and incentive compensation, etc.).

Variation in other institutions could explain why managerial agency costs aren't low enough. When it does, corporate law—even corporate law writ wide—no longer primarily determines the degree of separation.

A nation need not control insider machinations and motivate managers equally well; and to the extent it does one better than the other, concentration and diffusion are deeply affected: The diffusion decision is based on the *sum* of private benefits of control and managerial agency costs. Even if traditional corporate law drives private benefits to zero, concentration should persist if managerial agency costs are high.

Data are consistent. Several nations have, by measurement, good corporate law, but not much diffusion and hardly any separation. These nations also have a potential for high managerial agency costs if ownership and control separated: relatively weaker product market competition and relatively stronger political pressures on managers to disfavor shareholders.

The quality of a nation's corporate law cannot be the only explanation for why diffuse Berle-Means firms grow and dominate. Perhaps, for some countries at some times, it is not even the principal one.

Endnotes

Thanks for comments go to Lucian Bebchuk, Victor Brudney, John Coates, Einer Elhauge, Merritt Fox, Ronald Gilson, Jeffrey Gordon, Howell Jackson, Ehud Kamar, Reinier Kraakman, Curtis Milhaupt, Mitch Polinsky, and participants in workshops at Harvard Business School, the National Bureau of Economic Research, the Italian Securities Commission (CONSOB), the Sorbonne, and the Columbia, Harvard, Stanford, University of Southern California and Vanderbilt Law Schools. A parallel paper appears at Journal of Legal Studies 31: 233 (2002).

1. Private benefits also arise from pride in running and controlling one's own, or one's family's, enterprise. About this, corporate law has little direct impact.
2. To be clear, I am not speaking simply of corporate law as the "law-on-the-books," but as "law-on-the-books," including securities law, and the quality of regulators and judges, the efficiency, accuracy, and honesty of the regulators and the judiciary, the capacity of the stock exchanges to stymie the most egregious diversions, and so on. The best compendium of the legal and related institutions is in Black (2000).
3. Again, some private benefits are matters of taste, preferences for power, family recognition in a family firm, etc.
4. See Bebchuk (1999), who models the problem; see also Coffee (2001); La Porta et al. series.
5. The best-developed model of the corporate law problem begins by assuming a population of firms that is more valuable when diffusely owned than when privately-owned (see Bebchuk 1999). As such, its author does not have to address managerial agency costs, since these are assumed away as central for the population under discussion. But it is in that assumption though, we are saying here, that the critical calculus occurs in whether firms go public. (Not all other analyses of the relationship between corporate law and ownership diffusion confine their inquiry so adroitly.)
6. Gagliardi v. TriFoods Int'l, Inc., 683 A.2d 1049, 1052 (Del. Ch. 1996) (Allen, J.) (emphasis supplied).

7. 488 A.2d 858 (Del. Sup. Ct. 1985).
8. Del. Corp. Code § 102(b)(7).
9. See Joy v. North, 692 F.2d 880 (1982) (Winter, J.).
10. Thomson Financial (database) (accessed Oct. 2001). The comparison can be fine-tuned, by matching industries, firm-size, and other characteristics. But the persistence of the premium (the 10% gap is nearly constant over a couple of decades) suggests that refining the numbers will not change the fact that a substantial premium would persist even after American takeover law was perfected.
11. Not all firms will switch, of course. Path dependence and positional advantage will deter many. See Roe (1996). The point is that the pressures here from improving corporate law do not all point toward greater diffusion.
12. La Porta et al. series, and the followers. Economically less developed countries have added reasons why they have not developed securities markets. Good securities and corporate rules might come with wealth, and not the other way around.
13. Wall Street lawyers would have reservations about heavily using preemptive rights, cumulative voting, and the minimum percentage needed to call a special shareholder meeting—items not likely to be near the top of most American lawyers' lists of Delaware corporate law's most important legal protections— and of partly abandoning Delaware law for the index. (The index uses Delaware corporate law except on the minimum percentage needed to demand a meeting. Delaware allows firms to decide the issue by specifying a low percentage in their charter, a right that, I understand, firms rarely use. Sticking with Delaware here would have made Delaware corporate law protection look mediocre, when it is probably pretty good.) The point is not that Delaware is bad—the index probably hits the right bottom line—but that developing an accurate index is hard.

    For a critique more skeptical than mine of the index, see Vagts (2002). Vagts argues that the coding judgments for the German index are incorrect. For instance, although German stockholders are viewed as unable to vote by mail, most send their instructions in to their bank (by mail) and the bank then votes the stockholders. Hence, German corporate law is "better" than the index suggests. See also Milhaupt (2001: 2119–25) (coding judgments for the Japanese index are highly suspect).
14. The Italian number comes from the voting premium for dual-class common stock.
15. Franks and Mayer show that big blocks trade at an average premium of 13.85% over the price of the minority stock. Nonselling stockholders gain over time about 2.34%. That means that, net, the selling blockholder gets 11.61% more than the minority stockholders (from 13.85% minus 2.34%). Since the average

size of the block is 36.32% of the firm's issued stock, the new blockholder pays an extra 4.05% of the firm's value to the old blockholder, to the exclusion of the minority stockholders (from 36.32% of 11.61%). If this represented the total private benefits of control, then the private benefits would be about 3.8% of the firm's value. (If the firm's total value is 100 plus the private benefits of 4.05, the diversion would be 4.05/104.5, or .038).

16. The premium is the difference between block price and the trading value of the diffusely held stock. American blocks traded at a 20% premium over the price of diffuse stock, for blocks of (typically) one-fifth of the firm's stock. If the premium represents what the controller can grab for itself, the blockholder would be able to grab 4% of the firm's value (one-fifth of 20%). German blocks are larger, with many equal to half of the company's stock. A premium of 10% for half of the company, the typical numbers, indicates the controller could grab 5% of the firm's value for itself.

17. Other researchers recently found German bankers able to extract little in private benefits of control. Gorton and Schmid (2000a: 70).

18. It could fit with the poor corporate law theory if a) corporate law was poor, but b) big blockholders desisted from transferring value to themselves, while c) small blockholders would insist on massively transferring such value. Plausible, yes (big blockholders incur more deadweight costs if the transfers demean total firm value), but this confluence would seem implausible as accounting for all, or even most of, the doubling of value to minority stockholders of blockholding.

19. Nowak (2001) found a higher German voting premium.

20. Data measuring the value of the vote can be corrected to reflect that the minority voting stock represents the probability of joining a control group and not the direct value of control. The value of control rises or falls with what is needed to build the control block: in a country where 51% of the voting stock can control everything, the value of minority voting stock should approach that of nonvoting stock; but if there are two voting blocks of 40%, the minority voting stock's value should reflect the value of control. Sophisticated tests can approximate the correction (see Zingales 1994; Nenova 2000). Such calculations are inherently imprecise.

21. The density of dual class usage *could* indicate which propellant—private benefits or managerial agency costs—is central. If control is usually had via dual class stock (or pyramids) that might indicate that extraction of private benefits is primary. But this would be so only if the controller pulls his or her wealth out of the firm. If managerial agency costs are high, control with *some* financial commitment is important for firm value: if wealth constraints mean the controller cannot commit most of the family's wealth and still influence managers, then dual class could be privately efficient for managerial agency cost reasons.

22. We would have to be careful that we were not reading data in which *only* the control sale was regulated, while rampant shifts occurred elsewhere: If the relevant corporate law forced a mandatory bid for dispersed stock upon a control shift, the premium might be low, but incumbent controllers could still be otherwise shifting value. So the better data would measure the results before mandatory bids became common; or would measure control sales not subject to the mandatory bid, i.e., sales of less than the typical 30% trigger. This data does so.

23. The last column in Table 4.3 adjusts the premium for industry type: some industries are more likely to "naturally" protect dispersed shareholders, other industries are riskier for them. The adjustments refine the index but do not radically change the results: Austria and Italy still have the largest premiums; the U.S. and the U.K. are still at the protective end of the spectrum. Some of the middle range nations change rank: Germany and Finland look more protective; most other changes meander.

24. The index, a crude one, purports to measure both property rights and "the ability of individuals and businesses to enforce contracts" (O'Driscoll et al. 2001: 57). Cf. Levine (1999: 14–15, 20) (risk that government will not respect a contract it has signed: low for the United States, but *lower* for France, Germany, and Scandinavia).

25. Thus the United States has today a skewed distribution of wealth and income, but it has a very high demand of large-scale firms. In the nineteenth century the distribution was flatter, and, with the railroads creating a single huge market, the demand for large firms with widely gathered capital was even higher. If technology flattens and shrinks firms, then wealthy people can control them more easily than if the optimal scale is very large.

26. The importance of left-right economic politics is developed in Roe (2000; 2002).

27. Compare Milhaupt (1998): The extent the government retains control rights over firms can affect ownership structures.

28. The voting premium data described in table 4.2, however, do not predict separation as nicely as an index of corporate law rules; see table 4.4, suggesting that improvements to the commonly used qualitative index are possible. But we stay with the standard index, to show that even when using it, other considerations are needed to explain ownership separation.

References

Agnblad, Jonas, Erik Berglöf, Peter Högfeldt and Helena Svancar. 2001. Ownership and Control in Sweden—*Strong Owners, Weak Minorities, and Social Control. In The Control of Corporate Europe.* Fabrizio Barca and Marco Becht, eds. Oxford: Oxford University Press.

Barclay, Michael J. and Clifford G. Holderness. 1989. Private Benefits from Control of Public Corporations. *Journal of Financial Economics* 25: 371–95.

Baums, Theodor and Bernd Frick. 1999. The Market Value of the Codetermined Firm. In *Employees and Corporate Governance*. Margaret M. Blair and Mark J. Roe, eds. Washington, D.C.: Brookings Institution Press.

Bebchuk, Lucian Arye. 1999. A Rent-Protection Theory of Corporate Ownership and Control. Cambridge, Mass.: Harvard Law and Economics Working Paper (Discussion Paper No. 260.)

—— and Allen Ferrell. 1999. Federalism and Corporate Law: The Race to Protect Managers from Takeovers. *Columbia Law Review* 99: 1168–99.

Becht, Marco and Ailsa Röell. 1999. Blockholdings in Europe: An International Comparison. *European Economic Review* 43: 1049–56.

Bergström, Clas and Kristian Rydqvist. 1990. The Determinants of Corporate Ownership: An Empirical Study on Swedish Data. *Journal of Banking and Finance* 14: 237–53.

Bishop, Joseph W., Jr. 1968. Sitting Ducks and Decoy Ducks: New Trends in the Indemnification of Corporate Directors and Officers. *Yale Law Journal* 77: 1078–1103.

Black, Bernard S. 2000. The Core Institutions That Support Strong Securities Markets. *Business Lawyer* 55: 1565–1607.

—— and Reinier Kraakman. 1996. A Self-Enforcing Model of Corporate Law. *Harvard Law Review* 109: 1911–82.

Coffee, John C., Jr. 1999. The Future as History: The Prospects for Global Convergence in Corporate Governance and Its Implications. *Northwestern University Law Review* 93: 641–707.

——. 2001. The Rise of Dispersed Ownership: The Roles of Law and the State in the Separation of Ownership and Control. *Yale Law Journal* 111: 1–82.

Cusack, Thomas R. 1997. Partisan Politics and Public Finance: Changes in Public Spending in the Industrialized Democracies, 1955–1989. *Public Choice* 91: 375–95.

Deininger, Klaus and Lyn Squire. 1996. A New Data Set Measuring Income Inequality. *World Bank Economic Review* 10: 565–91.

Delaware Code Annotated (Michie).

DeMott, Deborah A. 1983. Current Issues in Tender Offer Regulation: Lessons from the British. *New York University Law Review* 58: 945–1029.

Demsetz, Harold. 1983. The Structure of Ownership and the Theory of the Firm. *Journal of Law and Economics* 26: 375–90.

Dooley, Michael P. and E. Norman Veasey. 1989. The Role of the Board in Derivative Litigation: Delaware Law and the Current ALI Proposals Compared. *Business Lawyer* 44: 503.

Dyck, Alexander and Luigi Zingales. 2001. Why are Private Benefits of Control so Large in Certain Countries and What Effect does this Have on their Financial Development (working paper, November 2001).

Edwards, Jeremy S. and Alfons J.Weichenrieder. 1999. Ownership Concentration and Share Valuation: Evidence from Germany (working paper).

Fama, Eugene F. 1980. Agency Problems and the Theory of the Firm. *Journal of Political Economy* 88: 288–307.

FitzRoy, Felix R. and Kornelius Kraft. 1993. Economic Effects of Codetermination. *Scandinavian Journal of Economics* 95: 365–75.

France. Art. 200. Decree No. 67–236 of March 23, 1967. Journal Officiel de la République Française, March 24, 1967, 2858.

France. Art. L225–252 Code de Commerce. (Art. 245. Law No. 66–537 of July 24, 1966 Journal Officiel de la République Française, July 26, 1966, 6420.)

Franks, Julian and Colin Mayer. 2001. Ownership and Control of German Corporations. *Review of Financial Studies* 14: 943–77.

Frick, Bernd, Gerhard Speckbacker and Paul Wentges. 1999. Arbeitnehmermitbestimmung und moderne Theorie der Unternehmung. *Zeitschrift für Betriebswirtschaft* 69: 745 (1999).

Gorton, Gary and Frank A. Schmid. 2000a. Universal Banking and the Performance of German Firms. *Journal of Financial Economics* 58: 29–80.

———. 2000b. Class Struggle Inside the Firm: A Study of German Codetermination. Cambridge, Mass.: National Bureau of Economic Research, October 2000. (Working Paper No. 7945.)

Holderness, Clifford G. 2001. A Survey of Blockholders and Corporate Control. *FRBNY Economic Policy Review*. Available at http://newyorkfed.org/rmaghome/econ-pol/2001/601hold.pdf.

Holmén, Martin and Peter Högfeldt. 1999. Corporate Control and Security Design in Initial Public Offerings. Stockholm: Stockholm School of Economics.

Iskander, Magdi, Gerald Meyerman, Dale F. Gray and Sean Hagan. 1999. Corporate Restructuring and Governance in East Asia. *Finance and Development* 36(1): 42–45 (March).

La Porta, Rafael, Florencio Lopez-de-Silanes, and Andrei Shleifer. 1999. Corporate Ownership Around the World. *Journal of Finance* 54: 471–517.

——— and Robert Vishny. 1997. Legal Determinants of External Finance. *Journal of Finance* 52: 1131–55.

———. 1998. Law and Finance. *Journal of Political Economy* 106: 1113–50.

———. 2000. Investor Protection and Corporate Governance. *Journal of Financial Economics* 58: 3–37.

Leser, Eric and Anne-Marie Rocco. 2000. Les Wallenberg veulent faire cohabiter capitalisme familial et mondialisation. Le Monde (Paris), November 24, 23.

Levine, Ross. 1999. Law, Finance, and Economic Growth. *Journal of Financial Intermediation* 8: 8–35.

Martins, Joaquim Oliveira, Stefano Scarpetta and Dirk Pilat. 1996. Mark-up Pricing Ratios in Manufacturing Industries: Estimates for 14 OECD Countries. Paris: OECD Econ. Dep't Working Paper No. 162.

Milhaupt, Curtis J. 1998. Property Rights in Firms. *University of Virginia Law Review* 84: 1145–94.

——. 2001. Creative Norm Destruction: The Evolution of Non-legal Rules in Japanese Corporate Governance. *University of Pennsylvania Law Review* 149: 2083–2129.

Modigliani, Franco and Enrico Perotti. 1997. Protection of Minority Interest and the Development of Security Markets. *Managerial and Decision Economics* 18: 519–28.

——. 1998. Security Versus Bank Finance: The Importance of a Proper Enforcement of Legal Rules. Cambridge: MIT Sloan School of Management.

Nenova, Tatiana. 2000. The Value of Corporate Votes and Control Benefits: A Cross-Country Analysis. Cambridge: Harvard University.

Nestor, Stilpon. 2000. Corporate Governance Trends in the OECD Area: Where Do We Go From Here? Paris: OECD. Working paper.

Nicodano, Giovanna and Alessandro Sembenelli. 2000. Private Benefits, Block Transaction Premiums and Ownership Structure. Turin, Italy: University of Turin. Working paper.

Nowak, Eric. 2001. Recent Developments in German Capital Markets and Corporate Governance. *Journal of Applied Corporate Finance* 14 (5): 35–48.

O'Driscoll, Gerald P., Kim R. Holmes and Melanie Kirkpatrick. 2001. *Index of Economic Freedom.* Washington, D.C.: The Heritage Foundation.

OECD. 1994. The OECD Jobs Study: Evidence and Explanations—Part II—The Adjustment Potential of the Labour Market. Paris: OECD.

——. 1999. Ad hoc Task Force on Corporate Governance, Principles of Corporate Governance. Paris: OECD.

——. Financial Market Trends. 1998. Paris: OECD.

Rock, Edward B. and Michael L. Wachter. 2001. Islands of Conscious Power: Law, Norms, and the Self-Governing Corporation. *University of Pennsylvania Law Review* 149: 1619–1700.

Roe, Mark J. 1994. *Strong Managers, Weak Owners: The Political Roots of American Corporate Finance.* Princeton, N.J.: Princeton University Press.

——. 1996. Chaos and Evolution in Law and Economics. *Harvard Law Review* 109: 641–68.

——. 2000. Political Preconditions to Separating Ownership from Corporate Control. *Stanford Law Review* 53: 539–606.

———. 2001. Rents and Their Corporate Consequences. *Stanford Law Review* 53: 1463–94.

———. 2003. *Political Determinants of Corporate Governance.* Oxford: Oxford University Press.

Sachs, Jeffrey D. and Katharina Pistor. 1997. Introduction: Progress, Pitfalls, Scenarios, and Lost Opportunities. In *The Rule of Law and Economic Reform in Russia.* Jeffrey D. Sachs and Katharina Pistor, eds. Boulder, Colo.: Westview Press.

Sachs, Jeffrey D. and Andrew M. Warner. 1998. Executive Summary. In *The Global Competitiveness Report.* Geneva: World Economic Forum.

Schmid, Frank A. and Frank Seger. 1998. Arbeitnehmermitbestimmung, Allokation von Entscheidungsrechten und Shareholder Value. *Zeitschrift für Betriebswirtschaft* 5: 453.

Shleifer, Andrei and Robert W. Vishny. 1986. Large Shareholders and Corporate Control. *Journal of Political Economy* 94: 461–88.

Shleifer, Andrei and Lawrence H. Summers. 1988. Breach of Trust in Hostile Takeovers. In *Corporate Takeovers: Causes and Consequences,* edited by Alan J. Auerbach. Chicago: University of Chicago Press.

Smith v. Van Gorkom, 488 A.2d 858 (Del. Sup. Ct. 1985).

Stein, Jeremy C. 1989. Efficient Capital Markets, Inefficient Firms: A Model of Myopic Corporate Behavior. *Quarterly Journal of Economics* 104: 655–69.

Stengel, Arndt. 1998. Directors' Powers and Shareholders: A Comparison of Systems. *International Company and Commerical Law Review* No. 2, 49.

Tunc, André. 1982. A French Lawyer Looks at American Corporation Law and Securities Regulation. *University of Pennsylvania Law Review* 130: 757–74.

Vagts, Detlev. 2002. Comparative Corporate Law—The New Wave. In *Festschrift for Jean-Nicolas Druey.* Rainer Schweitzer and Urs Gasser, eds. Zurich: Schulthess.

Witherell, William. 2000. Corporate Governance: A Basic Foundation for the Global Economy. *The OECD Observer,* Summer.

Zingales, Luigi. 1994. The Value of the Voting Right: A Study of the Milan Stock Exchange Experience. *Review of Financial Studies* 7: 125–48.

Part II

Convergence and Reform,
Europe and Asia

5 Regulation and the Globalization (Americanization) of Executive Pay

Brian R. Cheffins and Randall S. Thomas

A "global compensation imperative" is allegedly at work (Davis 2000) that can be alternatively dubbed "the Americanization of international pay practices" (Leander 1998a: 12). "As markets become truly global, you'll see the differences in compensation shrink," the managing director of an executive search firm has predicted (quoted in Flynn 2000). Or, as Kevin Murphy, a leading U.S. expert on managerial remuneration, has been quoted in the press as saying, "the rest of the world is moving to our pay model" (Johnston 1998).

This essay deals with the possible convergence trend on the executive pay front. The focus is on the contribution regulation is likely to make. As we will see, the manner in which executive compensation is dealt with by policymakers in a particular country could serve to foster or dampen a nascent convergence trend. We will also discover, however, that rules which seem important at first glance will not necessarily have a decisive impact.

The essay does not focus solely on regulations promulgated and enforced by public officials. It also takes into account rules and guidelines developed by private organizations to influence corporate conduct. This is because this sort of "soft law" is an increasingly important determinant of corporate behavior on an international basis.

One additional preliminary point requires mention. We will not assess in detail whether Americanization of executive pay would be a "good thing." Still, this essay makes a significant normative contribution by identifying obstacles regulators will need to address if they want to promote convergence and by drawing attention to rules that could be invoked to counteract the "global compensation imperative" if this was thought to be the better way to proceed.

The essay is organized as follows. Part I contrasts executive pay arrangements in the United States with those existing elsewhere. Part II discusses the potential trend toward convergence. Parts III and IV consider the impact legal regulation might have on this process. The effect which "soft law" could have is taken into account in Part V. Part VI draws upon the discussion in parts III to V to offer a synthesis of strategies available to policymakers in countries where Americanization of executive pay might be on the agenda.

I. Executive Pay Arrangements Around the World

With respect to compensation arrangements, American executives stand out as exceptional on an international basis and U.S. chief executive officers have particularly distinctive arrangements. Let us consider first aggregate pay by focusing on a study of worldwide remuneration compiled by Towers Perrin, a global management consulting firm. According to this study, which used an industrial company with approximately $500 million in annual sales as a benchmark, total annual remuneration for a U.S. CEO averaged $1,933,000 in 2001 (Towers Perrin 2001b: 20). This amount was more than double the average pay for CEOs in all of the other 25 countries surveyed and was more than triple the average in all but six (Argentina, Brazil, Canada, China/Hong Kong, Mexico, Singapore, and the United Kingdom).

With respect to managers other than CEOs, there is pay disparity between the U.S. and other countries, but it is not as great. Referring again to Towers Perrin data for 2001, America's human resource directors ranked at the top with total annual compensation of $449,000 annually (Towers Perrin 2001b: 21). Still, while CEO remuneration in the U.S. was more than double that in every other country, there were ten countries where human resource directors were paid at least half as much as their American counterparts.

Another important distinction between executive compensation in the U.S. and elsewhere is that pay is much more "incentivized" in American companies. With typical rank-and-file employees, most of their pay will be "fixed," meaning that they will be paid at a prescribed hourly, monthly, or annual level irrespective of contingencies such as firm performance. In contrast, with American chief executives, much of their compensation is variable in nature, in the sense that they only benefit if their company meets or exceeds prescribed targets. For instance, the Towers Perrin survey on worldwide remuneration pegged the annual bonus of a U.S. CEO at 56 percent of salary (Towers Perrin 2001b: 26). Moreover, variable compensation designed to function on a long-term basis (e.g. stock options and bonus plans with multi-year targets) constituted 161 percent of salary (Towers Perrin 2001b: 26).

Incentive-oriented pay is a considerably less important source of compensation for CEOs in other countries. According to the Towers Perrin survey on worldwide remuneration for 2001, with annual bonuses, there were only two jurisdictions (Australia and Venezuela) where the ratio of annual bonus to salary was higher than the 56 percent figure in the U.S. With long-term incentive pay, American CEOs stand alone. Only in Canada, at 90 percent, was the ratio of this form of compensation to salary close to the U.S. figure of 161 percent. The top European country—the U.K.—was far behind at 44 percent (Towers Perrin 2001b: 26).

The disparity involving long-term incentive schemes deserves further emphasis since it does a great deal to explain why American CEOs are better paid than their counterparts elsewhere. The same Towers Perrin survey indicates that a typical U.S. chief executive officer was awarded approximately $900,000 annually in the form of long-term incentive compensation. In only two of the other twenty-five jurisdictions dealt with in the study did *aggregate* annual CEO compensation come close to matching to this figure (Argentina at $879,000 and Mexico at $867,000) (Towers Perrin 2001b: 20).

Turning to executives other than CEOs, there again is a divergence between the U.S. and the rest of the world with respect to incentive-oriented pay but it is not as substantial as it is for chief executives. Referring once more to data from Towers Perrin, with human resource directors in the U.S., variable pay with a long-term aspect amounted to 66 percent of base salary (Towers Perrin 2001b: 27). This percentage was higher than in any other country. Still, unlike the pattern with CEOs, there were two jurisdictions (Malaysia and Singapore) where the relevant figure was relatively close (Towers Perrin 2001b: 27). Also, according to Towers Perrin data, as recently as 2000 the long-term incentive/base salary ratio was actually higher in these two countries than it was in America (Towers Perrin 2000: 25).

II. Evidence of Convergence Along U.S. Lines

To reiterate, the use of performance-related remuneration strongly distinguishes America's executive compensation arrangements from those in place elsewhere, particularly at the CEO level. There is evidence, however, which suggests that performance-oriented pay is becoming more popular outside the U.S. For instance, as the Towers Perrin survey of worldwide remuneration for 2001 shows, long-term incentive schemes are becoming an increasingly important element of overall compensation. Out of the 26 jurisdictions covered in the study, in 1996 there were 14 where the typical chief executive was not awarded variable compensation with a multi-year dimension. By 2001, there were only four (derived from Towers Perrin 2001b: 26–27). Moreover, in all of those countries where long-term incentive plans were in place in both 1996 and 2001, the ratio of this form of compensation to salary was higher in 2001.

Additional research Towers Perrin carried out for a 2001 report on stock options confirms that incentive-oriented pay with a long-term aspect is becoming increasingly commonplace outside the U.S. This study, which examined compensation patterns in large, domestic companies headquartered in 22 different countries, indicated that such remuneration was prevalent in only a minority of jurisdictions in 1997. It was predicted, however, that by 2003 it would be standard practice in almost all of the countries surveyed for companies to have a long-term incentive scheme in place for their top executives, with stock option plans being the most popular format (Towers Perrin 2001a: 4–5).

An important point to bear in mind with respect to possible convergence in the area of executive remuneration is that increased use of performance-related pay implies a shift to more generous managerial compensation. To understand why, it is necessary to appreciate that executives will, for good reason, have reservations about having their pay tied directly to shareholder return (Cheffins 1997a: 686). For instance, on diversification grounds, they will dislike having their pay linked to the performance of a company in which they have already tied up substantial human capital. Also, since the level at which an individual company's equity trades often fluctuates markedly, they will fear significant swings in income. Moreover, they will worry about having their remuneration tied to share prices, since factors unrelated to the skill and effort of a company's top people can influence its market standing.

Despite these various difficulties, companies that are seeking to recruit and retain good people do have scope to link managerial remuneration more closely with shareholder return if that is a key priority. The strategy to adopt is straightforward: offer a highly lucrative "upside." The logic involved is that a talented executive will accept the risks associated with having remuneration linked closely with shareholder return if the potential rewards are large enough (Cheffins 1997a: 686–87). The upshot is that if companies outside the United States are moving toward that country's model by using more performance-related compensation, there will be pressure to shift toward the sort of lucrative pay that currently distinguishes America's executives.

III. The Impetus for the Americanization of Executive Pay

Assuming that some sort of executive pay convergence might be occurring along American lines, what might be causing this? Changing share ownership patterns are one possible explanation. Share ownership in large U.S. business enterprises is widely dispersed because most are publicly quoted and only a minority have a significant blockholder. Britain's corporate economy is configured in a similar fashion (Cheffins 1999: 14–15). In contrast, in other major industrial countries concentrated share ownership is the norm (La Porta et al. 1997: 1137–38). There is, however, anecdotal evidence which indicates that the pattern is changing (Hansmann and Kraakman 2001: 449–59; Coffee 2001: 15–21) and such a trend could help to shift executive compensation arrangements in an American direction.

To elaborate, in a publicly quoted company with widely dispersed share ownership, a strong correlation between executive pay and corporate performance arguably is required to help address the agency cost problem that exists in such enterprises (Cheffins and Thomas 2001: 286, 308, 312). In contrast, in a firm where control is highly consolidated, monitoring can displace the need for performance-related compensation since the core shareholder(s) should have both the means and the motivation to discipline disloyal or ineffective managers (Cheffins 1999: 33; Park 2000: 246). Moreover, executives in companies with insider-dominated share ownership will be suspicious of incentive pay based on share price performance since price distortions arising from the small "free float" will mean the stock market is unlikely to be a reliable barometer of firm value (Abowd and Kaplan 1999: 156; Melis 2000: 353). The upshot is that in firms with concentrated ownership structures, executive pay logically will be configured differently than it is in the sort of firms that dominate the corporate economy in the U.S. The significance of evolving patterns of share ownership should now have come into focus: if dispersed ownership is becoming more common world-wide, some sort of shift to the U.S. model of executive pay can be expected to follow.

A second economic dynamic that could foster at least a partial executive pay transition is the growing internationalization of the labor market for executives. Allegedly, "[t]he dawn of the millennium is ushering in a true global marketplace for CEO's" (Lyons and Spencer 2000: 51). To the extent this is true, companies based outside the U.S. which want to recruit and retain managers that might otherwise go to a high-paying American company will feel under pressure to compete with respect to compensation (Vancouver Sun 1996; Dickson 2001).

An increasingly international market for corporate control constitutes a third factor that could help to foster a shift on the executive compensation front. Cross-border merger and acquisition activity has been booming for most of the past decade (Hansen 2000: 23–25). This trend has significant implications for managerial remuneration since a merger creates pressure for adoption of a single pay system for all top executives in the new entity (Fung 1999: 38; Romanchek 1999: 7). Most important for our purposes, when one of the companies involved is from the U.S., the momentum will be in an American direction.

Consider, for instance, a U.S. "target" that offers remuneration packages to its executives which are more lucrative than those in place for managers of the new foreign parent. A byproduct of the transaction will be potentially divisive pay inequities for senior management. The acquiror may then be under pressure to resolve the problem by increasing home-country executive compensation (Gross and Wingerup 1999: 30; Murphy 1999: 2497). Turning to American companies that are acquiring foreign business enterprises, the executives of a target probably will be paid much less than their counterparts in the U.S.. Under such circumstances, fear of harmful defections fostered by pay-oriented disgruntlement might well lead to a readjustment in an American direction (Romanchek 1999: 7, 14–15).

A significant increase in the number and size of companies that operate on a multinational basis (Branson 2000: 669, 672–75) is a fourth economic dynamic that could foster a shift toward the U.S. pay paradigm. To illustrate just one aspect of this, to the extent that multinationals headquartered in the United States seek to introduce a uniform remuneration policy internationally, this will promote the Americanization of executive pay. The effect will be most profound for host-country nationals actually employed by the American companies (Deresky 2000: 366–67). Also noteworthy, though, will be pressure brought to bear upon domestic firms seeking to recruit and retain talented managers who might otherwise move to the U.S. multinationals (Murphy 1999: 2497).

While various factors could be providing the impetus for the globalization of executive pay, it cannot be taken for granted that they will have a substantial influence in the near future. For instance, there is evidence which suggests that if a switch to dispersed share ownership is occurring, it will be gradual (Cheffins 1999: 35–36). Turning to the market for executive talent, full-scale international labor mobility probably remains some way off (Katz 1997; Plender 1999). With cross-border merger and acquisition activity, the recent decline in equity markets has done much to reverse the boom on this front (Larsen and Saigol 2001). Referring finally to multinationals, many do not seek to establish a uniform executive remuneration structure internationally but instead prefer to take into account domestic compensation norms, national tax considerations, and other local conditions (Fung 1999: 38).

The market-oriented dynamics just discussed are not the only factors that will influence the extent to which convergence occurs with respect to executive pay. Another variable that could be relevant is "culture." A common refrain is that the meritocratic and "winner-take-all" environment in the United States is more hospitable for lucrative, performance-oriented managerial pay than the milieu elsewhere (Fung 1999: 39; Gross and Wingerup 1999: 27; Orr 1999: 207). Even in English-speaking countries that are part of the same "country cluster" (Deresky 2000: 117–18), such reasoning is invoked to account for the discrepancy between domestic pay levels and those prevailing in the U.S. (Conyon and Murphy 2000: F667–68; Gay 1995). To the extent that "culture" in fact is a potent variable with respect to managerial compensation, "Americanization" will presumably be deterred to some degree.

Regulation is an additional factor that could influence executive pay convergence, though its precise impact will depend on the circumstances. Under certain conditions, rules affecting executive pay might promote the introduction of U.S.-style arrangements and in others they might act as a deterrent. In the next section we take into account these possibilities by considering potentially relevant corporate law rules. Then, in sections V and VI, we will examine certain other legal constraints and canvass the potential impact of "soft law." One object of our survey of regulatory options will be to provide policymakers with a "checklist" of strategies they might adopt once they have determined whether the Americanization of executive pay ought to be encouraged or discouraged.

IV. Corporate Law

A. Direct Regulation

Corporate law encompasses various types of legal rules that might influence the setting of executive pay. Statutory measures which stipulate specifically how executive pay arrangements should be structured—"direct regulation"—have the potential to address the issue in the most forthright manner. Past experiences in India offer a striking illustration of how far the law might go. The Companies Act of 1956 introduced various provisions that dictated how management was to be paid (for background, see Ramaiya 1971: li, lii, 15, 22, 337–40, 503–12). For instance, total managerial remuneration could not exceed 11 percent of a company's net annual profits. Also, the remuneration of directors acting in a managerial capacity could not be increased without government approval. The government issued guidelines concerning increases it would sanction, which included a ceiling on annual pay apparently based upon the prevailing salary of the President of India (Ramaswamy et al. 2000: 182).

The law on executive pay was liberalized somewhat in India in the early 1990s (Ramaswamy et al. 2000: 182; Ramaiya 2001: 1738–44, 2435–50, 2732–61). This served to bring the country closer into line with the prevailing practice since in industrialized countries corporate law typically does not dictate in any way the nature or scope of executive remuneration (Wymeersch 2001: 26). Still, direct regulation of executive pay does occur in some countries, albeit on a less rigorous basis than that which used to prevail in India. For instance, in some countries there is a rule prohibiting a company from paying more than a designated percentage of annual earnings to its directors; Argentina and the Philippines have laws of this sort (International Handbook 1996: 1, 4, 168). Also, certain jurisdictions have rules in place stipulating that executive pay must be "reasonable." Examples include Australia and Germany (Cheffins 1997a: 674; Cheffins 2001: 526).

In any country with detailed regulations such as those that existed in India, the rules in question likely would constrain in some measure a move toward the Americanization of executive pay. However, the sort of restrictions we just have considered probably do not constitute a serious obstacle. For instance, in Australia, in the years following the introduction of its "reasonable" remuneration rule in 1992, the country experienced an "enormous and well-publicized escalation in the rewards for CEOs" (Bosch 1998). Similarly, in Germany the requirement that compensation reasonably correspond to the services provided rarely causes logistical difficulties (Oppenhoff and Verhoeven 1999: §24.03[1][c][ii][B]). Moreover, since Argentina's chief executives are among the most highly paid in the world (Towers Perrin 2001b: 20), laws limiting director pay to a percentage of profits apparently do not impose serious constraints on lucrative compensation arrangements.

B. Breach of Duty and Related Causes of Action

Regardless of whether corporate legislation stipulates how executive pay arrangements are to be structured, judicial regulation is a theoretical possibility. This is because when a company's directors are responsible for setting executive pay, decisions they take can potentially be impugned on the basis that there has been a breach of duties of care, loyalty or good faith owed to the company (on the duties, see International Handbook 1996: 69–70; SJ Berwin & Co. 1997: 8, 16, 25–27, 34–35, 41–42, 49–51, 57, 67, 74; Neto and Levy 1998: 65–67). In the U.S., for example, derivative litigation has been used in numerous instances to challenge managerial remuneration arrangements. These suits are more frequently successful in closely held corporations, but even in publicly quoted firms they provide something of a check on managerial remuneration (Thomas and Martin 2001: 573–93).

Still, while the judiciary can theoretically regulate executive pay in certain instances, it is highly unlikely that suits for breach of duty will affect in a meaningful way any trend in favor of the Americanization of executive pay. Certainly, in the U.S. itself litigation has done little to stop dramatic overall increases in managerial remuneration (Thomas and Martin 2001: 601–2, 605). Part of the reason is that American judges have typically been reluctant to meddle in such a delicate area of corporate policymaking (Thomas and Martin 2001: 601–2). Their colleagues in other countries likely will share this deferent attitude (e.g., Cheffins 1997a: 674; Cheffins 2001: 527–28).

Moreover, even if judges in a particular jurisdiction were prepared to rule that the awarding of overly generous remuneration constituted a breach of

duties owed to a company, significant procedural constraints would probably deter litigation. In various civil law countries, shareholders do not have
any right to bring derivative actions (Stecher et al. 1997: 9–10). In others,
those interested in bringing proceedings must own a minimum designated
percentage of shares (e.g., 5 or 10 percent) before they can obtain standing
(Stecher et al. 1997: 9–10; Neto and Levy 1998: 65).

In a common law country, principles derived from English case law can
offer various exceptions to the principle that breaches of duty by directors
must be litigated through the medium of the company (Davies 1997: 670–76;
Ho 1998: 629–40). These exceptions, however, are narrowly focused and
most often are of little assistance to a disgruntled minority shareholder
(Cheffins 1997a: 315–16, 665–66). In some common law jurisdictions (e.g.,
Canada and Australia) the standing rules have been liberalized somewhat by
statute (Cheffins 1997b: 234–35; Prince 2000: 493–97). Still, the fact that
recovery is the right of the company rather than the shareholder conducting
the litigation will mean that investors will most often conclude that suing is
more trouble than it is worth (Cheffins 1997b: 256–58).

In a number of common law jurisdictions, the logistical difficulties just discussed can be sidestepped by relying on statutory measures that authorize the
judiciary to grant a remedy to a shareholder who has been unfairly prejudiced
by a company's actions (Peterson 1989ff.: § 18.15; Cheffins 1997a: 345; Ho
1998: 657–68). With such a provision, a minority shareholder can sue without
being concerned about the procedural constraints associated with derivative
litigation. Also, since recovery is the right of the shareholder seeking relief
rather than the company, the remedy granted can be attuned to the personal
considerations of the applicant. Still, while there is case law which indicates
that excessive remuneration can qualify as "unfairly prejudicial" conduct
(Peterson 1989ff.: §18.96; Defina 1994: 342–44), the judiciary has proved
reluctant to extend the application of the relevant statutory provisions beyond
closely held companies (Cheffins 1997a: 464; Ho 1998: 662, 667). As a result,
proceedings brought under the unfair prejudice remedy are unlikely to have a
significant impact in the type of business where globalization is most likely to
have an impact on executive pay, namely the publicly quoted company.

C. Shareholder Voting

Legally mandated shareholder voting constitutes another constraint on executive pay arrangements which corporate law can impose. It is common for a

company's board of directors to be assigned the lead role in determining executive pay (International Handbook 1996: 15, 26, 52, 76, 124, 147, 162, 206; Cheffins 1997a: 660; Cox et al. 1998: §11.4). At the same time, though, corporate legislation may stipulate that the shareholders have a say of some sort. For instance, in certain jurisdictions laws governing the issuance of equity and corporate "buy-backs" of shares mean that shareholders will have to pass a resolution endorsing the creation of stock options for top management (section IV, D, this essay).

The intention underlying the statutory provisions which give owners of corporate equity a vote presumably is to impose a check on excessive managerial remuneration. There is reason to doubt, however, whether rules on voting are of great practical importance. Start by considering companies with a controlling shareholder. Statutory measures that require remuneration issues to be put to a vote may effectively give the dominant investor a veto over changes falling within the scope of the relevant rules. On the other hand, a "core" shareholder will be well-situated to exercise influence on the executive pay front regardless of whether a shareholder resolution is specifically required or not.

What will be the situation in companies with dispersed share ownership? The experience in the U.S. and Britain, where a diffuse share ownership pattern is standard, provides guidance. In these two countries, the available empirical evidence suggests shareholder voting only functions as a potential check on executive pay when arrangements deviate far from the norm (Cheffins and Thomas 2001: 296, 306, 309–11). Again, certain countries where concentrated share ownership is the norm in large business enterprises may be shifting toward the more diffuse Anglo-American pattern (section III, this essay). The experience in the U.S. and the U.K. implies that this sort of shift would not cause shareholder voting to emerge as a significant determinant of executive pay.

D. Restrictions on the Distribution of Shares to Executives

When a company has established a share option plan on behalf of its executives, it must be in a position to satisfy its obligations when the options are exercised. The most straightforward procedure is to issue new shares to the option holders or to repurchase outstanding equity for sale to the executives (Cheffins 2001: 511). In many jurisdictions, however, the issuance of new equity is heavily regulated and/or share "buybacks" are prohibited except under special circumstances (e.g., Thorpe 1995: B62, D60–61, EC 88, F50, H48, P42, Q66). The effect can be that it is highly impractical for companies to make use of stock options.

The German experience is illustrative (Cheffins 2001: 511). The country's stock corporations are only permitted to issue and repurchase shares under tightly prescribed circumstances and satisfying option rights exercised by top executives traditionally did not qualify as an exception under the rules. As a result, firms could only make stock options available to executives by granting bonds that could be converted into shares of the company or had a warrant attached which granted the right to acquire shares upon its exercise. The situation was similar in Japan, Finland, and South Korea (Economist 1999: 13).

Since stock options are a pivotal aspect of the U.S. pay paradigm, rules that effectively preclude companies from using this form of remuneration inevitably will put something of a check on the Americanization of managerial compensation. Still, due to deregulation, such restrictions are of diminishing importance. During the late 1990s, Germany, Japan, South Korea and Finland all liberalized their statutory rules in a manner that now makes it feasible for corporations to grant conventional stock options to executives (Economist 1999: 13).

In these various countries, full deregulation was not implemented since shareholder approval does have to be obtained before matters can proceed (Kim and Lee 1999: 80, 85; Kawamura 1997: N-226–27; Grub 1999: 24–25). Still, since shareholder voting requirements do not appear to constitute a serious obstacle to change on the executive pay front, the law now constitutes less of a deterrent to the Americanization of executive pay than was the case previously. Indeed, large numbers of German, Japanese, and Korean companies have taken advantage of reform to begin granting stock option plans (Korea Herald 2000; Benes 2001; Woodruff 2001).

E. Disclosure

Though "direct regulation," shareholder litigation and shareholder voting requirements seem unlikely to influence the Americanization of executive pay and rules governing the distribution of corporate equity are apparently receding in importance, one set of corporate law rules could play a pivotal role. The measures in question are those that require corporations, on a periodic basis, to divulge publicly the remuneration arrangements in place for executives. Rules set down by America's Securities and Exchange Commission (SEC) that govern corporations which have distributed their shares to the public illustrate how matters can be handled. Under the SEC regime, a corporation must circulate annually a report that describes the firm's general approach to executive pay and offers a detailed individual breakdown of the compensation awarded to the CEO and the other four highest paid executive officers (Cheffins 1997a: 675–77).

The U.K., Canada, and Australia have disclosure rules that match the standards set down by the SEC or at least come fairly close (Conyon and Murphy 2000: F642-F643; Quinn 1999: 98). In other countries, though, disclosure regulation is lax. A common arrangement is that corporations eligible to join the stock market must identify in their accounts the aggregate remuneration of those serving as directors (International Handbook 1996: 4, 27, 77, 94, 106, 137, 201, 212; Romanchek 1999: 8). Companies are not required, however, to publish any details on individual directors.

The approach countries take toward the disclosure of executive pay will likely dictate to some degree the extent to which the sort of performance-oriented compensation packages that are prevalent in the U.S. become popular elsewhere. Shareholders might well want to promote increased use of variable managerial pay since incentivized remuneration can potentially reduce agency costs (Leander 1998a: 13; Cheffins and Thomas 2001: 286, 308, 311–12; Woodruff 2001). Disclosure regulation will likely affect the ability of investors to pursue this agenda. Shareholder intervention will become increasingly feasible as more data become available. Correspondingly, if companies are compelled to made available a wide range of information to investors, some sort of shift toward incentivized managerial compensation can be expected to follow (Iacobucci 1998: 497–501). The available Canadian empirical and anecdotal evidence supports this hypothesis (Iacobucci 1998: 502–3; Park 2001).

New disclosure laws also might foster a shift toward the U.S. compensation model by accelerating increases in executive pay. The catalyst will be that those who set remuneration will be able to find out readily the "market rate" offered by competitors in the same industrial sector and by firms of a similar size. Corporate pride and concern about recruitment and retention will in turn place pressure on these individuals to ensure that their company's executive pay arrangements are not "below average" (Bosch 1998; Thomas and Martin 1999: 1041–42). If all companies respond by seeking to match or exceed the "market rate," the inevitable result will be an upward "ratchet" in pay. Empirical work done in Canada lends support to this characterization of the effect of disclosure regulation (Park 2001).

It is ironic that increased disclosure might contribute to an American-style executive pay spiral. This is because those who are concerned that top managers are paid "too much" can be keen supporters of reform (Cheffins 1997a: 699). For instance, when the province of Ontario bolstered executive pay disclosure in 1993, a left-wing administration was in power that was concerned about the excesses of free-market economics. This led a columnist in a leading Canadian newspaper to speculate that the "real motivation" for reform "was to plunge the population into an egalitarian snit over the money paid to the capitalist scoundrels who run private-sector corporations" (Corcoran 1994). Matters did not quite work out as planned. As the same columnist observed in 2001, "So far, the only impact of the disclosure has been to drive compensation higher as companies now compete more aggressively for talent" (Corcoran 2001).

If it is true that extensive disclosure regulation provides a hospitable platform for a move toward American-style executive pay arrangements, then a potentially important trend is reform in those countries where the current regime is comparatively lax. The Towers Perrin stock options study discussed earlier indicates that in sixteen of the twenty-two jurisdictions covered, moderate or significant change is expected to the laws on disclosure (Towers Perrin 2001a: 15). Perhaps, then, "secrecy is on the way out for executive pay" (Woodruff 2000). If this turns out to be true, reform may well help to foster a shift toward the lucrative performance-oriented compensation packages that are prevalent in the U.S.

V. Other Legislation

A. Tax

While a diverse range of corporate law rules potentially could have an impact on the globalization of executive pay, other aspects of the law could also be relevant. Tax is one example. It may be, for instance, that the income tax rates payable by executives will help to dictate whether the sort of lucrative managerial compensation arrangements U.S. corporations offer will become increasingly prevalent elsewhere. More precisely, corporate executives are likely to be highly paid in a country where the top marginal tax rate (the rate applicable to any further taxable income) is low. The reason is that a typical company will seek to tailor compensation arrangements to match the preferences of its executives, who in turn will value generous financial compensation more highly in a liberal tax environment since they will be able to keep more of what they earn (Cheffins 1997a: 704). There indeed is historical and empirical evidence that indicates there is a correlation between lower income tax rates and higher executive pay (Abowd and Bognanno 1995: 85–87, 91–92, 95; Cheffins 1997a: 704), but there is also some conflicting data (Hall and Liebman 2000: 24–26).

Another circumstance where tax rules can potentially have an impact on the structure of executive pay arrangements concerns the use of stock options. Various countries have recently introduced reforms designed to reduce the tax burden for the individuals who receive this form of compensation (e.g., SJ Berwin 1999: 17, 19, 23, 25, 27, 31). A widely held belief is that taxation of recipients is an important determinant of stock option implementation (Towers Perrin 2001a: 10). Tax reform correspondingly might be promoting increased use of the sort of performance-oriented compensation that is popular in the U.S. (Woodruff 2001).

Abowd and Bognanno (1995: 92–95) have adduced empirical evidence covering twelve countries that casts doubt on the received wisdom on tax and stock options. It is important to note, though, that they focused on the position of individuals receiving stock options rather than the status of the corporate employer. Exceptionally, in the United States gains executives receive from exercising share options are typically deductible from corporate profits as an ordinary business expense (Johnston 1998; Hall and Liebman 2000: 5, Table 1). The special tax treatment in the U.S. has been proffered as at least a partial explanation for the exceptional popularity of executive share options in American companies (Conyon and Murphy 2000: F665). Still, it should not be taken for granted that America's unique tax treatment of stock options is highly influential. Instead, there is empirical evidence that suggests U.S. corporations which are not well-positioned to benefit from the tax deductibility of stock options use this form of compensation in much the same fashion as other firms (Hall and Liebman 2000: 18–20).

The situation with stock options is not the only instance where data from the U.S. suggest that tax rules which govern companies might not have the sort of impact on executive compensation that would be anticipated. In 1993, President Clinton fulfilled a campaign pledge to halt "excessive executive pay" by spurring changes to tax law that meant a corporation which paid an executive more than $1 million annually could only treat the expenditure as deductible for tax purposes if the additional compensation was "performance related" (Murphy 1995: 714, 738). Data collected in the years following indicates that this change to the law did very little to slow down increases in executive pay and only had a moderate impact on the balance between performance-related pay and salary (Hall and Liebman 2000: 22–24; Murphy and Oyer 2001: 32–34). This pattern, together with the evidence on the deductibility of stock options, suggests that policies which countries adopt on corporate tax may well not have a significant impact on whatever globalization trends exist in the area of executive compensation.

B. Labor Law

Compensation experts warn that the sort of incentive-oriented managerial compensation closely associated with the U.S. pay paradigm can potentially conflict with labor legislation. The problem is that various countries in Europe and Latin America have laws regarding "acquired rights" which might, over time, transform into an entitlement compensation designed to be conditional upon satisfaction of criteria related to corporate performance (Gross and Wingerup 1999: 29). Since companies will understandably be reluctant to grant performance-related remuneration that is likely to lose its incentive aspect, acquired rights laws could deter in some measure a move toward American-style executive compensation packages. Indeed, according to Towers Perrin research, rules of this type have a "very important" effect on the awarding of stock options in France and Mexico (Towers Perrin 2001a: 10).

The impact of "acquired rights" legislation should not, however, be overestimated. For instance, while stock option plans might constitute an "entitlement" under acquired rights legislation in some countries, they may not do so in others (Gates and Reid 1994: 29). Also, the experience in Brazil suggests that if major multinationals are using lucrative incentive schemes to lure managerial talent away from domestic companies, government officials may be prepared to level the playing field by relaxing enforcement of acquired rights laws in the managerial context (Leander 1998b).

VI. "Soft Law"

"Soft law" is an increasingly important determinant of corporate behavior on an international basis (Branson 2000: 670–71). The term can be defined for our purposes as rules and guidelines directed at corporations that have been promulgated by private organizations rather than by legislatures, government regulators, or judges. Under this definition, the fact that those formulating the relevant standards might be acting pursuant to a statutory mandate does not affect the "soft law" status of the relevant regulations. Hence, in a U.S. context, accounting standards developed by the privately organized Financial Accounting Standards Board (FASB) qualify as "soft law" even though the Board is exercising powers delegated to it by the SEC (Cheffins 1997a: 376–77). The situation is the same with listing rules that govern companies quoted on the New York Stock Exchange (NYSE) and NASDAQ since these exchanges formulate and enforce the relevant standards, albeit subject to SEC scrutiny (Karmel 2001: 339).

Shareholder voting is one issue relating to executive pay that "soft law" can address. For instance, the listing rules of the NYSE and NASDAQ stipulate that, subject to some exceptions, listed companies must obtain shareholder approval before introducing a stock option plan (Wagner and Wagner 1997: 12–13). Similarly, stock market rules in Australia, Hong Kong, and Singapore provide that shareholders must vote on the issuance of shares to directors under an employee incentive scheme (Lemberg and Keeler 2001: 36; Australian Stock Exchange 2002: §10.14).

Another issue "soft law" can address is disclosure. For instance, as events taking place in the United Kingdom illustrate, stock market listing rules can regulate the dissemination of information concerning executive pay. Currently, companies which have their shares listed for trading on the London Stock Exchange must comply with listing rules administered by the Financial Services Authority (FSA), a government regulator. Until 2000, however, the London Stock Exchange, a privately owned body, was responsible for promulgating and enforcing the listing rules, thus bringing these regulations within the "soft law" category. During the final few years when the London Stock Exchange was administering the listing rules as "soft law" the regulation of executive pay was expanded considerably (Smerdon 1998: 67–69, 72–80). A key change made in the mid-1990s was to require a quoted company to put before its shareholders a wide range of data on executive pay, including full details of the compensation package of each director holding an executive position.

Accounting standards configured as "soft law" can also govern public disclosure of information on managerial compensation. Indeed, recent events concerning stock options indicate that the accounting treatment accorded to managerial remuneration can generate considerable controversy. According to FASB guidelines, a company that awards stock options which do not have performance conditions attached does not have to set the "cost" against profits (Stabile 1999: 276–78). The relevant information does have to be disclosed in footnotes to the accounts. Still, since granting stock options to executives does not affect the "bottom line," U.S. accounting rules allegedly create a bias in favor of this form of compensation, at least when the options are of the "plain vanilla" variety (Murphy 1999: 2514–15). Indeed, many attribute the popularity of stock options in the U.S. to the treatment they receive under accounting rules (Bebchuk et al. 2001: 45) and there currently is a strong political campaign being waged to reverse the alleged bias (Broder 2002).

Still, while FASB guidelines might affect the form which America's executive remuneration takes, they do not explain why stock options are more popular in the U.S. than they are elsewhere. In those countries where accounting standards are promulgated, the pattern is that the granting of stock options does not affect the corporate "bottom line" (Accountant 2000: 18; Barker and Peel 2000; DeCloet 2002). Since the accounting bias in favor of stock options is present outside the U.S., other factors must account for the unique popularity of this form of compensation in America's publicly quoted corporations.

In addition to regulating shareholder voting and disclosure, "soft law" can set down guidelines for the determination of executive pay. For instance, during the mid-1990s, the London Stock Exchange's listing rules were amended to add a best practice code that instructed companies to have regard for pay and employment conditions elsewhere in the business (the "wider scene"), to avoid paying more than was necessary to hire talented executives and to follow detailed recommendations on the design of performance-related compensation (Smerdon 1998: 72–75). Companies governed by the listing rules were not obliged to comply with the guidance offered on the setting of executive pay but they were required to disclose the extent to which they were conforming with the relevant standards.

Aside from the intervention of the FSA as the relevant administrator, the position remains much the same now in Britain under an appendix to the listing rules referred to as the Combined Code (Financial Services Authority 2002: Section 1, paras. B1–B3, Schedule A). In the U.K., compliance with corporate governance codes backed by disclosure obligations has been substantial overall (Company Law Review Steering Group 2000: para. 3.129). As a result, it is sensible to infer that the U.K.'s best practice guidelines on executive pay have affected in some measure the configuration of managerial remuneration, even if they were originally developed as "soft law." Still, the point should not be pushed too hard. In the years following the issuance of instructions to take into account the "wider scene" and to avoid paying more than necessary to hire executives, managerial remuneration rose substantially in U.K. companies (Cheffins and Thomas 2001: 281).

Various corporate governance codes have been issued around the world during the past few years (Cheffins 2000: 13–14). These codes, which typically have been drafted by a committee of business leaders and/or stock market officials, offer guidance to publicly quoted corporations on various governance issues and quite often discuss the setting of executive pay. The British experience would seem to imply that these efforts could have a meaningful effect on managerial remuneration. Drawing any such inference, however, would be hazardous.

Enforceability is one reason why the use of "soft law" might well yield a different outcome outside Britain. Whereas in the U.K. the guidelines on executive pay had explicit backing from the London Stock Exchange's listing rules, in various other jurisdictions compliance with the corporate governance code is purely voluntary (Cheffins 2000: 14). Also, the guidance that is provided on incentive-oriented remuneration is typically much less detailed and specific than that offered in Britain, with the standard format being a few sentences stressing the importance of linking pay with performance (e.g., Peters Committee 1997: paras. 4.5–4.6; Committee on Corporate Governance 1999: para. 9.1; Committee for the Corporate Governance of Listed Companies 1999: para. 8.2). The upshot is that "soft law" guidelines on the determination of managerial remuneration are unlikely to have a significant impact on any trend in favor of the Americanization of executive pay.

VII. A Checklist for Policymakers

Generally speaking, executive compensation has not engendered strong debate around the world (Leander 1998: 12; André 1998: 159–61; Fanto

1998: 26). The United States, where top managers are paid much more than their counterparts elsewhere, stands as an exception to this trend (Murphy 1999: 2551–53), as does Britain (Cheffins and Thomas 2001: 278–82). Still, it may be that executive pay will move into the spotlight in various additional countries in the not-too-distant future (Betts 2002). The obvious catalyst would be the potential "global shakeup in executive comp" we have been considering here.

As we have seen, while there are factors promoting the Americanization of executive pay, it is not clear how strong any such trend is going to be. Still, since the U.S. pay paradigm has generated controversy in its country of origin, any sort of concerted shift toward this model likely would prompt vigorous debate in the various countries affected. The ensuing controversy would, in turn, likely put policymakers under something of an onus to address the situation.

Views on what should be done in response to the globalization of managerial remuneration would no doubt vary. There would, for instance, be those who would say that a shift in the American direction should be encouraged. Some might make the argument in defensive terms, asserting that domestic companies should take the steps required to ensure that talented nationals are not tempted to leave the country by U.S.-style pay. The case could also be made on more affirmative grounds by citing the heavy use of performance-oriented compensation in America's successful corporate economy. The argument on this count would be that the adoption of a highly "incentivized" approach to remuneration would provide a useful boost for companies that have, to this point, treated shareholders as "second class citizens" (Brull 1995; Kay 1998; Asian Wall Street Journal 1999).

On the other hand, the American approach to executive pay does have potential drawbacks. It may be that that the U.S. version of managerial compensation is an example of self-serving "rent extraction" by corporate executives rather than being the product of fair-minded efforts to align the interests of shareholders and executives (Bebchuk et al. 2001). Also, as events at scandal-ridden energy giant Enron Corp. arguably illustrate, executives who are anxious to cash in profitable stock options may be tempted to mislead the market so as to prop up the stock price until they can unload their shares (Samuelson 2002). Finally, in those countries where there is a strong egalitarian impulse, a growing gap between ordinary staff and the soaring fortunes of corporate leaders might well be viewed as objectionable on ethical grounds (Bryant 1999).

For a policymaker who has been called upon to address a potential Americanization of executive pay in his or her country and who has reached a conclusion on whether this trend should be fostered or not, this essay provides guidance on how to proceed. To illustrate, if the preferred option is to curb a shift in the U.S. direction, the analysis offered here suggests that introducing "direct" regulation of executive pay, strengthening directors' duties or imposing new shareholder voting requirements would not yield the desired outcome. Bolstering disclosure requirements would also be unwise; indeed this might have a counterproductive effect.

A policymaker who is seeking to blunt the Americanization of executive pay will find, moreover, that "soft law" does not constitute a particularly promising alternative. Again, in Britain corporate governance codes have had an appreciable impact on corporate conduct. Nevertheless, instructions to take into "the wider scene" and to avoid overpaying for executive talent have apparently fallen on deaf ears.

If a policymaker's objective is to constrain executive pay, a more direct cure would be to orchestrate an increase in the top marginal rate of income tax. This is because under the new conditions executives would know that they would keep less of what they earned and thus would not press as hard for lucrative remuneration. On the other hand, the politics of taxation are delicate and it is doubtful whether concern about the level of managerial compensation could ever provide a sufficiently strong political platform for a more progressive tax regime (Cheffins 1997a: 706–7).

Assume now that our policymaker has concluded that the preferred course of action is to foster a shift toward the U.S. executive pay model. Under such circumstances, introducing stronger disclosure requirements would be a prudent course to follow. The primary reason would be that shareholders, having additional information at hand, would be well situated to press for compensation packages that linked pay more closely with performance. Also, the fact that enhanced disclosure regulation might well foster an upward ratchet in executive pay would presumably be an acceptable byproduct of reform.

Another approach that a policymaker might adopt if he or she was favorably disposed toward U.S.-style executive pay would be to promote the unwinding of control blocks in domestic companies. All else being equal, a company with a "core" shareholder will probably have lower executive pay than its widely held counterpart and performance-oriented compensation will likely play a less important role. A popular thesis at present is that a country that wants to foster outside investment in domestic companies can "jump start" a move in this direction by enacting laws designed to protect minority shareholders (Cheffins 2002: 7–9, 21–22, 30). It is by no means certain whether any such attempt will succeed (Cheffins 2002: 19–22, 30–31). Still, for a country that does make a law-driven transition toward the sort of dispersed pattern of ownership that prevails in the U.S. and the U.K., a byproduct likely would be at least a partial shift toward the American model of executive pay.

Conclusion

This essay has discussed in general terms how executive pay arrangements differ between the U.S. and elsewhere, has described a potential Americanization trend, and has analyzed regulatory arrangements that might influence the pace of convergence. It has not sought to determine, however, whether a move toward the U.S. model of executive pay would be a "good thing." Instead, the purpose here has primarily been descriptive, namely identifying and discussing the variables likely to influence global managerial remuneration trends.

The analysis that has been offered here does have, however, significant normative ramifications. What has been provided is a checklist of regulatory options that policymakers outside the U.S. can take into account once they have formulated a view on the approach to take with executive pay. This means that, while those wondering whether the Americanization of executive pay would be a "good thing" will need to find their answers elsewhere, this essay offers valuable guidance for those have reached a tentative view concerning this question.

Acknowledgment

The authors are grateful for feedback provided at the Georgetown Law School's conference on Corporations as Producers and Distributors of Rents (October 2001), the British Accounting Association Special Interest Group on Corporate Governance conference held at Cardiff Business School (December 2001), the Business Associations section meeting at the Annual Meeting of the American Association of Law School (January 2002) and the conference on Global Markets, Domestic Institutions: Corporate Law and

Governance in a New Era of Cross-Border Deals held at Columbia Law School (April 2002). We also acknowledge very useful comments from Margaret Blair, John Core, Henry Hansmann, Saul Levmore, Robert Thompson and Michael Wachter.

References

Abowd, John M. and Michael L. Bognanno 1995. International Differences in Executive and Managerial Compensation. In *Differences and Changes in Wage Structures*. Richard B. Freeman and Lawrence F. Katz, eds. Chicago: University of Chicago Press.

——— and David S. Kaplan. 1999. Executive Compensation: Six Questions That Need Answering. *Journal of Economic Perspectives* 13: 145–68.

Accountant. 2001. Reform in Germany. *The Accountant*, July 21, 2000, 17–19.

André, Thomas J. 1998. Cultural Hegemony: The Exportation of Anglo-Saxon Corporate Governance Ideologies to Germany. *Tulane Law Review* 73: 69–171.

Asian Wall Street Journal. 1999. Pay Japan's Executives to Perform. *Asian Wall St. Journal.* April 12, 10.

Australian Stock Exchange. 2002. *Listing Rules.* Available at http://www.asx.com.au/ListingRules/LRIntro.shtm.

Barker, Thorold and Michael Peel. 2000. Companies Given No Choice on Revealing Share Options. *Financial Times* (London), July 21, 27.

Bebchuk, Lucian, Jesse Fried and David Walker. 2001. Executive Compensation in America: Optimal Contracting or Extraction of Rents. Harvard John M. Olin Discussion Paper Series, Discussion Paper No. 339/University of California at Berkeley School of Law, Public Law and Legal Theory Working Paper No. 75.

Benes, Nicholas. 2001. Japan's Coming Shareholder Revolution. *Asian Wall St. Journal.* February 14, 2001, 6.

Betts, Paul. 2002. Risk and Reward. *Financial Times* (London), February 16/17, 2002, 12.

Bosch, Henry. 1998. Looking in the CEO's Pay Packet Has a Cost. *Shares Magazine*, October, 61.

Branson, Douglas M. 2000. Teaching Comparative Governance: The Significance of 'Soft Law' and International Institutions. *Georgia Law Review.* 34: 669–98.

Broder, David S. 2002. Corporate Cake. *Washington Post*, April 21, B07.

Brull, Steven. 1995. Sony Links Executive Pay to Stocks. *Int'l Herald Tribune*, August 11, 11.

Bryant, Adam. 1999. American Pay Rattles Foreign Partners. *New York Times*, January 17, 1999, sec. 4, 1.

Cheffins, Brian R. 1997a. *Company Law: Theory, Structure and Operation*. Oxford: Oxford University Press.

———. 1997b. Reforming the Derivative Action: The Canadian Experience and British Prospects. *Company Financial and Insolvency Law Review* 1: 227–60.

———. 1999. Current Trends in Corporate Governance: Going From London to Milan via Toronto. *Duke Journal of Comparative and International Law* 10: 5–42.

———. 2000. Corporate Governance Reform: Britain as an Exporter. *Hume Papers on Public Policy* 8 (no. 1): 10–28.

———. 2001. The Metamorphosis of 'Germany Inc.': The Case of Executive Pay. *American Journal of Comparative Law* 49: 497–539.

———. 2002. Law as Bedrock: The Foundations of an Economy Dominated by Widely Held Public Companies. Unpublished working paper, forthcoming, *Oxford Journal of Legal Studies* 23: issue no. 1.

Cheffins, Brian R. and Randall S. Thomas. 2001. Should Shareholders Have a Greater Say Over Executive Pay?: Learning From the U.S. Experience. *Journal of Corporate Law Studies* 1: 277–316.

Coffee, John C., Jr. 2001. The Rise of Dispersed Ownership: The Roles of Law and the State in the Separation of Ownership and Control. *Yale Law Journal* 111: 1–82.

Committee for the Corporate Governance of Listed Companies (Italy). 1999. *Report; Code of Conduct*. Available at http://www.ecgi.de/codes/country_pages/codes_italy.htm.

Committee on Corporate Governance (Korea). 1999. *Code of Best Practice for Corporate Governance*. Available at http://www.ecgi.de/codes/country_pages/codes_korea.htm.

Company Law Review Steering Group. 2000. *Modern Company Law for a Competitive Economy: Developing the Framework*. London: Department of Trade and Industry.

Conyon, Martin J. and Kevin J. Murphy. 2000. The Prince and the Pauper? CEO Pay in the United States and the United Kingdom. *Economic Journal* 110: F640–F671.

Corcoran, Terence. 1994. Executive Pay is Not About Social Justice. *Toronto Globe & Mail*, May 14, B2.

———. 2001. Executive Hunting Season. *National Post*, April 3, C19.

Cox, James D., Thomas Lee Hazen and F. Hodge O'Neal. 1998. *Corporations*. Gaithersburg, NY: Aspen.

Davies, Paul L. 1997. *Gower's Principles of Modern Company Law*, 6th ed. London: Sweet and Maxwell.

Davis, Matthew E. 2000. Fast Forward: The Global Compensation Imperative. *ACA News*, May, 22-26.

DeCloet, Derek. 2002. Executives Want to Keep Their Options Open. *National Post*, April 19, FP3.

Defina, Andrew, Thomas C. Morris and Ian M. Ramsay. 1994. What is Reasonable Remuneration for Corporate Officers? An Empirical Investigation Into the Relationship Between Pay and Performance in the Largest Australian Companies. *Company and Securities Law Journal* 12: 341–56.

Deresky, Helen. 2000. *International Management: Managing Across Borders and Cultures*, 3rd ed. Upper Saddle River, NJ: Prentice Hall.

Dickson, Martin. 2001. Package Envy: Or the Curse of Keeping Up with the Yanks. *Financial Times* (London), April 28/29, 13.

Economist. 1999. The Best . . . and the Rest (A Survey of Pay). *Economist*, May 8.

Fanto, James A. 1998. France. In Arthur R. Pinto and Gustavo Visentini, eds., *The Legal Basis of Corporate Governance in Publicly Held Corporations: A Comparative Approach.*The Hague: Kluwer, 1–52.

Financial Services Authority. 2002. *Listing Rules*, Combined Code, Code of Best Practice. Available at http://www.fsa.gov.uk/ukla/1_listinginfo3.html.

Flynn, Julia. 2000. Pay for UK CEOs Trails U.S.; Consolidation May Bring Change. *Wall St. Journal Europe*, June 6, 28.

Fung, Shirley. 1999. How Should We Pay Them?. *Across the Board*, June, 36–41.

Gates, Jeffrey R. and David E. Reid. 1994. Translating Your ESOP Abroad. *Financial Executive*, July, 26–29.

Gay, Katherine. 1995. Canadian Pay Hampers CEO Talent Hunt. *Financial Post*, April 22, 57.

Gross, Steven E. and Per L. Wingerup. 1999. Global Pay? Maybe Not Yet. *Compensation and Benefits Review*, July–August, 25–34.

Grub, Maximilian. 1999. The Concept of Corporate Governance and Recent Developments in Germany. *Corporate Governance International* 4: 20–30.

Hall, Brian J. and Jeffrey B. Liebman. 2000. The Taxation of Executive Compensation. NBER Working Paper 7596.

Hansen, Fay. 2000. Global Mergers & Acquisitions Explode. *Business Credit*, June, 22–25.

Hansmann, Henry and Reinier Kraakman. 2001. The End of History for Corporate Law. *Georgetown Law Journal* 89: 439–68.

Ho, Betty M., 1998. *Public Companies and their Equity Securities*. The Hague: Kluwer.

Iacobucci, Edward M. 1998. The Effects of Disclosure on Executive Compensation. *University of Toronto Law Journal* 48: 489–520.

International Handbook. 1996. *International Handbook of Governance*. London: International Thomson Business Press.

Johnston, David Cay. 1998. American-Style Pay Moves Abroad. *New York Times*, September 3, C1.

Karmel, Roberta S. 2001. The Future of Corporate Governance Listing Requirements. *Southern Methodist University Law Review*. 54: 325–55.

Katz, Jan Hack. 1997. Competition Breeds Efficiency? Then Open the Executive Suite to the Free Market. *Los Angeles Times*, May 16, B9.

Kawamura, Akira. 1997. Introduction of Stock Option. *Journal of International Banking Law* 12: N-226-N-229.

Kay, Ira T. 1998. High CEO Pay Helps U.S. Economy Thrive. *Wall St. Journal*, February 23, A22.

Kim, Kon-Sik. and Choong-Kee Lee. 1999. South Korea. In *International Encyclopaedia of Laws: Corporations and Partnerships*. R. Blanpain and K. Geens, eds. The Hague: Kluwer.

Korea Herald. 2000. 105 Listed Firms Introduce Stock Options This Year. *Korea Herald*, October 20, Westlaw Allnews database: 2000 WL 27394960.

La Porta, Rafael, Florencio Lopez-de-Silanes, Andrei Shleifer and Robert Vishny. 1997. Legal Determinants of External Finance. *Journal of Finance* 52: 1131–50.

Larsen, Peter Thal and Lina Saigol. 2001. Annus Horribilis for Deal-Making Bankers. *Financial Times* (London), December 28, 19.

Leander, Tom. 1998a. The Global Shakeup in Executive Comp. *Global Finance*. August, 12–14.

———. 1998b. Latin Comp Joins the Fray. *Global Finance*. August, 27.

Lemberg, Jonathan and Kathleen Keeler. 2001. Equity Compensation: Bringing U.S.-Style Stock Option Plans to Asia. *International Financial Law Review*. October, Special Supplement: Private Equity and Venture Capital: A Legal Guide. 33–36.

Lyons, Denis B.K. and Spencer Stuart. 2000. International CEOs on the Rise. *Chief Executive*, February, 51–53.

Melis, Andrea. 2000. Corporate Governance in Italy. *Corporate Governance: An International Review* 8: 347–55.

Murphy, Kevin J. 1995. Politics, Economics, and Executive Compensation. 63 *University of Cincinnati Law Review* 63: 713–48.

———. 1999. Executive Compensation. In Orley Ashenfelter and David Card, eds., *Handbook of Labor Economics*. Amsterdam: Elsevier, 2485–2563.

——— and Paul Oyer. 2001. Discretion in Executive Incentive Contracts: Theory and Evidence. Unpublished working paper.

Neto, Eduardo S. and Jorge E.P. Levy. 1998. Brazil. In *International Encyclopaedia of Laws: Corporations and Partnerships*. R. Blanpain and K. Geens eds. The Hague: Kluwer.

Oppenhoff, Walter and Thomas O. Verhoeven. 1999. The Stock Corporation. In Dennis Campbell, ed., *Business Transactions in Germany*. New York: Matthew Bender.

Orr, Deborah. 1999. Damn Yankees. *Forbes*, May 17, 206–7.

Park, Yun W., Toni Nelson and Khalil M.Torabzadeh. 2000. Controlling Shareholder and Executive Incentive Structure: Canadian Evidence. *Canadian Journal of Administrative Sciences* 17: 245–54.

————. 2001. Executive Pay and the Disclosure Environment: Canadian Evidence. *Journal of Financial Research* 24: 347–65.

Peters Committee. 1997. *Corporate Governance in the Netherlands – Forty Recommendations*. Available on the internet at http://www.ecgi.de/codes/country_pages/codes_netherlands.htm .

Peterson, Denis H. 1989ff. *Shareholder Remedies in Canada*. Markham, Ont.: Butterworths.

Plender, John. 1999. Cult of the U.S. Manager. *Financial Times* (London), April 14, 19.

Prince, Peter. 2000. Australia's Statutory Derivative Action: Using the New Zealand Experience. *Company and Securities Law Journal* 18: 493–515.

Quinn, Michael. 1999. The Unchangeables—Director and Executive Remuneration Disclosure in Australia. *Australian Journal of Corporate Law* 10: 89–106.

Ramaiya, A. 1971. *Guide to the Companies Act (Act I of 1956 Amended Up to Date)*, 6th ed. Madras: Madras Law Journal Office.

————. 2001. *Guide to the Companies Act*, 15th ed. Agra: Wadwha.

Ramaswamy, Kannan, Rajaram Veliyath and Lenn Gomes. 2000. A Study of the Determinants of CEO Compensation in India. *Management International Review* 40: 167–91.

Romanchek, Robert A. 1999. Executive Compensation in a Global Merger. *ACA Journal*, First Quarter, 6–19.

Samuelson, Robert J. 2002. Stock Option Madness. *Washington Post*, January 30, 2002, A23.

SJ Berwin & Co., ed. 1997. *Directors' Responsibilities in Europe*. European Private Equity and Venture Capital Association Special Paper.

————. 1999. *Stock Options*. European Private Equity and Venture Capital Association Special Paper.

Smerdon, Richard. 1998. *A Practical Guide to Corporate Governance*. London: Sweet & Maxwell.

Stabile, Susan J. 1999. Motivating Executives: Does Performance-Based Compensation Positively Affect Managerial Performance?. *University of Pennsylvania Journal of Labor & Employment Law* 2: 227–85.

Stecher, Matthias W, Anita de Jong, Joren de Wachter and Clare Grayston. 1997. General Report. In *Protection of Minority Shareholders*. Matthias W. Stecher, ed. London: Kluwer.

Thomas, Randall S. and Kenneth J. Martin. 1999. The Effect of Shareholder Proposals on Executive Compensation. *University of Cincinnati Law Review* 67: 1021–81.

———— 2001. Litigating Challenges to Executive Compensation: An Exercise in Futility? *Washington University Law Quarterly* 79: 569–613.

Thorpe, Shaun W., ed. 1995. *Company Law in Europe*. London: Butterworths.

Towers Perrin. 2000. *Worldwide Total Remuneration 2000*.

————. 2001*a*. *Stock Options Around the World*.

————. 2001*b*. *Worldwide Total Remuneration 2001–2002*.

Vancouver Sun. 1996. CEO Shortage Sends Executive Salaries Soaring. *Vancouver Sun*, May 15, D3.

Wagner, Richard H. and Catherine G. Wagner. 1997. Recent Developments in Executive, Director, and Employee Stock Compensation Plans: New Concerns for Corporate Directors. *Stanford Journal of Law, Business & Finance* 3: 5–29.

Woodruff, David. 2000. A Vanishing European Taboo. *Wall Street Journal*, September 11, A28.

———. 2001. Europe, A Latecomer, Embraces Options. *Wall St. Journal*, May 15, 2001, A18.

Wymeersch, Eddy. 2001. Current Company Law Reform Initiatives in the OECD Countries: Challenges and Opportunities. Unpublished working paper.

6 Corporate Governance, Employees, and the Focus on Core Competencies in France and Germany

Michel Goyer

I investigate in this essay the responses of large French and German companies to the demands of Anglo-Saxon institutional investors for a clear strategic focus in their business strategy. The empirical evidence presented points to nationally specific patterns of change. Large French and German firms underwent a substantial institutional transformation in recent years in response to the demands of foreign investors, but they changed in different ways and without any strategic process of convergence. I compare the three leading theories of comparative corporate governance on the issue of refocusing: national institutionalist perspective, functional convergence, and the quality of law and the development of financial markets. I argue that the inclusion of the institutional arrangements of workplace organization constitute a critical variable to account for the divergent responses of large French and German companies, and substantially strengthen the theoretical insights of these three theories. The institutional arrangements of workplace organization in the two countries entail a path dependent transformation of national systems of corporate governance without relying on the notion of tight institutional complementarity. Moreover, the institutional arrangements of the workplace allow for the implementation of different mechanisms of functional convergence in France and Germany, with the consequence of reinforcing cross-national differences between these two systems.

The essay is organized as follows. In part I, I discuss the implications of the three leading theories of corporate governance for the prospects of a clear strategic focus by large French and German firms. Next, I present the empirical results associated with the responses of large companies in the two countries to the demands of Anglo-Saxon institutional investors. Third, I argue that the institutional arrangements of workplace organization constitute a critical variable to understand the different strategies followed by French and German companies. Fourth, I investigate the theoretical implications of the transformation of French and German corporate governance.

I. Theoretical Perspectives on the Dismantling of Conglomerates in France and Germany

Will the globalization of finance, investment, and trade lead to convergence across national systems of corporate governance? The arrival of Anglo-Saxon institutional investors on the European continent has led to a resurgence of interest in the issues of convergence and of the stability of national systems of corporate governance.[1] Two competing models of corporate governance have been thought to exist in separate spheres prior to the diversification policy of Anglo-American institutional investors (see Franks and Mayer 1997; LaPorta et al., 2000; Roe 2000 for reviews). The Anglo-Saxon model of corporate governance is characterized by a diffuse ownership structure, mutual and pension funds as key shareholders, high market transparency, active securities markets, and the importance of the market for corporate control. The continental European model of corporate governance has been associated with a concentrated ownership structure, banks and nonfinancial firms as major shareholders, low market transparency, underdeveloped securities markets, and the absence of hostile takeovers. The recent increases of foreign ownership and the occurrence of the first signs of the dissolution of ownership concentration of large French and German companies might render them vulnerable to the demands of their new owners. Anglo-Saxon institutional investors have pressed continental European companies in their portfolios to undertake substantial modifications of their corporate governance institutions to more closely resemble the arrangements and governing mechanisms found in their home country (Morin 1998: 34–48). Will the presence of new owners lead to a breakdown of cross-national differences, leading to convergence?

   The challenge posed by the rise of institutional investors as major shareholders of continental European companies is perhaps most visible on the question of the corporate strategy of the firm.[2] The process of refocusing on core businesses has become the new paradigm for economic success. Anglo-

Saxon institutional investors have expressed strong views against the maintenance of the conglomerate form due to its perceived overall inefficiency as an organizational form (Markides 1995). Conglomerates constitute an inefficient organizational form since they frequently use cross-subsidies from profitable divisions to shore up money losing ones (Porter 1987). Moreover, institutional investors have been adamant in seeing portfolio companies focus on a limited number of core competencies since most firms have succeeded in developing a world leadership position in only a small number of business activities (Prahalad and Hamel 1990). Finally, the sophistication of financial markets has severely diminished the importance of a key advantage of conglomerates, namely the diversification of risk across many activities. Institutional investors can readily diversify at much lower cost than conglomerates, since they do not have to pay a premium for acquiring shares (Bhide 1997: 112–17).

The demands of Anglo-Saxon funds are increasingly converging with the interests of French and German managers on the issue of corporate strategy. Foreign funds dislike the lack of transparency, cross subsidies between corporate divisions, and overall perceived inefficiency of conglomerates. The performance of conglomerates is particularly difficult for foreign investors to assess. As a result, conglomerates are penalized on financial markets. They suffer from a conglomerate discount, their stock market value being lower than the potential sum of their individual business segments (Berger and Ofek 1995; Comment and Jarrell 1995; Servaes 1996). The conglomerate discount of large German firms in the mid-1990s (approximately 20 percent) was roughly similar to that of diversified Fortune 500 companies in the 1980s (Lins and Servaes 1999). French and German managers possess strong incentives to demonstrate a strategic focus in order to avoid the discount. Undervalued companies constitute easier takeover targets (Davis et al. 1994). Moreover, managers also have an incentive to increase the stock market capitalization of their companies if they wish to conduct acquisitions via equity swaps. Lower market valuations would thus hurt them in the global M&A market (Coffee 1999: 649).

Despite the convergence of the preferences of managers and shareholders, however, the call for increased focus on core competencies constitutes a challenge for the position of employees in the firm. First, the dismantling of conglomerates entails the elimination of cross-subsidies among the divisions. Employees favor the mode of operation of conglomerates, whereby the central office can reallocate funds from fast growing units to poorer performing counterparts. Cross-subsidies among units allow growing segments to pick up slack from stagnant markets in resource utilization (Bhide 1997: 108). The increased focus on core competencies creates frictions with workers over the definition of the core business units and the uncertainties associated with divestiture of marginal units. Second, the dismantling of conglomerates entails the elimination of the internal labor market. In a conglomerate, employees can move from one unit to another in reaction to diverging performance (Doeringer and Piore 1985: 89–90). Third, conglomerates insulate firms from the pressures of capital markets—an outcome previously favored by both labor and management (Jensen 1993). The propensity to build corporate empires proved irresistible to managers—and fit very well with the preferences of employees. Fourth, the process of refocusing that took place in the United States in the 1980s provided employees with highly unpleasant lessons. The decade was characterized by a process of restructuring that resulted in portfolio reorganization through a concentration on core business activities and a rapid turnover of peripheral units (Davis et al. 1994: 548). The use of junk bonds and other newly created financial instruments exposed to the competitive forces of product and capital market pressures business units once protected by the conglomerate structure and the redistribution of funds through its central office. The restructuring process of the 1980s in the United States led to a significant transfer of wealth from employees to shareholders. The share of gross value added (GVA) occupied by labor declined substantially in the 1980s. In fact, a substantial proportion of the financial gains realized by shareholders was the result of the breach of implicit contracts between management and the workforces of both acquired and acquiring companies (Sheifler and Summers 1988). What are the prospects for the dismantling of conglomerates in France and Germany given the preferences of actors? I discuss the implications of the three theoretical perspectives of comparative corporate governance on the dismantling of conglomerates and the focus on core competencies: the institutionalist perspective, functional convergence, and the quality of law perspective on the development of financial markets.

A. Institutionalist Perspective

From the institutionalist perspective on comparative corporate governance, the dismantling of conglomerates in continental Europe is problematic.

Different institutions of corporate governance produce different consequences in terms of the mode of decisionmaking of firms, patterns of adjustment, and the distribution of value added among the various parties. In turn,
different institutional arrangements account for cross-national differences in
trajectories and their persistence over time despite the presence of common
challenges and pressures (Bebchuck and Roe 1999; Hall and Soskice 2001).
Institutions act as a filter to external sources of pressure. The concept of
institutional complementarity is central to the account of the lack of convergence across nations. Milgrom and Roberts (1990 and 1994) have best
developed the concept of complementarity, which refers to a relation
among a group of activities. The presence of institutional fit is determined
when an increase in any of the subset of activities results in an increase in
any or all of the remaining activities (Milgrom and Roberts 1990: 514). The
presence of institutional complementarity significantly contributes to the
resilience of domestic institutions since it provides for the internal cohesion
of the national system of corporate governance and constitutes a source of
economic efficiency. First, it increases the contribution of individual institutions to the overall effectiveness of the activities of the firm (Milgrom and
Roberts 1990 and 1994). The sustainability of a single institution is reinforced by its fit with the institutional structure of the other spheres of the
economy (Bebchuck and Roe 1999; Hall and Soskice 2001). In other words,
each institutional feature fits with the others and makes them more effective
than they would be on their own (Milgrom and Roberts 1994: 4). The
appropriate standard for evaluating the system is the aggregate institutional
configuration rather than the sum of the parts.

Second, institutional complementarity provides the fit with the conditions in an environmental niche that allow companies to achieve a position
of economic competitiveness in markets (Aoki 2001: 88). The comparative
advantage of a firm lies in achieving the proper match between its institutional organizational features and the requirements associated with specific
market niches (Sorge 1991). As a result, the piecemeal adoption of institutions is unlikely to work since it would break the existing complementarity
(Hall and Soskice 2001: 63–64; Milgrom and Roberts 1994: 11).

The feasibility of dismantling conglomerates in continental Europe is
limited according to the national institutionalist perspective. The process of
refocusing on core competencies might be difficult to implement. At the
very least, the American version of conglomerate dismantling needs to be
seriously amended. Two potential obstacles make it hard for European man-

agers to transform the conglomerate structure of companies. First, the political environment prevailing in continental Europe makes it difficult for managers to represent the interests of shareholders at the expense of employees. Distributional considerations force managers to forgo restructuring plans that would destabilize employment (Roe 2000: 539–53). The unbridled pursuit of shareholder interests might lead to political backlash (Roe 1998). Second, the institutions that facilitated the restructuring process in the United States—shareholder value norms, transparent accounting, the market for corporate control, and proxy fights—are seriously underdeveloped in continental Europe (Roe 2000: 553). The key institutional absence is the flexible labor market. The degree of investor protection is negatively correlated with employment protection across advanced industrialized nations (Pagano and Volpin 2000: 26–27). On every indicator of employment protection—notice and pay for no-fault layoffs, the definition of unfair dismissal, and procedural delays—continental European nations have greater obstacles to dismissals than their Anglo-Saxon counterparts.

B. Functional Convergence

Theorists of functional convergence share several assumptions with their institutionalist counterparts and recognize that the presence of institutional complementarity reduces the effectiveness of piecemeal change (Gilson 2001: 335–36). Nonetheless, these scholars argue that convergence across national systems of corporate governance is possible—and indeed, occurring—even in the absence of legislative reforms or institutional replication (Coffee 1999; Gilson 2001). The key insight behind this argument is that initial conditions and path dependency are not the only mechanisms influencing the behavior of companies. Firm strategy is also subjected to a powerful selection mechanism, namely competition (Gilson 1996: 332). If existing institutions do not allow domestic firms to compete with other systems of corporate governance, then functional convergence will take place.

Functional convergence can occur through two processes. First, institutions can change function but preserve their form (Gilson 1996; 2001). The implication of this process of functional convergence is that the link between institutional form and firm behavior might be less tight than originally conceived. Second, firms in different countries can converge through a process of migration and substitution (Coffee 1999: 679–82). For example, several foreign firms from systems of corporate governance that do not provide adequate protection for minority shareholders have listed on U.S. financial markets. This action constitutes a bonding mechanism as these foreign firms commit to the more demanding mandatory disclosure requirements prevailing in the United States. In particular, companies in systems of corporate governance that do not provide adequate legal protection for minority shareholders are more likely to issue American Depository Receipts on financial markets in the United States (Reese and Weisbach 2001). The implication of this process is that national institutions persist, but their importance diminishes (Coffee 1999: 652).[3]

The functional convergence perspective on comparative corporate governance has different implications for the issue of refocusing than the national institutionalist perspective. The lower stock market capitalization of continental European firms provides them with strong incentives to focus on a limited number of business activities. Given the spread of conglomerates in France and Germany (see Whittington and Mayer 2000), the conglomerate discount constitutes a quasi-universal problem for firms in these two countries. The inefficiency of the conglomerate form might act as a selection mechanism on the workings of national systems of corporate governance. Unfocused diversified firms have great difficulties in making acquisitions via equity swaps because of their reduced market capitalization and the reluctance of institutional investors to accept their shares (Coffee 1999: 641). This problem has become more acute in recent years since external growth through acquisitions has become an essential mechanism in the race for critical mass on world markets.[4] The implication of this perspective is that formal institutional stability can prevail through a change in functions performed by the various institutions of the corporate governance system (Gilson 1996; 2001).

C. Law, Private Benefits, and the Development of Financial Markets

From the legal perspective on the development of financial markets, the problem of undercapitalization of continental European companies is intimately linked to the agency problem, not primarily driven by the conglomerate discount. The fundamental issue in corporate governance concerns the protection of minority shareholders (LaPorta et al. 2000). The separation of ownership from control or the presence of a controlling owner requires the protection of minority shareholders if equity capital is to be provided. The research agenda of financial economists has increasingly focused on the existence of private benefits as the source of the underdevelopment of financial markets in continental Europe and as the manifestation of the violation of the rights of minority shareholders (see Zingales 1994; 1998). The existence of private benefits manifests itself by the willingness of a party to pay a premium in order to become a controlling shareholder of a company. The insight is that an investor pays a premium to gain control of a company since the private benefits from running it are not shared with other owners: increases in the equity stake through dilutive share issues, diversion of resources from the firm, synergy gains, and the ability to fix transfer prices between companies the controlling shareholder owns (Johnson et al. 2000: 22; Zingales 1998: 44–45).

How are private benefits relevant to this essay, which seeks to measure the extent to which large French and German companies meet the demands of Anglo-Saxon institutional investors for a clear strategic focus? The central theoretical insight of this literature lies in the potential increase in the stock market capitalization of the firm if the controlling shareholder credibly signals its willingness to stop expropriating from minority shareholders. Firms and national systems of corporate governance in which private benefits are substantial suffer from a trading discount by outside investors since the incentives of controlling shareholders lie in maximizing the value of their private benefits at the expense of the total market capitalization of the firm (Zingales 1998: 47). The implication is that legal rules can shape economic outcomes in a critical manner. The imposition of stringent disclosure requirements and greater financial transparency, the elimination of unequal voting rights, and strong stock market regulation can substitute for the dismantling of conglomerates as a strategy to increase the market capitalization of firms (Glaeser et al. 2001; Johnson et al. 2000). First, the imposition of stringent disclosure requirements acts as a form of monitoring on management since it requires the provision of detailed information on a regular basis (Fox 1998). The adoption of quarterly reports, for example, increases competitive pressures to adjust since it entails the publication of financial results by each individual corporate unit of the firm. Second, the effectiveness of regulators is contingent upon the presence of stringent disclosure requirements (Glaeser et al. 2001). The regulation of financial intermediaries—audit firms, banks, brokers, and others—as an alternative strategy to strict contract enforcement is facilitated by stringent disclosure requirements since they reduce monitoring costs. Third, greater financial transparency and the elimination of deviations from the one-share-one-vote principle decrease the ability of large shareholders to extract private benefits from the firm (Johnson et al. 2000). Such shareholders would find it more difficult to transfer resources from the company for their own private benefit or that of other companies they own and, thus, command a greater control premium for their shares (Zingales 1994). Fourth, strong stock market regulation acts as an obstacle for large owners seeking to increase their equity stake through the dilution of minority holdings (Johnson et al. 2000).

II. The Development of a Strategic Focus in France and Germany: An Empirical Evaluation

The reversal of the diversification strategy of large French and German companies is a recent phenomenon. The use of the conglomerate form, the internal organization of the firm based on the multidivisional structure, and the diversification in many related and unrelated business activities characterized large companies in France and Germany at least until 1994 (Whittington and Mayer 2000). This organizational structure was broadly similar to its counterparts in the U.K. and the U.S. (Dyas and Thanheiser 1976; Whittington and Mayer 2000).[5] From the point of view of labor, moreover, the conglomerate form allowed companies to stabilize employment, use up existing capital rather than downsize, and insulate management from the pressures of capital markets (Jensen 1993).[6] The diversification strategy and the multidivisional structure characterized these four advanced industrialized nations despite substantial diversity among their national systems of corporate governance.

The aim of this section is to track the evolution of the strategy of large French and German companies in the last 15 years. The following methodology is used. The sample consists of 28 currently listed non-financial French companies and 25 currently listed non-financial German firms (see tables 6.1 and 6.2). The sample firms are selected on the basis of the following two criteria: current level of foreign ownership higher than 15 percent and currently part of the largest 75 companies by stock market capitalization in their respective markets. The objective (and bias) of this sample selection is that sample firms are the most vulnerable to the demands of Anglo-Saxon institutional investors. The selection of these firms constitutes a critical test. If these

TABLE 6.1 Corporate Strategy of French Firms (1)

Company	1986	1990	1994	1998	2000
Accor	DIV	DIV	DIV	DIV	DIV
Air Liquide	DIV	DIV	DIV	DOM	DOM
Alcatel	DIV	DIV	DIV	DIV	DIV
Aventis (2)					SIN
Bic	DIV	DIV	DIV	DIV	DIV
Bouygues	DIV	DIV	DIV	DIV	DIV
Bull	SIN	SIN	SIN	SIN	SIN
Carrefour	DIV	DIV	DIV	DIV	DIV
Danone	DIV	DIV	DIV	DOM	DOM
Elf (3)	DIV	DIV	DIV	DIV	
Lafarge	DIV	DIV	DIV	DIV	DIV
Lagardere	DIV	DIV	DIV	DIV	DIV
LVHM	DIV	DIV	DIV	DIV	DIV
Lyonnaise des Eaux (4)	DIV	DIV	DIV		
Michelin	SIN	SIN	SIN	SIN	SIN
Moulinex	SIN	SIN	SIN	DOM	DOM
L'Oreal	DIV	DIV	DIV	DOM	SIN
Pechiney	DIV	DIV	DIV	DOM	DOM
Peugeot	DIV	DIV	SIN	SIN	SIN
PPR	DIV	DIV	DIV	DIV	DIV
Renault	SIN	SIN	SIN	SIN	SIN
Rhone-Poulenc (2)	DIV	DIV	DIV	DOM	
St-Gobain	DIV	DIV	DIV	DIV	DIV
Sanofi (5)		DOM	DOM	SIN	
Sanofi-Synthalabo					SIN
Schneider	DIV	DIV	DIV	DIV	DOM
Sodexho	DIV	DIV	DIV	DIV	DIV
Suez (4)	DIV	DIV	DIV		
Suez-Lyonnaise				DOM	DOM
Synthalabo (5)		DOM	DOM	SIN	
Thales-Thomson	DIV	DIV	DIV	DOM	DOM
Total (3)	DOM	DOM	DOM	DOM	
TotalElfFina					DOM
Valeo	DIV	DIV	DIV	DIV	DIV
Vivendi	DIV	DIV	DIV	DIV	DIV

Source: International Herald Tribune, French Company Handbook, various years; Whittington and Mayer (2000), The European Corporation, pp. 226–32; and annual report of companies, various years.

Abbreviations:

SIN (Single Business)

DOM (Dominant Business)

DIV (Diversified)

(1) Data on turnover are recorded for the following five years unless otherwise indicated: 1986, 1990, 1994, 1998, and 2000.

(2) Data are recorded for Rhone-Poulenc in 1986, 1990, 1994, and 1998. For 2000, data are recorded for Aventis.

(3) Data are recorded for Elf-Aquitaine and Total as separate companies for 1986, 1990, 1994, and 1998. Data for 2000 are recorded for TotalElfFina.

(4) Data are recorded for Lyonnaise des Eaux and Suez as separate companies for 1986, 1990, and 1994. Data for 1998 and 2000 are recorded for Suez-Lyonnaise des Eaux.

(5) Data are recorded for Sanofi and Synthalabo as separate companies for 1990, 1994, and 1998. Data for 2000 are recorded for Sanofi-Synthalabo.

TABLE 6.2 Corporate Strategy of German Firms (1)

Company	1986	1990	1994	1998	2000
Aventis (2)					SIN
Agiv	DIV	DIV	DIV	DIV	DIV
Babcock	DIV	DIV	DIV	DIV	DIV
BASF	DIV	DIV	DIV	DIV	DIV
Bayer	DIV	DIV	DIV	DIV	DIV
Beiersdorf	DIV	DIV	DIV	DIV	DIV
BMW	SIN	SIN	SIN	SIN	SIN
Continental	DIV	DIV	DIV	DIV	DIV
Daimler	SIN	DIV	DIV	SIN	SIN
Degussa	DIV	DIV	DIV	DIV	DIV
E-ON (3)					DIV
Henkel	DIV	DIV	DIV	DIV	DIV
Hoechst (2)	DIV	DIV	DIV	DIV	
Linde	DIV	DIV	DIV	DIV	DIV
Lufthansa	SIN	DOM	DOM	DOM	DOM
MAN	DIV	DIV	DIV	DIV	DIV
Merck	DIV	DIV	DIV	DOM	DOM
Metro			DIV	DIV	DIV
Preussag	DIV	DIV	DIV	DIV	DIV
Porsche	SIN	SIN	SIN	SIN	SIN
RWE	DIV	DIV	DIV	DIV	DIV
SAP	SIN	DOM	DOM	DOM	DOM
Schering	DIV	DIV	DOM	SIN	SIN
Siemens	DIV	DIV	DIV	DIV	DIV
Veba (3)	DIV	DIV	DIV	DIV	
Viag (3)	DIV	DIV	DIV	DIV	
Volkswagen	DIV	DOM	SIN	SIN	SIN

Source: Frankfurter Wertpapierborse, Borsenmitglieder, various years; Deutsche Informations Borse, DIB Aktienfuhrer Deutschland, various years; Frankfurter Allgemeine Zeitung Information Services, Germany's Top 300: a Handbook of Germany's Largest, various years; Monopolkommission, Hauptgutachen, various years; Whittington and Mayer (2000), The European Corporation, pp. 232–7; and annual report of companies, various years.
Abbreviations:
SIN (Single Business)
DOM (Dominant Business)
DIV (Diversified)
(1) Data on turnover are recorded for the following five years unless otherwise indicated: 1986, 1990, 1994, 1998, and 2000.
(2) Data are recorded for Hoechst as a separate company for 1986, 1990, 1994, and 1998. Data for 2000 are recorded for Aventis.
(3) Data are recorded for Veba and Viag as separate companies for 1986, 1990, 1994, and 1998. Data for 2000 are recorded for E.ON.

firms do not meet the preferences of Anglo-Saxon shareholders in regard to core competencies, then the rumors of the death of conglomerates in continental Europe would appear premature. The methodology used in this study is consistent with the one used by the Harvard program on the M-firm and its successors on the measurement of diversification (see Dyas and Thanheiser 1976; Whittington and Mayer 2000). The definition of diversification in these studies is based on turnover rates for the largest business.[7]

A single business strategy is defined by a minimum of 95 percent of turnover for the largest business activity. A dominant business strategy is characterized by a turnover rate between 70 and 95 percent for the largest business activity. Turnover rates below 70 percent for the largest business activity are associated with a strategy of diversification. I use the same classification scheme with five new years of data: 1986, 1990, 1994, 1998, and 2000.

The structural organization of large French and German companies underwent an important transition between 1994 and 2000. The results on the evolution of the diversification strategy of large French and German companies are presented in tables 6.1 to 6.4. The process by which large French and German companies stopped their diversification strategy differs on several key dimensions. First, the speed and extent of adjustment of the two countries are radically different. French companies have reduced their degree of diversification to a greater extent than their German counterparts. Radical restructuring characterizes the refocusing process in France while the corresponding trajectory in Germany is more incremental and limited. However, data on restructuring in France reveal substantial internal variation. The bulk of restructuring has been limited to private firms with a dispersed ownership structure. Family-owned companies have resisted demands for the dismantling of their conglomerate structure.[8]

Second, the trend away from diversification was accompanied by a lack of convergence in terms of financial transparency. The German system of corporate governance has been characterized in recent years by greater financial transparency through the adoption of international accounting standards (IAS or US-GAAP). In 1996, only nine of the country's largest 100 firms were using an international accounting standard. The same figure for 2000 is 64. The 24 firms in the 2000 sample use an international accounting standard. The French system of corporate governance, in contrast, has remained largely opaque. The number of companies using an international accounting standard among the country's largest 100 has risen from 35 in 1997 to 38 in 2000.

TABLE 6.3 Evolution of Corporate Strategy, France

1986 (27 Firms)	1990 (31 Firms)	1994 (31 Firms)	1998 (30 Firms)	2000 (28 Firms)
22 DIV (81.5%)	23 DIV (74.2%)	23 DIV (74.2%)	16 DIV (53.3%)	13 DIV (46.4%)
1 DOM (3.7%)	4 DOM (12.9%)	3 DOM (9.7%)	9 DOM (30.0%)	8 DOM (28.6%)
4 SIN (14.8%)	4 SIN (12.9%)	5 SIN (16.1%)	5 SIN (16.7%)	7 SIN (25.0%)

TABLE 6.4 Evolution of Corporate Strategy, Germany

1986 (25 Firms)	1990 (26 Firms)	1994 (26 Firms)	1998 (26 Firms)	2000 (25 Firms)
20 DIV (80.0%)	21 DIV (80.7%)	20 DIV (76.8%)	18 DIV (69.2%)	16 DIV (64.0%)
0 DOM	3 DOM (11.6%)	3 DOM (11.6%)	3 DOM (11.6%)	3 DOM (12.0%)
5 SIN (20.0%)	2 SIN (7.7%)	3 SIN (11.6%)	5 SIN (19.2%)	6 SIN (24.0%)

The figures for the CAC 40 index are even more modest. The adoption of an international accounting standard by companies currently part of the index rose from eight in 1996 to fourteen in 2000. Of the 28 French firms in the 2000 sample a mere ten use an international accounting standard. Finally, German companies have eliminated most infringements of the rights of minority shareholders (see table 6.5). Thus, speed of adjustment and transparency appear complementary. French firms have been more aggressive in the process of refocusing without being more transparent. German companies have become more transparent but have been relatively more modest in the process of dismantling conglomerates.

Third, the consequences of the process of refocusing on employment protection differ between the two countries. The slowly changing corporate strategy of German companies was a process negotiated with employees. The selling of non-core units did not represent the unilateral assertion of managerial authority in the conduct of corporate strategy. Works councils have negotiated comprehensive restructuring packages designed to allow the breakup of the firm without relying on an adjustment process based on dismissals and external labor flexibility. In other words, the pattern of refocusing that took place in the 1980s in the United States has not taken place in Germany. Since 1996, a little more than half of the 100 largest German companies have negotiated a "location agreement" or "employment pact" with their works councils (Streeck 2001: 26). These negotiated agreements entail the trading of wages for job security for two to four years—even if units of the firm are sold off. Of the 24 German companies included in the 2000

TABLE 6.5 Voting Rights (1996 & 1999)

| | France | Germany | Japan | UK | United |
| *Exception to one-share,* | *Top 120* | *Top 120* | *Top 250* | *Top 250* | *States* |
one-vote	*96–99*	*96–99*	*96–99*	*96–99*	*96–99*
% of firms with voting rights or ownership ceilings	20–22	3–2	0–0	1–1	0–0
% of firms with unequal voting rights	32–68	3–3	0–0	7–0	12–13

Source: Davis Global Advisors (2001: 52)

sample 20 signed agreements on the protection of existing employment. Moreover, slightly fewer than 20 firms have also included specific investment plans for the next two to four years in exchange for more flexible work shifts and a reduction of company premiums and wages (Kotthoff 1998; Streeck 2001: 27). Thus, the move toward core competencies took place in a context where labor was able to achieve employment guarantees and some influence over investment policy.

By contrast, the change in the corporate strategy of large French firms has entailed different consequences for employees. The move toward core competencies has been associated with a pattern of adjustment based on the overall exclusion of labor from the decisionmaking process. Formal agreements on the preservation of jobs have been rather limited. From 1994 to 1998, there were thirty-one agreements dealing with the preservation of jobs for firms with more than 500 employees (Dufour 2001: 100). Of the 28 French companies included in the 2000 sample, only nine signed deals on the preservation of existing employment. Moreover, there are two types of agreement reached on the preservation of employment: obligation of results and obligation of means. For firms with more than 500 employees, 22 signed agreements involving an obligation of results. The remaining nine only entailed an obligation of means (ibid.: 105).

Despite the divergent responses of large French and German firms to the demands of institutional investors for a clear strategic focus, they share one common element: the relative balance of acquisitions and divestitures in the move away from diversification between firms of the two countries is broadly similar. A focus on core business can be achieved by either M&A in a single line of activity or by divestitures of peripheral units. In a similar vein, diversification strategy can be the result of either M&A in unrelated business activities or by lack of divestitures of non-core units. French and German companies adopted a similar strategy between 1994 and 2000—the period where the move toward concentration on core business activities was more prevalent in both countries. The value of French acquisitions in this period in Europe and in the United States was $326.5 billion while divestitures amounted to $167.3 billion—for a surplus of $159.2 billion. The similar figures for Germany were $490.9 billion (acquisitions), $357.2 billion (divestitures), and $133.7 billion (surplus) (Mergers and Acquisitions, various issues). In both countries, acquisitions have been more important than divestitures in defining corporate strategy.

III. The Organization of Work, Corporate Governance, and Refocusing on Core Competencies

The empirical evidence on refocusing presented in the previous section points to nationally specific patterns of change that do not fully meet the predictions of any of the three leading perspectives on comparative corporate governance. Large French and German companies underwent a substantial institutional transformation in recent years—but they changed in different ways and without any strategic process of convergence. I do not want to reject the validity of the three perspectives on comparative corporate governance. Instead, I seek to build on them by highlighting the conditions under which they provide valuable theoretical insight to our understanding of the evolution of national systems of corporate governance. I argue that the institutional arrangements of the workplace constitute the critical variable that accounts for the differences in the pattern of change in the two countries. The institutional arrangements of workplace organization entail constraining and enabling forces on the ability of management to elaborate and implement the business strategy of the firm. It shapes a crucial issue of business strategy, namely whether the CEO and top managers can proceed to implement reorganization schemes in a unilateral manner or with the involvement of employees. In turn, the constraints placed on management contribute to the elaboration of their responses to the demands of Anglo-Saxon institutional investors. The mix of constraints and opportunities placed on managerial autonomy shapes the strategy adopted to deal with the problem of low stock market capitalization—dismantling of conglomerates or the introduction of greater financial transparency combined with elimination of deviations from the one-share-one-vote principle.

The organization of the workplace differs substantially between France and Germany (see Eyraud and Rozenblatt 1994; Géhin and Méhaut 1993; Maurice et al. 1986 for reviews). First, the countries are at opposite ends of the spectrum in the matching of jobs and worker competencies. The German economy is predicated on the presence of a majority of employees with certifiable skills. The qualification of workers determines the definition of jobs. The access to a majority of jobs in large firms is based upon the holding of a recognized diploma or qualification—most often acquired as part of a vocational training program. Training is very often a prerequisite for employment and promotion (Maurice et al. 1986: 65–73). By contrast, managers in France use their own criteria to define jobs to which employees adapt either in training programs (blue collar) or through the attainment of university diplomas (white collar). The relationship between training and promotion is reversed in France: Management selects workers to be promoted and then provides them with the appropriate training (ibid.: 77). The various attempts by state officials to impose the recognition of state vocational training as a prerequisite for holding jobs have encountered strong opposition from French employers (Culpepper 1998; Marsden 1999: 98).

These cross-national differences have been long standing. In 1970, only 27.6 percent of active males in Germany had no basic vocational training as compared to 79.7 percent in France. For the category of manual employees, 57.0 percent of German employees had completed a vocational training program as compared to only 26.0 percent in France (Maurice et al. 1984: 352–54). By 1995, the average number of trainees for large German firms (over 500 employees) was six per 100 workers with a retention rate of 85 percent. The corresponding figure for French companies was 2.2 per 100 workers in 1996 with a retention rate of 35 percent (Culpepper 1998: 286–301).

In addition, the prominent German training system is also relatively autonomous from managerial interference. The centrality of training in the German economy is legally based and protected from outside intervention (Muller-Jentsch 1995: 70–71). A high number of jobs require certifiable skills that are acquired in vocational training programs. The relevant chamber (industry or commerce) must certify the training programs of firms, and any change in the content of training certification—the modification of an existing certification or the introduction of a new one—requires the approval of a body of experts in which labor occupies half of the seats. The content of training programs in Germany is the outcome of a negotiated process between managers and employees. In other words, German companies are constrained on three fronts: skills are a prerequisite for jobs, management must provide the relevant training to employees, and the content of these programs must be certified by an outside body where labor possesses a veto.[9] Business associations and labor unions in Germany limit the ability of firms to pursue a unilateral strategy in this area. By contrast, boards of experts on training in France play a simple consultative role (Culpepper 1998: 278). No legal requirement to assign specific jobs to workers with certifiable skills is imposed on French firms. The content of training programs and the place of skilled workers in the production process in France represent areas of managerial prerogative. Thus, legal arrangements sustain the cross-national differences of institutional arrangements related to the match between job demands and employee competencies.

The second major difference in the institutional arrangements of the workplace between France and Germany concerns the autonomy of employees in the operation of the shop floor. The presence of extensive rules that regulate the nature of the tasks to be accomplished—rather than functions to be performed—characterizes the organization of the workplace in France (Marsden 1999: 103–4; Maurice et al. 1986: 60–65). The monitoring of employees and the implementation of the business strategy are accomplished through numerous sets of carefully defined rules designed to specify the exact terms of exchange among parties and to predict all types of behavior on the shop floor. The organization of work is divided into fragmentary tasks whose content is predetermined. Moreover, the skills of employees tend to be narrow and highly connected to tasks. The organization of the workplace in France results in a high supervisor-to-worker ratio and a strict division of authority between employers and the workforce (Maurice et al. 1986: 69–80). As a result, managers faced few constraints from the organization of work in the conduct of the business strategy of the firm.

By contrast, the monitoring of employees in Germany takes place through the application of rules to broad functions, rather than by trying to predict all contingencies on the shop floor. The role of vocational training is also central in this process. Employees are grouped according to the types of qualifications they possess, and tasks are organized according to their skill requirements (Marsden 1999: 38). As a result, the institutional arrangements of the workplace in Germany are characterized by blurred organizational boundaries, less segmentation, the involvement of employees in many tasks, greater autonomy of workers organized in teams, and reliance on noncontractual safeguards against the hazards of opportunism by workers (Kester 1992; Sorge 1991: 166). German workers are adaptable since the organization of the workplace favors the acquisition of broad-based skills (Maurice et al. 1986: 69–73; Streeck 1991). Thus, the organization of work in Germany places serious constraints on management in regard to the conduct of the business strategy of the firm.

The institutional arrangements of the workplace also constitute a source of opportunities for management, with substantially different incentives for French and German managers. The extent of segmentation of production activities shapes the ability of actors to participate in the conduct of business strategy. The organization of the firm in France is characterized by the sharp segmentation of activities and responsibilities between blue and white collar employees, a rigid system of rules, and the emphasis on narrow and specialized skills (Géhin and Méhaut 1993; Maurice et al. 1986; Sorge 1991). Employees have a limited view of the totality of the operations of the firm. The process of problem solving inside large French firms is management-led with the involvement of a few (internal or external) highly qualified technical specialists (Marsden 1999: 132). The French organizational system and its corresponding adjustment process entail the use of a flexible labor market for highly skilled specialists. Coordination by top management is the key characteristic of the adjustment process in France (Hancké 2001).

By contrast, the broad skills of German employees and blurred organizational boundaries provide them with a more complete view of the operations of the firm (Sorge 1991). There is greater scope for the involvement of skilled blue-collar workers in problem-solving activities in Germany (Maurice at al. 1986). German (and Japanese) firms exhibit a strong propensity to rely on task rotation, the use of which provides employees with a wide range of competencies that enable them to adjust to the many uncertainties of market fluctuations (Kester 1992; Streeck 1991: 15). The skills of employees shape their ability to solve problems that, in turn, present management with constraints on their ability to proceed in a unilateral manner.

IV. Theoretical Implications

The changing external environment has resulted in the imposition of a series of capital and product market pressures for large French and German companies. Top managers must devise solutions to reconcile the competencies of the firm with both the competitive requirements of markets and the demands of Anglo-Saxon institutional investors. Increasing the stock market capitalization of the firm has become a key objective for firms in this new environment. The different patterns by which the skills of employees are integrated into the firm constitute a critical variable to account for the conduct of business strategy. The argument is that the career strategies of workers are affected by the system of job classification that, in turn, shapes the delimitation of managerial authority. The institutional arrangements of the workplace provide serious constraints for German managers. The position and importance of training in Germany are both firmly protected by law. By recognizing the system of professional credentials, managers possess little autonomy in controlling the career strategies of workers. The pattern of such career strategies restrains the range of available business strategies. Management's room to maneuver by redeploying employees is limited. The development of new product lines entailing the hiring of employees with the requisite expertise is a negotiated process. Works councils possess a full veto over new hirings, thereby seriously curtailing the rapid dismantling of conglomerates. By contrast, the absence of professional training as criteria for holding jobs in France implies that other factors will matter. Managers possess considerable autonomy in determining the content of the system of job classification—and the organization of the production process—since formal credentials of training and professional qualifications are rarely used (Maurice et al. 1986: 66).

The multiplicity of strategic choices for managers facing capital and product market pressures and the occurrence of piecemeal institutional change constitute key theoretical insights of this essay. They cast serious doubts on the resilience of institutional complementarity since its presence has not been sufficient to prevent adjustment and the occurrence of institutional transformation. The transformation of the national systems of corporate governance of France and Germany has exhibited an element of institutional plasticity. The institutional arrangements of corporate governance of these two countries do not function solely as a mechanism through which external sources of pressure are mediated. The institutions themselves are undergoing a profound transformation. The empirical data presented here have shown that the transformation of corporate strategy in these two countries has been limited to a number of non-common areas. In other words, institutional change in the two countries has not been system-wide, but piecemeal. The link between the various institutional features of national corporate governance systems appears to be weaker than is commonly assumed. A subset of institutional features can change without affecting the rest of the system.

The role of institutions, however, is particularly useful in explaining the direction of change. Despite the presence of a range of potential strategies to a given problem, there are a limited number of responses available to firms and national systems of corporate governance. Some strategies are extremely difficult, if not possible, to pursue in a given institutional context. Moreover, the range of available responses is itself shaped by existing institutional arrangements of the workplace. In other words, national institutions mediate the impact of external stimuli but the presence of institutional complementarity does not inhibit adjustment. The process of change is institutionally embedded. In France and Germany, the mixture of constraining and enabling institutional features shaped the choice of strategy by top management. The transformations of the French and German systems of corporate governance are path dependent—but they do not rely on institutional complementarity as a source of divergence. The institutional arrangements of the workplace induced French and German managers to react in different ways to the demands of institutional investors for a clear strategic focus. Their divergent responses, however, entailed substantial but piecemeal institutional change.

The process of refocusing in France and Germany also provides some support for the functional convergence perspective. Large French and German companies have responded, albeit in different ways, to broadly similar capital and product market pressures. They have sought to deal with the problem of low stock market capitalization in their own nationally specific way. The forces of competition were influential in the process of adjustment despite the wide institutional diversity between the two countries.

The functional convergence perspective, however, neglects the importance of the processes of change. The achievement of functional convergence in one area through different institutional means does not provide a basis for further functional convergence. The differences in the process of refocusing in France and Germany are driven by differences in the institutional arrangements of the workplace. The outcome is that the achievement of functional convergence in one area increases the importance of institutions in other areas (e.g., the innovation system and labor relations). The different strategies adopted by French and German companies to tackle their lower level of stock market capitalization actually reinforced other cross-national differences. The key difference between the process of refocusing in the two countries was that it was negotiated in Germany, but unilaterally determined by management in France. The ability of German companies to issue credible commitments to their employees has not been affected by the process of refocusing. Job protection agreements were a major component of restructuring in Germany. By contrast, the French experience bears closer resemblance to that of the United States in the 1980s, whereby gains from restructuring came partly at the expense of employees, and the non-negotiated nature of change hindered the ability of firms to make credible commitments to employees (Shleifer and Summers 1988). The processes of refocusing in France and Germany left unchanged the institutional arrangements of the workplace that, in turn, shaped the business strategy of large firms. In other words, the occurrence of partial functional convergence in the two countries did not change their path dependent evolution. The implication is that functional convergence might be more difficult to achieve than institutional convergence.

The quality of law perspective on the development of financial markets provides substantial support for the German case and the family-owned sector in France. First, the adoption of greater financial transparency and respect for the rights of minority shareholders in Germany appear to have been adopted to deal with the problem of low stock market capitalization. Of the twenty-nine DAX 30 companies that have adopted an international accounting standard, only eight are listed in one form or another in the United States. By contrast, all CAC 40 firms with an international accounting standard are listed on American financial markets. The strategy of German companies constitutes a bonding mechanism, as these foreign firms commit themselves to the more demanding mandatory disclosure requirements prevailing in the United States without even raising funds from American financial markets. Second, the reluctance of French family-owned firms to adopt financial transparency and to remove deviations from the one-share-one-vote principle appear to be driven by the need to maintain private benefits. The size of private benefits in France is substantially higher than in Germany and is sustained by dual-class stocks with unequal voting rights (Nenova 2000: 30–35). Private benefits arise from the ability of a controlling shareholder to divert resources from the firm in order to achieve synergy gains and to fix transfer prices between owned companies (Johnson et al. 2000: 22; Zingales 1998: 44–45). The need to be present in many business activities in order to reap private benefits provides unambiguous incentives for family-owned firms in France to resist calls for the dismantling of the conglomerate form. Moreover, greater financial transparency would make it harder to pursue the strategies by which private benefits are extracted (Zingales 1998: 47).

Despite the theoretical insights associated with the legal perspective, a puzzle remains. What accounts for the reluctance of non-family-owned firms in France to adopt greater financial transparency and remove unequal voting rights? This question is appropriate given the lack of constraints on French managers for the elaboration and implementation of business strategy (Goyer 2001). The institutional arrangements of workplace organization in France allow for the concentration of power at the top of the firm. Large French companies chose to tackle the problem of the conglomerate discount rather than bonding themselves to the more demanding mandatory disclosure requirements of IAS and US-GAAP accounting standards.

I argue that the willingness of European companies to adopt greater financial transparency is significantly shaped by the participation of employees in the decisionmaking process. Opaque accounting standards have traditionally been part of the framework of institutional complementarity of corporate governance systems in continental Europe. Managers prefer that employees do not know how well the firm is doing since they will demand higher salaries (Roe 2000: 568). More transparent financial reporting would allow shareholders to better monitor management, but it might also lead to an increase in the influence of labor. On the other hand, greater financial transparency puts greater pressure on firms to adjust. In particular, quarterly reporting entails the release of financial information according to the various business units of the firm. Cross subsidies become more transparent and the internal labor market is harder to sustain. Financial transparency is characterized by a dual nature — the release of more information to employees combined with greater pressures for adjustment. The willingness of European companies to adopt greater financial transparency is shaped by the extent to which employees internalize the heightened requirements to compete. The assumption of responsibility for the economic performance of the firm by employees provides key incentives for management to adopt greater financial transparency.

The heightened competitive requirements associated with financial transparency are internalized by employees in Germany since they assume responsibility for the economic performance of the firm. The organization of the shop floor in Germany ensures the participation of workers at an early stage in the decisionmaking process (Maurice et al. 1986; Pistor 1999). The works councils are key actors in the implementation of restructuring measures (Muller-Jentsch 1995; Streeck 1991). By contrast, the exclusion of French employees from the decisionmaking process, combined with their ideological posture, reduces the incentives for management to adopt greater financial transparency.

The introduction of financial transparency in France would not likely lead to results similar to those obtained in Germany. The institutional organization of the workplace in France does not provide employees with the incentives to assume responsibility for the economic performance of the firm. The release of additional financial information is likely to increase the demands of workers for a greater percentage of the gross value added of the company without their involvement in painful restructuring processes. The evolution of the French system of corporate governance illustrates the opportunities and perils associated with a management-led strategy (Hall and Soskice 2001: 48).[10]

Conclusion

The theoretical contributions of this essay on the evolution of French and German corporate governance entail important implications for regulators. The effectiveness of regulatory reform of national systems of corporate governance should be viewed with skepticism on empirical and normative grounds. The advent of convergence across corporate governance systems is unlikely to occur unless it directly confronts the source of path dependence. The institutional arrangements of workplace organization in France and Germany led to the implementation of different mechanisms of functional convergence that, in turn, reinforced long-standing sources of divergence. In other words, some types of regulation will be more effective than others in eliminating cross-national differences. For example, European or French regulation on deviations from the one-share-one-vote principle would substantially hinder the extraction of private benefits of large, family-owned companies in France.

Moreover, regulatory reforms might be ineffective and unwise given the lack of evidence on the overall performance of different corporate governance systems. The institutional arrangements of workplace organization support different innovative capabilities for domestic firms. The institutional framework of France provides top management with the ability to respond quickly to changes in the competitive environment. Workplace organization in Germany enhances the ability of management to issue credible commitments to their employees. The processes of adjustment in France and Germany might entail different distributional consequences for domestic actors, but it is very difficult to argue for a specific process of reform in these countries that would result in economically superior outcomes. Rather, the ability of French and German companies to devise nationally specific mechanisms of functional convergence in response to the demands of foreign investors implies the superiority of firm-specific reform over national and supranational regulation.

Endnotes

I wish to thank Suzanne Berger, Richard Deeg, Miguel Glatzer, Peter Hall, Robert Hancké, Martin Hoepner, Simon Johnson, Curtis Milhaupt, Wolfgang Streeck, Richard Whittington, and the participants at the workshop on corporate governance and globalization held at Columbia Law School (October 2001) for comments on previous versions of the paper. The usual disclaimers apply.

1. The rise of foreign ownership in Europe's two largest economies—France and Germany—is impressive. In France, foreign investors owned 41.29% of the equity capital of CAC 40 firms in May 2001 (Adrien Tricornot, Qui sont les Propriétaires des Entreprises Européennes?, 22). In Germany, the similar figure for DAX 30 companies in 1999 was 28.5% (La Présence du Capital Étranger dans les Entreprises Françaises, 34).
2. I use the conventional definition of business and corporate strategy. Business strategy deals with the ways in which the firm competes within a particular industry or market. Companies can deal with market fluctuations, investment opportunities, and economic uncertainties in many ways. For example, the business strategy of the company can be based on quality differentiation or price competitiveness as a means to develop a position of competitive advantage. The firm's corporate strategy, in contrast, deals with the ways it manages its several business units together—the overall plan for a diversified company. The focus of corporate strategy is to create competitive advantage in each of the businesses it operates.
3. It is assumed that institutional replication will be the last stage of development across national systems of corporate governance. Formal convergence might be blocked by institutional, legal, and political barriers that prevent national systems of corporate governance from responding to the demands of changed circumstances (Gilson 2001: 356). Institutional convergence is unlikely to precede its functional counterpart.
4. Moreover, acquisitions have also become, for some companies, a strategy to develop new types of innovative capabilities through a geographical differentiation of their activities (see Kuemmerle 1999).
5. In the United States, conglomerates were dismantled during the takeover wave of the 1980s. The move toward a focus on competencies thus started about a decade earlier in the United States than in France and Germany (Davis et al. 1994).
6. British conglomerates were an exception to this dynamic. Job turnover was higher for British conglomerates than for their American, French, and German counterparts. I thank Richard Whittington for this point.

7. I use published materials to collect data on sales of French and German companies. The data for French firms were collected from the French Company Handbook published by the International Herald Tribune and from the annual report of companies. The data for German companies were collected from five sources: Frankfurter Wertpapierborse, Borsenmitglieder, various years; Deutsche Informations Borse, DIB Aktienfuhrer Deutschland, various years; Frankfurter Allgemeine Zeitung Information Services, Germany's Top 300: a Handbook of Germany's Largest; Monopolkommission, Hauptgutachen, various years; and annual report of companies, various years. I discarded from the sample companies for which a lack of unanimity on the importance of the largest business activity was prevalent among the sources consulted.

8. Among the 14 family-owned French firms, nine remain diversified companies (Accor, Bic, Bouygues, Carrefour, Lagardere, LVHM, PPR, Sodexho, Valéo) and only five have either a dominant or single corporate strategy (Danone, Michelin, Moulinex, L'Oréal, Peugeot). For the six privatized firms with a dispersed ownership structure, only Alcatel remains a diversified company while the remaining five firms (Aventis, Elf-Total, Péchiney, Suez-Lyonnaise des Eaux, Thales) have either a dominant or single strategy.

9. German companies are constrained on a fourth front: hiring policy. Works councils possess a full veto power over the hiring of new workers. As a result, German companies cannot unilaterally pursue a business strategy based on the redeployment of the firm's resources to new activities combined with the hiring of new employees. By contrast, works councils in France simply possess information rights on hiring matters.

10. I do not want to argue that the introduction of financial transparency in continental Europe is more likely to occur in countries where employees are involved in the conduct of the business strategy of the firm. The adoption of greater financial transparency is driven by many factors, of which the behavior of employees is one. The extraction of private benefits by a large owner or by managers strongly militates against transparency (Zingales 1998: 47). Instead, I simply want to suggest that a well-organized labor force is not incompatible with financial transparency.

References

Aoki, Masahiko. 2001. *Toward a Comparative Institutional Analysis*. Cambridge: MIT Press.

Bebchuk, Lucian and Mark Roe. 1999. A Theory of Path Dependence in Corporate Ownership and Governance. *Stanford Law Review* 52: 127–70.

Berger, Phillip and Eli Ofek. 1995. Diversification's Effect on Firm Value. *Journal of Financial Economics* 37: 39–65.

Bhide, Amar. 1997. Reversing Corporate Diversification. In *Studies in International Corporate Finance and Governance Systems: A Comparison of the U.S., Japan, and Europe.* Donald Chew, ed. New York: Oxford University Press.

Coffee, John. 1999. The Future as History: The Prospects for Global Convergence in Corporate Governance and its Implications. *Northwestern University Law Review* 93: 641–707.

Comment, Robert and Greg Jarrell. 1995. Corporate Focus and Stock Returns, *Journal of Financial Economics* 37: 67–87.

Culpepper, Pepper. 1998. Individual Choice, Collective Action, and the Problem of Training Reform: Insights from France and Eastern Germany. In *The German Skills Machine: Comparative Perspectives on Systems of Education and Training.* Pepper Culpepper and David Finegold, eds. New York: Berghahn Books.

Davis, Gerald, Kristina Diekmann, and Catherine Tinsley. 1994. The Decline and Fall of the Conglomerate Firm in the 1980's: the De-Institutionalization of an Organizational Form. *American Sociological Review* 59: 547–70.

Davis Global Advisors. 2001. *Leading Corporate Governance Indicators.* Washington, D.C.

Doeringer, Peter and Michael Piore. 1985. *Internal Labor Markets and Manpower Analysis.* Armonk, NY: M. E. Sharpe

Dufour, Fabienne. 2001. *Les Clauses de Garantie d'Emploi dans les Accords d'Entreprise Donnant-Donnant.* In Le Salarié, l'Entreprise, le Juge et l'Emploi. Jean-Yves Kerbourch and Christophe Willmann, eds. Paris: La Documentation Française.

Dyas, Gareth and Heinz Thanheiser. 1976. *The Emerging European Enterprise: Strategy and Structure in French and German Industry.* Boulder: Westview Press.

Eyraud, François and Patrick Rozenblatt. 1994. *Les Formes Hiérarchiques: Travail et Salaires dans Neuf Pays Industrialisés.* Paris: La Documentation Française.

Fox, Merritt. 1998. Required Disclosure and Corporate Governance. *Law and Contemporary Problems* 62: 113–27.

Franks, Julian and Colin Mayer. 1997. Corporate Ownership and Control in the U.K., Germany, and France. *Journal of Applied Corporate Finance* 9: 30–45.

Géhin, Jean-Paul and Philippe Méhaut. 1993. *Apprentissage ou Formation Continue? Strategies Éducatives des Entreprises en Allemagne et en France.* Paris: L'Harmattan.

Gilson, Ronald. 1996. Corporate Governance and Economic Efficiency: When do Institutions Matter? *Washington University Law Quarterly* 74: 327–45.

———. 2001. The Globalization of Corporate Governance: Convergence of Form or Function. *American Journal of Comparative Law* 49: 329–57.

Glaeser, Edward, Simon Johnson, and Andrei Shleifer. 2001. Coase Versus the Coasians. *Quarterly Journal of Economics* 116: 853–99.

Goyer, Michel. 2001. Corporate Governance and the Innovation System in France, 1985–2000. *Industry and Innovation* 8: 135–58.

Hall, Peter and David Soskice. 2001. Introduction: Varieties of Capitalism. In *Varieties of Capitalism: The Institutional Foundations of Comparative Advantage.* Peter Hall and David Soskice, eds. New York: Oxford University Press.

Hancké, Robert. 2001. Revisiting the French Model: Coordination and Industrial Restructuring in the 1980's. In *Varieties of Capitalism: The Institutional Foundations of Comparative Advantage.* Peter Hall and David Soskice, eds. New York: Oxford University Press.

Jensen, Michael. 1993. The Modern Industrial Revolution, Exit, and the Failure of Internal Control Systems. *Journal of Finance* 48: 831–80.

Johnson, Simon, Rafael LaPorta, Florencio Lopez-de-Silanes, and Andrei Shleifer. 2000. Tunelling. *American Economic Review* 90: 22–27.

Kester, W. Carl. 1992. Industrial Groups as Systems of Corporate Governance. *Oxford Review of Economic Policy* 8: 24–44.

Kotthoff, Hermann. 1998. *Mitbestimmung in Zeiten Interssenpolitischer Ruckschritte. Industrielle Beziehungen* 5: 76–100.

Kuemmerle, Walter. 1999. The Drivers of Foreign Direct Investment into Research and Development. *Journal of International Business Studies* 30: 1–24.

LaPorta, Rafael, Florencio Lopez-de-Silanes, Andrei Shleifer, and Robert Vishny. 2000. Investor Protection and Corporate Governance. *Journal of Financial Economics* 3–27.

Lins, Karl and Henri Servaes. 1999. International Evidence on the Value of Corporate Diversification. *Journal of Finance* 54: 2215–2239.

Markides, Constantinos. 1995. *Diversification, Refocusing, and Economic Performance,* Cambridge: MIT Press.

Marsden, David. 1999. *A Theory of Employment Systems: Micro-Foundations of Societal Diversity.* New York: Oxford University Press.

Maurice, Marc, Francois Sellier, and Jean-Jacques Silvestre. 1984. Rules, Contexts and Actors Observations Based on a Comparison Between France and Germany *British Journal of Industrial Relations* 22: 346–63.

——. 1986. *The Social Foundations of Industrial Power: A Comparison of France and Germany.* Cambridge: MIT Press.

Mergers and Acquisitions, monthly.

Milgrom, Paul and John Roberts. 1990. The Economics of Modern Manufacturing: Technology, Strategy, and Organization, *American Economic Review.* 80: 511–528.

——. 1994. Complementarities and Systems: Understanding Japanese Economic Organization. *Estudios Economicos* 9: 3–42.

Morin, François. 1998. *Le Modele Français de Détention et de Gestion du Capital.* Paris: Les Éditions de Bercy.

Muller-Jentsch, Walter. 1995. Germany: from Collective Voice to Co-Management. In *Works Councils: Consultation, Representation and Cooperation in Industrial Relations.* Joel Rogers and Wolfgang Streeck, eds. Chicago: University of Chicago Press.

Nenova, Tatiana. 2000. The Value of Corporate Votes and Control Benefits: A Cross-Country Analysis. Working Paper, Department of Economics, Harvard University.

Pagano, Marco and Paolo Volpin. 2000. The Political Economy of Corporate Governance. Working Paper #29, Center for the Studies in Economics and Finance, University of Salerno.

Pistor, Katharina. 1999. Codetermination: A Sociopolitical Model with Governance Externalities. In *Employees and Corporate Governance.* Margaret Blair and Mark Roe, eds. Washington, DC.: Brookings Institution Press.

Porter, Michael. 1987. From Competitive Advantage to Corporate Strategy. *Harvard Business Review* 65(3): 43–59.

Prahalad, C.K. and Gary Hamel. 1990. The Core Competence of the Corporation. *Harvard Business Review* 68: 79–91.

La Présence du Capital Étranger dans les Entreprises Françaises. 1999. Les Echos. Oct. 8/9, 34

Reese, William and Michael Weisbach. 2001. Protection of Minority Shareholders Interests, Cross-Listing in the United States, and Subsequent Equity Offerings. Cambridge, MA: NBER Working Paper #8164.

Roe, Mark. 1998. Backlash. *Harvard Law Review* 98: 217–41.

———. 2000. Political Preconditions to Separating Ownership from Corporate Control. *Stanford Law Review* 53: 539–606.

Servaes, Henri. 1996. The Value of Diversification During the Conglomerate Wave. *Journal of Finance* 51: 1201–25.

Shleifer, Andrei and Lawrence Summers. 1988. Breach of Trust in Hostile Takeovers. In Alan Auerbach, ed. *Corporate Takeovers: Causes and Consequences.* Chicago: University of Chicago Press.

Sorge, Arndt. 1991. Strategic Fit and the Societal Effect: Interpreting Cross-National Comparisons of Technology, Organization and Human Resources. *Organization Studies* 12: 161–90.

Streeck, Wolfgang. 1991. On the Institutional Conditions of Diversified Quality Production. In *Beyond Keynesianism: The Socio-Economics of Production and Full Employment.* Egon Matzner and Wolfgang Streeck, eds. Brookfield, VT: Edward Elgar.

———. 2001. The Transformation of Corporate Organization in Europe. In *Institutions et Croissance.* Robert Solow, ed., Paris: Albin Michel.

Tricornot, Adrien. 2001. Qui sont les Propriétaires des Entreprises Européennes? Le Monde, June 15, 22.

Whittington, Richard and Michael Mayer. 2000. *The European Corporation: Strategy, Structure, and Social Science*. New York: Oxford University Press.

Zingales, Luigi. 1994. The Value of Voting Right: A Study of the Milan Stock Exchange Experience. *Review of Financial Studies* 7: 125–48.

———. 1998. Why it's Worth Being in Control. In *The Complete Finance Companion*. George Bickerstaffe, ed. London: Pitman Publishing.

7   Convergence on Shareholder Capitalism

An Internationalist Perspective

Jeffrey N. Gordon

This essay tries to move the corporate governance convergence debate away from the familiar arguments over efficiency and politics toward what I will call the international relations perspective: that the pace of convergence in corporate governance will depend crucially on a country's or, perhaps more importantly, on a group of countries' commitment to a project of international economic and political integration. Two examples drawn from the evolution of German shareholder capitalism over the 1990s will illustrate the argument.

The convergence debate is usually presented in terms of competing efficiency and political claims. Convergence optimists assert that an economic logic will promote convergence on the most efficient form of economic organization, usually taken to be the public corporation governed under rules designed to maximize shareholder value (see e.g., Hansmann and Kraakman 2001). Convergence skeptics counterclaim that organizational diversity is possible, even probable, because of path dependent development of institutional complementarities whose abandonment is likely to be inefficient (see e.g., Bebchuck and Roe 1999). The skeptics also assert that existing elites will use their political and economic advantages to block reform; the optimists counterclaim that the spread of shareholding will reshape politics. These considerations are obviously important, yet the debate thus far omits a crucial variable: state-level choices over strategies of corporate governance convergence (or divergence) based on their effects in integrating (or not) the country within transnational systems of economic and political life.

These choices are usually the product of elite opinion with differing degrees of democratic ratification. In other words, convergence may proceed or be hindered irrespective of efficiency considerations at the corporate level, or even irrespective of conventional domestic politics, depending on the role that convergence plays in an explicitly state level transnational drama (compare, e.g., Milhaupt 1998: 1148).

On this view shareholder capitalism, a term intended to reference the Anglo-American model of public ownership and strong equity markets, is particularly well-suited as the optimal convergence form not necessarily because of organizational or productive efficiencies but because it offers the best hope for the control of economic nationalism, the tendency toward which is a major obstacle to the transnational integration project. Shareholder capitalism serves this end by reducing the role of the state in economic decision-making, by decentralizing such decisions at the level of the firm and by subjecting such firm-level decisions to a neutral, transnational standard of the share price. In particular, shareholder capitalism opens up the contestability of corporate control. This is particularly important in relation to cross-border combinations, which are crucial to the integration project. Cross-border mergers can create entities of optimal size and scope for transnational enterprise. But apart from achieving efficient scale, cross-border mergers can build businesses that are conduits for the transnational free flow of capital, goods, services, and people, and, no less, a transnational attitude.

Nevertheless, cross-border mergers entail a special sort of risk. The government of the state of the target's organization will be legitimately concerned that investment and divestment decisions will be influenced by economic nationalism benefiting the state of the acquiror's organization. Will the acquiror show home country bias in decisions regarding location of facilities, layoffs, or downsizings? To put it more simply: Will the minister insist that the new plant be located in Lyon rather than Düsseldorf?

What best protects against the potential for such economic nationalism is the mutual vulnerability to takeover bids by both putative acquiror and target that is the hallmark of shareholder capitalism. To see this, assume the acquiror begins to show significant home country bias. This inefficiency in the acquiror's operations will lead to a fall off in shareholder value that would create an opportunity for a control entrepreneur, if the acquiror were also exposed to the potential for a hostile bid. In other words, exposure of firms to the threat of hostile takeover on roughly equal footing will help constrain economic nationalism while permitting very valuable cross-border merger activity. This is not to say that exposure to takeovers is a complete solution to the economic nationalism problem. A government could make payments or provide subsidies to cover the costs to the firm of economic nationalism and thus protect shareholder value. But such payments might be fiscally infeasible, they could be matched by a competing government, and, of course, such payments could be forbidden by the transnational regime. Takeover vulnerability makes it harder for a government to promote economic nationalism simply by imposing the costs on shareholders.

To repeat: cross-border mergers are critical to the transnational project not only, or even principally, because of efficiency considerations. Rather, they create organizations that make important decisions from a transnational perspective and, in so doing, give extra meaning to the transnational project. On this view, the push for convergence on shareholder capitalism, including public firms with relatively dispersed ownership, has an extra dimension. To control economic nationalism it is not sufficient merely to privatize former state-owned enterprises. Public share ownership, which gives rise to firms of relatively greater mutual takeover vulnerability, is also an important element. Some have argued that concerns of economic nationalism cut the other way: that governments will have less sway over the managers of private firms or public firms with concentrated ownership because shareholders in such firms are better able to police managerial behavior. In my view, the behind-the-scenes deal-making between governments and concentrated or private owners—the national elite—in the service of economic nationalism is, over the long term, more likely to resist solution than such pressure brought against the managers of public firms. Managers of widely held public firms succumbing to costly government pressure will face public equity market responses and will be unprotected by concentrated owners. Quid pro quos with public firm actors to compensate firms against the cost of economic nationalism will be more visible and easier to police in a transnational system. For example, in the case of private or concentrated ownership, the government can reward a controlling shareholder through a seemingly unrelated transaction; it would be impossible to reward all shareholders in a public firm in the same way. Finally, the evolving international share ownership of public firms will, over time, make economic nationalism seem more anachronistic.

This essay develops this argument in the context of the evolution of German shareholder capitalism in the 1990s. First I will sketch out some of the quantitative evidence on the extent of convergence on the shareholder model in Germany. This bears on the debate between the convergence optimists and skeptics about the plasticity of corporate systems. In general the data show significant movement in Germany toward the shareholder model in a relatively short period of time. Still, judgment must be reserved on exactly how full or empty this particular glass is, and, even more important, how durable is the 1990s' legacy in the face of the post-2000 downturn in stock markets.

Then I will briefly develop two examples in which the project of transnational economic and political integration did in fact affect the pace of convergence. The first example is the way in which the European Union Telecommunication Directive helped trigger the privatization of Deutsche Telekom, which in turn led the German government, eager to obtain a high price, to promote shareholder capitalism by cultural, market, and legal intervention. So here the transnational project promotes convergence beyond what could have been expected solely from efficiency considerations.

The second example is the way that economic nationalism by its EU partners in the protection of state champions led Germany to pull back from ratification of the "board neutrality" position of the proposed 13th Company Law Directive on Takeovers. Instead, Germany adopted a takeover law that permits the supervisory board to approve defensive measures without a shareholder vote. This can be understood, I argue, as a move of "aggressive reciprocity" in the trade negotiation sense—a raising of barriers by Germany with the goal of precipitating a negotiation that will in the end produce lower barriers and a more level playing field. This move, played out in pursuit of transnational integration, will lead away from convergence in the short run and, like many such acts, may produce a degenerate spiraling away from the cooperative outcome and, ultimately, less convergence. In both of these cases, simple economic efficiency and the standard political stories may play a subsidiary role to overarching transnational objectives.

I. Some Evidence on Convergence in Germany, 1990–2000

The German corporate governance system is marked by some features that at the beginning of the 1990s were quite different from the Anglo-American model. For example: As a formal legal matter, German public corporations are governed by a two-tier board structure: a supervisory board that consists of outsiders and a managing board that consists of the firm's key operating officers. Under the truly different feature of "co-determination," half the supervisory board seats are filled by labor representatives. The ownership structure has also been distinctive. A comparatively large portion of GDP is produced by relatively small or medium-sized privately owned firms, the *Mittelstand*. Few large public firms are held by dispersed shareholders. Instead, most public firms are dominated by one or a small number of large blockholders—families, other companies, and financial institutions. The share ownership structure is part of a larger pattern of German political economy in which households have tended not to own stock but rather to invest in bonds and life insurance and in which relatively little corporate finance is provided by public markets, especially public equity markets.

What has been the extent of the change in the 1990s? Although some of the structural differences persist, most notably the two-tier board and co-determination, there has been significant evolution in German capital markets, ownership structure, legal rules, and cultural attitudes. It seems premature to say that these changes make for a regime shift, but the importance of this evolution toward shareholder capitalism should not be gainsaid.

One important measure of change is the increased level of initial public offerings. Most directly, the potential to do an IPO opens a new channel of finance that is, almost by definition, sensitive to shareholder interests. But the increased availability of such a capital-raising route also reflects various institutional developments, including new laws, that foster and protect shareholder interests generally, and cultural changes that encourage investors to make investments through direct share ownership. In other words, a change in the potential supply of public equity capital not only enhances shareholder capitalism—extends its reach—but also indicates the spread of background conditions for its success. As table 7.1 indicates, there has been a sharp increase in the number of IPOs over the period. Early in the decade and consistent with the 1980s, there were an average of 15–20 IPOs annually. The number of IPOs exploded toward the end of the decade, when many high tech startups went public on a newly formed German rival for NASDAQ, the Neuer Markt. As table 7.2 illustrates, IPOs provided increasingly larger infusions of equity capital over the period, not just in absolute dollar terms, but normalized for increases in GDP. As in the United States, there has been a significant fall-off in IPOs both in number and in dollar amount after 2000. But Germany's first exposure to the IPO cycle is part of the conditioning of sophisticated capital markets.

TABLE 7.1 Number of Initial Public Offerings (1990–99)

1990-92	1993-95	1996	1997	1998	1999	Total	Total new/ total 1990
51	39	20	35	67	168	380	69.3%

Source: Van der Elst (2002: Table 7).

TABLE 7.2 Equity raised by IPOs as percent of GDP (1990–99)

1990-92 avg.	1993-95 avg.	1996	1997	1998	1999	1990–99 avg.
0.10%	0.11%	0.65%	0.15%	0.20%	0.91%	0.25%

Source: Van der Elst (2002: Table 8).

Another measure of the penetration of shareholder capitalism is the increasing importance of equity to the portfolios of individuals, both as "stock" and "flow." This is another measure of the supply side—the willingness of individuals to acquire and hold equity assets. As graph 7.1 shows, the value of household ownership of public equity as a percentage of total financial assets significantly increased during the 1990s. Graph 7.2, which tracks equity acquisitions as a percent of total household financial asset acquisition, generally reflects significant equity additions over the period, with a surge in the post-1996 period. Undoubtedly some of this increase came from the increase in stock market values in the period; hence the flattening of the curve in the 1999–2000 period. But nevertheless, by the end of the decade, most of the marginal gain in household wealth derived from public equity. Even if some portion of the increase derives merely from appreciation of existing equity holdings rather than new purchases, it still draws the connection between household wealth and shareholder value. This connection helps establish a political economy favorable to further developments favorable to shareholder capitalism.

This evidence of a strengthening of the demand for equity capital is also reflected in the significant increase in the number and percentage of share-

GRAPH 7.1 Household Public Equity Assets as Percentage of Total Household Financial Assets

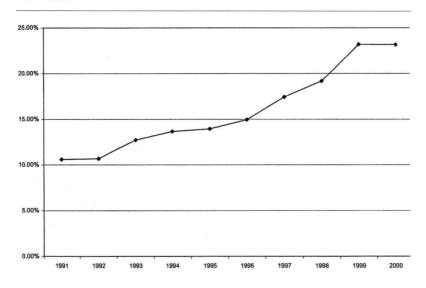

GRAPH 7.2 Household Public Equity Acquisitions as Percentage of Total Household Financial Asset Acquisitions

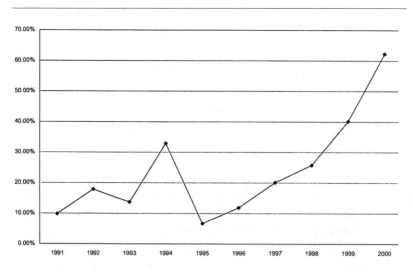

Source: Deutsche Bundesbank (2001); own calculations

holders in Germany (see table 7.3). Equity mutual funds became a particularly popular way for individuals to participate in the stock market, much as in the United States, especially as banks worked to migrate their customers from relatively low yielding savings accounts into bank-managed stock mutual funds. Growing from essentially negligible importance in the early 1990s, equity mutual funds became as important a vehicle for equity investment as direct stock ownership (see table 7.4). By the end of the decade, the penetration of stock ownership including ownership of equity mutual funds increased almost four-fold over the prior level (table 7.5).

One classic way to think of the influence of shareholder capitalism is in terms of ownership structure. Concentrated ownership is associated with

TABLE 7.3 Shareholders in publicly traded companies (in 000's; as percentage of population)

Year	1988	1992	1994	1996	1997	1998	1999	2000
No.	2,229	2,661	2,736	2,675	2,767	3,218	3,775	5,121
% pop	4.9	4.2	4.4	4.2	4.4	5.1	5.9	8.0

Source: DAI Factbook (2001).

TABLE 7.4 Shareholders in Stock Mutual Funds (in 000's; as percentage of population)

Year	1997	1998	1999	2000
No.	1,751	2,458	3,582	6,601
%pop	2.8	3.9	5.6	10.3

Source: DAI Factbook (2001) (Time series begins in 1997).

TABLE 7.5 Shareholders in public companies (including through employee stock ownership plans) and in mutual funds (including "mixed funds") (in 000's; as percentage of population)

Year	1992	1994	1996	1997	1998	1999	2000
No.	2,229	2,661	2,736	5,601	6,789	8,231	11,828
% pop	4.9	4.2	4.4	8.9	10.7	12.9	18.5

Source: DAI Factbook (2001) (Combines Tables 7.3 and 7.4) Pre-1997 years do not include mutual fund owners and so may not be strictly comparable.

insider governance systems, dispersed ownership with outsider governance systems. Often the debate about convergence comes down to a question about the persistence of that particular systemic difference. The best evidence suggests that there has been a significant increase in the number and percentage of public firms in Germany with dispersed ownership. In 1990, approximately 10 percent of the public firms were either widely held or otherwise lacked a 25 percent "blocking" shareholder (Jenkinson and Ljungqvist 2001: 405). By 1999, approximately 25 percent of a larger number of public firms were widely held (Van der Elst 2002). This is a significant change that would be unlikely in the absence of the development of better minority shareholder protection and in the gradual unwinding of the cross-holding inducements of the insider system.

Another familiar way of illustrating the increasing importance of equity to a country's political economy is the ratio of market capitalization to GDP. As might be expected, this ratio significantly increased for Germany over the period, from approximately 20 percent in 1991 to 67 percent in 2000. As graph 7.3 also shows, however, Germany's ratio increased at approximately the same rate as for other EU countries, suggesting common phenomena that enhanced shareholder capitalism throughout the EU, including but not limited to the rapid appreciation in public equity values in the latter part of the decade.[1] Perhaps of greatest interest is graph 7.4, which compares the market capitalization/GDP ratios of Germany and the UK, widely regarded as the European leader of shareholder capitalism, and shows a narrowing of the gap as the decade progresses. This comparison, which controls for stock market appreciation that would be common to both countries, suggests a significant element of convergence in Germany on the shareholder model.

The convergence question can be framed at many different levels, as the prior data make us aware. One question is whether the managers of an existing set of public firms are more likely to seek to maximize shareholder value in ways that predictably should lead to a higher stock price for a given underlying cash flow. That question leads us to think about possible convergence in governance arrangements and, perhaps even more important, convergence in ownership structures that affect how a particular set of legal rules will play out in practice (and what legal rules will be chosen). But another question is the extent to which the economy is organized through public firms: how much economy activity is guided by managers who are exposed to capital market signals. Germany's relatively low market capitalization/GDP

GRAPH 7.3   Ratio of Market Capitalization to GDP: Germany vs. EU (Value-Weighted)

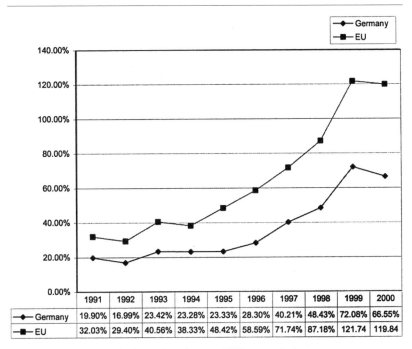

	1991	1992	1993	1994	1995	1996	1997	1998	1999	2000
◆ Germany	19.90%	16.99%	23.42%	23.28%	23.33%	28.30%	40.21%	48.43%	72.08%	66.55%
■ EU	32.03%	29.40%	40.56%	38.33%	48.42%	58.59%	71.74%	87.18%	121.74	119.84

Source: Federation of European Stock Exchanges (2001); own calculations.

ratio and yet its convergence toward the UK may say less about the governance or ownership structure of public firms (that is, changes in the market capitalization of the cash flows of firms that are already public) and more about the evolution of the German economy toward a system in which much more of the activity is conducted by public firms. Germany has been famous for its *Mittelstand,* its medium size enterprises, mostly family owned, which account for an unusually large part of its economy activity. The changing market capitalization/GDP ratio may indicate the shrinking of this sector. Even if the ownership structure of large German firms has not radically changed in the 1990s, convergence may express itself even more importantly in the increasing extent to which public firms account for economic activity—because even classic insider governance of a public firm will be more sensitive to stock market signals than a private firm. As more of

GRAPH 7.4 German Market Cap/GDP vs. English Market Cap/GDP

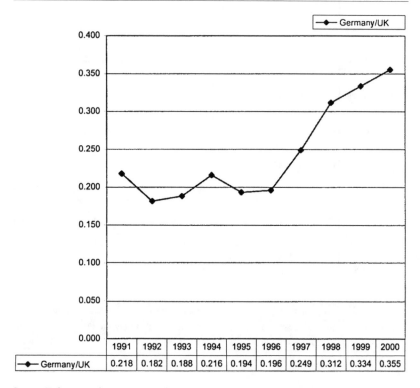

	1991	1992	1993	1994	1995	1996	1997	1998	1999	2000
Germany/UK	0.218	0.182	0.188	0.216	0.194	0.196	0.249	0.312	0.334	0.355

Source: Federation of European Stock Exchanges (2001); own calculations.

the economy is exposed to such signals, it is bound to affect governance even at insider firms.

The empirical conjecture from the market capitalization/GDP ratio is borne out by directly tracing the importance of public companies to German GDP over time. We collected data on the sales of the largest 50 German companies over the 1991–2000 period, determined which of those companies were public, and then mapped a ratio of those large public company sales to GDP. (Sales and GDP are not strictly comparable, since the latter is a value-added measure). As graph 7.5 shows, this ratio increases significantly over the period, especially in the latter half of the decade, from 30 percent to nearly 70 percent. A number of possibilities suggest themselves:

GRAPH 7.5 Sales of German Public Companies in Top 50 as a percentage of
GDP

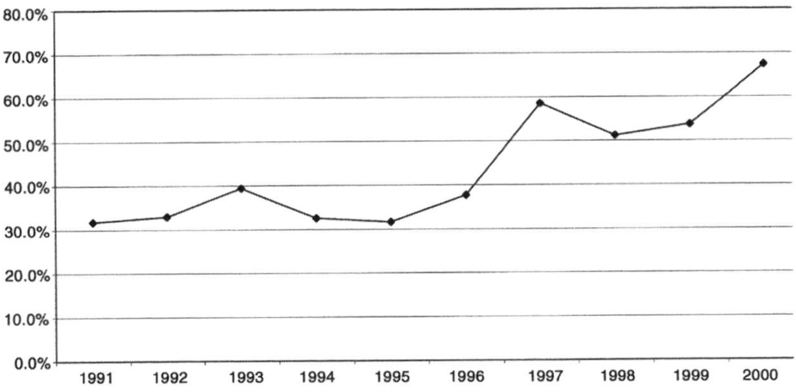

Source: ELC International; own calculations.

public firms are growing faster than private firms (suggesting the value of
capital market signals and pressure for the firm's performance), public firms
are acquiring private firms, perhaps using their appreciated stock as acquisition currency, or formerly private firms are going public as part of the
increasing number of German IPOs.

All these various quantitative indicators are imperfect proxies for the measurement of what is, in any event, an imprecisely defined category, "shareholder capitalism." Nevertheless the indicators are trending in the same
direction over the period in Germany, suggesting the existence of important
institutional shifts that are promoting convergence. Undoubtedly many of
the efficiency-related reasons offered by convergence optimists contributed
to these changes in Germany. In particular, as equity capital increasingly
becomes the most mobile factor of production, it is not surprising to see
movement toward shareholder-tilted regimes and more convergence in corporate structure and governance. Still, as two examples from Germany discussed in the next section illustrate, states have objectives beyond short-run
efficiencies. They may promote convergence because of its importance in
transnational economic and political integration; more remarkably, they
may resist convergence for the same reason.

II. The Privatization of Deutsche Telekom and the Fostering of Shareholder Capitalism

The privatization of Deutsche Telekom in 1996, the largest-ever initial public offering by a European company, is a powerful example of how a state's pursuit of transnational integration can promote corporate convergence on a faster timetable and to a greater extent than predicted even by the efficiency claims of convergence optimists. The transaction succeeded in placing a large amount of stock, 40 percent of the total issuance worth approximately $5 billion, with German retail purchasers. Nearly 2 million Germans subscribed to the offering, including 400,000 who had never previously owned shares.

In one sense the transaction is not so remarkable. The privatization of state-owned enterprises (SOEs) swept the world in the 1980s and 1990s, stimulated by the privatization successes of Thatcherite Great Britain. Countries were particularly eager to sell shares in their telecommunications SOEs because of high market valuations. But Germany did not generally participate in this privatization wave, in part because a smaller share of significant economic enterprise was state-owned. Why was Telekom the great exception? In addition to other considerations, the transaction was triggered by the EU's new telecommunications regime, which ended Deutsche Telekom's privileged monopoly position and made privatization irresistible.

In order to secure the success of the privatization from a financial point of view, German political and business elites promoted shareholder capitalism much more vigorously than otherwise would have been the case. The Deutsche Telekom transaction became a moment of high social mobilization, in which an idea that was the province of the elites was successfully argued to the populace generally. The immediate effect was obvious: a high price for Deutsche Telekom shares. But there were immediate secondary effects as well: for example, the quick ramping up of a new stock market aimed especially at raising equity from public shareholders for high-tech startups, the Neuer Markt, modeled on NASDAQ; the development of German corporate law in a public shareholder-protective direction, and the acceptance of an unprecedented hostile bid for a German public company, the Vodafone takeover of Mannesmann. In other words a significant push toward convergence on the model of shareholder capitalism derived at least in part from a step motivated by Germany's pursuit of transnational integration within the EU framework. Even if these social and institutional developments are set in wet concrete, at risk in the post-2000 stock market swoon, including the fall of the "T-share" below the initial offering price and the somewhat heavy-handed government intervention to force the resignation of the incumbent CEO,[2] the point remains that convergence moved further and faster because of the international relations choices of German decisionmakers, not simply the purported efficiencies of the organizational form.

A. The Opening of European Telecommunications to Competition

In 1987 the EU started down the road of telecommunications liberalization that concluded a decade later, January 1, 1998, in the full opening of national telecommunications markets to competition, including services, networks and equipment. The process began with a "Green Paper" issued by the European Commission that focused on the importance of telecommunications:

> The strengthening of European telecommunications has become one of the major conditions for promoting a harmonious development of economic activities and a competitive market throughout the Community and for achieving the completion of the Community-wide market for goods and services by 1992 (Toward a Dynamic European Economy—Green Paper 1987).

At the time of the Green Paper in 1987, telecommunications in most European countries was the province of a "post-telephone-telegraph" entity (PTT) within the government that was both the monopoly operator and regulator of telecommunication services. The Commission's initial regulatory actions (undertaken in 1988) were first, to require a separation between the telecommunications operator and the regulatory authority; second, to restrict the scope of the telecommunications monopoly to voice telephony and infrastructure (but not new services); third, to liberalize the telecommunications equipment markets by requiring open procurement and interconnection with nonproprietary equipment; and fourth, to facilitate increased competition by new entry through "open network" access to the basic infrastructure. The Commission also pushed for "harmonized" equipment standards and transmission standards that would sustain a trans-European market. There were multiple reasons for this agenda, including the special role that efficient telecommunications would play in knitting together the economic and political life of the European Union as well as the realization that a large common market would facilitate the rollout of cutting edge telecommunications services and products. The economies of scale and scope would be particularly important in the competition with U.S. telecommunications equipment manufacturers.

The process of telecommunications liberalization received additional impetus from the 1992 Maastricht Treaty, adding Article 129b to the Treaty of Rome, which called for the "establishment and development of trans-European networks in the areas of transport, telecommunications and energy infrastructure." High-level EU conferences subsequently endorsed a "Trans-European Networks" project whose aims were not only economic but also "intended to support the EU's goal of social and economic cohesion" (Johnson and Turner 1997: 18–20). Thus there were dual objectives. Rapid development of integrated telecommunications networks was seen as crucial to the development of the "single European market," because this sort of infrastructure would make it easier and cheaper for firms to coordinate economic activity across nominal national borders. Integrated telecommunications networks would enable greater economic payoff from the existing reduction in legal and practical barriers to intra-EU activity and in turn would create greater demand for further reduction. But it was also understood that telecommunications liberalization would help foster the dense communications exchange that creates integration and cohesion. After a 1992 Commission review (and in light of the Maastricht Treaty), the Council of Telecommunication Ministers decided in July 1993 on full liberalization of the European telephony market by January 1, 1998.[3]

Mobile telephony was quickly opened to full competition (despite its competitive threat to the landline voice monopoly) and by January 1, 1998, all telecommunications services and networks were opened to competition. In accord with the call of Article 129b, there ultimately proved to be two crucial elements to the regulatory program: standard setting to enhance the creation of interstate networks and anti-monopoly competition policy—in particular, the breakup of state domination of telecommunications services and networks—and guaranteed cost-based access to the existing infrastructure. The goal was to substitute competition for economic regulation. This in turn led over time to state divestment of ownership over telecommunications assets. In 1987 most telecommunications services were provided by the state-owned monopolist in most EU countries; by 2000 most of these companies were privatized (although in many cases governments retained substantial stakes) (see Curwen 1997: 73–90).

B. Germany's Response to EU Telecommunications Reform

As of the late 1980s Germany's monopoly telecommunications carrier was one arm of the Deutsche Bundespost, the German PTT, which included the post office and a public credit union. The Bundespost was operated as a separate entity for budgetary purposes and was headed by the Minister of Posts and Telecommunication, a cabinet member of the government. Its employees were federal civil servants.

Germany's first response to the new EU telecommunication policy and directives could be described as minimalist. "Post Reform I," adopted in 1989,[4] separated the regulatory functions from entrepreneurial activity, gave a new telecommunications entity a small amount of entrepreneurial freedom, and partially opened the telecommunications market. More specifically, the three activities of the Bundespost were converted into separate entities explicitly set up as "businesses" with a managing board and a supervisory board in the fashion of the two-tier board structure for private corporations. The autonomy of the telecommunications entity, "Deutsche Telekom," was quite limited, however. The Ministry appointed managing board members as well as supervisory board members, and although the ostensible purpose of Post Reform I was to separate "sovereign" and "entrepreneurial" decisionmaking, the Ministry wore both hats. Moreover, under the Post Reform I structure, Deutsche Telekom profits went to cross-subsidize losses at the postal office and the credit union and were also subject to an additional 10 percent tax going to the Federal Treasury. Additionally, in the period Deutsche Telekom was obliged by government mandate to make a heavy (DM40 billion) investment in the telecommunications infrastructure of the former East Germany.

The emphasis in the Maastricht Treaty (1992) on telecommunications and the ensuing Commission directives calling for complete liberalization of telecommunication markets by 1998 made it clear that the Post Reform I regime did not sufficiently address the status of Deutsche Telekom. The coalition government (Christian Democrats and Free Democrats) and Deutsche Telekom management vigorously promoted privatization as the necessary next step to equip Telekom to compete in the liberalized environment. Privatization would serve many ends for Deutsche Telekom: new equity to overhaul its networks (and to complete the modernization of the East), flexibility to downsize and reorient its workforce, freedom to pursue cross-border alliances, and stimulus for an entrepreneurial and innovative spirit in the company. The matter was complicated by the government's desire to privatize all three functions of the Bundespost and by the need to obtain a constitutional amendment, since Article 87 of the Grundgesestz was read as requiring direct government provision of postal services, including telecommunications, rather than mere regulation to that end. A constitutional amendment required a two-thirds approval in both houses of the German parliament, which gave the Social Democrats (SPD) a veto. An important SPD ally, the Post Trade Union, strongly opposed privatization because of the threat to employment security and perks, and others were concerned about the loss of the "Bügerpost" ("citizens' post") ideal of high-quality universal service. Nevertheless the case for privatization of Deutsche Telekom in light of the EU-wide telecommunications policy proved decisive and led to the adoption in 1994 of "Post Reform II,"[5] which formally privatized the three Bundespost business entities.[6]

On January 1, 1995 Deutsche Telekom became a private corporation subject to the general German corporate law, the Aktiengesetz, but 100 percent owned by the government. Its management was entirely separate from the other two former Bundespost entities and its financial responsibility to them ended. It became subject to the general system of taxation. In other words, although Deutsche Telekom was regulated as a public utility, meaning some government involvement in rate-setting and other terms of service, it was financially independent and accountable for its financial results. Of particular importance, Post Reform II explicitly contemplated the sale of a substantial stake in the company through a public offering, so the goal was not just formal privatization but the creation of a publicly owned company. The legislative history established that the government would not try to sell its shares until 2000, to protect the company's access to equity markets.

C. The Privatization of Deutsche Telekom and Shareholder Capitalism

So the forces flowing from EU integration were an important catalyst in the privatization of Deutsche Telekom. To be sure, state-owned telecommunication utilities were favorite candidates for privatizations throughout the world, and Deutsche Telekom would have faced the same competitive and capital-raising pressures that led to other such transactions. Yet the EU liberalization added to that pressure, in no small part by triggering privatizations of virtually every state-owned European telecommunications company. Privatization in Germany was politically a close case and certainly the timing owed much to the EU project.

But what is the connection between the decision to privatize Deutsche Telekom and the promotion of shareholder capitalism in Germany? The privatization could have been handled in different ways. For example, in more typically German fashion, the shares could have been placed with German financial intermediaries and other institutional investors, with some small distribution of shares to the public. Instead, the Deutsche Telekom transaction came to be the vehicle by which various elites who favored shareholder capitalism were able to enlist the government and other elements of the elite in what became a moment of high social mobilization that changed the institutional and political landscape.

Independent of the Telekom question, many important elites had come to believe that the development of shareholder capitalism was important for German's economic development.[7] Germany was eager to replicate the success of Silicon Valley in spinning out technological innovation that produced high-end jobs as well as superior investor returns. An active stock market that provided a successful entrepreneur and the venture capitalist intermediary with a lucrative exit strategy through an initial public offering seemed integral to the Silicon Valley model.[8] Yet initial public offerings historically were rare in Germany—only ten in all of 1994, and the stock markets were famously illiquid and volatile. This stemmed in large part from the reluctance of public retail investors to take on the risk associated with stock purchases, especially IPOs. For example at the beginning of 1996 (the year of the Deutsche Telekom transaction), only 5 percent of Germans owned common stock, as opposed to 18 percent of the British and 21 percent of Americans. From a balance sheet perspective, in Germany common-stock holdings accounted for 6.9 percent of household assets, in Britain, 9.1 percent, and in the U.S., 18.7 percent, at the beginning of 1996. In general German investors preferred bonds to stocks and also heavily invested through life insurance policies.

Various elites also saw development of shareholder capitalism as necessary to address pension problems arising from German demographics. The relative aging of the population as the birthrate declined was beginning to undermine the existing pension system, in which workers looked almost exclusively to the state for a generous defined benefit pension payment. Ultimately, financial solvency would require at least partial replacement of the state plan, funded from tax revenues on a "pay as you go" basis, by a private contributory plan, whose payout would depend upon its investment returns. Appropriate equity investments could deliver greater long-term returns than fixed-income investments and thus make the shift more politically palatable; fostering shareholder capitalism would help investors obtain better outcomes in contributory plans.

Finally the government (and the management) had a particular reason to sell Deutsche Telekom shares to the public rather than to financial intermediaries and other institutions. As became clear as the transaction unfolded, this would maximize the sale price for the shares. Since the proceeds were flowing directly to the company, this would increase the value of the government's remaining 76 percent stake and of course make more funds available for corporate purposes. Maximization of shareholder value became visibly important shortly after the transaction, when the government arranged partial "sales" of its stake to an affiliated financial institution, the Kreditanstalt für Wiederaufbau (Credit Bank for Reconstruction) over three successive years, 1997–99. The sales, which amounted to a 25 percent interest in Deutsche Telekom, helped address budgetary shortfalls that were made critical by the need to satisfy the participation criteria for "economic and monetary union," the common EU currency regime.

D. How the Deal Was Sold to the German Public and to the Institutions

Once the decision to privatize Deutsche Telekom was taken, the transaction planners followed what appears to be a two-pronged strategy to obtain a high price for the offering: work hard to enhance retail demand for the offering by the German public and take other measures that would lead institutional investors to buy in the aftermarket to bolster the price. In contrast to privatizations in countries such as Britain and France, where shares were often sold at a significant discount to comparable private equity offerings, the Deutsche Telekom offering was fully priced, yet the price came to be supported by the structure of demand generated by the transaction planners.

The planners knew that they had a substantial uphill battle to transform German attitudes toward stock ownership. For example, in June 1996 *Focus* magazine reported survey results that 57 percent of Germans did not want to buy Telekom shares "under any circumstances." "Otto-Normal-Anleger has a panicking desire to stay as far from stock market risk as possible," preferring federal bonds and savings accounts. *Focus* noted that if anything, Germans had less appetite for equity risk than before: In the 70s, every tenth German owned shares; in 1996, less than half that number did (*Focus* 1996:180). The Telekom offering prompted considerable speculation about the sources of German investment caution (see, e.g., Schmidbauer et al. 1996: 15).[9] There were a number of economic and purely promotional steps taken to bolster retail German demand. On the economic side, German retail purchasers were given a small 1.75 percent discount (up to a maximum of 300 shares per investor) and, to discourage "flipping" of shares, were promised "loyalty shares," one bonus share for each ten shares continuously held for a three-year period. To appeal to risk-averse German investors, the company announced that it expected to pay a 2 percent dividend in 1997 and a 4 percent dividend in 1998. Taking into account the tax credit for the corporate level tax paid on dividends that was available to German (but not foreign) purchasers, that would produce a 1998 yield above then prevailing long-term German bond yield.

Beginning in March 1996 Deutsche Telekom undertook an extensive promotional campaign that helped make stock ownership seem a natural, even fashionable, investment choice among those who had traditionally looked for fixed-income investments. The year-long campaign cost DM85 million. Early on the company established a toll-free telephone number for prospective investors to talk about the stock market generally or Deutsche Telekom specifically and circulated glossy brochures on both the stock market and the company. This was followed up by a "blitz of print ads, radio spots and television commercials proclaiming 1996 as the year of the Telekom share, . . . set to the Cole Porter tune 'Who Wants To Be a Millionaire'" (Ascarelli 1996). The commercial endorsers included the star of a popular TV detective series.

Perhaps the high moment was a nationally televised awards program hosted in September at Deutsche Telekom's headquarters in which CEO Ron Sommer gave out prizes to contestants who had assembled the best-performing stock portfolios over a three-month period. The "T-share" became a brand name, and people would signal one another with hands in a "T." There was undoubted giddiness to the national mood, captured by the headline on one commentary: "Run on the Telekom shares: 500 Mark gain is sure; Buy, buy, buy. Why students and pensioners alike are suddenly interested in bulls and bears" (Boeker 1996). Indeed, the hoopla prompted a complaining editorial from a leading national newspaper about the lack of serious discussion (FAZ 1996: 15).[10] The marketing campaign was an obvious success: eventually 3.2 million people responded with some level of interest, more than half of whom subscribed for shares.

The German commercial banks also played a significant role in steering German investors into the offering. Enlisting the banks' support was important, because in many cases share purchases would be funded with money that might otherwise go into certificates of deposit or other bank products. Thus it seems that all of the major German banks were members of the underwriting syndicate.[11] As further encouragement to the banks, the retail purchaser incentives described above were limited to investors who purchased through an account maintained at one of the participating banks in the German part of the offering.[12]

Many of the banks apparently organized special programs to encourage retail purchase of Deutsche Telekom shares. For example, Dresdner Bank offered a special interest rate (5 percent vs. 2 percent) for funds set aside in a special account to purchase shares. Commerzbank advertised special "T-Share" savings accounts, which accumulated more than DM100 million. Commerzbank also offered a "risk-free" way of buying shares, the so-called "Safe T": customers could deposit the shares in trust until the day after the Deutsche Telekom 2002 annual meeting (six years later!) with the option of receiving the shares or the initial public offering price. In turn, during the trust period, the bank would receive annual dividends (and the associated tax credit) and voting rights in the shares.

These promotional efforts were remarkably successful. The offering was five times oversubscribed. As this demand became apparent in the period before the definitive offering documents, it undoubtedly strengthened the resolve of Deutsche Telekom to set a high offering price and led to a lowering of the discount that retail purchasers eventually received. Earlier in the marketing process, a discount of up to 5 percent had been discussed; as noted, the final figure was 1.75 percent.

But the transaction planners also understood that a truly successful offering required substantial institutional participation worldwide. Ultimately Germany wanted to sell off substantial amounts of its remaining interest in a secondary offering. Deutsche Telekom also wanted to be able to access the equity capital markets for corporate purposes or to spin off parts of its business, or to engage in merger activity, all of which would go better with a substantial institutional following.

Thus the company organized a global public offering that included a leading U.S. underwriter, Goldman, Sachs, as a "global coordinator" along with local favorites Deutsche Bank and Dresdner Bank. The issue was vigorously marketed by dozens of banks in the underwriting syndicate to 3,700 institutional investors throughout the world by way of sixty road shows and presentations in thirty cities. In addition to its primary listing on the Frankfurt Stock Exchange (and several German regional exchanges), the stock was listed on the New York Stock Exchange (where it would trade as ADRs) and the Tokyo Stock Exchange.

If German retail demand could be described as overwhelming, worldwide institutional demand was not. The matter came down to price. The underwriting syndicate banks initially proposed a price range of DM20 to DM25. Deutsche Telekom insisted on a price range of DM25 to DM30, which many institutional investors felt could not be supported on the fundamentals, notwithstanding the marketing push at the retail level. The eventual offering price of DM28.50—despite retail bookbuilding and "when issued" (or "gray market") trading that would have supported at least DM30—was something of a concession to institutional investors.

Deutsche Telekom's organization of the underwriting syndicate seems to have been an important factor in its ability to achieve a high price for the offering. Virtually every significant bank in Germany and, indeed, throughout much of the world, was given a place in the syndicate. The offering was deemed to be subject to the "gun-jumping" rules of the US securities laws, which meant that the syndicate banks were disabled from any public comment on the offering from the time of its preliminary announcement to the breakup of the syndicate after the offering was launched. The effect was to quash the possibility of high-profile analyst reports that might have cast doubt on the DM28.50 price. As one commentator put it, "By getting all the players on your side, there is effectively no opposing team around to argue about miscalculating company value or overpricing the deal" (Corporate Money 1997).

The scene on Monday, November 18, 1996, the day that Deutsche Telekom opened for trading on the Frankfurt Stock Exchange was striking. "'The Stock Market Is Bubbling,' cheered a banner front-page headline in the mass-market *Bild*" (Walsh 1996). Mounted policeman kept control of the crowds that gathered outside. Deutsche Telekom had erected a corporate promotional sculpture—"71 big, flashing lighted cubes in Telekom's new official color, magenta—which incongruously covered most of the plaza in front of the stately renaissance facade of the Frankfurt Stock Exchange" (ibid.). Demand for the offering, led by German retail demand, led to an increase in the public offering from 500 million to 600 million shares, to the underwriters' exercise of their over-allotment or "greenshoe" option to sell another 90 million shares, and to an enlargement of the special employee allocation to a total of 23.7 million. The ultimate offering, 713.7 million shares, netted the company approximately DM19.4 billion (US $12 billion). The day's trading (including special after hours trading on the electronic exchange IBIS) ended at DM32.58, up 14 percent.

Ultimately German investors received a 67 percent allocation, 60 percent of which (meaning 40 percent of the entire offering) went to German retail customers, 14 percent went to the Americas, mostly the U.S., 8 percent for Britain, 6 percent for continental Europe, and 5 percent for Asia and the rest of the world. The original plan had called for only a 25 percent placement with the German retail public. Shareholder capitalism in Germany had received a major boost.

E. Evidence that Shareholder Capitalism Took Deeper Root Following the Transaction

One might ask how the Deutsche Telekom transaction counts as much of an advance of shareholder capitalism in Germany when there are so many features that fit with the established insider governance system. After all, the government remained as 76 percent owner with an understanding that it would preserve its majority stake at least until 2000. Even after another primary offering, a secondary offering of German government stock, and a stock acquisition of a major U.S. firm (VoiceStream Wireless), the government owned 43 percent (as of year end 2001). The supervisory board was designated with five-year terms in 1995; virtually the entire board was recently reelected for another set of five-year terms. It takes a 75 percent shareholder vote to remove a supervisory board member, meaning the government has a veto over removal. This means that, as a practical matter, Deutsche Telekom is protected from a hostile takeover bid. Moreover, the initial public offering was sold as much on its risk-avoidance steadiness as on the risk-taking upside. As noted above, the company virtually promised a high dividend payout that would be comparable to a bond yield.

Nevertheless the Deutsche Telekom privatization was a turning point (if not necessarily an irreversible one) because it demonstrated that it was possible to raise large amounts of equity capital from German retail investors. The promotional effort succeeded in its most ambitious project: to sell to the

German public the idea of stock market-investing generally, not just the T-share in particular. It achieved a necessary precondition for the development of shareholder capitalism because it showed the potential benefit of institutional change: access to large amounts of capital, no strings attached. The availability of public equity capital demonstrated by the Deutsche Telekom transaction fit well with a corresponding change in the availability of public debt via the growth of public bond markets in Germany, and then, after EMU, the explosive growth of a European bond market. Insider governance lost its privileged position in the supply of outside capital.[13]

The Deutsche Telekom transaction also changed the politics of shareholder capitalism in Germany. It added at least a half-million people to the German shareholder rolls and, even more important, heightened the saliency of shareholder value and shareholder protection. An idea that had been held by certain business and academic elites was transformed into an element of popular understanding. Moreover, the transaction gave the German government a direct interest in public shareholder protection. Much as the "entrepreneur" in the classic Jensen and Meckling account of agency costs, the government bore the costs of the corporate governance arrangements. The market price of the initial and subsequent offerings of Deutsche Telekom stock (including the government's secondary offerings) would reflect (with an appropriate discount rate) the public shareholder protections that would apply after the government lost its control position. Thus the government came to have a distinct budgetary interest in better protection of public shareholders.

Evidence for the impact of the Deutsche Telekom privatization on the rise of shareholder capitalism is found in a number of places: the supply side and demand side for equity capital, institutional changes that facilitated public offerings (most particularly the Neuer Markt), changes in the legal infrastructure of public shareholder protection, and, perhaps most dramatically, the change in the response to hostile takeover activity, as reflected in the widespread belief that the outcome of the Vodafone hostile bid for Mannesmann was a question of shareholder choice.

1. *Quantitative Evidence on Supply and Demand of Equity Capital.* Review the previously presented empirical evidence on corporate convergence in Germany over the 1990s. In almost every case there is a kink in the curve after 1996. The number of IPOs and amount raised as a percentage of GDP increased markedly after 1996 (tables 7.1 and 7.2 above). The accretions of household public equity assets (graphs 7.1 and 7.2 above), the num-

ber of shareholders in public companies (tables 7.2 and 7.5), the very existence of stock mutual funds (table 7.3)—these indicators too took a sharp upward turn after 1996. The most vivid evidence of change is the post-1996 shift in the ratio of stock market capitalization to GDP in Germany vs. the UK (graph 7.4). The ratio is essentially unchanged early in the 1990s; the sharp upward turn after 1996 reflects a German catch-up. There were undoubtedly many other codeterminants of these trends, but the timing of the changes does suggest the importance of the Telekom public offering.

2. *The Launch and Flourishing of the Neuer Markt.* The Neuer Markt was established by the Deutsche Börse in 1997 as a NASDAQ competitor in the launch of initial public offerings for high technology companies of minimal seasoning. The main "official" exchange of the Deutsche Börse was a notoriously inhospitable place for initial public offerings, because of listing rules that required several years of profits and other signs of financial soundness. In offering a home for "young growth companies" the Neuer Markt substituted disclosure and transparency for seasoning. For example, its rules required an issuing prospectus on an international standard, IAS or GAAP accounting standards, and periodic reporting, quarterly and annually, also on an international standard.

The Neuer Markt was very successful, especially in light of the prior German history. It opened for business in March 1997 and the pace of IPOs rapidly increased, from 13 in 1997, to 43 in 1998, reaching 133 in 1999, and 139 in 2000. As of 2001, more than 340 companies were listed on the Neuer Markt, 56 of them headquartered outside of Germany. Unlike the "official" market, individual investors were especially vigorous market participants, owning approximately 50 percent of the free float of listed companies.[14]

The impetus behind the Neuer Markt may have come from Germany's concern about Silicon Valley, but this turn to shareholder capitalism might not have been possible without the prior Deutsche Telekom transaction. The creation and ultimate success of a German market for high-tech IPOs depended on equity investor demand and liquidity, which in turn depended on the participation of retail investors. Neither industrial companies nor financial institutions were likely to buy significant shares for their own account (since these startup firms were certainly not going to be governed on the insider model). Unlike the U.S., Germany had no cash rich pension funds. Thus retail demand, either through mutual funds or direct purchases, was going to be crucial, and while the Deutsche Börse worked very hard to attract foreign market participants, a high level of German participation would be essential. The Deutsche Telekom transaction proved that Germans would buy stock and, in the huge marketing push, it persuaded many Germans that equities were a legitimate part of an investment portfolio. Undoubtedly the appreciation in the DAX and the by-then famous appreciation of the NASDAQ index played a critical role in the successful launch of the Neuer Markt, but the prior success of the Telekom IPO was a powerful reassurance.

3. *Legal Reform.* Following the Telekom transaction, there were a number of reforms that added to public shareholder protection and increased the exposure of public firms to capital market pressures. The most important of these changes was the 1998 Act on Control and Transparency of Enterprises (KonTraG).[15] The legislation was adopted in response to a number of high-visibility monitoring failures by supervisory boards, in particular, instances of apparent negligence by "hausbank" representatives on supervisory boards. The legislation was also designed to cut back the traditional bank influence over the proxy system of dispersed public companies and to limit various antitakeover strategies at German firms. In particular, the Act strengthened the monitoring capacity and responsibility of the supervisory board, limited the voting prerogatives of a bank that owns more than 5 percent of the shares of a particular firm, and prohibited creation of super-voting stock or caps on voting rights, which protected public shareholders by restricting the separation of voting rights from cash flow rights.

Passage of the Act seems strongly influenced by the Telekom IPO. The reform package had been first presented in 1994 in response to an emerging consensus about the weakness of the governance system for public companies, underscored by dissatisfaction expressed by international institutional investors. But managers were unhappy with the governance interventions and in particular the limits on a favorite antitakeover protection of capped voting. The banks also resisted the cutback in their influence. The Telekom IPO changed the dynamic in two ways. First, the government would obtain immediate budgetary benefits from corporate law that better protected public shareholders. It was then planning to sell a significant part of its stake in Telekom to the KfW, a government affiliate, to help achieve the budget deficit targets that were a precondition for joining the EMU, and, like any selling shareholder, wanted to book the highest possible sale price. Like the classic entrepreneur, it bore the cost of governance arrangements. Second, the popular mobilization on behalf of shareholder capitalism associated with the Telekom transaction significantly added to the urgency of the legislation and its popular appeal. Public shareholder protection became a populist cry and a political winner.

4. *The Acceptance of Vodafone's Hostile Bid for Mannesmann.* Perhaps the most visible evidence of a shift toward shareholder capitalism in Germany in the course of the 1990s was the change in public and elite response to hostile takeover bids: away from shock, even horror, at the disruption of established relationships toward grudging acceptance of shareholder choice. This evolution is vividly illustrated by the contrasting outcomes of Pirelli's failed bid for Continental in 1991 and Vodafone's successful bid for Mannesmann in 1999. In both cases, the hostile bidder was a foreign raider; in both cases the target was embedded in the German industrial establishment. If anything, the Vodafone bid was much brasher, since the UK bidder was an upstart (founded in 1985) and the German target, founded almost 100 years earlier, exemplified German industrial prowess as well as economic adaptability. Moreover, the size of the transaction, $180 billion, and the acceptance of acquiror's stock as consideration, suggested that size didn't matter when it came to takeover protection. Thus the takeover of Mannesmann, apparently the first successful hostile tender offer for control of a German public corporation, both reflected a transformation and may hasten a further one.

Continental/Pirelli. In September 1990 Pirelli, the Italian tire manufacturer approached the German tire manufacturer Continental with what Americans would call a "bear hug."[16] The overture was ostensibly friendly. Pirelli and Continental were the fourth and fifth largest tire manufacturers in the world, each with about an 8 percent market share and each with significant production in Europe and North America. Significant overcapacity in the worldwide tire industry made a compelling case for economic rationalization and consolidation. But Pirelli said its offer was backed by a "support group" of German and Italian investors that held more than 50 percent of Continental's stock, and so the overture carried the implied threat of action against managerial resistance. As a precondition to negotiations, Continental's management insisted on a standstill agreement, which Pirelli rejected. Continental then deemed the offer "hostile."

The details of the ensuing financial and legal battle boiled down to this: Deutsche Bank organized a "blocking coalition" of the German industrial establishment (including Allianz, Deutsche Bank, Dresdner Bank, BMW, Volkswagen, and Daimler Benz) that successfully thwarted the Pirelli bid. As the Economist put it, "Corporate Governance in Germany: Our Crowd" (The Economist 1991: 66).[17]

Mannesmann/Vodafone. The Vodafone takeover bid of Mannesmann, although like the Pirelli bid for Continental a cross-border hostile bid, proceeded to an entirely different conclusion. Mannesmann management pursued no preclusive defensive measures, sought no defensive blockbuilding by industrial or financial allies, and turned down political help that might have been forthcoming. Instead, it argued the merits of its strategy against the Vodafone alternative, an argument pitched to its shareholders and the equity markets. Its capitulation came when it became clear that Mannesmann's shareholders found Vodafone's offer economically compelling.

Mannesmann, founded in 1890 as a manufacturer of metal tubes, had by the late 1990s morphed into one of Europe's largest telecommunications companies. Vodafone's hostile bid, launched in November 1999, arose from a fierce competition to establish a pan-European telecommunications network. The takeover battle was fought on the public stage, a war of dueling CEOs arguing for public shareholder support, since Mannesmann's ownership was genuinely dispersed. Pivotally, however, the CEOs were on the same side of another argument: that hostile bids were not inherently illegitimate and that the ultimate decision was for the shareholders.

Much had changed in Germany since the failed Continental bid, especially in the post-Telekom privatization period. Telekom itself had raised another $11 billion in a primary offering. The Neuer Markt had taken off. Perhaps most important in practical terms, German firms had been acquirors in high visibility transnational takeovers of British firms: Rolls Royce (VW), Rover (BMW) and Orange (Mannesmann); U.S. firms: Bankers Trust (Deutsche Bank) and Chrysler (Daimler); even Italian firms: Omnitel, Infostrada (Mannesmann). German firms had also suffered from the nationalist policies of others, for example, Deutsche Telekom's thwarted bid for Telecom Italia.

Thus, perhaps surprisingly, there seemed to be relatively little political traction in opposing the takeover bid. Indeed, Chancellor Schröder's efforts to intervene were met with harsh criticism. He was initially quoted as indicating that the market should decide: "Whoever wants to buy a British company—like Mannesmann with Orange—can't say: We're allowed, but they're not" (Boston 1999). But then in apparent response to pressure from SPD party leaders, he began tacking in opposition: "Hostile takeovers destroy an enterprise's culture. They harm the target, but also, in the medium-term, the predator itself." He played the nationalism card: "I much prefer Franco-German cooperation because it is friendly" (Wall St. J. 1999:

A18). But his comments ignited a storm of criticism in Germany, England, and elsewhere, and ultimately played no role in the transaction.

In sum, the Deutsche Telekom privatization played an important, even crucial role in the evolution of shareholder capitalism in Germany. Yet efficiency considerations, while important, were not the catalyst for the transaction. Rather, it was the decision of the German government to pursue transnational economic and political integration. A sale was virtually compelled by the EU telecommunications policy—a policy that the German government itself had helped create. Having decided to sell, the government wanted to receive full value, which in turn required a large public offering and the fostering of ancillary legal and cultural institutions that would support the features of shareholder capitalism. It would be wrong to overstate the extent to which the German corporate model has converged on shareholder capitalism. Yet convergence trends are reflected in undeniable post-1996 changes, and they owe much to decisions taken on the international relations dimension.

III. The Collapse of the 13th Directive and Germany's New Stance on Target Defenses

The second example of the way international relations decisions affect corporate convergence points in the opposite direction: how Germany's pursuit of transnational integration led it away from a convergence strategy in its rejection of the 13th Company Law Directive and its new stance on target defensive tactics.

A. The Collapse of the 13th Directive

The 13th Directive was a proposal for EU-wide regulation of some of the critical terms of takeover bids, requiring particularly that a shareholder acquiring control make a "mandatory bid" for the remaining shares and prohibiting board efforts to "frustrate" a hostile bid through defensive measures undertaken without shareholder approval. The 13th Directive would thus lead to a board neutrality/shareholder choice regime to govern hostile bids throughout the EU. By summer 2000, when it came up for final vote, the 13th Directive had proceeded through more than a decade's gestation and

Germany had been one of the proposal's staunchest and most constant supporters.

But the world had changed for corporate Germany: Vodafone had just successfully completed its hostile takeover of Mannesmann, after an Anglo-American style hostile tender offer. The 1998 corporate law reforms eliminated many important takeover barriers from the German corporate code. Moreover, in December 1999 the German government made a surprise proposal to repeal the capital gains tax on shareholdings of corporations. The repealer, adopted in July 2000 and effective as of January 1, 2002, would make it possible for firms to dispose of their substantial cross-holdings (approximately 15 percent of German stock market capitalization) without a ruinous tax penalty (an estimated 52 percent rate on realized gains). Indeed, many believed that the high tax rate had artificially locked in the web of corporate cross-holdings that characterized the German political economy. Regardless of the past role of the insider stakes, many financial firms wanted to dispose of their corporate holdings, invested capital on which they earned a substandard rate of return, in order to reposition themselves for competition in the global economy. Deutsche Bank, for example, had already spun off its corporate holdings into a separate subsidiary in anticipation of a selloff or spinoff. Law firms rushed to staff up for what was anticipated to be a "big bang" of merger and restructuring activity in Germany beginning in 2002.

Germany had moved profoundly toward shareholder capitalism. The upshot of Vodafone/Mannesmann seemed to be that a hostile takeover bid, even for the largest firms, was for the shareholders to resolve. The consequence of the tax law change was that the state would no longer provide an artificial barrier to the unwinding of inefficient control positions. Perhaps corporate blockholders would merely reshuffle the cards among themselves in the traditional German pattern of transactions in control, but after the successful hostile tender offer in Vodafone, the door was now open to genuine outsider bids, including foreign bids. If the banks were refashioning themselves as investment banks and the corporate blockholders were sellers at the right price, then the complementarities that sustained concentrated ownership would disappear and a new form of ownership structure would emerge. German managers and unions were obviously concerned about these various possibilities, which would disturb existing economic and political settlements. The board neutrality position of the 13th Directive thus became the center of an intense lobbying effort to persuade the government to oppose the entire directive. A particularly effective supplicant was Ferdinand Piech, the CEO of Volkswagen, whose supervisory board was once chaired by Chancellor Schröder. (Recall that Schröder was also once prime minister of Lower Saxony, which held a 20 percent VW stake.)

But there was a separate concern, which could not be dismissed as mere self-seeking protectionism: the "level playing field" problem. At the same time that the European Parliament was in its final deliberations on the 13th Directive, the EU Advocat General issued a surprising blanket rejection of several actions brought by the European Commission before the European Court of Justice against "golden shares" held by member countries that protected privatized former SOEs (Financial Times 2001).[18] The Commission had contended that golden shares, which give governments veto rights over significant share acquisitions, recapitalizations, takeovers, and other fundamental transactions in privatized companies, violated the EU rules and treaties on competition policy and the free movement of capital. The Advocat General's opinion (which did not bind the ECJ but which is ordinarily persuasive) sustained Portugal's requirement of ministerial approval for a 10 percent stock acquisition in any privatized company, France's requirement for ministerial approval of a stock acquisition above a certain threshold in Elf Aquitaine, the oil company, and Belgium's requirement of ministerial approval, on a national interest test, of an acquisition of a significant stake in the Société Nationale de Transport par Canalisations, a transportation utility.[19]

Countries like France, Italy, and Spain, had undertaken large-scale privatizations of SOEs in the 1990s and retained golden shares in some of the most substantial enterprises in the country.[20] By contrast, Germany's privatization program was relatively small (except for Deutsche Telekom) because the level of prior state ownership was much less, and, as to the privatized firms, Germany did not retain a golden share. Thus Germany faced a situation in which large acquisitive enterprises might pursue hostile cross-border acquisitions of German firms, secure in the knowledge that they were shielded from countermeasures by the golden shares. Moreover, on occasion SOEs, totally protected from a takeover bid, had pursued cross-border acquisitions.

The importance of cross-border mergers to the integration of the European economy and ultimately its political economy was well understood. The single market called out for firms large enough to achieve appropriate scale economies. It was foreseeable that this might entail the consolidation of facilities or divestments or downsizings, which might mean that a given firm would direct resources to one particular country, and away from another, despite the origins of the constituent firms. As I argued above, the risk to the project of economic and political integration is economic nationalism, mercantilism redux in the making of those resource allocation decisions. Economic geography matters. It would quickly become intolerable if French acquirors (for example) of German targets began to shift facilities and resources to French venues in response to explicit or implicit direction of the French government, to bolster French jobs at the expense of German jobs. Yet this was the threat of the golden shares.

Mutual vulnerability in the market for corporate control was important protection against nationalist behavior. An inefficient diversion of resources to France would be punished in the capital market—which cares about cash flow not favor curried with the Minister—and would send a signal to a control entrepreneur. The behavior of the management would be appropriately constrained. But this feedback system would be at serious risk in the case of a firm in which France retained a golden share. In other words, a golden share interferes with the mutual vulnerability that assures the credibility of the non-national basis for resource allocation.

The point was more general. Golden shares exemplified the wide ranging problem of national law (voting caps, for instance) that protected the control position of national economic elites who were susceptible to entreaties and expectations about favoritism on national grounds. Even if the French government was not a shareholder it might be tempted to exert nationalist pressure on controlling shareholders or perhaps intercede with managers in the diffusely held firm. It is the mutual vulnerability to the market for corporate control that checks those tendencies. Thus, local takeover protection, which is hardly limited to golden shares, may encourage and sustain the economic nationalism that disrupts economic and political integration.

Thus the "level playing field" objection was the special concern that now drove German resistance to the 13th Directive, which it had strongly advocated over the prior decade (Meller 2001a).[21] In other words, the standard story of private rent-seeking by managers and unions does not do justice to the other compelling issue at stake: the prospects for economic and political integration.

The unexpected Advocat General opinions on golden shares came down on July 2. The European Parliament took up the 13th Directive almost immediately thereafter. It failed on a tie vote, 273–273, on July 4, 2001; the German members were crucial swing voters.

B. Germany's New Takeover Law

Even before the final vote on the 13th Directive, Germany moved to adopt a law regulating takeovers. It had previously operated without one, relying instead on a voluntary Takeover Code (*Übernahmenkodex*) adopted in 1995 based on the English City Code. As of 1997 approximately 80 percent of the DAX 30 companies but only 60 percent of the MDAX companies had agreed to comply (see Baumann 1998: 659–65). Foreign offerors, however, rarely tied themselves to the Code and there was no enforcement machinery (see generally Kirchner and Painter 2002). The Mannesmann transaction and the prospect of bids stimulated by the unwinding of blockholdings after the tax law change put takeover legislation on the agenda.

In many respects the initially proposed legislation tracked the 13th Directive in its then current form, adding additional protection for workers, and, more controversially, confining the making of exchange offers to companies that listed on a European exchange. The May 2000 draft also contained the provision that Germany was then pushing for in the Directive, namely, permission for pre-bid shareholder authorization of defensive measures.

In draft legislation as of October 2001, the exceptions to board neutrality were relatively narrow. In addition to actions that a "prudent and diligent manager" would otherwise take, or a search for a competing bid (a "white knight"), management could employ only those particular defensive measures that had obtained shareholder approval *prior* to the announcement of the bid, and only to the extent that the specific measures had been authorized by a vote of at least 75 percent of the share capital. The authorization period was limited to eighteen months.[22] Lightning struck. In a draft of November 8, 2001, from the government's public finance committee, a remarkable addition to management board authority appeared: *"actions which have been approved by the target's supervisory board."*[23] In other words, the supervisory board is to be empowered to approve target defensive measures without any shareholder approval whatsoever. This appears to eliminate the general shareholder veto as well as the shareholder veto over particular defensive measures. The supervisory board is well insulated from pressures that might produce independent scrutiny of the requested defensive measures on behalf of shareholder interests. Recall that half the members of the supervisory board are employee representatives and that even shareholder representatives are elected for five-year terms, removable only upon a 75 percent shareholder vote. The actions of the supervisory boards are subject to the usual fiduciary duties under German company law of care and responsibility in acting in the company's best interest, but Germany does not have a robust tradition of judicial review of board action, certainly not in the quick-paced timeframe of a contested bid, nor does it permit contingent-fee litigation, which has policed fiduciary duty compliance in the United States. The new legislation, effective January 2002, may well unleash a broad range of target defensive measures in contested takeover bids in Germany. There is at least one important exception: the protection of preemptive rights under German company law (and the EU Second Company Law Directive) will almost certainly rule out a U.S.-style poison pill, which depends upon the discriminatory allocation and exercise of share rights.[24]

One way to understand Germany's protectionist move in the Takeover Act is as frustrated response to the 13th Directive's failure to promote adequate European-wide takeover regulation, in particular the failure to address the level playing field problem. The Takeover Act can be seen as a move in a trade negotiation, an example of "aggressive reciprocity." When trading partners fail to lower barriers, one response is to raise your own. This move, which imposes costs on partners as well as oneself, may stimulate a negotiation to achieve the first best cooperative outcome, a mutual lowering of barriers. In the context of cross-border mergers, the way for Germany to promote its objective of economic and political integration, and its strategy of mutual vulnerability to control transactions, is to raise its barriers. This is what added takeover protection does: in permitting new target defense measures it raises the barriers to obtaining control of German-based firms. Such a move makes hostile transactions—both entirely domestic and cross-border—more difficult, and in that sense may be seen as a step away from shareholder capitalism. So in this context the desire for economic and political integration slows down the move to shareholder capitalism.

The standard rent protection and domestic interest group stories told by convergence skeptics are undoubtedly a significant contributor to Germany's anti-takeover move, and represent to that extent a resistance to shareholder capitalism on the Anglo-American model. But there is an important additional element that may be pivotal. The ambition for transnational economic and political integration is shaping Germany's attitudes to shareholder capitalism, for the most part toward convergence but here, crucially, a move away. Ultimately it may be that Germany's aggressive reciprocity evokes a cooperative response, a joint move toward easier cross-border bids. But the attainment of that first-best outcome may not be possible in light of the political economy of Germany's partners. The result may be a degenerate equilibrium of increasing takeover protection and more economic nationalism. In effect, the trade negotiation may fail, leaving trade war in its wake. Member states may also understand the economic and political integration that shareholder capitalism will bring, and may resist it for precisely that reason. The point is that the divergence away from shareholder capitalism, much like the convergence in the wake of the Deutsche Telekom privatization, needs telling not just in the terms of the standard stories of efficiency and politics, but as part of a country's international aspirations, its conscious effort to pursue (or avoid) a greater sense of union with its neighbors.

Conclusion

This essay has tried to insert a "wedge" into the customary debate about convergence, in particular the importance of the supranational impulse. This concern may run quite differently from more traditional expressions of efficiency concerns and domestic politics. The power of this impulse and its potential to push toward a convergence on shareholder capitalism is made manifest by the European Commission's latest effort to revive the 13th Directive. As part of the Parliamentary debate, the Commission agreed to convene a "High Level Group of Company Law Experts" to address some of the open issues, in particular, the level playing field concerns that ultimately proved fatal to the Directive. That Group issued the Report of the High Level Group of Company Law Experts on Issues Related to Takeover Bids in January 2002. It is a bold proclamation on behalf of European economic integration, the role that shareholder capitalism plays in its achievement, and the importance of eliminating national barriers to control transactions.

The Report states:

> An important goal of the European Union is to create an integrated capital market in the Union by 2005. The regulation of takeover bids is a key element of such an integrated market.
>
> Many European companies will need to grow to an optimal scale to make effective use of the integrating internal market. . . . Takeover bids are a means to achieve this for those engaged in business of both bidder and target.

Takeover barriers existing in various Member States more often tend to result in control over listed companies being uncontestable. . . . this is undesirable in the European context [even if done in the U.S.], as an integrated capital market has to be built up in order for business to fully benefit from and make effective use of the integrating internal market in Europe (Report of the High Level Group of Company Law Experts 2002: 18, 19, 41).

In order to render this objective operational, the Report calls for a new directive that reaffirms the importance of board neutrality and shareholder choice. But its crucial move is to call for the overcoming of golden shares and most other barriers to control via a novel "breakthrough" provision that lets holders of a majority or required supermajority (but in no event more than 75 percent) of cash flow rights to take over the firm. The Report summarizes its conclusions in this area as follows:

Companies will be required to disclose complete information about their capital and control structures. . . . After announcement of the bid, the board of the offeree company should not be permitted to take actions frustrating a takeover bid on the basis of a general meeting authorisation given prior to the bid. . . . A rule should be introduced which allows the offeror to break-through mechanisms and structures which may frustrate a bid . . . in the case of a takeover bid which achieves such a measure of success as clearly to justify this [but not more than] 75% of the risk bearing capital of the company on the date of the completion of the bid. . . . Provisions in the articles of association and other constitutional documents deviating from the principles of shareholder decisionmaking and proportionality between risk bearing capital and control shall be overridden (ibid.: 42–43).

If implemented, such a program would substantially increase the control contestability of corporations in the EU. It would work a revolution in EU corporate governance and a revolution in much else besides. So Germany's "aggressive reciprocity" in rejecting the prior draft of the 13th Directive and its adoption of a Takeover Law with raised takeover defenses has been perhaps a catalytic event. It has led to a call for a much more powerful directive that would use the market in control—shareholder capitalism in its most direct form—as the vehicle for economic and political integration.

Endnotes

This chapter draws from a longer work, "Corporate Convergence and Supranationalism: The Evolution of German Shareholder Capitalism, 1990–2000," available on SSRN, which documents many of the factual assertions in this chapter. I appreciate comments on earlier drafts from Mathias Baudisch, Theodor Baums, Zohar Goshen, Ed Iacobucci, and Peter Mülbert and the research assistance of Sven Hodges, Wulf Kaal, and Virginia Tent.

1. One candidate would be the privatization of SOEs, which accounted for a much larger share of the economy in many other EU countries (e.g., France, Italy, Spain) and whose impact in jump-starting a shareholder culture was significant (see generally Megginson and Netter 2001; Boutchkova and Megginson 2000).
2. See Karnitschnig and Rhoads (2002). Moreover, problems in policing disclosure violations in the Neuer Markt have led to the folding of that exchange into the main Frankfurt markets. See note 14 below.
3. 93/C 213/01, OJ C 213/1, 06.08.1993. There were certain transition periods of 2 or 5 years for certain smaller states.
4. Gesetz zur Neustrucktierung des Post und Fernmeldewesens und der Deutschen Bundespost (Postruckturgetsetz) (PostStrukturG), vom 08.06.1989, BGBl.I/1989, S. 1026 ff; vgl. Buchner, JA 1990, 194 ff; Hermann, ZPT 9/1991, 8 ff. The stated objectives of Post Reform I were: The promotion of competition in the telecommunications market by introducing new regulatory conditions, and a restructuring of the Deutsche Bundespost by separating the sovereign from the entrepreneurial tasks and by implementing a market-oriented business organization to ensure that it can fulfill the infrastructure obligations and improve its performance in competitive markets.
5. Postneuordnungsgesetz (PTNeuOG) vom 14.09.1994, BGBl, I/1994, S. 2325 ff.
6. For a useful summary of some of the politics of Germany's path to telecommunications liberalization, see Naik and Boston (1999).
7. Some of this follows Gordon (1999).
8. For a comparison of venture capital markets in the U.S. and Germany, see Black and Gilson (1998: 246–52).
9. Psychoanalyst Wolfgang Schmidbauer's article traces the campaign for German shareholding back to Adenauer's plan against communism—class warriors should become economic citizens of a real economic democracy. Schmidbauer asserts that Germans never had healthy stock markets like the French and the British in the nineteenth century and that Hitler fueled anti-Semitism with

claims that Jewish capitalists undermined the economy. Schmidbauer adds that the Depression and the two lost wars compounded this fear of risk.

10. "Telekom's offering is only months away and despite lots of advertising, there is still not enough deciding information. It's time for the image campaign to turn into an information campaign. People should care a lot about the future of the telecoms market, the result of layoffs in productivity, and the future position of Deutsche Telekom in the national and international markets. So far, T does not stand for transparency" (FAZ 1996: 15; Virginia Tent, trans.).

11. German banks are "universal banks," meaning that unlike U.S. banks of the time, they could directly underwrite securities.

12. Deutsche Telekom Prospectus (1996: 13).

13. A monopoly on debt finance provided insider financial institutions with a conduit for rents that justified the monitoring expenses of the insider system. The greater development of public debt markets gave managers the means to "cheat"—i.e., to obtain market rate capital—and to work free of the double threat behind insider monitoring: not only trouble in the board room but in corporate finance as well. In turn, the banks have turned from a "hausbank" to an "investment bank" model and have been lessening their traditional company ties. Deutsche Bank, for example, reduced its supervisory board seats from 29 to 17 over the 1996–98 period and helped Krupp in its hostile takeover bid for Thyssen (on whose supervisory board it sat) (Hoepner 2001).

14. An account of the Neuer Markt as evidence of the change in German shareholder culture in the 1990s would be incomplete without discussion of the Neuer Markt's problems and the September 2002 decision of the Deutche Börse to shut it down by year end 2003. Instead, the Börse will create a technology segment for its main market, based on disclosure requirements similar to the Neuer Markt (though supported by a better enforcement regime), and a technology-focused index.

The Neuer Markt had come under sharp criticism not only because of the sharp decline in share values over 2000–2002, but also because of price volatility, which led to allegations of price manipulation, and cases of outright fraud in publicly issued financial reports. Characteristically for a market which gained credibility through high-quality listing standards, the interested parties initially pursued tightening the standards. Subsequent commentary focused particularly on enforcement mechanisms, in light of the importance of credibly accurate and honest disclosure in investor evaluation of unseasoned companies. The absence of an omnibus antifraud provision like Section 10b of the 1934 Securities Exchange Act and the ambiguous legal status of disclosures filed under private listing standards created an enforcement deficit. This enforcement question was addressed by the enactment in 2002 of the Fourth Financial Markets Promotion Act, which gives the Börse the delegated power to put its listing requirements—including the elements of a high-quality disclosure regime—into public law, an improvement in enforceability that should enhance investor confidence.

The Börse will use its new power to create a "Prime Standard" segment of its market based on extensive disclosure on the international standard that will include most of the significant firms now traded on the main exchange as well as the Neuer Markt companies which will be included in the technology segment. The new segment preserves the Neuer Markt's general strategy but replaces the Neuer Markt as a listing and trading venue in recognition of the Neuer Markt's credibility problems. More important than the demise of the Neuer Markt is the persistence and spread of its disclosure-based listing strategy, and the augmentation of private efforts to create a high-quality disclosure regime with a public enforcement backstop. These are both important elements in drawing and creating conditions for the development of public equity markets and ultimately to the spread of diffusely owned firms.

15. Gesetz zur Kontrolle und Transparenz im Unternehmensbereich, Bundesgesetzblatt I vom. 30.04.1998, 786 ff; see also Baums (1998).

16. This account draws from Baums (1993). See also Jenkinson and Ljungqvist (2001: Appendix).

17. After identifying other situations of aggressive tactics in the German mergers market, the Economist concluded: "Foreigners can win control of German firms, but usually only when the target company is in trouble and when no leading German firm objects to the acquisition. . . . But when Germans decide a national asset is at stake, and the old-boy network starts buzzing, a foreign buyer's chance of victory is almost always low" (The Economist 1991: 66).

18. The action was particularly a surprise because of a May 2000 decision of the European Court of Justice, which struck down golden shares maintained by Italy in Telecom Italia and ENI. For more information on EU Advocat General's opinion, see Opinion of Advocat General Ruiz-Jarabo Colomer, Cases C-367/98, C-483/99, C-503/99 and Morris and Galbraith (2000) (includes an English translation of opinion).

19. Ironically, a year later the ECJ rejected the Advocat's advice in a series of decisions that viewed golden shares as presumptively restricting the free movement of capital and thus requiring a demonstration of a precisely tailored scheme for the national interest to be protected. The Court rejected both Portugal's and France's laws while sustaining Belgium's (see Commission v. France 2002; Commission v. Portugal 2002; Commission v. Belgium 2002).

20. A large percentage of share issuance in the EU is a consequence of privatization of SOE's, in which governments often retain a significant ownership stake (Jones et al. 1999). For example, in the case of France, four large privatized companies (France Telecom, TotalFina, STMicr, and BNP) account for 20

percent of the market capitalization of the Paris Bourse. In Italy, the comparable figure for the Rome exchange is 36 percent (TI, TIM, ENEL, ENI) (See
Megginson and Netter 2001: table 11, using firms in the Global 1000).

21. See also Meller (2001b), quoting Lehne as saying the directive "would not produce a level playing field for cross-border investment, it would create a complete
imbalance in Europe." Germany wanted the board neutrality provision amended
to permit boards to get blanket authority from shareholders good for up to five
years for target defenses, i.e., eliminating the need to put specific defenses for a
specific bid to shareholder vote. A spokesperson noted the various protective provisions in other national laws, singling out golden parachute provisions. "This is a
level-playing-field argument in favor of the German government's new position."
Indeed, the "Daily Notebook" of the European Parliament for July 4, 2001,
describes the defeat of the 13th Directive in these terms: "Parliament has therefore in effect followed the recommendation made by its rapporteur Klaus-
Heiner Lehne (EPP-ED, D), who opposed the conciliation agreement mainly
on the grounds that the requirement for the board of a company which is the
object of a takeover bid to refrain from taking defensive action until it has consulted its shareholders could only be justified if a 'level playing field' existed.
Since, according to Mr. Lehne, there is no level playing field either at [the]
international or European level and the joint text resulting from the Conciliation committee did not resolve this problem, he argued that the conciliation
agreement should be rejected" (Europarl Daily Notebook 04–07–2001).

22. Draft of a Bill on the Regulation of Public Offers for the Acquisition of Securities and the Regulation of Takeovers (Wertpapiererwerbs-und Übernahmegesetz—WpÜG) (Cleary Gottlieb Steen and Hamilton transl.) (Section 33).

23. Section 33(1) (Thaeter and Frederick transl.). So Sec. 33(1) reads: "After
announcement of a decision to make an offer, up to the publication of the
results of the offer, the management board may take no actions that could frustrate the offer. This does not apply [to certain actions] . . . as well as for actions
which have been approved by the target's supervisory board."

24. German law requires a 75 percent vote for the limitation of preemptive rights
[AktG §186(4)] and requires an explicit written explanation before the share-
holder vote. A poison pill has rarely, if ever, been put to shareholder vote in the
U.S. principally on the belief that the shareholders would reject it.

References

Ascarelli, Sylvia. 1996. IPO Campaign Aims To Dip Into Pockets Of German Savers;
Deutsche Telekom Will Offer Toll-Free Line, Brochures To Snag Private
Investors. *Wall Street Journal*, March 22, 1996. Available on Westlaw at 1996
WL-WSJ 3095874.

Baumann, Karl-Herman. 1998. Takeovers in Germany and EU: Regulation, Experience and Practice. In *Comparative Corporate Governance: The State of the Art and Emerging Research*. Klaus Hopt et al., eds. Oxford, U.K.: Clarendon Press; New York: Oxford University Press.

Baums, Theodor. 1993. Hostile Takeovers in Germany: A Case Study on Pirelli vs. Continental A.G., Univ. of Osnabrück, WP 3/93 (May 1993). Available at http://www.jura.uni-osnabrueck.de/institut/hwr/arbeitsp.htm.

——. 1998. Corporate Governance in Germany—System and Current Developments. Univ. of Osnabruck, WP (1998). Available at http://www.uni-rankfurt.de/fb01/baums.

Bebchuk, Lucian and Mark. J. Roe. 1999. A Theory of Path Dependence in Corporate Ownership and Governance. *Stanford Law Review* 52: 127–70.

Black, Bernard S. and Ronald J. Gilson. 1998. Venture Capital and the Structure of Capital Markets: Banks versus Stock Markets. *Journal of Financial Economics* 47: 243–77.

Boeker, Alexander. 1996. Süddeutsche Zeitung (SZ), Oct. 28, 1996, Muenchen section. (Virginia Tent transl.).

Boston, William. 1999. Hostile Deal Could Breach German Resistance—Mannesmann Has Weapons In Vodafone Contest, But Others Hang Back. *Wall Street Journal*, Nov. 17, 1999, p. A 17. Available on Westlaw at WL-WSJ 24922274.

Boutchkova, Maria and William Megginson. 2000. Privatization and the Rise of Global Capital Markets, FEEM WP 53 (July 2000).

Commission v. Belgium, C-503/99 (June 4, 2002).

Commission v. France, C-483/99 (June 4, 2002).

Commission v. Portugal, C-367/98 (June 4, 2002).

Corporate Money. 1997. Banks Bow to Price Pressure. January 29, 1997. Available on Westlaw at 1997 WL 9405629.

Curwen, Peter J. 1997. *Restructuring Telecommunications: A Study of Europe in a Global Context*. New York: St. Martin's Press.

Deutsche Aktien Institut (DAI) Factbook, April 2001.

Deutsche Bundesbank, Financial Accounts for Germany, 1991–2000 (Special Statistical Publication No. 4) September 2001.

Deutsche Telekom Prospectus for the Offering of 85,000,000 Ordinary Shares in the form of American Depository Shares, November 17, 1996

Draft of a Bill on the Regulation of Public Offers for the Acquisition of Securities and the Regulation of Takeovers (Wertpapiererwerbs-und Übernahmegesetz—WpÜG) (Cleary Gottlieb Steen and Hamilton transl.).

Draft of a Bill on the Regulation of Public Offers for the Acquisition of Securities and the Regulation of Takeovers (November 8, 2001) (Wertpapiererwerbs-und Übernahmegesetz—WpÜG) (Cleary Gottlieb Steen and Hamilton transl.) (Thaeter and Frederick transl.).

The Economist. 1991. Corporate Governance in Germany: Our Crowd. Feb. 23, 1991.

Europarl Daily Notebook: 04–07–2001. Available at www.europarl.eu.int/press /index_publi_en.htm (follow links under Daily Notebook).

European Commission 1987. Towards a Dynamic European Economy—Green Paper on the Development of the Common Market for Telecommunications Services and Equipment. Report COM 87(290 final).

Federation of European Stock Exchanges. 2001. Market Statistics.

Financial Times. 2001. EU Advocat General Would Allow 'Golden Shares,' July 3, 2001.

Focus Magazin. 1996. Telekom-shares: A People Agrees. No. 24, June 10, 1996, p. 180 (Virginia Tent transl.).

Frankfurter Allegemaine Zeitung (FAZ) 1996. T as in Transparency. June 18, 1996, p. 15 (editorial).

Gesetz zur Kontrolle und Transparenz im Unternehmensbereich, Bundesgesetzblatt I vom. 30.04.1998, 786 ff.

Gesetz zur Neustrucktierung des Post und Fernmeldewesens und der Deutschen Bundespost (Postruckturgetsetz) (PostStrukturG), vom 08.06.1989, BGBl.I/ 1989, S. 1026 ff; vgl. Buchner, JA 1990, 194 ff; Hermann, ZPT 9/1991, 8 ff.

Gordon, Jeffrey N. 1999. Pathways to Corporate Convergence? Two Steps on the Road to Shareholder Capitalism in Germany. *Columbia Journal of European Law* 5: 219–41.

Hansmann, Henry and Reinier Kraakman. 2001. The End of History for Corporate Law. *Georgetown Law Journal* 89: 439–68.

Hoepner, Martin. 2001. Ten Empirical Findings on Shareholder Value and Industrial Relations in Germany (Max-Planck-Institute for the Study of Societies WP 05/2001) (available on SSRN).

Jenkinson, Tim and Alexander Ljungqvist. 2001. The Role of Hostile Stakes in German Corporate Governance. *Journal of Corporate Finance* 7: 397–446.

Johnson, Debra and Colin Turner. 1997. *Trans-European Networks: The Political Economy of Integrating Europe's Infrastructure.* Houndmills, Basingstoke Hampshire: Macmillan.

Jones, Steven L., William L. Megginson, Robert C. Nash and Jeffrey M. Netter. 1999. Share Issue Privatizations as Financial Means to Political and Economic Ends. *Journal of Financial Economics* 53: 217–53.

Karnitschnig, Mathew and Christopher Rhoads. 2002 CEO Ron Sommer Is Forced to Leave Deutsche Telekom. *Wall St. Journal,* July 17, 2002, A1.

Kirchner, Christian and Richard W. Painter. 2002. Takeover Defenses under Delaware Law, the Proposed Thirteenth EU Directive and the Proposed German Takeover Law: Comparison and Recommendations for Reform. *American Journal of Comparative Law* 50: 451–76.

Megginson, William L. and Jeffry M. Netter. 2001. From State to Market: A Survey of Empirical Studies on Privatization. *Journal of Economic Literature* 39: 321–89.

Meller, Paul. 2001a. Europe Plan on Mergers Hits a Snag; Germany Switches on Crucial Element. *New York Times*, May 3, 2001, at D1.

———. 2001b. European Parliament Rejects Measure to Ease Takeovers. *New York Times*, July 4, 2001.

Milhaupt, Curtis J. 1998. Property Rights in Firms. *Virginia Law Review* 84: 1145–1194.

Morris, John E. and Robert Galbraith. 2000. Trying to Kill the Golden Share. *Corporate Control Alert*, June 2000.

Naik, Gautam and William Boston. 1999. Telecoms Liberalization: A Year of Competition. *Wall Street Journal Europe*, Jan. 8, 1999. Available on Westlaw at 1999 WL-WSJE 5504578.

Opinion of Advocat General Ruiz-Jarabo Colomer, Cases C-367/98, C-483/99, C-503/99.

Postneuordnungsgesetz (PTNeuOG) vom 14.09.1994, BGBl, I/1994, S. 2325 ff.

Report of the High Level Group of Company Law Experts on Issues Related to Takeover Bids, Jan 10, 2002.

Schmidbauer, DeutsWolfgang, Anneliese Hieke and Christian Baulig, 1996. "Volkstrauma shares." *Die Woche*, Nov 22, 1996, p. 15 (Virginia Tent transl.)

Van der Elst, Christoph. 2002. The Equity Markets, Ownership Structures and Control: Towards and International Harmonisation? (Financial Law Institute, Univ. of Ghent, WP 2000–4) Available at http://www.law.rug.ac.be/fli/WP/wp2000–04.pdf, forthcoming in E. Wymeersch, ed. Company Law and Financial Markets.

Wall Street Journal, Anglo-Saxons at the Gates. Nov. 24, 1999, p. A 18 (editorial). Available on Westlaw at 1999 WL-WSJ 24923243.

Walsh, Mary Williams. 1996. "High Marks Frenzied Deutsche Telekom Trading Ushers In New Era." *Los Angeles Times*, Nov.19, 1996. Available on Westlaw at 1996 WL 12757682.

8 Off the Books, but on the Record

Evidence from Italy on the Relevance of Judges
to the Quality of Corporate Law

Luca Enriques

Participants in the debate on law and finance[1] unanimously agree on at least two points. First, law does matter, as a necessary condition or, at the very least, a useful tool for the development of financial markets. Even Roe (this volume), who questions the idea that law is a precondition to the separation of ownership and control, admits that "[g]ood corporate law lowers the cost of operating a large firm [since it impedes insider machinations]; it is good for a nation to have it." Second, the relevant factor is not "law on the books" as much as the combination of law and its enforcement mechanisms (e.g., Pistor et al. 2000: 328). La Porta et al. (1999) are also well aware of the need to take enforcement into account in their oft-cited statistical analysis. The hypothesis they test is whether in countries with bad law on the books as gauged by their shareholder rights indexes, "active and well-functioning courts . . . step in and rescue investors abused by the management," finding that "legal families with investor-friendlier laws are also the ones with stronger enforcement of the laws. Poor enforcement aggravate[s], rather than cure[s], the difficulties faced by investors in the French-civil-law countries" (La Porta et al. 1998: 1140, 1145).

If these two points of agreement, self-evident as they may seem today, hold true, then for a better understanding of the relationship between law and finance it is helpful to inspect the interaction between the law on the books and its enforcement by judges.

After showing how poor enforcement may render "good" corporate law—
that is, law that protects minority shareholders—on the books irrelevant, (section I.A), I explain how, as La Porta et al. (1999) also sensed, good corporate law
"off the books" may in theory develop in any jurisdiction, no matter how bad its
statutory law (section I.B). I then show what kind of corporate law rules may
best contribute to the absence of such a positive development (section I.C).

Next, the analysis focuses on corporate law judges, to identify the requisite skills and tendencies judges must have in order for corporate law on the
books (bad or good) to be good "off the books" (section I.D). I argue that, in
order to provide a good corporate law landscape, a country must have honest
and sophisticated judges who: (1) show no deferential attitude toward insiders when conflict-of-interest situations are involved; (2) are endowed with
the "nose" to sense what really is at stake among the litigants and the real
causes of the dispute that has led the plaintiff to bring suit; (3) do not partake
of a formalistic legal culture; (4) are concerned with the impact of their
decisions on the future behavior of corporate actors in general.

To illustrate the relevance of these characteristics, after providing some
background information on shareholder litigation and Italian judges' style
(part II), I analyze how the most specialized court in Italy for corporate law
cases decides them (part III). The analysis casts a negative light on Italian
corporate law judges, and, by implication, confirms the negative picture of
Italian corporate law frequently found in the literature.[2]

I. Corporate Law "Off the Books" and How Judges (May) Shape It

This part highlights the central role of judges in shaping the legal environment for corporate actors (investors, blockholders, managers) and how corporate law on the books may influence the way in which judges perform
their role. This may produce a better understanding of which legal features
really matter for corporate governance, and of what policymakers interested
in improving a country's securities markets by legislative reform can do.

A. How Bad Judges Can Spoil Good Law

At the most basic level, there is widespread agreement that a certain degree
of judicial honesty and effectiveness (in terms of speed and practical

enforceability of court decisions) are necessary elements of a sound corporate law system (La Porta et al. 1998: 1140; Black 2001a: 790–91, 807).
Their absence is a real problem today mainly in developing countries
(Buscaglia and Dakolias 1999). In the richer countries, including continental Europe, judges are sufficiently honest and the judicial system is broadly
efficient, at least in corporate cases. This fact, which is reflected to some
extent in the La Porta et al. (1999) data,[3] also holds for Italy, which scores
last in corruption and second to last (just above Spain) in judicial efficiency
among countries with above average GDP (La Porta et al. 1998: 1142–43).
In fact, according to a recent study, corruption of judges in Italy is a rare
phenomenon (Savona and Mezzanotte 1998: 46). Even the undeniable
length of Italian trials[4] is less important in corporate cases, where parties
often ask for injunctive remedies or preliminary decisions, after which they
usually abandon the case (Galletti 2001). Such rulings can usually be
obtained in a matter of weeks, or at worst months (Stanghellini 1999: 36).

   Of course, honesty and speed alone are not enough. Even a quick and
honest judiciary can spoil "good" corporate law on the books. Most legal systems provide for fiduciary duties under one name or another (e.g. Enriques
2000a: 302–3), but judges' inclination to strictly enforce them differs greatly.[5]
The most interesting case in point is Japan, where the American corporate
law draftsmen, in introducing the requirement of board approval for conflict-
of-interest transactions (Article 265 of the Japanese Commercial Code),
clearly "intended to import . . . principles that would be recognized by any
common lawyer as involving essentially fiduciary standards" (Nakajima 1999:
51). However, "in considering whether there has been a conflict of interest,
Japanese judges have shied away from attempting any detailed analysis of the
facts let alone attempting to lay down any principles of general application"
(ibid.).

B. How Good Judges May Fix Things Up (Even in Civil-law Systems)

While it is plain that "bad" judges may spoil good laws, the reverse is somewhat counterintuitive but no less true. At a time when English and American corporate law on the books provided no protection against unfair self-
dealing, it was the courts that extended the fiduciary obligations of agents
and trustees to corporate directors (Black 2001b). Some scholars argue, however, that judges can remedy the shortcomings in corporate law only in common law systems. In this view, civil law systems, marshalling their codes of

bright line rules to eliminate all gaps in the law, minimize the opportunity for judicial discretion and innovation, and thus limit the development of "better" corporate law (Coffee 2001b: 62; Johnson et al. 2000).

This view of civil law systems as limiting judges' ability to forge new rules reflects the ideology of the civil law tradition more than the actual functioning of such systems. Civil law codes certainly contain bright line rules, but they also contain general clauses (*Generalklauseln*, in German, *clausole generali*, in Italian)—standards that must be specified by judges case-by-case.[6] Moreover, in some instances civil law judges create new standards themselves or extend the application of existing ones to areas other than those explicitly provided by the codes. A codified law is no obstacle to this process.[7]

Consider two examples drawn from corporate law in support of this proposition, one from Germany and one from Italy. The German corporation statute (*Aktiengesetz*) says nothing about whether shareholders have a reciprocal duty of loyalty (*Treuepflicht*), but the Supreme Court, following a protracted scholarly debate (*e.g.*, Wiedemann 1991), has ruled that this duty does exist and requires that majority shareholders take the interests of minority shareholders into account in exercising their corporate powers.[8] A similar evolution can be observed in Italy, where no explicit statutory provision restricts the discretion of majority shareholders in exercising their voting rights on resolutions regarding dividends, new issues of shares, or liquidation.[9] Italian courts have invalidated resolutions on these matters when they were convinced that the resolutions harmed minority shareholders and had no legitimate business purpose. The courts have based their decisions either on the grounds that majority shareholders had abused their voting powers or, under another construction, that they had violated their duty of good faith to other shareholders.[10]

C. Which Substantive and Procedural Rules on the Books May Prevent the Rise of Good Corporate Law Off the Books?

It may be argued that a bad corporate law system is also one that does not give minority shareholders access to justice, such as by denying standing in derivative or class actions. In a system with procedural barriers to the protection of minority shareholders, it is impossible for judges to develop a friendlier legal regime, because they will decide no corporate law cases involving disputes between minority shareholders and insiders. One can reply, first, that convergence between common law and civil law systems in this regard is already under way (Hertig forthcoming: 16). Second, and more importantly, no corporate law in the world is so hostile to minority shareholders as to provide no legal remedy at all. In section II, I will show how even Italian corporate law, so often dubbed unfriendly to minority shareholders, gives them at least two ways to call the court's attention to misconduct by majority shareholders or managers. However, as we shall also see, these avenues are often "ostensible," meaning that minority shareholders, lacking the standing to ask a court to judge the specific behavior that purportedly harmed them, must challenge other courses of action or decisions, alleging some unrelated or collateral violations of the law and hoping that the judge will see through the case and take the real rights and issues into account in her ruling.[11]

The foregoing analysis carries three implications: First, when corporate law on the books is bad in terms of access to justice for minority shareholders, judges need to be comparatively more interventionist and better at understanding (and possibly more willing to take into account) the true rights and wrongs behind the dispute. Second, there will often be no way for the judges to tackle the real issue—fairness to minority shareholders—and hence to develop coherent and comprehensive case law lending substance to the duty of loyalty. Third, as it is more difficult to bring suit, judges will gain less experience in the core corporate law area of fiduciary duties and thus find it harder to develop a "a textured situation sense respecting the problems of fiduciary duty in corporation law" (Allen 2000: 73). Consequently, corporate law will be less expressive[12] and its enforcement will be less frequent.

This problem is even more acute for "bad" corporate law jurisdictions lacking contingency fees or the standard "American rule" that each side bears its own legal fees (Hertig forthcoming: 16; Coffee 1999a: 6–7). In other words, in these jurisdictions the law does not provide the incentives necessary for derivative suits and class actions to be brought frequently enough to deter insider misconduct. The consequence may be an even lower level of corporate law enforcement (Hertig forthcoming: 3, 16) and, as noted above, greater difficulty for courts in becoming sufficiently skilled in corporate law matters, and more precisely in understanding whether a specific transaction or resolution is fair. In itself, however, the lack of legal instruments providing these incentives does not absolutely prevent courts from developing a more friendly corporate law environment.

One last comment on the development of corporate law expertise is appropriate. If the substantive and procedural rules in place make it harder for courts to develop such expertise, then the judges themselves will feel they lack legitimacy to take an active role in corporate law issues, or to second-guess behavior and business decisions of insiders, however tainted they may be. Why? Judges may fear making incorrect decisions, or they may be aware that they cannot grasp the technicalities of the business transactions under review. Thus, they will be anxious to apply substantive or procedural rules barring the review of business decisions for fairness.

D. Assessing the Quality of Corporate Law Judges: Some Relevant Features

As a corollary to these reflections, this section identifies the most relevant features to be taken into account in order to assess the quality of a legal system's corporate law judges.

1. *Honesty, rapidity, and expertise.* We have seen that the honesty of judges and the rapidity of the courts are basic preconditions for a good corporate law system. A third relevant feature, as suggested, is a sufficient degree of sophistication and business expertise on the part of judges (Black 2001a: 791).[13]

2. *No deference in conflict-of-interest cases.* Business expertise, however, is not enough. Suppose that in a country with equity markets dominated by a few families, or networks of managers and families due to pyramids, cross-holdings and other deviations from the one-share-one-vote principle,[14] the government succeeded in hiring as judges the most prominent transactional lawyers. No matter how long their mandate, they could be expected to be quite lenient in judging their former clients' behavior, practices, and transactions. These transactions will presumably resemble those that the judges structured in their former capacity as transactional lawyers. Moreover, the judges will likely have personal or social ties with many corporate insiders.

This scenario shows how business expertise is a necessary, but not a sufficient condition for the courts to protect minority shareholders' interests. Also needed, then, are unawed judges, who feel legitimacy to review the merits of insider transactions and decisions. In short, judges must not hesitate to strike down such transactions and resolutions whenever they "stink badly enough."[15]

3. *Capacity to identify real rights and wrongs.* Judges should develop a good nose also for the real rights and wrongs underlying the specific facts alleged by the parties.[16] In other words, judges should be endowed with the curiosity to learn the whole story of the corporation involved in the dispute, to discern the role played by each party, and their relations with one another, in order to understand who may have acted opportunistically and, more generally, what actually went wrong. In short, they should be willing and able to learn all "the particulars of the case" and "to be directly open to arguments based upon moral precepts of fairness and justice" (Allen 1992: 17). This feature is especially important for closely held companies, in which disputes among shareholders often involve relationships of personal trust and opportunistic behavior by one shareholder-manager to the detriment of another who typically has made firm-specific human capital investments (Easterbrook and Fischel 1991: 229–30). This same feature is generally central, as already suggested, in legal systems that restrict access to justice for minority shareholders.

4. *Antiformalism.* Judges should be immune from a formalistic legal culture, which unfortunately still predominates in many civil law countries (*e.g.*, Zweigert and Kötz 1998: 122–23). Antiformalism is a precondition to the ability to play a creative role in evaluating the real rights and wrongs behind the dispute.

Furthermore, when the law requires corporate actors to comply with certain formalities, which may be unnecessary in smaller companies and are thus often disregarded,[17] frivolous suits may well be brought simply to extract side-payments from the corporation or from majority shareholders. When such suits are brought, good judges should construe formalities as narrowly as possible. A narrow construction will also reduce the burdens such rules impose on businesses. But in countries that restrict minority shareholders' ability to bring suit, minority shareholders may allege the violation of rules of this kind for want of more direct access to the courts. In such cases, judges should be ready to play the formalist and rule in favor of the plaintiff, if they are satisfied that given the peculiarities of the case and the possibility of opportunistic conduct by insiders, they may strengthen the plaintiff's bargaining position or punish the insider misconduct.[18] In other words, good corporate law judges working under "bad" substantive and procedural rules should be ready to be "functionally" formalistic.

5. *Concern for spill-over effects.* Finally, good corporate law judges should be concerned with the message their decisions send to corporate actors on

what is (im)permissible and (un)fair. In other words, judges should always be conscious that their decisions mold corporate actors' behavior and, more specifically, affect their incentives to act cooperatively instead of opportunistically.[19]

E. Conclusions

Corporate law off the books, even in civil-law systems, may be good or bad, irrespective of the quality of corporate law on the books, depending on the quality of judges. However, it will be harder for judges to remedy shortcomings in the law when substantive or procedural rules limit minority shareholders' ability to bring suit against insiders. In any event, to evaluate the quality of judges, one should assess their: (1) integrity and the speed of the judicial system in deciding cases; (2) business expertise; (3) independence from corporate insiders; (4) ability to understand where rights and wrongs actually lie; (5) antiformalism; (6) concern for the behavior-molding potential of their decisions.[20] In part III, I will evaluate the "quality" of decisions by Italy's most important court for corporate matters on the basis of the last four of these criteria.

II. Shareholder Litigation and Judicial Style in Italy

This part introduces the empirical analysis of the Milan court's corporate law decisions found in part III. First, I examine the remedies available to minority shareholders under the law. Next, since the "style" of Italian judges and the system by which cases are reported differs greatly from their U.S. and other common law counterparts, I provide clarification on how the sample of cases to be analyzed was collected, and why many cases proved to be irrelevant for purposes of analysis.

A. Shareholder Litigation in Italy

Under Italian corporation law,[21] directors are elected by the shareholders' meeting for terms not longer than three years, and may be removed with or without cause (Di Sabato 1999). The shareholders' meeting has much broader powers than, for instance, its American counterpart (see Campobasso 1999: 298). This fact allows us to better understand the importance of the power that any shareholder has under Article 2377 of the Italian Civil Code to bring suit—formally against the corporation, de facto against its majority shareholders—to nullify resolutions the shareholder has not voted for, if they violate the law or the corporation's bylaws. This power may be exercised only up to three months from the day on which the voidable resolution was passed. However, there is no statute of limitations if the resolution has an "illicit or impossible object."[22] While legal scholars widely debate the meaning of "illicit object," the courts have consistently held that the term covers all resolutions violating laws aimed at protecting a general interest, rather than simply the interests of shareholders (see Campobasso 1999: 341, citing cases). Since rules concerning the process of approving shareholder resolutions (like those on how to call the meeting, how to conduct it, how to express votes) are thought to be exclusively in the interest of shareholders, courts have also introduced a third category of invalidity unknown to the Italian Civil Code—"nonexistence," which applies when a resolution passes under the cloud of serious procedural irregularities.[23] This development, providing another example of creativity by civil law judges, stems from judges' willingness to provide some protection for minority shareholders who, perhaps through no fault of their own, had not brought the Article 2377 suit before the expiration of the three-month statute of limitations.

It is interesting to note that courts have voided resolutions approving false or unclear financial statements.[24] Since the financial statements of closely held corporations in Italy are seldom impeccable, minority shareholders quite frequently challenge their approval in court.[25] This is a good example of "ostensible" minority shareholder litigation. In fact, these suits commonly bear no relation to the grievance of the plaintiff-shareholders against majority shareholders or directors (Enriques 2001). Rather, the threat of or refusal to settle such suits is an effective bargaining tool, because they have potentially serious consequences for the corporation and its directors, which, in closely held corporations, are normally the majority shareholders.[26]

Another reason for the relative frequency of this kind of action, however, is simply that non-ostensible remedies are often unavailable under Italian law. What actually happens if a minority shareholder's grievance relates to violations of fiduciary duties or, more broadly, to opportunistic behavior by insiders? The most obvious remedy, the derivative suit, is not allowed in privately held corporations, and it is available only to shareholders of listed corporations representing at least 5 percent of the voting shares, a threshold "too high to allow this procedure to be an effective tool for minority shareholders."[27] In closely held corporations, outside bankruptcy, liability suits against directors must be authorized by the shareholders. Majority share-holders may cast their vote in such resolutions, unless they are themselves the directors against which the suits are to be brought.[28] It is therefore very rare for directors to be summoned as defendants in liability suits, unless the company goes bankrupt (see Stanghellini 1995: 169–70).

One provision of Italian corporate law might have been construed by judges as allowing derivative suits, had they desired to do so. In fact, Article 2395 of the Italian Civil Code reads: "The provisions of the preceding arti-cles[29] do not affect the right to compensation for damages of an individual member or third person who has been directly injured as a result of malice, fraud or negligence of the directors."[30] This provision has been consistently construed as not allowing recovery of damages by shareholders if the dam-age is a consequence of misconduct which harms the shareholder *as a shareholder*.[31] Courts deciding on Article 2395 suits have regularly held for the defendant-directors in cases in which shareholders used the Article 2395 action as if it provided a derivative remedy.[32] This construction, like all mat-ters of legal interpretation, is not without alternatives. It has been argued that an interpretation more consistent with the basic principles of Italian tort law would allow individual shareholders to recover against directors dam-ages suffered as shareholders (Stanghellini 1995: 172).

Whether or not the dominant construction of Article 2395 is defensible, the provision is of little help to minority shareholders suffering from insider misconduct. What other remedies exist? If the board of directors adopts a resolution that prejudices an individual shareholder's right, she may chal-lenge the resolution in court. But a comprehensive analysis of the case law in this area shows that in only one instance has the court invalidated a board resolution challenged by a minority shareholder (Irrera 2000: 113–30), sug-gesting that this is not a very effective remedy.

The final remedy available to minority shareholders, and one which is frequently used (Stanghellini 1995: 173), is the complaint against serious irregularities in the management of the company. According to Article 2409 of the Italian Civil Code,

> If there is a well founded suspicion of serious irregularities in the dis-charge of the duties of the directors and auditors, shareholders repre-senting at least one-tenth of the company's capital can complain of these facts to the court.
>
> The court, after hearing the directors and auditors in chambers, can order an investigation of the company's management . . . .

If irregularities are found to exist, the court may grant any appropriate precautionary remedy and call the shareholders' meeting for the consequent resolutions. In the most serious cases, [the court] may remove directors and auditors and appoint a temporary administrator, determining his powers and the term of his office.

The temporary administrator may bring a liability action against directors and auditors.

. . . . The public prosecutor may petition the court for the remedies provided for in the present Article.[33]

For listed corporations, standing in an Article 2409 proceeding has been extended to shareholders representing 5 percent of the voting shares,[34] to the board of auditors[35] (in the case of serious irregularities in the discharge of directors' duties), and to the Consob, the Italian securities regulatory agency (in the case of serious irregularities in the discharge of auditors' duties).[36]

A few comments on this provision will be useful before proceeding with the analysis. The threat of an Article 2409 complaint is an effective bargaining tool in the hands of minority shareholders. Since the approval of false financial statements is deemed to be a serious irregularity (Tedeschi 1988: 197), the same considerations made above with regard to challenges of resolutions approving financial statements apply. Moreover, the temporary administrator appointed by the court has the legal status of a public official (ibid.: 253), and hence has the duty to report any criminal offense discovered in discharging assigned duties. More generally, "the operations of . . . companies usually suffer as a result of court inspection pursuant to Article 2409" (Stanghellini 1999: 37).

The law affords courts great latitude in determining the appropriate measures to stop serious irregularities and to counteract or mitigate their harmful consequences (Tedeschi 1988: 236). In theory, then, courts may play a very important and creative role in the Italian corporate governance landscape, at least in closely held companies, in which minority shareholders may more easily reach the relevant threshold.[37] In practice, however, it is extremely rare for courts to order precautionary remedies of any kind. Typically, they simply appoint a temporary administrator or call the shareholder meeting, if they do anything at all (Marcinkiewitz 1990: 521–22).

Finally, although the temporary administrators do sometimes bring liability suits against directors and auditors, often the shareholders' meeting, by vote of the majority shareholders, authorizes the directors elected after the temporary administrator has left office to settle or abandon those suits.[38]

In summary, four judicial remedies are available to minority shareholders in cases of oppression or opportunistic behavior by insiders: the action against void or voidable shareholders' resolutions; the liability suit in the rare case that shareholders have suffered harm directly from directorial conduct; the action against board resolutions that prejudice individual rights; and the complaint against serious irregularities in the management of the company, which may lead (though regularly with no practical positive outcome for minority shareholders) to a liability suit against the directors.

Frequently, then, legal remedies allowing minority shareholders to challenge a specific opportunistic course of action are unavailable. Minority shareholders will then try to proceed with other, ostensible, remedies, at least to strengthen their bargaining position against insiders. In certain instances, shareholders may choose an ostensible remedy in the presence of other remedies more closely related to the opportunistic act, simply because the former is a more effective bargaining tool. Thus, quite commonly in Italy shareholder suits have nothing to do with the real cause of the dispute, and the real rights and wrongs are difficult to perceive for the judge, let alone for the reader of the judge's decision, as I show in the following section.

B. A Few Remarks on the "Italian Style"

Before proceeding with the empirical analysis, recall that there is a striking difference between judicial opinions in common law jurisdictions and in Italy and other civil law systems. As an American comparative law scholar aptly pointed out a few decades ago, "[t]he civil law judge is not a hero-figure (or a father figure), as he tends to be in England or in the United States" (Merryman 1966: 586). Italian judges are "just another kind of civil servant" (ibid.: 589), selected usually without any prior significant professional experience on the basis of a written and oral exam in which candidates deal exclusively with legal subjects (Oberto 2001). They perform their duties in a cultural environment in which the traditional view that judges do not make law still prevails.[39]

The style of Italian judicial opinions "is closely imitative of doctrinal writing," (Merryman 1966: 586–87) which, in turn, is still dominated by "abstractness, conceptualism, and cultural agnosticism," (ibid.) at least in certain areas like corporate law.[40] It follows that "in the writing . . . of opinions the abstractness and conceptualism of the doctrine are prominent. The factual emphasis, the concreteness, common lawyers associate with judicial writing is absent in the Italian. Opinions often contain no coherent statement of the facts of the case," instead reading "more like excerpts from treatises or commentaries on the codes than the reasoning of a court in deciding a concrete case" (ibid.: 592).

Why do opinions often contain no coherent statement of the facts? A legal explanation for this lies in the procedural rules that describe the requisite content of a valid judicial opinion. As a leading Italian civil procedure scholar points out, these rules require the exposition only of those facts and evaluations that enable counsel to appeal the decision and facilitate the appellate judge's work (Taruffo 1988: 187–88). In other words, these rules justify judges' habit of writing opinions for an audience consisting solely of the parties' lawyers and the appellate judge.[41] It is no wonder that the statement of facts is often incomprehensible to an outsider.

Outsiders' access to the facts of cases is even more problematic because there are no complete collections of judicial opinions, except for those of the Supreme Court and the Constitutional Court. Law journals publish selected judicial opinions, but generally in abridged form. Very often, "at the point where the facts might be found, one encounters the disheartening term 'omissis,' signifying that a part of the opinion is omitted. The emphasis, rather than on the facts, is on the production of the polished maxim (*massima*), and this abstract and conceptual statement, divorced from the factual context out of which it arose, may be the only part of the opinion to be published."[42]

This reflects the propensity of Italian legal scholars, practitioners and judges toward conceptualism and abstractness. The effect of this widespread faith in legal "maxims" on judges' legal discourse is "to reduce legally relevant facts to the minimum in the interest of abstract order at the expense of pragmatic concreteness, the rule at the expense of the exception, the category or class at the expense of the individual" (Merryman 1966: 587).[43]

A final clarification: Although there is formally no *stare decisis* doctrine in Italy (ibid.: 588), there is general consensus that precedents "do in practice have some effect on future cases" (ibid.: 591). In fact, opinions frequently cite prior decisions of the Supreme Court as well as of lower courts (ibid.: 605–6) and usually adhere to the rules of law (maxims) extrapolated from those prior decisions, similar to the practice of common law judges.[44]

This is certainly not the ideal background for an empirical investigation of how Italian corporate law judges perform in terms of lack of deference, ability to identify real rights and wrongs, antiformalism, and concern for spill-over effects, since such an evaluation obviously requires knowledge of the facts. Nevertheless, I attempt precisely such an evaluation in the next section.

III. Italian Corporate Law off the Books: Evidence from Milan

A. The Sample

In order to evaluate the "quality" of Italian corporate law judges, I have gathered all 123 opinions issued by the Milan Tribunal, the court of first instance, published in law journals between 1986 and 2000[45] involving (1) suits brought by shareholders under Articles 2377–79 of the Civil Code[46] (73 decisions); (2) shareholder suits challenging board of directors' resolutions (2 decisions); (3) liability suits brought by the corporation against directors outside bankruptcy (11 decisions); (4) individual liability suits brought by shareholders against directors (13 decisions); and (5) Article 2409 complaints brought by shareholders (27 decisions).[47]

There are two reasons for choosing the Milan court. First, the Milan Tribunal has "[a] leadership role in the corporate area. . . . [and] is generally regarded as the most specialized in Italy" (Stanghellini 1999: 35). Hence, the analysis of its decisions should provide the most sanguine picture possible of the "quality" of Italian corporate law judges. This is justified by the fact that any Italian corporation may choose the Milan court as the forum for its corporate law controversies simply by inserting a clause in the corporate statute to that effect. Second, Milan is the financial and business heart of the country, and home to many of the major Italian corporations.[48] The decision to evaluate opinions of a first instance court is justified not only because litigation at this stage is more centered upon the facts, but also because corporate law cases in Italy are relatively rarely appealed.[49]

Of the 123 decisions gathered, 61 involved *società per azioni* (of which 13 were listed on the Milan Stock Exchange) and 57 *società a responsabilità limitata*, while in five cases the legal form of the company involved was unspecified. Only 26 decisions proved useful for the inquiry. Of the other 97 cases, 45 were written or reported in such a way as to make it impossible to understand the facts of the case. The remaining cases were irrelevant, most often because the decision dealt exclusively with a specific matter of statutory interpretation, showing no particular sign of formalism or antiformalism.[50]

B. The Cases

Due to space constraints, I will describe the most revealing decisions in the text and refer to the other cases in the footnotes. Needless to say, the small number of relevant decisions does not allow for meaningful quantitative analysis.

1. *How do Milan corporate law judges decide on self-interested transactions/resolutions?* Eighteen decisions in the sample may provide an answer to this question. I first report those rejecting the plaintiff's claim and condoning the insiders' behavior. Next, I will describe the cases that may to some extent support the claim that Italian judges are prepared to use their discretion to counter insider abuses.

a. Deferential judges? In *Cavaggioni v. Rotondo,*[51] the plaintiff-shareholder filed an Article 2409 complaint alleging that the majority shareholder and sole director of Athena s.r.l. had entered into a self-dealing transaction. Specifically, he had caused Athena to acquire an undertaking heavily burdened with short-term debts from Chartour s.r.l., a company which he also controlled.[52] Although the director had succeeded in postponing the entrance of new minority shareholders into the company, clearly in order to avoid any interference with the transaction, the Court found no basis for suspicion of serious irregularities, since the plaintiff had provided no evidence that the transaction "considered as a whole," had harmed the corporation.[53]

In *Serafini v. Tosi,*[54] the plaintiff had asked the court to issue a preliminary injunction against a shareholder resolution authorizing a parent-subsidiary merger. The plaintiff alleged that the resolution had been approved by a vote of the majority shareholder, a corporation owning roughly 90 percent of the shares, and was hence voidable for violation of Article 2373 on shareholders' conflict of interest, or because the majority shareholder had abused its voting power. After dismissing the conflict-of-interest issue with a formalistic argument, the Court denied any abuse of power by the majority shareholder, on the grounds that a finding of abuse of powers "requires evidence of the majority's fraudulent intent to harm other shareholders to its own or to third parties' advantage; it is very difficult to prove this with regard to the share exchange ratio of a merger, since the law imposes disclosure and procedural obligations (i.e., the obligation to deposit the merger project and all the relevant documents in the company register and the obligation to ask an accountant for a fairness opinion) such as to discourage any fraudulent intent."[55]

In *Ferrara v. Torpia*,[56] the court rejected an Article 2395 liability suit brought by an individual shareholder against directors, on the ground that the damage suffered by the shareholder was indirect. In dictum, it also stated that the shareholder would have had no recovery in light of the intrinsic merits of the claim. The shareholder alleged that the board of directors, after seeking the advice of the corporation's outside counsel, had decided not to take action to challenge an allegedly illegitimate arbitration award concerning a dispute with another corporation. One of the controlling shareholders of the latter corporation was a defendant-director of the former corporation. The court stated that the board's decision, "corroborated by the very relevant advice of the same lawyer who had defended the corporation in the arbitration proceeding, cannot be criticized in terms of its legality, . . . as it was taken in observance of the criteria of professional diligence which directors have to abide by in the discharge of their duties."[57] In other words, the court applied the business judgment rule to a resolution in which one of the two joint-controlling shareholders was interested, and attached considerable weight to the advice of a lawyer whose independence was far from self-evident, as he had been appointed by the directors—that is, by the controlling shareholders.

A fourth case, *Milan v. Trema Gestione*,[58] is the most striking example of the respectfulness of Italian judges toward dubious insider behavior. Trema Gestione s.r.l. brought a liability suit against its former director, Alberto Milan, as a counterclaim on an action for damages brought by the latter, who had been removed from office. In the court's words:

> While it is uncontested that Milan used credit cards issued in the name of the corporation, it is completely unproven that he abused them. In order to prove it, it is not enough to state that the credit cards were used in order to pay for "goods and services having nothing to do with the discharge of his duties," "in vacation resorts or anyway in localities having nothing to do with those in which the corporation had an interest or was doing business;" nor is it enough to state that they were used to pay for "other persons accompanying him and hav-

ing no relationship with the corporation." . . . It is, in fact, uncontested that Milan was the leading man not only of the corporation, but also of the whole Financière Trema group, and that—as the corporation itself has declared—in the discharge of his duties, he might act "with wide discretion and absolute freedom." It is, then, perfectly plausible that negotiations for this or that transaction, the contacts with prospective clients, the relationships with third parties connected somehow with his duties as a director, may have taken place also in holiday resorts, and that he may have paid for highway tolls and hotels, even luxury ones, perhaps offering a meal in this or that restaurant, giving small gifts or paying for other "entertainment" expenses. None of these expenses can be deemed unrelated to Milan's activity as a director and the broad management powers entrusted to him; and [the corporation] has produced no specific evidence to prove that this or that expense was in fact unrelated to his activity.[59]

Apparently, the acquisition of such goods and services in holiday resorts did not "stink badly enough" for the judge to place the burden of proof on the defendant or at least to alleviate the plaintiff's burden by evaluating the director's behavior more severely.[60]

In *FIN.GE.M. v. Montedison (1)*,[61] the court had to decide whether sufficient information had been given to shareholders in connection with their approval, as required by law,[62] of the settlement of a liability suit between the company and its former directors. The settlement had been negotiated as part of a broader agreement by which a consortium of banks had acquired a controlling stake in the Montedison corporation from the Ferruzzi family, whose holding companies at the top of their pyramidal group were insolvent (Penati and Zingales 1997). The new controlling shareholders and the directors they had appointed potentially had a conflict of interest: the grant of a generous settlement agreement to former directors, most of whom were members of or had close relations with the Ferruzzi family, may have been designed to reduce the acquisition price (Enriques 2000b: 255–56). The court held that directors had properly informed shareholders of the settlement agreements, by distributing a report on those agreements at the meeting. Directors had declared that the full text of the agreements was available for shareholders requesting it, and "the report [had] exhaustively illustrate[d] the *basic* and *qualifying* clauses of the agreements."[63] Furthermore, the directors had provided sufficient clarifications to the shareholders upon request and, in any case, the shareholders should have asked to read the full text of the agreements or to postpone the meeting, if they felt that they were not sufficiently informed.[64] The shareholders had only themselves to blame if they had not done so.[65] The next section discusses the Milan Tribunal ruling overturning this decision, clarifying how strongly biased in favor of the directors and controlling shareholders the court was in this decision.

b. No deference? To be sure, there are cases in which the court found transactions or resolutions to be unfair, or otherwise found for the plaintiff-shareholder. In two cases, *Barbiani v. Compagnia Latina di Assicurazioni*[66] and *Cavalli v. GAIC*,[67] the court, petitioned for a preliminary injunction against parent-subsidiary mergers, ruled the share exchange ratio for the mergers unfair, since the directors had failed in both cases to take relevant data into account.

These holdings, however, did not lead to the issuance of a preliminary injunction. In both cases the court ruled that shareholders had not provided evidence of irreparable damage.[68] Thus, the practical effect of the rulings was nil.

In *FIN.GE.M. v. Montedison (2)*,[69] the court dealt with the same case as in *FIN.GE.M. v. Montedison (1)*,[70] but ruled very differently. The court found it "perplexing" that the directors had not made public all the documents concerning the settlement agreement prior to the day of the meeting, in light of their importance to the corporation. In fact, this settlement ended a dispute with the former controlling family, which had mismanaged the company, bringing it almost to insolvency and severely damaging the corporate image.[71] Even more perplexing, the court found, was the fact that although shareholders at the meeting had immediately asked to see the full text of the settlement agreements, they were only made available hours later. At that point, the directors read a summary of the agreements, implicitly suggesting that they contained all pertinent information, when in fact the summary omitted material information.[72]

FIN.GE.M. v. Ferruzzi[73] was also decided in favor of the plaintiff-shareholder who had sued the former directors of a listed corporation for damages. FIN.GE.M. alleged that it had invested in the corporation, and failed to divest, on the basis of annual reports which turned out to be false. Among other things, the reports did not mention or properly account for a number of transactions draining money from the corporation and its subsidiaries to the controlling family.[74] It was an easy case factually and given the identity of the defendants, all members or associates of the Ferruzzi family, which had fallen into disgrace after the collapse of their business empire. However, the court ruled in favor of the plaintiff on a series of highly controversial legal issues, such as the causal link between factual omissions in the annual reports and the damage suffered by the shareholder.

In *Iniziative Finanziarie v. Baraldi*,[75] the court found for the plaintiff corporation in an Article 2393 liability suit against directors.[76] Iniziative Finanziarie alleged that the directors had overpaid for shares representing a controlling stake in a corporation called I.C.C.U. Containers, as part of a transaction with another corporation, which in turn was controlled by the controlling shareholder of Iniziative Finanziarie.[77] The court held that the price paid for the shares was excessive, based on an expert opinion which relied on balance-sheet data. In response to the obvious objection by one of the defendant-directors that expected profits, not balance sheet data, should be used to determine the value of the shares, the court stated that the contention was "arbitrary," since, as the expert also stated, it ignores the "correct legal and technical criteria" to be applied in order to appraise shares.[78] It also noted that the expert's valuation was in line with the price of the shares on an unofficial and highly illiquid exchange called Terzo mercato, not taking into account any control share premium. It is hard to say whether the court simply deferred to a faulty expert opinion, never doubting its merits, or whether it also took into account the fact that a "stinking" conflict-of-interest transaction was involved. In any event, the decision illustrates the unfamiliarity of Milan judges (and their experts) with basic notions of finance.

Finally, in *Tonani v. Viscontea*,[79] two shareholders together holding 10 percent of a company's shares had challenged a resolution increasing the share capital. The resolution had passed by a vote of the majority shareholders (who were also the directors), after the court, at the request of the plaintiffs, had ordered the inspection of the corporation pursuant to Article 2409. The increase in capital left the minority shareholders with a difficult choice: they either had to increase their investment, although they were clearly at odds with the controlling shareholders, or they would lose standing in the Article 2409 proceeding, since they would fall below the 10 percent threshold of Article 2409. The court voided the resolution, holding that it had been passed for the exclusive purpose of reducing the minority shareholders' stake in the corporation and thus of depriving them of standing in the Article 2409 proceeding. The majority shareholders had thus abused their voting power, as indicated by the fact that the meeting was called just after the Article 2409 judicial hearing of the directors.[80]

2. Do the Milan court judges care for the real underlying rights and wrongs? Italian corporate law opinions never begin with a brief history of the corporation involved, a description of its business, or the personal relationships among its shareholders, as is normally the case in Delaware opinions.[81] In the decisions gathered for the present analysis, the background of the cases revealing the reasons why the plaintiff brought suit is seldom reported.[82] This is especially true of the earlier decisions in the sample. In no decision issued before 1997 are the background reasons for the dispute disclosed. In most cases, therefore, it is impossible to determine whether the court took real rights and wrongs into account. In a few opinions, however, one gets the impression that the court did so, based on a tension between the facts as explicitly related by the judge and the outcome of the case. In other words, several seemingly anomalous judgments may be explained by an implicit evaluation of the merits by the judge. This finding appears less conjectural when one considers that most of these cases dealt with excessive director compensation in closely held corporations.

In Italy, as elsewhere, for tax reasons, profits in closely held firms are distributed to shareholders in the form of director employee compensation (Weigmann 1991: 793; Easterbrook and Fischel 1991: 229). This is fine with the shareholders as long as they get along and serve as directors of the corporation. If circumstances change, and shareholders begin to disagree for business or personal reasons, the majority shareholder(s) normally dismiss the minority shareholders from the board but continue to distribute all profits as directors' compensation (Weigmann 1991: 793–94). In that situation, minority shareholders find themselves owning shares worth almost nothing, while the value of any firm-specific human capital investments they may have made plummets.

In *GE.VI v. ME.AL.*, two minority shareholders challenged a shareholder resolution determining directors' compensation. They alleged that the resolution was passed by the vote of self-interested majority shareholders (a director and her husband) and that the compensation was excessive. The court held the compensation packages excessive on the grounds that they exceeded the company's profits for the year and that the director's involvement in the company had been limited, with much of the management in the hands of her husband, an officer of the company.[83] There is no Italian law prohibiting a company from compensating directors unless it reports gross profits (Jaeger 1987). Thus, it is highly probable that the judge felt that where one group of shareholders was excluded from the management of the company, it was unfair for the other group to obtain all the profits.[84]

As suggested earlier, in more recent decisions the real dispute is sometimes revealed and seems to be implicitly taken into account by the court.[85] In *Innenz v. Fiduciaria Sant'Andrea*,[86] one of the two 50 percent shareholders of a corporation challenged the other's repeated refusal to approve the financial statements and appoint new directors. As the decision makes clear, the two shareholders disagreed over the strategy of their joint venture. The plaintiff argued that the refusal to approve the financial statements and the appointment of directors was an abuse of the voting right. The court rejected the claim because the defendant consistently provided specific reasons for the negative vote on the financial statements, and the refusal to appoint new directors was justified by the substantial strategic disagreement between the shareholders. Since an abuse of the voting right exists only where a shareholder's exclusive aim is to harm other shareholders, the fact that the vote was properly justified excluded a finding of abuse.[87] Whatever the general implications of such a holding,[88] the court appears to have correctly resolved this dispute. In fact, as the court acknowledges,[89] deadlock may cause the dissolution of the corporation.[90] Yet this is the outcome the shareholders had implicitly agreed upon in the event of serious disagreement, as indicated by their decision to each hold 50 percent of the shares.[91]

Another case in which the background disagreement is not only well described in the opinion but also duly taken into account in the judgment is *Cornelli v. Fratelli Cornelli*.[92] The case involved two corporations, Fratelli Cornelli, a forwarding agent, and Cotras, a transportation company. The shareholders of both were members of the same family. Alberto Cornelli was the majority shareholder of Fratelli Cornelli, which had as minority shareholders other family members. These, in turn, were the majority shareholders of Cotras, in which Alberto Cornelli had a minority stake. Fratelli Cornelli often used Cotras for transport. Cotras had financial problems, and its majority shareholders proposed that Fratelli Cornelli modify the terms of the transport agreements between the two companies in favor of Cotras. Alberto Cornelli refused. At the annual meeting of Fratelli Cornelli, the minority shareholders made use of the voting ban under Article 2373 and authorized a liability suit against Alberto Cornelli and his son, also a director of the company. They alleged that Alberto Cornelli had engaged in self-dealing transactions by employing his son and in purchasing a luxury car, despite the allegedly critical financial condition of Fratelli Cornelli. Alberto Cornelli challenged the shareholders' resolution in court, alleging, in turn, that the employment of his son, *per se*, was not harmful to the corporation, unless it was shown that his son was overpaid. He also denied any personal use of the luxury car. The court found for Alberto Cornelli, noting that the minority shareholders had a conflict of interest in the resolution, since they had presumably taken advantage of the situation to persuade him to accept the proposed changes in the agreements with Cotras.[93]

3. *Do the judges have a formalistic mentality?* We have seen that formalism is still a pervasive mental habit of Italian legal scholars, judges, and practitioners, even in the corporate law area. It would be surprising to find that the Milan Tribunal judges do not share this mind-set. After all, their decisions are reviewed by an appellate court and, indirectly, by a Supreme Court also of this mind-set (Enriques 2001: 91). I have searched the decisions in the dataset for symptoms of either formalism or antiformalism. It is quite possible that I failed to identify signs of antiformalism, since antiformalistic judgments and constructions are consistent with common sense, and so might more easily go unnoticed. In any case, I found only one relevant example of antiformalism as against five cases showing formalistic thinking on the part of the judges.

The antiformalistic decision is *Cavalli v. GAIC*. After solving a complex legal issue in favor of the plaintiff, the court held that the exchange ratio in a merger was unfair. The court held that a certain provision protecting the right of holders of nonvoting shares to privileged treatment vis-à-vis holders of voting shares, literally not applying to merger transactions, ought to be applied to them as well. Otherwise, as the court held, the nonvoting shareholders' right to privileged treatment would be nullified.[94]

Sviluppo Immobiliare v. Reale[95] is the most striking example of formalistic reasoning by the Milan court. A corporation brought a liability suit against its internal auditors. The defendants alleged that the shareholders' resolution authorizing the suit had been taken during an irregular shareholders' meeting, because the present shareholders (representing 100 percent of the capital) had failed to properly deposit their share certificates with a bank or the corporation's registered agent at least five days prior to the meeting, as required by a 1962 law.[96]

In fact, the share certificates had not been deposited because employees of the corporation's registered agent (plausibly the very auditors subject to the liability suit) had refused to accept them in deposit without justification.

According to the court, the shareholders should have obtained a declaration from a notary that it was impossible to deposit the share certificates, and deposited them elsewhere.[97] Failing this, the court held that the shareholders' resolution was "nonexistent"[98] and rejected the liability suit on this ground.[99]

Formalistic thinking about corporations is also illustrated by decisions denying that Article 2373 applies to resolutions approving parent-subsidiary mergers by a vote of the parent. For example, in *Serafini v. Tosi*, the plaintiff argued that the resolution was voidable because the majority shareholder, who was of course interested in setting the exchange ratio most favorable to itself, had voted, in violation of Article 2373 of the Italian Civil Code. The court denied that a conflict of interest between a shareholder and the corporation may arise with regard to a resolution concerning the share exchange ratio in a merger, because "not only majority shareholders have an interest in a certain exchange ratio, but also minority shareholders have an interest which is of course opposite to that of majority shareholders, while the corporation is indifferent to the exchange ratio, which only involves personal relationships among its shareholders."[100] The reasoning underlying this opinion is that regardless of the exchange ratio, the assets of the corporation are not affected: the assets are the same after the transaction, even though they have become part of a larger entity.[101] This conclusion implicitly denies that the purpose of the corporation is to maximize shareholder wealth. It does so without considering whether rejecting the shareholder primacy norm is wise or unwise from a policy perspective. Instead, it simply partakes of the view, popular among Italian judges,[102] that a corporation is a real entity with its own purpose, distinct from the shareholders' interests. This is not surprising, since, as will be shown below, Milan judges are indifferent to the effects their decisions may have on corporate actors and on society as a whole.

4. Are the judges concerned with spill-over effects? As is well known, common law judges in general are inclined to consider the effects that their rulings may have on society, or at least on the actions of people who may find themselves in a similar situation.[103] A good illustration of this concern can be found in Justice Cardozo's oft-cited description of trustees' obligations in *Meinhard v. Salmon*:

A trustee is held to something stricter than the morals of the market place. Not honesty alone, but the punctilio of an honor the most sensitive, is then the standard of behavior. . . . Uncompromising rigidity

has been the attitude of courts of equity when petitioned to undermine the rule of undivided loyalty by the 'disintegrating erosion' of
particular exceptions. . . . Only thus has the level of conduct for fiduciaries been kept at a level higher than that trodden by the crowd. *It
will not consciously be lowered by any judgment of this court.*[104]

Trying to find any similar concern in an opinion by a Milan judge is an
exercise in futility. Judges never express concern for how a decision might
influence the behavior of corporate actors, nor do they ask themselves
whether, for example, holding a director not liable in a specific case might
send the wrong message to other corporate directors. Of course, one cannot
rule out the possibility that they do engage in such reasoning, simply failing
to *express* it in their opinions. The fact that courts do not give voice to this
concern, however, is itself a negative feature of Italian corporate law and
governance, as the signals judges send indiscriminately to corporate actors
through their decisions are vague and obscure.[105]

One may think that judges' lack of concern for spill-over effects is related
to the absence of a formal *stare decisis* doctrine in Italy. Judges do not need
to worry that they are establishing a precedent and hence do not consider
that they may be guiding future business decisionmaking. However, we have
seen that in Italy precedents do have considerable persuasive power on
judges. This is confirmed by the Milan Tribunal's frequent citation of its
own prior decisions.[106]

In the face of judges' silence concerning these grounds, one may examine the decisions in our sample to see whether judges do in fact send the
"right" messages to corporate actors. This sort of analysis can only be
sketched out here. Some of the decisions described above construing
abstruse legal rules so as to impose cumbersome formalities on corporate
actors are not the best products of a corporate law judge.

Some interesting implications can be drawn from challenges of resolutions approving parent-subsidiary mergers passed by the vote of the parent.
We have seen that the Milan court takes for granted that the parent may vote
at the subsidiary's meeting called to approve the merger.[107] Further, as seen
above, the court consistently refuses to grant a stay against the merger, holding that minority shareholders damaged by the share exchange ratio may
later recover damages in an ordinary action. Thus, under the Milan case
law, majority shareholders can unilaterally proceed with a parent-subsidiary
merger and set the terms of the deal. If the terms are unfair, minority share-

holders must bring an ordinary action for damages. Since the damage to individual shareholders is normally small, while the cost of suing (in the absence of class actions, contingency fees and the American rule) is high, even substantially unfair mergers may proceed without compensation to minority shareholders. In other words, it is highly doubtful whether the liability rule applied by the Milan Tribunal to this kind of self-dealing transaction is efficient in light of all relevant factors, including the efficacy of the judicial system and the disciplinary role of markets and social norms.[108]

Conclusion

If corporate law matters to corporate governance and finance, then in order to assess the quality of the law in any given country, one must look at corporate law off the books—the characteristics of corporate law as applied by judges and other relevant public officials. This essay has provided an assessment of Italian corporate law based on an analysis of a sample of decisions by the Italian court most specialized in corporate law. I have tried to evaluate the quality of the judges by examining: (1) how deferential they are to corporate insiders; (2) how keen they are to understand, and possibly take into account, the real merits of the case before them; (3) the degree of antiformalistic reasoning revealed; (4) their concern for the effects their decisions have on corporate actors generally.

It is fair to say that this analysis casts a negative light on Milanese (and by extension, all Italian) corporate law judges. We have seen egregious cases of deference to corporate insiders, especially with regard to parent-subsidiary relationships. Furthermore, few opinions are drafted so as to allow the reader to understand the actual nature of the dispute and whether a party had acted opportunistically. In any case, it appears that courts rarely take into account the substantive reasons for the dispute. I have also described cases in which the court has relied on very formalistic arguments. Finally, there is no sign that judges care about the signals they send to corporate actors and the incentive effects of their decisions on directors and shareholders.

These conclusions, in turn, confirm the negative assessment of Italian corporate law and governance so often found in the literature. Arguably, a similar analysis of many other legal systems would provide comparable results. It may be useful, then, not only for Italian corporate governance but for other countries, to consider how policymakers could change the land-scape of bad corporate governance off the books.

First, a revision of corporate law on the books would be helpful. Access to justice for minority shareholders should be made easier and more "direct" by enabling them to challenge self-interested transactions in court. As argued in section I.C, this would reduce the incentives to bring ostensible suits, making it easier for courts to address the real issues. It would also enable judges to gain experience with such cases and thereby develop a good nose for corporate misconduct. Statutory provisions maintaining point-less formalities should be eliminated, so that attention is not diverted from more substantive issues.

Policy initiatives more directly targeted at corporate law judges would seem to take much more time to be effective, as their effectiveness will cru-cially depend upon changes in a country's (legal) culture. It would obviously be useful to have judges devoted exclusively or at least predominantly to cor-porate law. Needless to say, in order to have more specialized judges, they must be trained to handle complex corporate cases, and exposed to at least basic notions of corporate finance, accounting, and business administration. Acquiring more knowledge in these areas should also enhance their sense of legitimacy to second-guess the self-interested decisions of corporate actors.

Yet changing a judiciary's deferential attitude toward corporate insiders and reducing formalism in the construction of the law will be very difficult. After all, corporate insiders are often wealthy and powerful. Most Italians, not simply corporate law judges, have a deferential attitude toward the wealthy and powerful. Moreover, judges in Italy and other civil law jurisdic-tions share a formalistic approach to law with most practicing lawyers and legal scholars. As law students, they were taught to be formalistic. Later, they were selected as judges thanks to their skills in formalistic reasoning and the application of rules. Policymakers may find few effective tools to deal with such cultural features, at least in the short term. It is far more realistic to expect that changes in national (legal) culture will be the product of global-ization and competitive forces.

Endnotes

The author thanks Ferruccio Auletta, Fabrizio Barca, Marcello Bianchi, Fabrizio Cafaggi, Danilo Galletti, Amir Licht, Jon Macey, Curtis Milhaupt, Alan Palmiter, Matteo Rescigno, Walter Santagata, Gianni Sofri, Lorenzo

Stanghellini, Marcello Tarabusi, and participants at workshops at the University of Siena and at the Columbia Law School, for helpful comments on previous versions of this paper and Marco Corradi, Federico Mucciarelli, and Alessandro Pomelli for their valuable research assistance. Usual disclaimers apply.

1. This debate, as old as that on the public corporation (see Berle and Means 1933), was recently revived by works by La Porta et al. (esp. 1997, 1998) (arguing that good legal investor protections are a necessary condition for the development of strong capital markets, on the basis of statistical analysis showing that ownership is more dispersed and capital markets more developed in countries having a common law origin than in those having a French civil law origin).

2. See, e.g., Shleifer and Vishny (1997: 742); Macey (1998: 140) (In Italy "[t]here is a complete absence of protection for minority shareholders"). Italy scored poorly in La Porta et al.'s indices, especially the antidirector rights index (see La Porta et al. 1998: 1131). To be sure, La Porta et al.'s data are not very accurate with regard to Italy. In fact, contrary to that data, proportional representation on the board is allowed (and even mandated for privatized companies since 1994: see Bianchi et al. 2001: 185) in Italy no less than in the U.S. (where the cumulative voting system is permitted, but rarely used). Also, the assignment of a "0" for Italy under the "Oppressed minority" heading is rather arbitrary, since the Article 2409 procedure discussed below has been in place since 1942. It is interesting to note that in 1998, after La Porta et al.'s data were collected, the Italian Government enacted a corporate law reform strengthening minority shareholders rights (Legislative Decree 25 February 1998, No. 58). With the improvements introduced by this statute, Italy would now score 5 in La Porta et al.'s antidirector rights index, the same as the U.S. and the U.K.

3. La Porta et al. 1998: 1141–43.

4. See, e.g., Istituto di Studi e Analisi Economica (2001).

5. See Shleifer and Vishny (1997: 752).

6. See di Majo (1988: 305–8).

7. See Hertig (forthcoming: 15); Delebecque (1998: 68–69); Cafaggi (2001: 61–62).

8. The Supreme Court first stated this principle in the 1988 case *Linotype* (103 BGHZ 185), then confirmed it in the 1995 case *Girmes* (129 BGHZ 137) and in the 1999 case *Hilgers* (44 Aktiengesellschaft 517 [1999]).

9. See Campobasso (1999: 327–28). This is the leading corporate law textbook in Italy and reports as "dominant and correct" the view that Article 2373 of the Italian Civil Code, which renders voidable a shareholder resolution passed by

the vote of a shareholder who has an interest in conflict with that of the company, if the resolution would bring damage to the company, does not apply to resolutions on whether to distribute dividends, to issue new shares, or to liquidate the company. Under Italian corporate law, the power to decide these issues is assigned to the shareholder meeting.

10. Campobasso (1999: 327–28) (citing a number of opinions by the Italian Supreme Court—Corte di Cassazione).

11. In such cases, minority shareholders normally expect to gain from the judge's decision a stronger bargaining position against insiders to reach a settlement. This is especially the case for closely held corporations.

12. On the expressive function of judge-made law see Cooter (1998).

13. Of course, it is always true that "judges are not business experts" (*Dodge v. Ford Motor Co.*, 204 Mich. 459, 508 [1919]), but some judges undeniably have less business expertise than others.

14. This is the picture of an average country's equity markets. The U.S. and U.K., with their large number of independent public companies, are the exception. See, e.g., La Porta et al. (1999).

15. U.S. practitioners refer to the fairness test as applied by Delaware judges as the "smell test." As Yablon (1991: 502) puts it, "if the terms of the underlying transaction stink badly enough, the courts will find a way to abrogate any procedural protection supplied by the business judgment rule."

16. See also Hansmann and Kraakman (forthcoming: 26) ("judges must . . . understand the possible motivations, both legitimate and illegitimate, of corporate actors").

17. In some continental European countries, even medium-sized firms adopt the form of the public limited corporation, even though the law may be quite strict and burdensome (see Rojo 1993: 6–7).

18. Of course, judges in these cases must be careful to write opinions that allow future judges to identify functionally formalistic reasoning that may not be appropriate in other cases.

19. See Barca (1998: 8); Fisch (2000: 1079); Allen (1997: 895) ("the elemental purpose of corporation law is the facilitation of cooperative activity that produces wealth").

20. Predictability is noticeably absent from this list of relevant features. Arguably, this is not such an essential feature, as the unpredictability of Delaware judges' decisions suggests. See, e.g., Fisch (2000: 1078–79); Allen (2000: 72).

21. Unless otherwise specified, the description that follows covers all three legal forms of corporations under Italian law: the *società per azioni* (or joint stock company or corporation), the *società a responsabilità limitata* (or limited liability company), and the *società in accomandita per azioni* (an infrequent form in which some of the shareholders carry unlimited liability and have a right to be directors of the corporation). The legal regimes for the latter two legal forms

"borrow from that of the societ[à] per azioni, the only one of the three that is complete and self-standing:" Stanghellini (1995: 99).

It is important to note here that a sweeping reform of Italian corporate law and shareholder litigation is currently under way. It is too early to judge whether this reform will make corporate law on the books "better" in terms of minority shareholder protection, let alone to evaluate its impact on the quality of Italian corporate law as actually enforced.

22. Article 2379, Civil Code (Italy).

23. Campobasso (1999: 338–40) (providing examples of irregularities judged to produce the nonexistence of the resolution, such as when a shareholder meeting had never been convened, or when the resolution had been passed by the vote of a non-shareholder).

24. See Campobasso (1999: 435–47) for references to the relevant case law. Article 2365 of the Civil Code (Italy) provides that financial statements must be approved at the annual shareholders meeting.

25. A conspicuous body of "accounting" case law has developed in the last 40 years or so. See, e.g., Colombo (1994: 440–44, 450–54) for references. However, it is very difficult to bring this kind of suit for shareholders of listed corporations. Article 157, Legislative Decree 25 February 1998, No. 58 (which has taken the place of the slightly less restrictive Article 6, Legislative Decree of Mar. 31, 1975, No. 136), provides that, if the certified accounting firm has approved the financial statements, the resolution of the shareholders' meeting approving the financial statements may be challenged on the grounds that they fail to conform to the provisions governing their preparation, only by shareholders representing at least 5 percent of the share capital.

26. It is a criminal offense for directors to present false financial statements (see Articles 2621 and 2622, Civil Code [Italy]). The judge finding that the statements are false has a duty to report the facts to the public prosecutor (see Article 361, Criminal Code [Italy]).

27. Cheffins (2000: 35). See also Bianchi and Enriques (2001: 38).

28. Article 2373, Para. 3, Civil Code (Italy). In order to avoid the prohibition on voting in such resolutions, shareholder-directors are normally well advised not to own their shares personally (see Stanghellini 1995: 172), but to use trust-like devices, nominees or holding companies.

29. Specifically, Article 2393's requirement that the shareholders' meeting authorize liability suits.

30. Translation by Colussi (1993: 163).

31. See Bonelli (1985: 313), who refers to the nearly unanimous legal scholarship siding with the courts on this issue.

32. See, e.g., Judgment of Sept. 7, 1993, No. 9385, Cass. Civ., 1994 Giurisprudenza commerciale II, 365 (Negretti vs. Chiaretti).

33. Translation by the author.

34. Or a smaller fraction at the company's discretion. No company has lowered the threshold, however (see Consob 2001: 28).

35. Italian law assigns the audit function in corporations to a separate board (*collegio sindacale*), composed of three or more auditors, and requires that its members be independent of the board of directors. See Articles 148–154, Legislative Decree, February 25, 1998, No. 58, for listed corporations and Articles 2397–2408 Civil Code (Italy) for unlisted firms.

36. See Articles 128, 145, Para. 6, and 152, Legislative Decree 25 February 1998, No. 58.

37. While it is not rare for prosecutors to file such actions (pursuant to Article 2409, Para. 5), sometimes also on the behalf of minority shareholders representing less than the required percentage (see, *e.g.*, Tedeschi 1988: 212–13), seldom if ever have they filed the complaint against directors of a listed corporation, where it might be very difficult for minority shareholders to reach the 5 percent (10 percent before 1998) threshold.

38. See Cottino (1999: 456). Settlement agreements and decisions to abandon the case may not be authorized by the shareholders' meeting if shareholders representing at least 20 percent of the capital are opposed (Article 2393, Para. 4, Civil Code [Italy]). But this may not be necessary in order to frustrate the liability suit, as the case *Mondialpunte v. Lovati* aptly shows. See Decision of January 17, 1991, Tribunal of Milan, 1991 *Giurisprudenza italiana* I, 2, 563, in which the court rejected a liability suit brought by the temporary administrator on the simple grounds that, after the end of the temporary administration, the corporation, again in the hands of the majority shareholders, simply failed to provide evidence substantiating the charges against directors. Hereinafter, decisions cited only by party name are decisions from the Tribunal of Milan.

39. See Taruffo (1988: 209) (noting that the style of judicial opinions reveals that Italian judges still see themselves as bureaucrats and "mouths of the law" rather than as "problem solvers").

40. See Enriques (2001: 91). There are, of course, notable exceptions: in the last two decades an increasing number of corporate law scholars have approached the law and economics methodology. For references to some of the main recent works in this area, see Sanfilippo (2000: 49–63).

41. See Preite (1988: 976–77).

42. Merryman (1966: 587); Galgano (1988: 506–8).

43. It is worth noting that this way of thinking is especially critical within the corporate law field. As Macey (1989: 1697–98) points out, good corporate law relies crucially upon a mix of flexible statutes and active courts engaging in "case by case analysis because of the necessity for close attention to the specific fact patterns." Especially in the corporate governance arena policymakers "cannot benefit shareholders by developing rules that successfully regulate whole

classes of transactions," since these will prove to be inevitably either overinclusive or underinclusive.

44. Sbisà (1989: 521).

45. The decisions were identified by searching the CD-ROM "Repertorio del Foro Italiano 2000–2001," Ed. 1.0, June 2001.

46. The sample does not include challenges to resolutions approving financial statements, because of the high level of technicality of the accounting issues decided.

47. The full list of cases is on file with the author. One case decided an action challenging both a shareholder resolution and a board of directors' resolution. In two cases, the same decision decided both an action brought under Article 2377 and an Article 2395 individual liability suit.

48. More than one quarter of Italian listed corporations have their seat in Milan. Consob data on Italian listed corporations, 2001 (on file with the author).

49. Of the 26 cases which have proved useful for the analysis, one was an appeal (*Fingem v. Montedison [2]*) of another case among the 26, while of the remaining 24, only 2 were decided by the Milan Court of Appeals according to the CD-ROM "Repertorio del Foro Italiano 2000–2001," Ed. 1.0, June 2001. It is possible, however, that some of the appeals were never published or had not been decided by June 2001.

50. See, *e.g.*, *Spalletti Trivelli v. Gallarati Scotti* (Decision of Nov. 11, 1993), 1994 Giurisprudenza commerciale Part 2: 866 (deciding on the validity of a resolution introducing a right of first refusal in the bylaws). The finding of a large number of opinions not useful to the analysis is disturbing, but falsifiable.

51. Decision of June 26, 1986, 1987 Foro Padano Part 1: 402 (Manfrin, J.).

52. Under Italian law, the acquirer of an undertaking (*azienda*) is liable for the debts resulting from its books. Article 2560, Civil Code (Italy).

53. *Cavaggioni v. Rotondo*: 405. The Milan Court of Appeals reversed this judgment: see *Cavaggioni v. Rotondo* (Decision of Oct. 28, 1986, 1987 Foro Padano I, 402 [Milan Court of Appeals]). Two similar cases are *Finter v. Immobiliare Cassinazza* (Decision of July 3, 1986, 1987 Le Società: 144 [Gilardi, J.]) and *GE.VI v. ME.AL.* (Decision of June 29, 1992, 1993 Giurisprudenza italiana Part 1.2: 234 [Marescotti, J.]).

54. Decision of Jan. 20, 1998, 1998 Le Società: 811 (Tarantola, J.).

55. Ibid.: 813. The obligations mentioned in the text are imposed by Articles 2501-*bis* and 2501-*quinquies*, Civil Code (Italy). A similar case is *Aliverti v. Immobiliare Isaia Volontè* (Decision of Apr. 21, 1986, 1986 Le Società: 869 [Marescotti, J.]).

56. Decision of Mar. 2, 1995, 1995 Giurisprudenza italiana Part 1.2: 618 (Riva Crugnola, J.).

57. Ibid.: 622.

58. Decision of May 18, 1995, 1996 Le Società: 68 (Gilardi, J.).
59. Ibid.: 70.
60. See also *Brichetti v. Nuova COI* (Decision of Apr. 27, 1989, 1989 Giurisprudenza italiana Part 1.2: 932 [Quatraro, J.]).
61. Decision of Sept. 12, 1995, 1996 Giurisprudenza commerciale Part 2: 827 (Quatraro, J.).
62. Article 2392, Para. 4, Civil Code (Italy).
63. *FIN.GE.M. v. Montedison (1)*: 833.
64. Ibid. According to Article 2374, Civil Code (Italy), "[i]f members in attendance, who aggregate one-third of the capital represented at the meeting declare themselves not sufficiently informed on the matters to be dealt with in a resolution, [they] may request that the meeting [be] postponed for not more than three days" (translation by Colussi [1993: 151]).
65. *FIN.GE.M. v. Montedison (1)*: 832–33.
66. Decision of Sept. 25, 1995, 1996 Giurisprudenza italiana Part 1.2: 77 (Tarantola, J.).
67. Decision of Sept. 28, 1995, 1996 Giurisprudenza italiana Part 1.2: 77 (Manfrin, J.).
68. Together with preliminary evidence that the action is well founded (*fumus boni juris*), the plaintiff petitioning for a preliminary injunction must provide evidence of the risk of irreparable damage, if required to wait for a court's decision in an ordinary proceeding (*periculum in mora*). See Article 700, Civil Procedure Code (Italy).
69. Decision of Oct. 31, 1995, 1996 Giurisprudenza commerciale Part 2: 828 (Tarantola, J.).
70. The plaintiff in *FIN.GE.M. v. Montedison (1)* had asked for a preliminary injunction, which had been denied. The October 31 decision was the appellate decision on the denial.
71. See *FIN.GE.M. v. Montedison (2)*: 838.
72. Another decision in favor of the minority shareholder on an issue of procedural fairness is *Giuliani v. Le Forane* (Decision of Feb. 8, 1988, 1998 Le Società: 707 [Marescotti, J.]).
73. Decision of Oct. 21, 1999, 2000 Giurisprudenza italiana: 554 (Sperti, J.).
74. Ibid.: 559–62, providing an impressive catalogue of misappropriation practices in which the controlling shareholders had engaged.
75. Decision of Mar. 2, 1995, 1995 Giurisprudenza italiana Part 1.2: 706 (Marescotti, J.).
76. In all likelihood the suit had been brought after a change in control. The opinion does not clarify this point, however.
77. *Iniziative Finanziarie v. Baraldi*: 713.
78. Ibid.

79. Decision of June 9, 1994, 1996 Giurisprudenza commerciale Part 2: 273 (Marescotti, J.).
80. Ibid.: 276–77. A case similar to this is *Megamoda v. Provasoli* (Decision of May 13, 1994, 1994 Le Società: 1389 [Marescotti, J.]).
81. See, e.g., *Shreiber v. Pennzoil Co.*, 419 A.2d 952 (Del. Ch. 1980).
82. Possibly, in some proceedings the parties themselves make no reference to these real reasons. But this is no less a consequence of the courts' lack of interest in them than a justification for the courts' silence.
83. *GE.VI v. ME.AL.*: 242.
84. Very similar cases are *Terracciano v. F.r.o.m.m.* (Decision of Sept. 17, 1987, 1987 Giurisprudenza commerciale Part 2: 797 [Quatraro, J.]) and *Casterida v. Immobiliare V.O.R.* (Decision of Nov. 20, 1995, 1996 Giurisprudenza commerciale Part 2: 825 [Riva Crugnola, J.]).
85. See *Bonfiglio* (Decision of Jan. 16, 1998, 1998 Le Società: 806 [Tarantola, J.]) and *Fiordelli v. CO.MO.I. s.i.m.* (Decision of Jan. 18, 1999, 1999 Giurisprudenza italiana: 2112 [D'Isa, J.]).
86. Decision of June 2, 2000, 2000 Il Foro italiano Part 1: 3638 (D'Isa, J.).
87. Ibid.: 3642–43.
88. One may fear that an abuse of the voting right will almost never be found to exist, if the judge must be satisfied that the shareholder aimed exclusively (i.e., in the absence of any appreciable interest) at harming the other shareholders (see Enriques 2001: 89).
89. *Innenz v. Fiduciaria Sant'Andrea*: 3641.
90. See Article 2448, No. 3, Civil Code (Italy) (providing that a corporation dissolves in case the shareholder meeting is unable to work, e.g., in the case of a deadlock).
91. This is even more apparent if one considers that Italian law does not provide for exit remedies except in very peculiar circumstances. See Enriques (2001: 81).
92. Decision of July 26, 1997, 1998 Giurisprudenza italiana: 93 (D'Isa, J.).
93. Ibid.: 94.
94. *Cavalli v. GAIC*: 86–87.
95. Decision of Jan. 27, 1986, 1986 Le società: 609 (Quatraro, J.).
96. See Article 4, Law No. 1745, of Dec. 29, 1962. This provision had been enacted as a defense for incumbents against creeping acquisitions. But the rule also applies to closely held corporations, for which it has no purpose. See Enriques (2001: 92).
97. *Sviluppo Immobiliare v. Reale*: 613.
98. See *supra* text accompanying note 23.
99. *Sviluppo Immobiliare v. Reale*: 613–14. The court had to resort to nonexistence because the auditors had failed to challenge the resolution within three months: it was hence too late to declare the resolution simply voidable. Two

other cases showing a high degree of formalism are *Biocoral v. Borgonuovo Sim* (Decision of Feb. 5, 1998, 1998 Giurisprudenza italiana: 1429 [D'Isa, J.]) and *Mazzoni v. Saeco* (Decision of June 23, 1988, 1989 Giurisprudenza commerciale Part 2: 248 [Marescotti, J.]).

100. *Serafini v. Tosi:* 812–13.
101. See also *Aliverti v. Immobiliare Isaia Volontè.*
102. See Enriques (2000b: 162–63). And see also *Terracciano v. F.r.o.m.m.:* 798.
103. See, e.g., Fisch (2000: 1079–81) and Allen (1997: 903), both with specific regard to Delaware corporate law judges.
104. 249 N.Y. 458, 464 (1928) (emphasis added).
105. See Barca (2001: 13).
106. See, e.g., *Terracciano v. F.r.o.m.m.:* at 802; *Innenz v. Fiduciaria Sant'Andrea,* at 3642; *Mazzoni v. Saeco:* 252 and 257; *Biocoral v. Borgonuovo s.i.m.:* 1430. A civil law theorist might object that it is not the judge's duty to decide which rules are best for corporate actors, or to send appropriate messages to the business world; the judge's duty is to apply the law, not to make it. Making law is the legislature's function. Yet this is not a realistic view, in Italy or elsewhere (Mengoni 1994; Merryman 1966).
107. See especially *Serafini v. Tosi:* 813.
108. See Goshen (2000: 23–33).

References

Allen, William T. 1992. Speculations on the Bicentennial: What Is Distinctive about Our Court of Chancery? In *Court of Chancery of the State of Delaware, 1792–1992:* 13–19.

———. 1997. Ambiguity in Corporation Law. *Delaware Journal of Corporate Law* 22: 894–903.

———. 2000. The Pride and the Hope of Delaware Corporate Law. *Delaware Journal of Corporate Law* 25: 70–78.

Barca, Fabrizio. 1998. Some Views on U.S. Corporate Governance. *Columbia Business Law Review* 1998: 1–24.

———. 2001. La riforma incompiuta del governo societario italiano: Un'introduzione. *Stato e mercato:* 3–16.

Berle, Adolf A. and Gardiner C. Means. 1933. *The Modern Corporation and Private Property.* New York: Macmillan, reprint 1982.

Bianchi, Marcello, Magda Bianco, and Luca Enriques. 2001. Pyramidal Groups and the Separation Between Ownership and Control in Italy. In *The Control of Corporate Europe.* Fabrizio Barca and Marco Becht eds. Oxford: Oxford University Press.

Bianchi, M. and L. Enriques. 2001. Corporate Governance in Italy after the 1998 Reform: What Role for Institutional Investors? In Quaderni di Finanza Consob, No. 43. Available at http://papers.ssrn.com/sol3/papers.cfm?abstract_id= 203112.

Black, Bernard S. 2001a. The Legal and Institutional Preconditions for Strong Securities Markets. UCLA Law Review 48: 781–855.

———. 2001b. The Core Fiduciary Duties of Outside Directors. Asia Business Law Review 33: 3–16.

——— and John C. Coffee, Jr. 1994. Hail Britannia?: Institutional Investor Behavior under Limited Regulation. Michigan Law Review 92: 1997–2087.

Bonelli, Franco. 1985. Gli amministratori di società per azioni. Milano: Giuffrè.

Buscaglia, Edgardo and Maria Dakolias. 1999. An Analysis of the Causes of Corruption in the Judiciary (World Bank. Working paper).

Cafaggi, Fabrizio. 2001. Riforma del diritto societario: Il ruolo delle "clausole generali." Stato e mercato: 45–77.

Campobasso, Gian Franco. 1999. Diritto commerciale, 2, Diritto delle società (4th edition). Torino: Utet.

Cheffins, Brian R. 2000. Current Trends in Corporate Governance: Going from London to Milan Via Toronto. Duke Journal of Comparative and International Law 10: 5–42.

Coffee, John C., Jr.. 1999a. Privatization and Corporate Governance: The Lessons from Securities Market Failure. Journal of Corporation Law 25: 1–39.

———. 1999b. The Future As History: The Prospects for Global Convergence in Corporate Governance and Its Implications. Northwestern University Law Review 93: 641–707.

——— 2001a. Do Norms Matter? A Cross-Country Evaluation. University of Pennsylvania Law Review 149: 2151–77.

———. 2001b. The Rise of Dispersed Ownership: The Roles of Law and the State in the Separation of Ownership and Control. Yale Law Journal 111: 1–82.

Colombo, Giovanni E. 1994. Il bilancio d'esercizio. In G.E. Colombo and G.B. Portale eds., Trattato delle società per azioni, vol. 7.1: 23–573. Torino: UTET.

Colussi, Franco (transl.). 1993. The Italian Civil Code. Labour. Milano: Giuffrè.

Consob. 2001. Relazione per l'anno 2000. Dati e analisi. Roma: Istituto Poligrafico e Zecca dello Stato.

Cooter, Robert. 1998. Expressive Law and Economics. Journal of Legal Studies 27: 585–608.

Cottino, Gastone. 1999. Le società. Diritto commerciale, vol. 1.2 (4th edition). Padova: Cedam.

Delebecque, Philippe. 1998. Il ricorso dei giudici alle clausole generali in Francia. In Luciana Cabella Pisu and Luca Nanni eds., Clausole e principi generali nell'argomentazione giurisprudenziale degli anni Novanta: 65–72. Padova: Cedam.

di Majo, Adolfo. 1988. *Delle obbligazioni in generale*. Bologna-Roma: Zanichelli Editore and Soc. Ed. del Foro Italiano.

Di Sabato, Franco. 1999. *Manuale delle società* (6th edition). Torino: Utet.

Easterbrook, Frank H. and Daniel R. Fischel. 1991. *The Economic Structure of Corporate Law*. Cambridge: Harvard University Press.

Enriques, Luca. 2000a. The Law on Company Directors' Self-Dealing: A Comparative Analysis. *International and Comparative Corporate Law Journal* 2: 297–333.

——. 2000b. *Il conflitto d'interessi degli amministratori di società per azioni*. Milano: Giuffrè.Enriques, Luca. 2001. *Il nuovo diritto societario nelle mani dei giudici: una ricognizione empirica, Stato e mercato*: 79–105.

——. 2001. *Il nuovo diritto societario nelle mani dei giudici: una ricognizione empirica, Stato e mercato*: 79–105.

Fisch, Jill E. 2000. The Peculiar Role of the Delaware Courts in the Competition for Corporate Charters. *University of Cincinnati Law Review* 68: 1061–1100.

Galgano, Francesco. 1988. *Dei difetti della giurisprudenza, ovvero dei difetti delle riviste di giurisprudenza. Contratto e impresa*: 504–9.

Galletti, Danilo. 2001. E-mail to the author, 21 February (on file with the author).

Goshen, Zohar. 2000. Voting and the Economics of Corporate Self-Dealing: Theory meets Reality. Working Paper. Available at http://papers.ssrn.com/sol3 /papers.cfm?abstract_id = 229273.

Hansmann, Henry and Reinier Kraakman. Forthcoming. What is Corporate Law? In *The Anatomy of Corporate Law. A Comparative and Functional Approach*, Reinier Kraakman et al., eds. Oxford: Oxford University Press.

Hertig, Gérard. Forthcoming. Convergence of Substantive Law and Convergence of Enforcement: A Comparison. In *Convergence in Corporate Law: The Emerging Questions*. Jeffrey N. Gordon and Mark J. Roe, eds. Cambridge: Cambridge University Press.

Irrera, Maurizio. 2000. *Le delibere del consiglio di amministrazione*. Milano: Giuffrè.

Istituto di Studi e Analisi Economica. 2001. *Rapporto trimestrale* (April).

Jaeger, Pier Giusto. 1987. *Ancora sulla determinazione del compenso degli amministratori: conflitto d'interessi, commisurazione al "fatturato," principio di "ragionevolezza." Giurisprudenza commerciale* Part 2: 797–810.

Johnson, Simon, Rafael La Porta, Florencio Lopez-de-Silanes, and Andrei Shleifer. 2000. Tunnelling. *American Economic Review* 90 (2): 22–27.

La Porta, Rafael, Florencio Lopez-de-Silanes, and Andrei Shleifer. 1999. Corporate Ownership Around the World. *Journal of Finance* 54: 471–517.

—— and Robert Vishny. 1997. *Law and Finance*. Legal Determinants of External Finance. *Journal of Finance* 52: 1131–55.

—— 1998. Law and Finance. *Journal of Political Economy* 106: 1113–50.

Macey, Jonathan R. 1989. Courts and Corporations: A Comment on Coffee. *Columbia Law Review* 89: 1692–1702.

———. 1998. Italian Corporate Governance: One American's Perspective. *Columbia Business Law Review* 1998: 121–44.

Marcinkiewitz, Andrea. 1990. Condizioni per l'ispezione della società. *Le Società*: 521–23.

Mengoni, Luigi. 1994. L'argomentazione orientata alle conseguenze. *Rivista trimestrale di diritto e procedura civile*: 1–18.

Merryman, John H. 1965. The Italian Style I: Doctrine. *Stanford Law Review* 18: 39–65.

———. 1966. The Italian Style III: Interpretation. *Stanford Law Review* 18: 583–611.

Nakajima, Chizu. 1999. *Conflict of Interest and Duty. A Comparative Analysis in Anglo-Japanese Law*. Den Haag: Kluwer Law International.

Oberto, Giacomo. 2001. Recrutement et formation des magistrats: le système italien dans le cadre des principes internationaux sur le statut des magistrats et l'independence du pouvoir judiciaire. *Rivista di diritto privato*: 717–52.

Penati, Alessandro and Luigi Zingales. 1997. Efficiency and Distribution in Financial Restructuring: The Case of the Ferruzzi Group. CRSP Working Paper No. 466. Available at http://papers.ssrn.com/sol3/papers.cfm?abstract_id=224439.

Pistor, Katharina, Martin Raiser, and Stanislav Gelfer. 2000. Law and Finance in Transition Economies. *The Economics of Transition* 8: 325–69.

Preite, Disiano. 1988. Osservazioni a Trib. Milano, 9 novembre 1987 (in tema di conflitto d'interessi del socio e azione sociale di responsabilità). *Giurisprudenza commerciale* Part 2: 969–77.

Rojo, Angel. 1993. La sociedad anónima como problema. In Pietro Abbadessa and Anjel Rojo eds., *Il diritto delle società per azioni: Problemi, esperienze, progetti*: 1–25. Milano: Giuffrè.

Sanfilippo, Pierpaolo M. 2000. *Funzione amministrativa e autonomia statutaria nelle società per azioni*. Torino: Giappichelli.

Savona, Ernesto U. and Laura Mezzanotte. 1998. *La corruzione in Europa*. Roma: Carocci Editore.

Sbisà, Giuseppe. 1989. Certezza del diritto e flessibilità del sistema (la motivazione della sentenza in common law e civil law). *Contratto e impresa*: 519–25.

Shleifer, Andrei and Robert W. Vishny. 1997. A Survey of Corporate Governance. *Journal of Finance* 52: 737–83.

Stanghellini, Lorenzo. 1995. Corporate Governance in Italy: Strong Owners, Faithful Managers. An Assessment and a Proposal for Reform. *Indiana International and Comparative Law Review* 6: 91–185.

———. 1999. Family and Government Owned Firms in Italy: Some Reflections on an Alternative System of Corporate Governance. Paper presented at the Corporate Group Meeting Symposium, Venice, 25–26 June. On file with the author.

Taruffo, Michele. 1975. *La motivazione della sentenza civile*. Padova: Cedam.

———. 1988. *La fisionomia della sentenza in Italia*. In *La sentenza in Europa. Metodo, tecnica e stile*: 180–214. Padova: Cedam.

Tedeschi, Guido U. 1988. Il controllo giudiziario sulla gestione. In G.E. Colombo and G.B. Portale eds., *Trattato delle società per azioni* vol. 5: 189–303. Torino: UTET.

Weigmann, Roberto. 1991. Compensi esagerati agli amministratori di società a base ristretta. In *Giurisprudenza italiana* Part 1.2: 793–802.

Wiedemann, Herbert. 1991. *Zu den Treuepflichten im Gesellschaftsrecht*. In *Festschrift Heinsius*: 949–66. Berlin: de Gruyter.

Yablon, Charles M. 1991. On the Allocation of the Burden of Proof in Corporate Law: An Essay on Fairness and Fuzzy Sets. *Cardozo Law Review* 13: 497–518.

Zweigert, Konrad and Hein Kötz. 1998. *Introduction to Comparative Law* (3rd edition). Oxford: Clarendon Press.

9   Institutional Change and M&A in Japan

Diversity Through Deals

Curtis J. Milhaupt and Mark D. West

The potential effects of globalization have emerged as a central focus of the corporate law and governance debate. Some scholars argue that national corporate governance systems are converging toward a homogeneous corporate law and governance model (Hansmann and Kraakman 2001). Others claim that despite the pressures of global markets, local institutions will block the emergence of a uniform corporate governance system (Bebchuk and Roe 1999). While the debate has yielded interesting theoretical ideas, ultimately the extent to which national systems are converging is an empirical question that can be resolved only with the appearance of data over time.

In this essay, we take a different approach to the question of how globalization is affecting corporate governance. Rather than looking at diversity or homogeneity among various national systems, we consider the potential for convergence toward a particular governance technology—the market for corporate control—to increase diversity within a given system. Specifically, we examine the role of takeovers—a feature commonly associated with the "Anglo-American" model of corporate governance—in promoting a corporate governance regime in Japan that expands managerial options and is more readily adaptable to the competitive needs of firms in different industries.

We begin by applying in the corporate governance setting two related and underappreciated insights from other fields. Economic theory holds that there is no universally efficient corporate organizational model; rather, different firms in different industries require diverse organizational forms (Aoki

1995a: 30; Demsetz and Lehn 1985; see also Aoki 2000: 18; Aoki 1995b: 330). Organizational behavior and related literature provides evidence that heterogeneous groups outperform homogeneous ones (Robbins 2001: 235–36; Hong and Page 2001). Combining these insights, we argue that corporate governance systems that promote, or at least do not impede, organizational diversity are more likely to produce firms that are adaptable, receptive to new governance technologies, make effective decisions, and avoid shackling by inefficient norms. Thus, our first claim is straightforward: diversity within a corporate governance system is a virtue.

We are using the term "corporate governance" to mean the range of formal and informal mechanisms by which corporate decisions are made, monitored, and effected. It is the structural environment for corporate decisionmaking. "Diversity" for our purposes means "differences in problem solvers' perspectives and heuristics—variations in how people encode and search for solutions to problems" (Hong and Page 1998: 2). The literature suggests that two types of corporate governance diversity are beneficial: interfirm diversity, as firms or industries select the governance tools most appropriate to their competitive environment, and intra-firm diversity, as boards and other key decisionmaking units draw upon a range of problem solvers. Corporate governance diversity, then, cannot be confined to a single metric, but instead refers to variation not only in structural features such as board size and composition, but also in such areas as methods of finance, stakeholder relations, and decisionmaking processes.

The second step of our argument is that a specific corporate governance tool—an active market for corporate control—is an effective way to promote these beneficial forms of diversity. To date, commentators have viewed mergers and acquisitions (M&A) almost exclusively as a disciplining mechanism. Largely overlooked, however, is the potential for takeovers to broaden managerial outlook, expand strategic option sets, match governance technology with production processes, and contribute to a more robust market for legal innovation.

We explore this new perspective with reference to Japan. As most readers are aware, historically Japan has had little takeover activity. Yet this prosaic fact obscures a multitude of unexplored issues. We show that an institutional environment much more highly textured than the conventional focus on cross-shareholding would suggest contributed to a homogenous approach to corporate governance in Japan. For a time, this governance system matched the production technology and competitive needs of Japanese firms extremely well. But as the political economy, technology, and competitive environment changed, the lack of mergers and acquisitions left Japanese firms without a crucial adaptation mechanism, reinforcing continued adherence to practices designed to complement a system that no longer functioned effectively. Through institutional reform, Japan has in recent years taken steps to stimulate the market for corporate control. The preliminary results suggest that corporate actors have responded to the new institutional set, and that a more flexible formal environment for corporate decisionmaking—one in which mergers and hostile takeovers are both possible and valued as a strategic option—has spawned innovation and variation in governance practices ranging from board composition to transaction structure and the use of the courts.

Analyzing the Japanese experience with the market for corporate control also suggests that two prominent theories in comparative corporate governance literature may be misleading or incomplete. The first, the "functional substitutes" theory, holds that all national corporate governance systems must basically solve the same set of problems, and functional substitutes exist across systems as means to solve this problem set. While persuasive on a general level, this theory masks some important points. First, unless systems are infinite in their plasticity, perfect substitutes are unlikely to exist. Second, in a world of institutional complementarity, how a problem is addressed affects the development and operation of other institutions. We apply these insights to two ostensible hallmarks of Japanese corporate governance: main banks and cross-shareholding.

Another prominent perspective, the "law and finance" theory advanced in a series of empirical works by Rafael La Porta et al. predicts that the quality of legal protections for minority shareholders is an important determinant of corporate governance patterns around the world (La Porta et al. 1997, 1998, 1999). Strong legal investor protections, they assert, lead to more dispersed share ownership and larger capital markets. Yet, as we will demonstrate empirically both with evidence from Japan and the results of our own regression analysis using La Porta et al.'s data, the impact of law on corporate governance is more ambiguous and complex than this influential econometric model suggests.

We hasten to add several caveats. Our claim is not that takeovers are universally beneficial; clearly some deals destroy value. Nor do we claim that takeovers are the sole, or necessarily the primary, mechanism through which firms achieve diversity in corporate governance. Even in Japan during the time period we examine, takeovers are by no means the only factor at work. Finally, our claim that intra-firm diversity is beneficial is not an implicit endorsement of statutes mandating the use of outside directors. By definition, firms need flexibility from the legal system to attain the governance structures that best suit their needs. Our claims are simply that an active market for corporate control is beneficial in ways that have not previously been recognized, and that this insight has important consequences both for institutional design issues and the convergence debate.

The essay proceeds as follows. Part I discusses the theoretical foundations of the gains from organizational diversity, and describes how institutions conducive to an active market for corporate control improve the prospects of reaping those gains. Part II examines the historical (absence of a) market for corporate control in Japan. We present the most complete domestic and comparative data available on Japanese takeover activity. The data belie the claim that while hostile deals are rare, friendly deals are plentiful. In part III, we link the historically low level of M&A activity to low-quality financial disclosure as well as overly protective corporate law and tender offer regulations. We then show how these same features correlate to the lack of diversity in Japanese corporate practices, as an inflexible and high-cost environment led firms to adopt uniform governance techniques. Part IV first discusses recent institutional changes in the Japanese market for corporate control and the ensuing increases in M&A activity. Next, preliminary evidence is presented indicating that a deal-friendly environment correlates with increased governance innovations, a proliferation of non-standard corporate practices, and increased legal development. Part V discusses implications of our findings for the "functional substitutes" and "law and finance" theories.

I. Gains from Diversity and the Market for Corporate Control

Commentators engaged in the convergence debate have thus far ignored some important questions. For example, what are central characteristics that any corporate governance system should contain? By what mechanism(s) might those features be transmitted from system to system?

A starting point for analyzing these questions is the work of economists Harold Demsetz and Kenneth Lehn, who argue in essence that there are no central corporate governance characteristics. Because "the structure of corporate ownership varies systematically in ways that are consistent with value maximization," the management structure that works in one firm may not work best everywhere (Demsetz and Lehn 1985).

Extending this insight, economist Masahiko Aoki has contributed important ideas that have yet to be utilized by participants in the convergence debate. Aoki theorizes that organizational diversity is a virtuous characteristic for economic systems. In a series of articles, Aoki argues that "maximum economic gains may be realized by implementing different organizational forms that correspond to the specific nature of each industry" (Aoki 2000). Diversity can be achieved by accommodating these forms.

The claim that diversity is a key feature of successful systems draws support from several sources. Organizational behavior scholars who study corporate demography, for example, note that two very successful U.S. industries, high tech in Silicon Valley and entertainment in Hollywood, are characterized by diverse organizational forms and high rates of demographic turnover (Carroll and Hannan 2000: xx–xxii). Increased organizational diversity in the beer and wine industry may explain increased consumption in the United States (ibid.). Corporate demographers note that the United States "stands out as extremely diverse," in organizational forms, while "the Soviet Union, before the collapse of state socialism, stood at the other pole" (ibid.: 2). Thus, "the more diverse the population, the more likely that organizational structures exist that can deal effectively with the unexpected environmental events" (ibid.: 8).

Other studies provide more theoretical support for these claims. Economists Lu Hong and Scott Page (1998, 2001) have produced a model demonstrating that diversity among problem solvers increases the ability to solve difficult problems. "Being boundedly rational," they note, "only stifles good decisions if we are boundedly rational in the same way" (Hong and Page 2001: 17). In biology, variation is a prerequisite for evolution (Kauffman 1993). Oliver Williamson (1996: 102), drawing on the work of Hayek and Barnard, claims that "adaptability is the central problem of economic organization." If so, then plasticity and variation are desirable—even essential—traits of a successful economic environment.

In perfectly competitive markets, diversity might be achieved naturally. As Demsetz (1983) theorizes, firms that survive in the long run will be those that have picked appropriate management structures. But even Demsetz recognizes—and offers quantitative evidence in support of the claim—that "systematic regulation reduces the options available to owners" (Demsetz and Lehn 1985: 161).[1] By limiting managerial options, regulation and other factors diminish a system's ability to attain diversity. Again, Aoki elaborates and extends Demsetz's point: "The combined effect of such factors as the bounded rationality of individuals, evolutionary pressures, and institutional complementarity is a tendency for a more or less homogeneous organizational convention to be adopted throughout a particular economy. However, different organizational conventions will evolve in different nations" (Aoki 2000: 131). Numerous recent studies highlight the tendency toward national convergence of organizational forms and corporate governance practices (Davis 1991; Filgstein 1985; Kobayashi and Ribstein 1996; Mizruchi 1989).

Accordingly, a central question is how to prevent homogenizing institutional and evolutionary pressures from discouraging the optimal corporate governance diversity within national systems and within individual firms — diversity that might arise naturally in a perfectly competitive environment. One promising path toward organizational diversity is provided by the market for corporate control. Literature on the market for corporate control is vast, but most commentators make the same point: takeovers mitigate agency problems. The threat of job loss for inefficient managers posed by a market for corporate control provides powerful incentives to advance shareholder interests (Easterbrook and Fischel 1991; Jensen and Ruback 1983; Manne 1965).[2]

The literature discussed above, however, suggests a powerful alternative rationale for merger activity in general, and cross-border mergers in particular: promotion of organizational diversity both within and across firms. We hypothesize that increased merger activity correlates with heightened managerial, transactional and legal innovation, as new perspectives are introduced into firm governance by the clash of perspectives between bidders and incumbents, and those clashes themselves spawn an expanded set of approved transactional and legal responses. Some of the gains may come from the enhanced discipline that exposure to global "best practices" brings. The motivation for our study, however, is the point that the best practice is one that properly aligns governance institutions with the needs of specific firms, not the adoption of a one-size-fits-all model.

To be sure, an active market for corporate control is not the only way of achieving diversity in a system.[3] We simply argue that international convergence toward an active market for corporate control may be one powerful way to endogenize a healthy level of diversity within economic systems.

To explore this new perspective, we now turn to Japan. Aoki, along with many others, saw the main bank and stable shareholding—institutions deeply rooted in the old political economy of Japan—as an alternative to the market for corporate control. One key—but overlooked—consequence of this prevailing organizational mode was relative homogeneity in governance structures. For a time, it did not matter, because this system of corporate governance matched the production needs and technology of Japanese firms extremely well. But those needs have changed and the main bank system has largely ceased to function, giving rise to an important natural experiment: How will the old system adapt, what institutions will grow up in its place, and what are the implications for corporate governance?

II. Japanese M&A in Historical and Comparative Perspective

It will come as no surprise to most readers that Japan has not experienced much merger activity in the postwar period. So low is the level of activity in the world's second largest economy, however, that it demands deeper exploration than has been provided to date. Using a variety of official and unofficial sources of data, in this part we examine merger activity in Japan.

A. Merger Data

1. *Official data.* Until January 1999, the Antimonopoly Act required that every merger and asset sale be reported to the Japan Fair Trade Commission. Figure 9.1 shows the number of notifications received by the JFTC from 1969 to 1989 (Kōsei Torihiki Iinkai, various years).

These data, which show only about 1,000 mergers per year, may significantly overstate the level of merger activity in Japan. The JFTC data include mergers of tiny firms (including limited liability companies and limited partnerships) and intra-group mergers.[4] In the 1980s, for example, nearly two-thirds of all merger notifications were for mergers between firms with assets of less than ¥1 billion ($10 million U.S. at current exchange rates). About 95 percent of all mergers were for firms with assets of less than ¥50 billion ($500 million), and ¥100 billion mergers ($1 billion) averaged in the single digits (Yamazaki 1995). The figure also shows that Japan has not experienced significant merger "waves" as in the United States. Although asset

FIGURE 9.1 Merger and Asset Sales Reported, 1968–1989

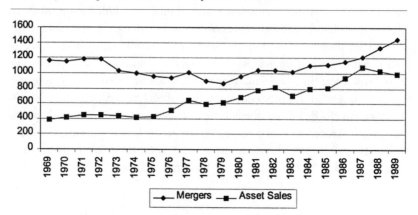

sales increased over the twenty-year period, mergers, at least by this measure, have remained at a relatively constant level.

2. *Private data.* Several unofficial sources of merger data are more instructive. Recof LLC, a Japanese M&A boutique, maintains merger data that exclude both intra-group mergers and transactions that involve changes only in preexisting equity positions, such as from majority to minority. Although these data are less comprehensive than the JFTC figures, they are likely to be a better indication of significant merger activity. These data show a gradual increase from 182 transactions in 1985 and 256 in 1989 (Recof 2001: 38).

Thomson Financial maintains data on the number of merger announcements in Japan. From 1990 to 1994, purely domestic ("in-in") M&A averaged fewer than 100 transactions per year, with a gross average value of about ¥800 billion ($8 billion). During the same period, foreign acquisitions of Japanese firms ("out-in") averaged only about 50 transactions per year, with a total average value of only ¥50 billion ($500 million) (Thomson Financial Securities Data Reports, various years).

These data indicate that Japanese M&A activity is minuscule in comparison to U.S. levels. According to Mergerstat (various years), the average number of U.S. merger announcements from 1990 to 1994 was 2,437, with a total average annual value of $135 billion. Even the U.S. data from as far back as 1963, the earliest on record in Mergerstat, are approximately 900 percent higher than the highest figures recorded for Japan at the peak of the economic bubble. In 1990, Japanese merger activity was approximately 0.4 percent of its GDP[5] in comparison to the U.S. figure of 1.8 percent.[6]

B. Tender Offers

Although the disparity between total merger activity in the U.S. and Japan is large, a comparison of tender offers in the two countries is even more striking. From 1971 to 1990, a total of three tender offers were made in Japan. By contrast, Mergerstat, defining tender offers as those seeking more than 10 percent of a target's shares and excluding self-tenders, recorded 218 tender offers in the United States for 1988 alone.

C. International Comparisons

Lest one conclude that these disparities simply reflect the oversized U.S. market for corporate control, data indicate that Japan's M&A activity is extremely low by any international measure. In a ranking of targets by nation, Japan had a 0.6 percent market share in 1997 (behind South Africa, Malaysia, and Bermuda) (Thomson Financial, Merger Yearbook). In 1998, on the basis of M&A transaction value as a percentage of GDP, China's market for corporate control was three times larger than that of Japan; Australia's was twenty times larger; and the U.S. market was forty-six times larger (Raupach-Sumiya 2000: 9).

III. Institutional Foundation for Takeovers and Corporate Governance

Existing literature has provided incomplete answers to two basic questions on takeovers in Japan. First, why is merger activity so low? Academic explanations to date have focused almost exclusively on cross-shareholding. Second, what are the consequences of the absence of a market for corporate control? Only the agency cost issue has been discussed, followed by the ubiquitous reference to main bank monitoring. In this part, we uncover underlying reasons why deals are difficult, and expose the relationship between internal monitoring and homogeneous corporate governance practices in Japan.

A. *Obstacles to a Market for Corporate Control*

A recent report on corporate governance in leading economies assigns to Japan its second lowest rating on takeover barriers (meaning that they are among the most formidable in the world, behind only the Netherlands)(Davis Global Advisors 2001: 67–69). The report notes that "visible, formal takeover defenses are not always as potent as those present by custom and practice that are invisible and informal. Japan, for instance, has the fewest variations in defenses against takeovers, but those it does feature are strong enough—thanks to unwritten rules of the market—to stop nearly all unwelcome bids" (ibid.: 64). The report identifies three almost universal and nearly insurmountable barriers in Japan: core shareholders, cross-shareholding, and targeted stock placements to white knight investors.

In our view, these "barriers" are not root causes of low M&A activity, but instead are symptomatic of more fundamental, and less well understood, obstacles to the efficient transfer of corporate assets in Japan. Our task here is to explain the institutional factors that underlie these anti-takeover practices and to deepen understanding of the often-discussed barriers.

We begin with a startling fact: the average premium paid for shares in a tender offer in Japan is negative. We arrive at this conclusion by analyzing all fifty-nine tender offers made between 1990 and 2000 for which complete data are available.[7] Building on a dataset and methodology used by Merrill Lynch, we compared the offer price to the target's stock price on the day preceding the offer. So calculated, the average premium is –4.72 percent. Perhaps more important than the average is the distribution of premiums, which reveals a stark division between deals with positive premiums and deals with negative or zero premiums. Twenty-nine deals had negative or zero premiums, while thirty had positive premiums. The average positive premium was 24.5 percent, while the average negative premium was –37.4 percent.[8]

Compare these figures with those of other large economies for the same period. Average premiums (by month) for European targets in 1999 ranged from 4 to 25 percent over the market price the day before the offer was announced. For U.S. targets in the three months ending in January of 2000, the average premium over the price one week before announcement of the offer was 35 percent (Kirchner and Painter 2000).

At least two interrelated explanations for the prevalence of below-market tender offers in Japan are likely.[9] First, the quality of financial information appears to be low (see West 1999). In such an environment, it may be rational for a bidder to pay a negative control premium to compensate for uncertainty. Second, the takeover procedures codified in the Securities Exchange Act, ostensibly designed to protect investors, may create incentives that actually work to the disadvantage of minority shareholders. We take up these explanations in turn.

Limited financial disclosure has historically played a large role in dampening the market for corporate control in Japan, particularly by limiting foreign acquisitions of Japanese firms (Scott 1998). Historically, public financial disclosure of useful information has been very limited. For example, consolidated financial statements were not mandatory until very recently, so liabilities and underperforming assets could be taken off a firm's balance sheet by moving them into subsidiaries. Curiously, many Japanese financial analysts focused only on parent companies, so stock prices did not necessarily reflect the corporate group's complete financial situation. Financial assets were recorded at cost. Pension liabilities were not required to be disclosed. Cash flow data were limited, and there was general unfamiliarity with discounted cash flow analysis (Merrill Lynch 2000: 19). Moreover, both internal and external auditing practices tended to be minimalist and forgiving (Fukao 1998: 404–6).

Limited information obviously raises the cost (reduces the number) of takeovers. Valuation is difficult, and concerns over undisclosed liabilities are hard to quell. The efficient transmission of information is all the more problematic because Japan has traditionally had few professional advisors specialized in mergers and acquisitions. Due diligence thus simultaneously becomes absolutely crucial and exceedingly difficult and time consuming (Zaloom and Kawai 2000).

Tender offer procedures have served as a second structural impediment to takeovers. Tender offers were technically unregulated prior to the enactment of legislation in 1971, but no offers were made, at least in part because the lack of a legal framework caused many legal advisors to question their legality (see Kanda 1995: 609). From 1971 until 1990, a ten-day waiting period and prior review of all offers by the Ministry of Finance were required, on the theory that Japanese courts would be reluctant to enjoin legally defective offers due to unfamiliarity with the new procedure (Tatsuta 1983: 178–79). As a prominent Japanese commentator has noted, this rationale reveals distrust of the judiciary and overconfidence in administrative agencies (ibid.). Not surprisingly, as noted above, only three tender offers were made during this period.

In 1991, Japan instituted a mandatory bid rule patterned after (but more stringent than) London's City Code. This rule (Shōken Torihiki Hō, [Securities Exchange Act], § 27–2(1)[4]) requires that any off-exchange offer, the acceptance of which would result in the acquisition of more than 33.3 percent of the target's shares, be made through a tender offer to all shareholders. The rule is designed to protect minority shareholders by ensuring that they receive a pro rata share of any control premium, and to ensure disclosure of even a "private" purchase where a major shareholder would emerge (Kanda 1998).

In fact, even Japanese policymakers acknowledge that the supposedly shareholder-protective mandatory bid rule has had adverse consequences (JETRO 2000: 84–85). In particular, while the mandatory bid rule may deter some inefficient bids, it has two unintended consequences that may work to the disadvantage of minority shareholders. First, the rule may dampen beneficial tender offer activity by increasing uncertainty and cost for erstwhile acquirers, who must incur the expense and unpredictability of a tender offer even to pass a relatively low shareholding threshold. This is particularly problematic because a tender offer cannot be used as the first of a two-step acquisition process to acquire 100 percent control of the target, since under Japanese law minority shareholders cannot be squeezed out for cash. Thus, often there may be little advantage to obtaining more shares than necessary to surpass the critical 33.3 percent level at which major corporate transactions can be vetoed.[10]

Second, because once the mandatory bid rule is triggered the tender offer must be made to all shareholders, it may be difficult for large blockholders to achieve liquidity. The probability that the blockholder will be able to cash out completely declines as the premium increases, since the premium will encourage other shareholders to tender, and shares must be accepted on a pro rata basis. Accordingly, both acquirers and blockholders seeking liquidity have incentives to make "prearranged" tender offers at prices below prevailing market prices to ensure that other shareholders do not tender into the offering (Merrill Lynch 2000: 30). We found that all twenty-one cases in which the negative premium exceeded 10 percent were prearranged by the bidder and a blockholder—usually founding shareholders, shareholding executives, or stable shareholding group companies. While we lack specific evidence, we assume these shareholders may be willing to accept lower prices because of inside information, various forms of side payments, or an inability to demand prevailing market prices for large blocks in low-float Japanese markets.

An additional and related obstacle to M&A similarly grows out of the shareholder-protective stance of the Commercial Code. Several attributes of the Code make takeovers relatively unattractive. As noted above, there is no legal authority for cash-out or short-form mergers, so it is not possible to eliminate minority holdouts in the back end of a two-step acquisition (see Kanda 1998). Perhaps more importantly, historically the Code has not provided managers with the flexibility to craft U.S.-style defensive mechanisms such as the poison pill. If it did, presumably those measures would be reviewable by the courts and would have to be removed if found to be inconsistent with directors' duties to the corporation and its shareholders.[11] The lack of such litigation, however, has left the scope of directors' duties in Japan ambiguous (see Kanda 1994: 68). Ironically, the absence of law-based takeover mechanisms leaves risk-averse Japanese managers few alternatives but to resort to the draconian, relationship-based defense of cross-shareholding, which is generally unreviewable by the courts. Quite plausibly, firms would have avoided or unwound unprofitable cross-shareholding investments if managers had been more secure in their ability to respond to unsolicited bids through legal devices.

One further potential obstacle to M&A remains to be addressed. It is often said that social and cultural distaste for the sale of corporate control, based on shame or corporate paternalism toward employees, is a major impediment to M&A in Japan. As one of us has previously argued (Milhaupt 2001), the social norm denigrating takeovers as unethical may have emerged as a substitute for a more fully developed and efficient set of ground rules for M&A activity. Here, the parallels with the United States are instructive. Prior to 1968, takeover activity in the United States was essentially unregulated. A social norm against hostile bids developed. Statutory and common law regulation of takeovers eventually proliferated, but in ways that did not completely shut down takeover activity. Deals were done, law was made. The ground rules for takeovers became clearer, and the norm virtually vanished (see Lipton and Rowe 2002).

Japan's historical path differs. As in the United States, the legal vacuum surrounding takeovers led to a social norm against hostile bids. In Japan, however, specific anti-takeover regulation did not appear. Instead, the social norm was buttressed by relationship-based takeover defenses. Unlike U.S. regulation, the Japanese response virtually eliminated takeover activity. In the absence of takeovers, corporate legal development was slow, and the underlying norm denigrating the market for corporate control was reinforced.

B. Governance Traits

In this section, we show how this same institutional setting that constrains takeovers also contributes to a one-size-fits-all approach to corporate governance in Japan. A range of evidence indicates that many large Japanese firms have adopted strikingly similar—indeed one might say highly stylized—approaches to corporate governance. The point is not that the precise approach to these practices matters a great deal to corporate success. Rather, it is that Japanese firms appear to have adopted uniform practices without a compelling economic rationale for doing so. If the diversity theory outlined above has merit, this is not an optimal approach to corporate governance.

1. *Low Disclosure*. Low quality disclosure in Japan, as discussed above, contributes to the lack of takeovers. It also leads to widespread adoption of several corporate practices:

- Shareholders' meetings. In 1997, 95 percent of first-section Tokyo Stock Exchange firms held their shareholders' meeting on the same Thursday in June (West 1994: 799). In 1990, 83.6 percent of all firms ended their meetings in less than 30 minutes (Shōji Hōmu Kenkyūkai 1990: 79). Both are measures to prevent heckling activity by *sokaiya* (racketeers) who, as one of us has argued elsewhere (West 1994), prey on corporate secrets that result from institutionally encouraged low levels of disclosure.
- Fiscal year. In 1996, 85 percent of first-section Tokyo Stock Exchange firms ended their fiscal year in March (Tokyo Stock Exchange 1997: 25). All ten major national banks issued their annual reports on May 24 (Choy 1996).

2. *Commercial Code Rules*. The inflexible character of the Commercial Code, which until recently virtually eliminated the possibility of takeover defenses beyond relationship-based shareholding, also encouraged conformity in other corporate governance practices.[12]

- Auditors. All firms have statutory auditors designed to monitor management's compliance with law, regardless of their efficacy or the availability of substitutes, because they are mandated by the Commercial Code.

- Board committees. Few firms have formal committees of the board for significant matters such as executive compensation and audits, because they were not recognized by the Code until 2003. Indeed, the Code (Section 260[2]) prohibits the delegation of "important" board functions.
- Share transactions. Share repurchases and stock splits are heavily regulated by the Commercial Code and historically have not been viable options for pursuing corporate strategy (West 1994: 809 & n. 51).
- Organizational concerns. Until December 1997, holding companies were prohibited by the Antimonopoly Act, and similar structures were heavily regulated by intra-group cross-shareholding limits under the Commercial Code (Sections 211-2, 241[3]). Although some companies found ways to avoid the ban, it rendered impermissible many corporate structures that are common elsewhere.
- Executive compensation. Cash compensation is relatively low by international standards, leaving less room for variation (see Abowd and Kaplan 1999: 146). Intra-industry executive compensation is virtually identical among leading firms, at least in part because large compensation packages and performance-based pay, which could create variation, remain rare (see Nakamoto 1998).

3. Other homogeneous practices.

- Dividends. Japanese dividends typically have no correlation to earnings, and are instead based on a fixed percentage of par value (Fatemi and Rad 1994). In 1990, 24.7 percent of Tokyo Stock Exchange companies issued dividends of exactly five yen per share (equal to 10 percent of the standard fifty-yen par value). Another 19.1 percent issued dividends of exactly ten yen per share. More than 90 percent of all TSE firms paid dividends ranging from five to ten yen (Zenkoku Shōken Torihikijo Kyōgikai 2000).[13]
- Boards of directors. Postwar Japanese boards of directors have followed a well-established convention of large size, internal promotion, and lack of independent members (Corporate Governance Committee 1998: 41–42). This convention is likely the result of widely held beliefs about the board's proper structure and role as

employee representatives, which are reinforced by an environment devoid of takeovers (Milhaupt 2001).

- Advisors. Independent professional advice on corporate transactions is in short supply, raising problems both of access and uniformity of opinion. Severe state-set limitations on the number of
  licensed attorneys and the historical shortage of transactional work
  contribute to a dearth of attorneys with expertise in corporate matters. As a result, a short list of prominent attorneys and law firms
  handle virtually all sophisticated transactional work in Japan.
  Accounting advice is also limited, a phenomenon that may correlate with low quality information disclosure.[14]

- Share ownership patterns. Stephen Prowse (2000) compared the
  ownership concentration of nonfinancial firms in Germany,
  Japan, the United States, and the United Kingdom. The mean
  percentage of shares held by the five largest shareholders in Japan
  is 33.1 percent, more than in the U.S. (24.4 percent) or the U.K.
  (20.9 percent), but far less than in Germany (79.2 percent). The
  interesting difference from our perspective, however, lies in the
  range of shareholding patterns in the various countries. Prowse
  reports that while Germany has a range of 5 percent to 100 percent, with a standard deviation from the mean of 31.7, Japan's
  range is 10.9 percent to 85 percent, with a standard deviation of
  only 13.8, the smallest in the sample. In short, Japanese firms have
  less variation in ownership structure than firms in other leading
  economies.

C. Consequences

One consequence of the rules and practices discussed above can be seen in
figure 9.2, which illustrates the ratio of bust-up value to market capitalization
for 779 nonfinancial Tokyo Stock Exchange firms. As the figure indicates, in
2000 approximately 13 percent of these firms were trading below their bust-
up value.[15] In other words, more than one of every eight public firms in Japan
was worth more in liquidation than under current management. In the
1980s, there were U.S. firms trading below bust-up value. In contrast to the
U.S. situation, however, there is no market action in Japan to dismantle
these firms. Despite the obvious potential to profit by acquiring and then

FIGURE 9.2   Ratio of Bust-up Value to Market Capitalization, 2000

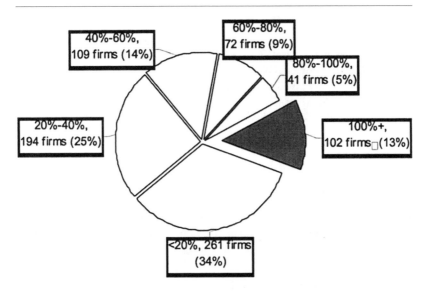

selling off the assets of these firms, bids are rare, suggesting that the transaction costs involved are prohibitive.

Indeed, this intuition is reinforced by evidence from firms that do merge. Table 9.1 shows the time required from announcement date to closing for six recent, well-publicized Japanese and U.S. financial firm mergers. As the table shows, time to closing for major deals is five to ten times longer in Japan than in the United States. At least in the case of Mizuho, commentators have pointed directly to institutional barriers, such as the Commercial Code requirement of approval of two-thirds of shareholders, as the cause of the delay (Smith 2002).

These data indirectly suggest an important relation between the lack of mergers and the lack of diversity in Japanese corporate governance. Because strategic differences among competitors in Japan are minimal, firms compete primarily on the basis of operational efficiency, leading to severe profit pressures (Porter et al. 2000: 78–91). An active market for corporate control could serve as a natural corrective to this problem both by weeding out unprofitable firms and by providing managers with strategic options to distinguish their firms from rivals. But transaction costs prevent many inefficient firms from being acquired, while the lack of differentiation among

TABLE 9.1 Time from Announcement to Closing, U.S. and Japan

Country	Firm	Time Required
Japan	Mizuho Financial Services (DKB/Fuji/IBJ)	31 months
Japan	Mitsui Sumitomo Bank	19 months
Japan	Sumitomo Fire & Marine/Mitsui Fire & Marine	20 months
U.S.	Chase/JP Morgan	4 months
U.S.	Travelers Group/Solomon Smith Barney	2 months
U.S.	Morgan Stanley/Dean Witter	3 months

Source: Goldman Sachs data, in Hattori (2001: 23).

competitors reduces the potential for synergistic gains from mergers. In this manner, the lack of M&A in Japan, a product of institutional constraints, is inextricably linked with homogeneity in the corporate governance environment.

Within this linkage, however, lies potential. As the next part shows, primarily through deregulation and liberalization, institutions can be manipulated to invigorate the market for corporate control, which in turn can increase diversity among stakeholders, and create new options for strategic competition and firm governance.

IV. New Institutions, More Deals, New Governance

We begin this part by surveying some key legal and accounting changes brought about in Japan's changing political economy. We then examine the impact of the new institutions on M&A activity, and reassess Japanese governance practices. We conclude by explaining why the pessimistic response of observers to the recent reforms is unwarranted.

A. New Institutions

1. *Legal/Regulatory Reforms.* Japan's Commercial Code was amended more extensively in the 1990s than in any other period since the Occupation. Many of the significant reforms were designed to improve corporate governance.

- *Holding Companies.* In 1997, the Occupation-imposed ban on "pure" holding companies was eliminated. This change should have several important benefits for Japanese firms (see Aoki 2000: 133–40). It will promote management reorganization through spin-offs, mergers, and corporate reorganizations. But it will also provide useful legal separation between strategic and operating units of the firm, and allow firms to differentiate personnel management systems. Firms may retain conventional "Japanese" employment patterns where useful, while introducing more diverse arrangements in other subsidiaries. Removal of the ban on financial holding companies will also facilitate reorganization of the financial industry into functionally diverse groups offering banking, securities, and insurance products and services.
- *Share-for-Share Exchanges.* The Commercial Code was revised in 1999 to introduce share-for-share exchanges. This reform produces several benefits. Share exchanges can be used to create wholly owned subsidiaries. Capital gains taxes are not owed at the time of the share exchange. Time-consuming and expensive valuation procedures to protect creditors mandated by the Commercial Code for ordinary mergers are not required. Minority shareholders can be forcibly excluded from the subsidiary (although they become shareholders of the parent).
- *Spin-offs and Split-offs.* A new statutory scheme provides a flexible framework for separating business units from parent companies. Among other benefits, court-appointed auditors are no longer required to value assets before transfers can be effected.
- *Corporate Reorganizations.* A Civil Rehabilitation Act, enacted in 2000, may promote acquisitions of financially troubled firms by providing more flexible and efficient reorganization procedures than its predecessor statute. It is now possible to do a pre-packaged bankruptcy, with the reorganized firm emerging under new ownership.
- *Stock Options.* Beginning in 1997, the Commercial Code formally authorized the issuance of stock options to certain firm employees. According to a Nikko Securities/Towers Perrin survey, the number of listed companies issuing stock options has nearly quadrupled from 121 in 1998 to 463 in 2001, up from zero in 1997 and representative of about one-sixth of listed companies

(see Record 463 Firms Offer Stock Options 2001). As forms of executive compensation change, managers may increasingly discover incentives to "sell out" and encourage fellow shareholders to transfer control to a bidder. This process may alter the social cost/benefit calculus for managers, which traditionally has weighed heavily against the sale of corporate control.[16]

- *Shareholder Monitoring.* A seemingly technical change in procedural law in 1993 that lowered the cost of filing derivative suits led to a major increase in this form of shareholder monitoring. Japanese shareholders brought approximately twenty derivative suits between 1950 and 1990. By contrast, 245 derivative suits were pending in 1999 (West 1994; 2001a). While the Japanese derivative suit mechanism suffers from the same attorney's-fee-based incentive distortions that plague such suits in the United States (West 2001a), this shift toward heightened shareholder monitoring may place greater pressure on managers to explain to their shareholders actions such as declining to pursue a strategic alternative presented by a suitor. Moreover, institutional investors, whose managers must answer to their own shareholders and beneficiaries, will likely face increased pressure to sell into an attractive offer, regardless of long-term relationships with the target firm.

2. *Accounting Reforms.* Japanese accounting standards have been revised significantly in the past several years to bring them substantially into conformity with international accounting standards. More stringent standards for consolidated accounting were introduced in fiscal year 1999. Mark-to-market accounting for financial assets was introduced in fiscal year 2001. Pension liabilities are reflected on balance sheets as of fiscal year 2001. Cash flow statements were introduced in fiscal year 1999.

Assuming audit practices improve as well, these reforms can be expected to have a significant impact on corporate governance. The new rules enhance management transparency and provide powerful new incentives for restructuring or divesting underperforming assets. Perhaps most significantly, these reforms enable cross-country comparisons of financial statements between foreign and Japanese companies, which assists due diligence and valuation efforts. In the past, lack of international accounting comparability was a major obstacle to cross-border M&A in Japan.

B. More Deals

Merger activity in Japan has increased significantly in recent years. Our sense, confirmed in discussions with practitioners, is that institutional reforms are a significant cause of the increase. Although still small in comparison to deal activity in the United States, the increase in the number, size, and structure of transactions in recent years is striking.

1. *Merger data.* As in part II, we examined data from two private sources: Recof LLC and Thomson Financial. Both measures show marked increases in the 1990s, as shown in figure 9.3.[17] The Recof data, which showed approximately 250 mergers and acquisitions of Japanese firms in 1989, surpassed 300 in 1991, 400 in 1997, and 500 in 1997. The trend continues: Recof reports 847 transactions in 1999, 1,241 in 2000, and 1,348 in 2001 (Recof 2001; 2002).

The Thomson Financial data show a significant increase in domestic M&A. "In-in" M&A, which averaged fewer than 100 transactions per year during 1990–1994, with a gross average value of about ¥800 billion ($8 billion), reached over 1,300 transactions in 1999, with a gross transaction value of ¥13 trillion ($130 billion). The number of "out-in" transactions, which averaged only about fifty per year during 1990–1994, with a total average value of only ¥50 billion ($500 million), increased to 227 transactions with a value of ¥3 trillion ($30 billion) in 1999. Japanese M&A has fared comparatively well even in global recession; while the worldwide M&A market fell by 45 percent the from the first quarter of 2001 to the first quarter of 2002, the Japanese market fell by only about 2.5 percent (Thomson Financial 2002b).

There are no data available on the specific legal mechanics of each deal. But some mergers, such as the giant Mizuho Financial Group alliance that combined Dai-Ichi Kangyo Bank, Fuji Bank, and the Industrial Bank of Japan, have used the holding company structure. The newly established share exchange system also appears popular; one source lists seventeen such transactions in 1999 and another twenty-five in the first six months of 2000, involving such firms as Sony, Matsushita, Isuzu, and Toyota (Kikuchi 2000a: 118–19). In the first fiscal year that spin-offs were legally permitted, more than 200 such transactions occurred (Kaisha Bunkatsu 2002), including several combinations that would have not been undertaken absent the change (Kaisha ha Kōshite Henshin Saseru 2002).

FIGURE 9.3 Number of Deals Involving Japanese Targets, 1993–2000

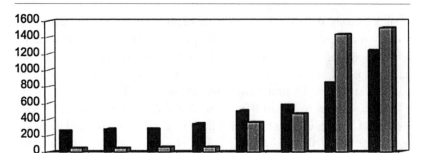

Although Mergerstat data for the U.S. remain considerably higher than the Japanese data, the gap shows signs of narrowing. Mergerstat shows a huge increase in U.S. M&A activity, from 2,997 transactions in 1994 to 9,278 in 1999, with a corresponding increase in transaction value from $226 billion in 1994 to $1.42 trillion in 1999. The U.S. market, in other words, was three to five times larger in 1999 than in 1994. The Japanese market, by contrast, grew by more than ten times during the same period. The increase may also be seen relative to gross domestic product. As noted above, in 1990 Japanese merger activity was approximately 0.4 percent of GDP. In 1999, Japanese merger activity was approximately 3.3 percent of GDP. In the ranking of targets by nation, Japan moved from a 0.6 percent market share in 1997 to a fifth-place 4.5 percent market share in 1999 (Thomson Financial, Merger Yearbook), and to 5.5 percent in the first quarter of 2002 (Thomson Financial 2002b).

2. *Tender offer data.* Tender offers likewise surged in the 1990s. Although only three tender offers were consummated in the 1970s and 1980s, by our count, sixty-four tender offers were made in the 1990s. The average annual transaction value rose from approximately ¥30 billion ($300 million) in 1994 to nearly ¥250 billion ($2.5 billion) in 1999 (Kikuchi 2000a: 36). Although these measures continue to pale in comparison to the U.S. figure of 799 completed tender offers for the same period (Mergerstat 2000: 39), it

is apparent that significant increases in tender offer activity have recently occurred in Japan.

C. New Forms of Governance?

It is too early to document fundamental changes in organizational heterogeneity among Japanese firms, and we acknowledge the imprecision of the data available at this stage. Still, incremental changes in at least five areas are preliminary indications of potentially more fundamental future trends toward diversity. Although many factors contributed to the changes detailed below, their form and timing suggest interrelations both with institutional changes and with the increased merger activity that those changes engendered.

1. *Boards of directors.* In the mid-1990s, many companies began to consider altering the composition of their boards through a reduction in size and the inclusion of outside directors. Survey data show an increase in firms displaying particular interest in reducing the number of directors from 28.6 percent to 46.2 percent from 1998 to 2000 (Tokyo Shōken Torihikijo 2000). Of the firms reducing their boards, 79.9 percent scaled back to fewer than 10 directors. By May 2001, 38.8 percent of first-section Tokyo Stock Exchange firms had added outside directors to their boards (Shagai Torishimariyaku 38% ga Sennin 2001). Moreover, diversity among board members is beginning to draw attention as a desirable distinguishing characteristic for Japanese firms (Diversity Distinguishes IY Bank 2001).

2. *Officers.* Beginning in 1997, many corporations, in concert with reductions in board size, added a new corporate governance organ: the executive officer. Executive officers, an organ not formally authorized by the Commercial Code until 2003, were attractive because they had decisionmaking power but were not subject to derivative suit liability in the same manner as directors. As Milhaupt (2001) has noted, executive officers went from being a Sony innovation in 1997 to a fixture at over 200 firms by 1999. Survey data confirm that 71.4 percent of responding firms had adopted such a mechanism (Shōji Hōmu Kenkyūkai 1999).

Additional changes may soon be seen at the CEO level. Due in part to the success of Brazilian-born auto executive Carlos Ghosn of Renault in reviving Nissan Motor Company, other firms have appointed foreigners to top positions. Many Japanese companies have begun the "search for the perfect Ghosn clone" (Tanikawa 2001).

3. *Cross-shareholding.* Cross-shareholding ratios, which began to decline in the early 1990s, reached an all-time low in 2000 (Nissei Kiso Kenkyūjo 2001), down from 18.39 percent by value and 14.52 percent by number of shares in 1987 to 10.64 percent (by value) and 10.10 percent (by number) in 2000. The long-term holding ratio, which includes not only confirmed cross-holdings but also one-sided stable shareholdings involving financial institutions, also reached new lows in 2000, falling from 45.77 percent by value and 43.36 percent by number of shares to 33.0 percent and 31.34 percent in 2000.

The decline in cross-shareholding reflects the erosion of one important practice that bred conformity in several areas of corporate conduct. More significantly, it may lead to further innovations in corporate governance as individual firms respond to a variety of new stakeholders, some of which will emerge as acquisitions become possible. In light of these changes, the managing director of the Federation of Economic Organizations (Keidanren) has called for further corporate and securities law revisions to reflect the "diversification of financial supply," characterized by such newly invigorated sources as venture capital (Nakamura 2000: 20).

4. *Employment relations.* Intriguing evidence on increased diversity in employment relations is provided by researchers Christina L. Ahmadjian and Gregory Robbins (2000), who found statistically significant correlations between levels of foreign ownership and changes in downsizing, asset divestiture, and gross executive bonuses during the periods 1975–1981 and 1991–1997. Although the primary independent variable in their study was foreign ownership and not merger activity per se, these findings tentatively suggest that an active market for corporate control that includes cross-border acquisitions would further increase the type and range of corporate practices in Japan. The findings on downsizing and divestiture are particularly interesting because corporate norms are said to constrain such actions by Japanese managers.

5. *Corporate practices.* As the work of Ahmadjian and Robbins suggests, firms with substantial foreign investment are more likely to deviate from conventional Japanese governance practices. As a crude test of this hypothesis, we compared the corporate governance characteristics of two sets of firms: (1) the 11 Tokyo Stock Exchange first-section firms listed by NLI Research Institute as having a shareholding ratio of foreigners by net investment in excess of 33 percent, and (2) the 25 public Japanese firms identified

by Daiwa Research Institute as the top candidates for takeover (Kikuchi 2000b: 61). The Daiwa rankings are determined strictly by an accounting formula that does not take into account corporate governance factors.[18]

We examined four corporate governance measures: number of directors, number of outside directors, number of executive officers, and the filing of a derivative suit against directors.[19] The results are provided in Table 9.2.

Although caution is obviously required in interpreting data from such a small sample, as the table shows, firms with substantial foreign ownership are much more likely to have outside directors, to separate monitoring and decisionmaking functions through use of the executive officer system, and to be free of shareholder derivative litigation.[20] Recent case studies also suggest that Japanese firms are becoming more responsive to foreign investors, even if takeovers remain difficult (see Singer 2001).

Other evidence also suggests a proliferation of approaches to corporate governance:

- *Outside advisors.* By the late 1990s, firms had begun to actively seek outside consulting advice, and they sought it from more varied sources. In 2001, foreign investment banks such as Goldman Sachs dominated the league tables, comprising six of the top ten financial advisors of announced deals involving Japanese targets, and eight of the top ten advisors in deals with Japanese targets, acquirers, or ultimate parents (Thomson Financial 2002a). While

TABLE 9. 2 Corporate Governance Characteristics

Measure	>33% Foreign Firms	Takeover-Likely Firms
Average Number of Directors	14.9	13.5
Percentage of Firms with Fewer than 15 Directors	73%	76%
Average Number of Outside Directors	0.9	0.56
Percentage of Firms with Outside Directors	45%	28%
Average Number of Executive Officers	4.8	0
Percentage of Firms with Executive Officers	18%	0
Percentage of Firms with Directors as Derivative Suit Defendants	0	16%

Japanese players like Nomura continue to be strong (ibid.), foreign
advice is significant because foreign investment banks currently
appear to be a principal device by which new governance technology is transmitted in Japan.

- *Dividends.* Although most companies continue to base dividends
  on share par value, considerable variation has arisen. In 1990, 24.7
  percent of Tokyo Stock Exchange companies issued dividends of 5
  yen per share. In 1999, that figure had fallen to 16.3 percent. The
  percentage of companies issuing dividends between 5 and 10 yen
  per share fell from 90 percent to 63.7 percent. The change in distribution cannot be attributed entirely to economic downturn;
  although the percentage of companies issuing no dividends rose
  from 7.7 percent to 20.5 percent, the percentage of companies
  issuing dividends of more than 10 yen per share rose from 23.7
  percent to 30 percent for the same period (Zenkoku Shōken
  Torihikijo Kyōgikai 2000). More companies are also issuing dividends on a consolidated basis (see Kigyō no Haitō Renketsu Be-su
  ni Henshin, Keiei to Shōhō no Mujun Kaishō 2001).

- *Share Repurchases.* In 1995, a total of five companies implemented share repurchases. In 1998, following Commercial Code
  revisions, 1,179 companies announced buybacks, and 186 implemented them in that year (Yasui 1999: 26; Zhang 2000). Buybacks
  by listed companies in fiscal 2001 exceeded 2.3 trillion yen (about
  $20 billion) for more than two billion shares, an increase of nearly
  100 percent over fiscal 2000 (Jisha Kabu Kai Baizō 2 Chō Enchō
  2002).

- *Shareholders' meetings.* Although most firms continue to hold
  their meetings on the same Thursday in June, some limited variation has begun to occur. For the first time in two decades, the percentage of Tokyo Stock Exchange firms holding their meetings on
  that date fell to 80 in 2001 (Kabunushi Sōkai, Hachiwari ga 28
  Nichi Kaisai 2001). In part because of increased shareholder
  activism, and in part because of increased pressure from the
  courts,[21] the length and conduct of meetings have begun to vary.
  While 83.6 percent of firms in 1990 ended their meetings in less
  than 30 minutes (Shōji Hōmu Kenkyūkai, 1990: 79), only 57.8
  percent of firms did so in 2000 (Shōji Hōmu Kenkyūkai 2000: 91).

Although not tremendous changes, these data at least tentatively suggest erosion of previously homogeneous practices.

- *Case studies.* Anecdotally, there is also growing evidence that foreign acquisitions are inspiring innovations in many areas of corporate practice in Japan. Consider two brief examples among many: (1) Mazda, under Ford control, modified the widely used "ringi" corporate decisionmaking approach, in which proposals proceed up a long, formal ladder of managerial approvals. The number of approvals was reduced to three from more than twenty, and the entire process was transferred to the internet (Fields 2001). (2) AXA, the French insurance group, "totally transformed" failing Japanese life insurer Nippon Dantai by eschewing the asset stripping approached followed by U.S. rivals in Japan and reorganizing the firm from within. It hired a new team of managers who had been successful in a wide array of industries including commercial banking, automotives, and Silicon Valley high tech (Arnaud 2001). Within one year of the acquisition, new clients were up 28 percent, premiums were up 5 percent, and AXA's name recognition in Japan increased from 9 percent to 50 percent (ibid.; Kadri 2001).

These examples are particularly interesting because the acquirer's success appears to derive from the application of fresh ideas to existing Japanese practices, rather than wholesale adoption of foreign management concepts.

D. The Reality of Reform

Many academic and other observers doubt the effectiveness of legal reforms in altering Japanese corporate behavior (Columbia Conference 2001; Root 2001). More generally, commentators, asserting cultural or other reasons, voice skepticism that legal change is effective in Japan and doubt the utility of the government's recent reform efforts (Lochner 2001; Miwa and Ramseyer, this volume).

The evidence presented here, however, suggests that such pervasive skepticism may be unwarranted. We have shown that in M&A, as in other areas of corporate governance, actors in Japan respond voraciously to changes in their legal and transaction cost environments. Some of the increase in M&A activity is plainly attributable to macroeconomic factors, as distressed firms are sold at bargain prices.[22] This type of activity presumably will decline once the most troubled companies have been restructured. But evidence suggesting a broader opening of the market for corporate control does exist. While distress was present in one-third of the largest Japanese deals in the first half of 2001, the other two thirds were motivated by globalization and consolidation trends (Stead 2001).

Three informal indications of a broader development of the market can also be found: hostile takeover attempts for firms that could not be characterized as financially troubled have been made in the past two years, including one purely domestic bid, many investment banks are no longer discouraging foreign clients from hostile bids (Ishibashi 2000), and large numbers of Japanese managers are seeking professional advice on defensive measures.[23] Anecdotal though it may be, this evidence suggests a potential social norm shift, as Japanese corporate actors begin to view takeovers as a viable and enduring part of the landscape.[24] These developments, taken together with the formulation of major reforms to the Commercial Code,[25] indicate that the corporate governance environment in Japan, and the social norms than underlie it, have been altered to a degree that would have been unimaginable just five years ago.

The implications of these developments extend beyond corporate governance. The nascent market for corporate control also portends changes in traditional patterns of lawmaking and enforcement, buttressing our claim that deal structure and legal development are intimately linked. Commercial Code amendment and interpretation have long been the province of a small group of legal scholars and Ministry of Justice officials, who convened advisory committees to study—often for years—the propriety of potential amendments (West 2001b). Under this process, the law changed, but at a snail's pace and seldom in response to the exigencies of market transactions—"policy pushed," rather than "demand pulled" reform (Shishido 1999). Directorial duties to investors, particularly in respect to contests for control, remain largely untested and unclear. But as commentators have remarked, "[i]f hostile M&A is coming to Japan, it is only [a matter of] time before its courts will answer such questions" (Zaloom and Muraoka 2000). There is already substantial debate among legal scholars and practitioners over the permissible scope of defensive measures. As these issues are eventually addressed through litigation and legal innovation, it seems inevitable that the Japanese courts will assume a more prominent role in corporate law development.

V. Implications

In this part, we examine the implications of our findings for two prevalent perspectives on comparative corporate governance: the "functional substitutes" theory and "law and finance" theory.

A. Functional Substitutes in Comparative Corporate Governance

For more than a decade, the conventional wisdom has held that "bank oversight replaces the market for corporate control in Japan" (Macey and Miller 1995: 81). A significant exception was Gilson and Roe (1993), who qualified the conventional wisdom by pointing out that main banks may not constrain the waste of free cash flow as well as hostile takeovers.

Our analysis, however, has suggested a serious problem with the conventional wisdom. The data show that many Japanese firms ripe for takeover in fact do not attract the attention of main banks. Thus, main bank-led restructurings are not a perfect substitute for an efficient market for corporate control. More centrally for our purposes, we have presented evidence suggesting that the market for corporate control is not simply a monitoring device; it is also a port of entry for outsiders with new perspectives on the firm, and an engine for legal innovation that displaces inefficient norms. Main banks, with their deep ties to conventional corporate and regulatory practices, simply cannot provide these benefits.

Just as bank monitoring cannot fully substitute for the market for corporate control, cross-shareholding is an imperfect substitute for takeover defenses formally based on a country's corporate law. By definition, informal, relationship-based defenses such as cross-shareholding are impervious to legal challenge. As a result, they persist in isolation from judicial review, no matter how damaging to shareholders or other stakeholder interests, even if their sole purpose is management entrenchment. Law does not readily adapt to market imperatives, and the transaction costs of doing deals remain high.

This analysis of the Japanese experience has implications for the convergence debate. Agnostics have taken the position that whether or not formal convergence among national systems takes place, functional convergence is likely. But it is unlikely that institutional forms in major economic systems contain sufficient plasticity to permit complete convergence of function (see Coffee 1999: 641). As the relationship between main banks and takeovers suggests, even if similar problems are addressed in different ways, functional overlap is incomplete and the choice of mechanism has major structural implications for the system as a whole.

B. Takeovers and Investor Protections

The "law and finance" argument advanced by La Porta et al. holds that countries with high quality legal protections for investors have more dispersed share ownership and larger capital markets (La Porta et al. 1997, 1998). Because takeovers are more likely to occur in countries where shares are widely dispersed and capital markets are large, all else being equal, the "law and finance" logic appears to dictate that countries with good legal protections for investors would have more takeover activity.[26]

We argued above that economic success depends in part on matching governance technologies to firms, not on abiding by one-size-fits-all rules. More specifically, we also argued that corporate law that is too protective of minority shareholders (or at least law that favors formal procedural protections over disclosure and self-help) can stifle the market for corporate control and limit the gains from diversity in corporate governance. Both claims are in tension with the imputed predictions of the La Porta et al. model.

On each point, we have presented substantial evidence from Japan that raises serious doubts about the universality of "law and finance" logic. A skeptic, however, might argue that Japan, for cultural or other reasons, is somehow unique. Accordingly, we move beyond Japan to explore the correlation between legal regimes and M&A activity in the global context. To do so, following the La Porta et al. methodology,[27] we construct a series of regressions of corporate control market measures on estimates of the quality of investor protection and several control variables.

La Porta et al. use such factors as ownership concentration and stock market capitalization as dependent variables. In our regressions, we use as dependent variables two separate measures of the corporate control market.

Merger Value is the dollar value in millions of announced transactions in which a majority interest (tender offers, leveraged buyouts, and spin-offs) or a remaining interest (squeeze-outs) was involved in each country. Merger Deals is the number of such transactions. Both measures are from The Merger Yearbook, published by Thomson Financial Securities Data Publishing.[28] La Porta et al. based their study on 49 countries; the Merger Yearbook contains data on only 38 of those countries. Because the omitted countries are small markets, it is unlikely that our results would differ significantly if those countries were included.[29]

Our primary independent variables are identical to the ones used by La Porta et al. in their 1997 regressions: Origin, Antidirector Rights, and One-share = One-vote. To determine which shareholder rights are most likely to affect control transactions, we then disaggregate "Antidirector Rights" into its component parts: One-share = One-vote, Proxy-by-Mail, Shares Blocked Before Meeting, Cumulative Voting, Oppressed Minorities Mechanism, and Percentage of Share Capital to Call an Extraordinary Shareholders' Meeting (La Porta et al. 1996). Consistent with the regressions in La Porta et al., we also control for GDP growth, the logarithm of real GNP, and the rule of law. With respect to each of the independent variables, we have adopted the La Porta et al. variables and 1997 data values for analytical compatibility.[30] All variables are described in table 9.3.

Table 9.3 examines the determinants of merger activity. Not surprisingly, GNP is significant; larger economies have more and larger mergers than small economies. In both specifications for the two dependent variables, GDP growth and rule of law are insignificant. Legal origin matters in only one specification, and there it is only marginally significant. These findings are interesting, given that La Porta et al. have emphasized the legal explanation for variations in corporate governance, particularly the asserted difference in legal protections for investors provided by civil versus common law systems. The rule of law (at least as measured by La Porta et al.) and legal origin do not seem particularly noteworthy when one analyzes their impact on fundamental corporate transactions, as opposed to concentration of ownership.

Controlling for these variables, in two specifications, we find a marginally significant positive correlation for Antidirector Rights to Merger Value, and a significantly positive correlation to Merger Deals. These correlations are not surprising: bids are more likely to be made and accepted when shareholders possess legal rights that may be exercised contrary to the interests of managers.

TABLE 9.3 Determinants of Mergers

Independent Variables	Dependent Variable: Merger Value		Dependent Variable: Merger Deals	
GDP Growth	−3226.699	−1498.411	−41.926	−25.244
	(9561.611)	(9725.162)	(110.891)	(113.382)
Log GNP	68025.745***	61905.798**	907.567***	822.874***
	(18129.251)	(18828.601)	(210.255)	(219.515)
Rule of law	−386.502	3841.614	6.394	45.408
	(11242.793)	(11933.536)	(130.389)	(139.128)
French origin	−19987.532	−104598.9	694.328	−1433.430*
	(59868.642)	(68006.092)	(−.123)	(792.855)
German origin	−83705.435	−150618.3	−1311.751	−2001.841*
	(70229.778)	(88661.658)	(814.492)	(1033.670)
Scandinavian origin	−26951.137	−58610.96	−554.197	−868.263
	(76276.155)	(86421.069)	(884.615)	(1007.548)
One-share = one-vote		14735.104		136.197
		(50577.319)		(589.660)
Antidirector rights	38304.719*		488.310**	
	(20153.489)		(233.731)	
Proxy by mail		34870.461		571.926
		(69441.903)		(809.594)
Shares blocked before meeting		−52850.615		−782.185
		(83316.123)		(971.348)
Cumulative voting		169554.05**		1958.336**
		(56904.838)		(694.908)
Oppressed minorities mechanism		−37995.605		−421.261
		(51652.409)		(602.194)
Percentage of share capital to call an extraordinary shareholders' meeting		3411.882		27.947
		(13240.893)		(694.370)
Intercept	−850282.4***	−686844.0**	−11155.895***	−8294.333**
	(230330.55)	(234539.63)	(2671.265)	(2734.401)
Adjusted R^2	.334	.343	.435	.436
Observations	38	38	38	38

TABLE 9.3 Determinants of Mergers *(Continued)*

Ordinary least squares regressions of the cross-section of 38 countries. *Merger Value* is the dollar value of announced transactions in which a majority interest (including tender offers, leveraged buyouts, and spin-offs) or a remaining interest (squeeze-outs) was involved in each country. *Merger Deals* is the number of such transactions. *Origin* identifies the legal origin (English, French, German, or Scandinavian of the Company Law or Commercial Code of each country. *GDP Growth* is the average annual percent growth of per capita gross domestic product for the period 1970–1993. *Log GNP* is the logarithm of the Gross National Product in 1994. *Rule of law* is an assessment of the law and order tradition in the country. Average of the months of April and October of the monthly index between 1982 and 1995. Scale from 0 to 10, with lower scores for less tradition for law and order. *One-share = one-vote* equals one if the Company Law or Commercial Code of the country requires that ordinary shares carry one vote per share, and 0 otherwise. *Antidirector rights* is an index aggregating the following 5 shareholder rights, formed by adding 1 for each variable. The index ranges from 0 to 5. *Proxy by mail* equals one if the Company Law or Commercial Code allows shareholders to mail their proxy vote, and 0 otherwise. *Shares blocked before meeting* equals one if the Company Law or Commercial Code allows firms to require that shareholders deposit their shares prior to a General Shareholders' Meeting, thus preventing them from selling those shares for a number of days, and 0 otherwise. *Cumulative voting* equals one if the Company Law or Commercial Code allows shareholders to cast all of their votes for one candidate standing for election to the board of directors, and 0 otherwise. *Oppressed minorities mechanism* equals one if the Company Law or Commercial Code grants minority shareholders either a judicial venue to challenge the management decisions or the right to step out of the company by requiring the company to purchase their shares when they object to certain fundamental changes, such as mergers, assets dispositions and changes in the articles of incorporation. The variable equals 0 otherwise. *Percentage of Share Capital to Call an Extraordinary Shareholders' Meeting* is the Minimum percentage of ownership of share capital that entitles a shareholder to call for an Extraordinary Shareholders' Meeting. Equals one if the percentage is less than or equal to 10% (the sample medium), and 0 otherwise. Standard errors are shown in parentheses.
*, **, and *** indicate significance at the 90 percent, 95 percent, and 99 percent levels, respectively.

In the other two specifications in table 9.3, we include the One-share = One-vote variable (as per La Porta et al.; see La Porta et al. 1997: 1141[31]) and disaggregate "Antidirector Rights" into its five subsidiary components. When the independent variables are disaggregated, we find that the positive correlation for Antidirector Rights appears to be driven almost exclusively by the Cumulative Voting variable, which is positive and significant. All other correlations were insignificant, and several were negative — including oppressed minorities mechanisms.[32]

We have no definitive explanation for the correlation between cumulative voting and merger activity. Cumulative voting enables minority shareholders to elect their own representatives, and those representatives are more likely than other board members to seek or respond to takeover bids. Another possible explanation is that firms with cumulative voting have relatively weak boards. Weak boards could conceivably lead to more merger activity, either because the market for corporate control tends to replace weak managers, or because those managers lack shareholder backing to maintain effective defensive devices. Alternatively, the correlation may be affected by some lurking or confounding variable not included in our regressions.

The point of this exercise is that the relation between corporate activity and law is not easily expressed. La Porta et al. and the genre of literature they inspired link the quality of law to relatively static phenomena—shareholding patterns and the size of a country's capital markets. But when M&A, a fundamental corporate activity and a more fluid phenomenon, is examined, the relationship between the legal environment and corporate outcomes becomes much more complex.

These findings, tentative to be sure, are nonetheless consistent with the basic lessons we derive from Japan's experience with takeovers and corporate governance: for takeovers, as in other areas of corporate governance, institutions do indeed matter. But a "high quality" institutional environment for the efficient transfer of corporate assets cannot be equated simply with statutory protections for minority investors.

Conclusion

In this essay, we have posited that diversity in corporate governance is a virtue, and that the market for corporate control, far from being exclusively a monitoring mechanism, is useful in increasing diversity within economic systems and within firms. We have explored this new perspective through a detailed examination of new data on Japanese markets and institutions. We find that historically, the institutionally determined lack of M&A in Japan is integrally linked to a homogeneous corporate governance environment.

Notwithstanding the predictions of skeptics who doubt the efficacy of Japanese legal change, reform of "institutions for deals" in Japan is helping to transform the corporate landscape. These developments may lead to more effective monitoring of Japanese management. Perhaps even more importantly, M&A may spawn managerial and legal innovations incubated in the clash of perspectives between bidder and incumbent that motivates the takeover attempt. Although far from conclusive, the recent evidence suggests that increased organizational diversity may indeed be on Japan's horizon.

The Japanese experience with takeovers and corporate governance yields insights for several prominent comparative corporate governance debates. First, the evidence from Japan indicates that the functional substitute theory is incomplete. In crucial respects, main banks do not substitute for takeovers, and cross-shareholding differs markedly from defensive tactics derived from corporate law. Second, the evidence from Japan, combined with our analysis of La Porta et al. data in the takeover context, suggest that the strength of legal protections for minority shareholders can be a misleading gauge of important corporate governance practices. Finally, convergence optimists and pessimists alike may benefit from greater attention to the important issue of how a desirable economic trait, such as organizational diversity, can be transmitted from one system to another.

Endnotes

The authors thank Ron Gilson, Marc Goldstein, Jeffrey Gordon, Zohar Goshen, Ed Iaccobuci, Amir Licht, Ronald Mann, Hugh Patrick, Adam Pritchard, Mark Ramseyer, and Anthony Zaloom for comments and stimulating questions on earlier drafts. This chapter was presented at the American Law and Economics Association Annual Meeting, the Asian Institute of Corporate Governance at Korea University, the Bank of Japan, Columbia Law School, Kyushu University, and the University of the Pacific McGeorge School of Law. The authors also gratefully acknowledge the substantial contributions of numerous investment bankers, attorneys, and government officials in Japan who provided data and insights. West thanks the Nippon Life Insurance Company's endowment at the University of Michigan Law School for generous support.

1. Though not addressed by Demsetz and Lehn, achieving intra-firm diversity is likely hobbled by collective action problems among shareholders. While a diverse board may be efficient, shareholders might lack the information needed

accurately to match board composition with the firm's decisionmaking needs (see Bebchuk and Roe 1999: 167).

2. Several non-agency cost explanations have also been offered, but these focus on synergy gains (see Black and Grundfest 1988; Romano 1992) or market failures (see Easterbrook and Fischel 1991: 1751–85). Perhaps the closest analogue to our diversity perspective is the view of takeovers as an "equilibrating" or "adaptive" mechanism that is engaged when technological change alters the efficient boundaries of the firm, making a reshuffling of assets economically desirable (Gilson 1992).

3. We do not argue that diversity *always* leads to optimal, or even necessarily efficient, results. As Hong and Page (1998) note, diversity of problem solvers may be problematic if people disagree on outcomes, miscommunicate, or have differing incentive structures. Moreover, while diversity may contribute to success, it may also be the cause of failed mergers in specific cases (Robbins 2001: 603).

4. Of 126 Tokyo Stock Exchange firm mergers and acquisitions between 1992 and 1995, 77, or 61.1 percent, were combinations of a parent and a subsidiary (see Yamazaki 1995: 30). By our count, 53 of the 126 combinations were between firms with elements of the same name. Unlike the German situation (see Franks and Mayer 2001), we find no evidence in Japan of large block trades substituting for the market for corporate control.

5. Calculated using Thomson Financial data and GDP measures from the Japanese Economic Planning Agency.

6. Calculated using Mergerstat data and GDP measures from the U.S. Bureau of Economic Analysis.

7. A complete data set is available in a longer version of this essay, available at http://www.papers.ssrn.com/abstract = 290744.

8. Dyck and Zingales (2002) find that Japan has an average control premium of minus 4 percent, the only country in their 39-country sample with a negative figure.

9. A third explanation is also possible: pre-bid market prices may reflect leaked information regarding the bid.

10. Under the Commercial Code, most major corporate actions, including mergers, require the approval of holders of two-thirds of the corporation's shares. Thus, 33.3 percent is a critical "blocking stake" in a Japanese firm, often tantamount to outright control.

11. See, e.g., Shūwa K.K. v. K.K. Chūjitsuya, 1989 (voiding target management's white knight stock placement as unfair where "primary purpose" of issuance was to dilute holdings of bidder and to maintain control over the company).

12. Japan's corporate law regime is unitary. Unlike the situation that exits in the United States, there is no competition for corporate charters. As a result, any mandatory corporate law provisions are therefore truly mandatory, in the sense

that corporations cannot evade them without incorporating in a jurisdiction outside of Japan. Recent incorporations of Japanese firms in Hawaii suggest that some corporations do just that (Moffett 2002).

13. The Modigliani-Miller theorem holds that dividends are irrelevant in perfect capital markets (Miller and Modigliani 1961). We do not claim that Japanese dividend policies are systematically inefficient, only that they are homogeneous without any compelling rationale for such broad uniformity.

14. In 1988, Japan had only 8,000 CPAs, compared to approximately 250,000 in the United States and 65,000 in the United Kingdom (Ballon and Tomita 1988: 170). In the same year, all major Japanese banks and securities houses combined had a total of only 338 M&A staff (Kester 1991: 9).

15. Source: Nomura Research Institute (2001). Bust-up value is defined as cash and cash equivalents + investment securities—short and long-term debt. Calculated for 779 nonfinancial Tokyo Stock Exchange Firms as of November 2000.

16. Holmstrom and Kaplan (2001: 136) cite stock option plans as a major cause of "management's acceptance of the shareholder perspective." Still, most Japanese option plans are not performance-based. Most of those that are performance-based are linked to profits, not share price.

17. Sources: Thomson Financial, Merger Yearbook (various years); Recof (2001; 2002).

18. The formula was (cash – long term securities – sales × 5% + investment securities (not including those of affiliates) + unrealized capital gains on stock × 60% + land × 50% + unrealized capital gains on land × 30% – interest-bearing debt)/price.

19. The first three factors are from Nihon Keizai Shinbunsha (2000). Derivative suit information from lists in Shiryōban Shōji Hōmu (2001).

20. A recent empirical study of Japanese listed companies finds that the presence of outside board members correlates significantly with improved performance, but executive officer presence correlates in some sectors with poor performance, perhaps because the system is often adopted at companies that anticipate liability. Ōyanagi and Sekiguchi (2001).

21. See Takashi v. Shikoku Denryoku (1996) (finding practice of seating employees in front to regulate meeting times to be unlawful).

22. Some corporate governance changes may also be attributed to the downturn, as management has lost some ability to credibly commit to future returns (Fukao 2001).

23. Milhaupt interviews with Tokyo-based M&A specialists affiliated with both Japanese and U.S. investment banks, June 2000.

24. The diversity through takeovers idea is consistent with studies that show corporate performance gains in Japan after mergers (see Kang et al. 2000; Kruse et al. 2002).

25. Recent amendments to the Commercial Code allow large corporations to opt out of the statutory auditor system in favor of independent audit, nomination and compensation committees of the board, provide for the formal recognition of executive officers, and expand permissible issuance of stock options.

26. This interpretation of La Porta et al. is consistent with Pagano and Volpin (2000). We find the opposite implication from the La Porta et al. research—that takeovers would be rare where legal protections are good because they force managers to operate firms in an efficient and shareholder-regarding manner—far less plausible.

27. We use the La Porta et al. methodology for solely for data compatability, and do not endorse their measurement techniques (see Milhaupt 2001: 2119–25).

28. For Merger Value, minimum = 204.5, maximum = 901773.2, mean = 4122.29, standard deviation = 145915.7. For Merger Deals, minimum = 12, maximum = 11190, mean = 645.55, standard deviation = 1836.29.

29. We omitted Colombia, Ecuador, Jordan, Kenya, Nigeria, Pakistan, Sri Lanka, Turkey, Uruguay, Venezuela, and Zimbabwe.

30. The alternate use of a combination of data from other years did not significantly affect results.

31. We found no changes in any specification as a result of inclusion or exclusion of the One-share = One-vote variable or of another La Porta et al. variable, domestic firms per capita.

32. Dyck and Zingales (2002: 32, 35) find that "countries with more anti-director rights have lower private benefits of control." But the statistical significance of that finding vanishes when extra-legal factors are included. To compare their results with ours (among other things, they did not disaggregate the anti-director rights variable as we do), we ran a third multivariate regression, using block premia data from Dyck and Zingales (2002) on 34 of our 38 sample countries as the dependent variable. We found no significant correlation to any variable in either specification.

References

Abowd, John M. and David S. Kaplan. 1999. Executive Compensation: Six Questions that Need Answering. *Journal of Economic Perspectives* 13: 145–68.

Ahmadjian, Christina L. and Gregory E. Robbins. 2000. A Convergence of Capitalism? Foreign Shareholders and the Spread of Investor Capitalism to Japan. Unpublished working paper.

Aoki, Masahiko. 1995a. *Keizai Shisutemu no Shinka to Tagensei* [Evolution and Diversity of Economic Systems].

———. 1995b. An Evolving Diversity of Organizational Mode and Its Implications for Transitional Economies. *Journal of the Japanese and International Economies* 9: 330.

———. 2000. *Information, Corporate Governance, and Institutional Diversity: Competitiveness in Japan, the USA, and the Transitional Economies*. Oxford: Oxford University Press. Translated by Stacey Jehlik.

Arnaud, Regis. 2001. Nothing Axa-dental about Success, *Far Eastern Economic Review*, March 22, p. 48.

Ballon, Robert J. and Iwao Tomita. 1988. *The Financial Behavior of Japanese Corporations*. Tokyo: Kodansha.

Bebchuk, Lucian Ayre and Mark J. Roe. 1999. A Theory of Path Dependence in Corporate Ownership and Governance. *Stanford Law Review* 52: 127–70.

Black, Bernard and Joseph Grundfest. 1988. Shareholder Gains from Takeovers and Restructuring Between 1981 and 1986. *Journal of Applied Corporate Finance* 1: 5–15.

Carroll, Glenn R. and Michael T. Hannan. 2000. *The Demography of Corporations and Industries*. Princeton: Princeton University Press.

Choy, Jon. 1996. Japanese Executives Still Not Sharing with Shareholders, JEI Report, July 12.

Coffee, John C., Jr. 1999. The Future as History: The Prospects for Global Convergence in Corporate Governance and Its Implications. *Northwestern University Law Review* 93: 641–707.

Columbia Conference. 2001. The New Rhetoric and Realities of Corporate Governance, panel discussion at Corporate Japan: The Beginning of a New Era?, held March 23.

Corporate Governance Committee. 1998. Corporate Governance Principles—A Japanese View, May 26.

Davis, Gerald F. 1991. Agents without Principles? The Spread of the Poison Pill through the Intercorporate Network. *Administrative Science Quarterly* 36: 583–613.

Davis Global Advisors. 2001. Leading Corporate Governance Indicators 2000.

Demsetz, Harold. 1983. The Structure of Ownership and the Theory of the Firm. *Journal of Law and Economics* 26: 375–90.

——— and Kenneth Lehn. 1985. The Structure of Corporate Ownership: Causes and Consequences. *Journal of Political Economy* 93: 1155–77.

Diversity Distinguishes IY Bank, *Nikkei Weekly*, June 11, 2001. p. 13.

Dyck, Alexander and Luigi Zingales. 2002. Private Benefits of Control: An International Comparison. NBER Working Paper 8711.

Easterbrook, Frank H. and Daniel R. Fischel. 1991. *The Economic Structure of Corporate Law*. Cambridge: Harvard University Press.

Fatemi, Ali M. and Alireza Tourani Rad. 1994. Stock Return Variation and Expected Dividends: The Far Eastern Experience. In 11B *Studies in the Financial Markets of the Pacific Basin*. Theodore Bos and Thomas A. Fethersten eds. Greenwich: JAI Press.

Fields, Mark. 2001. Remarks of President of Mazda Motor Corporation, at Columbia University, March 23.

Filgstein, Neil. 1985. The Spread of the Multidivisional Form Among Large Firms, 1919–1979. *American Sociological Review* 50: 377–91.

Franks, Julian and Colin Mayer. 2001. The Ownership and Control of German Corporations. *Review of Financial Studies* 14: 943–77.

Fukao, Mitsuhiro. 1998. Japanese Financial Instability and Weaknesses in the Corporate Governance Structure. *Seoul Journal of International Economics* 11: 381–422.

———. 2001. Japan's Lost Decade and Weaknesses in Its Corporate Governance Structure, paper presented at Symposium: Japan's Lost Decade: Origins, Consequences, and Prospects for Recovery, at University of Michigan, March 22, 2002.

Gilson, Ronald. 1992. The Political Ecology of Takeovers: Thoughts on Harmonizing the European Corporate Governance Environment. *Fordham Law Review* 61: 161–92.

——— and Mark J. Roe. 1993. Understanding the Japanese Keiretsu: Overlaps Between Corporate Governance and Industrial Organization. *Yale Law Journal* 102: 871–906.

Hansmann, Henry and Reinier Kraakman. 2001. The End of History for Corporate Law. *Georgetown Law Journal* 88: 439–68.

Hattori, Nobumichi. 2001. Tayōka suru Nihon Kigyō no Saihen Sukiimu [How Ever-Diversifying Japanese Corporations can Restructure]. *Shōji Hōmu* 1599: 11–25.

Holmstrom, Bengt and Steven N. Kaplan. 2001. Corporate Governance and Merger Activity in the United States: Making Sense of the 1980s and 1990s. *Journal of Economic Perspectives* 15: 121–44.

Hong, Lu and Scott E. Page. 1998. Diversity and Optimality. Unpublished working paper.

———. 2001. Problem Solving by Heterogeneous Agents. *Journal of Economic Theory* 97: 123–63.

Ishibashi, Asako. 2000. Former MITI Official Part of New Wave of Vocal, Aggressive Shareholders. Nikkei Weekly, June 3, 2000, at 1.

Japan External Trade Organization (JETRO). 2000. Trends in Japan's M&A Market.

Jensen, Michael C. and Richard S. Ruback. 1983. The Market for Corporate Control: The Scientific Evidence. *Journal of Financial Economics* 11: 5–50.

Jisha Kabu Kai Baizō, 2 Chō Enchō, [Share Repurchases Double to Exceed 2 trillion], *Nihon Keizai Shinbun*, April 28, 2002, p. 1.

Kabunushi Sōkai, Hachiwari ga 28nichi Kaisai [80% to Hold Shareholders' Meetings on 28th], *Nihon Keizai Shinbun*, June 9, 2001, p. 1.

Kadri, Francoise. 2001. AXA Builds Up Strength in Japan Despite a Harsh Climate for Insurers, *Agence France-Presse*, May 28, available at WL 2415657.

Kaisha Bunkatsu: 1nen de 200 ken [200 Spin-Offs in One Year], *Nihon Keizai Shinbun*, March 31, 2002, p. 1.

Kaisha ha Kōshite Henshin Saseru [Corporations Will Change Thusly], *Shūkan Tōyō Keizai*, Apr. 6, 2002, pp. 42, 43–45.

Kanda, Hideki. 1994. Kabunushi Daihyō Soshō ni Kansuru Rironteki Sokumen [The Theoretical Side of Shareholder Derivative Suits]. *Jurisuto* 1038: 65–71.

——. 1995. Developments in Japanese Securities Regulation: An Overview. *International Lawyer* 29: 599–614.

——. 1998. Comparative Corporate Governance Country Report: Japan. In Klaus J. Hopt et al. eds., *Comparative Corporate Governance: The State of the Art and Emerging Research*. New York: Oxford University Press.

Kang, Jun-Koo, Anil Shivdasani and Takeshi Yamada. 2000. The Effect of Bank Relations on Investment Decisions: An Investigation of Japanese Takeover Bids. *Journal of Finance* 55: 2197–2218.

Kauffman, Stuart A. 1993. *The Origins of Order: Self-organization and Selection in Evolution*. New York: Oxford University Press.

Kester, Carl W. 1991. *Japanese Takeovers: The Global Contest for Corporate Control*. Boston: Harvard Business School Press.

Kigyō no Haitō Renketsu Be-su ni Henshin, Keiei to Shōhō no Mujun Kaishō [Companies Changing to Consolidated Dividends, Eliminating Contradiction Between Management and Commercial Code], *Nihon Keizai Shinbun*, June 12, 2001. p. 17.

Kikuchi, Masatoshi. 2000a. TOB, *Kaisha Bunkatsu ni yoru M&A Senryaku [M&A Strategy: Takeovers and Spin-offs]*. Tokyo: Tōyō Keizai Shinbunsha.

——. 2000b. TOB Sareyasui Kigyō 25sha [25 Easily Taken-over Companies], *Ekonomisuto*, March 14, pp. 60–62.

Kirchner, Christian and Richard W. Painter. 2000. Towards a European Modified Business Judgment Rule for Takeover Law. *European Business Organization Law Review* 2: 353–400.

Kobayashi, Bruce H. and Larry E. Ribstein. 1996. Evolution and Spontaneous Uniformity: Evidence from the Evolution of the Limited Liability Company. *Economic Inquiry* 34: 464–83.

Kōsei Torihiki Iinkai ed., *Kōsei Torihiki Iinkai Nenji Hōkoku [Annual Report of JFTC]*, various years.

Kruse, Timothy A., Hun Y. Park, Kwangwoo Park and Kazunori Suzuki. 2002. Post-Merger Corporate Performance: Evidence from Japan. Unpublished working paper.

La Porta, Rafael, Florencio Lopez-de-Silanes, and Andrei Shleifer. 1999. Corporate Ownership Around the World. *Journal of Finance* 54: 471–517.

—— and Robert Vishny. 1996. Law and Finance. NBER Working Paper 5661.

——. 1997 Legal Determinants of External Finance. *Journal of Finance* 52: 1131–55.

——. 1998. Law and Finance. *Journal of Political Economy* 106: 1113–50.

Lipton, Martin and Paul K. Rowe. 2002. Pills, Polls and Professors: A Reply to Professor Gilson. *Delaware Journal of Corporate Law* 27:1–35.

Lochner, Philip. 2001. Corporate Japan: Beginning of a New Era? Conference held at Columbia University, March 23.

Macey, Jonathan R. and Geoffrey P. Miller. 1995. Corporate Governance and Commercial Banking: A Comparative Analysis of Germany, Japan, and the United States. *Stanford Law Review* 48: 73–112.

Manne, Henry G. 1965. Mergers and the Market for Corporate Control. *Journal of Political Economy* 73: 110–20.

Mergerstat, *Mergerstat Review*, various years.

Merrill Lynch, 2000. Regarding Mergers and Acquisitions Environment in Japan.

Milhaupt, Curtis J. 2001. Creative Norm Destruction: The Evolution of Nonlegal Rules in Japanese Corporate Governance, *University of Pennsylvania Law Review* 149: 2083–2129.

Miller, Merton H. and Franco Modigliani. 1961. Dividend Policy, Growth and the Evaluation of Shares. *Journal of Business* 34: 411–33.

Mizruchi, Mark S. 1989. Similarity of Political Behavior among Large American Corporations. *American Journal of Sociology* 95: 401–24.

Moffett, Sebastian. 2002. Japan's Entrepreneurs Say Hawaii Offers a Better Business Climate. *Wall St. Journal*, Oct. 15, p. A16.

Nakamoto, Michiyo. 1998. Executive Pay, *Financial Times*, Dec. 18, p. 16.

Nakamura, Yoshio. 2000. Shōhō Zenmen Kaisei e no Kihontekina Shiten [Basic Views on Commercial Code Revision]. *Shōji Hōmu* 1574: 17–23.

Nihon Keizai Shinbunsha. 2000. *Kaisha Nenkan [Corporate Yearbook]*. Tokyo: Nihonkeizai Shinbunsha.

Nissei Kiso Kenkyūjo. 2001. Kabushiki Mochiai Jōkyō Chōsa 2000nendo Ban [1999 Cross-Shareholding Survey].

Nomura Research Insitute. 2001. Unpublished data on ratio of bust-up value to market capitalization.

Ōyanagi, Kōji and Ryōsuke Sekiguchi. 2001. Ko-pore-to Gabanansu to Kigyō Gyōseki to no Kankei [The Relation Between Corporate Governance and Firm Performance]. *Shōji Hōmu* 1594: 14–22.

Pagano, Mario and Paolo Volpin, 2000. The Political Economy of Corporate Governance. CSEF Working Paper No. 29.

Porter, Michael E., Hirotaka Takeuchi and Mariko Sakakibara. 2000. *Can Japan Compete?* Houndmills, Basingstoke, Hampshire: Macmillan.

Prowse, Stephen. 2000. Corporate Governance: Emerging Issues and Lessons from East Asia. World Bank Group Paper.

Raupach-Sumiya, Jorg. 2000. Growing M&A Activities and their Impact on Japan's Corporate System (slides from presentation of the German Institute for Japanese Studies at the University of Tokyo, June 5).

Recof LLC. 2001. Mergers and Acquisitions Report, Aug.

———. 2002. http://www.recof.co.jp/01_market/index.htm.

Record 463 Firms Offer Stock Options, *Daily Yomiuri*, June 19, 2001, p. 14.

Robbins, Stephen P. 2001. *Organizational Behavior* (9th ed.). Upper Saddle River, New Jersey: Prentice-Hall.

Romano, Roberta. 1992. A Guide to Takeovers: Theory, Evidence and Regulation. *Yale Journal of Regulation* 9: 119–80.

Root, Hilton L. 2001. Asia's Bad Old Ways, *Foreign Affairs* 80(2): 9–14.

Scott, Berkeley. 1998. M&A Japan: An Update from Morgan Stanley, *Business Insight Japan*, at http://japan-magazine.com/1998/nov/bijpana-www.zashi/dm2.htm.

Shagai Torishimariyaku 38% ga Sennin [38% Choose Outside Directors], *Nihon Keizai Shinbun*, June 16, 2001, p. 1.

Shiryōban Shōji Hōmu. 2001. *Shiryōban Shōji Hōmu* 202: 178.

Shishido, Zenichi. 1999. Reform in Japanese Corporate Law and Corporate Governance: Current Changes in Historical Perspective. *American Journal of Comparative Law* 49: 653–78.

Shōji Hōmu Kenkyūkai. 1999. Kabunushi Sōkai Hakusho [White Paper on Shareholders' Meetings]. *Shōji Hōmu* 1234: 3–118.

———. 1999. Shikkō Yakuin Seido ni Kansuru Ankeeto Shūkei Kekka [Summary of Results of Survey Regarding Executive Officers]. *Shiryōban Shōji Hōmu* 182: 26–39.

———. 2000. Kabunushi Sōkai Hakusho [White Paper on Shareholders' Meetings]. *Shōji Hōmu* 1579: 3–125.

Shūwa K.K. v. K.K. Chūjitsuya, Tokyo District Court, 1317 *Hanrei Jihō* 28 (July 25, 1989).

Singer, Jason. 2001. Bridgestone Provides Case Study in Japan's Liberalization, *Wall Street Journal*, May 30, p. A19.

Smith, Charles. In Japan, M&A Accelerates, but Hurdles Remain, *The Daily Deal*, Jan. 3, 2002. Available in LEXIS.

Stead, Gary. 2001. Remarks at ACCJ, Tokyo, June 18.

Takashi v. Shikoku Denryoku, *Shōji Hōmu* 1440: 39, Supreme Court, Nov. 12, 1996.

Tanikawa, Miki. 2001. Imitating Mr. Ghosn in Japan, *New York Times*, May 20, sect. 3, p. 2.

Tatsuta, Misao. 1983. Proxy Regulation, Tender Offers, and Insider Trading. In *Japanese Securities Regulation*. Louis Loss et al., eds. Tokyo: University of Tokyo Press.

Thomson Financial. 2002a. Japanese M&A Hits Low of US $65 Billion, Jan. 16, 2002. Available at http://www.tfibcm.com/league/pdfs/MA/4Q2001/Docs/4Q01JapanesePR.PDF.

———. 2002b. Japanese M&A: Stayin' Alive, April 4, 2002. Available at http://www.tfibcm.com/league/pdfs/MA/1Q2002/PR/1Q02JapanesePR.PDF.

———. Merger Yearbook, various years.

———. Securities Data Reports, various years.

Tokyo Shōken Torihikijo. 2000. Kooporeeto Gabanansu ni Kansuru Ankeeto no Chōsa Kekka ni Tsuite [Results of Corporate Governance Survey] (Nov. 30).

Tokyo Stock Exchange. 1997. Fact Book 1996.

West, Mark D. 1994. The Pricing of Shareholder Derivative Actions in Japan and the United States. *Northwestern University Law Review* 88: 1436–1507.

———. 1999. Information, Institutions, and Extortion in Japan and the United States: Making Sense of *Sokaiya* Racketeers. *Northwestern University Law Review* 93: 767–817.

———. 2001a. Why Shareholders Sue: The Evidence from Japan. *Journal of Legal Studies* 30: 351–82.

———. 2001b. The Puzzling Divergence of Corporate Law: Evidence and Explanations from Japan and the United States. *University of Pennsylvania Law Review* 150: 527–601.

Williamson, Oliver E. 1996. *The Mechanisms of Governance*. New York: Oxford University Press.

Yamazaki, Katsuya. 1995. Jōjō Kaisha no Saikin no Gappei, Eigyō Jōto tō ni kansuru Jittai Chōsa [Survey of Recent Corporate Mergers and Acquisitions]. *Shōji Hōmu* 1405: 25–36.

Yasui, Takahiro. 1999. Corporate Governance in Japan, OECD Paper, March 3, 1999.

Zaloom, Anthony E. and Kanako Muraoka. 2000. Judgment Call Asian M&A: Go With What Works. *The Daily Deal*. May 15, p. 15.

——— and Satoshi Kawai. 2000. Negotiated Acquisitions in Japan: The Rules are Different. *M&A Lawyer* 4: 24–26.

Zenkoku Shōken Torihikijo Kyōgikai. 2000. Kigyō Gyōseki oyobi Haitō no Jōkyō [The Status of Corporate Performance and Dividends].

Zhang, Hua. 2000. Share Repurchases in Japan: Market Reaction and Actual Implementation. Unpublished working paper, available at http://www.efmaefm.org/hzhang.pdf.

10 Financial Malaise and the Myth of the Misgoverned Bank

Yoshiro Miwa and J. Mark Ramseyer

As the century opens, we blame the international financial malaise on lax banking regulation. With the nearly global ideology of democracy what it is, we blame the government when we have half a chance.[1] Banks handle nothing if not finance, and they do seem to be in trouble. In the U.S., bad regulatory design arguably drove the savings and loan fiasco. Within Japan, maybe the same thing ruined the banks.

We blame it on rich managers. With the global rhetoric of populism what it is, we blame the rich even without half a chance. The rich are different from us, and at various turns in the last century Americans blamed John D. Rockefeller, Michael Milken, and Bill Gates. Japanese blamed the Mitsui, Sumitomo, and Iwasaki families. The rich do seem to be wreaking havoc in Russia. Maybe they did the same in Japan.

We blame it on bad "corporate governance," and in imagining this nightmare we implicate both the spineless regulators and the avaricious rich. Absent well-performing firms, economies will not rebound. Absent good governance, firms will not perform well. And maybe absent stringent regulatory frameworks, greedy managers will install the lackadaisical governance structures that generate the lackluster performance we see today.

Or so the self-styled public intellectuals declare. But is it so? Public intellectuals have been wrong before. Did managers indeed cause the malaise by wheeling and dealing beyond the law? Or did the intellectuals yet again round up their usual suspects?

To explore these issues, we focus on Japan. Arguably, the crisis and recession began there. Arguably, they remain as intractable there as anywhere.

Arguably—at least the blond institutional investors peddling the CalPERS gospel in Tokyo so claim (Kamiya 1999: 130)—they demand the same solution there that they demand everywhere else.

Whatever did cause the international malaise (and we offer no hypothesis), it was not bad corporate governance. Indeed, by standard economic theory it could not have been bad governance, for competitive capital and product markets drive firms to adopt efficient governance mechanisms or die. Without a governance structure that promotes investor returns, a firm faces higher capital costs. Unable to expand as cheaply as its rivals, it faces higher product or service market costs. Eventually, its competitors drive it out of business. In such a world, proposals to improve corporate governance are $20 bills on sidewalks: either ideas firms have already adopted, or ideas that would fail.

To apply this logic to the current malaise, we first summarize the literature tying the crisis to corporate governance (section I). We then trace the implications of basic economic theory (bad governance cannot account for the depression; section II). We ask whether the malaise is systemic or sector-specific (sector-specific, we conclude), and which sectors have suffered most severely. We take data from a major, badly depressed sector (banking) and examine the tie between performance and governance. The results, we find, closely track basic theory we introduced earlier (section III, appendix). Finally, we ask whether the recession resulted from the deregulation in the financial services industry. No, we answer, and explain why not (section IV).

I. Governance and the Recession

"The 1990s," several prominent economists recently observed, "turned out to be a traumatic decade for Japan." As the "unemployment rate soared," it became "Japan's 'lost decade.' " The trauma had begun in 1990 with the fall in stock and land prices. Prices had been high before, but not—these economists argued—because of "economic fundamentals." Instead, they had been high because of a "classic speculative bubble" (Cargill et al. 2000: 11, 14; but see Garber 2000).

When prices fell, banks that had lent money on the now-depressed real estate found their loans uncollectible. As they lost their funds, firms that relied on them found themselves without access to cash. By 1997, the financial crisis had spread across Asia. Appearing first in Thailand, it soon engulfed South Korea and Indonesia. By the end of the century, it had reached even Russia and Brazil.

Still, a fall in asset prices—whether a burst bubble or no—should not cause a ten-year recession. Several observers (we discuss the literature in more detail below) blame the economy's failure to rebound on bad corporate governance. Typically, they cite the decline of the "main bank system." Japanese firms, they explain, for years borrowed from many banks but maintained one as their "main bank."[2] That bank lent the most to the firm, and monitored it on behalf of other lenders. As Japan deregulated its capital markets in the 1980s, firms increasingly switched from bank finance to the newly available sources. By so doing they cut their dependence on their main bank. In the process, they reduced both the bank's access to the information it needed to monitor the firm, and its incentive to do so.

By cutting main bank monitoring, these observers continue, Japan eliminated the one mechanism that might seriously have checked managerial folly and greed. Although managers in U.S. firms answered to shareholders, Japanese managers had long ignored the stock market. Although U.S. managers answered to a corporate control market, Japanese managers faced none. As the "reliance on debt capital" by Japanese firms falls, predicted management scholar Michael E. Porter (1995: 94), "main banks will take a diminished role . . . as effective monitors of companies. . . . The lack of effective monitoring will accentuate existing weaknesses of the Japanese system." By the close of the decade, concluded sociologist Bai Gao (2001: 19), "the weak control and monitoring of corporations" in Japan had contributed decisively to the disaster.

II. Governance and Performance

A. Demsetz-Lehn in Theory

And yet, for reasons economists Harold Demsetz and Kenneth Lehn explained in 1985, this corporate governance talk should leave one troubled. Elsewhere, we discuss why the "main bank system" never existed anywhere but in the academic imagination (Miwa and Ramseyer 2002a; contra Milhaupt 2002). Yet whether with a main bank system or no, firms that maintain underperforming governance arrangements should face higher costs in the capital market. That penalty should in turn raise their product or service market costs. Over time, such firms should not survive (Demsetz and Lehn 1985; Miwa and Ramseyer 2002c; see Miwa 1999: 1229).

Demsetz and Lehn made the point in the context of the Berle-Means (1932) debate—were public American firms at a competitive disadvantage because their dispersed ownership patterns allowed managers to shirk undetected? They argued no, but their logic applies more broadly: given competitive capital markets, firms with ownership or governance structures that do not minimize investor costs will tend to go out of business. In that context, any reforms academics might propose were either reforms firms had already incorporated, or ideas that would not work.

The point is not that firms consciously choose their ownership structure to maximize shareholder returns. Rather, firms that do maximize those returns will raise new capital more cheaply. Over time, such firms will disproportionately tend to survive. In equilibrium, the firms that persist will tend to be those that choose ownership and management structures that increase investor returns.

What is more, because the efficient governance structure is specific to a firm, scholars who tie observed firm profitability to governance structures will find no relationship. Recall the logic. Firms with inefficient structures will fail and drop out of the sample. If so, then a firm for which a given structure promotes shareholder returns will tend to persist, while a firm for which the same structure generates losses will tend to disappear. Although a particular structure may well lower shareholder returns at most firms, that point will not appear in the data since only the firms at which it increases returns will tend to survive.

Despite occasional debates about its empirical implications (Morck et al. 1988; Morck et al. 2000; McConnell and Servaes 1990; Holderness et al. 1999), the logic behind the Demsetz-Lehn hypothesis remains unchallenged. Recently, empiricists have confirmed its application to the U.S. (Cho 1998; Hermalin and Weisbach 1991; Himmelberg et al. 1999). In a related article, we do the same with Japan (Miwa and Ramseyer 2003b). Toward that end, we ask how firms responded to the late 1940s *zaibatsu* dissolution program—an exogenous shock to the prewar ownership equilibrium. Almost immediately, the firms subject to the dissolution began reconcentrating their ownership. A year after the close of the occupation (1953), they had not yet completed the process, and firms with dispersed shareholdings still earned lower profits than their peers. By 1958, the equilibrating process was largely complete. The formerly zaibatsu firms had reconcentrated their ownership (though at different levels than twenty years earlier), and the observable correlation between ownership concentration and profitability had vanished.

B. Demsetz-Lehn Applied

1. *Cross-shareholdings.*—(a) *Generally.* For most proposals to "improve" Japanese governance, the Demsetz-Lehn hypothesis poses devastating implications. According to a variety of writers, the desultory Japanese economic performance reflects the nefarious effect of widespread cross-shareholding arrangements. Suppose, however, that these arrangements cut shareholder returns at a given class of firms. Those firms should incur a penalty on the capital market when they try to raise funds. Suffering when they need to expand, over time they should "wither away." If the cross-shareholdings impose a net cost on the constituent firm shareholders, firms with the arrangements should tend to disappear.

In fact, the cross-shareholding arrangements are not disappearing, for there were no arrangements to vanish. Take the principal roster of Japanese corporate groupings from their putative heyday in 1965 (Keizai chōsa kai, various years). Among the Sumitomo *keiretsu* of 48 nonfinancial firms, only 11 pairs of firms had at least a one percent stake in each other; among the Mitsui *keiretsu* of 48 firms, only six pairs did; among the Sanwa *keiretsu* of 36 firms, only six pairs; among the Mitsubishi *keiretsu* of 46 firms, only four; among the Fuji *keiretsu* of 45 firms, only three; and among the Daiichi *keiretsu* of 29 firms, only two pairs. As we explain at length elsewhere (and subject to the qualifications detailed there), cross-shareholding in Japan was a myth from the start (Miwa and Ramseyer 2001; 2002b).[3]

Between the financial and nonfinancial firms, more cross-holdings exist—but not because anyone tried to exchange the shares. Given that Japanese banks can legally hold stock (unlike banks in the U.S. until 1999; see Glass-Steagall Act, 48 Stat. 162 [now partially repealed]), prudent banks will diversify their assets into a broad equity portfolio. Given that the standard *keiretsu* roster selects group members from among a bank's principal borrowers (Miwa and Ramseyer 2002b), banks will have the best information about those firms that the roster lists as group members. If they invest in ways that economize on information costs, they will tend to buy stock in those members. And if the borrowers in turn occasionally invest in their banks, cross-holdings will ensue. Crucially, they will not ensue because anyone tried to insulate his firm from stock market pressure. They will ensue because firms prudently and efficiently diversified investments.

2. *Outside directors.* — (a) *Generally.* Stock-exchange-listed Japanese firms seldom have many outside directors. Instead, they choose their directors from their senior managerial ranks, from their customers or suppliers (like banks), or from the government. Might the absence of many outsiders generate bad governance? So, again, do argue journalists, academics, politicians, and institutional investors. Throughout 2001, reformers talked of requiring by statute all large firms to install outside directors (Kamiya 2001: 69).

The ostensible logic behind the proposal resembles the logic behind its U.S. equivalents. Insiders will not scrutinize the actions their golfing buddies take, the story goes. Instead, they will help them shunt firm perquisites to themselves.[4]

Alas, the reformist agenda again misses the logic of competitive capital markets.[5] Firms that insiders manipulate for private gain will earn investors less money. Systematically delivering a lower return, they will suffer on the capital market and find that the funds to operate or expand come at a higher price. Facing higher capital costs, over time they will tend to disappear. In equilibrium, only firms that deliver competitive returns will endure.

Remember, outside directors do not just bring benefits. They come at a cost, for generally they know little about firm dynamics. They may be independent of everyone at the firm, but only because they know nothing about them. For exactly that reason, U.S. firms long retained few outsiders.

(b) *Outside directors and derivative suits.* Although U.S. firms have more outside directors now, they did not hire them to improve their governance. Were that the case, capital market pressure would have induced them to hire the outsiders decades ago. Instead, in their eagerness only recently to hire outsiders they reflect the receptivity U.S. judges now show toward derivative and shareholder class action litigation. As corporate law scholar Roberta Romano (1991) explained, virtually all these suits involve extortionate claims that generate attorney fees but no shareholder returns. For firms facing such claims, outside directors offer substantial benefits: by routing potential conflicts of interest through a committee of nominally independent outsiders, the firms can insulate themselves from virtually all duty of loyalty claims. For such firms (which is to say, for almost all listed firms), outside directors offer cheap insurance against the plaintiffs' securities bar.

Until recently, Japanese law imposed on derivative claimants a formidable set of costs, and virtually no shareholders filed suit (West 1994). Over the past few years, courts and legislators have begun to dismantle those burdens (West 2001). Even if the proposed legislation to require outside directors does not pass, firms may well start hiring outsiders anyway. They would not be hiring them because outsiders improved management. They would be hiring them because outsiders helped insulate them from fraudulent derivative litigation.

(c) *Retired bureaucrats.* Scholars offer cross-cutting theories about bureaucrats-turned-directors. On the one hand, several argue that the retired bureaucrats retain their loyalty to the government and help it monitor the banks (or other firms) to which they retired.[6] Because the bureaucrats earn no (present or future) compensation from the government, this reverses their incentives.

On the other hand, economists Akiyoshi Horiuchi and Katsutoshi Shimizu (2001) suggest that banks hire retired bureaucrats to buy regulatory largess. Perhaps, they write, the firms hire them to keep someone on staff who can negotiate regulatory favors.[7] To test this hypothesis, they collect data on more than 120 regional banks from 1985 to 1989.[8] They then regress the log of the firms' bad loan ratio in 1996 on the presence of a retired Ministry of Finance (MoF) or Bank of Japan (BoJ) bureaucrat. The presence of an ex-MoF bureaucrat during the 1980s was indeed associated with a higher fraction of bad loans in 1996, they find. The practice of taking retired bureaucrats constituted, they conclude (ibid.: 590), "implicit collusion to enable banks to expand risk-taking activities."

"Corrupt" as public intellectuals may consider all this, for shareholders it potentially represents corporate governance as it should be. If retired bureaucrats perform as Horiuchi and Shimizu suggest, then their presence on a board may indeed reduce regulatory compliance. It will also, however, boost shareholder returns.

3. *Financial disclosure.*—Many observers argue that the lackluster Japanese performance follows from the lenient financial disclosure rules. Since the postwar occupation, Japanese law has imposed costly disclosure requirements analogous to the 1933 Securities Act (15 U.S.C. §§ 77a, et seq.). According to the reformists, though, on several counts the Japanese rules are less onerous than their U.S. analogues. Perhaps that is true, perhaps not. We have not tried to gauge the relative stringency of the securities disclosure rules in the two countries.

Yet the reformers assert that because of the lax Japanese disclosure rules, investors cannot monitor the firms, and the firms find it harder to raise funds.[9] Disclosure is the currency of governance, and governance the means to investment. Absent disclosure governance will not function, and absent governance investors will not part with their funds.

Unfortunately, the reformers again miss the logic of competitive securities markets (in this case, a logic classically explained by George J. Stigler, 1964). To investors, disclosure brings benefits: information they want to know. They can either acquire the information individually, or invest in a firm that produces the information for everyone. If a firm collects, assembles, and disseminates it, shareholders incur costs. As a result, whether a firm produces the information itself or its investors do so privately, investors foot the bill. If either the production of the information entails scale economies or the information is a firm-specific public good, they gain by having the firm produce the information collectively. If not, then public disclosure yields no net benefits.

With information, more is not necessarily better than less.[10] Even if the production of information involves scale economies or public goods, investors will not want all information. They will want only cost-justified information. Beyond that point, they suffer a net loss from any additional information.

Given these principles, the optimal level of disclosure is that level generated in competitive securities markets.[11] In such markets, firms that disclose information up to but only up to the cost-justified level incur the lowest capital market costs. They produce and expand most cheaply. By contrast, firms that produce either too much information or too little suffer a capital market hit. They eventually change their strategy or go out of business. By this logic, when the law mandates disclosure beyond the level firms produce voluntarily, it necessarily mandates information that investors value less than the cost to the firm of disclosing it. Otherwise, after all, the firm would have disclosed the information voluntarily to attract them.

What then do we make of reformist claims that disclosure in Japan is too low? Nothing. Maybe the optimal level of disclosure in the U.S. is higher than in Japan. Maybe the disclosure levels do not differ in fact. And maybe the U.S. accounting and legal cartels controlling the securities registration process enjoy more political clout than their Japanese counterparts. The bar generally is less powerful in the U.S. than in Japan (Ramseyer 1986), but the securities sub-bars could well be otherwise. To generate rents for themselves, maybe U.S. lawyers and accountants demanded disclosure requirements beyond the levels that benefit their clients.

Then again, maybe any differences reflect relative political clout within the securities industry. Lower-tier securities analysts everywhere probably prefer more disclosure to less. Because investors bear the cost of the disclosure, mandatory disclosure lowers the informational advantage sophisticated analysts can offer. If lower-tier analysts have less political power in Japan than in the U.S., that too could generate more lax disclosure rules in Japan.

4. *Objections.*—(a) *Mutual insurers.* Surely, many readers will claim, such a corrosively stock-market-based theory cannot apply to mutuals. Yet mutual life-insurance firms are prominent among bank shareholders, they observe. If mutuals control the banks but do not maximize profits, then neither should the banks (Hanazaki and Horiuchi 1998: 8–10).

Unfortunately, this observation misses the product market incentives that mutuals face. At any given level of contractual benefit, consumers choose from among life insurance contracts by price. A mutual insurance firm can offer a given level of benefits at a competitive price only if it effectively invests the premiums it receives. If it systematically buys underperforming stock, it will earn a lower return than a firm that invests in market-performing stock. Over time, the former will offer less attractive prices than the latter. Over time, competition in the insurance product market will tend to drive the former out of business.

(b) *Government guarantees.* That the government guaranteed deposits and allegedly promised to rescue troubled banks affects none of this. In the late 1980s, it insured deposits of up to 10 million yen per depositor (Nihon ginkō 1995: 124). Simultaneously, claim many observers, it informally promised not to let banks fail. One might wonder about the latter, as it did let them fail once it faced hard times in the 1990s. Nonetheless, law professors Curtis J. Milhaupt and Geoffrey P. Miller (1997: 8) accurately capture the received wisdom when they characterize Japanese banking regulation "as a 'convoy' system of regulation" in which "the group is allowed to move no faster than its slowest members," and the government focuses on "the avoidance of failure by financial institutions." As game theorist Masahiko Aoki (2000: 150) put it, "the expectation that the government is responsible for the control of financially distressed banks, either through bailing-out or an arrangement of acquisition by healthier banks, was generally shared and taken for granted."

According to economists Masaharu Hanazaki and Akiyoshi Horiuchi (1998: 15–16), these government guarantees eviscerated corporate governance. The deposit insurance and promised rescues "deprived investors," they write, "of incentives to monitor the performance of individual banks." In the process, they "hindered the development of market mechanisms to discipline bank management."

In truth, the policies did nothing of the sort. To be sure, they raised the possibility—indeed probability—of moral hazard. If times were good the shareholders made money, but if times were bad the government paid the bill. Under such conditions, shareholders obviously had an incentive to increase risk. Crucially, they did not have any lesser incentives to monitor the firm. Although the government changed the risk level that maximized firm profits, it did not reduce their incentive to ensure that managers selected that (now higher) optimal risk level. Neither did it reduce their incentive to ensure that managers took other profit-maximizing steps.

(c) *Competitive restraints.* Nor is any of this changed by the restrictions on competition. Again, Hanazaki and Horiuchi (1998: 19) speak for many scholars when they cite the "interest rate controls and restrictions on new entry into banking," and suggest these restraints weakened bank governance. However faithfully they capture the standard wisdom, they again mischaracterize the industry itself.

First, the loan interest rate controls did not bind. In recent research, we investigate the effect that these rate ceilings had. Even in the 1970s, they did not constrain (Miwa and Ramseyer 2003a). From time to time, observers have suggested that banks circumvented the controls by requiring debtors to maintain low-interest deposits at the bank. If true, the ploy could have ratcheted up the effective interest rates. In fact, the loan interest rate caps were so porous that banks rarely demanded them. Even without the "compensating balances," they charged market-clearing rates.

Second, the entry restrictions did not shape competition. As of the early 1990s, Japanese firms chose from among 140-plus banks.[12] With that many rivals, the industry was competitive, new entrants or no. To be sure, only the three long-term credit banks (and a few other financial institutions) could issue debentures and in general only the seven trust banks could serve as trustees on any trusts their clients wanted. Otherwise, the market was largely open to all—hardly what Milhaupt and Miller characterize as "extreme compartmentalization."[13] In any case, money is nothing if not arbitrable. Given the possibility of arbitrage, even harsher regulations than this would have had little effect.

(d) *The corporate control market.* And none of this hinges on any "corporate control market." Nearly four decades ago, Henry G. Manne (1965) tied the market for corporate control to efficient managerial incentives. Ever since, many legal (and occasionally economic) academics have suggested that without a thriving takeover market managers will indulge their greed and indolence. Eyeing few hostile acquisitions in Japan, they posit inefficient governance. Only with the help of their "main bank," they explain, do shareholders keep their managers in check. Only in the "main bank," as Paul Sheard famously put it, does Japan have a "substitute mechanism for [the] 'missing' takeover market."[14]

Help as the prospect of a takeover may to constrain managers, firm efficiency does not hinge on it. The takeover is not a prerequisite to efficient management. Instead, it is one mechanism among several by which market competition moves assets to their most productive use. In an academic environment that castigated takeovers as wasteful and irresponsible, Manne explained how they could facilitate productive efficiency. He did not posit rampant agency slack without them.

Takeovers or no, a firm sells good products cheap or—eventually—dies. To make those products it needs capital, and to raise the capital it must convince investors to part with their money. Whether as debt or as equity, however, investors will invest only if promised a market return. Absent efficient governance, that promise will be hard to keep.

In any case, the Japanese government never imposed high costs on tender offers anyway. Until 1971, it regulated them not at all. Since then, it has merely imposed on acquirers a framework modeled on the Williams Act. Although the framework does raise the cost of an acquisition, it raises it little—if any—more than the Williams Act itself (Ramseyer 1987; contra Milhaupt and West, this volume).[15] The point is crucial, because the incentive effect of the corporate control market does not hinge on the *number* of takeovers (if most firms are well-managed, after all, there will be few takeovers even in an unregulated market—simply because there will be few plausible targets). It hinges only on the *potential* for takeovers. Sans regulatory interference, that potential will remain high.

In crucial ways, moreover, hostile takeovers and friendly mergers are substitutes, and there have always been plenty of mergers in Japan (Ramseyer 1987; contra Milhaupt and West, this volume). In the former, a would-be acquirer obtains the target shares by paying target shareholders a premium.

In the latter, it does so by bribing target managers to deliver the firm. The bribe is a fiduciary duty breach, to be sure. Disguised as a consulting agreement or other high-salary low-work contract, it is also unpoliceable. Suppose an acquirer could more efficiently run a firm than its incumbent managers. Whether it offers the target shareholders a premium or those senior managers a consulting contract, it will obtain the firm. Either way, the target's assets will move to the entrepreneurs who can most efficiently exploit them.

III. The Recession

A. *Pervasive or Sectoral?*

Speculative bubble or new information—we will not guess what caused real estate prices to climb so precipitously in Japan in the late 1980s and fall so disastrously a few years later (see, *e.g.*, Chirinko and Schaller 2001; Ueda 1990). Perhaps investors tried to play a bubble. Perhaps they updated their information about future rental streams. Perhaps some investors did one, some the other, and some a bit of both. What matters for our purposes is that prices rose, and then fell. At the six largest cities (with prices indexed at 100 for March 1990), they rose from 24.5 in March 1980 to 33.6 in March 1985. After hitting 100 in March 1990, they fell to 54.7 by March 1995. The fluctuation was particularly pronounced for commercial real estate: from 16.7 in 1980 to 25.6 by 1985, 100 in 1990, and then to 41.7 by 1995 (Nihon fudōsan 1998).

Within the real-estate industry, this fluctuation caused massive losses. Obviously, those who bought high and sold low lost money, but the loss was a simple transfer: assets moved to those who had sold high. More inefficient were the projects driven by future projections. On the basis of high expected rentals, contractors and developers (they at least seem not to have thought the prices a bubble) began golf courses, houses, office towers. When expected future demand fell, many of them found their finished projects unmarketable and their unfinished ones not worth completing. For the economy, they generated a dead-weight loss.

Not only did developers and construction firms lose when the demand for real estate fell; so did those who lent them the money they lost. Particularly when they borrowed nonrecourse by pledging the real estate, the firms could walk away from the loan. Effectively, they forced a sale to their creditors. Those creditors then lost additional funds if—after the price collapse— they lent extra money to try to help the debtors recover.

GNP did grow during the 1990s, even if at a slow pace (Hayashi and Prescott 2001), and other than the firms that either bought real estate or lent to those that did, many firms remain healthy at the core. To see this, first take indexed stock prices for Tokyo Stock Exchange listed firms (we follow the Tokyo Stock Exchange's classification of firms by industry; note that anomalies occasionally arise through changes in the classification scheme). The effect of the real estate collapse appears directly. Among the ten sectors with the lowest share prices relative to 1986, four were involved directly in real estate (agriculture, mining, real estate, and construction), and two more were invested heavily in such firms (securities and banking).

By contrast, the firms whose stock prices rose fastest since 1986 included firms in several of the sectors most central to the Japanese economy. Stock prices in the automobile (transportation equipment) industry, for example, rose 86 percent between 1986 and 1998 (tire manufacturers catalogued under "rubber" grew even more rapidly). Machinery, pharmaceuticals, and electrical products posted less dramatic results (9 percent, 16 percent, and 18 percent), but still showed growth. Economists Fumio Hayashi and Edward Prescott (2001) find no evidence that firms were unable to exploit profitable investment opportunities because of a credit crunch. All this hardly shows a boom, but neither does it suggest an economy facing a governance crisis. (See table 10.1.)

B. Corporate Governance in Banking

1. *Introduction.*—If basic economic theory suggests that the roots of the crisis lie not in issues of governance, consider data from the banking industry—the largest of the 10 sectors doing the worst in table 10.1. Coupling data on corporate performance with those on corporate governance, ask whether the proposed governance changes would likely improve economic outcomes.

We describe our data, variables, and econometric estimates in more detail in the appendix. As explained there, we take financial data on 56 regional banks from 1977 to 1995 and explore the effect of a wide variety of governance variables on bank performance.

2. *Geography.*—The tests confirm the decisive effect of the real estate market. According to our regressions, metropolitan banks did well in the 1980s and poorly in the 1990s. In the early 1980s, banks headquartered in the greater Tokyo and Nagoya areas earned higher returns; in the early

TABLE 10.1 Stock Prices and Market Capitalization, 1998 relative to 1986

Industries	Stock Price 98/86 (%)	Market Capitalization 98/86 (%)	1998
Securities	37	*	3616
Communication	50	*	16229
Air transp.	52	42	1149
Agriculture	53	62	244
Mining	53	51	279
Real Estate	54	47	2835
Petroleum ref 'g	56	54	1647
Construction	58	61	7185
Textiles & app.	66	73	3691
Banks	70	*	32979
Glass & cement	71	72	3300
Gas & elec. util.	71	53	14152
Marine transport.	75	74	863
Nonferrous metals	77	68	2984
Wholesale	77	*	7814
Warehousing	80	82	660
Foods	85	107	9376
Metal Products	85	110	1830
Pulp & paper	86	97	1666
Chemicals	89	*	13810
Iron & steel	90	84	4056
Insurance	91	*	4804
Land transport.	98	128	12066
Misc. services	104	271	7879
Misc. finance	105	*	6519
Machinery	109	148	9491
Retail	112	*	15002
Pharmaceuticals	116	*	12804
Electrical prod.	118	122	40275
Misc. manuf.	121	146	6792
Precision instr.	130	80	2457
Transp. equip.	186	176	24039
Rubber	265	262	2688

Note: Weighted average of 1998 stock price relative to 1986 stock price (in %), followed by 1998 market capitalization relative to 1986 market capitalization (in %), followed by 1998 market capitalization (in billion yen).

* Entry omitted either because the data are not available, or because they are potentially misleading due, for example, to changes in TSE classifications (e.g., by 1998 the TSE had split Chemicals into Chemicals and Pharmaceuticals) or to major changes in the firms included (e.g., the listing of the former national telephone monopoly NTT in Communication).

Sources: Tōkyō shōken torihiki jo, Shōken tōkei nempō [Securities Statistics Annual] (Tokyo: Tōkyō shōken torihiki jo, various years).

1990s, those headquartered in Osaka earned lower returns, and those in Tokyo suffered a greater fraction of bad loans. Crucially, the price of metropolitan real estate rose more dramatically than rural real estate in the 1980s, and fell more dramatically in the 1990s. Because the metropolitan banks loaned to borrowers who invested in urban real estate, they did better than rural banks in the 1980s and worse in the 1990s.

3. *Cross-shareholdings.* — Suppose, as reformers routinely argue, that Japanese managers exchange blocks of stock with business partners to evade the pressure of the capital market. If so, then firms with large portions of stock held by lead shareholders should earn lower returns than their rivals.

In fact, firms with large block shareholders do not underperform. Consistently, the percentage of stock held by the top ten shareholders has no significant effect on shareholder returns. Although theorists continue to debate whether block shareholdings improve firm performance, we note here that the effect probably varies by industry, by market, by personalities. Demsetz and Lehn suggest that firms will choose the shareholding structure that maximizes their expected performance. If so, then the *observed* relation between shareholding patterns and firm performance will be insignificant. Such is what we observe.

4. *Financial shareholders.* — Reformers also argue that financial institutions hurt bank performance when they buy bank stock. Fundamentally, they claim that these institutions do not themselves maximize profits. If they hold bank stock, neither will they pressure those banks to maximize. Following the Demsetz-Lehn hypothesis, we suggest instead that the effect will vary by firm, and that the firms that tend to survive will be those that approach their firm-specific optimal level of financial shareholding. If so, then the level of financial-institution shareholding should have no observable effect on shareholder returns. Again, such is what we observe.

5. *Outside directors.* — Reformers write that Japanese firms could substantially improve their performance by adding outsiders to their boards. Yet if many firms are selecting suboptimal numbers of outside directors, then those with more outsider directors should outperform those with fewer. By contrast, we reason that firms that could profit from outside directors will already have hired them. Since firms earn a competitive return or eventually die, those with more outsiders on their boards should do no better than those with fewer (Miwa and Ramseyer 2002c).

Once more, so the data suggest. Whether in the 1980s or 1990s, banks with more outside directors do no better than those with fewer. If outsiders promoted the "social responsibility" that reformists so cherish, one might also have thought they would prevent moral hazard. Not so. As of 1996, banks with more outside directors had no smaller a fraction of bad loans than the others (for an analogous study of other large Japanese firms, see Miwa and Ramseyer 2002c).

6. *Retired bureaucrats.* — Horiuchi and Shimizu (2001) claim that by hiring retired MoF bureaucrats (they find no effect with BoJ bureaucrats) Japanese banks bought regulatory forbearance. In effect, through these officials they could negotiate their way out of unpleasant regulatory predicaments. Accordingly, firms with retired bureaucrats were more likely to raise the risk level of their portfolios, and exploit the government's deposit insurance and rescue commitment.

Horiuchi and Shimizu do not suggest that banks without retired bureaucrats could have improved their performance by hiring them, and rightly so. Like other facets of corporate governance, this too is endogenous. Firms should hire retired bureaucrats when retired bureaucrats improve expected performance, and do without them when they would not. In equilibrium, those with retired bureaucrats will then earn shareholder returns no higher than those without. Our results again confirm this logic: like Horiuchi and Shimizu, we find that banks with retired bureaucrats earn no more than those without.

Yet where Horiuchi and Shimizu argue that banks with retired MoF officials had a larger fraction of bad loans in their 1996 portfolios, we find no such results. Instead, we find that the presence of retired bureaucrats at a bank had no significant effect on its loan portfolio. If ex-bureaucrats facilitated moral hazard, it does not appear in our data.

IV. The Significance of Deregulation

A. Introduction

This debate poses implications not just for corporate law reform, but for regulation and de-regulation more generally. For if some scholars see the source of the current financial malaise in corporate governance, some also see its genesis in the 1980s deregulation of financial services. According to these scholars, it was through that deregulation that Japanese firms came to raise funds through avenues outside banks.[16] As they did, either managers escaped the disciplining effect of "main bank monitoring" and then failed (a theory we summarize in subsection B, below), or banks turned to riskier borrowers who then failed (subsection C, below). By either hypothesis, the political implications are obvious: increased competition need not create a healthy economy; deregulate without the appropriate governance-related infrastructure and disaster can strike even the healthiest economy.

B. Aoki

Game theorist Masahiko Aoki ties the current malaise to a deregulation-induced decline in "main-bank monitoring."[17] As Japan loosened bond-market restrictions, Aoki argues, firms became "less reliant on bank loans and [were] freed from the bank's implicit and explicit intervention" (Aoki 2000: 91). Increasingly, they raised their funds directly on the capital market and diversified their remaining bank debt among multiple banks. In the process, they "diminished the flow of information from firms to main banks, and consequently diminished the bank's ability to perform interim monitoring." Ultimately, "a vacuum in the external discipline over Japanese firms" resulted. Banks could no longer keep managers in line, and newly freed managers made risky bets that went bad (ibid.: 91, 98).

Others echo the hypothesis. Economic historian Hideaki Miyajima (1998: 57), for example, claims in a recent study:

[D]uring the bubble economy period corporate governance . . . was characterized by a conspicuous decline in main bank monitoring. . . . In the absence of a market-based system of control such as that found in the United States, Japan was left without an effective system for monitoring and disciplining the top managements of large Japanese firms.

Similarly, Gao (2001: 38) asserts that the 1980s liberalization, coupled with the lingering effects of the 1970s recession, led to a changed relation between banks and firms such that "the banks' monitoring of big corporations deteriorated further. Having lost their leverage over big corporations, banks could not monitor them closely even had they wanted to do so."

Unfortunately for this hypothesis, the firms that failed in the 1990s were rarely firms that had turned to the bond market. Indeed, if bond-market firms had been the ones to fail rather than bank-loan firms, Japan would not have the banking-sector crisis it does. The firms that could sell bonds in the 1980s were the blue-chip firms, and what were blue-chip firms then largely remain solvent today. The firms that defaulted in the early 1990s were instead those tied to real estate: developers, contractors, and construction firms. Generally smaller and often unlisted, most of them would have been unable to tap the bond market if they had tried (Miwa and Ramseyer 2001: 382–84).

C. Hoshi-Kashyap

Economists Takeo Hoshi and Anil Kashyap (1999) similarly argue that the malaise traces its roots to deregulation, but not to a failure in main-bank monitoring. Rather, they reason that the deregulation caused a shift in bank-loan strategy. According to them, deregulation enabled blue-chip firms to raise disintermediated funds; these firms increasingly abandoned banks; and banks responded by turning to riskier firms that then failed. "[B]etween 1983 and 1989," they explain, "the Japanese bond market blossomed, per-mitting many internationally known companies to tap the public debt mar-kets for the first time." As a result, the banks "lost many of their borrowers in a very short period of time."[18] "[T]he bank mortgage lending business became more attractive," explain Milhaupt and Miller (1997: 29), "when banks began to lose corporate finance business to the capital markets in the mid-1970s and 1980s." To make up the lost business, banks turned to real estate developers. Those developers failed when the market crashed, and banks then found themselves saddled with losses.

To show how blue-chip firms left banks, Hoshi and Kashyap (1999: 148, table 5) examine the ratio of bank debt to assets among the biggest listed manufacturing firms. That ratio, they note, fell from 36 percent in 1970 to 32 percent in 1980. From 32, it fell to 13 percent by 1990, and there it has roughly remained since. "As the banks started to lose their customers to cap-ital markets, they went after small firms." The result was a "portfolio shift: increasing loans to the real estate industry" (Hoshi and Kashyap 1999: 163).

Ratios mislead here, for the banks did not lose their customers, and bond issues do not explain the shift into real estate loans.[19] At root, any decline in loans to these listed manufacturing firms was simply too small to have driven any substantial shift in bank loans. From 1983 to 1989, bank loans to all listed manufacturing firms fell 6.6 trillion yen (see table 10.2). During the same period, the total loans made by Japanese banks increased monotoni-cally by 174 trillion yen. Even loans to listed firms increased year by year. At the "city banks" alone, total loans increased by 71 trillion. Banks did not shift into real estate because their loans to their traditional clientele fell, for traditional clients as a whole apparently did not cut their loans. They shifted because they captured huge increases in loanable funds.

TABLE 10.2 Bank Loans, by Borrower Category

| | All Firms | | | Listed Firms | | | | | Manufacturing | | | | | |
	Total	Const	Manuf	Total	Const	Retail	Real Est	Total Manuf	Chem	Oil & Coal	Steel	Mach.	Elec Goods	Transp Equip
1980	1346	73	430	564	33	116	13	267	40	27	55	15	21	36
1981	1484	80	468	604	33	120	14	285	42	32	56	16	22	39
1982	1640	88	501	641	33	131	16	295	43	29	61	16	22	42
1983	1810	100	523	657	34	139	16	293	43	24	64	15	22	43
1984	2021	114	553	665	36	150	16	280	42	21	63	15	20	40
1985	2228	127	582	675	39	154	18	280	43	17	65	16	22	37
1986	2444	135	576	690	40	158	20	282	41	17	66	16	25	37
1987	2686	140	550	717	41	184	25	268	38	17	60	16	28	34
1988	2882	148	539	770	45	242	30	252	35	17	46	16	27	36
1989	3551	192	591	813	44	298	35	227	30	18	35	16	26	32
1990	3760	200	592	857	52	288	45	255	32	27	33	18	34	35
1991	3857	216	600	899	71	279	50	275	37	25	33	20	38	39
1992	3930	234	592	932	81	275	52	293	40	23	37	21	40	42
1993	4776	298	766	937	92	242	54	296	43	21	41	20	36	44
1994	4784	307	748	937	93	240	54	290	42	20	42	19	38	39
1995	4845	311	726	928	90	232	54	279	41	19	38	20	36	36

Notes: Figures are in 100 billion yen. Figures for "all firms" give the loans and discounts through the banking accounts of all banks. They thus exclude loans through trust accounts, and loans from such sources as life insurance companies and government institutions. Note that in 1990 when manufacturing firms borrowed 59.2 trillion yen through their banking accounts, they borrowed only 2.2 trillion yen through trust accounts. Figures for "listed firms" include (non-securitized) loans from all sources.

Sources: Tōyō keizai shimpō sha, ed., Kigyō keiretsu sōran [Firm Keiretsu Overview] (Tokyo: Tōyō keizai shimpō sha, various years); Nihon ginkō, ed., Keizai tōkei nempō [Economic Statistics Annual] (Tokyo: Nihon Ginkō, various years).

Conclusion

Since the start of the 1990s, vast tracks of the capitalist expanse have flirted with financial disaster. Few wealthy economies flirted so dangerously as Japan. Idolized and feared for much of the 1980s, Japanese firms have been ridiculed and shunned for much of the ensuing 1990s.

Did the source of the malaise lie in the governance structures these very firms adopted? Contrary to several corporate observers, we suggest not. Like firms in the U.S., firms in Japan face competitive capital, service, product, and labor markets. Govern themselves inefficiently, and they find themselves punished when they ask for capital. Given that capital market constraint, the firms that survive will tend disproportionately to be those with governance structures adapted to their markets, their industries, their personnel. Given that constraint, blaming the firms for the malaise is blaming the victim all over again.

Consider the reforms academics propose: unwind cross-shareholdings, hire outside directors, disclose more financial data—and if firms refuse, legislate them offers they cannot refuse. A draconian litany that embodies nothing so much as the government-can-do-no-wrong conceit in the academic tradition, it leaves unanswered—indeed, unasked—the classic Chicago workshop question: if the reforms are so great, why did firms that ignore them so thoroughly earn so much for so long (Miwa 1999: 1228–29)? If cross-shareholdings, inside boards, and nondisclosure harmed investors, why did Japanese firms that indulged those characteristics succeed so spectacularly for decades? Should they not have found themselves penalized in the capital market? Unable to raise funds competitively, should they not have disappeared?

In Japan, the recession hit banks among the hardest. To ask whether bad governance caused the malaise, we explore the relation between governance and performance among 50-odd banks. We find: that banks with outside directors did no better than those without; that banks with concentrated shareholding networks did no worse than the others; that banks owned disproportionately by financial institutions did no worse than the others; that retired bureaucrats did not add value or raise risk levels; and that the financial crisis did not trace its roots to the deregulatory steps in the 1980s. At least according to this banking industry data, bad governance did not cause the malaise. Statutes to change that governance would do nothing to end it.

Appendix: Econometric Estimates

A. Data

To explore the association between corporate governance and firm performance, we assemble selected board and financial data for 56 regional
banks, from 1977 to 1996 (for an analogous study of other large Japanese
firms, see Miwa and Ramseyer 2002c). We limit ourselves to regional banks
to maintain a relatively homogenous sample. Although smaller than the
large money-center banks (known as the "city banks"), these regional banks
are still substantial firms. By focusing on them rather than the money-
center banks, we are also able to explore the effect of retired bureaucrats on
firm performance. These bureaucrats were disproportionately concentrated
in the regional banks. In 1986, only two of the city banks had MoF officials
in positions of representative director or higher. Only three had BoJ officials.

    We obtain our shareholder return data from the *Kabushiki tōshi shūeki
ritsu* (Nihon shōken), our bad loan data from *Kin'yū bijinesu* (96 nen 1996)
and all other data from the the *Kigyō keiretsu sōran* (Tōyō keizai).

B. Variables

1. Dependent variables.—

Return on Investment (ROI): Total annual shareholder returns on investment (annual rate of appreciation in stock price plus dividends received) for
1980–85, 1985–90, and 1990–95.

    Loan Growth: Growth in loans (in percent, calculated from book value)
at the bank, for 1977–81, 1981–86, and 1986–89.

    Bad Loans: The percent of a bank's total loans catalogued as bad loans by
the staff of *Kin'yū bijinesu* in 1996. Following Horiuchi and Shimizu (2001),
we also run our regressions using the log of bad loans. The results remain
qualitatively similar.

2. Explanatory variables.—

Outside Dir: The number of outside directors on a firm's board. We also
used a dummy variable equal to 1 if the firm had any such directors, and
obtain qualitatively similar results. We include variables for 1981 (Regs.
3[a]-3[c], 4[a]-4[f]) and 1989 (Regs. 3[d]-3[i], 4[g]-4[i], 5[a]-5[e]).

MoF Alum: 1 if the bank included as a representative director (*jōmu torishimariyaku* or higher) one or more retirees from the central management (*kanbu*) of the Ministry of Finance (MOF); 0 otherwise. We include variables for 1981 (Regs. 3[a]-3[c], 4[d]-4[f]) and 1986 (Regs. 3[d]-3[i], 4[g]-4[i], 5[a]-5[e]). We use the comparable figures for 1977 in Regs. 4(a)-4(c), but for reasons of data availability use all (not just representative) directors in defining the variable. Following Horiuchi and Shimizu, we use a dummy for this variable. We reason that regulatory clearance (the Horiuchi-Shimizu hypothesis) is something one director could handle as well as several.

BoJ Alum: Analogously defined for the Bank of Japan.

Top 10 S/h: The percentage of a bank's shares held by the ten shareholders holding the most bank stock. We include variables for 1977 (Regs. 4[a]-4[c]), 1981 (Regs. 3[a]-3[c], 4[d]-4[f]) and 1986 (Regs. 3[d]-3[i], 4[g]-4[i], 5[a]-5[e]).

Fin S/h: The percentage of a bank's shares held by the financial institutions listed among the bank's top 10 shareholders. We include variables for 1977 (Regs. 4[a]-4[c]), 1981 (Regs. 3[a]-3[c], 4[d]-4[f]) and 1986 (Regs. 3[d]-3[i], 4[g]-4[i], 5[a]-5[e]).

Geographical dummies: 1 if a bank was headquartered in Tokyo, Osaka, or Nagoya; 0 otherwise. Note that these are the locations where the price of real estate most radically escalated in the late 1980s.

Sm Firm Fin: The percentage of a bank's loans to firms classified as small- or medium-sized by the Ministry of International Trade and Industry in 1989.

We include selected summary statistics in Table App 10-1.

C. Results

In general, stock market returns on investment will most accurately capture any effect governance has on shareholder welfare. For that reason, we urge readers to focus on our regressions using Returns on Investment as the dependent variable (table App. 10-3). Because of the collinearity among some of the independent variables (see table App. 10-2), we report the results of several different combinations of these variables. At least hypothetically, to the extent that shareholders can observe any bad governance structures, stock market returns may not reflect the effect those structures have on firm performance. Suppose that a group of firms maintains a systematically inferior set of governance structures, and that the structures are ones an acquirer could not remove. In such a world, investors will anticipate the negative effect of the structures, and discount the price they pay for the stock ex ante. In equilibrium, they will then earn a competitive market return on the stock ex post. Other than with governance structures imposed by regulation, we do not believe this occurs. As we have explained in the body of this essay, entrepreneurs can indeed launch takeovers in Japan, and if bad governance structures were in place they would have had strong incentives to do so. They have not.

Nevertheless, to deal with the possibility that shareholders might anticipate the effect of nonremoveable, observably bad governance structures, we add regressions using a bank's loan portfolio as the dependent variable. We then ask which banks grew most rapidly before the 1990 real-estate price peak (table App. 10-4), and which banks found themselves with the largest portfolios of bad loans after that peak (table App. 10-5)? To the extent strategies that maximize profits correlate with those that generate growth or affect loan quality (obviously a less-than-perfect correlation), the results are consistent with the theory we outline above: variations in governance among firms do not explain variations in performance.

We stress several points. First, most of our significant results are a function of geography rather than governance. More specifically, our results reflect the greater volatility of urban (we focus on the Tokyo, Osaka and Nagoya metropolitan centers) over rural real estate. Because banks disproportionately lent to local borrowers and took local real estate as collateral, urban bank performance reflected that volatility. During the early 1980s, Tokyo and Nagoya banks earned noticeably higher shareholder returns than banks generally (Regs. 3[a]-3[c]); in the early 1990s, Osaka banks earned lower (Regs. 3[g]-3[i]). Similarly, Osaka banks grew rapidly in the late 1970s (Regs. 4[a]-4[c]), Tokyo banks in the early 1980s (Regs. 4[d]-4[f]), and Tokyo, Osaka and Nagoya banks in the late 1980s (Regs. 4[g]-4[i]). By 1996, however, the Tokyo banks had amassed a larger fraction of bad loans than banks generally (Regs. 5[a]-5(e)).

Second, smaller firms also showed higher variance in performance during this period. Accordingly, banks that financed smaller firms grew faster than other banks in the late 1970s (Regs. 4[a]-4[c]), but by 1996 those loans had disproportionately gone bad (Regs. 5[c]-5[d]).

Last, the coefficients on the governance variables are seldom significant, and even when significant show no coherent pattern. Most basically, the data exhibit no sign that outside directors improve performance. Indeed, in our stock market returns regressions, the signs are not even in the right direction (table App. 10-3). The coefficient on the presence of Bank of Japan alumni on a bank's board is similarly insignificant. The coefficient on the presence of Ministry of Finance alumni is correlated only with loan portfolio growth in the late 1970s (and then only at the 10 percent confidence level; Regs. 4[a]-4[c]), and is otherwise insignificant. Holdings by top 10 shareholders are associated with high growth rates in the late 1980s (Reg. 4[h]) but not otherwise. Holdings by financial shareholders are associated with high growth in the early 1980s (Reg. 4[d]; 10 percent confidence level), but not otherwise.

Endnotes

We received helpful comments from David Weinstein and participants in presentations at Harvard and Columbia Universities. We gratefully acknowledge the financial assistance of the Center for the International Research on the Japanese Economy and the Business Law Center at the University of Tokyo, the John M. Olin Center in Law, Economics and Business at the Harvard Law School, and the Sloan Foundation.

1. On the mistaken tendency to ascribe responsibility to the Japanese government for economic performance, see Miwa and Ramseyer (2002d; 2003c).
2. *See generally* Aoki et al. (1994); Sheard (1994, 1989). For a critique of this literature, see Miwa and Ramseyer (2001: chs. 1, 5; 2002a; 2003a).
3. Many observers cite cross-holdings in the mid-70 percent range. These are not the figures for cross-shareholdings, but rather for corporate shareholdings more generally.
4. In fact, the reformers proffer a more mottley set of reasons: e.g., that outside directors will increase managerial efficiency and corporate social responsibility as well. See Kamiya (2001: 69) (discussing draft bill).
5. I.e., the logic behind Demsetz-Lehn. It also misses the more general logic against mandatory corporate law terms, articulated most forcefully in Easterbrook and Fischel (1991). See generally Miwa and Ramseyer (2002c).
6. *E.g.,* Aoki et al. (1994: 31): "When a bank is judged to be poorly managed and to need drastic organizational and asset restructuring, typically the MOF arranges for a retired high-ranking MOF bureaucrat to enter as a director. . . ." However, continue Aoki et al. (ibid.: 32), the "flow of personnel is not limited to the trouble-shooting cases." Instead, "[h]ealthy banks are willing to accept ex-

bureaucrats for various reasons, including as a means of gaining access to valuable information from, and to exert influence on, the regulatory authorities."

7. This also explains why the private firms would hire these ex-bureaucrats, a point made more informally in Ramseyer and Rosenbluth (1993).

8. Apparently, to the regular regional banks, they add the so-called "type-two regional banks"—successors to the prewar mutual credit lotteries known as *mujin*. Because of the sample heterogeneity that this causes, we focus only on regular regional banks.

9. West (1999) even uses the lack of disclosure to explain how and why gangsters commandeer shareholder meetings in Japan.

10. For expositional simplicity, we focus exclusively on the costs associated with simple disclosure. We ignore here the many costs associated with *regulating* and *mandating* disclosure—costs such as shifts in the type of information disclosed, the disclosure of information benefiting competitors but not shareholders, or the reduced informativeness of the information in a heavily regulated environment caused by fears of liability.

11. All this holds even when the information is unfavorable. If a firm refuses to produce information that investors would ordinarily value, investors will presume the worst—and their competitors will encourage them to adopt that presumption. To avoid their adopting that presumption, firms will produce even information that is negative.

12. As of March 1993, there were 11 "city" (money-center) banks, 64 regional banks, 66 "type-2" regional banks, 3 long-term credit banks, and 7 trust banks. There were no legal distinctions among the first three of these categories. In addition, there were a wide variety of other financial institutions (see generally Kusumoto 1994).

13. Millhaupt and Miller (1997: 6). Regional banks may have "specialize[d] in local lending to small business" (ibid., 7), but (other than the effects of the ministry's approval process for banches), this specialization was not regulatorily driven.

14. Sheard (1989: 407); see Aoki (2000: 64): "the neoclassical market for corporate control was eliminated as a prevailing system in Japan. What took its place was stable shockholding by corporate stockholders centered around a main bank."

15. Modeled on the 1933 Illinois Business Corporations Act, the Japanese corporations code imposes no particularly onerous costs on mergers. See Ramseyer and Nakazato (1999: ch. 5).

16. In Miwa and Ramseyer (2003a), we explain how this exaggerates the unavailability of non-bank funds during the period before deregulation. *See also* Miwa and Ramseyer (2001: chs. 1, 5, 6).

17. Directly, albeit more tentatively than we present in the abbreviated summary here.

18. Hoshi and Kashyap (1999: 143–44). Miyajima (1998: 53) similarly writes: "with the amount of loans to large Japanese firms decreasing drastically from the mid-1970s onward, city banks attempted to diversify their clientele by shifting their focus from manufacturing to service industries (real estate and construction), pursuing the business of small and medium-sized firms, and expanding their international operations."

19. Miwa and Ramseyer (2001: ch. 6). The listed manufacturing firms that cut their bank loans in the 1980s–90s were not the firms in the strongest sectors. From 1983 to 1995, the largest percentage declines were in oil (20.3 percent, or 488 billion yen), nonferrous metals (23.5 percent, or 498 billion), glass (24.3 percent, or 283 billion yen), and steel (40.6 percent, or 2.6 trillion yen). Significantly, these were declining sectors that are currently losing equity as well. Consider the table 10.1 stock market capitalization test: the percentage change from 1986 to 1998. By this measure, the oil industry lost 44 percent of its equity value over the period, nonferrous metals lost 23 percent, glass lost 29 percent, and steel lost 10 percent.

References

Aoki, Masahiko. 2000. *Information, Corporate Governance, and Institutional Diversity: Competitiveness in Japan, the USA, and the Transitional Economies.* Oxford: Oxford University Press.

———, Hugh Patrick and Paul Sheard. 1994. The Japanese Main Bank System: An Introductory Overview. In Masahiko Aoki and Hugh Patrick, eds., *The Japanese Main Bank System: Its Relevance for Developing and Transforming Economies.* Oxford: Oxford University Press.

Berle, Adolph, Jr. and Gardiner C. Means. 1932. *The Modern Corporation and Private Property.* New York: MacMillan.

Cargill, Thomas F., Michael M. Hutchison and Takatoshi Ito. 2000. *Financial Policy and Central Banking in Japan.* Cambridge: MIT Press.

Chirinko, Robert S. and Huntley Schaller. 2001. Businenss Fixed Investment and "Bubbles": The Japanese Case. *American Economic Review.* 91: 663–80.

Cho, Myeong-Hyeon. 1998. Ownership Structure, Investment, and the Corporate Value: An Empirical Analysis. *Journal of Financial Economics* 43: 103–21.

Demsetz, Harold and Kenneth Lehn. 1985. The Structure of Corporate Ownership. *Journal of Political Economy* 93: 1155–77.

Easterbrook, Frank H. and Daniel R. Fischel. 1991. *The Economic Structure of Corporate Law.* Cambridge: Harvard University Press.

Gao, Bai. 2001. *Japan's Economic Dilemma: The Institutional Origins of Prosperity and Stagnation.* Cambridge: Cambridge University Press.

Garber, Peter M. 2000. *Famous First Bubbles: The Fundamentals of Early Manias*. Cambridge: MIT Press.

Hanazaki, Masaharu and Akiyoshi Horiuchi. 1998. A Vacuum of Governance in the Japanese Bank Management. University of Tokyo Faculty of Economics Discussion Paper CIRJE-F- Dec. 29.

Hayashi, Fumio and Edward C. Prescott. 2001. The 1990s in Japan: A Lost Decade. Unpublished paper.

Hermalin, Benjamin E., and Michael S. Weisbach. 1991. The Effects of Board Composition and Direct Incentives on Firm Performance. *Financial Management* 20: 101–12.

Himmelberg, Charles P., R. Glenn Hubbard and Darius Palia. 1999. Understanding the Determinants of Managerial Ownership and the Link Between Ownership and Performance. *Journal of Financial Economics* 53: 353–84.

Holderness, Clifford G., Randall S. Kroszner and Dennis P. Sheehan. 1999. Were the Good Old Days That Good? Changes in Managerial Stock Ownership since the Great Depression. *Journal of Finance* 54: 435–69.

Horiuchi, Akiyoshi and Katsutoshi Shimizu. 2001. Did Amakudari Undermine the Effectiveness of Regulator Monitoring in Japan? *Journal of Banking and Finance* 25: 573–96.

Hoshi, Takeo and Anil Kashyap. 1999. The Japanese Banking Crisis: Where Did It Come from and How Will It End? NBER Macroeconomics Ann. 1999: 129–201.

Kamiya, Takafusa. 1999. Shagai torishimariyaku no juyō to kyōkyū [The Supply of and Demand for Outside Directors]. *Jurisuto* 1155: 129–37.

Kamiya, Takayasu. 2001. Kōkai kaisha no kikan [The Mechanisms of the Public Corporation]. *Hōgaku kyōshitsu*, 251: 69–75.

Keizai chōsa kai, ed. Various years. *Keiretsu no kenkyū* [Research on the Keiretsu]. Tokyo: Keizai chōsa kai.

Kusumoto, Hiroshi, ed. 1994. *Nihon no kin'yū gyōsei, kanchō, kin'yū kikan.* [Japanese Financial Administration, Bureaucracy, and Institutions]. Tokyo: Tōyō keizai shimpō sha.

Manne, Henry G. 1965. Mergers and the Market for Corporate Control. *Journal of Political Economy* 73: 110–20.

McConnell, John J. and Henri Servaes. 1990. Additional Evidence on Equity Ownership and Corporate Value. *Journal of Financial Economics* 27: 595–612.

Milhaupt, Curtis J. 2002. On the (Fleeting) Existence of the Main Bank System and Other Japanese Economic Institutions. *Law and Social Inquiry* 27: 425–37.

—— and Geoffrey P. Miller. 1997. Cooperation, Conflict and Convergence in Japanese Finance: Evidence from the "Jusen" Problem. *Law and Policy in International Business* 29: 1–78.

Miwa, Yoshiro. 1999. Corporate Social Responsibility: Dangerous and Harmful, Though Maybe Not Irrelevant. *Cornell Law Review* 84: 1227–54.

—— and J. Mark Ramseyer. 2001. *Nihon keizairon no gokai: "keiretsu" no jubaku kara no kaihō* [Misunderstandings in the Theory of the Japanese Firm: Liberation from the Spell of the "Keiretsu"]. Tokyo: Tōyō keizai shimpō sha.

——. 2002a. The Myth of the Main Bank: Japan and Comparative Corporate Governance. *Law and Social Inquiry* 27: 401–424

——. 2002b. The Fable of the Keiretsu. *Journal of Economic and Management Strategy* 11: 169–224.

——. 2002c. Who Appoints Them, What Do They Do? Evidence on Outside Directors from Japan. Harvard Law School John M. Olin Center for Law, Economics, and Business, Working Paper 374.

——. 2002d. *Sangyō seisaku ron no gokai: kōdō seichō no shinjitsu* [Misunderstandings About Industrial Policy: The Truth About High Growth]. Tokyo: Tōyō keizai shimpō sha.

——. 2003a. Directed Credit? Capital Market Competition in High-Growth Japan. *Journal of Economic and Management Strategy* (forthcoming).

——. 2003b. Does Ownership Matter: Evidence from the Zaibatsu Dissolution Program. University of Tokyo Faculty of Economics. *Journal of Economic and Management Strategy* 12: 67–89.

——. 2003c. Capitalist Politicians, Socialist Bureaucrats? Legends of Government Planning from Japan. *Antitrust Bulletin* (forthcoming).

Miyajima, Hideaki. 1998. The Impact of Deregulation on Corporate Governance and Finance. In Lonny E. Carlile and Mark C. Tilton, eds., *Is Japan Really Changing its Ways? Regulatory Reform and the Japanese Economy*. Washington, D.C.: Brookings Institution.

Morck, Randall, Masao Nakamura and Anil Shivdasani. 2000. Banks, Ownership Structure, and Firm Value in Japan. *Journal of Business* 73: 539–67.

——, Andrei Shleifer and Robert W. Vishny. 1988. Management Ownership and Market Valuation: An Empirical Analysis. *Journal of Financial Economics* 20: 293–315.

Nihon fudōsan kenkyū jo, ed. 1998. Shigai chikakaku shisū [Price Indices for Metropolitan Real Estate]. Tokyo: Nihon fudōsan kenkyū jo.

Nihon ginkō kin'yū kenkyū jo, ed. 1995. *Shimpan: waga kuni no kin'yū seido* [New Edition: Our Country's Financial System]. Tokyo: Nihon ginkō.

Nihon ginkō, ed. Various years. *Keizai tōkei nempō* [Economic Statistics Annual]. Tokyo: Nihon ginkō.

Nihon shōken keizai kenkyū jo, ed. Various years. Kabushiki tōshi shūeki ritsu [Rates of Return on Common Stocks]. Tokyo: Nihon shōken keizai kenkyū jo.

Porter, Michael E. 1995. [Comments], in Mitsuhiro Fukao, *Financial Integration, Corporate Governance, and the Performance of Multinational Companies.* Washington, D.C.: Brookings Institution.

Ramseyer, J. Mark. 1986. Lawyers, Foreign Lawyers, and Lawyer-Substitutes: The Market for Regulation in Japan. *Harvard International Law Journal* 27: 499–539.

———. 1987. Takeovers in Japan: Opportunism, Ideology and Corporate Control. *UCLA Law Review* 35: 1–64.

——— and Frances M. Rosenbluth. 1993. *Japan's Political Marketplace.* Cambridge: Harvard University Press.

——— and Minoru Nakazato. 1999. *Japanese Law: An Economic Approach.* Chicago: University of Chicago Press.

Romano, Roberta. 1991. The Shareholder Suit: Litigation without Foundation? *Journal of Law, Economics and Organization* 7: 55–87.

Sheard, Paul. 1989. The Main Bank System and Corporate Monitoring and Control in Japan. *Journal of Economics, Behavior and Organization* 11: 399–422.

———. 1994. Reciprocal Delegated Monitoring in the Japanese Main Bank System. *Journal of Japanese and International Economies* 8: 1–21.

Stigler, George J. 1964. Public Regulation of the Securities Markets. *Journal of Business* 37: 117–42.

Tōkyō shōken torihiki jo, ed. Various years. *Shōken tōkei nempō* [Securities Statistics Annual]. Tokyo: Tōkyō shōken torihiki jo.

Tōyō keizai shimpō sha, ed. Various years. *Kigyō keiretsu sōran* [Firm Keiretsu Overview]. Tokyo: Tōyō keizai shimpō sha.

Ueda, Kazuo. 1990. Are Japanese Stock Prices Too High? *Journal of Japanese and International Economies* 4: 351–70.

West, Mark D. 1994. The Pricing of Shareholder Derivative Actions in Japan and the United States. *Northwestern University Law Review* 88: 1436–65.

———. 1999. Information, Institutions, and Extortion in Japan and the United States: Making Sense of *Sokaiya* Racketeers. *Northwestern University Law Review* 93: 767–817.

———. 2001. Why Shareholders Sue: The Evidence from Japan. *Journal of Legal Studies* 30: 351–82.

96 nen 3 gatsu kessan, ginkō sōgō rankingu [Consolidated Bank Rankings, March 1996], *Kin'yū bijinesu*, Sept. 1996, pp. 48–78.

TABLE APP-1 Selected Summary Statistics

	n	Min	Mean	Max
A. *Dependent Variables:*				
ROI				
1980-85	42	6.1	17.8	36.9
1985-90	46	13.5	20.3	34.0
1990-95	55	-20.2	-7.4	5.3
Loan Growth				
1977-81	48	158.1	193.8	257.8
1981-86	48	119.2	150.4	180.1
1986-89	54	115.5	142.5	175.1
Bad Loans (1996)	56	.74	2.77	7.86
B. *Independent Variables:*				
Outside Dir				
1981	49	0	2.5	5
1989	56	0	2.9	7
MoF Alum				
1977	56	0	.357	1
1981	56	0	.286	1
1986	54	0	.357	1
BoJ Alum				
1977	56	0	.500	1
1981	56	0	.446	1
1986	56	0	.393	1
Top 10 S/h				
1977	48	11.3	22.7	41.6
1981	48	13.3	24.4	43.3
1986	54	15.5	25.2	40.7
Fin S/h				
1977	48	2.3	15.7	38.3
1981	48	4.3	17.4	36.7
1986	54	6.1	19.1	34.5
Tokyo	56	0	.179	1
Osaka	56	0	.107	1
Nagoya	56	0	.089	1
Sm Firm Fin	56	58.1	77.7	90.2

Sources: Tōyō keizai shimpō sha, ed., Kigyō keiretsu sōran [Firm Keiretsu Overview] (Tokyo: Tōyō keizai shimpō sha, various years); Nihon shōken keizai kenkyū jo, ed., Kabushiki tōshi shūeki ritsu [Rates of Return on Common Stocks] (Tokyo: Nihon shōken keizai kenkyū jo, various years); 96 nen 3 gatsu kessan, ginkō sōgō rankingu [Consolidated Bank Rankings, March 1996], Kin'yū bijinesu, Sept. 1996, at 48.

TABLE APP-2 Selected Correlation Coefficients

A. *For 1980-85 ROI Regressions:*

	BoJ Alum	MoF Alum	Outsid Dr	Top10 S/h	Fin S/h
BoJ Alum	1.00				
MoF Alum	.06	1.00			
Outsid Dr	.23	.36	1.00		
Top10 S/h	.22	.11	.31	1.00	
Fin S/h	.10	.20	-.01	.32	1.00

B. *For 1985-90 and 1990-95 ROI Regressions:*

	BoJ Alum	MoF Alum	Outsid Dr	Top10 S/h	Fin S/h
BoJ Alum	1.00				
MoF Alum	-.09	1.00			
Outsid Dr	.21	.23	1.00		
Top10 S/h	.22	.09	.37	1.00	
Fin S/h	.10	.20	.12	.27	1.00

Sources: See Table App-1.

TABLE APP-3 Return on Investment

	3(a)	3(b) 1980-85	3(c)	3(d)	3(e) 1985-90	3(f)	3(g)	3(h) 1990-95	3(i)
Outsid Dr	-.265	-.369	-.532	-.404	-.333	-.287	-.254	-.182	-.279
	(0.35)	(0.50)	(0.77)	(0.68)	(0.58)	(0.52)	(0.46)	(0.32)	(0.56)
MoF Alum	-1.807	-1.841		-.637	-.738		.154	.137	
	(0.89)	(0.91)		(0.40)	(0.47)		(0.10)	(0.09)	
BoJ Alum	-1.035	-.696		.884	.759		.536	.625	
	(0.56)	(0.38)		(0.62)	(0.53)		(0.37)	(0.44)	
Top10 S/h		-.115			-.025			-.099	
		(0.76)			(0.18)			(0.73)	
Fin S/h	.091			-.060		.084	-.027		
	(0.63)			(0.49)		(0.05)	(0.23)		
Tokyo	7.788**	9.773**	8.216**	.665	.253		-1.064	-.807	-1.181
	(2.65)	(3.58)	(3.64)	(0.30)	(0.13)		(0.47)	(0.37)	(0.61)
Osaka	-4.911	-3.164	-4.403	4.755	4.696	3.993	-6.459**	-6.300**	-6.300**
	(1.27)	(0.81)	(1.26)	(1.57)	(1.49)	(1.53)	(2.72)	(2.66)	(2.94)
Nagoya	5.068*	5.043*	5.216*	-2.589	-2.489	-2.390	-.448	-.423	-.425
	(1.80)	(1.80)	(1.96)	(1.17)	(1.12)	(1.12)	(0.19)	(0.18)	(0.19)
S Firm Fin	-.127	-.120	-.107	.158	.149	.158	-.136	-.134	-.156
	(0.35)	(0.92)	(0.87)	(1.44)	(1.38)	(1.63)	(1.22)	(1.22)	(1.60)
Adj R2	0.27	0.27	0.31	0.02	0.01	0.08	0.10	0.11	0.16
n	41	41	42	44	44	44	53	53	55

Notes: The dependent variable is Return on Investment. The regressions are ordinary least squares. The table gives the coefficient, followed by the absolute value of the t-statistic in parentheses. * — statistically significant at the 10 percent level, two-tailed test; ** — statistically significant at the 5 percent level, two-tailed test. All equations include a constant term, not reported.
Sources: See Table App-1.

TABLE APP-4 Loan Regressions —Portfolio Growth during 1977-89

	(4a)	(4b) 1977-81	(4c)	(4d)	(4e) 1981-86	(4f)	(4g)	(4h) 1986-89	(4i)
Outside Dr	1.327 (0.68)	.966 (0.49)	2.828 (1.51)	-.357 (0.25)	-.753 (0.51)	-.628 (0.46)	1.822 (1.47)	1.348 (1.09)	1.720 (1.43)
MoF Alum	9.933* (1.94)	10.245* (1.96)		.787 (0.20)	1.689 (0.42)		-2.645 (0.74)	-1.742 (0.51)	
BoJ Alum	6.460 (1.26)	6.261 (1.20)		-2.580 (0.72)	-2.221 (0.59)		-4.215 (1.27)	-4.332 (1.35)	
Top10 S/h		.385 (0.97)			.166 (0.55)			.683** (2.24)	
Fin S/h	.462 (1.26)			.500* (1.79)			.401 (1.47)		
Tokyo	-4.621 (0.61)	-2.614 (0.36)	2.958 (0.44)	17.526** (3.06)	21.555** (3.89)	22.767** (4.67)	15.357** (3.12)	15.537** (3.44)	18.229** (4.07)
Osaka	17.554** (2.28)	16.715** (2.14)	19.658** (2.50)	5.471 (0.96)	5.537 (0.93)	5.529 (0.97)	10.205* (1.84)	9.026 (1.67)	8.992* (1.69)
Nagoya	-2.010 (0.26)	-1.988 (0.25)	-5.135 (0.64)	8.924 (1.52)	8.885 (1.46)	9.306 (1.58)	11.678** (2.13)	11.489** (2.16)	11.512** (2.10)
S Firm Fin	.748** (2.13)	.742** (2.10)	.740** (2.03)	.227 (0.86)	.248 (0.91)	.258 (0.97)	.037 (0.14)	.054 (0.22)	.136 (0.55)
Adj R2	0.32	0.32	0.27	0.33	0.28	0.32	0.33	0.37	0.33
n	48	48	48	48	48	48	54	54	54

Notes: The dependent variable is Loan Growth. The regressions are ordinary least squares. The table gives the coefficient, followed by the absolute value of the t-statistic in parentheses. * — statistically significant at the 10 percent level, two-tailed test; ** — statistically significant at the 5 percent level, two-tailed test. All equations include a constant term, not reported.

Sources: See Table App-1.

TABLE APP-5 Loan Regressions—Portfolio Quality (Bad Loan Ratio) in 1996

	5(a)	5(b)	5(c)	5(d)	5(e)
Outside Dir	.030 (0.17)	.002 (0.01)	.098 (0.59)		
MoF Alum	.481 (0.97)	.583 (1.20)		.707 (1.49)	
BoJ Alum	-.712 (1.55)	-.687 (1.51)			-.705 (1.61)
Top 10 S/h	.047 (1.09)				
Fin S/h	.041 (1.08)				
Tokyo	1.416 (2.08)**	1.525 (2.37)**	1.539 (2.47)**	1.621 (2.89)**	1.790 (3.16)**
Osaka	.906 (1.18)	.817 (1.07)	.869 (1.17)	.601 (.80)	1.077 (1.49)
Nagoya	-.837 (1.10)	-.853 (1.13)	-1.027 (1.33)	-.999 (1.32)	-.979 (1.29)
Sm Firm Fin	.043 (1.21)	.047 (1.32)	.059 (1.77)*	.068 (2.07)**	.048 (1.51)
Adj R2	0.20	0.20	0.17	0.20	0.21
n	54	54	56	56	56

Notes: The dependent variable is Bad Loans. The regressions are ordinary least squares. The table gives the coefficient, followed by the absolute value of the t-statistic in parentheses. * — statistically significant at the 10 percent level, two-tailed test; ** — statistically significant at the 5 percent level, two-tailed test. All equations include a constant term, not reported.

Sources: See Table App-1.

11 Revamping Fiduciary Duties in Korea

Does Law Matter to Corporate Governance?

Kon-Sik Kim and Joongi Kim

A provocative debate in comparative corporate governance discourse concerns the question, which factors—law, social norms, market pressure, or others—matter more in corporate governance reform? Korea offers an interesting example for that debate. A general consensus has emerged among policymakers and scholars that Korean corporate governance needs to make the transition to a more capital market-oriented system (Johnson, et. al. 2000; KFSC and KFSS 2000). The question remains, however, what role should law play in achieving this transformation?

Several conflicting views exist on this subject. Economists Raphael La Porta et al. have indicated empirically that deep capital markets cannot develop without investor protections (La Porta et. al. 1997; 1998; 2000). Implicitly at least, this work stresses the importance of legal reforms to corporate governance.[1] Some legal scholars, by contrast, are more skeptical of the impact of corporate law on corporate finance and governance. The skeptics emphasize that market pressure plays a more significant role (see, e.g., Easterbrook and Fischel 1991). Fischel and Bradley (1986) even suggest that legal mechanisms such as fiduciary duties and derivative actions are overrated in their utility. Eisenberg (1999) and Cooter and Eisenberg (2001) suggest that managerial behavior can be better restrained through social rather than legal norms. Coffee (2001) concludes that the importance of private ordering through self-regulation should be emphasized relative to legal change.

In this essay, we examine the role of law—particularly the law of fiduciary duties—in Korean corporate governance, and suggest that the foregoing scholarly positions are in less tension than they may first appear. We will argue that in the early stages of corporate governance reform, the law, at least as represented by the fiduciary duties of directors, plays a critical role. Social norms, private ordering through self-regulation, and market-based pressure are undoubtedly important as well, but we assume that the foundation of corporate governance reform begins with law-based discipline. Dispersed ownership and a capital-market orientation have not fully developed without an effective legal system for corporate governance.[2]

Fiduciary duties of directors are the most important legal protection common law systems provide to shareholders. Fiduciary duties provide the means to minimize the potential for expropriation and the conflict between managers and shareholders. During the Asian financial crisis in late 1998, Korea amended its Commercial Code (KCC) to explicitly establish a "fiduciary duty" of directors.[3] According to the policymakers in charge of revising the KCC, this new provision was meant to establish an Anglo-American style fiduciary duty (Ministry of Justice 1999).[4] The primary purpose of introducing this duty explicitly was to help minimize the acute conflicts of interest that arise out of the controlling shareholder's domination of corporate decisionmaking in Korea. While legislatively transplanting a concept such as a fiduciary duty might be relatively simple, many obstacles must be overcome before such concepts effectively function within a country's corporate governance system (Berkowitz et al. 2003). The real challenge is to make fiduciary duty protections effective.

Focusing on the fiduciary duty of directors, this essay will seek to highlight the importance of a comprehensive legal infrastructure in bringing about corporate governance reform. It will describe why, in the initial stages, such a legal infrastructure is critical to the development of an effective fiduciary duty concept and how such an infrastructure can contribute to deeper, more liquid securities markets. It will show that Korea is finally beginning to formulate a more effective corporate governance structure following the recent establishment of a comprehensive legal infrastructure based upon fiduciary duty.

This essay begins in part I by exploring the nature of the agency problem in Korea. It discusses controlling shareholders' disproportionate influence on Korean firms and the complicated ownership structure of conglomerates. The various means that existed in the past to reduce agency costs, such as social norms, organizational structure, market pressure, and legal structure, will be reviewed. Part II explains the legal infrastructure needed to make the

fiduciary duty of directors function more effectively. It reviews the significance of the recent establishment of an express fiduciary duty for directors
and explains the limitations on the effective application of fiduciary rules. It
also highlights the elements necessary to strengthen fiduciary duties, including effective private enforcement, the possibility of disgorgement of
improper gains, and the role of the judiciary and attorneys. Part III shows
how the basic legal infrastructure helped shape the contours of fiduciary
duty in Korea and spurred corporate governance reform in several landmark
cases. The conclusion summarizes the results of these developments.

I. Agency Problems and Governance Mechanisms in Korea

A. *Disproportionate Corporate Control by Clans*

While the emphasis might vary among countries, the main goal of corporate
law is to minimize the potential for expropriation by insiders. According to
the classic hypothesis of Berle and Means (1932), as the ownership of large
corporations becomes more dispersed, shareholders have less ability and
incentive to act as controlling owners; in their place, managers with marginal ownership stakes begin to dominate the corporation. Berle and Means
emphasized that under a governance structure of divided ownership and
control, it is necessary to establish appropriate monitoring mechanisms to
ensure that managers do not neglect the interests of shareholders. In many
other countries, however, especially those that follow a civil law tradition,
ownership and control have not separated, and blockholders have remained
in control.

The governance structure of Korea's large, family-controlled conglomerates called *chaebol* (which are the focus of this essay) initially resembled this
latter and more prevalent type of blockholder model where controlling
shareholders maintained concentrated ownership positions. Because controlling shareholders held large blocks of stock, they had an interest in
increasing the firm's stock price. To this extent, their interests were aligned
with those of the minority shareholders. Under this structure, the agency
problem was not pronounced, and strong external controls were not particularly important.

Over time, however, the ownership structure of *chaebol* firms has
changed. Founder-shareholders and their families maintained control over

management, but their ownership positions as represented by cash flow rights declined dramatically (see figure 11.1). Personal ownership stakes, including family interests, fell to less than 5 percent in most *chaebol*. Despite these dwindling economic stakes, the owners maintained control over voting rights through cross-ownership structures or pyramidal shareholding schemes (KFTC 2001; La Porta et al. 1999). Through these mechanisms, on average controlling shareholders dominated approximately 40 percent of the total voting rights in their firms through a web of cross shareholdings. Following the financial crisis, cross shareholdings increased further, and the disparity between a controlling family's cash flow rights and its voting rights widened significantly (Jang 2000).

FIGURE 11.1 Intra-Conglomerate Shareholding at Top 30 Chaebol (1983–2000)

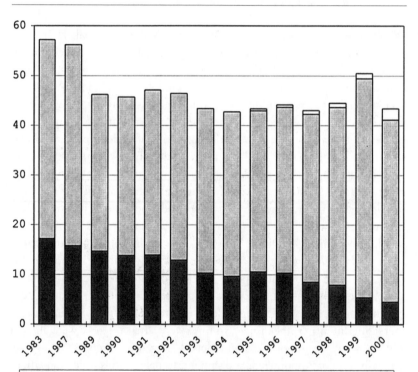

The ownership structure of major Korean firms has been altered further with the rise in both domestic and foreign institutional ownership. Unfortunately from a corporate governance perspective, most domestic institutional investors are direct affiliates of *chaebol* or rely upon them for business, and thus remain captive and passive monitors.[5] Foreign institutional investors now own close to 30 percent of the stock market.[6] They are marginally more willing to take action, but are constrained by factors such as a complicated proxy process operating through custodians (Kim and Kim 2001).

Overall, this complex ownership structure of Korean firms aggravates the agency problem and the conflicts of interest between the controlling and non-controlling shareholders. The controlling shareholders maintain governance rights that far exceed their cash flow rights. Insulated from accountability, they rule unchallenged within their *chaebol* empires, irrespective of performance.[7] Controlling shareholders inevitably have a propensity to favor their personal interests over the interests of the noncontrolling shareholders. The severe gap between cash flow rights and voting rights effectively led Korea to become a country with "dispersed ownership." Anomalously, however, despite the severity of the agency problem, investor protections remained weak.

B. Internal Governance Structure

The agency problem discussed above can be structurally monitored through a range of control mechanisms. These mechanisms include direct restraints such as fiduciary duties, shareholders' meetings, boards of directors and audit committees, and various other factors like market pressure. This section will focus on internal corporate governance mechanisms; external factors and fiduciary duties will be covered in subsequent sections.

As in other countries, corporations in Korea are composed of various organs, such as the general shareholders' meeting, the board of directors, representative directors, and statutory internal auditors. These organs are supposed to work together to reduce conflicts in a system of checks and balances. If each corporate organ performs its assigned function properly, agency problems or the potential for expropriation would be mitigated. Until recently, however, this internal corporate structure failed to function adequately, primarily due to the dominance of controlling shareholders. For instance, shareholders' meetings were mere formalities, and only recently have become a more serious forum for discussion (Kim 2000).

The board of directors of most companies consisted of individuals loyal to the controlling shareholder, which compromised their ability to act as monitors. Formal board meetings themselves were seldom held, and even if convened, substantive discussions rarely occurred. Controlling shareholders could further their interests at will because they dominated the decision-making process.

To rectify this situation, the government recently required all publicly held companies to appoint outside directors, and certain large companies must also establish audit committees in place of the statutory auditor.[8] The mere presence of independent directors can act as a restraint against a controlling shareholder's pursuit of self-interest. An audit committee consisting solely of outside directors theoretically can be more effective in reducing potential conflicts than a statutory auditor, a position typically occupied by senior managers before they retire.

From this perspective, the recent reforms mandating the appointment of outside directors and audit committees are positive developments. In practice, however, strengthening internal governance through these reforms alone is difficult, as much depends on the independence and competence of the persons involved. Unfortunately, statistics show that the controlling shareholders have selected the outside directors more than 70 percent of the time (Korean Listed Companies Association 2001). While large companies must elect outside directors through nominating committees, invariably the preferences of the controlling shareholder and management determine who is elected. In fact, until recently shareholders could not even make a shareholder proposal to nominate a candidate for consideration by this committee. Similarly, audit committees are generally composed of outside directors who tend to be faithful to management.

Many observers are therefore skeptical of the efficacy of the outside director and audit committee system. Furthermore, the perception of outside directors has been sullied by several recent scandals (see Chosun Ilbo 2000).[9] Yet most of the criticism appears to be based on unrealistic expectations. While not yet apparent, the benefits of these reforms will no doubt increase as outside directors become more comfortable and knowledgeable about their role as fiduciaries. In several isolated but significant recent cases, outside directors of leading companies have played critical roles in safeguarding internal corporate governance, a promising sign that is emboldening the outside directors of other firms to become more active.[10]

C. The Market as a Controlling Mechanism

The pursuit of personal interests by controlling shareholders can also be minimized through stronger market-based controls, such as a more competitive product market, a more fluid labor market for managers, and more active capital and corporate control markets (Eisenberg 1998). However, the only market-based control that has been functioning even to a limited extent is the product market. Heavily dependent on exports, Korean firms have long faced competitive pressure in international markets. In the future, as Korea's domestic market continues to liberalize, domestic-oriented corporations will also be subject to similar pressures. The remaining market mechanisms have been relatively underdeveloped, largely by design of economic policymakers, who have sought to protect domestic firms. Controlling shareholders have been, and still remain, relatively free from managerial, capital, and takeover market pressures (Kim 2000).

For example, a flexible labor market for managers has not yet developed in Korea. In order for more lateral movement by professionals to occur, business practices must become more transparent and accountable. Otherwise, personal loyalty will still be preferred over managerial competence, and managers will continue to be recruited from within the firm. Increased accountability and greater potential risk will lead competent managers to be less willing to condone expropriation by controlling shareholders, thereby sacrificing themselves. Thus, increased managerial transparency and accountability will contribute to the development of a management labor market.

Recently, the merger and acquisition market in Korea has received considerable attention. The conflicts between controlling and minority shareholders could be substantially mitigated if the external corporate control market acted as an effective source of discipline. While replacing controlling shareholders through mergers and acquisitions might not be the most efficient means of discipline, an active merger and acquisition market can contribute to the reduction of agency costs. Hostile mergers and acquisitions could be attempted where the controlling shareholder's ownership stake is relatively small and the stock is trading at a substantial discount to asset values. In the past, hostile takeovers were unfathomable events in faraway countries, but they are becoming more familiar concepts in Korea.

Nevertheless, the corporate control market remains weak. Controlling shareholders can rely on a host of defensive measures, including staggered boards, three-year tenures for directors, private placements of convertible bonds, and the acquisition of treasury shares.[11] Another critical barrier to hostile takeovers is the lack of information. Although accounting standards are improving, financial reports are still not widely trusted. Acquisitions often falter because vast contingent liabilities surface unexpectedly during the due diligence process. Furthermore, many observers and policymakers remain skeptical of the efficacy of hostile tender offers, and public hostility persists.[12] At present, large *chaebol* and foreign investors remain the only viable potential acquirers in Korea. Six of the seven tender offers made between the end of the financial crisis and October 2001 were launched by foreign companies (Hong 2001; Kim 1999).

The product, labor, and corporate control markets may indirectly restrain controlling shareholders, but the capital market is a key monitoring mechanism. The Korean academic community has not devoted serious attention to the relationship between agency problems and the capital market. In general, the more effectively capital markets function, the less severe agency problems are in the corporate setting. Since investors are wary of firms whose controlling shareholders have poor reputations or disproportionate voting rights, the shares of these firms are discounted and their credit ratings suffer.

In the past, when banks offered generous financing to corporations on the basis of collateral or political connections, a decline in share price or credit rating was not necessarily a serious problem. As corporations increasingly rely on the capital markets, however, maintaining investor confidence to minimize financing costs is becoming critical. In the United States, for instance, the practice of appointing outside directors and retaining independent accounting firms to perform audits emerged, not because of direct statutory requirements, but because of the voluntary decisions of the corporations themselves to maintain investor confidence. Controlling shareholder abuse tends to be more limited in the United States not only because of its strong legal protections, but also because of the pressure of its well-developed capital market. While still minimal, such tendencies are beginning to appear in Korea. A classic example may be the recent splintering of the giant Hyundai Group. It suffered a critical loss of confidence in the market following several near fatal business decisions and the dramatic succession fight carried out by two of the founder's sons (Kirk 2000).

Managers of Korean firms are now paying more attention to share prices. With the era of industrial policy based upon generous credit coming to an end, costs associated with direct financing are becoming crucial issues for Korean firms. Accordingly, corporations are gradually being affected by market pressure to restrain controlling shareholder expropriation and to improve their ownership structures. Controlling shareholders are less sensitive to share price because they usually do not intend to cash out their shares, and they are legally prohibited from holding stock options.[13]

D. Fiduciary Rules

While the need to minimize the conflicts of interests of controlling share-holders in Korea has increased, internal firm controls as well as external controls based on market pressures have remained weak. Therefore, the role of fiduciary duties has become even more important. Under Korean law, a director has the "duty of care of a good manager."[14] Commentators have disputed the meaning of this duty, particularly when compared with the fiduciary duties of directors under U.S. law.[15] One view is that the duty of care of a good manager is the functional equivalent of the fiduciary duties imposed on directors under U.S. corporate law.

The concept of the good manager duty, however, has undeniably been underdeveloped in comparison to the concept of fiduciary duty under Anglo-American law. This may be due to various factors, but the inherent vagueness of the concept is not a persuasive reason. As noted previously, during the Asian financial crisis in late 1998, the "fiduciary duty" of directors was explicitly established by law, with the intention of replicating the Anglo-American concept.[16] The KCC now offers an explicit basis upon which to develop an effective jurisprudence in line with Anglo-American law. Perhaps the ultimate significance of the "new" duty is that the judiciary, managers, practitioners, and investors have all become more aware of the concept.

Before the establishment of an express fiduciary duty, several existing provisions provided a basis for a U.S.-style fiduciary duty. The KCC, like the laws of many other countries, had provisions designed to restrain managerial misconduct with respect to self-dealing and competition with the corporation. A self-dealing provision required board approval of transactions between the corporation and a director acting on his or a third persons' behalf.[17] An anti-competition provision required board approval before a director could enter into a transaction falling within the same line of business as the corporation.[18] A director who desired to become a director of another corporation engaged in the same line of business also needed to obtain board approval. A director violating the duty of a good manager or one of the more specific provisions mentioned above is liable to the corporation for any resulting damages.[19] If a director fails to fulfill these duties intentionally or through gross negligence, the director is liable even to third parties.[20] These provisions were buttressed further by the express fiduciary duty.

II. The Importance of Legal Infrastructure Surrounding Fiduciary Duties

The persistent lack of strong, market-based constraints in Korea has increased the importance of law-based corporate governance reform. This section describes the recently established legal infrastructure related to fiduciary duties, which is designed to promote governance reform. We first discuss the legal changes themselves and the implementation and enforcement processes. We then offer suggestions to improve the legal infrastructure.

A. Inadequate Restraint of Controlling Shareholders

A serious flaw in Korean corporate law was that controlling shareholders remained outside the formal legal framework. The KCC provisions related to self-dealing, competition with the corporation, and liability to the corporation (among others), lacked the concept of a "controlling shareholder," and thus applied only to statutory organs such as the director or statutory auditor.[21] In larger *chaebol*, controlling shareholders merely assumed nonstatutory titles such as "chairperson" to avoid the responsibility that would come with the assumption of formal positions such as representative director or director.

Conceivably, the controlling shareholder could be held accountable indirectly by imposing liability on individual directors of the various affiliated corporations. But this would not only be harsh for the directors involved, but also ineffective as a deterrent to self-interested behavior. Directors typically are salaried employees with no real choice but to be loyal subordinates of the controlling shareholder, ready to assume responsibility on its behalf. This significant gap in the legal framework failed to attract the serious attention of academics, practitioners or policymakers.

The problems surrounding this legal gap, however, reached new heights during the financial crisis. Controlling shareholder accountability was identified as one of the five critical corporate areas in need of reform (Black

2001a). In 1998, Article 401–2 was added to the KCC to bring controlling shareholders within the legal framework. While the term "controlling shareholder" was not used, persons who participate in the business conduct of the corporation are now subject to the same liabilities as those imposed on directors. However, because the new article focuses on a person's conduct rather than his status, controlling shareholders can still avoid liability if they do not exercise control. It thus covers persons who participate in the management of a corporation by directly instructing the directors, or by indirectly instructing the directors through such entities as the controlling shareholder's office (ibid.).[22] Such persons will assume the liability of a director if they are deemed to have influence and have given instructions to management. Influence can derive from share ownership, but it may also be based upon other sources. Banks and large corporate customers or suppliers in dominant positions could qualify as having influence.[23]

Despite the progress reflected in this reform, Article 401–2 has several limitations. First, to impose liability on a party for the business conduct of a corporation, the party must have committed an act that affected the corporation. In the case of a controlling shareholder, the plaintiff must establish that the controlling shareholder gave instructions to a manager. Proving this is virtually impossible, however, because explicit instructions are rare. A senior manager's competence is often evaluated according to his ability to anticipate the controlling shareholder's implicit preferences and to act in pursuit of those interests. Thus, some have argued that Article 401–2 has only symbolic meaning and little deterrent effect (Tsche 1998). From this perspective, Article 401–2 actually creates a perverse incentive for the controlling shareholders not to openly participate in managerial decisionmaking.

As enacted, Article 401–2 also does not properly cover controlling shareholders who engage in self-dealing or transactions that compete with the company. It only covers the types of conduct that will lead to liability as a director, such as liability to the corporation (Art. 399), liability to a third party (Art. 401), and derivative suits (Art. 403). Similarly, unless the controlling shareholder is also a director of the corporation or it can be established that the controlling shareholder gave instructions to management, the controlling shareholder can avoid liability.

Most of these problems could be resolved if a broad de facto director concept were adopted in relation to controlling shareholders. A person who has participated regularly in the conduct of a business, for instance, could be regarded as a de facto director, resulting in the imposition of various duties and liabilities applicable to directors. As long as it could be demonstrated that a controlling shareholder gave instructions to a director on a regular basis, specific instructions for an individual act would not have to be shown. Moreover, unlike Article 401–2, all the provisions related to fiduciary duties, such as self-dealing, could be applied through the application of a de facto director concept. This expansion in the scope of duties would not require statutory change and could be achieved through judicial interpretation. Ironically, while the potential for such a judicial interpretation remains, the adoption of Article 401–2 has to some extent reduced the probability that the courts would take this broad approach.

The controlling shareholder problem could also be significantly addressed by expressly recognizing a fiduciary duty of such shareholders. This would allow courts to play a more active role in cases of expropriation. A growing number of Korean corporate law scholars advocate explicitly recognizing such a duty, and several leading scholars have argued that controlling shareholders are already subject to fiduciary duties (e.g., Chung 2000; Tsche 1987). Courts should recognize such a duty despite the absence of an explicitly statutory provision. Most notably, the highest civil court of Germany (*die Bundesgerichtshof*) in 1988 reversed its long-standing position and issued a decision recognizing fiduciary duties for a controlling shareholder despite the absence of an express statutory provision under German law.[24]

Despite its limitations, Article 401–2 is a significant attempt to fill the legal gap governing the conduct of controlling shareholders. Controlling shareholders can now be held legally accountable for their involvement in a business decision, and the passage of this provision promoted awareness of this potential source of liability.

B. Board Approval for Breaches of Fiduciary Duty

As in many other countries, under Korean law, directors may carry out conflict-of-interest transactions if they obtain board approval. Unlike the situation under U.S. law, however, without board approval the transaction is in principle invalid, regardless of its fairness. Of course, for director approval to be valid, the board must be properly informed and disinterested. There are several problems with this approval process.

First, to be properly informed, directors should have an affirmative duty to disclose personal conflicts of interest to the board. Such disclosure is critical to Anglo-American fiduciary law, but it is not expressly required in Korea. Because approval by an uninformed board should be invalid, this type of disclosure duty should be inferred, or preferably required by law.

Second, a broad definition of interestedness is essential. In the U.S., inside directors and executive officers can be considered interested even if they do not have a direct stake in the decision, because courts take into account such factors as pecuniary, familial, or professional interest. Approval is effective only when it is obtained from truly disinterested directors. Therefore, U.S. companies have an incentive to select directors without any potential to be considered "interested" (Black 2001). In Korea, however, a much narrower definition has been used that allows directors to vote as long as they do not have direct personal interests in the transaction. Thus, where a controlling shareholder enters into a transaction with the company, all the directors are eligible to participate in the board vote, even though the outcome is a foregone conclusion. From this perspective, the new mandatory outside director requirement raises the hope that these decisions will be made by more independent boards.

The KCC does allow individual companies to adopt stricter provisions in their articles of incorporation. Therefore, companies can require outside director approval in specified circumstances, and some firms have already adopted this approach. The more management covets the trust of the capital market, the more it will voluntarily adopt such provisions. The fact that such provisions can seldom be found, however, signifies that most companies still do not pay much attention to capital market forces.

C. Lack of Private and Public Enforcement; Weak Legal Remedies

According to one assessment, "[s]hareholder suits are the primary mechanism for enforcing the fiduciary duties of corporate managers" (Kraakman et. al. 1994: 1733; contra Fischel and Bradley 1986). Adopted in Korea in 1962, the shareholder's derivative suit was deemed to be a crucial means for minority shareholders to hold managers accountable for abuses or negligence. In reality, however, it failed to function as anticipated, and no derivative suits were publicly recorded until 1997. Actions for breach of fiduciary duty were therefore literally nonexistent.

A primary reason for the lack of such private enforcement was the 5 percent shareholding requirement imposed on a plaintiff shareholder. This requirement was in effect for more than thirty-five years. Since the average market capitalization of listed companies in 1997 was 62.3 billion won ($69 million), this requirement meant shareholders had to hold, in the aggregate, 3.1 billion won ($3.5 million) in shares to launch a derivative action, making it all but impossible given collective action problems. In 1998, the 5 percent limit was finally reduced to 1 percent. The Securities Exchange Act was thereafter repeatedly amended, and shareholders of listed firms holding 0.01 percent of the shares for six months may now file a derivative suit (Art.191–13[1]). Despite these reforms, and in contrast with Japan's experience following similar changes to the procedural environment (see West 1994), the number of derivative actions remains small. Less than a dozen cases have been filed since the initial legal reform in 1998.

Remedies available for violations of fiduciary duties have also been limited. They consist only of compensatory damages, invalidation of a conflict-of-interest transaction or, more fundamentally, removal of the director. This contrasts sharply with U.S. law, where breaches are reviewed under equity principles and remedies are fashioned flexibly. Allowing shareholders of Korean firms to sue for disgorgement of a director's improper gains would be an important reform, because it would serve as a considerable deterrent to abuse. Under Korean law, however, this type of remedy has been recognized only for violations of the prohibition against establishing a competing business.[25] An even more aggressive approach would be to impose punitive or treble damages, in light of the difficulty plaintiffs encounter in discovering, maintaining an action for, and proving a breach of fiduciary duty (Cooter and Freedman 1991).

Some reforms, however, have attempted to address the costs shareholders incur in bringing derivative actions. For example, plaintiff shareholders can now seek reimbursement from the company for reasonable litigation costs.[26] Courts determine the reasonable amount of attorney fees that the company should pay successful plaintiffs. Contrary to the loser-pays rule applicable in other civil litigation, in a derivative action, a losing shareholder is not liable for the loss caused to the company by the action, unless it was brought in bad faith (Art. 405[2]). Despite these developments, it is unlikely that Korean judges will be as generous as their U.S. counterparts in respecting contingency fee agreements, and it is premature to presume that aggrieved shareholders and their attorneys will now have sufficient incentive to bring derivative actions.

In the case of direct actions, a critical problem has been whether share-holders must pursue their claims individually or through an opt-in system of consolidating plaintiffs. In other words, Korea still does not allow class actions, a critical flaw in its enforcement regime. While the government plans to introduce class actions, pressure from business groups is currently restricting application to certain types of securities fraud, and not breaches of fiduciary duty.[27]

In terms of public enforcement, until recently, prosecutors and regulators have rarely pursued liability for breaches of fiduciary duties by corporate managers. Even when prosecutors have sought to hold managers account-able, they have not necessarily been consistent in their application of the law. For example, in two recent cases, representative directors of two medium-sized companies were indicted and found guilty of embezzling company funds for causing the company to issue private placements of bonds with warrants to themselves at extraordinary discounts.[28] By contrast, in a nearly identical case, the directors of a leading *chaebol* company were not indicted even though they caused their firm to issue bonds with warrants to the chairman's son and daughters, bestowing on them several hundred million dollars in gains (Jang and Kim 2002).

One of the most promising developments in public enforcement can be found in the recent activities of the Korea Deposit Insurance Corporation (KDIC) and the Korea Fair Trade Commission (KFTC). In the wake of the financial crisis, KDIC began to pursue liability against those responsible for the problems, much like the U.S. Federal Deposit Insurance Corporation fol-lowing the savings and loans crisis. In 1999, KDIC filed civil liability actions against 222 executives from 53 financial institutions for a total of 263.1 billion won ($202 million). In 2000, civil actions were filed against 1,287 executives from 157 financial institutions for a total of 5 trillion won ($3.85 billion). The KDIC also filed 1,560 injunctions to freeze 274.7 billion won ($211 million) in 1999. In 2000, it filed 1,812 injunctions to freeze 670 billion won ($515 million) in assets of allegedly liable former executives (KDIC 2000).

Similarly, since 1998, the KFTC has brought a string of investigations resulting in fines against leading *chaebol* for improper inter-conglomerate trading. For instance, the top five *chaebol* were fined $170 million from 1998 to 2000 for over $16.2 billion in illegal insider transactions. Together, the work of the KDIC and KFTC are among the most far-reaching regula-tory actions ever taken to hold corporate executives accountable for their decisions, and they are unprecedented in their scope and severity.

D. Role of Judges and Other Legal Practitioners

Ultimately, however, judges and other legal practitioners play a critical role in enforcing and applying fiduciary duty. Given the many ways in which managers can expropriate funds from shareholders, it is vital that the courts hold them accountable using a flexible and general concept such as fiduciary duty. Under the common law tradition, the courts developed fiduciary duties out of a need to devise a way to resolve disputes equitably. The question is why continental courts did not develop a similar jurisprudence of fiduciary duties. Some theorize that continental systems, with their comprehensive and sophisticated legal codes, tend to downplay or distrust judicial lawmaking (e.g., Mattei 1997: 81–83). Ultimately, the differences between continental courts and common law courts are not as great as is commonly thought (ibid.). Even in France, where distrust of the judiciary has a long tradition, judges have played a considerable role in developing jurisprudence.[29] Similarly, Korean judges often do not hesitate to exercise considerable discretion.

Yet Korean courts have been passive and conservative in applying fiduciary duties. For instance, a basic remedy for breach of fiduciary duty is to nullify the relevant transaction. Korean courts, however, have displayed a tendency to overemphasize the concerns surrounding "stability of the marketplace." Their failure to nullify the new issues and private placements of convertible bonds in several recent cases such as Hanwha Merchant Bank and Samsung Electronics are classic examples (Kim 2000: 315; Jang and Kim 2002: 91). In the *Samsung Electronics* case, shareholders claimed that a private placement of bonds with warrants of several hundred million dollars was issued to the children of the controlling shareholder at a considerable discount. Despite acknowledging the unnecessary nature of the transaction and the private benefits to the controlling shareholder's family, the court refused to nullify the disputed issuance of securities out of concern for the "stability of the marketplace," even though the converted shares were still held by the family members. In both the *Hanwha* and *Samsung* cases, the courts were excessively cautious; stability of the marketplace should not have been a consideration because the shares were not transferred to third parties.[30]

Several reasons can be cited for the apparent passiveness of Korean courts in regard to staking out the boundaries of fiduciary duties and providing the necessary remedies to aggrieved shareholders. First, given the sheer lack of lawsuits, courts have not been given enough opportunity to develop precedent. Second, the enormous workload makes judges reluctant to enter unfamiliar territory and apply "new" concepts such as fiduciary duties, leading them instead to be conservative. Third, the judicial system relies upon attorneys to take the lead in unraveling sophisticated business decisions made by directors and bringing claims for violations of fiduciary duties. Yet few attorneys represent shareholders, and they lack experience in this area of practice. In fact, a leading public interest group that advocates minority shareholders rights has brought the only significant shareholder actions to date (Kim and Kim 2001).

IV. Landmark Cases Following Legal Reform

The recent legal reforms have led directly to several landmark cases that have become crucial in shaping corporate governance in Korea. Several shareholder derivative actions holding managers liable for breaches of fiduciary duties have sent shockwaves throughout the Korean business community. The following cases demonstrate the importance of legal infrastructure in developing fundamental corporate governance concepts.

A. Korea First Bank

The historic litigation involving Korea First Bank (KFB) illustrates the multiple layers of legal problems that have thwarted shareholders from holding directors accountable for fiduciary duty violations, and the importance of legal reforms in improving corporate governance. In 1997, a group of shareholder activists attracted fifty-two minority shareholders of KFB and gained widespread public attention by filing the first reported shareholder derivative suit in history. The Seoul District Court eventually found the KFB directors liable for 40 billion won ($44.4 million) plus interest.[31]

The Court held that the directors not only violated their "duty as a good manager," but also their "fiduciary duty" toward the bank. In its own terms, the court first stressed the basics of the business judgment rule, noting that managers need to take risks and deserve discretion in making business decisions. The court found that as long as the managers were within the bounds of a businessperson's rational choice and faithfully fulfilled their duty, they would not be held responsible for decisions that subsequently led to corporate losses. The court held, however, that a breach of fiduciary duty will be found "when based on the relevant facts, from the perspective of an average businessperson, in the decision making process a director *commits an error that cannot be excused and that exceeds the scope of his discretion.*"[32] The court added that any directors who failed to disapprove of such decisions would also be found liable.

In their defense, the KFB directors claimed that their decision to extend loans to the controversial Hanbo Group (which later imploded following a string of poor business decisions and heavy loan commitments to firms in saturated markets) deserved to be protected as fully informed business judgments. They further argued that all the necessary board approvals were obtained and that they anticipated in good faith that Hanbo would be a rewarding client in the long run. Some directors even suggested that they should not be held liable because they merely followed the dictates of the President of the bank.

Contrary to the directors' arguments, however, the facts overwhelmingly showed that the KFB directors breached their fiduciary duty. Not only did they receive bribes in return for the questionable loans, they also made more than 1 trillion won ($1.2 billion) in loans that were largely unsecured. Among the other critical facts that the court cited were that the directors were fully informed of Hanbo's dire situation and potential risk of default and still failed to take any appropriate protective measures, that they disregarded continuous warnings by their own loan officers, and that they all approved the decisions without raising any objections.

For the first time in history, most managers in Korea came to realize that they had a fiduciary duty and that they could be held liable for breaching it. The decision is noteworthy in several respects. First, the case would not have been possible without the amendment lowering the minimum shareholder ownership requirement. Second, overwhelming evidence showed that the directors violated their fiduciary duty, but cases with such egregious facts and blatant, intentional malfeasance are rare. Third, the case would not have been possible without the involvement of the shareholder activist group noted above (Kim and Kim 2001). Fourth, the case was possible only because shareholders had access to evidence brought forth in a criminal investigation following the sensational collapse of the Hanbo Group.[33] It would have been practically impossible for shareholders to acquire the requisite evidence in the absence of the criminal investigation.

As noted above, the decision sent shockwaves throughout the cozy Korean business community. As testimony to the impact of the case, for the first time companies began purchasing directors and officers (D&O) liability insurance. The number of companies with D&O insurance dramatically increased from one in 1996, to five in 1997, 105 in 1998, and 320 by 1999

(Financial Supervisory Service 2000). For the first time, the insurance industry was able to sell a product to corporate managers based on the perception of potential legal risk and accountability.

B. Samsung Electronics

On December 27, 2001, an even more significant judgment was rendered against Samsung Electronics (SE), Korea's flagship company.[34] In this case, minority shareholders won a derivative action against Kun-Hee Lee, the Samsung Group chairman and controlling shareholder, and various managers of SE. The controlling shareholder and nine directors were found liable for approximately $75 million. The critical fiduciary duty-related claims of the case involved the acquisition of an ailing affiliated company called E-Chon Electric and the discounted sales of stock to another affiliated company.[35]

The district court's finding with regard to SE's acquisition of E-Chon Electric bears a striking resemblance to the landmark U.S. case *Smith v. Van Gorkom*.[36] For the first time, an important standard regarding the limitations of the business judgment rule was established in Korean corporate law. The court found SE's managers liable for losses resulting from the acquisition of the ailing target, E-Chon Electric, because they did not engage in any substantive review of the financial or operational status of the company during the acquisition process, and hastily approved the acquisition in the absence of any factors requiring urgency. Furthermore, the court criticized SE's continued participation in several equity issuances even after E-Chon Electric became defunct. SE ultimately suffered more than 190 billion won ($146 million) in losses. The second claim involved the sale by SE of the shares of one affiliated company to another at a 74 percent discount on the price at which SE had purchased the shares just eight months earlier.[37] This sale in effect siphoned off SE's assets to support the affiliate.

A problematic part of the case, however, is the court's holding that Samsung chairman Kun-Hee Lee was not liable because he did not participate in the relevant board meetings. The court held that a director's failure to attend board meetings, by itself, does not constitute a breach of duty. It stated that a director would not be liable for a board's decision unless the director "did not participate when the director knew or could have known that the decision in question was being made." Proving that a director knew or should have known of an improper board decision will usually be difficult, as this case illustrates. The court found that evidence on this issue was insufficient, even though Chairman Lee was not only the controlling share-holder and a director, but arguably had an obligation to be aware of such significant information, especially since no record exists of him regularly attending board meetings. Under this rule, directors will have a perverse incentive not to attend board meetings where controversial decisions are being made, in order to avoid liability. Therefore, the court's application of the "could have known" standard is overly narrow.

Furthermore, the court held that if a company carries out an illegal act without a board decision, the directors are not liable unless they were aware of the act and made no attempt to prevent it. The court thus dismissed this prong of the plaintiff's claim because board knowledge was not proven. It is possible that the SE directors did not know of the particular transaction, but lack of knowledge should not automatically serve to exculpate a director, particularly the representative director. At the very least, the court should have justified its decision by finding, for example, that the size of the transaction in question did not reach a level that would have prompted the directors to seek full board approval.

Despite these problems, the SE decision was far more significant than the KFB case. The KFB decision involved a defunct bank, whereas SE is Korea's flagship company. The court in the SE case made it clear that even managers of the largest and most profitable companies could be held liable for decisions made against shareholder interests. Therefore, regardless of the ultimate outcome of this case, which is currently on appeal, it sent a powerful message to the securities market and to foreign investors. As expected, manager groups in Korea have vigorously protested and campaigned against the court's assessment of liability. Yet most of these reactions stem from their lack of understanding of the basic preconditions to business judgment rule protection. At the same time, SE's managers deserve some sympathy, because in many regards they were following standard Korean corporate procedures. Even for the most ardent critics of the decision, however, it would be difficult to argue that such practices are compatible with Korea's recent efforts to improve its corporate governance and develop its financial markets.

Conclusion

In recent years, the potential for expropriation has become a critical problem in Korean corporations. An increasingly dispersed ownership structure without the requisite internal corporate governance protections or market-based constraints has led to many problems. Spectacular corporate failures provided the spark for the 1997 financial contagion to spread to Korea. The recent collapse of more than a dozen of Korea's largest *chaebol*, including the $80 billion failure of the Daewoo Group and the splintering of the Hyundai Group, testify to the fragility of Korean firms.[38]

Despite significant obstacles, Korea has moved closer to a shareholder-centered governance model. Following the financial crisis, Korea adopted a host of legal reforms and its corporate governance system shifted dramatically toward a capital market-oriented system. In line with the vast legal changes, for instance, capital market-based equity financing by the thirty largest *chaebol* rose from 69 trillion won in 1997 to 155 trillion won by 2000, and their debt-to-equity ratio fell from 519 percent in 1997 to 171 percent in 2000. The corporate governance spectrum has become quite diverse, with professional managers finally taking the helm in many leading companies.

While a full discussion is beyond the scope of this essay, many theories exist as to why Korea was able to adopt its various reforms. The prevailing view holds that the negative external shock of the financial crisis and the corporate governance reforms imposed by the International Monetary Fund and World Bank spurred significant change. In comparison, corporate governance reform in Japan has lagged, primarily because that country managed to escape acute illness from the Asian contagion. The primary concern in Korea today is that following the rebound of the economy and in the absence of external impetus, the momentum for reform is subsiding too quickly.

It would also be naïve to assume that these legal reforms toward a more shareholder-oriented model have immediately effectuated a substantive change in corporate governance practices.[39] In the largest *chaebol* conglomerates, the controlling shareholders still functionally retain their unchallenged authority as in the past. As evidence of the fact that actual corporate practices lag behind the spirit of the reforms, Korean companies still remain markedly undervalued in terms of their earnings and assets relative to non-Korean companies (Gill 2001; PriceWaterhouseCoopers 2001). Enforcement remains an important issue, and efforts to improve implementation of legal reforms must continue.

Ultimately, a capital market-oriented system will arrive when managers not only refrain from directly infringing shareholder rights, but also actively seek to pursue maximization of shareholder value. Legal reforms and fiduciary duties alone will not provide incentive for managers to pursue this type of affirmative strategy. Managers must feel pressured by the capital markets, particularly to enhance share prices. One of the biggest differences between controlling shareholders and top managers in Korea and those in countries with advanced capital markets is their interest in share prices. Korean controlling shareholders remain less interested in share price than in maximizing their private benefits of control.

Despite several pessimistic perspectives on the role of law in corporate governance, we have argued in this essay that the significance of legal reforms must not be overlooked. We have sought to show how the new legal infrastructure, especially principles relating to fiduciary duties, is helping to minimize controlling shareholder pursuit of private benefits of control. Legal reforms, particularly in the early stages of transitional economies, play an important function in restraining managers from unbridled pursuit of private interests. They also contribute to the formation of a social norm against the maximization of private benefits of control. While this social norm remains weak in Korea, it will gradually act as another informal means of monitoring managerial decisions.

The precise aim of fiduciary duties is to reduce the private benefits of control. Once the private benefits of control are minimized, controlling shareholders have less incentive to maintain control. Once managers pursue the interests of shareholders based on pressure from the capital markets, the significance of fiduciary duties diminishes. Ultimately, fiduciary duties can be viewed as a necessary pillar in corporate governance reform and the transition to a capital market-oriented system.

Endnotes

The authors would like to like to express their thanks to Curtis Milhaupt, Hwa Jin Kim, and Jeongmin Lee for their comments and assistance in preparing this article.

1. For a discussion emphasizing the importance of legal infrastructure, see Black (2001).
2. Coffee (2001) suggests that private action through self-regulation is also critical. Cheffins (2001) finds that the U.K.'s stock markets were able to develop even though legal protections for shareholders were lacking.
3. Article 382–3 of the Commercial Code, entitled "The Fiduciary Duty of Directors," provides that "directors must carry out their official duties in a faithful

manner on behalf of the corporation according to the law and the articles of incorporation." In contrast, officers and controlling shareholders are not subject to an explicit fiduciary duty.

4. The U.S. occupation forces brought about the inclusion of an explicit fiduciary provision in Japan's Commercial Code, presently Article 254–3, in 1950. Although Korea's modern Commercial Code, enacted in 1962, largely followed Japan's Commercial Code, for some reason this explicit fiduciary duty provision was not included.

5. In the spring of 2001, for example, during the proxy process to solicit votes for an outside director candidate proposed by minority shareholders at a leading company, most institutional investors who had initially disclosed publicly that they would support the candidate abruptly reversed their positions, buckling under pressure from the *chaebol* and their affiliates (Jang and Kim 2002).

6. Foreigners now own majority stakes in premier companies such as Samsung Electronics, SK Telecom, Hyundai Motors, and Kookmin Bank.

7. This was aggravated because a strong perception existed that many of the *chaebol* became "too big to fail" and the government often needlessly prolonged their impending collapse despite clear signs of mismanagement and abuse.

8. The Korea Stock Exchange first required listed companies to have at least one outside director beginning in February 1998 and in January 2000. The Securities Exchange Act was amended to require that at least 25 percent of the board must consist of outside directors. Companies with more than 2 trillion won in assets not only must have at least 50 percent outside directors nominated by an outside director nominating committee, but must also have an audit committee. The number of outside directors was 1,418 as of 2000 (Korea Listed Companies Association 2000).

9. In one case, outside directors received preferential loans from the company to purchase nontendered shares following a rights issue leading to "in the money options."

10. The outside directors of Hyundai Heavy Industries (HHI) forced the company to file a suit against a Hyundai Group affiliate for indemnification after HHI was forced to make substantial payments based on a put option on the affiliate's behalf. The Seoul District Court ruled in favor of HHI. Seoul District Court, Judgment No. 2000 Kahap 54623 (January 25, 2002).

11. Securities Exchange Act, Art. 189–2.

12. For a contrasting view, see Kim (2002).

13. Securities Exchange Act, Art. 189–4, Para. 1; Art. 84–6, Para 1, Implementing Decree.

14. KCC, Art. 382 II, Civil Code, Art. 681.

15. A similar debate exists in Japan.

16. Revised Commercial Code (Corporation Section), Commentaries: 46.

17. KCC, Art. 398.

18. Ibid., Art. 397(1).

19. Ibid., Art. 399(1).
20. Ibid., Art. 401(1).
21. Article 398 concerning self-dealing, Article 397 regarding competition with the corporation, and Article 399 relating to liability to the corporation all address misconduct by "directors."
22. Although drafted mainly with individuals in mind, Article 401–2 should be construed as applying where the controlling shareholder is a juridical person (i.e. a corporation) (Lee 2001: 603–9).
23. If the creditor bank exercised its influence over the corporation to dispose of the corporation's property to a third party under terms unfavorable to the corporation, the creditor bank may be held liable (ibid.: 607). Some scholars believe that even government officials exercise such influence. It is questionable, however, whether officials may be held liable as participants for conduct carried out to implement a government policy, although they may be liable under the National Compensation Law.
24. BGHZ 103, 184. For a comment on this famous decision, see Lutter (1989).
25. Japan's newly proposed trust law explicitly includes a provision that would allow repatriation of profits obtained in violation of trustee's fiduciary duties. Arts. 22, 27.
26. Art. 405; SEL, Art. 191–13, Sec. 6.
27. Ministry of Justice (November 2, 2001).
28. Seoul District Court (Judgment of Aug. 30, 2001); Busan High Court (Judgment of May 2001).
29. Mattei (1997: 85). Examples include "astreinte" under French Law and the "general power of injunctions" under Italian law.
30. Seoul High Court, Judgment No. 68 Na 4608 (June 23, 2000).
31. Seoul District Court, Judgment No. 97 Kahap 39907 (July 24, 1998); Kim (2000).
32. Seoul District Court, Judgment No. 97 Kahap 39907 (July 24, 1998), emphasis added.
33. The ensuing criminal investigation revealed that KFB directors received bribes in return for favorable loan decisions. The disclosures eventually brought down eight senior politicians, aides to then President Young Sam Kim, and also led to the arrest of President Kim's own son.
34. Suwon District Court, Judgment No. 98 Kahap 22553 (Dec. 27, 2001).
35. Another claim involved Kun-Hee Lee's bribery of a former Korean President. Such illicit "political contributions" were common corporate practice in the past but the court held that these acts, although carried out "on behalf of the interests of the company," actually harmed the company. No one now questions the criminality of such acts. A claim for improper support for another affiliated company was denied.
36. Smith v. Van Gorkom, 488 A.2d 858 (1985).

37. The SEC followed the valuation method for unlisted stock as provided under the Inheritance and Gift Tax Law, but the court held it should have been calculated based on the total asset value. The court focused its attention on the correct valuation of the stock, and did not sufficiently consider the fact that the transaction was with an affiliated company.

38. Since 1997, as many as 12 of the top 30 *chaebol* conglomerates have collapsed. OECD (2001: 131).

39. It is probably premature to call Korea's corporate governance world class. But see Kim (2002) (arguing that "the Korean corporate governance system successfully adapts to the best practice model accepted by global standards"). See Black et al. (2001).

References

Berkowitz, Daniel, Katharina Pistor and Jean-Francois Richard. 2003. Economic Development, Legality and the Transplant Effect. *European Economic Review* 47: 165–95.

Berle, Adolph and Gardiner Means. 1932, 1968 (rev.). *The Modern Corporation and Private Property*. New York: Harcourt, Brace & World.

Black, Bernard. 2001. The Legal and Institutional Preconditions for Strong Securities Markets. *UCLA Law Review* 48: 781–855.

———. 2001a. Corporate Governance in Korea at the Millennium. *Journal of Corporation Law* 26: 537–45. ["Ministry of Justice Report "]

Busan High Court (Judgment of May 2001).

Cheffins. 2001. Does Law Matter? The Separation of Ownership and Control. *Journal of Legal Studies* 30: 459–84.

Chosun Ilbo. 2000. Outside Director System in Need of Mending. August 25.

Chung, Dong-Yoon. 2000. *Hwoisabop* [Corporate Law], Sixth Ed. 208. Seoul: Bopmunsa.

Coffee, John C., Jr. 2001. The Rise of Dispersed Ownership: The Roles of Law and the State in the Separation of Ownership and Control. *Yale Law Journal* 111: 1–82.

Cooter, Robert and Melvin A. Eisenberg. 2001. Norms and Corporate Law; Fairness, Character, and Efficiency in Firms. *University of Pennsylvania Law Review* 149: 1717–33.

——— and Bradley Freedman. 1991. The Fiduciary Relationship: Its Economic Character and Legal Consequences. *NYU Law Review* 66: 1045–75.

Easterbrook, Frank and Daniel R. Fischel. 1991. *The Economic Structure of Corporate Law*. Cambridge: Harvard University Press.

Eisenberg, Melvin A. 1998. The Modernization of Corporation Law: An Essay for Bill Cary. *University of Miami Law Review* 37: 187, 203–4.

———. 1999. Corporate Law and Social Norms. *Columbia Law Review* 99: 1253–92.

Financial Supervisory Service. 2000. On file with authors.

Fischel, Daniel and Michael Bradley. 1986. The Role of Liability Rules and Derivative Suits in Corporate Law: A Theoretical and Empirical Analysis. *Cornell Law Review* 71: 261–97.

Gill, Amar. 2001. *Saints and Sinners: Who's Got Religion?* CLSA Emerging Markets, CG Watch: Corporate Governance in Emerging Markets (April).

Haesul [Commentaries]. 1999. Ministry of Justice. (in Korean).

Hong, Bokki. 2001. *Hyun-dae-sang-sa-bup-ron-jip* [Recent Events Surrounding Tender Offers and Several Problems Concerning the Current Securities Laws].

Jang, Hasung. 2000. An Analysis of the Effects of Corporate Restructuring after the Economic Crisis. (Korea University, unpublished paper).

——— and Joongi Kim. 2002. Nascent Stage of Corporate Governance in an Emerging Market: Regulatory Change, Shareholder Activism and Samsung Electronics. *Corporate Governance* 10: 84–95.

Johnson, Simon, Peter Boone, Alasdair Breach and Eric Friedman. 2000. Corporate Governance in the Asian Financial Crisis. *Journal of Financial Economics* 58: 141–86.

Kim, Hwa-Jin. 1999. *M&A and Corporate Control* (in Korean), 3rd ed. Seoul: Bakyoungsa.

———. 2002. Toward the 'Best Practice' Model in a Globalizing Market: Recent Developments in Korean Corporate Governance. *Yearbook Law and Legal Practice in East Asia*, vol. 5. London: Sweet & Maxwell.

Kim, Jooyoung and Joongi Kim. 2001. Shareholder Activism in Korea: How PSPD Used Legal Measures to Improve Corporate Governance. *Journal of Korean Law* 1: 51–76.

Kim, Joongi. 2000. Recent Amendments to the Korean Commercial Code and Their Effects on International Competition. *University of Pennsylvania Journal of International Economic Law* 21: 273–330.

Kirk, Don. 2000. As Korean Heirs Feud, An Empire is Withering; Changes and Frail Finances Doom the Old Hyundai. *New York Times*, April, 26, p. 1

Korea Deposit Insurance Corporation (KDIC). 2000. Annual Report.

Korea Fair Trade Commission (KFTC). 2001. *Sijang Kyungjae Changdalui Baljachui: Gongjung-guraewuiwonhwoi 20 Nyunsa* [A Chronicle of Promoting a Market Economy: 20-Year History of the Fair Trade Commission]. Seoul: Korea Fair Trade Commission.

Korea Financial Supervisory Commission (KFSC) and Korea Financial Supervisory Service (KFSS). 2000. *Financial Reform and Supervision in Korea.* Seoul.

Korea Listed Companies Association. *Saoeisa Tongye* [Statistics of Outside Directors] 2001.

Kraakman, Reinier, Hyun Park and Steven Shavell. 1994. When Are Shareholder Suits In Shareholder Interests? *Georgetown Law Journal* 82: 1733–75.

La Porta, Rafael, Florencio Lopez-de-Silanes, and Andrei Shleifer. 1999. Corporate Ownership Around the World. *Journal of Finance* 54: 471–517.

—— and Robert Vishny. 1997. Legal Determinants of External Finance. *Journal of Finance* 52: 1131–55.

——. 1998. Law and Finance. *Journal of Political Economy* 106: 1113–50.

——. 2000. Investor Protection and Corporate Governance. *Journal of Financial Economics* 58: 3–27.

Lee, Cheol Song. 2001. *Hoesabop Gangeui* [Corporate Law Lectures], 9th ed. Seoul: Bakyoungsa.

Lutter, Marcus. 1989. Die Treupflicht des Aktionaers. *Zeitschrift fuer das gesamte Handels-und Wirtschaftsrecht* 153: 446.

Mattei, Ugo. 1997. *Comparative Law and Economics*. Ann Arbor, MI: University of Michigan Press.

Ministry of Justice. 1999. *Gaejung sangbop (hwoesapyun)* [Revised Commercial Code (Corporation Section)].

Ministry of Justice (November 2, 2001). Hearing on Establishing Securites Related Class Actions.

Organisation for Economic Cooperation and Development (OECD). 2001. Economic Surveys. Paris: OECD.

PriceWaterhouseCoopers. 2001. The Opacity Index, www.pricewaterhousecoopers.com.

Seoul District Court, Judgment No. 2000 Kahap 54623 (January 25, 2002).

Seoul District Court (Judgment of Aug. 30, 2001).

Seoul District Court, Judgment No. 97 Kahap 39907 (July 24, 1998).

Seoul High Court, Judgment No. 68 Na 4608 (June 23, 2000).

Smith v. Van Gorkom, 488 A.2d 858 (1985).

Suwon District Court, Judgment No. 98 Kahap 22553 (Dec. 27, 2001).

Tsche, Kiuon, 1987. *Shin hoesabopron* [A New Treatise on Corporation Law], 3rd ed. Seoul: Bakyoungsa.

——. 1998. Reform of KCC for Recovering from the Current Economic Crisis (Part 2), *Popryul shinmun* (Legal Times) (Seoul), April 16, p. 14.

West, Mark D. 1994. The Pricing of Shareholder Derivative Actions in Japan and the United States. *Northwestern University Law Review* 88: 1436–1507.

12 Global Markets and Parochial Institutions

The Transformation of Taiwan's
Corporate Law System

Lawrence S. Liu

Taiwan offers an interesting case for a discussion of global markets and domestic institutions. Taiwan began to develop its economy in the early 1960s, after a reasonably successful land reform program by the Nationalist Kuomintang (KMT) government in the 1950s. The KMT-controlled Republic of China (ROC) government had retreated to Taiwan in 1949 after losing the civil war to China.[1] Despite its impressive economic achievements in the fifty years since the KMT government went to Taiwan, a curious dichotomy persists: While Taiwan has its eyes on global markets, its corporate law system and financial markets remain parochial. Taiwanese businesspeople are entrepreneurial and outgoing, but the Taiwanese government is becoming more introverted and rigid. Indeed, this dichotomy is a long-term weakness for Taiwan, which for the first time (in Taiwanese and Chinese history) had a peaceful transition of government when a candidate from the Democratic Progressive Party (DPP), former Mayor of Taipei, Chen Shui-bian, won the March 2000 presidential election after the KMT splintered.

Despite Taiwan's accession to the World Trade Organization (WTO) in 2002, its government now faces new challenges. For example, President Chen faced a global recession and a lack of confidence in Taiwan, which registered negative growth for the first time since the first oil crisis in the early 1970s. Also, after a decade of opening up Taiwan's financial market, which coincided with its democratization, Taiwan finds its financial market in a dire situation. The problems in the financial market are illustrated by an increase in nonperforming loans (NPLs), reluctance to lend because of the shrinking market value of collateral, and lack of innovation.[2] In the industrial sector, inadequate confidence in the new government led to reduced domestic investment and an exodus of funds for direct and portfolio investment abroad. Despite political stagnation in cross-strait relations, the economies of Taiwan and coastal China are being integrated. High-tech and service companies have lobbied the government to ease restrictions on entry into China, before it is too late to reap early-mover advantages as foreign investors.

These powerful forces have compelled Taiwan to change. Indeed, there has been a transformation of its corporate law system in the years since the martial law decree was lifted in 1987. As discussed below, Taiwan's complex political economy has significantly shaped its corporate law system. Specifically, Taiwanese development strategies encouraged the formation of a corporate law system resembling codified industrial policy. For national security and public-choice reasons, Taiwan did not develop a public financial market to fund national development. Until the early 1990s, the government controlled virtually all the banks. Globalization and democratization, however, have forced open the financial and other service-sector markets, while manufacturing has been relocated offshore. As a result, parochial legal and government institutions in Taiwan, including its archaic and inefficient corporate law system, are undergoing a complete makeover.

I. The Political Ecology of Taiwan's Corporate Law and Development Strategies

A. *Taiwan's Corporate Ecology*

Taiwan's corporate law system is an integral part of its political system. Taiwan's political economy determined its national development strategies, which in turn informed the corporate law. In this political economy, four parochial institutions—political governance, industrial organization, corporate governance, and judicial involvement—fit together to form an "ecology" of governance. For decades, this ecology stressed stability before growth. Legal and other public institutions were established to meet these goals. The foundation of the government's legitimacy was not the market for political control, but economic growth. Taiwan maintained a dual eco-

nomic system: all-out export promotion and import substitution in key sectors. The government also created incentives for high savings, which were
channeled into investment through government-owned banks, and it generally suppressed the financial market. Courts were allowed to handle routine
contract and property disputes, but were not in a position to check the power
of agencies and bureaucrats. The courts did not develop the expertise, nor
were they needed, for the protection of investors at large.

By the mid-1980s, strains appeared in this paradigm, as the four parochial
institutions all began to change. Political actors were affected by democratization, which began in the late 1980s, and led to a precocious polity and
emerging civil society. The private sector became stronger, more efficient,
and more assertive. The diplomatically isolated government was forced by
globalization to provide market access and reduce intervention. A securities
market finally began to take shape in the 1990s, with high-tech firms taking
the lead in accessing the emerging market for cheaper funds to meet international competition. In a decade, the ratio of equity to all financings
increased from 14 percent to 28 percent, and corporate governance became
a relevant and pressing issue. In the real economy, tariffs were reduced and
domestic sectors were opened. The judiciary has been involved in the resolution of an increasing array of social issues since the 1990s. As a result of
these institutional changes, Taiwan's corporate law system has been transformed.

B. Cross-Strait Relations

The most important factor affecting Taiwan's corporate law system is its relationship with China, which is linked to Taiwan by cultural ties but separated
from it by a gulf of political differences. A corollary of this difficult relationship was the imposition of martial law in Taiwan, which was maintained for
forty years for political and security reasons. Martial law had a profound
impact on Taiwan and its economy. Government procrastination in lifting
martial law resulted in long-term adjustment costs in the form of a bossy and
rigid government mentality, archaic economic and financial laws with wide
discretion given to the executive branch (checked, ironically, in the past by
pro-growth political strongmen), and disregard for due process. Martial law
also fostered public disrespect for law.

The lifting of martial law in 1987 ushered in a new era of democracy in Taiwan. Taiwanese legislators and other officials elected in the post–martial law era, however, are not free from rent-seeking activities. Since many of them are personally involved in business, they thwarted efforts to enhance financial supervision. For example, in the 1990s it took eight years for the Legislative Yuan to enact an important amendment to the Securities and Exchange Law (SEL), because some legislators with interests in financial firms filibustered measures designed to give Taiwan's Securities and Futures Commission (SFC) more investigative powers.[3]

The diplomatic isolation imposed on Taiwan by China has had adverse effects as well. While Taiwanese businesspeople are active everywhere, Taiwanese government officials stay behind. Ironically, when Taiwanese companies globalize, they often go to China. Taiwan is one of the largest investors in China, and the government estimates that about US$40–50 billion of capital has flowed from Taiwan to China. Initially driven by a 40 percent currency appreciation forced on Taiwan as a result of fixed exchange rates and huge trade surpluses, this migration of capital started in the late 1980s, beginning with small and medium sized enterprises (SMEs) in Taiwan's old economy. Since 2000, Taiwan's high-tech companies have followed. In short, for Taiwan, "globalization" means Sinification. Schizophrenia is inherent in this equation. How much economic integration with a hostile China can Taiwan tolerate politically?[4]

C. Foreign Exchange Control and Foreign Investment Law Shield

Owing to Chinese hostility, Taiwanese authorities have long felt the need to maintain a firewall between themselves and the world. This explains Taiwan's enactment of the Statute for the Administration of Foreign Exchange (SAFE) in the late 1950s and, more importantly, the failure to repeal it even after Taiwan began to enjoy huge trade surpluses and hoard huge reserves in the early 1980s. To be sure, under U.S. trade pressure Taiwan removed foreign exchange control measures on trade-account transfers, on the same day martial law was lifted in 1987. However, Taiwan has maintained controls over inbound and outbound capital-account transfers. In this way, Taiwan maintained barriers to cross-border mergers, acquisitions, joint ventures, and restructuring, and created incentives for "round-tripping" by some domestic firms to evade tax and other regulations, such as populist-oriented rules mandating ownership diversification in some industries.[5]

The need to maintain a distance between itself and the outside world also explains why Taiwan has imposed restrictions on foreign investment. Taiwan has always regulated foreign direct investment through a foreign investment approval (FIA) process. Concerns over political stability also delayed plans to open up Taiwan's capital market to foreign portfolio investors for almost a decade. Before the early 1980s, launching a foreign portfolio investment program was impossible, and in any event foreign institutional investors were not interested in Taiwan. In 1984 Taiwan created a small, four-member mutual fund industry on a pilot basis. It was not until the early 1990s that Taiwan grudgingly expanded foreign investment in its securities market, through a Qualified Foreign Institutional Investors (QFII) program controlling the qualifications, amount and, until 2000, percentage of investment by foreign portfolio investors in each listed Taiwanese company. In other words, foreign investment laws were used as a shield, and were superimposed on Taiwan's corporate laws.

D. Moral Virtue of Promoting Manufacturing

Another factor that informed Taiwan's economic policy, and thus its corporate law system, was infatuation with manufacturing. Manufacturing activity virtually defines the role of the state and business in Taiwan. The first generation of economic policymakers in postwar Taiwan clearly attached a sense of priority to developing manufacturing, especially for the export sector. They saw it as the way for Taiwan to survive, earn scarce foreign exchange, and create full employment. In the half century that followed, this priority has become a moral virtue; manufacturing was sacrosanct. Until 1990, tax incentives were granted only to manufacturing companies.

In 1995 the Taiwan government launched an economic reform program called the Asia-Pacific Regional Operations Center (APROC) Initiative. One of the debates under this initiative was whether the infatuation with manufacturing should be balanced against the need to develop and strengthen the financial sector. The traditional view has been that financial services are speculative in nature. The redeeming value of the financial services industry is its support for the manufacturing sector. Thus finance always serves a secondary function. By the mid 1990s, however, many in academia and the business community began to espouse a different view, arguing that the traditional approach is too rigid, and that financial suppression actually has hurt the competitiveness of the manufacturing sector. They also argued that the financial sector in Taiwan was overregulated but undersupervised, resulting in numerous financial scandals. Therefore, it was actually quite perverse to allow the financial sector to open up without an enlightened and balanced regulatory policy. But the traditional school has thus far persisted. Moreover, the Asian financial crisis in the late 1990s and the exodus of Taiwanese companies into China has further solidified the government's resolve to upgrade into high-tech manufacturing so as to maintain Taiwan's competitiveness and national security.

E. Reliance on the "Civil Law" Approach

The "civil law approach" has seriously set back the corporate law system in Taiwan. Entrenched bureaucrats argue that Taiwan has a civil law system, and should follow the corporate and financial codes in Germany and Japan. It seems anomalous that a technical distinction between the common law and the civil law traditions could have so much influence on regulatory philosophy, corporate governance, and financial regulation. Aided, however, by the martial law past, the perceived need to keep China and the unstable world at bay, and the moral virtue attached to promoting the manufacturing sector, the civil law approach as practiced in Taiwan played readily into the hands of bureaucrats resisting change (Liu 2001a; 2001b; 2001c).

The "civil law approach" essentially means strong faith in state control, and takes the form of pervasive licensing for business establishment and comprehensive rules governing business operations. The bureaucratic process focuses on perceived fairness and is extremely formalistic. Regulators place more emphasis on creditor protection than shareholder welfare, and stress minority shareholder welfare in the name of shareholder democracy. There is also a public-choice cast to this bureaucratic approach, because bureaucrats are concerned with allegations of favoritism, a crime since the martial-law era that has become an easy label in a feisty and precocious democracy like Taiwan's. Staying with the more petrified, risk-averse civilian system helps government officials avoid such allegations.

While bureaucrats may have a political pretext to avoid inquiries into issues of first principles, civilian-trained scholars are happy to supply the legal framework for this cautious approach. These scholars see the civil law approach as an intellectual crusade to protect the sunk costs of their investments in comparing codes and writing doctrinal treatises. Therefore, they are not interested in the possible lesson from La Porta, et al. (1997; 1998; 2000) that common law jurisdictions have stronger corporate governance systems. When leading civil law jurisdictions deviate from tradition in modifying their systems, Taiwanese scholars explain away these changes as politically driven. For example, the European Union rules, which changed the traditional corporate law rules in Germany, are viewed as a way to achieve unity at the expense of intellectually pure legal arguments. Recent changes in Japan are viewed as a quick fix to save the country from a crisis.

Legal education has not helped to enrich the policy debate. The civil law approach to teaching in Taiwan has been very doctrinal, emphasizing the "right" answer to the legal issue at hand. When legal scholars do take different positions, their debates involve extremely technical arguments on esoteric aspects of the law. Scholars also write the questions for the two examinations used by the government to admit members of the legal profession (lawyers, judges, prosecutors) and qualify bureaucrats. The passage rates for these exams are extremely low, encouraging students to spend large amounts of time on rote memorization, at the expense of a more well-rounded legal education.

Most law instructors in Taiwan have no real-world practical experience, and indeed avoid such experience as potentially corruptive of their intellectual purity. In their view, corporate law need not bear any relationship to modern theories of finance. Worse yet, when Taiwan began a precocious, noisy and wayward process of democratization in the 1990s, many bureaucrats with the capacity to reform the system from within were afraid to be drawn into politically charged policy arguments. The "civil law approach" thus conveniently became a pretext with which to resist reform proposals when bureaucrats themselves refused to change.

F. Weak Judiciary and Its Impact on Corporate and Financial Reform

As a byproduct of authoritarianism, Taiwan's courts were suppressed in the martial law era. The courts were moderately capable of handling regular civil and commercial disputes, although they have suffered from congestion. However, in most cases involving challenges to agency action under the Administrative Litigation Law, the state prevailed. In other words, the courts could not prevent the state from engaging in burdensome, and even illegal and capricious, economic regulation. This situation has improved with the democratization of Taiwan beginning in the late 1980s, as courts began to invalidate agency actions more frequently, and to provide better-reasoned arguments in support of their decisions.

Taiwan's courts, however, are still incapable of dealing with investor-protection disputes arising under the corporate and financial laws. Taiwan's civil litigation process, for example, requires that the plaintiff advance to the district court one percent of the claim as court fees under a loser-pays system. For de novo appeals to the appellate courts, the appellant must pay an additional one percent, and a final review on legal grounds entails a 1.5 percent court fee. In addition, there is no class-action mechanism. However, in recent years, following several scandals, a nonprofit foundation called the Securities and Futures Institute (SFI), which is supported by the Taiwan SFC, has developed a practice of "piggyback" group litigation. The SFI solicited individual shareholders to ride on the coattails of the criminal prosecutions arising out of these scandals. As shown by this brief overview, law enforcement in the area of investor protection is unpredictable and uneven. When scandals are made public, prosecutors rush to bring criminal cases. Civil relief, however, is inadequate and, as such, not a credible deterrent to managerial misconduct.

Taiwan's courts are weak in another important sense: judges are professionally trained after passing state examinations, and become judges almost directly after graduation from undergraduate law faculties. Most judges, therefore, lack real-world experience, and have an inadequate understanding of economic and financial matters. In the law faculty curriculum, courses on corporate, banking, and securities laws are viewed as unimportant for those wishing to sit for state qualifying examinations for the judiciary. Indeed, until the Taiwan stock market came alive in 1986, not many law instructors were interested in, or even capable of, teaching these courses.

The civilian inquisitorial system of trying cases in Taiwan adds interesting twists to judicial proceedings involving corporate law or economic and financial issues: judges can behave like authoritarian, yet ignorant mandarins. The lack of discovery rules also means that the plaintiff will have difficulty overcoming the information asymmetry problem typical in financial disputes. Since the 1990s there has been better interaction between financial regulators and the judiciary to familiarize the latter with the essence of corporate and financial laws. Still, bureaucrats with regulatory authority over corporate, securities and financial matters are not confident that there is adequate judicial competency. Therefore, they conveniently argue that laws are too important to be left to the judges. Hence, the argument goes, deregulation will lead to more manipulation and "disorderly market conduct."

G. A Scoreboard of State-Society Disconnect

According to a 2001 Organization for Economic Cooperation and Development (OECD) report on technological developments, on a purchasing power parity (PPP) basis, Taiwan's 1999 GDP reached US$437 billion, and its per-capita GDP reached US$20,000, putting Taiwan between Italy and Spain. Taiwan has fared well in the first stage of its postwar economic development. However, there is now an alarming state-society disconnect. Taiwan has matured into an economically advanced country, yet its legal and government institutions remain underdeveloped. There are now two Taiwans: public-sector Taiwan and private-sector Taiwan.

This disconnect is revealed in Taiwan's schizophrenic scores on competitiveness and market openness ratings. Private-sector Taiwan has risen to prominence. In the 2001–2002 Global Competitiveness Report issued by the World Economic Forum (2002), among seventy-five countries surveyed, Taiwan ranked seventh in overall growth competitiveness. Public-sector Taiwan, however, showed laggard performance. In the same report, Taiwan ranked eleventh in bureaucratic competence, twenty-ninth in trust in politicians, thirty-third in government red tape, thirty-seventh in organized crime, forty-fifth in judicial independence, and sixty-sixth in continuity of policies. By the government's own account, its executive branch is bloated and inefficient.[6] This dichotomy has strained the country's corporate law system, an important interface between the two Taiwans.

III. Modernizing Taiwan's Corporate Law System

A. Rigid and Archaic Corporate Law System

Taiwan's corporate law system is closely linked to global exploration beginning in the fifteenth century, and reflects extensive legal borrowing.[7] Many substantive rules in the Company Law are relics of commercial law reform in the late Qing dynasty.[8] At the same time, the Company Law is based principally on German and Japanese corporate law. As a result, Taiwan's Company Law benefits from the "learning externality"—increasing returns from transplanting a body of law and related case law and scholarly commentary.[9] However, through such transplantation, Taiwan is also constrained by the same defects that exist in the German and Japanese corporate laws on which it is based.[10]

The difficulty of valuing a corporate enterprise and aversion to risk explain why many of Taiwan's corporate finance rules are so rigid. Many rules relating to corporate operations are a disguised form of industrial policy. Together, the legal framework for corporate finance shows a formidable distrust of private activities and market forces. This is surprising and counterintuitive, as Taiwan is generally considered very open and global in orientation. As the following analysis will make plain, however, many institutions in the traditional Taiwanese corporate law system are parochial and rigid. Moreover, while Taiwan has been reasonably successful in transplanting the American venture capital industry and practice from Silicon Valley to the Hsinchu Science Park, legal restrictions comparable to those in Japan have also constrained how venture capital transactions can be structured.[11]

One important byproduct of the "civil law approach" discussed above is the emphasis on form over substance. One classic example is the inflexible way in which codified rules are written, making adaptation to new market conditions or new behavioral patterns difficult. Examples of the lack of emphasis on substance include the definition of control and beneficial ownership in the context of the opaque labyrinth of family holdings and cross ownership prevalent in Asia, including Taiwan. The same rigidity was exemplified in the period from 1997 to 2000, when several Taiwanese listed companies fell into financial difficulty in part because insiders used wholly owned subsidiaries to buy back their own stock. The SFC initially took the unthinkable position that since its jurisdiction under the SEL extended only to listed companies, it could do nothing about these unlisted subsidiaries!

Similarly, Taiwan's Criminal Code, Civil Code, and case law treat corporations rather than their shareholders as the direct victims of criminal breach of trust and criminal embezzlement. As such, aside from enforcement cost factors, shareholders in Taiwan face formidable barriers, even at the conceptual level, in seeking direct redress for civil and criminal liabilities. This example illustrates that the rigidity of this approach is even stronger in procedural rules designed to protect rights afforded by Taiwan's corporate laws.

Codes of procedure in civil law jurisdictions including Taiwan were not written for group remedies or representative litigation; they were designed for traditional one-on-one dispute resolution. As Liu (2001b) has shown, Taiwan has had moderate success in simulating securities class actions with the support of prosecutors and regulators like the SFC. Modernizing Taiwan's corporate law system, therefore, became a priority since the 1990s.

B. Reform Agenda and Agency Competency

The Ministry of Economic Affairs (MOEA) enforces Taiwan's Company Law, whereas the SFC, which is a part of the Ministry of Finance, enforces the SEL. Historically, there have been overlaps between these two laws. Unlike the federal-state division between disclosure rules (in the federal securities laws) and substantive rules (in the state corporate laws) in the United States, the SEL and the Company Law are both primarily substantive and heavy handed in their orientation. The SFC is generally faced more directly with a strong demand by public companies to modernize Taiwan's corporate law rules, and has a much larger professional staff. Therefore, the SFC is more proactive than the MOEA in setting the reform agenda. The MOEA has been in a catch-up mode vis-à-vis the reform program since the late 1980s. Both agencies, however, tend to rely on onerous and formalistic rules rather than allowing competitive market forces to alleviate their regulatory burden.

Another important, albeit mislabeled agency, the Council for Economic Planning and Development (CEPD), has become more interested in corporate law reform since the late 1990s. The CEPD, a council of ministers serving as the policy coordination body for the cabinet, historically was the agency that administered American aid in the 1950–60s. It has had a more open mentality than some other agencies, and since the 1980s it has pushed for deregulation and privatization. In addition, the CEPD has never been an industry or market regulator, making it much less entrenched by vested interests.

In 1999–2000 and 2002, the CEPD awarded research contracts to reform Taiwan's corporate law system. This author was the chief consultant for the 1999–2000 CEPD corporate law overhaul and the chief draftsman of the 2001 Corporate Mergers and Acquisitions Law (CMAL) bill proposed by the CEPD. The corporate law overhaul substantially influenced the 2001 Company Law amendment, which had previously been proposed by the

MOEA in a much less aggressive form in 1999. The CMAL was enacted in early 2002, and introduced profound changes to the mergers and acquisitions environment in Taiwan.

C. Formation and Operating Rules

Infatuation with formalism in Taiwan has produced a cumbersome and nontransparent environment for corporate mechanics. For example, formalism led to the view that a corporation must be a society (*Gesellschaft*, or *societé*) of shareholders. Until its amendment in 2001, the Company Law prohibited one-shareholder companies. A company was required to have at least seven shareholders, six of whom often could hold a single share to comply with this requirement. A tacit concern was that a one-shareholder company was a per se abuse of the limited liability regime. This rule contributed to the nominee culture of Taiwan, since every new investment started with several nominees. The government's elaborate corporate registration system, discussed below, made matters worse by undermining prudential corporate governance standards like fiduciary duty and transparency.

The Company Law follows the civil law approach of requiring a minimum capitalization of NT$1 million (about US$30,000) reflecting a strong concern with creditors' rights (see, e.g., Enriques and Macey 2001). The regulators justified this rule by pointing out that many small companies (and their auditors) forge initial balance sheets to show paid-up capital, which is then somehow siphoned off or returned to the investors. This rule, however, placed too much emphasis on initial paid-up capital at the expense of net worth. In any event, the capital adequacy rule does not function as intended for small- and medium-sized enterprises. The small amount of the statutory minimum paid-up capital, combined with the historical risk aversion of state-owned banks, have led to the practice of requiring key shareholders, directors, and supervisors to guarantee corporate debt.

Perversely, however, this rule has become deeply embedded in the regulatory culture of Taiwan. So much so that regulators often use the minimum capitalization test as an (often futile) entry barrier to various regulated businesses, such as banking (NT$10 billion or about US$300 million), integrated securities (NT$1 billion, or about US$30 million), and telecommunications (NT$40 billion, or about US$1.3 billion). An ineffective creditor protection rule has metastasized into an ineffective barrier to market access.

Capital rules have also been used in other ways. Until pressure from globalization in the 1990s led to abolition of the provision, the Company Law limited an operating company's "reinvestment" in other firms to 40 percent of its paid-in capital. This was an important industrial policy restriction designed to reinforce Taiwan's infatuation with manufacturing, suppress the financial sector, and implement the SFC's bias against holding companies. If this restriction had not been relaxed, large Taiwanese companies wishing to acquire foreign firms would have been constrained by investment barriers imposed by their own government. Oddly, however, the old 40 percent rule was recently reincarnated as the ceiling for China-bound loans and investment by listed Taiwan companies.

Corporate rules have been similarly ineffective in dealing with the problems of corporate groups, which were formed by large Taiwanese firms in the 1990s.[12] In 1997 the Company Law was amended to introduce affiliated company rules influenced by comparable German legislation. The purpose of the affiliated companies law was to control abusive conduct by parent companies in a corporate group and thereby avoid expropriation of minority shareholders and creditors. Although well intended, these rules missed the central issue—the role of directors (including independent directors) in bringing about better corporate governance in Taiwan. In addition, in 2001 the MOF succeeded in achieving passage of a Financial Holding Company Law (FHCL) so as to allow universal banking in Taiwan. Listed banks, securities and insurance firms have since restructured into financial holding companies, increasing the group structure of the economy.

Finally, the Company Law traditionally circumscribed the scope of business permissible to firms. A company could engage only in businesses listed in the business scope clause of its articles of incorporation, which had to be approved by the MOEA. This "positive listing" requirement allowed various agencies to control and implement their industrial policy and market restriction programs. The Company Law as amended in 2001 now follows a "negative listing" approach recommended by the CEPD, giving businesses flexibility to engage in any profit-seeking activities unless specifically prohibited by regulation.

The CEPD scored its biggest victory in obtaining relaxation of the costly but largely useless corporate registration rules of the Company Law. Under these rules, registration was required from corporate cradle to grave. Companies (or their shareholders) had to apply for registration when they were formed and dissolved. This was legitimate, although the registration require-ment often served as a de facto approval process. Registration was also required to effect changes to the business scope, charter, capital (as a result of increase, reduction or mergers), responsible persons (directors, supervi-sors and managers), bond offerings, locations, and other miscellaneous cor-porate housekeeping matters. Specific requirements for registration have now been eliminated from the Company Law.

D. Corporate Finance Rules

Taiwan's securities market became relevant to its economic growth in the late 1980s. And by the 1990s, accessing international capital markets was an important means of financing for large Taiwanese firms. Yet, as this section will demonstrate, Taiwan's corporate law system is fraught with archaic cor-porate finance rules.

Founded in 1965, the Taiwan Stock Exchange (TSE) saw its TAIEX break 1,000 points for the first time in 1986. By 1989, however, it had shot up to over 12,000 points. Companies, mostly consisting of high-tech firms, rushed to the market to raise funds in the 1990s. In 1994, Taiwan had 313 TSE-listed companies, with only 14 others listed on the GreTai Securities Market (or GTSM, Taiwan's over-the-counter trading market). By then, close to 5.5 mil-lion Taiwanese citizens already had brokerage accounts for TSE trading, and about 16,000 citizens maintained accounts for GTSM trading. By 2002, more than 900 companies were listed on the TSE and GTSM. More than 12.3 million individuals (out of a total population of 23 million) maintain accounts for TSE trading, and more than 7.5 million maintain accounts for GTSM trading. Stock investment has become a national phenomenon.

By the end of the twentieth century, raising funds abroad became more important for Taiwanese companies. Taiwan's listed firms began to access the international market in the early 1990s by offering convertible bonds (CBs) and global depositary receipts (GDRs). For example, in 1997 Taiwan listed companies raised about NT$5.950 trillion in 317 offerings, of which thirty-one foreign offerings for CBs and GDRs raised NT$1.230 trillion (20.75 percent of the total). For 2000, out of a total of 215 offerings for NT$6.869 trillion, 54 foreign offerings raised NT$3.937 billion (57.31 per-cent).

The legal system, however, has not kept pace with these developments in corporate finance. The remainder of this section details the problems in the legal environment. For example, Taiwanese policymakers are infatuated with par value, a meaningless concept. Worse yet, total par value is registered with the MOEA, magnifying disinformation about firm value. This rule created a problem in the years 2000–2001, when the per-share market capitalization of many listed companies dropped below the par value. The 2001 amendment to the Company Law, therefore, removed the traditional prohibition against issuing new shares at a price below the par value for listed firms. Other restraints on corporate finance, however, continue to be based on the infatuation with par value. Taiwanese companies have not been allowed to issue freely convertible bonds, because conversion would change the par-value capitalization. Likewise, all convertible preferred shares in Taiwan must have a one-for-one conversion ratio into common shares. Until the 2001 amendment, the Company Law prohibited setting different prices for new shares so as to prevent perceived unfairness. But this rule also prohibited efficient price discrimination. For example, once Taiwan's SFC began to adopt a partial book building system for public offerings in the 1990s, all such offerings technically violated the one-price rule.[13]

Legal constraints have also curtailed use of the preferred share as a financial instrument. Because of the perception that preferred shares are similar to debt, there are Company Law restrictions on issuing these shares when the issuer has prior-year losses or when the dividend rate would not match the after-tax net profit of prior years. Put differently, specific financial covenants are embedded in the Company Law as a mandatory cushion for capital adequacy. As a result, the preferred share has not become an attractive financial instrument. Venture capital investments in Taiwan must be structured using contracts for put or call options with founders and key shareholders of the startup company, an imperfect substitute for preferred stock.

Even though venture capital investment in Taiwan is done primarily through common shares (which limits contractual flexibility), Taiwan's VC industry has performed amazingly well since it was establsihed with government assistance in 1984. There were 191 government-registered VC funds by the end of 2000, which raising over NT$130 billion (US$3.6 billion). More than NT$92.5 billion was invested in Taiwan, which led to more than NT$900 billion (US$25 billion) of investment in Taiwan's high-tech sector. By the end of 2000, 117 VC-invested companies were listed on the TSE, and 104 VC-invested companies were listed on GTSM.

In addition, 88 Taiwan VC-invested American companies were listed on the NASDAQ.[14]

On the debt side, bond offerings also have been very uncommon. One important reason is that until early 2002, a 0.1 percent securities transfer tax was levied on corporate bond trading.[15] Convertible securities such as convertible preferred and convertible bonds were unheard of until the 1990s. Even during the 1990s, these so-called "new" financial instruments were subject to a number of restrictions such as conversion ratio and frequency of conversions.

Moreover, because the Company Law requires an issuer to have strong financial capability, these debt securities are essentially unavailable to issuers in a distress situation. This restriction could make it difficult, for example, to ameliorate the challenge facing Taiwan in recapitalizing its weak banks. In the 2000 amendment to the SEL and 2001 amendment to the Company Law, at least the gearing ratio for issuing bonds was doubled.

In view of these obstacles, the CEPD recommended streamlining the capital registration system and permitting debt-equity swaps. Both proposals were accepted by the MOEA and the SFC and reflected in the 2001 Company Law amendment. However, the MOEA and the SFC objected to repealing the financial track record and financial covenant provisions in the Company Law governing the issuance of these securities. They therefore missed an opportunity for reform. As Taiwan begins to deal with its banking crisis and explore ways to recapitalize its financial institutions, it needs to provide a template of more sophisticated capital structure to would-be investors. Currently, even though the MOF follows the multi-tiered capital principles under the Basle capital adequacy accord, its banks still largely rely on common shares and deposits to fund their lending operations. In the future, this means of funding will not be sustainable.

Traditionally, Taiwan's Company Law has provided only for straight (fixed), capital. As mentioned above, corporate registration rules made it difficult to issue truly convertible bonds. Likewise, the Company Law did not explicitly accommodate the issuance of convertible bonds, warrants, or options. Since the Company Law did not contain any provisions governing these equity securities, the validity of contracts with the issuers granting such securities has been in doubt. In 2000, an SEL amendment finally permitted all public reporting companies to issue warrants and options.

The Company Law had a requirement that companies exceeding a certain level of paid-up capital determined by the MOEA (historically set at

NT$200 million) offer their shares to the public. This rule, reflecting a socialist strand of Taiwan's economic development policy, was designed to accelerate the ownership diversification of industrial companies. There is a comparable mandatory public offering rule in the SEL, added in 1988.[16] At CEPD's urging, the 2001 Company Law amendment essentially dropped this requirement.

The Company Law guarantees that employees will receive certain bonuses in the form of stock dividends at par value out of the company's net income after tax. Again, this rule reflects socialist concepts, treating employees as holders of preferred shares. The government loses revenue on these transactions because the basis for taxation is the arbitrary par value instead of the market value of the shares distributed.[17]

When a company issues new shares for cash, the Company Law requires that 10–15 percent of the offering be allocated to its employees. However, this requirement, which again displays moderately socialist overtones, is not very efficient or effective. First, unless a company needs new capital and issues new shares for cash, employees have no right to subscribe for shares. Second, the anti-discrimination feature of the one-price rule mentioned above applies to employees as well, so they may not receive any discount on their shares. Thus, employees of Taiwanese firms may not reap the benefits contemplated by the statute.

As a substitute incentive to employees, founders often transfer their own shares to employees at preferential prices. In this way, rigidity in corporate capital structure can force owner-managers to do more for other stakeholders like employees, because owners stand to gain more by circumventing these rigid rules and co-opting other stakeholders. If they work around the legal rules, they can implement employee incentives and accelerate the initial public offering schedule. But psychologically, owner-managers may also seek compensation for sacrificing their interests to motivate employees, and this may take the form of favorable related-party transactions. In the end, minority shareholders bear the cost in the form of expropriation.

Until the 2001 Company Law amendment, only employees of the issuing company were entitled to this preemptive subscription right. Employees of subsidiaries were not eligible, as the Company Law followed a formalistic approach. This rigidity created a problem for Taiwanese companies wishing to take over foreign companies, particularly in the high-tech sector. A case in point is an acquisition by a group of Taiwan government and private investors of NYSE-listed Wyse Technology, then a leader in monitor manufacturing, in 1988–89. The clever solution in that case was the use of an off-shore company to "warehouse" the parent company's shares to fund employee stock options.

Finally, the Company Law has historically prohibited corporate share buybacks except when dissenting shareholders sought appraisal remedies or to cancel debt owed to the company. This was changed by the 2000 SEL amendment, which now allows corporate buybacks primarily to "protect the interest of shareholders," a euphemism for boosting the shares of publicly listed companies in a downward market.[18] In addition, the SEL amendment also implemented a new employee stock option system. Companies may buy back and retain treasury shares to meet the exercise of options granted to employees, which is now permitted under this amendment. However, following the European model, the SEL as amended only permits a publicly listed company to buy back up to 10 percent of its total issued and outstanding shares.[19]

IV. Corporate Governance and the Market for Corporate Control

For cultural reasons and owing to the nature of family business, ownership of large Taiwanese firms remains concentrated even after their shares have been publicly listed. Industrial policy and financial regulation have affected Taiwan's corporate profile as well. When Taiwanese SMEs focused on exports and large Taiwanese firms (including state-owned enterprises) operated in a closed domestic market, they did not need corporate governance. However, after the TSE became active in the late 1980s, and with the opening of the domestic market, corporate governance has become very relevant. Indeed, for most of the 1990s regulators were often more concerned with strengthening corporate governance than relaxing corporate finance rules.

The Taiwan government, however, has not carefully considered its own role. In addition to exercising strong merit-review oversight of listed firms, the government itself has become a market participant. Government representatives sit on the boards of publicly listed state-owned enterprises undergoing privatization, and to boost the market, the government buys shares through public and private pension funds it controls. Despite the growth in investor sophistication and trading volume on the Taiwan securities market since the late 1980s, work to improve corporate governance has just begun.

A. *Election of Directors and Supervisors*

The board of directors is the centerpiece of any corporate governance system. In Taiwan, directors and supervisors are elected from among the shareholders in separate elections. Supervisors are somewhat like the *Aufsichrat* under the two-tier board system of the German *Aktiengesetz*. But they more closely resemble the *kansayaku* system under the Japanese Commercial Code. In other words, the Taiwanese board of directors and supervisors have a horizontal, rather than vertical (or two-tiered), relationship. In addition, in Taiwan, supervisors act in their individual capacity. Therefore, there is no supervisory "board."

The board of directors does not go through a nominating committee process. Indeed, the Company Law does not authorize the establishment of committees. It only permits a board of managing directors to be established if the board is perceived to be too big. As a result, Taiwanese companies rarely set up committees within the board of directors. As of this writing, the SFC is reviewing a proposed rule requiring the establishment of various board committees. Yet the validity of committee resolutions will be in doubt, as neither the Company Law nor the SEL explicitly authorizes them.

By law, the same person may not stand for election as both a director and a supervisor, to avoid a conflict of interest. In practice, however, candidates for directors and supervisors are often supporters of the same group of insiders (or more specifically, the chairman of the board), and they rarely perform an independent role. The Company Law makes the chairman of the board the statutory representative of a company. This rule, coupled with Confucian culture, effectively makes the chairman king of the corporate empire. In sum, even though Taiwan companies have become very global, the composition and practice of their boards of directors remains very parochial.

B. *Institutional Directors and Supervisors*

Legal entities in Taiwan such as governmental organs and corporations may become directors and supervisors. They are entitled to appoint individuals as candidates, or run for election as an entity and then appoint representatives to perform the director or supervisor role on their behalf. This institutional director/supervisor rule gives rise to a significant agency problem: While directors and supervisors are elected to serve the company (and its share-holders), these institutional appointees are loyal to the entities with which they are affiliated. In addition, representatives can be reappointed up to the maximum three-year term.[20] While this rule allows flexibility for closely held companies, it creates significant corporate governance problems for public or widely held companies, and undermines the requirement, mentioned above, of separate elections for directors and supervisors.

The CEPD consultants saw this institutional director/supervisor rule and its consequences as a major weakness of Taiwan's corporate governance system. They therefore unanimously recommended repealing this rule for public companies. Yet the MOEA, SFC and the Executive Yuan rejected this recommendation. While they understand the nature and enormity of the problem, the Taiwan government (under both political parties) has used this rule to control state-owned enterprises and other government-affiliated companies. The government cannot break itself of this habit.

C. Fiduciary Duty and Independent Directors

The owner-manager's fiduciary duty strikes at the core of the corporate governance problem in Taiwan. Fiduciary duty, however, has not become an important corporate law principle in Taiwan until recently. Taiwan is not unique in this regard. By following the Japanese Commercial Code model for its Company Law, Taiwan has suffered from the same problems as Japan, such as lack of independent directors and weak corporate governance (American Chamber of Commerce 2001). The same unfamiliarity with fiduciary concepts exists in Germany and the transition economies that transplanted German law. As a cultural matter, the duty of loyalty seems to be downplayed in the Asian civil law jurisdictions as a result of the prevalence of family control and ownership concentration. Family or kinship substitutes for legal duties. In addition, as a technical matter, the lack of a body of trust law in the civil law tradition may explain the underdevelopment of fiduciary duty principles in the civilian system. This is vastly different from the common law jurisdictions, where directors are held to a higher level of fiduciary conduct.[21]

By contrast, the duty of "due care as a good manager" is a core concept in the contract of "mandate" under the civil law system, which governs the legal relationship between directors (and supervisors) and the companies they serve. By virtue of this duty, directors are held to a professional negligence standard for their performance. This contrasts with the business judgment rule, which in the United States prevents judges from imposing liability ex post for non-reckless director conduct performed in good faith. Theoretically, there is no such judicial deference toward directors in Taiwan.

It is surprising that a jurisdiction with low corporate governance performance like Taiwan has more stringent textual requirements for the directors' duty of due care than the United States. In fact, the situation regarding fiduciary duties is exactly the reverse of the U.S. corporate law regime, where courts give careful scrutiny to breaches of the duty of loyalty, but do not second-guess poor business decisions by directors.

Although Taiwan's civil code jurisprudence is vague on the duty of loyalty, breach of trust and embezzlement are crimes under the Criminal Code. Therefore, in cases involving serious corporate misconduct, prosecutors can invoke criminal fiduciary duty law. Similarly, serious violations of the SEL are criminally prosecuted. In fact, for most of the 1990s, Taiwan relied on criminal sanctions for major securities law violations to ensure a minimum level of accountability among corporate insiders. However, decriminalization (at least of technical violations) has been a trend in post-martial law Taiwan. Therefore, civil fiduciary duty law needs to be developed. The 2001 Company Law amendment now explicitly imposes an American-influenced fiduciary duty on directors, supervisors, and other executive officers. Codification, however, is just the beginning, and it will take time for a fiduciary culture to set in and for fiduciary duty case law to be developed.

Another problem with the underdevelopment of the concept of fiduciary duty in Taiwan is uncertainty as to whom the duty is owed. The essence of fiduciary duty is to serve the best interest of all shareholders. Yet in Taiwan, fiduciary duties are owed to the *company* served by the directors and supervisors. Form again prevails over substance, as shareholders are viewed as distinct from the company, which is a separate legal entity. This view is inconsistent with the 1997 amendment to the Company Law, which added a German-style affiliated enterprises law. This puzzling distinction has another ramification: it removes fiduciary duty considerations from the mergers and acquisitions context, because shareholders may completely sell off their financial stakes in the company. The problem arises because if fiduciary duties are owed to the company (not the shareholders) and the company disappears as a result of a merger, the fiduciary duties are extinguished. Thus, the rigid view that the recently transplanted fiduciary duty is owed only to the company does not help foster a market for corporate control.

Codification of the fiduciary duty of directors and supervisors is welcome. Realistically, however, it is difficult to expect them to discharge this duty faithfully if they are supported or appointed by insiders. Therefore, the Taiwan government has considered requiring independent directors since the early 1990s, and particularly after the Asian financial crisis.[22] One fundamental issue related to the debate over independent directors in Taiwan is whether to part with the civil law tradition of using supervisors to oversee the performance of directors. Indeed, supervisors in a dual-board regime are intended to function much like independent directors in a unitary board system. Therefore, some experts argued that functional convergence was more practical than formal convergence.

Following the Asian financial crisis, however, there is now a stronger emphasis on electing independent directors as a substitute for the two-tiered board. Korea, for example, has opted for a mandatory independent director regime for large listed companies, while apparently abandoning any hope of reforming the supervisor system (Kim 2000). In August 2001, the China Securities Regulatory Commission (CSRC) followed suit with a set of guidelines requiring that all listed companies in China have two independent directors and that by July 2003, one-third of the board of such companies should be consist of independent directors. The CSRC did not hesitate to impose this system on top of the supervisor regime.

Since the early 1990s, the Taiwan Stock Exchange and GTSM have routinely negotiated with companies applying for initial public offerings to install independent directors. Often, family-owned companies would agree to install an independent director after the initial public offering. However, the ostensibly independent director was often close to the insiders, and was not viewed by the market as truly independent. Moreover, once listed, these companies would once again elect a majority of family members or affiliates to the board in the next election (Chen 2000).

In early 2002, the TSE and GTSM strengthened the independent director requirement in their listing rules at the request of the SFC. Under the new rules, each company seeking a public listing must have two independent directors and one independent supervisor, each of whom must have at least five years experience in law, business, or finance. At least one of the independent directors and the supervisor must be an accounting or finance professional. The SFC also instructed that a talent database be set up to assist newly listed companies recruit independent directors and supervisors. In addition, independent directors must now take continuing education courses. Following a German-inspired rule, they may not serve as directors of more than five companies concurrently.

The SFC's laudable independent director initiative has generated controversy. Some scholars and insiders of old economy companies argue that the SFC does not have statutory authority under the SEL to impose this requirement, as it would limit insiders' voting rights to elect themselves as directors. Moreover, in light of the high risks and unclear benefit of board service, it is unclear whether capable candidates will come forward. It is clear, however, that the SFC will pursue this new program vigorously. Shortly after the SFC launched this program, it asked the TSE and GTSM to draft comprehensive best practice corporate governance guidelines, which were jointly adopted in October 2002. One success story on the independent director issue is Taiwan Semiconductor Manufacturing, Taiwan's high-tech leader and a corporate governance role model, which has attracted several internationally known scholars and corporate executives to its board.

D. Shadow Directors and Shadow Supervisors

The CEPD consultants recommended adoption of the "shadow director" or de facto director doctrine found in British and other Commonwealth jurisdictions (Davis 1997). In the United States, a similar corporate law concept of "deputization" exists in the case law. These doctrines hold that if a person performs the function of a director, even if not formally elected as such, he or she will be treated as a director under the law. The reason for recommending this proposal is simple: a nominee culture, often aided by formalist legal requirements, prevails in Taiwan. True insiders use front men to serve as directors and supervisors in their place. In regulated industries such as financial services, there is an even more flagrant practice of using managers and former government officials to serve as directors and supervisors. This proposal, viewed as radical by the authorities responsible for corporate law reform, was not pursued.

E. Related-Party Transactions, Self-Dealing, and Other Manipulative Conduct

After lifting martial law in 1987, the top priority in enforcing Taiwan's corporate law has been to vigorously pursue related-party transactions, self-dealing, insider trading, short-swing trading, and other manipulative conduct. To this end, the 1988 SEL amendment drew inspiration from American securities law by adding rules requiring prior reporting and limiting the daily selling volume of insiders, in addition to the preexisting rule generally prohibiting off-exchange transactions. The SEL also authorizes the SFC to require directors and supervisors collectively to hold a minimum number of shares while in office.[23] The SFC also uses the SFI, a nonprofit foundation set up and supported by the SFC, as an innovative way to enforce the strict-liability disgorgement rule against short-swing trading.[24] The 1988 SEL amendment also added an important and much more elaborate rule against insider trading, copying extensively from the American Insider Trading Sanctions Act of 1984, including a treble damages provision.

From 1998 to 2000, a number of scandals involved insiders of publicly listed companies literally stealing from the firms without much pretense. Many of the scandals involved transactions in land or unlisted shares with affiliates. More flagrant conduct involved the chairman of the board, the legal representative of the company under the Company Law, siphoning funds from the company through loans, or simply through notes of instruction to the corporate treasurer.

These incidents showed that the 1997 Company Law amendment to transplant the German-influenced affiliated enterprise rules were not effective, primarily because no single "parent" company could be found. In 2000, the SFC secured an SEL amendment providing for up to seven years imprisonment of any individual who causes a public company to engage in a materially adverse transaction at other than arms' length.

In the late 1990s, it became fashionable for listed companies to set up unlisted investment holding companies (which, under then-prevailing SFC interpretations, were not subject to the SEL), to buy parent company shares on margin and without disclosure. Insiders then pledged the shares, trading at artificially high prices, to banks in exchange for loans in order to realize the gains. But when the market tumbled in 1998–2000, this practice brought down many listed companies.

A study of 42 "land-mine" companies that failed during the late 1990s shows several interesting patterns. Compared with a sample of normal companies in the same industry, they had a much stronger tendency for the chairman of the board to double as the President and CEO as well. Insiders also tended to dump shares in an "end period" game when the company went down (Ko 2002). This study also classified the improper conduct contributing to their downfall into thirteen categories.[25] Twenty-six of the firms engaged in three or more counts of manipulative conduct. The most notorious of these firms engaged in eight counts of corporate misconduct. In convicting the defendants, the district court judge wrote an unprecedented opinion of more than one million words.

Regulators had to learn the hard way to improve their enforcement tools. One example was cross investment and churning through captive subsidiaries to support parent company share price. Although the Company Law had prohibited share buybacks, the MOEA and SFC could not invoke this rule because a subsidiary rather than the listed parent was undertaking the buyback. The 2001 Company Law amendment now prohibits such cross investment. Even as reformed, however, the law remains weak because it does not stipulate any criminal or administrative sanctions for violations.

F. Derivative Actions and Class Actions

In the 1970s, Taiwan amended its Company Law by copying the derivative action rule from Japan, even though this concept originated from the United States. However, in a departure from both the Japanese and the American models, to invoke this derivative action remedy against directors, the company has required a group of minority shareholders to collectively own 5 percent of the outstanding shares of the company continuously for one year.[26] Demands to sue directors must first be made on the supervisors. If the supervisors fail to act on such demands, qualifying minority shareholders may bring a derivative action.

Taiwan's Judicial Yuan has been considering the introduction of class actions as a part of its overhaul of the civil justice system in Taiwan. It has jurisdiction over amendments to the Code of Civil Procedure. However, Taiwan's judges, including senior judges at the top of the Judicial Yuan, are notoriously conservative and slow in attempting any reform. Class actions have been viewed as the epitome of the litigious American society. Unless this conservative view is changed, it will remain difficult to use derivative actions and class actions to challenge director conduct in Taiwan. As noted above, one innovative solution to these problems is the nonprofit foundation supported by the SFC. This foundation purchases a trading unit of the shares of all listed companies and solicits other investors to bring suit when there are major, criminal infractions of the SEL or Company Law. These civil law suits ride on the coattails of the criminal complaint of the prosecutors. The effectiveness of this kind of piggyback securities class action system, however, is limited (see Liu 2001b). In July 2002 an Investors Protection Act was enacted to institutionalize this kind of public interest litigation.

G. Disclosure

In the last ten years, Taiwan has improved disclosure requirements under the SEL, along with the SFC and TSE rules. These improvements include the quantity, scope, accuracy, and timeliness of disclosure. However, the quality of disclosure still requires improvement. For example, the bottom quartile of a 2001 Standard & Poor survey of the transparency of the top 100 Asian listed companies was mostly occupied by Taiwanese firms (Hastings 2001). Although the Taiwanese accounting profession has created linkages with international accounting firms and largely follows American accounting and auditing conventions, their professional standards are in need of improvement. In a purely domestic context, disclosure has not been viewed as important to improving corporate governance, because financial information would be drowned out by the herd mentality and the speculative approach to stock market investing. Foreign institutional investors, however, who focus more on research and are subject to fiduciary duties in their home countries, are changing the impression that disclosure does not pay.

The American style of disclosure has clearly influenced securities regulation in Taiwan since the early 1990s. In addition to importing U.S. disclosure principles, Taiwan has "exported" listed companies, which offer American Depositary Receipts or Global Depositary Receipts in the United States. In Taiwanese legal practice, there is now a clear pattern of doing "Western-style due diligence" in such offerings and cross-border M&A transactions.

H. Proxy Contests

Taiwan has deliberately avoided building a market for corporate control. Ownership concentration has been comparatively high, as Taiwan is essentially still at the stage of entrepreneurial capitalism. Traditionally proxy rules were lax and favored incumbent owner-managers. This is hardly surprising in light of the government-business coalition in Taiwan's past industrial policy, and the need to maintain a façade of social harmony for political and cultural reasons. Before the 1990s, proxies were often bought. The SFC finally overhauled the proxy rules to prohibit vote buying in the late 1990s as part of an anti-crime campaign to deal with "professional shareholders" (equivalent to *sokaiya* in Japan). However, some listed companies have over-reacted by holding shareholders meetings in inconvenient locations to discourage these activities.

Other problems will likely limit the role of proxy contests as a means of improving corporate governance in Taiwan in the near term. Individual investors are still unsophisticated, appreciating small gifts from management at the shareholders meeting more than good corporate performance. And the infamous Article 17 of the SFC Proxy Rules, which generally instructs mutual fund mangers to vote for resolutions put forward by the board, continues to favor incumbents.[27]

I. Mergers and Acquisitions

Mergers and acquisitions of Taiwan public companies, especially cross-border deals, were rare until the late 1990s. Even as of 2002, there have been only two public tender offers in Taiwanese history. Both were successful, but by narrow margins.

Corporate, tax, securities, banking, pension, and antitrust laws were all in need of reform in order to foster a vibrant M&A market. Indeed, in this area, Taiwan recently adopted some important changes in law and government regulations. Interestingly, these changes were first effected in financial services regulation, a tightly controlled sector and an unlikely candidate to plant the seeds of reform. However, by the late 1990s the Taiwan government recognized that there was a financial crisis, reflected in the worsening nonperforming loan problem and the saturated financial market. As a result, the MOF rather than the MOEA became a champion of corporate law reform, and endorsed many recommendations that had been rejected by the MOEA less than a year before. Two important pieces of legislation, the Financial Institutions Mergers Act (FIMA) and the Financial Holding Companies Law (FHCL), were the forerunners in changing the way M&A transactions involving financial firms were regulated and structured. The third was a comprehensive Corporate Mergers and Acquisitions Law (CMAL), which made even more changes to facilitate M&A transactions.

There was also urgency for M&A law reform in the industrial sector. For example, Acer Incorporated, Taiwan's flagship information technology company, announced in late 2000 that it wanted to split itself up into two companies—an original equipment/design manufacturing business, and the Acer-brand business. But the plan was troubled by a host of issues, the most important of which was that Taiwan's Company Law did not contemplate this type of corporate division. Acer was losing competitiveness, because as a Taiwan company it was subject to rigid M&A rules prohibiting efficiency-enhancing restructurings.

The CMAL overhauled these rules, permitting tax-free reorganizations for the first time. The use of cash as consideration in mergers (to enable cash-out mergers) as well as short-form mergers (to streamline integration) were also permitted. The CMAL also allowed triangular mergers, corporate divisions (or de-mergers), and share exchanges. Income tax consolidated reporting was introduced to facilitate averaging of gains and losses among constituent companies. Where an M&A transaction is involved, the mandatory public offering rule of the SEL and the preemptive subscription rules of the Company Law do not apply. Taiwan must now also modify the TSE and GTSM listing rules that prohibit listings by holding companies. The 2002 SEL amendment follows the British mandatory bid rule and repealed the requirement of prior SFC approval before a tender offer could be launched. However, for fear of antagonizing individual investors, the SFC did not transplant the British mechanism for minority squeeze-outs even after 90 percent of the shares are tendered, leaving some doubts as to how to deal with the hold-out problem.[28]

An improvement of the CMAL over other existing laws is the express imposition of a fiduciary duty on directors and other officers in the M&A context. In contrast to the express fiduciary duty provided by the 2001 Company Law amendment, in an M&A transaction, directors and officers owe the duty to all shareholders, not just the company they nominally serve. Hopefully, with this change, substance will triumph over form. Also, for public companies, the CMAL requires independent financial experts to render fair price opinions in M&A transactions.

The CMAL also addressed post-acquisition governance issues where the acquisition is less than a complete buyout. To this end, it authorizes voting trusts, share transfer restrictions and joint governance arrangements, subject to disclosure obligations and a minority shareholders' appraisal remedy where public companies are involved. These rules override previous judicial interpretations challenging the validity of such agreements and arrangements. In addition, to facilitate strategic alliances the CMAL permits all companies, private or public, to increase their corporate buyback quota to 20 percent of issued and outstanding shares.

Deregulation remains the focus of the CMAL. To this end, in a qualified asymmetrical merger the surviving company would not need to hold a shareholders meeting to approve the merger. By the same token, the CMAL permits short-form mergers and mergers between domestic and foreign companies. This pierces the foreign investment law shield, which had made Taiwan's corporate law system rigid and parochial. CMAL also relaxed cumbersome notice requirements of the Civil Code and Company Law.

Conclusion

Taiwan's experience suggests that for it and other emerging markets, the corporate law system is very much a part of the national political economy. That is, corporate and securities laws exist as part of an ecology involving industrial organization, development strategies, industrial, labor, and fiscal policy, bureaucratic interests, and politics. All politics are local, but local politics can be checked by the need to globalize. The need for survival and international visibility dictates a balance between stability and growth. Stability concerns dictate certain types of rigid corporate and financial laws. But rigidity makes Taiwanese firms less competitive, so that new laws must be devised to preempt or replace existing laws.

Taiwan has been ambivalent toward globalization. More international contact makes Taiwan stronger politically in its sustained struggle with China. The more internationalized Taiwan firms become, however, the less control the Taiwan government can assert over them. The current challenge is even more daunting. Globalization for some Taiwan companies could mean assimilation into the Greater China market. Thus, for the Taiwan government, political considerations will always loom large in corporate and financial reform.

Democratization in Taiwan since the late 1980s has been the catalyst that challenged the existing ecology. With democratization came the opening of the financial sector, which became less bank-centered and more market-centered. However, Taiwan's laws and legal culture have yet to fully follow this paradigm shift. Taiwan pushed political and economic reforms virtually simultaneously in the 1990s. As a result, there were bound to be tradeoffs. Thus far, Taiwan's precocious democratization has paid limited economic development dividends. Yet globalization is serving as an impetus for improving corporate governance and constraining undue domestic political pressures resisting reforms.

Sadly, the courts have been a reticent and irrelevant constituency in much of the improvement of the corporate law system and financial market in Taiwan. Taiwan's judiciary has just emerged from the martial law past, and its first step in the reform process since the late 1980s has focused on the political agenda like legislative and electoral reform. Even though Taiwanese judges are becoming more activist on many issues and have permitted a greater scope for justiciability and standing in recent years, they seem uninterested and unprepared for a meaningful debate on their role in improving Taiwan's corporate law system.

Globalization intensifies competition among firms and the domestic institutions within which they operate. The Taiwanese have always had a crisis mentality and survival instinct. As told in this essay, corporate law reform received an unexpected boost from the MOF, simply because it realized a financial storm was taking shape in Taiwan. Perhaps in this crisis mentality and survival instinct lies hope for further institutional reforms to improve Taiwan's parochial corporate law system as an integral part of its globalization program.

Endnotes

The author drafted and took part in reviewing some of the legislative bills discussed in this essay. The views expressed herein are his alone.

1. Taiwan is formally known as the Republic of China (ROC), which was founded in Mainland China in 1912.

2. For the first time the Taiwan government took over 36 community financial institutions, which were virtually bankrupt, in late 2001 (Guyot 2001).

3. The SEL was enacted in 1968 with the advice of an American advisor, George Ferris, borrowing from the U.S. Securities Act of 1933 and Securities Exchange Act of 1934.

4. As a result of this tension, Taiwan authorities have used 40 percent of net worth as the ceiling for China-bound investment by listed companies in Taiwan. The source of this regulatory concept is the reinvestment restriction in the Company Law, discussed below.

5. Round-tripping refers to the practice of local investors converting currency into foreign currency, establishing a foreign company, and investing in the local economy as a "foreign" investor.

6. According to the Directorate General of Budget and Statistics, in the 1990s, civil service personnel costs averaged 4.7% of Taiwan's GDP. The comparable 10-year average for Singapore, Japan, Korea and America was 5%, 0.8%, 2.2% and 1.9% (See Chou 2001).

7. Baskin and Miranti (1997).

8. For a history of Republican Chinese company legislation in the early 1900s, see Kirby (1995).

9. See Liu (1997).

10. American Chamber of Commerce in Japan (2001).

11. For a discussion of legal constraints on the development of the Japanese venture capital industry, see Milhaupt (1997).

12. See Chung-Hwa Credit Institute (2001). Of the approximately one million registered companies in Taiwan as of 1999, 4,317 were part of an affiliated business group. As of that same year, a total of 195 groups of companies employed more than one million people, or about 10.78% of the workforce (compared with 111 groups employing about 277,000 persons, or 5.40% of the workforce in 1973) (Ibid.: 37–39).

13. Previously, there was no real underwriting in Taiwan. In order to achieve fairness, interested public investors were asked to draw lots (often for one trading unit each, that is, 1000 shares) when there was oversubscription. The SFC also regulated the public offering price through a four-factor weighted formula, which even included the prevailing one-year savings deposit rate. As a result, the price discovery mechanism of book building simply did not exist.

14. Taiwan Venture Capital Association (2001).

15. The same tax for equity trading was 0.3% of the gross selling price. This is more advantageous than a capital gains tax, which has been suspended since 1988 and for political reasons is not likely to be reinstated.

16. Perversely, this rule received some American influence: Section 12(g) of the Securities and Exchange Act of 1934 imposes public disclosure obligations on

companies having both a minimum amount of assets and a minimum number of shareholders.

17. Taiwan's high-tech companies were challenged abroad for dumping because, under generally accepted accounting principles in markets like the United States, such after-tax bonuses would be imputed as labor costs to the companies involved and added to their production cost. In the late 1990s, American competitors of Taiwan chip manufacturers alleged that the latter had dumped SRAM chips into the U.S. market. The allegations rested, in part, on the granting of such bonus shares.

18. This rule was prompted in part by the 1996 cross-strait crisis, when China fired missiles in an attempt to influence Taiwan's first presidential election by popular vote, and the Taiwan stock market almost crashed.

19. The 2001 Company Law amendment now permits non-public companies to buy back 5% of outstanding shares to fund employee stock options.

20. This maximum term for directors and supervisors (subject, theoretically, to removal powers) was influenced by the pro-business rule of the Japanese Commercial Code.

21. To be sure, Taiwan's Company Law disqualifies directors from voting on matters involving personal interest and from engaging in competitive business unless the conflict is waived by the shareholders through informed consent. However, the existence of institutional directorships and the use of holding companies aligned with, but which do not technically appoint, institutional directors in a legal culture stressing form over substance has eviscerated the enforcement of this rule.

22. The SFC has been more aggressive than the MOEA in advocating this requirement. The CEPD consultants did not propose a system of independent directors, as the experts had heated debates on the direction and pace of reform in 1999–2000.

23. The SFC has a weighted scale under this rule (from 15% to 5% for directors, and 1.5% to 0.5% for supervisors, based on paid-in capital).

24. Notably, this rule *compels* the company to seek disgorgement from insiders, leaving no discretion to acquiesce or settle. This institute would buy and hold at least one trading unit (1,000 shares) of all shares listed in Taiwan so as to be able to take enforcement actions if listed companies fail to compel disgorgement (Liu 2001b). The computerized market monitoring by TSE and GTSM once every six months and the strict liability regime have made such claims relatively easy and risk-free to enforce. According to Vice Chairman Wu of the Taiwan SFC, as of June 2001, this institute had taken on 1,971 cases and forced the disgorgement of NT$750 million (more than US$21 million) (Wu 2002).

25. Among the 42 companies, 25 engaged in public-market price support, 8 engaged in illegal nonsettlement of securities trading (usually when the market

turned against them), and 13 engaged in cross investment (that is, corporate buybacks through captive subsidiaries). Sixteen firms engaged in related-party transactions, 10 gave improper check guarantees to others, and insiders in 18 firms simply siphoned corporate funds. Six engaged in illegal lending, 10 borrowed more than they could repay, 9 had bad investments in other projects. Five of them had excessive expansion, 5 used other companies for backdoor shelf listing, 2 got into control contests, and 12 had mismanaged their business (Ko 2002).

26. The 2001 Company Law amendment reduced the shareholding threshold to 3%, which is still too high to be meaningful.

27. Article 17 requires that Taiwan mutual fund management companies vote in the best interests of unit holders *"and for the candidates and proposed resolutions put forward by the board."* This rule does not apply, *"and their own board may decide otherwise, if the listed companies engage in bad management activities to the detriment of the company and shareholders."* The rule further provides that, unless foreign institutional investors give definitive instructions on how to vote, they are deemed to support proposals by the board of the listed companies.

28. Lack of a minority squeeze-out mechanism has created problems elsewhere. For example, Vodafone had difficulty restructuring Mannesmann after acquiring it in 2000 (Editorial 2001).

References

American Chamber of Commerce in Japan. 2001. US-Japan Business White Paper. Tokyo: American Chamber of Commerce in Japan.

Baskin, Jonathan Barron and Paul J. Miranti, Jr. 1997. *A History of Corporate Finance.* Cambridge: Cambridge University Press.

Chen, Kuo-Wei. 2001. 384 Listed Companies in Mainland China by Q1/2001. *China Times.* June 1, p. 14 (Chinese).

Chen, Weng-Ho. 2000. Study of Effective Exercise by Exterior Directors and Supervisors of Listed Companies. Taipei: TSEC Monthly Review, vol. 456 no. 1, p. 9, April 2000 (Chinese).

Chou, Huei-Ru. 2001. "Bloated Government." Taipei: China Times. September 12, p. 21 (Chinese).

Chung-Hwa Credit Institute. 2001. Business Groups in Taiwan Special Edition, Taipei: Chung-Hwa Credit Institute (Chinese).

Davis, Paul L. 1997. *Gower's Principles of Modern Company Law,* 6th ed. London: Sweet and Maxwell.

Editorial. 2001. Living in the Past: German Takeover Laws Need an Update. 2001. *Asian Wall Street Journal.* August 28, p. 8.

Enriques, Luca and Jonathan R. Macey. 2001. Creditors Versus Capital Formation: The Case Against European Legal Capital Rule. *Cornell Law Review* 86: 1165–1204.

Guyot, Erik. 2001. Taiwan Grants Full Guarantees to 36 Banks. *Asian Wall Street Journal*, August 13, pp. 1, 3.

Hastings, Kirsh. 2001. Survey Ranks of Transparency: Companies from Australia and Singapore Are Rated Superior. *Asian Wall Street Journal*. November 16, 2001, p. 4.

Kim, Joongi. 2000. Recent Amendments to the Korean Commercial Code and Their Effects on International Competition. *University of Pennsylvania Journal of International Economic Law* 21: 273–330.

Kirby, William C. 1995. China Unincorporated: Company Law and Business Enterprises in Twentieth-Century China. *Journal of Asian Studies* 54: 43–63.

Ko, Chen-En. 2002. Framework for Corporate Governance and Development Trends. Speech to Taiwan Academy of Banking and Finance, Taipei (Chinese).

La Porta, Raphael, Florencio Lopez-de-Silanes, Andrei Shleifer and Robert W. Vishney. 1997. Legal Determinants of External Finance. *Journal of Finance* 52: 1131–50.

——. 1998. Law and Finance. *Journal of Political Economy* 106: 1113–55.

——. 2000. Investor Protection and Corporate Governance. *Journal of Financial Economics* 58: 3–27.

Liu, Lawrence S. 1997. The Law and Political Economy of Capital Market Regulation in the Republic of China on Taiwan. *Law and Policy in International Business* 28: 813–856.

——. 2001a. A Perspective on Corporate Governance in Taiwan. *Asian Business Law Review* 31: 29–37.

——. 2001b. Simulating Securities Class Actions: The Case in Taiwan. *Corporate Governance International* 3: 4–12.

——. 2001c. Chinese Characteristics Compared: A Legal and Policy Perspective of Corporate Finance and Governance in Taiwan and China. Social Science Research Network. (http://papers.ssrn.com/sol3/papers.cfm?abstract_id=273174).

—— and Tian-Jy Chen. 2001. The Role of Law and Legal Institutions in Asian Economic Development: The Case of Taiwan, Pattern of Change in the Legal System and Socio-Economy, Harvard Institute for International Development Discussion Paper No. 663.

Milhaupt, Curtis. 1997. The Market for Innovation in the United States and Japan: Venture Capital and the Comparative Corporate Governance Debate. *Northwestern University Law Review* 91: 865–98.

Organisation for Economic Cooperation and Development (OECD). 2001. Main
    Science and Technology Indicators, Paris: OECD.
Taiwan Venture Capital Association. 2001. Taiwan Venture Capital Association
    Annual Report, Taipei: Taiwan Venture Capital Association (Chinese).
World Economic Forum. 2002. The Global Competitiveness Report 2001–2002.
Wu, Dan-Jieh. 2002. Corporate Governance Under Secruities Regulation Rules.
    Speech to Taiwan Academy of Banking and Finance. Taipei (Chinese).

Part III

Globalization and the
Capital Markets

13 The Impact of Cross-Listings and Stock Market Competition on International Corporate Governance

John C. Coffee, Jr.

Today, there are an estimated 150 securities exchanges trading stocks around the world (see Vision Test 2001). Soon, this number is likely to shrink radically. Indeed, this was the U.S. experience at the beginning of the twentieth century when over 100 securities exchanges in the United States operated, until they were compelled to consolidate or simply shut down, as improved communications and transportation systems lowered the informational cost barriers that had sustained them. Today, the two great forces reshaping the contemporary world—globalization and technology—appear to be forcing a similar consolidation. Because globalization has lowered the barriers to cross-border capital flows, including in particular traditional restrictions on foreign investments in domestic stocks, and because technology has made instantaneous information flows feasible, securities markets can now compete on a global basis that never previously was possible. As a result, issuers, particularly those in emerging economies, have a choice of markets on which to list their securities and raise equity capital.

Predictably, once this competition begins, a natural consequence will be a wave of mergers, consolidations, and related alliances among securities markets. But where does this process end? Many who have studied this new competition have assumed that the winners (or at least the survivors) in this consolidation process will be those who can offer the greatest liquidity, or the lowest trading costs, or the most advanced technology. Some believe that this competition will inherently result in a "winner-takes-all" contest that will leave only a few large pools of liquidity in major international financial centers (see DiNoia 2001). The premise here is that "liquidity attracts liquidity" (ibid.: 55), and thus larger markets should drain order flow and liquidity from smaller markets, ultimately leaving them hollowed-out shells.

This essay resists the claim that competition will produce uniformity or any single winner. Because the cross-border competition among securities markets typically involves markets operating under different regulatory regimes, an inherent regulatory competition underlies this competition among markets. The more closely one examines the actual motives and behavior of cross-listing firms, the more one finds that considerations of corporate governance and access to equity finance dominate their decisions. Because firms have very different preferences about governance, however, competition produces specialization, rather than homogenization. This essay will argue that this regulatory competition will both (i) restrain the centralizing forces that others see as leading to a natural monopoly of a few dominant "super-exchanges," and (ii) improve corporate governance by increasing the protection of minority shareholders, at least in those markets most subject to competitive pressure.

Although the term "regulatory competition" has been much used in recent debates over securities regulation, the form of regulatory competition that has in fact developed over only the last half dozen years is very different from that envisioned by its academic proponents. These proponents, convinced that securities markets are often overregulated and skeptical of the motives of public regulators, have advocated a system of "issuer choice" under which each issuer could choose the regulatory regime under which its securities would trade.[1] Thus, issuers incorporated in a U.S. jurisdiction and trading on the New York Stock Exchange could elect to be governed as to their disclosure standards by the laws of India, Taiwan, or Switzerland. By forcing different regulatory regimes into competition, "issuer choice" in the view of its proponents would enable firms to engage in a regulatory arbitrage that would prune out-of-date or inefficient regulation, leaving only that degree of regulation sophisticated market participants would design for themselves.

In fact, however, the regulatory competition that has actually developed involves not issuers choosing a regulatory regime from a menu of available options, but rather issuers cross-listing on an international securities market—and thereby opting into additional and usually higher disclosure and corporate governance standards. Two critical differences distinguish this system from the "issuer choice" model: first, issuers choose a market *and* a regulatory regime together and cannot sever their choice of market from their choice of regulatory principles. Thus, it is impossible to enter a strong and deep market, while observing only the laws governing a thin or primitive market. Second, the issuer cannot "exit" its home jurisdiction in a manner that truly escapes that jurisdiction's potentially more stringent regulation. Initially, this essay finds that strong legal standards today attract, rather than repel, issuers who are cross-listing. Indeed, when one examines the actual movement of issuers and listings across jurisdictions, the dominant pattern has been a pronounced migration of listings and trading to exchanges in jurisdictions that are noted for their strong protection of minority shareholders (Jackson and Pan 2001). By opting for a higher disclosure regime, the migrating firms enhance their share price and become able to raise additional equity at lower cost.

This finding that migrating firms are opting into stronger, more mandatory legal standards is, of course, consistent with a new and important academic literature that argues that liquid and deep securities markets develop only in jurisdictions that protect the rights and expectations of minority shareholders (La Porta et al. 1998; 1999).[2] Still, even if the need to assure minority investors that they will be adequately protected underlies the contemporary race among foreign firms to cross-list on U.S. exchanges, one cannot fairly leap from this conclusion to a broader scenario under which intermarket competition produces an all-encompassing, regulatory "race to the top." Not only is the world more complicated and path dependent than such a simple Darwinian competitive model suggests, but, more important, such a scenario misunderstands the normal impact of competition. Put simply, competitive pressures tend to produce not uniformity, but specialization and fragmentation.

Particularly in the case of securities markets, any assumption that competition will produce uniformity ignores that the universe of firms that use securities markets divides radically into those with concentrated ownership versus those with dispersed ownership (La Porta et al. 1999). Concentrated ownership firms tend to behave differently than dispersed ownership firms, with the former often acting to maximize the private benefits of control for its controlling shareholders, while the latter tend to act to maximize their share price in the market. As a result, these different types of firms are likely to have correspondingly different attitudes toward exchanges that impose stronger legal protections for minority shareholders. Specifically, recent research shows that those firms that migrate to "high disclosure" exchanges will be disproportionately composed of firms with high growth prospects that require equity finance to be realized (Doidge et al. 2001), while those that decline to migrate will be firms with controlling shareholders who would prefer to maximize their receipt of the private benefits of control, rather than to maximize the share price of their publicly held, minority shares. As a result, a dual equilibrium becomes possible under which "high" and "low" disclosure exchanges persist, side by side, reflecting the fact that firms with both concentrated and dispersed ownership will also persist, side by side.

This picture becomes even more complex once we recognize that the process of competition among markets does not end with the decision of some firms to cross-list abroad. Rather, as national and regional markets lose liquidity and trading volume to international exchanges, a political reaction has sometimes followed. In those countries where the local brokerage and securities industry has been most adversely affected by the migration of cross-listing firms, legislative and regulatory reforms have been recently adopted seeking to raise governance and disclosure standards in order to stem the flight of firms and trading to foreign markets. This political response is also a form of regulatory competition, although not the sort envisioned by proponents of "issuer choice." As a result, the ability of controlling shareholders in at least some emerging markets to retain the traditional private benefits of control may increasingly be challenged. In short, there is a trade-off: firms with concentrated ownership may wish to persist in their traditional system of corporate governance, but the viability of their market is threatened unless the exodus of trading to international exchanges can be stemmed.

Organizationally, this essay is divided into five parts. Part I begins with an overview of developments in the international securities markets, with a particular focus on the appearance and development of the cross-listing phenomenon. Part II then turns to the obvious questions that the rapid growth in international cross-listings poses: why do firms cross-list? What is the source of the gains that cross-listing produces for these firms? Two competing explanations will be assessed: (1) a market segmentation explanation, and (2) a corporate governance or "bonding" hypothesis. Once, it was assumed that cross-listing was basically a means of integrating segmented markets and thus enabling the issuer to access trapped pools of liquidity. A newer interpretation is today emerging that cross-listing may also be a bonding mechanism by which firms incorporated in a jurisdiction with weak protection of minority rights or poor enforcement mechanisms can *voluntarily* subject themselves to higher disclosure standards and stricter enforcement in order to attract investors who would otherwise be reluctant to invest (or who would discount such stocks to reflect the risk of minority expropriation) (see Coffee 1999; Stultz 1999). Although both explanations have some validity, the second or "bonding" explanation has the greater predictive power for the future, because the barriers that once segmented markets have largely eroded, thus reducing the need for issuers to enter distant markets to access trapped pools of liquidity.

Parts III and IV focus on the changes impacting securities markets globally and what strategies individual exchanges can pursue to become more successful competitors. Part V examines the new form of regulatory competition that appears to be developing and ultimately recommends what the author terms an "exit-less" model for regulatory competition.

I. An Overview of Market Competition

Head-to-head, intermarket competition among stock exchanges was and remains rare.[3] In the past, most firms simply listed on their home country exchange, which was generally a public or a quasi-public entity that possessed a *de facto* monopoly. Historians can point to a few counterexamples (see. e.g., DiNoia 2001), but these prove little.

A. *Cross-listing: The Dominant Competitive Technique*

By far, the principal mechanism that produces competition among market centers has been the issuer's decision to cross-list its stock on a foreign exchange, typically in the United States. Cross-listing on a United States exchange is usually effected by the issuer first establishing a depository receipts facility (typically, with a major U.S. bank). The bank will hold shares of the foreign issuer and issue depository receipts to U.S. investors, who will thereby achieve the convenience of dollar-denominated trading. These depository receipts then may (or may not) be listed on a U.S. exchange or Nasdaq.

During the 1990s, the popularity of American Depository Receipts (ADRs) soared. In 1990, 352 depository receipt programs from 24 countries were in effect in the United States, but by 1999, this number had grown to

1,800 programs from 78 countries—an increase of more than 500 percent (Claessens et al. 2000: 17). The combined market capitalization of these companies exceeded $6 trillion at the end of 1999 (ibid.). Correspondingly, the number of foreign companies listed on the two principal U.S. stock markets (the NYSE and Nasdaq) grew from 170 in 1990 to more than 750 in 2000 (or roughly a 450 percent increase) (Davis and Marquis 2001). As of April, 2001, more than 970 non-U.S. firms were listed on the NYSE, Nasdaq or the Amex (Gruson 2001: 187). During the 1990s, trading of ADRs grew by 22 percent a year, reaching $758 billion in 1999 (Davis and Marquis 2001). While depository receipts are primarily used simply to list a stock in a foreign market, their listings can also be accompanied by equity offerings in the foreign market. In 1999 alone, a record $22 billion was raised in the U.S. markets through the issuance of depository receipts, which brought the total equity capital raised during the 1990s through this method to $133 billion (ibid.).

The impact of cross-listings has been particularly pronounced on the NYSE. As table 13.1 below shows, foreign listings on the NYSE have grown from approximately 2 percent of all NYSE listings in 1975 and just over 5 percent in the early 1990s to nearly 17 percent by 2002. As the table also indicates, foreign listings have more than quadrupled since 1990, while domestic listings on the NYSE have actually declined every year since 1998.

The NYSE's recent inability to attract a net increase in domestic listings, while its foreign listings have soared over the same period, suggests that a NYSE listing does something for a foreign issuer that it does not do for a domestic issuer. Within the U.S., the NYSE's trading technology (which still relies on an open outcry system on an actual trading floor and is significantly less computerized than its chief rival, Nasdaq) strikes many as relatively antiquated, and firms listed on Nasdaq have shown less interest in recent years in moving up to the NYSE once eligible for listing there. But for the foreign issuer, the NYSE still offers a critical advantage: its reputation as the leading repository of high disclosure standards and market transparency. Here, it clearly outranks its leading international competitor for listings, the London Stock Exchange (LSE). The NYSE's relative success against the LSE suggests that reputation may be more important than technology—at least for firms that cross-list.

Why did the rate of foreign listings in the U.S. suddenly accelerate in the 1990s? Initially, the sudden growth in popularity of ADRs in the early 1990s was a consequence of state privatizations of formerly state-owned enter-

TABLE 13.1 Foreign Listed Companies on the New York Stock Exchange

Year	Total Listing	Foreign	Domestic	Foreign listings as % of total listings
1975	1557	33	1524	02.12%
1980	1570	37	1533	02.35%
1985	1541	54	1487	03.5%
1990	1174	96	1678	05.4%
1991	1885	105	1780	05.6%
1992	2089	120	1969	05.7%
1993	2361	153	2208	06.5%
1994	2570	216	2354	08.4%
1995	2675	247	2428	09.0%
1996	2907	304	2603	10.5%
1997	3047	356	2691	11.7%
1998	3114	379	2735	12.2%
1999	3025	406	2617	13.4%
2000	2862	434	2428	15.2%
2001	2798	462	2336	16.5%
June 30, 2002	2796	468	2328	16.8%

Source: This table is an abbreviated version of a table in Macey and O'Hara (2001). Additional data have been added for 2001 and 2002, which is taken from the NYSE's website.

prises, which swept across Europe and South America, beginning in the late 1980s. More generally, however, there was a world-wide explosive growth in stock market capitalization during the 1990s. Expressed in terms of the ratio of market capitalization to GDP, Claessens et al. (2002: 11) find that this ratio increased from a mean (median) percentage of 31 (18) percent in 1990 to 62 (34) percent in 2000. While rich countries outperformed poor countries, the direction was positive everywhere.

1. *The Impact on Local Markets.* As stock markets grew exponentially during the 1990s, firms listed in the local market also listed abroad. Indeed, the ratio of market capitalization listed abroad to total market capitalization rose even more dramatically than did the ratio of market capitalization to GDP, particularly in emerging markets (ibid.). Although a foreign listing does not necessarily imply that trading will also shift to the foreign market, trading during the 1990s did in fact follow the migration of listings, at least in the

case of "middle-income" countries (which category includes most emerging market economies in Asia and Latin America). For these countries, the ratio of trading abroad to total trading rose over the decade of the 1990s "from a few percentage points to some 40 percent in 2000" (ibid.: 13).

On the positive side of the ledger, foreign listings enabled firms in emerging markets to raise vast amounts of equity capital. On the negative side of the ledger, the adverse impact on local markets from cross-listings comes into clearest focus when we examine the special case of Latin American markets. In 1989, only two Latin American companies were cross-listed, but by January, 1999, this number had grown to 106 (Hargis 2000). This increase seems best explained by the fact that companies found, over this period, that cross-listing increased the value of their firm and enhanced the liquidity of their stock (Miller 1999). Indeed, the market capitalization of the four principal Latin American stock exchanges soared from $66 billion in 1990 to $439 billion in 1996 (or over 650 percent).

But, along the way, something else happened: stock turnover increased, and trading migrated from Latin American countries to the United States. By 1999, over 87 percent, 54 percent, 62 percent and 71 percent of the Mexican, Argentine, Chilean and Brazilian stock market indices, respectively, were available for trading in the United States in the form of ADRs (Hargis 2000: 103). Even more dramatically, trading moved to the United States, as table 13.2 shows:

If one looks at the year 1995, one sees from this table that the value of Mexican, Argentine, and Chilean ADRs traded in the United States was greater than the total value of all stocks traded in their respective domestic markets in that year. Only Brazil seemed exempt from this domination, and, even in its case, 1996 was the first year in which U.S. trading became proportionately significant (it has since increased substantially).

2. Who Cross-Lists? The evidence shows that firms establishing depository facilities in the United States come heavily from emerging market economies (Miller 1999). In 2001, when ADR issuances fell sharply in the wake of terrorism and uncertainty, emerging market issuers accounted for 73 percent of new ADR issuances, with Asian companies representing more than half this total (Karmin 2001). A basic difference also seems to distinguish the motivation for cross-listings: European countries often cross-list in the U.S. to gain a currency with which they can make stock-for-stock acquisitions of U.S. companies, whereas emerging market companies tend to be interested simply in raising equity capital.

TABLE 13.2 Growth in U.S. Trading In Proportion to Domestic Trading
(in millions)

	1990	1993	1994	1995	1996
Argentina					
Domestic trading value:	852	10,339	11,372	4,594	4,382
U.S. trading value:	0	6,125	12,612	15,679	12,445
Turnover ratio (%)	26.1	37.4	65.0	53.6	37.7
Brazil					
Domestic trading value:	5,598	57,409	109,498	79,186	112,108
U.S. trading value:	0	96	284	3,284	25,801
Turnover ratio (%)	34.2	57.8	58.0	55.9	63.2
Chile					
Domestic trading value:	783	2,796	5,263	11,072	8,460
U.S. trading value:	92	2,369	7,210	11,600	9,584
Turnover ratio (%)	6.4	11.6	18.3	30.7	27.3
Mexico					
Domestic trading value:	12,212	62,454	82,964	34,377	43,040
U.S. trading value:	2,577	37,307	83,496	54,400	29,391
Turnover ratio (%)	45.2	49.7	127.8	97.9	67.9

Source: This table is taken from a fuller table in Hargis (2000: 102).

In this light, the Latin American experience, which saw trading also migrate to the U.S. in the wake of the earlier migration of listings, may also generalize to other emerging market issuers, but not to European issuers. On the other hand, Latin America may be unique in that trading on its exchanges overlaps in time closely with the trading hours of U.S. markets. This is important because the presence or absence of "flow back" (i.e., the return of trading to the home country) probably predicts the degree to which a jurisdiction is pressured to reform its corporate governance in the wake of issuers migrating to the U.S. (see Pulatkonak and Sofianos 1999).

B. IPOs in International Markets

Issuers can go one step beyond cross-listing on a foreign exchange; they can do their initial public offering and listing on such an exchange and simply ignore their host country exchanges. This would not seem a logical step for most young companies because they have greater visibility in their home country, where price discovery can naturally occur more quickly and with lower transaction costs. Nonetheless, the case of Israeli firms shows that it is possible for firms in one country to abandon their home market and adopt the U.S. market, as approximately 96 Israeli firms are now listed on Nasdaq (Rock 2001).

C. Satellite Markets and Market Networks

A final mechanism for increased competition among market centers involves exporting the international market to other areas of the world through satellite operations or a network of affiliations. Although Nasdaq has essentially done this, opening branches in Europe and Japan, the success of this tactic remains in doubt, both because it involves significant startup and operating costs and because it encounters resistance from entrenched local interests. Clearly, it is a strategy beyond the financial capacity of many exchanges, which generally have limited capital resources.

In this light, the alternative and more logical means of extending the competitive range of an exchange may be to buy, merge, or affiliate with the leading local exchange. This appears to be the New York Stock Exchange's strategy: namely, to negotiate affiliations with other exchanges and seek cross-listings. Probably the leading example of growth through merger is Euronext, a combination of the Paris, Amsterdam, and Brussels exchanges, which the Lisbon exchange is also scheduled to join in 2002. Almost concomitantly with the creation of Euronext, the Deutsche Boerse and the London Stock Exchange negotiated a similar merger, only to see it ultimately collapse over control issues. O.M. Gruppen Inc., the owner of the Swedish exchange, later made an unsuccessful hostile bid for the London Stock Exchange, thereby foreshadowing the likelihood that as exchanges are privatized, their control may become increasingly contestable in the market.

Market consolidation—either through mergers or, more likely, through network alliances—seems the most likely scenario for the future, with relatively few exchanges seeking to cross national borders and establish outposts in foreign jurisdictions. Over the near future, affiliations among market centers may increase and begin to be negotiated with the same competitive intensity as were diplomatic alliances in the nineteenth century—in both cases based primarily on the fear that those who are left out will become the most vulnerable.

II. Why Do Firms Cross-List?: The Competing Explanations

To this point, it has been argued that cross-listing is the dynamic and destabilizing force that will move liquidity from local exchanges to international "super-markets," thereby impelling a consolidation among market centers. But this explanation leads to an obvious further question: what motivates firms to cross-list?

The answer may seem obvious: firms can increase their value through cross-listing. The evidence here is relatively clear (see Doidge et al. 2001; Miller 1999; Foerster and Karolyi 1999). But this answer only leads to a further question: why do stock prices increase when firms cross-list? Here, there are two competing explanations, one old and one new. The traditional explanation was that cross-listing broke down market segmentations and allowed the firm to reach trapped pools of liquidity (e.g., Jayaraman et al. 1993; Forester and Karolyi 1999). Segmentation of markets because of investment barriers (e.g., taxes, regulatory restrictions, or informational constraints) creates an incentive for firms to cross-list in order to achieve market integration. Economic theory has long suggested that stock prices should rise for firms in segmented markets that cross-list (see e.g., Merton 1987). A variation on this basic theory has suggested that, as cross-listing increases the shareholder base, the firm's risk is shared among more shareholders, which reduces the firm's cost of capital (Foerster and Karolyi 1999: 988–95). For a time, the empirical evidence seemed to confirm this explanation because abnormal returns incurred by cross-listing firms seemed to rise and then decline post-listing (ibid.: 993–95). Until recently, little evidence suggested that a dual listing actually increased firm value (Miller 1999: 104).

But at least one recent study has found a different pattern: cross-listing results in positive abnormal returns that are statistically significant and that do not dissipate post-listing (ibid.). Unlike earlier studies, this study focused on the announcement date of the decision to cross-list, not the actual listing date. The announcement date is clearly the theoretically more appropriate date because the market should react to news of the expected improvement, and frequently there is an appreciable delay between the announcement and the actual listing. In addition, this study found that the abnormal returns were considerably greater in magnitude when the firm cross-listed on the NYSE or Nasdaq than when the firm just established a depository receipt facility in the United States and listed only on an over-the-counter market. Although these findings are not necessarily inconsistent with the market segmentation hypothesis, they better fit an alternative hypothesis that this essay will call the "bonding hypothesis."

A. The Bonding Hypothesis

Essentially, the bonding hypothesis posits that cross-listing on a United States market is a strategy by which the firm credibly commits itself to respect minority shareholder rights and to provide more complete disclosure. Listing on a U.S. exchange has this effect because (i) the listing firm becomes subject to the enforcement powers of the SEC; (ii) investors acquire the ability to exercise effective and low-cost legal remedies (such as a class action and the derivative action) that are not available in the firm's home jurisdiction; (iii) the entry into the U.S. commits the firm to provide more complete financial information and to reconcile its financial statements to U.S. generally accepted accounting principles (GAAP); (iv) securities analysts will more closely monitor the firm once it cross-lists; and (v) institutional investors can and do negotiate minority protections if the firm wishes to make an initial public offering in the U.S.

Beyond the strictly legal requirements, entry into the U.S. equity markets also exposes the foreign issuer to the scrutiny of "reputational intermediaries," including U.S. underwriters (if the issuer undertakes an initial public offering in the U.S., as is frequently the case), auditors, debt rating agencies, and securities analysts. Finally, the foreign issuer becomes subject to any listing requirements imposed by the U.S. exchange on which it lists. Although U.S. exchanges do impose significant corporate governance requirements on domestic firms that regulate board structure and protect shareholder voting rights, they have largely waived these substantive corporate governance requirements in the case of foreign issuers (American Bar Association 2002). The SEC has acquiesced in this pattern.[4] As result, such increased minority protection as results from listing in the U.S. comes principally from SEC disclosure requirements and from public and private enforcement, but not from the U.S. exchanges, themselves. Indeed, the broad exemption afforded by U.S. exchanges to foreign issuers from the listing requirements that they apply to domestic companies represents a new and important barrier to efforts by emerging markets to upgrade their corporate governance standards.

Because the only mandatory changes incident to entering the U.S. markets relate to disclosure, the bonding hypothesis must postulate that improved disclosure can be a functional substitute (albeit an imperfect one) for higher substantive standards of corporate governance. To the extent that this premise is accepted, then listing in the United States resembles a bonding mechanism, which reduces the potential for the expropriation of minority investors. This essay will both defend this proposition that enhanced disclosure can be a second-best substitute for governance reform and argue that entry into the U.S. markets should require foreign issuers to meet the local governance standards applicable to domestic companies.

As a matter of theory, the idea that a credible promise of improved disclosure should produce a positive stock price reaction is neither surprising nor unorthodox. Economic theory has long predicted that the more credibly a firm commits itself to increased levels of disclosure, the more this action should reduce the informational asymmetry component of the firm's cost of capital (Diamond and Verrechia 1991; Baiman and Verrechia 1996).

B. The Case for Bonding

Evidence supporting the bonding hypothesis tends to fall under four distinct headings, each of which will briefly be examined.

1. *The Market Reaction to Cross-listings.* An initial source of evidence consists of studies of the stock market's reaction to a U.S. cross-listing by a foreign firm. Although there are numerous such studies, most do not consider the possibility that a U.S. cross-listing serves to protect and assure minority investors, and only one study has carefully focused on the market reaction around the announcement date, rather than the often much later date of the actual listing. Miller (1999: 111) found positive abnormal returns on the announcement of a prospective U.S. listing, without any subsequent post-listing dissipation of those returns. Alone, this is significant because proponents of the segmentation hypothesis have long interpreted their theory to predict that post-listing expected returns would decline because investors would accept a reduced rate of return with greater liquidity. More importantly, Miller (1999) also found that the stock price performance of foreign firms that established a depository receipt facility depended heavily on

whether they also listed on an exchange or Nasdaq. Those that did not experienced only modest positive abnormal returns, while, in sharp contrast, those that also listed on the NYSE or Nasdaq experienced much larger positive abnormal returns, which were in fact more than double those of the firms that did not list. Finally, foreign firms that only did private placements under Rule 144A in the U.S. market and then listed on PORTAL, a special electronic market restricted to large institutional investors, had the smallest abnormal returns.

Why are these differences significant? Here, it is necessary to understand that a foreign firm wishing to access the U.S. capital markets by establishing a depository receipt facility has a choice of essentially four options. First, it can establish only a "Level I facility," which means that while a U.S. bank, or other agent, will hold its shares and issue receipts reflecting interests in them to investors, trading in these receipts will be conducted only on the over-the-counter market (typically, in the so-called "pink sheet" market). Secondly, the foreign firm can again establish a depository receipt facility, but now the firm lists its ADR securities on an exchange or Nasdaq (this is called a "Level II" facility). Third, the foreign firm can establish the same depository facility, list its securities, and in addition conduct an underwritten public offering in the U.S. markets—in effect, entering the primary market as well as the secondary market (this is known as a "Level III" facility). Finally, one last alternative is to conduct a Rule 144A private offering (which does not entail SEC registration or sales to public retail investors) and then list these securities on PORTAL, which is a private electronic market on which only very large institutional investors can trade (who are known as "Qualified Institutional Buyers" or "QIBs").[5] This last technique is sometimes referred to as a "RADR" (that is, a Rule 144A offering of ADRs), and it does not involve any entry into the public markets (either the primary or secondary markets) in the U.S.

Legally, there are important differences between these various levels. Basically, firms that establish only a depository facility without listing on an exchange or Nasdaq (a "Level I" facility in the standard parlance of securities lawyers) are not required to become "reporting companies" under the U.S.'s federal securities laws, need not reconcile their financial statements in accordance with U.S. GAAP, and need not file Form 20-F with the SEC.[6] Rather, an exemptive SEC rule (Rule 12g3–2[b]) permits unlisted foreign private issuers to simply continue to file the same documents that they file with their home country regulator and/or stock exchange with the SEC. In short, from a corporate governance perspective, little of significance happens when only a Level I facility is created; there is no upgrading in the quality of financial disclosure and no bonding of any consequence. In contrast, when a foreign firm lists on a U.S. stock exchange or with Nasdaq, it must become a reporting company, must annually file Form 20-F with the SEC, and must reconcile its financial statements to U.S. GAAP. In addition, it becomes subject to SEC oversight and to private enforcement in the U.S. courts through class and derivative actions. In short, there are meaningful corporate governance changes, and thus the Miller (1999) findings support the interpretation that the market has responded to these changes by increasing the firm's share price.

Finally, when a foreign firm both establishes a depository facility in the U.S., lists on a stock exchange, and makes a public offering of securities in the U.S. (i.e., a Level III facility), Miller (1999: 117) found a much stronger positive market reaction than when the firm simply listed on an exchange or Nasdaq (i.e., a Level II facility). Intriguingly, this is in sharp contrast to the normal U.S. experience in which public firms announcing a public offering of equity typically experience an abnormal *negative* stock price movement (Masulis and Korwar 1998). Further complicating the picture is another finding in Miller (1999): when foreign firms sell equity in the U.S. markets in a private transaction under Rule 144A, there is a negative price reaction, while in contrast U.S. firms increase shareholder wealth on average by making private placements.[7] The apparent paradox then is that while a public sale by a foreign issuer in the U.S. market increases firm value, a private sale does not, whereas the reverse is true in both cases for domestic issuers.

Curious as this pattern may seem, it makes sense from a corporate governance perspective. By making a public registered sale in the U.S., a foreign issuer voluntarily subjects itself to the strict liability provisions of Section 11 of the Securities Act of 1933. In principle, this gives added credibility to what it says (because it faces high liability for any material misrepresentation or omission). In contrast, a foreign issuer that merely lists on the NYSE or Nasdaq faces antifraud liability only under Rule 10b-5, which places on the plaintiff the burden of proving the defendant's fraudulent intent (or "scienter"). The difference between strict liability versus liability only for statements made with fraudulent intent is ultimately a difference in the degree to which the firm has "bonded" itself to tell the truth. Also, a public offering in the U.S. involves the preparation of a detailed registration statement, which will provide more current information than the typical Form 20-F. Arguably, the positive market reaction to a public offering by a foreign firm reflects both the value of more information and enhanced credibility. In contrast, the market segmentation theory cannot explain the sharp increase in stock value that listed firms experience when they make a public offering in the U.S. because market segmentation has already been broken down by the earlier point on which the firm lists on Nasdaq or the NYSE.

2. *The Cross-Listing Premium.* A second source of data involves a comparison of the foreign firms that do cross-list in the U.S. versus those that do not. Doidge et al. (2001) focused not on stock price reaction but on the valuations of foreign firms that cross-list in the United States in comparison to a control group that did not so cross-list. They find that "the firms listed in the U.S. have a Tobin's q ratio that exceeds the q ratio of firms from the same country that do not list in the U.S. by 16.5% on average (ibid.: 1). This valuation difference, which they call the "cross-listing premium," depends significantly on the particular form of listing chosen and is largest for exchange-listed firms.

If this evidence does not necessarily favor one explanation over the other (because an exchange listing does increase the firm's liquidity consistent with the market segmentation theory, while requiring the issuer to reconcile its financial statements to U.S. GAAP is consistent with the bonding theory), two additional factors suggest at least a closer fit with the bonding hypothesis:

First, firms "from countries with poorer accounting standards" were found "more likely to list in the U.S." (ibid.: 21). This makes sense from a bonding perspectives, because a U.S. listing would uniquely signal for such companies that their accounting had been upgraded. Second, those firms that not only cross-listed on an exchange but also raised equity capital in connection therewith (i.e., a level III facility) had a "significantly higher premium" (ibid.: 24). Again, because an exchange-listed firm already has high liquidity, this added premium for capital raising efforts suggests that the fact of SEC registration and the use of a U.S. underwriter are interpreted by the market as further and persuasive evidence that the issuer has credibly committed itself to a full disclosure policy.

3. *Post-Listing Behavior: Common Law Firms Versus Civil Law Firms.* Although the foregoing stock price studies did not consciously seek to test the bonding hypothesis (and indeed may have been unaware of it), one study has made a deliberate effort to test this explanation by comparing firms incorporated in common law jurisdictions to civil law jurisdictions. The

premise to this comparison is the well-known assertion made by La Porta et al. (1998; 1999) that the civil law provides inferior protection for minority shareholders. If this is true, then it would also logically follow that firms incorporated in civil law jurisdictions would gain more from cross-listing in the United States.

Reese and Weisbach (2002) examined the composition and post-listing behavior of foreign firms that cross-listed in the United States, and concluded that the evidence tends to corroborate the bonding hypothesis. In particular, firms that cross-list in the United States significantly increase their equity offerings thereafter, and those firms that enter the U.S. from civil law jurisdictions with presumptively weaker corporate governance protections are more likely conduct subsequent offerings in their home jurisdictions. This suggests, they conclude, that while common law firms may come to the U.S. simply to tap its markets, civil law firms come to "bond"—to earn a credential that enables them to sell equity at home.

The reverse side of this coin has been investigated by Pagano et al. (2002), who find that the number of U.S. companies cross-listing in Europe shrank over the 1986 to 1997 interval (despite continued expansion by U.S. firms in Europe). Moreover, European firms cross-listing in the U.S. behaved very differently from European firms cross-listing on other European exchanges. European firms cross-listing in the U.S. pursued a strategy of rapid expansion fueled by high leverage before the listing and made large equity offerings after the listing. They also tended to be in high-tech industries. In contrast, European firms cross-listing in Europe did not grow at a more rapid rate than a control group and did not tend to make equity offerings after the offering, but rather increased their leverage after the cross-listing. They conclude that "the motivation for a U.S. listing appears to be the need for an equity infusion by rapidly expanding, highly leveraged companies that plan to expand their sales internationally and/or belong to high-tech industries" (ibid.: 29). Although this finding is consistent with the bonding hypothesis, it suggests that those firms that enter the U.S. market from a particular country differ distinctively from those firms in that same country that do not enter the U.S., quite apart from the fact that those that do enter the U.S. may provide greater legal protection or more credible disclosure to their shareholders. As next discussed, this *ex ante* difference between listing and non-listing firms requires some reinterpretation of the bonding thesis.

4. Flow back and Market Share. That a foreign firm lists on the NYSE or Nasdaq does not imply that its common stock will principally trade there (as opposed to on its home country exchange). In most cases, the allocation of trading between the NYSE and the home country exchange is constrained by an inherent limitation in the nature of the securities traded: the NYSE will trade the issuer's ADRs, while the home country exchange will trade the issuer's ordinary shares. This was not the case, however, when DaimlerBenz AG merged in a share-for-share exchange with Chrysler Corporation in 1998. Rather, DaimlerBenz carefully designed a new security—a Global Registered Share—that could trade and settle on both the NYSE and the Frankfurt Stock Exchange (and other exchanges). Freed from the usual constraints that restrict flow back, 95 percent of the trading in the DaimlerChrysler promptly flowed back to Frankfurt. Yet, DaimlerBenz had elaborately negotiated its listing on the NYSE only a few years earlier and had undergone the painful experience of converting its earnings from German to U.S. GAAP, which transition had turned a reported profit (under German principles) into a loss (under U.S. GAAP). In short, Daimler management saw a U.S. listing as important to it, but its shareholders still preferred to trade in Germany. Such evidence suggests that, although the U.S. listing was useful to Daimler, its value lay not in breaking down market segmentation or in improving liquidity, but in serving as a mechanism for bonding. Without a NYSE listing, Daimler could not have made a major U.S. acquisition for stock, because U.S. shareholders would not be satisfied with holding a foreign, risky, and illiquid security in lieu of their former Chrysler shares. Still, the need to assure U.S. shareholders that they were protected against expropriation did not require that trading actually occur in the U.S., and it quickly migrated back to Germany.

This phenomenon of "flow back" thus supports the bonding hypothesis, because it shows that the value of a U.S. listing may have little to do with improving liquidity. However, it also implies that a U.S. exchange may have little incentive to cause foreign issuers to bond in this fashion, because the U.S. exchange does not necessarily capture the value of the trading in that stock.

C. The Case Against Bonding

The simple bonding story also has its critics, who raise variations on the following themes:

1. Litigation Risk. One skeptical response has been that increased enforcement risk associated with a U.S. listing has been exaggerated. A detailed study by Siegel (2001) argues that SEC actions against foreign firms listed in the U.S. have been rare.

This evidence is, however, far from dispositive, either on the empirical or theoretical level. First, the SEC has recently brought high-profile enforcement actions against foreign firms listed on U.S. exchanges, and private class actions involving foreign companies listed in the United States have similarly been filed and settled at significant cost to the foreign defendants. Second, as with other administrative agencies, the SEC's litigated actions resemble the tip of the proverbial iceberg. More enforcement occurs through informal contacts, warnings, and administrative enforcement than through litigated actions.

On the level of theory, it is a fundamental mistake to believe that the deterrent threat of a legal standard can be reliably inferred from evidence about the actual rate of apprehension or the actual severity of sanctions. Deterrence theorists have long recognized that the population to be deterred has only limited and generally inaccurate knowledge of the "true probabilities" of a detection (Zimring and Hawkins 1973). More important is the manner in which the legal threat is communicated. Here, the corporate bar in the United States is the government's natural ally, because it maximizes its own importance by focusing its client on the possibility of SEC enforcement (and thus on the need to consult closely with U.S. counsel). Moreover, the basic message communicated by U.S. counsel that there are legal risks associated with entering the U.S. is one that much of the world already understands, because the United States is widely perceived by foreign firms and their officers as a litigation-crazed environment in which almost any dispute ends up in court. Overstated as this perception possibly may be, it is the subjective perception that counts for deterrence purposes.

Although perceptions can be debated, harder, more quantitative evidence also exists that entry into the U.S. capital markets exposes the foreign firm to a significantly heightened risk of litigation. Seetharaman et al. (2002) find that when U.K. firms access the U.S. capital markets, their auditors raise their fees, and the increase reflects the difference in risk across the two legal regimes. Further, no such increase occurs when U.K. firms access other capital markets. Because auditors are only secondarily liable (with the issuer being the primary violator in a securities fraud case), then, if auditors charge more because of U.S. liability exposure, it logically follows that the issuer also faces an equivalent or greater increase in its exposure to liability. Finally, because the U.K. legal system shares obvious similarities with the U.S. system, it also seems logical that companies incorporated in civil law countries, which lack any such similarities, would experience an even greater relative increase in their litigation exposure on entry into the U.S. capital market.

Accordingly, even if some foreign firms still engage in fraud after cross-listing in the U.S., most firms (and their auditors) perceive themselves as exposed to significantly greater litigation risk on entry to the U.S. capital markets. All that is necessary for the bonding hypothesis to have validity is that the defendant's perceived risk of liability rises at least marginally with its entry into the U.S. markets, not that the SEC or private enforcers will always be omniscient or vigilant policemen. If, as a result, the controlling persons of the foreign issuer provide superior disclosure or consume less private benefits of control, even if they do so only marginally upon their firm's entry into the U.S., then the share value of the public shares in such companies should logically rise (and it does).

2. *The Comparability Problem.* A second problem with the simple bonding story may require greater reformulation of this thesis. Here, the problem is that when we compare firms that cross-list into the U.S. from any given country with those firms in that same country that do not, we are essentially comparing apples and oranges. Even prior to their entry into the U.S. markets, these two classes of firms were different. Recent studies suggest that that firms cross-listing in the U.S. have higher growth prospects (and hence higher a Tobin's q) (Doidge et al. 2001; Pagano et al. 1999).

This finding makes obvious sense because it explains a motivation for cross-listing: to obtain the higher valuations that those growth prospects would command if the issuer's public statements were deemed credible by the market. The firm with such prospects needs the certification that entry into the U.S. market provides far more than does the firm without such prospects. Also, such an issuer may need an equity infusion in order to finance those growth prospects, and this will be obtained with less dilution if the issuer provides its new minority shareholders with superior legal protections. Both these reasons in turn explain why controlling shareholders might be willing to forego some private benefits of control: namely, they expect to gain more from enhanced valuations than they lose in private benefits.

Yet, this interpretation implies that firms cross-listing into the U.S. receive higher valuations because they have superior growth prospects. The implicit claim by cross-listing firms that they have high growth prospects is made credible precisely because the controlling shareholders will be sacrificing some measure of private benefits. Hence, the positive stock price reaction to cross-listing in the U.S. is not exclusively a reaction to bonding. Rather it is mixed response to bonding (i.e., superior legal protections) and the implicit signal of superior earnings growth. No simple formula seems possible by which to allocate the stock price reaction between these two categories.

This interpretation suggests that the bonding hypothesis explains some of the motivation to list on a U.S. exchange or Nasdaq, but that we cannot measure with precision the actual price reaction attributable to bonding.

3. *The Market Bubble Explanation.* Finally, one last reason for skepticism about bonding must be at least acknowledged. Some of the motivation to cross-list in the U.S. could be explained by the claim that the equity market in the United States experienced a bubble during the latter half of the last decade. On this premise, foreign issuers rushed to cross-list in the U.S. to participate in stock market valuations not attainable elsewhere (because they were irrational). Although this premise could have some partial explanatory power, it cannot easily explain the decade-long migration of foreign issuers to the U.S. Nor has it been only high-tech firms that have cross-listed. Finally, high stock market valuations also characterized other markets outside the United States during this period (emerging markets may have had even more unrealistic valuations prior to the 1997–1998 Asian financial crisis). The bubble hypothesis works only to the extent that there is a relative disparity in valuations between the U.S. and other markets that cross-listing exploits. At most then, the bubble hypothesis should lead us to be cautious about how much of the valuation premium inherent in cross-listing should be attributed to the bonding effect.

III. The Current Competitive Landscape: Can Foreign Markets Compete?

Is the migration of issuers toward international (and mainly U.S.) markets irreversible? Or can foreign markets compete at protecting minority shareholder rights? This section will survey the institutional and legal developments that will shape and constrain the emerging competition among securities markets.

A. The Trend Toward Demutualization

Historically, securities exchanges in the U.S. and generally elsewhere have operated as nonprofit mutual or membership organizations. As such, they behaved more like sluggish monopolies than dynamic entrepreneurs. That pattern is, however, rapidly changing. Since 1993, a number of exchanges have demutualized, and more have announced plans to do so.

What will demutualization imply for competition and consolidation? When organized as a membership or mutual organization, the governance of American stock exchanges generally gave the specialists and certain market-making members control of the price, quality, and range of services offered by the exchange (Karmel 2001). With demutualization comes a more simplified governance structure in which the interests of the new shareholders are likely to dominate over those of the constituent groups within the exchange who formerly exercised veto power. Shareholders in turn will predictably wish to maximize the share value of their investment, and so will look favorably both upon acquisition and merger proposals and innovation generally. This does not mean that such proposals will necessarily be accepted (managements of private corporations in the U.S. and elsewhere have a long history of blocking them), but the rate of merger and acquisition activity seems likely to grow and, independently, the profitability of the exchange will become the dominant consideration.

B. The Shaky Status of Exchanges in Transitional Economies

The prospects for many transitional stock markets are not encouraging. Claessens et al. (2000: 16) predict that even by 2005 and "under the best possible policy outcomes," only six of the twenty-six transitional economies will have securities markets with market capitalizations equal to 25 percent or more of GDP—a level that is more or less the median for other emerging markets today. Market turnover is also predicted to remain low in most transitional economies, with only a minority approaching the 50 percent level needed to assure liquidity (ibid.). Low liquidity then seems an endemic problem for these exchanges.

To achieve economies of scale sufficient to produce decreasing costs in the processing of trades, some estimate that a securities market needs to have a market capitalization in excess of $15 billion (ibid.: 18). On this basis, only four transitional economies are likely to reach this point by 2005: the Czech Republic, Hungary, Poland, and Russia. This analysis suggests that trading costs will remain comparatively high on most smaller markets, further inhibiting their ability to compete on an international level. In turn, this may motivate issuers on these markets to seek other trading venues, even if they are not interested in improving their corporate governance.

This bleak picture does not establish that smaller markets will necessarily fail. For political reasons, including nationalistic pride, some may be subsidized, much as national flag airlines have been. But the combined impact of demutualization and poor economic prospects suggest that others will seek alliances, including mergers. Although mergers have been admittedly rare to this point, a precedent has been set by the three Baltic exchanges (Estonia, Latvia, and Lithuania), which have merged and also established a linkage with the Helsinki Stock Exchange. All in all, it is difficult to describe a future for securities exchanges in traditional economies that does not involve radical consolidation. Even regional exchanges may find it hard to survive—unless they are either (1) subsidized by the state, or (2) establish a "brand name" that attracts listings.

C. A Success Story?: The Experience of New "High Standards" Markets

The foregoing bleak description of the stock markets in transitional economies suggests that the odds are stacked formidably high against any new entrant. But two counter-examples need to be considered before a serious evaluation is possible. In both Germany and Brazil, new "high standards" markets have been recently established by existing exchanges in an effort to halt the migration of listings and trading to the U.S.

1. *The Neuer Markt.* Established in 1997 by its parent, the Deutsche Boerse, the Neuer Markt swiftly became Europe's dominant market for high-growth firms, both in terms of number of listings and market capitalization (Leuz 2001: 8–9). Indeed, in so doing, it has outdistanced earlier established rivals (such as Easdaq, which eventually was acquired by Nasdaq), and has so far successfully resisted Nasdaq's own efforts to achieve dominance in the European market.

Intended as a market for high-growth firms, the Neuer Markt has adopted a unique style by advertising itself as "the most regulated market in Europe"

(Fuhrmans 2000). Whenever possible, it regularly stresses its high disclosure and transparency standards, which it has continued to update. Listing eligibility on the Neuer Markt requires that an issuer: (1) adopt either IAS or U.S. GAAP; (2) publish quarterly financial reports within two months after each quarter; (3) hold at least one analyst conference per year; (4) prepare and publish audited annual financial statements no later than three months after the end of its fiscal year; (5) have a minimum free float of 20 percent; (6) adhere to a six-month lock-up period following its initial public offering before insiders can sell their shares; and (7) disclose all share transactions by managers, the company, and supervisory board members. In addition, the contents of the required IPO prospectus are also elaborately specified (Leuz 2001: 8–9).

In substance, these requirements are more rigorous than those specified either by its parent, the Deutsche Boerse, or, more surprisingly, by the SEC which permits foreign issuers to file only its Form 20-F. The Neuer Markt's strategy initially appeared to work: it quickly grew from only two listed companies in 1997 to 302 in 2000 and acquired a market capitalization of $172 billion in only three years (Fuhrmans 2000). Only a handful of exchanges had larger capitalizations. Still, the Neuer Markt was plagued by scandals and watched its market capitalization fall sharply in 2001 and 2002 with the worldwide decline of high-tech stocks. Interestingly, its major listed companies pressured it for higher standards and the purge of more questionable listed firms (see Boudette and Kueppers 2001). Nonetheless, in 2002, its parent, the Deutsche Boerse, announced its intent to close the Neuer Mart in 2003 and replace it with a new listing section on its own exchange (Landler 2002). Ultimately, the fate of the Neuer Markt probably shows not that heightened listing standards cannot work, but that there are network externalities that link firms listed on the same market and that cause stronger firms to wish to escape association with weaker ones.

2. *The Novo Mercado.* If the Neuer Markt was the product of Europe's desire to emulate Nasdaq and create an indigenous nursery in which to grow young high-tech companies, Brazil's Novo Mercado was the product of the massive migration of local firms to the United States and the consequent decline in liquidity in Latin America markets. The Sao Paulo Stock Exchange (BOVESPA), Brazil's largest, was adversely affected by these developments and perceived the inadequacies in Brazil's protection of minority shareholders to be a principal factor inhibiting the development of its securities market (Jordon and Lubrano 2002: 21).

Frustrated in attempts to secure legislative reform, BOVESPA instead decided to follow the example of the Neuer Markt. Indeed, it invited U.S.

institutional investors to participate in the design of the listing rules for this new exchange in order to assure that they would be "investor friendly" (Karmin and Karp 2002). Its goal was less to create a specialized incubator for high-tech companies than a "high corporate governance" listing section that would be open only to issuers that voluntarily elected to subscribe to its stricter rules.

To list on the Novo Mercado, the issuer has to accept major corporate governance reforms and, among other things, obligate itself not to issue non-voting shares and to grant "tag along" rights under which noncontrolling shareholders would be accorded the same right to sell their shares and on the same terms as a controlling shareholder. Issuers were also given the option of listing on either of a less restrictive Level One and Level Two segments, which intermediate designations required greater disclosure, but not substantive governance reforms (and, in particular, did not ban the use of nonvoting shares). The Novo Mercado's listing rules were officially announced in December 2000, but it was not until February 2002 that the first (and still the only) company listed on its highest listing segment (Jordan and Lubrano 2002: 22), which requires full compliance with its corporate governance reforms. As of April, 2002, some nineteen companies had listed under the less rigorous standards of its Level One category and applications were pending for Level Two, both of which require only greater transparency and disclosure (ibid.).

What does this weak (or at least equivocal) response suggest about the desire to bond? At a minimum, it implies that a new exchange or listing segment will face difficulty in competing with the stronger "reputational brand" of the NYSE. Firms who list on the NYSE also obtain the practical ability to effect an initial public offering, while the feasibility of such an offering remains in doubt in Brazil. Such "high standards" exchanges may therefore appeal only to firms who do not qualify for an NYSE listing or who find the expenses associated with cross-listing to be prohibitive. Yet, it is noteworthy (and perhaps ironic) that the Novo Mercado has essentially leapfrogged the NYSE by precluding the use of nonvoting shares (while the NYSE continues to list foreign firms with nonvoting classes of stock).

D. The "New" Regulatory Competition

The Novo Mercado was essentially a response by the BOVESPA to the inability of Brazil to enact meaningful corporate governance reform legislation. Yet, since 2000, the major Latin American markets—Argentina, Brazil, Chile, and Mexico—have enacted significant corporate governance reform legislation, after decades of inaction (Jordon and Lubrano 2002: 22). Mexico supplies the best illustration of this common pattern. As earlier noted, Mexico experienced a migration of listings and trading volume to the NYSE that was at least as significant as that experienced by Brazil. In response, in April 2002, pursuant to earlier enacted legislation delegating the requisite power to them, Mexico's National Commission on Banking and Securities, in combination with the Mexican Stock Exchange and the Mexican Association of Market Intermediaries, substantially revised its rules on tender offers in order to strengthen the rights of minority shareholders and accord them a proportionate share of control premiums (Authers 2002: 24). Under this reform, nonvoting shares now enjoy full "tag-along" rights in the event of takeover offers. Specifically, the new rules require that all purchases of between 30 and 50 percent of the voting stock must be accompanied by a tender offer for all share classes at the same price, and all offers to acquire more than 50 percent of the voting stock must be accompanied by a tender offer for 100 percent of all shares in all classes. While the rules do not prohibit nonvoting shares, they were intended to create an incentive to cause issuers to abandon their existing structure of multiple share classes, and some issuers have already responded by doing so. In turn, the goal of this effort was to make "local and foreign investors feel more secure about investing in Mexican equities" (ibid.: 24, quoting Renato Grandmont of Deutsche Bank Securities in New York).

Still, the irony in the Mexican experience is that, while the benefits of improved corporate governance will be felt principally by Mexican firms (which in theory should be able to raise more equity and at lower cost with improved governance), the impetus for these reforms has come not from Mexican corporations (which could have adopted them voluntarily), but from the Mexican securities industry (which was the principal loser from cross-listings). The indifference or even hostility of many Mexican firms to corporate governance reform is understandable, because improved governance implies reduced private benefits of control, and controlling shareholders may anticipate that these lost benefits will exceed the value to them of any improvement in their firm's stock price. Nonetheless, political reforms may come for the unexpected reason that the controlling shareholders' self-interest eclipses the local securities market in a globalizing world.

IV. How Markets May Compete: Rival Scenarios

To this point, it has been argued that the world of securities markets is in flux: exchanges are privatizing; issuers are cross-listing; some markets may fail; and others may consolidate by any of several techniques. Finally, the latest development is that some legislatures are responding to the loss of trading to international exchanges by enacting reform legislation. But will this new competition produce a race to the top or to the bottom? As next examined, a plausible case can be made for either scenario.

A. The "Race to the Top" Scenario

The case for governance reform as a strategy to increase the competitiveness of a market center is easily made. Although comparative studies of corporate governance in the United States have not been able to correlate "higher" standards of governance with improved market value, the reverse has been true in the case of emerging markets. Several studies have shown that firms with higher quality governance have higher market values (see Durney and Kim 2002; Black 2001). Similarly, the cost of capital appears to be lower for firms that make fuller disclosure (see, e.g., Doebele 2001: 22).

The "race to the top" scenario must face, however, some important objections. First, exchanges may not benefit by establishing themselves as high quality, "high disclosure" exchanges if the trading in the foreign issuers that list on these exchanges still flows back to the issuer's home country exchange. Such flow back is common, as shown by the DaimlerChrysler experience, and it may accelerate as firms come to replace ADRs with global shares that can settle in either country. If a foreign issuer can list on the NYSE, and yet the majority of the trading in its stock eventually flows back to the issuer's home country exchange, the NYSE gains less from such a listing than from a comparable domestic listing. This may explain why the NYSE has long been more willing to waive listing requirements that it applies to domestic issuers in the case of foreign issuers. Because both it and its dealers gain less from such a listing and because the NYSE must compete with a foreign exchange for trading volume, the NYSE logically has less incentive to pursue or monitor foreign listings.

Second, the increase in stock value associated with listing on a "high disclosure" exchange may mean little to controlling shareholders, who are more focused on retaining the private benefits of control, as next discussed.

B. The "Race to the Bottom" Scenario

The alternative perspective begins with the recognition that firms with controlling shareholders may not wish to upgrade their disclosure or governance practices because controlling shareholders enjoy (and do not wish to reduce) high private benefits of control. For controlling shareholders, what is particularly important is the ability to receive a control premium that is based on their participation in the firm's voting rights, rather than on their typically lower participation in the firm's cash flow. On any given exchange outside the U.S. and the U.K., firms with controlling shareholders are likely to be in the majority and would be able to outvote those firms that wished to upgrade the local exchange's governance or disclosure requirements if these reforms seemed likely to challenge their ability to receive the traditional private benefits of control. Even a privatized exchange would be unlikely to seek to raise its governance standards for listed companies if this effort were likely to cause the delisting of a significant number of listed companies. Hence, a powerful coalition of entrenched forces appears ready to resist governance reform in most markets.

Dealers also may have little innate desire to upgrade transparency or disclosure standards. Bloomfield and O'Hara (2000) note several examples in which nontransparent exchanges seem to have dominated transparent ones. In particular, the London Stock Exchange was able to outcompete the Paris Bourse for large block traders by permitting dealers to delay the reporting of such block transactions for as much as several days. So much of the block trade volume migrated from Paris to London that the Paris Bourse was eventually compelled to change its trade reporting rules to match those of London.

These objections do not imply, however, that the world will remain static; rather, they suggest that there are institutional rigidities that reforms will have to accommodate.

C. Combining the Scenarios: A Mixed World of High and Low Disclosure

Assume for a moment that the controlling shareholders of many listed issuers outside the U.S. and the U.K. would prefer to enjoy the private benefits of control, rather than maximize their market valuations through bonding. On this assumption, can additional "high disclosure" markets emerge?

The answer is that we have already witnessed how a "high disclosure" exchange can appear in such an environment. Both in Europe and Latin America, the appearance of the Neuer Markt and the Novo Mercado, respectively, shows that "low" and "high" disclosure change can coexist. But their creation also shows that the old markets will resist change, as applied to them. Precisely because the Deutsche Boerse, the parent of the Neuer Markt, and BOVESPA, the parent of the Novo Mercado, were unwilling or unable to upgrade their own listing standards significantly, they instead founded new markets, in one case as a wholly owned subsidiary and in the other as a special listing section. In so doing, they offered an additional alternative to their clients without forcing any listed firm to change its governance or face delisting. This approach is likely to be repeated.

For those firms that do list on a Neuer Markt, Novo Mercado, or some similar infant exchange, the rationale for listing will be essentially that the expected gains to their controlling shareholders from being able to finance "high growth" investment opportunities with equity capital exceed the expected losses in foregone private benefits of control. Typically, cross-listing firms will be companies with high growth prospects that require equity capital because they are already highly leveraged. Pagano et al. (1999) report that this was basically the profile of European firms that cross-listed in the United States during the 1986 to 1997 period that they studied.

High growth prospects are not the only reason that a firm might migrate to a "high disclosure" exchange, even at the cost to its controlling shareholders of foregoing some of the private benefits of control that they previously enjoyed. An alternative scenario starts from the fact that, as the worldwide barriers to product market competition have fallen, firms are increasingly forced either to grow to global scale or to accept the fate of being acquired by a competitor (Coffee 1999: 676–83). For example, an auto maker based in Sweden or Germany was faced with the choice, after the integration of the European market, of either expanding its activities to a European-wide scale or expecting that its rivals that did so would soon dwarf it and realize probable economies of scale and scope. The most ambitious firms in the industry might even expand to become world-wide manufacturers (as clearly some U.S., German, and Japanese producers have done). In this process of expansion to global scale, the quickest, most logical mechanism for expansion is the cross-border merger or acquisition. This scenario principally fits many European firms that have recently cross-listed in the U.S., while in contrast emerging markets firms that have cross-listed have been generally smaller and more motivated by the desire to finance high growth opportunities.

On this playing field of cross-border mergers, firms with dispersed ownership that are listed on "high disclosure" exchanges have a distinct advantage. Their stock will predictably trade at less of a discount to reflect the lesser prospect of expropriation by controlling shareholders. Other things being equal, they will find it easier to make acquisitions with equity securities. To be sure, firms with concentrated ownership can make acquisitions for cash, but there may be a ceiling on magnitude of cash acquisitions that are feasible. For example, one has difficulty imagining Daimler acquiring Chrysler for $50 billion in cash, and hence the prior decision of Daimler to list on the New York Stock Exchange may have been a necessary prerequisite to this transaction being accomplished. Other recent large acquisitions (including British Petroleum's 1999 acquisition of Amoco for $48 billion, Ford's purchase of Volvo, and the Exxon/Mobil merger) seem also to strain the limits of practical finance if these were attempted as cash transactions. The point is not simply that stock for stock acquisitions are easier, but that firms that maximize the value of their publicly held shares can make acquisitions at less dilutive cost to themselves. As a result, firms listed on "high disclosure" exchanges are more likely to be the survivors and acquirers, rather than the targets, in the wave of acquisitions that the drive for global scale entails.

Even if "high disclosure" exchanges can thus attract listings from high growth or acquisition-oriented companies and even if some controlling shareholders would willingly abandon some private benefits of control to achieve these ends, one practical issue remains: Has the U.S. already monopolized the market for "high disclosure" exchanges? The weak response to the creation of the Novo Mercado may suggest that other new entrants will similarly find it hard to compete against the strong "reputational brands" of the NYSE and Nasdaq. Still, a residual market may remain to the extent that many issuers cannot satisfy the listing standards of the NYSE or Nasdaq or find a U.S. listing too costly.[8]

In this light, regional "supermarkets" might develop from exchanges that already had relatively high disclosure standards and could offer greater credibility to companies incorporated in jurisdictions perceived by investors as having weak governance standards. Conversely, firms less interested in attracting minority investors (but still desiring some degree of liquidity) might trade only on lower-disclosure exchanges (such as the Korean or Shanghai Stock Exchanges).

This prediction has two implications: First, high and low disclosure exchanges should both persist, each attracting a different core constituency of issuers. Second, the fiercest competition will likely be between those regional exchanges that aspire to attract dual listings from issuers originally listed on smaller exchanges; for example, the Australian and Singapore exchanges in Asia and the London Stock Exchange and Euronext in Europe seem natural competitors (although natural competitors can, of course, merge or collude). Although single-country exchanges will probably endure in large-market countries (e.g., Korea in Asia or Milan in Italy), they seem likely to progressively lose trading volume to the regional "super-markets." Exchanges in small-market countries (i.e., many of the transitional stock exchanges) will either close, consolidate, or be subsidized by the state. Whatever the outcome, they will lose liquidity.

If some exchanges wish to upgrade their disclosure standards to attract listings (or to organize a subsidiary market that does so), what specific reforms should they adopt? The Neuer Markt has already shown that quarterly reporting and use of U.S. or International GAAP can be required. Beyond these obvious requirements, institutional investors will probably most want "tag along" rights: namely, the right to share on proportionate terms in any control premium. Both the recent Mexican reforms and a similar, although less successful, legislative struggle in Brazil indicate that this is the corporate governance reform that most divides controlling shareholders and institutional shareholders. Effectively, conferring this right reduces the significance of the disparity between cash flow and voting rights that characterize many firms in emerging markets.[9]

Is it realistic to expect exchanges outside the United States to attempt to adopt anything resembling the NYSE's old "one share, one vote" rule? Although both the Novo Mercado and the Mexican Stock Exchange have done so, it is uncertain whether others will follow. Put differently, so long as the NYSE will allow foreign firms to list their nonvoting shares on it, there may be little willingness on the part of cross-listing foreign firms to upgrade their substantive corporate governance.

D. Other Competitors: Who Else Can Offer Bonding Services?

Can any mechanism or certification process other than an exchange listing credibly assure investors that a foreign corporation possessed adequate corporate governance to protect minority investors from expropriation? The answer is almost certainly yes, but whether such new entrants will in fact emerge is very speculative. The most likely scenario under which a new competitor could enter the scene would be if international brokerage firms sought to offer bonding services, in effect certifying to their clients that selected foreign issuers, investigated by them, would protect the expectations of minority shareholders. If such representations were credible, brokerage firms could perform a role that would eliminate the need for foreign issuers to migrate to the U.S. markets. Although the transaction costs might be lower in such an organizational structure, this approach would require investors to accept the idea of brokers as reputational intermediaries, whose assurances carried real value, and it would invite courts to enforce this representation. Today, at least, it seems unlikely that investors would accept, or that brokers would be willing to make, such representations.

V. How Should Regulatory Competition Be Structured?

The efforts by emerging markets to develop new "high disclosure" markets and to upgrade their corporate governance standards is motivated both by the obvious desire to spur economic development and by the equally obvious fear that, in the absence of reform, their securities markets will wither away, as trading migrates to international exchanges. These efforts are complicated, however, by a long-standing position of the U.S. exchanges and the SEC: they do not require foreign firms that list in the U.S. to satisfy the same listing requirements as domestic firms. As a result, when a foreign market such as the Novo Mercado seeks to upgrade its governance standards, it encounters resistance (or at least apathy) from its audience of potential listed companies that know they can list in the U.S. and obtain both greater liquidity and lower governance requirements. The unwillingness of U.S. exchanges to impose governance or voting listing requirements on foreign listed firms thus surfaces as a barrier to improved governance in emerging markets; indeed, it may create a perverse form of regulatory competition in which U.S. exchanges in effect underbid their competitors in terms of substantive governance requirements.

The appropriate response does not require treating all foreign issuers identically with U.S. companies. Rather, the practical test might look to the volume of trading in the U.S. If the foreign issuer has a higher level of trading in the U.S. than on any non-U.S. exchange, then such an issuer should not be able to escape U.S. listing standards that are intended to protect the investors who trade on U.S. exchanges. Conversely, if the issuer listed ADRs on the NYSE that account for, say, only 10 percent of its total trading, the U.S. has less justification for seeking to impose its standards on a security that has only a limited presence in U.S. markets. This proposed standard also recognizes that there could someday develop conflicts between what exchanges in different jurisdictions require, thereby making it impossible to comply with both.

Above all, this approach would end the prospect that U.S. exchanges could become a haven for firms willing to make higher and more detailed disclosure, but still seeking to utilize nonvoting stock in order to preserve the private benefits of control for its controlling shareholders.

Recent experience shows that some forms of regulatory competition may be desirable. For example, the higher disclosure and governance standards adopted by both the Neuer Markt and the Novo Mercado are clearly the product of a competitive desire to attract listings. In addition, recent legislation adopted in Brazil, Mexico, and elsewhere seems clearly intended to upgrade local corporate governance in order to stem the migration of trading and listings abroad (Jordon and Lubrano, 2002). But if this form of regulatory competition is desirable, why should we not go further and adopt the "issuer choice" approach that several commentators have endorsed under which an issuer could trade on any exchange using the disclosure and governance standards of any recognized jurisdiction? This essay will give three brief reasons for rejecting "issuer choice" and then describe an alternative model to issuer choice that it calls "exit-less" regulatory competition:

1. *Complementarity.* Because investors do not evaluate individual stocks in isolation, but rather compare them, it is desirable that any market have a set of common standards and rules that facilitates investor comparison. Under "issuer choice," one U.S.-incorporated company could adopt Italian accounting and disclosure standards; another Greek; and a third Korean. While each set of standards may be internally consistent, they are not externally comparable. Hence, these three companies could have performed very similarly, but appear very different. The claim here is not that one set of accounting standards is necessarily superior to another, but that a common standard is better than diverse and noncomparable standards (Coffee 1999). Similarly, the spread of English as the language of business does not reflect the natural superiority of English, but rather the natural desirability of a

common standard language. To be sure, markets can function without such a common standard, but they are less transparent and more costly for investors to use.

2. Strong Laws Encourage Economic Development. The available empirical evidence suggest that adopting and enforcing a prohibition against insider trading significantly reduces the cost of capital (Bharrachayra and Daouk 2002). Such a finding is consistent with the broader proposition advanced by La Porta el al. (1998; 1999) and others that strong laws protecting minority investors are a precondition to financial development. Given this evidence, consider now the impact of the "issuer choice" approach to securities regulation. If issuers could opt to be governed by a non-U.S. legal regime, even though they were listed on the NYSE, some might well opt for the law of a jurisdiction that does not prohibit insider trading. Proponents of "issuer choice" will, of course, respond that an issuer that did so would be penalized by the market and would experience an appropriate discount in its share value. Perhaps, it would. But this does not respond to the more basic point that an externality has arisen: the immunity conferred on some firms to engage in insider trading may affect the cost of equity capital for all firms trading in that market. Rather than research the laws of numerous jurisdictions, skeptical investors may simply assume that they were vulnerable to insiders misappropriating material, nonpublic information, and so adjust prices downward in response. Moreover, there is also the prospect that the ability of some persons to engage in lawful insider trading may induce others to similarly engage in this behavior, even if it were illegal in their case. In effect, the moral foundations of the norm against insider trading are undercut.[10]

3. Reputational Brands. The foregoing example involving insider trading can be generalized to apply to most other forms of disclosure deficiencies. If some firms are permitted to trade in the market making less than the prescribed level of disclosure, there is a potential effect on other issuers, who may incur a higher cost of equity capital as a result. Essentially, this is why the NYSE developed listing standards, beginning in the late nineteenth century. Put simply, it recognized that to develop a "reputational brand," it had to exclude those unwilling or unable to comply with its "high quality" standards (Coffee 2001a). In short, issuer choice is incompatible with the idea of a market developing a "high standards" reputation. Yet, ironically, only those markets that have developed such a brand name have developed into major international market centers with deep liquidity.

Where then does the dividing line lie between desirable and undesirable forms of regulatory competition? Proponents of "issuer choice" favor a form of regulatory arbitrage that is designed to allow firms to escape undesired regulation. Such an approach makes sense from a policy perspective only if one believes firms are systematically subject to overregulation. Yet, the form of regulatory competition that one actually observes today and that is inherent in cross-listing involves opting into higher standards (at least in the case of disclosure rules). This form of regulatory competition can be called "exitless," because the issuer does not escape its home jurisdiction laws and rules. That is, even if the market center to which the issuer cross-lists has lower disclosure standards, the issuer will still be required to make disclosures to its home jurisdiction regulator. This form of competition can generate bonding, but not a regulatory arbitrage designed to weaken legal rules. At best, it is desirable; at worst, it is benign.

Conclusion

One underlying question that has not yet been squarely faced unites many of the themes considered in this essay: How much does law matter? This article's answer is that law matters a lot—but only to some. The cross-listing phenomenon that accelerated during the 1990s shows that many firms do wish to upgrade their corporate governance and for an easily understood reason: to gain access to equity capital, either to finance high growth investment opportunities that could not be financed domestically or to facilitate strategic mergers and acquisitions. Yet other firms that have not cross-listed appear to be indifferent to this prospect of higher market valuation, and again it is for an understandable reason: because higher market valuation would be offset by reduced private benefits of control to their controlling shareholders. The firms that do and do not cross-list appear then to be as different as proverbial apples and oranges. As a result, different forms of securities markets, each catering to a different clientele, appear likely to persist.

Endnotes

This essay has been presented at a variety of workshops and conferences, including the Ninth Annual Singapore Conference on International Business Law, the Law and Economics Workshop at Harvard Law School, the 2002 Ibmec Business School conference in Sao Paulo, Brazil, the 2001 Brookings-Wharton Conference on Financial Services, the Second Annual Asian Corporate Governance Conference in Seoul, Korea in

2002, and the Columbia Law School Conference on "Global Markets, Domestic Institutions: Corporate Law and Governance In a New Era of Cross-Border Deals" in 2002. The author wishes to acknowledge helpful comments from commentators and participants at each of these conferences. A longer version of this chapter was published in the Columbia Law Review (2002).

1. Typically, proponents of "issuer choice" view this approach as initiating a process of regulatory arbitrage that would pare back excessive over-regulation (see Romano 1998; 2001; Choi and Guzman 1998). Contra Fox (1999).

2. This author has been skeptical as to whether this "legal explanation" can truly account for the appearance of the separation of ownership and control in Anglo-American countries (see Coffee 2001a; 2001b). Nonetheless, this author strongly agrees with the thesis that "law matters" and that minority legal protections can affect share value (see Coffee 1999).

3. A distinction needs to be drawn here between competition for listings, which is more common, and competition for trading supremacy in the same security. Thus, the NYSE, Nasdaq and the Amex have long competed for listings, but until recently did not trade the same stocks.

4. See Securities Exchange Act Release No. 24,634 (June 23, 1987).

5. Rule 144A ("Private Resales of Securities to Institutions"), 17 C.F.R. 230.144A, exempts resales made by the initial purchasers of securities to "Qualified Institutional Buyers," who generally must manage a portfolio in excess of $100 million in order to so qualify, from the registration requirements of the Securities Act of 1933. PORTAL is an electronic secondary market operated by the National Association of Securities Dealers (NASD) in which only QIBs may trade.

6. Form 20-F is the SEC form for foreign issuers corresponding to Form 10-K, which domestic issuers must file once they become subject to Section 13 or 15(d) of the Securities Exchange Act of 1934. Unlike domestic issuers, foreign private issuers need only file Form 20-F within six months after the end of their fiscal year. Basically, Form 20-F requires the same financial information as Form 10-K, but permits the foreign issuer to file this information in accordance with non-U.S. GAAP principles, if a reconciliation to U.S. GAAP is included.

7. In contrast, an earlier study of U.S. firms making private placements finds that they result in an average increase in shareholder wealth of 4 percent (Wruck 1989).

8. LaPorta et al. (1998: 512) conclude that "a New York listing is prohibitively expensive for many companies." If so, regional exchanges have a niche.

9. Assume that a firm has both Class A and Class B shares and that only the Class A shares have voting rights, while the cash flow rights belong 25 percent to

Class A and 75 percent to Class B. Today, an acquiring corporation would logically direct its control premium exclusively to the holders of the Class A shares. But if "tag along" rights exist, either under the corporation's charter or applicable law, this premium would have to be shared with the Class B shareholders, with the same premium paid to all. This reform could cost the Class A shareholders 75 percent of the premium that would otherwise have gone to them alone and will predictably be resisted by them.

10. Normative consensus may be the critical factor underlying "strong" corporate governance (Coffee 2001b).

References

American Bar Association. 2002. Section in Business Law, Committee on Federal Regulation of Securities, Special Study on Market Structure, Listing Standards and Corporate Governance (May 17, 2002).

Authers, John. 2002. Mexico Moves to End Class Warfare: New Rules on Tender Offers Will Boost the Voting Rights of Minority Stockholders. *Financial Times*, May 2, 2002.

Baiman, Stanley and Robert E. Verrechia. 1996. The Relation Among Capital Markets, Financial Disclosure, Production Efficiency and Insider Trading. *Journal of Accounting Research* 34: 1–22.

Bhattachayra, Utpal and Hazem Daouk. 2002. The World Price of Insider Trading. *Journal of Finance* 57: 75–108.

Black, Bernard. 2001. Does Corporate Governance Matter?: A Crude Test Using Russian Data. *University of Pennsylvania Law Review* 149: 2131–50.

Bloomfield, Robert and Maureen O'Hara. 2000. Can Transparent Markets Survive? *Journal of Finance* 55: 425–59.

Boudette, Neal and Kueppers, Alfred, Frustrated Neuer Markt Members Push for Tightening Listing Rules. *Wall Street Journal*, July 11, 2001, at C-2.

Choi, Stephen and Andrew Guzman. 1998. Portable Reciprocity: Rethinking the International Reach of Securities Regulation. *Southern California Law Review* 71: 903–51.

Claessens, Stijn, Simeon Djankov and Daniela Klingebeil. 2000. Stock Markets in Transition Economies. World Bank Financial Sector Discussion Paper No. 5 (Sept. 2000).

———, Daniela Klingebeil and Sergio L. Schmukler. 2002. Explaining the Migration of Stocks from Emerging Economies to International Centers (World Bank Working Paper 2002).

Coffee, John C., Jr. 1999. The Future As History: The Prospects for Global Corporate Convergence in Corporate Governance and Its Implications. *Northwestern University Law Review* 93: 641–707.

——. 2001a. The Rise of Dispersed Ownership: The Roles of Law and the State in the Separation of Ownership and Control. *Yale Law Journal* 111: 1–82.

——. 2001b. Do Norms Matter? A Cross-Country Evaluation. *University of Pennsylvania Law Review* 149: 2151–77.

Davis, Gerald F. and Christopher Marquis. 2001. Are U.S. Stock Markets A Pathway to Global Governance Convergence? (Working Paper 2001).

Diamond, Douglas W. and Robert E. Verrechia. 1991. Disclosure, Liquidity and the Cost of Capital. *Journal of Finance* 46: 1325–59.

DiNoia, Carmine. 2001. Competition and Integration Among Stock Exchanges in Europe: Network Effects, Implicit Mergers and Remote Access. *European Financial Management* 7: 39–72.

Doebele, Justin. 2001. We Won't Be Bullied, We'll Sue! *Business Times Singapore*, April 28, 2001, at 22.

Doidge, Craig, G. Andrew Karolyi, and Rene Stulz. 2001. Why Are Foreign Firms Listed in the U.S. Worth More? (Working Paper August, 2001).

Durney, Art and E. Han Kim. 2002. The Effects of Growth Opportunities and External Financing on Corporate Governance: Theory and Evidence (Working Paper 2002).

Foerster, Stephen R. and G. Andrew Karolyi. 1999. The Effects of Market Segmentation and Investor Recognition on Asset Prices: Evidence from Foreign Stocks Listing in the United States. *Journal of Finance* 54: 981–1013.

Fox, Merritt B. 1999. Retaining Mandatory Securities Disclosure: Why Issuer Choice Is Not Investor Empowerment. *Virginia Law Review* 85: 1335–1419.

Fuhrmans, Vanessa. 2000. Playing By the Rules: How Neuer Markt Gets Respect. *Wall Street Journal*, August 21, 2000, at C-1.

Gruson, Michael. 2001. Global Shares of German Corporations and their Dual Listings on the Frankfurt and New York Stock Exchanges. *University of Pennsylvania Journal of International Economic Law* 22: 185–283.

Hargis, Kent. 2000. International Cross-listing and Stock Market Development in Emerging Economies. *International Review of Economics and Finance* 9: 101–22.

Jackson, Howell and Eric Pan. 2001. Regulatory Competition in International Securities Markets: Evidence From Europe in 1999. *Business Lawyer* 56: 653–91.

Jayaraman, Narayanan, Kuldeep Shastri and Kishore Tandon. 1993. The Impact of International Cross Listings on Risk and Return: Evidence from American Depository Receipts. *Journal of Banking and Finance* 17: 91–103.

Jordon, Cally and Mike Lubrano. 2002. How Effective Are Capital Markets in Exerting Governance on Corporates?: Lessons of Recent Experience with Private and Public Legal Rules in Emerging Markets (Working Paper April 2002).

Karmel, Roberta. 2001. The Future of Corporate Governance Listing Requirements. *SMU Law Review* 54: 325–56.

Karmin, Craig. 2001. Foreign Concerns' New Issuances of ADR's Fell Sharply this Year. *Wall Street Journal*. December 19, 2001, at C-13.

—— and Jonathan Karp. 2002. Brazilian Market Tries Friendly Approach. *Wall Street Journal*, May 10, 2002 at C-1.

Landler, Mark. Gernman Technology Stock Market to be Dissolved. *New York Times*, September 27, 2002, at W-1.

La Porta, Rafael, Florencio Lopez-de-Silanes, Andrei Shleifer. 1999. Corporate Ownership Around the World. *Journal of Finance* 54: 471–517.

—— and Robert Vishny. 1998. Law and Finance. *Journal of Political Economy* 106: 1113–55.

Leuz, Christian. 2001. IAS versus U.S. GAAP: A (New) Market Based Comparison (Working Paper 2001).

Macey, Jonathan and Maureen O'Hara. 2001. The Economics of Stock Exchange Listings Fees and Listing Requirements (Working Paper September 2001).

Masulis, Robert W. and Ashok N. Korwar. 1986. Seasoned Equity Offerings: An Empirical Investigation. *Journal of Financial Economics* 15: 91–118.

Merton, Robert. 1987. Presidential Address: A Simple Model of Capital Market Equilibrium With Incomplete Information. *Journal of Finance* 42: 483–510.

Miller, Darius P. 1999. The Market Reaction to International Cross-Listings: Evidence from Depository Receipts. *Journal of Financial Economics* 51: 103–23.

Pagano, Marco, Ailsa Roell, and Josef Zechner. 2002. The Geography of Equitly Listings: Why Do Companies List Aboard? *Journal of Finance* 57: 2651–94.

Pulatkonak, M. and G. Sofianos. 1999. The Distribution of Global Trading in NYSE-Listed Non-U.S. Stock. NYSE Working Paper 99–03 (March 1999).

Reese, William A. and Michael S. Weisbach. 2002. Protection of Minority Shareholder Interests, Cross-Listings in the United States, and Subsequent Equity Offerings. *Journal of Financial Economics* 66: 65–104.

Rock, Edward. 2001. Greenhorns, Yankees and Cosmopolitans: Venture Capital, IPOs, Foreign Firms and U.S. Markets. *Theoretical Inquiries in Law* 2: 711–44.

Romano, Roberta. 1998. Empowering Investors: A Market Approach to Securities Regulation. *Yale Law Journal* 107: 2359–2430.

Seetharaman, Ananth, Ferdinand A. Gull and Stephen G. Lynn. 2002. Litigation Risk and Audit Fees: Evidence from UK Firms Cross-Listed on U.S. Markets. *Journal of Accounting and Economics* 33: 91–115.

Siegel, Jordan. 2001. Can Foreign Firms Bond Themselves Effectively By Submitting to U.S. Law? MIT Working Paper (September 10, 2001).

Stultz, Rene M. 1999. Globalization, Corporate Finance, and the Cost of Capital. *Journal of Applied Corporate Finance* 12(3): 8–25.

Vision Test: Nasdaq's Drive to Build Global Exchange Hits Some Major Potholes. *Wall Street Journal*, June 25, 2001, at C-1

Wruck, Karen. 1989. Equity Ownership Concentration and Firm Value: Evidence from Private Equity Financing. *Journal of Financial Economics* 23: 3–28.

Zimring, Franklin and Gordon Hawkins. 1973. *Deterrence: The Legal Threat in Crime Control*. Chicago: University of Chicago Press.

14 Coming to America?

Venture Capital, Corporate Identity,
and U.S. Securities Law

Edward B. Rock

Venture capital is all the rage. The success of Silicon Valley across all the relevant dimensions has provided a vision of gold at the end of the rainbow. A region with no significant natural resources other than nice weather and a nontrivial risk of earthquakes became the richest borough in the land.

Success breeds imitation. Now, in addition to Silicon Valley, we have Silicon Alley (NY), Silicon Bog (Ireland), Silicon Wadi (Israel), Silicon Fen (Cambridge, England), Silicon Glen (Edinburgh to Glasgow, Scotland), Silicon Alps (Carinthia, Austria), among others (Silicon Wannabes 1999). Social planners everywhere ask how they can establish a venture-capital–fueled startup sector with the dynamism and success of Silicon Valley. Indeed, perhaps worrisomely, it reminds one of the ambition of every nation, fifty years ago, to build a steel industry!

As the burgeoning literature on Silicon Valley and its imitators makes clear, there is no single secret of success, and no obvious way to clone it.[1] One finds more and less successful venture-capital–fueled "clusters" around the U.S. and abroad in very different contexts. While there are significant similarities, there are also different styles.

In this essay, I want to focus on two main issues that have not been addressed in the literature, both of which revolve around the IPO exit option. First, I argue that Taiwan and Israel—the two most important non-U.S. clusters—represent two interestingly different models of international VC financing. As we know, venture capital depends sensitively on the existence of an exit strategy, with the two principal exits being sale to a larger firm and going public on a market that offers sufficient amounts of capital at satisfactory valuations.[2] As I discuss in more detail below, in Taiwan the primary IPO exit route is the local Taiwan Stock Exchange, while in Israel the primary IPO exit route is the NASDAQ. Interestingly, casual empiricism suggests that one does not observe intermediary cases where, say, half of the IPOs are on the local exchange and half on NASDAQ. This pattern is consistent with several different explanations. It could be, I argue, the result of a "separating equilibrium" in which a single market emerges as the preferred exit option. In such a circumstance, high-quality offerings are likely to congregate in a single market, while firms raising capital in other markets will be perceived to be of lower quality. It could also, however, result from simple liquidity or clientele concerns: it could be that the greatest appetite for Taiwan issues has been on the Taiwan Stock Exchange while NASDAQ valuations for Israeli startups typically trump those available on other exchanges. Figuring out which explanation is correct is important in understanding the nature of international competition among stock exchanges.

Second, I argue that for countries that choose (or end up with) the NASDAQ as their primary IPO exit, U.S. securities law assists this process in some surprising and little noticed ways. Using the NASDAQ as an exit option has implications for how a company presents itself to the investor community. In particular, it provides an incentive for firms to "pass" as regular U.S. companies. U.S. securities regulation draws a distinction between U.S. companies and "foreign private issuers," and imposes reduced disclosure obligations on the foreign firm. Although the goal of this regulatory distinction was to make U.S. listings more attractive for existing foreign firms, a happy byproduct is a mechanism for identifying oneself as "American," even when the company's main centers of activity are off shore. As I detail below, this is an aspect of the structure that Israeli companies liberally exploit.

I. Exits

Venture capitalists provide financing and a bundle of non-financial services (Gompers and Lerner 1999). They provide early-stage capital to new enterprises. They provide management advice to the entrepreneurs. They provide industry contacts in the various markets in which the firm operates. In this role, they may provide assistance in making customer introductions (product market); identifying and hiring critical personnel (labor market); and securing additional financing, identifying strategic partners, acquiring other firms or being acquired by them, or tapping public capital markets (capital market).

These noncapital inputs have special value to early-stage companies. As the firm matures, VCs need to exit in order to deploy their capital and expertise elsewhere. In addition, exit is critical to the investors in the VC funds as a way of realizing returns and of measuring VC performance. As a result, exit—either through the sale of the firm to another firm or through an IPO—forms a critical aspect of the venture capital process.

A. Models of Venture Capital Exits: Domestic and Offshore

Venture capital has traditionally been a "local" business. The nonfinancial services provided, including membership on the board of directors, are both labor intensive as well as market specific. Evidence indicates that venture firms tend strongly to invest in companies within an easy drive (Gompers and Lerner 1999: 180–82). As VC has spread and evolved, it has retained this "local" flavor, although what counts as "local" may be industry rather than geographically specific.[3]

But the intrinsically local nature of the VC business does not mean that the exit options need to be local as well. After all, capital is mobile and many markets are international. A priori, there is little reason to think that the range of the exit options should correspond with the scope of the VCs' activities.

The Israeli experience makes this point dramatically. As I've described elsewhere, Israeli venture capitalists and portfolio firms have had success selling portfolio firms to non-Israeli acquirers as well as going public on the NASDAQ (Rock 2001).[4] For Israeli venture capital, the preferred IPO exit option is, without a doubt, the NASDAQ. Although some firms have gone public on the Tel Aviv Stock Exchange (TASE), and other firms on other "technology" exchanges like the Neuer Markt (while it existed) or the London Stock Exchange's New Issue Market, it is clear that the preferred market is the NASDAQ. What is most interesting about this phenomenon is that Israeli venture capital has managed to piggy back onto the NASDAQ and its concomitant advantages: NASDAQ valuations; NASDAQ order flow and liquidity; access to U.S. institutional investors; and NASDAQ-listed shares that can be used for acquisitions.

If Israel provides one model, Taiwan provides another. Taiwan and Israel are two of the more important clusters of technology companies and venture capital. In many ways, they are similar. They both have very active venture capital sectors, which feed into and are fed by a very active technology sector. Both sectors were jump-started through similar government programs. In 1991, the Israeli government established the state owned Yozma Venture Capital Ltd., with total capital of $100 million. Yozma co-invested as a minority partner, investing 40 percent of the total capital of each fund up to $8 million. Moreover, the private partners had an option to buy out Yozma's interest under favorable terms. Observers attribute the establishment of nine prominent funds with about $200 million in capital to the program, which ended in 1997.[5] In Taiwan, the government likewise provided seed funds to prospective venture capital firms, and created tax incentives for the venture capital industry (Saxenian and Li 2002).

Taiwan and Israel are similar across other dimensions as well. In both cases, there are a large number of expatriates who have succeeded as high-tech entrepreneurs in Silicon Valley.[6] In both cases, expatriates have been active in spurring the development of local venture capital. In both cases, "repatriates" and "astronauts" (individuals who live in both Silicon Valley and Taiwan/Israel and spend hours on airplanes moving back and forth) have been important in the development of the local technology sector. In both cases, there is a large pool of technologically sophisticated graduates who, by world standards, are inexpensive.

Yet, despite these similarities, the venture capital sectors are strikingly different when it comes to exit. While Israel piggy-backs onto the NASDAQ, the Taiwanese exit option is largely through the Taiwan Stock Exchange. NASDAQ currently lists eighty-eight "Israeli" companies.[7] Until recently, very few of these even had secondary listings on the Tel Aviv Stock Exchange (Licht 2001). Recently, in order to encourage dual-listings, Israel has changed its law to accept a NASDAQ listing (and the accompanying disclosure required under U.S. securities law) as sufficient to satisfy the requirements for a TASE listing. It is still too early to tell how successful this initiative will be in attracting companies to the TASE. European markets have recently begun to attract Israeli listings, although they are still largely insignificant. For example, as of January 1, 2002, there were eight Israeli companies listed on the Neuer Markt with a total market capitalization of 252 million euros.[8]

By contrast, NASDAQ only identifies three Taiwanese companies (one of which, ASE Test, is actually incorporated in Singapore). Only one of these—ASE Test, a partially owned subsidiary of Advanced Semiconductor Engineering—has in fact done a public offering in the U.S. The other two have a listing through an ADR facility. There are three large publicly traded Taiwanese companies with ADR listings on the NYSE: Taiwan Semiconductor Manufacturing Corporation (TSMC), Advanced Semiconducter Engineering (ASE) and United Microelectronics (UMC).[9] In addition, there are some other companies listed as Singapore companies that are holding companies for Taiwanese firms, such as GigaMedia. Finally, there are some companies listed as "Cayman Island" companies that are in fact holding companies for Taiwanese companies. No matter how one counts, there are not very many Taiwanese companies listed on NASDAQ. The Taiwan Stock Exchange is the prime IPO exit option for Taiwanese technology companies.

One hears a variety of explanations for this difference. Some trace Israel's use of the NASDAQ to the 1994 crash of the Tel Aviv Stock Exchange, from which it has never quite recovered. Others point out that NASDAQ is where the money is.

There are a number of possible explanations for the reliance of Taiwanese venture capital on the Taiwan Stock Exchange for IPO exits. One potential explanation is that valuations on the local exchange were, or are, sufficiently optimistic to make it an attractive market, or at least sufficiently attractive to reduce the pressure to invest resources in developing a path to an alternative market. A second explanation could be that various features of the formal and informal Taiwanese regulatory structure make it difficult for Taiwan companies to go public on a foreign exchange (see Liu this volume).

Regulatory barriers, however, cannot be the full explanation, as there are some Taiwanese companies that choose, and are able, to go public on NASDAQ. The preferred mode seems to be through the establishment of a holding company. For example, both ASE Test, Inc., a $1.3 billion integrated circuit testing company and a part of the Taiwanese ASE Group, and GigaMedia, a Taiwanese broadband company, are Singapore holding companies whose shares are directly listed on the NASDAQ.[10] By contrast, companies like Macronix and Siliconware Precision Industries went public on the TSE, and subsequently obtained dual-listing on NASDAQ through an ADR facility.

One can also find examples of NASDAQ-listed companies whose nationality is ambiguous. A nice example is Integrated Silicon Solutions. Two Taiwanese engineers working in Silicon Valley, K. Y. Han and Jimmy Lee, founded the company, using Asian contacts to raise capital and sell products. Eventually, Han moved back to Taiwan and continued to build the business there. ISSI is incorporated in Delaware, listed on the NASDAQ, and has operations in both Silicon Valley and the Hsinchu science park in Taiwan (Saxenian 1999). NASDAQ does not list it as a "Taiwan" company.

Whatever the full explanation, the Taiwan experience identifies a second model for the development of a non-U.S. venture capital sector. Taiwan's success makes clear that piggy-backing onto NASDAQ is not necessary. Indeed, a variety of factors affect the listing decision. If local valuations are sufficiently "optimistic," one would guess that other factors (language, geographic proximity, familiarity with the regulatory environment) would likely push toward an IPO on local markets.

An interesting potential intermediate model is a regional exit option like the Deutsche Boerse's Neuer Markt, NASDAQ Europe, or the London New Issues Market, which have emerged as European high-tech markets, serving a similar role to NASDAQ. With their European scope, they are neither entirely offshore, like Israel's use of NASDAQ, nor entirely domestic, like Taiwan's use of the TSE.

B. Stickiness and the Implications for Stock Exchange Competition: Market Niches

Now we get to an interesting feature of the different models. In none of these cases does one find an active venture capital sector with more than one IPO exit market: Israel uses NASDAQ; the U.S. uses NASDAQ; Taiwan uses the TSE; Europe seemed to prefer the Neuer Markt until its demise. What one does not observe is a domestic venture capital sector where IPO exits are substantially split among various exit markets (domestic or off shore). What might be going on here?

There are several possible explanations. Developing an IPO exit option is costly. Investors need to develop a comfort level with underwriters, issuers, the quality of disclosure, and other protections. Underwriters need to develop reputations. Venture capitalists need to establish relationships with underwriters, and so forth. In the Israeli context, one finds U.S. institutions

investing in Israeli-based venture capital funds, U.S. investment banks opening offices in Tel Aviv, and hiring U.S. trained Israelis. One likewise finds
U.S. or multinational investment banks developing specialties in the marketing of Israeli securities to U.S. institutional investors.

Once these investments are made, a particular market will assume a certain prominence. This prominence can play out in different ways. First, once
the path is forged, issuers can compare valuations in different markets and
choose the best terms. If, thereafter, one market maintains its prominence, it
may mean that investors on that market are simply willing to pay more. Why
an American institutional investor would be willing to pay more for a share of
an Israeli startup on NASDAQ than on the Tel Aviv Stock Exchange may
reflect nothing more than language, currency effects, and familiarity.

But the salience of the one market paradigm could play out differently. If
issuers go public on some other market, the obvious question in investor's
minds will be "why"? Is it that the people who know—the underwriters on
the principal IPO market—have information leading them to refuse to take
the company public? If the choice to go public on some other market sends
this sort of signal to investors, then issuers will be branded as second rate or
substandard if they go public elsewhere, unless they have a convincing
explanation. This, in turn, will drive firms to try to make it on the preferred
exchange, which will further solidify that exchange's preeminent position.

This story is consistent with the historical developments in both Taiwan
and Israel. One explanation for the migration of Israeli firms to NASDAQ is
the crash of the Tel Aviv Stock Exchange in 1994. This came at a critical
period in the evolution of Israeli venture capital, and its success is in part a
tribute to Israeli venture capitalists' success in finding an alternative exit
option. In other words, the Israeli VCs seem to have made a virtue of necessity.[11] Having paved the way to NASDAQ, Israeli venture capitalists say that
the best companies typically go public on NASDAQ. They take companies
public elsewhere—on the TASE or in Europe—if they cannot make it on
the NASDAQ or if there are special circumstances (e.g., if the product market is in Europe, a European IPO is more likely).

By contrast, the Taiwanese VCs have had a much more favorable exit
option in the local Taiwan Stock Exchange. As a result, they have not had
the same need to invest in building bridges to NASDAQ. The interesting
question is whether Taiwanese firms that seek to go public on NASDAQ
rather than the TSE raise questions in the minds of investors. Are they perceived as inferior to those that go public on the TSE. Alternatively, on the

assumption that it is harder to convince NASDAQ investors than local investors, are they viewed as superior?

If going public on a less salient market sends a negative signal, then it can create stickiness in competition among exchanges (see Coffee, this volume). If this type of signaling actually takes place, then once an exchange establishes itself as a high-quality exchange for IPO listings, its reputation will provide an advantage in its competition with larger and often better financed exchanges. It may be that if NASDAQ had expanded into Europe earlier, it could have become the preeminent European technology exchange. Arriving late, however, it seemed to face an uphill battle in displacing the Neuer Markt, not only because of entrenched interests of market participants, but also possibly because of the signaling effects produced when firms choose to list on a new entrant in the competition among exchanges. This stickiness may partially explain NASDAQ's difficulties in expanding abroad. It should be noted that this is a story about IPOs and not dual listings, which raise substantially different issues.

This stickiness—even if present—should not be exaggerated. At some point, if the Taiwanese VC sector continues to succeed, the local market for IPOs may become saturated. Firms wishing to raise capital may find that they have little choice but to look abroad for other sources of capital, and to invest in paving a path to an alternative market, like NASDAQ. Once that path is paved, the equilibrium may flip, with NASDAQ becoming the preferred IPO exit option.

I now turn to how a company does that.

II. Coming to America

As we have seen, using the NASDAQ as an IPO exit option is hardly necessary for a successful, non-U.S. technology sector. Indeed, it may be that the Israeli practice of going public on NASDAQ simply emerged out of necessity, as the collapse of the TASE in 1994 removed it as a plausible exit option at a critical moment in the development of Israeli venture capital. But the Israeli experience proves that the barriers to cross-border capital flows are not so high that it is impossible for a start-up in country X to expect to go public on the NASDAQ. If that is the route a company (or country?) chooses, how does it happen? How do foreign companies come to America?

With the increasing internationalization of the securities markets in the last twenty years, foreign company access to U.S. capital markets has become a hot topic for the Securities and Exchange Commission, securities regulators around the world, and commentators (see Fordham Symposium 1994). Each of the three principal ways in which foreign companies can access U.S. capital markets (private placements, public offerings, and listing on a US exchange) has been discussed at length (see, e.g., Decker 1994).

But these discussions—like the SEC's attention—have largely focused on established, publicly traded foreign companies that seek to enter the U.S. capital markets, and publicly traded U.S. companies that seek to move into foreign capital markets. I want to focus on a different and, to my knowledge, largely ignored facet of the same phenomenon: the young (usually technology) company that considers coming to the U.S. for capital-raising and listing purposes, often at the IPO stage. In other words, I focus on the interaction between the regulatory framework and cross-border transactions at the start-up frontier. What is most interesting is how start-ups can use the framework established for large publicly traded companies to their advantage.

A. The Legal Framework I: SEC Structure

The SEC has focused a great deal of attention on the globalization of capital markets. Aware that some foreign firms do not list on U.S. exchanges because of a reluctance to comply with the full set of U.S. disclosure requirements, the SEC has sought to make it easier for foreign firms. From the SEC's perspective, there is a tension.[12] On the one hand, it believes that U.S. investors need the protections of disclosure regulation at least as much for foreign firms as domestic firms. On the other hand, if the U.S. regulations are applied without any modifications, U.S. investors will lose the opportunity to invest in those foreign firms unwilling to comply.

To reconcile this tension, the SEC has modified the disclosure obligations for foreign firms. Simplifying somewhat, the structure is as follows.[13] Foreign firms that wish to be listed on a U.S. exchange must register their securities with the SEC by filing an Exchange Act registration statement, and subsequently must file annual reports on Form 20-F. Foreign firms that want to issue securities in the U.S. must register those securities under the Securities Act using Form F-1, unless they qualify for forms F-2 or F-3. This parallels the Securities Act integrated disclosure system for domestic companies with Forms S-1, S-2, and S-3. Several accommodations have been made to encourage listing by foreign firms. For example, interim reporting follows home country practice, rather than quarterly reports. Thus, most foreign firms will not file an equivalent to the quarterly Form 10-Q. Foreign firms are also exempt from the proxy rules and the insider reporting and short swing trading provisions of Section 16. Executive compensation need only be reported in the aggregate, if that is permitted in the home country.[14] Foreign firms need not prepare their financial statements using U.S. GAAP, so long as they use a comprehensive body of generally accepted accounting principles. In such cases, the reports must include a reconciliation of significant variations from U.S. GAAP. In addition, foreign firms need not provide "line-of-business" or segment data.[15] Finally, foreign private issuers are not subject to Regulation FD restricting "selective disclosure."

The existence of this two-tier structure creates some problems for the SEC. Principally, it worries about leakage: U.S. firms seeking to take advantage of the lower disclosure requirements by passing themselves off as foreign firms. The regulatory structure guards against this possibility through its definition of "foreign private issuer."

The Exchange Act defines a "foreign private issuer" to be any foreign issuer (other than a foreign government) except an issuer where:

1. More than 50 percent of the issuer's outstanding voting securities are directly or indirectly held of record by residents of the United States; and

2. Any of the following: (i) The majority of the executive officers or directors are United States citizens or residents; (ii) More than 50 percent of the assets of the issuer are located in the United States; or (iii) The business of the issuer is administered principally in the United States.[16]

This definition prevents, for example, a Silicon Valley firm, of which Americans directly or indirectly hold a majority of the shares, from incorporating in the Cayman Islands as a means of avoiding the full reach of U.S. disclosure regulations. Such a firm would not be considered a foreign private issuer, and would thus be subject to the full panoply of securities law obligations.

When publicly traded foreign private issuers enter the U.S. capital market, either through a stock exchange listing or a public issuance of shares, they typically do so by means of ADRs (American Depositary Receipts). An ADR "is a receipt issued by a U.S. depositary bank, such as The Bank of New York, that actually represents the shares that are held overseas" (Velli 1994). It works as follows. Suppose a U.K. issuer, listed on the London Stock Exchange, lists its ADRs on the New York Stock Exchange. When an American investor wants to buy an ADR, the broker looks first to see if any are for sale. If not, the broker buys shares in London and deposits those shares with the depositary bank, which then issues ADRs to the investor. When an American investor wants to sell ADRs, the process works in reverse: the broker first looks to see whether there are any buyers for the ADRs on the NYSE and, if not, sells the underlying shares on the LSE, thereupon canceling the ADR.

B. The Legal Framework II: Incorporation

There are no appreciable difficulties under U.S. law for a foreign firm that wishes to incorporate in the U.S. Indeed, Delaware makes a concerted effort to attract such incorporations.

Under Delaware law, "any person, partnership, association or corporation, singly or jointly with others, and without regard to such person's or entity's residence, domicile or state of incorporation, may incorporate or organize a corporation."[17] Incorporating in Delaware is quick and easy. Indeed, for an extra fee of $500, a corporate filing can be completed within two hours.[18]

Delaware markets Delaware incorporation all over the world. Delaware's Secretary of State leads international missions explaining Delaware's advantages as a corporate domicile, often with the assistance of the governor. In both Taiwan and Israel, local facilitators assist companies that wish to incorporate in Delaware.

In addition, Delaware corporation law itself minimizes the logistical difficulties of locating a headquarters outside of the state of incorporation. Under Delaware law, neither board meetings nor shareholders' meetings must be held in Delaware.[19] Directors may participate in board meetings by conference call.[20] Indeed, the only presence a Delaware corporation must have within Delaware is a designated "registered office" and "registered agent" whose main function is to receive service of process.[21] As one would expect, there are firms that perform this function for hundreds of Delaware corporations. The Delaware Division of Corporation's website helpfully provides a long list of firms that stand ready to play this role, filing the paper work for incorporation, providing the relevant forms and even, for an extra charge, creating a lovely corporate seal.[22]

C. A Curious Byproduct: Unrestricted Immigration

How, then, does this structure provide a smooth route to passing as American? As described above, the SEC system of regulating foreign issuers anticipates three types of firms: the major or "world class" foreign company; the unscrupulous foreign company seeking to prey on U.S. investors; and U.S. companies seeking to escape from U.S. disclosure burdens. The goal of the regulatory structure is to allow U.S. investors access to the Daimlers of the world, who, without some regulatory relief, would simply not enter the U.S. market, while protecting U.S. investors from unscrupulous foreign firms, and preventing U.S. firms from exploiting the relaxed disclosure regime available to foreign issuers. The key to the SEC's accommodation is its distinction between regular issuers and "foreign private issuers."

But here we see an interesting and unanticipated (but not inconsistent) result of this regulatory structure. By distinguishing between "regular" companies and "foreign private issuers," it provides an extremely easy way for a firm to identify itself as a "regular" U.S. firm, so long as the firm is willing to assume the burdens that come with that choice.

To see how this works, we need to take a step back. If one starts from the assumption that only publicly traded foreign issuers are interested in entering the U.S. market, then it is easy to conclude, as many have, that the only way for foreign firms to enter is through an ADR facility. At a 1994 Fordham symposium on "Entering the U.S. Securities Markets: Opportunities and Risks for Foreign Companies," there was an interesting exchange between Joseph Velli, head of Bank of New York's ADR business and a leading figure in the ADR world, and an unidentified audience member. The audience member asked what type of foreign issuer is best suited for a direct listing on a U.S. exchange as opposed to an issuance of ADRs (Fordham Symposium 1994: Panel I Discussion).

Velli's response was interesting:

> There is an awful lot of confusion about this. In fact, I am told almost every day, "We don't want to list our ADRs in the United States; we

want to list our shares." The fact of the matter is that, excluding Canada, non-U.S. companies . . . are looking at the possibility of direct listings—but right now, if a non-U.S. company wants to list in the United States, they have to use ADRs. There really isn't a choice.

There have been a few Chinese companies who have formed shell companies in Bermuda and then listed their shares, not ADRs, directly in the United States. There have been a couple of other cases where European companies have done that. But they're not listing the company; they are forming a separate company and listing that company. Essentially, they are listing a U.S. company in the U.S. marketplace. Everywhere else—France, Spain, Italy—they all use ADRs (ibid: S70).

For already established, public companies, Velli is correct. Absent creating a separate class of stock for the U.S., the way a foreign public firm lists its common stock in the U.S. is through ADRs. Once the firm has chosen to enter with ADRs, it is then subject to the foreign issuer disclosure standards. It is also instantly identifiable as a "foreign" firm.

But what about the foreign company that, for whatever reason, does not want to be immediately identifiable as a foreign firm? That, I take it, is the desire of the firms noted by Velli, seeking a direct listing of shares (rather than ADRs) on a U.S. exchange. While Velli is right that direct listings by already public, "world class" foreign companies are unworkable, these constraints need not apply if the firm identifies the goal of being American early in its life-cycle.

If one chooses early enough, the very same regulatory structure that provides reduced disclosure burdens for "foreign private issuers" allows foreign firms that do not want to be labeled as foreign to choose to enter the U.S. market as a "regular" company. Indeed, it is quite easy to do so. The standard route is simple and effective: incorporate the startup in Delaware; identify the U.S. office as headquarters; keep the accounts in accordance with U.S. GAAP from day one; draft major documents in English; go public on NASDAQ as a regular (i.e., U.S.) company; and deemphasize foreign connections in the investor relations efforts. Indeed, as we'll see below, a company can accomplish nearly the same thing if it is incorporated abroad.

The regulatory structure not only permits this, it actually encourages firms to do so. Under the securities laws, entering as a "foreign private issuer" is permissive, not mandatory. The definition is designed to prevent leakage outward (firms that are "really" U.S. firms seeking to present themselves as foreign private issuers) not inward (foreign firms seeking to present themselves as U.S. firms). Because the U.S. follows the "internal affairs" doctrine, under which the law of the state of incorporation applies to all issues related to the corporation's internal affairs, state corporate law assists the efforts of firms seeking to "pass." Delaware is thrilled to attract incorporations from abroad (and with them, increased franchise tax income and similar benefits).

Note an interesting aspect of Delaware's welcome mat: there is no requirement that the shareholders of a new Delaware corporation be U.S. citizens or permanent residents. From one perspective, this is an obvious aspect of international capital markets. But, from another perspective, it may seem quite odd and counterintuitive: an Israeli or Taiwanese entrepreneur, resident in Israel or Taiwan, who does not have U.S. citizenship or permanent residency, can establish a Delaware corporation, with its headquarters in Silicon Valley, Hsinchu, or Tel Aviv. If the entrepreneur wants to come to the U.S. to work in the Silicon Valley office, or to visit customers or investors, he or she will need an appropriate visa, as with any other foreign national who wishes to visit or work in the U.S. But none of those requirements interfere with the foreign national who will work in the Tel Aviv or Hsinchu research and development facility.

D. Exploiting the Opportunity

The opportunity that U.S. law provides to foreign firms to pass themselves off as U.S. firms is not a mere theoretical possibility. It is exploited every day and is the hallmark of the Israeli success in tapping the NASDAQ. In this section, I want to focus on two leading Israeli technology companies that have pursued two variations on this approach: Mercury Interactive; and Check Point Software Technologies. I then turn to an intriguing Taiwan example, Integrated Silicon Solution, Inc.

My point is not that there are no large, publicly held Israeli or Taiwan companies with secondary listings on U.S. markets. In fact, there are such firms.[23] Rather, I want to explore the alternative route that allows firms to choose to fly below the market's radar.

1. *Mercury Interactive.* Mercury Interactive provides "integrated performance management solutions that enable businesses to test and monitor their Web-based applications."[24] It was founded in 1989 by Aryeh Finegold, an Israeli born entrepreneur. In the early 1980s, after working for Intel, Finegold started one of the first "Israeli" companies in Silicon Valley, Daisy Systems Inc. Later in the 1980s, Finegold returned to Israel, bringing with him his experience and contacts. From the beginning, Mercury was tailored for NASDAQ. It went public in 1993 on the NASDAQ national market and, as of February 2002, had a market capitalization of approximately $3 billion.[25] During 2001, it traded at between $18 and $100 per share, with recent prices at around $35 per share.[26]

All of Mercury's investor relations efforts work together to project an image of a Silicon Valley technology company. For example, Mercury's SEC disclosure documents give little hint that it has more than a casual relationship with Israel. It is incorporated in Delaware, its principal executive offices are in Sunnyvale, California and, so far as the SEC is concerned, it is as American as Coca Cola. If one examines Mercury's Form 10-K for the fiscal year ending December 31, 2000, one discovers, on page 6, that Mercury's primary research and development facility is located near Tel Aviv. Interestingly, this is presented as an advantage, not as a risk factor:

> Our primary research and development group is located near Tel Aviv, Israel. Performing research and development in Israel offers a number of strategic advantages. Our Israeli engineers typically hold advanced degrees in computer-related disciplines. Operation in Israel has allowed us to enjoy tax incentives from the government of Israel. Geographic proximity to Europe, a strategic market for Mercury, offers another key advantage.[27]

The description of its personnel is consistent with this image of an international technology company:

> As of December 31, 2000, we had a total of 1,418 employees, of which 634 were based in the Americas and 784 were based internationally. Of the total, 941 were engaged in marketing, sales and related customer support services, 316 were in research and development, and 161 were in general and administrative and operations support functions.[28]

The description of the executive officers is likewise silent on the Israeli connection. Although Amnon Landan, the president, CEO, and chairman of the board is Israeli, there is no mention of that fact in the 10-K. Similarly, Moshe Egert's Israeli origins are not mentioned. Turning to Mercury's proxy statement, one finds that its five directors are: Kenneth Klein, Igal Kohavi, Amnon Landan, Yair Shamir, and Giora Yaron. All but Klein are Israeli, but their Israeli roots are conspicuously not emphasized.[29]

The descriptions of the "Israeli" members of the board bristle with indications that the directors are insiders in Israeli business, especially high tech. According to the proxy statement, Kohavi has served as chairman of the DSP Group (David Gilo's Silicon Valley-based operation) and Chairman of Polaris, an Israeli-based venture capital fund. Yair Shamir is a former CEO of Elite, the Israeli food products company, an identity that provides a slightly discordant link to the old economy but that reflects the extent to which in Israel, "old economy" firms have engaged in venture capital investments.

To the insider, the Israeli connections are obvious. More interesting, however, is what is not mentioned. There is no mention of military rank or undergraduate degrees. There is no mention of where the directors live. There is no mention of where the board meetings are held. In addition, one is never told whether the Israelis live in Israel or Silicon Valley. With the number of Silicon Valley ex-Israelis involved in technology companies, it would be easy to assume that the same is the case with Mercury's Israelis.

Mercury Interactive's website carries forward this same strategy.[30] On the homepage, there is no mention of Israel at all. Likewise, the "Company" page is entirely silent. All press releases carry the Sunnyvale, California dateline. The only contact addresses or numbers are in the U.S.

As judged by analysts' reactions, Mercury has been spectacularly successful in its efforts to "pass" as a normal, Silicon Valley technology company. In the Merrill Lynch analyst updates, Mercury is categorized as "United States: Server & Enterprise Software" (see, e.g., Shilades and Goldmacher 2000). In the Multex Stock Snapshot, Israel is not mentioned even once.[31] Mercury is identified as a U.S. corporation, with headquarters in Sunnyvale. Similarly, in the Multex ACE consensus estimate (a summary of analyst recommendations), there is again no mention of Mercury's Israeli connection.[32] Mercury is a Yankee company and, to the analysts, every bit as American as the Silicon Valley firms founded by expatriate Israelis. Indeed, in 1999, Mercury appeared as number 36 on *Fortune* Magazine's list of "America's Fastest Growing Companies" (Daniels 1999: 90).

In operational terms, one cannot determine whether Mercury is "really" an Israeli company or a U.S. company. Like many technology companies, Mercury has operations all over the world. Like many technology companies, Mercury has significant R&D facilities outside the U.S. Like many technology companies, Mercury has foreign-born founders, directors and top executives. Like many technology companies, the U.S. is Mercury's single most important market, but it also sells in Europe and Asia. Indeed, what Mercury teaches is that there may be little meaning to the question whether a firm is "really" Israeli or "really" American.

2. *Check Point.* Check Point Software Technologies is the leading provider of Internet network security products. Unlike Mercury Interactive, it is incorporated in Israel rather than Delaware. Like Mercury, however, it went public on the NASDAQ. Unlike Mercury, it has taken advantage of its "foreign private issuer" status making its periodic disclosure under the Exchange Act on Form 20-F. Since going public in 1996, its shares have traded in the range of $11.50 per share to $237 per share. As of February 2002, its stock was trading at around $30 per share and it had a market capitalization of around $7 billion.[33]

Check Point thus represents a direct rebuttal of the claim that the only way that foreign private issuers can be listed on U.S. markets is through an ADR facility. If a foreign private issuer targets NASDAQ as its primary listing, then going public on the NASDAQ with a direct listing seems to be the dominant strategy.

Check Point's listing on NASDAQ is accompanied by a coordinated investor relations strategy which, while not denying the Israeli connection, hardly trumpets it. How does Check Point project this image? Like Mercury, the Check Point board is small and technology-oriented. Three co-founders of the company serve on the board. In addition to the three insiders, there are two venture capitalists and a European technology guru. The financial statements, audited by an Ernst & Young affiliate, are prepared in accordance with U.S. GAAP.

Check Point's website almost completely ignores its Israeli connections.[34] All press releases carry the dateline of the Redwood City, California headquarters. In the boilerplate description of the company that appears in press releases, there is no mention of Israel. Contact numbers are the California office.

How do analysts view Check Point? Like Mercury, Check Point is largely treated as a "regular" company. When one looks at the analyst reports, one finds either no mention of the firm being Israeli, or a cursory reference — e.g., "Israel-based Check Point" (Morgan Stanley Dean Witter).[35]

The success of this strategy can be seen in a recent *Forbes* article. In 1998, as the NASDAQ bubble began to inflate, Forbes identified forty-six prominent Web-related stocks, many of which were already selling at outrageous multiples (Yen 2001). Two years later, in December, 2001, Forbes looked back and asked whether anything justified the hype. As it turns out, Check Point was the best performer of the group. For our purposes, however, even more interesting is that Forbes viewed Check Point as yet another (particularly successful) Silicon Valley company:

> The best performer: Check Point Software Technologies (nasdaq: CHKP—news—people). A $1,000 investment in Check Point is now worth $7,552, for a price gain of 655%. This Redwood City, Calif.-based firm develops Internet security infrastructure. Check Point lived up to its promise as a high growth company: Sales have increased to $426 million in 2000 from $142 million in 1998. In the same time period, earnings jumped to $221 million from $70 million.

Of course, the truth is that Check Point is a Ramat Gan based firm, not a Redwood City, California based firm, a fact that one could discover by checking *Forbes'* link to its stock section. Indeed, Forbes itself recognized Check Point's Israeli base when it put Check Point's founder Gil Shwed on the cover of its "World's Billionaires" issue (Goldman 2002: 103–6 and cover). The point is not whether or not *Forbes'* fact checkers blundered. Rather, the point is that Check Point, like Mercury, achieved its goal of being perceived to be a Silicon Valley based company.

Could Check Point have had equal success with an ADR program and a primary listing on the Tel Aviv Stock Exchange? Does 20-F reporting make it harder? It is hard to know. My claim is not that entering the U.S. capital markets as a regular reporting company rather than as a 20-F company is necessary to be accepted on NASDAQ. Nor is my point that companies that come in through ADRs rather than direct listing of shares cannot be accepted in the U.S. markets. Neither claim is likely to be true. Rather, my point is that the existing institutional and regulatory structure — largely designed to attract world-class foreign publicly held companies to list their shares on U.S. exchanges and to raise capital in the U.S.—provides, at the same time, an invitation to startups to present themselves as "regular" companies rather than foreign companies. Indeed, the more frequent and prominent the entry of foreign world class publicly held companies—companies like Daimler, Deutsche Bank, or Deutsche Telecom, which are indelibly linked in investors' consciousness to particular countries—the easier it is for a Mercury or a Check Point to distinguish itself from the "foreigners" on U.S. exchanges.

3. *Integrated Silicon Solution.* AnnaLee Saxenian tells the story of Integrated Silicon Solution's founding:

> K. Y. Han is typical. After graduating from National Taiwan University in the 1970s, Han completed a master's degree in solid state physics at the University of California at Santa Barbara. Like many Taiwanese engineers, Han was drawn to Silicon Valley in the early 1980s and worked for nearly a decade at a series of local semiconductor companies before joining his college classmate and friend, Jimmy Lee, to start Integrated Silicon Solutions, Inc. (ISSI). After bootstrapping the initial start-up with their own funds and those of other Taiwanese colleagues, they raised more than $9 million in venture capital (Saxenian 1999: 57–58).

Saxenian goes on to describe how they raised the venture capital from Asian sources, and then mobilized their professional and personal networks in both Taiwan and the U.S. to build the company. They hired many Chinese engineers, targeted Taiwanese motherboard manufacturers as customers, and established manufacturing operations in Taiwan's Hsinchu Science-Based Industrial Park. Eventually, Han moved back to Taiwan, although he "still spends an hour each day on the phone with Jimmy Lee and he returns to Silicon Valley as often as ten times a year" (ibid: 59).

ISSI went public on NASDAQ in 1995. As of January 30, 2002, it had a market capitalization of $314 million.[36] ISSI's Form 10-K identifies it as a Delaware corporation with its principal place of business in Santa Clara, California.[37] As one flips through the 10-K, it looks like a successful, Silicon Valley semiconductor memory company.

It is not that references to Taiwan are absent. For example, one learns that ISSI's manufacturing is performed by Taiwan foundries, and that ISSI keeps an eye on manufacturing from its Taiwan office. Similarly, one discovers that ISSI has investments in Taiwan firms and recently took a Taiwanese subsidiary public on the Taiwan Stock Exchange.[38] In addition, like other firms which manufacturer in Taiwan, ISSI is subject to a certain amount of political risk, whether from the People's Republic or from U.S. anti-dumping proceedings.[39] In other words, the presentation of ISSI in its 10-K is of a U.S. firm with operations in Taiwan and elsewhere.

ISSI's website is to the same effect.[40] Throughout, ISSI is identified as a "Silicon Valley" company which, of course, it is. In the "about ISSI" section, the company's first milestone is "Silicon Valley start up—1988." In its corporate profile, it identifies itself as follows: "Integrated Silicon Solution, Inc. (ISSI) designs, develops and markets high performance memory semiconductors throughout the world. The Silicon Valley-based high tech company is one of the largest producers of SRAMs in North America."[41] It trumpets its "unique foundry partnerships" with Taiwan semiconductor foundries.[42]

In describing the management team, the website thoroughly obscures Jimmy Lee's Taiwanese origins:

> Jimmy S.M. Lee is ISSI's Chairman, Chief Executive Officer and co-founder. He has held this position since October 1988. He also served as ISSI's president until May 2000. He has served as a director of Integrated Circuit Solution, Inc. since September 1998 and of NexFlash Technologies, Inc. since October 1998. Prior positions include engineering manager at International CMOS Technology from 1985 to 1988; design manager at Signetics Corporation from 1983 to 1985; and project manager at Toshiba Semiconductor. Mr. Lee has a Masters degree in electrical engineering from Texas Tech University.[43]

ISSI is followed by three analysts, which is more or less normal for a company of its size. MSN's Money Central report, an easily and widely available research source for investors, contains no indication that ISSI is other than a Santa Clara–based company. The "company description" depicts ISSI as a U.S. company that subcontracts manufacturing in Asia:

> Integrated Silicon Solution, Inc. (ISSI) wants its integrated circuits to solve electronics manufacturers' memory problems. The company makes static random-access memory chips (SRAMs, used in computers, networking equipment, instrumentation, and telecommunications), dynamic RAMs (DRAMs, for set-top boxes, disk drives, and other applications), specialized read-only memories, and voice record-

ing chips. Almost half of sales come from outside the US; top customers—either directly or through distributors and contract manufacturers—include Cisco Systems and 3Com. ISSI farms out its manufacturing to factories in Asia. The company's SRAM products account
for two-thirds of sales.

Thus, as with Israeli-born entrepreneurs, Taiwanese-born entrepreneurs
can choose their corporation's nationality. While ISSI is arguably more
Santa Clara than Hsinchu, that is the product of an early choice. Little
stands in the way of another entrepreneur who might choose to shift the balance more toward Hsinchu.

D. The Absence of Effective Barriers to Corporate Immigration

Can it be so easy to choose your corporate citizenship? In this section, I
explore the potential barriers.

1. *The Domestic Side: Why No Protectionism?* As described above, the
U.S. "corporate" immigration policy is very different from its individual
immigration policy. While U.S. law imposes all sorts of restrictions on foreign individuals who wish to become American citizens, there is an entirely
open door policy for firms. If a firm anywhere in the world wishes to be
American, Delaware stands ready to assist, and no one erects any barriers.

From a social perspective, such an open door policy is easy to defend.
Encouraging foreign firms to locate as much of their capital and operations
in the U.S. makes America richer. To the extent that Israeli firms choose to
incorporate in Delaware, to pay Delaware taxes and fees, and to hire
Delaware lawyers, who would complain? Moreover, to the extent that this
decision makes it more likely that the company will locate significant operations somewhere in the country, it seems unlikely to have negative consequences for the U.S.

But many of these advantages are generic advantages to free trade—
advantages that often are met by opposing arguments and interests. Who
might be disadvantaged by an open door policy toward corporate immigration, and why don't we see them objecting? There are two potential losers.
First, to the extent that the open door policy makes it easier for such firms to
tap U.S. capital markets, their competitors in those markets might plausibly

be disadvantaged. Second, to the extent that such a policy makes it easier for such firms to sell products in the U.S., their domestic product market competitors might likewise suffer.

Now, perhaps, we can see why there is no substantial opposition to such a policy. Both the capital and product markets are so intensely competitive regardless of corporate immigration that the effects of an open door policy are unlikely even to be felt. Moreover, even if there is some slight effect, the magnitude is likely to be so small—and the difficulty of organizing opposition in such a fragmented market so large—that no one is likely to even try. Here we see yet another difference between the technology sector and icons of the "old economy" like steel.

2. *The Foreign Side.* If the U.S. is untroubled by the wholesale immigration of foreign corporations, one does not find the same indifference abroad. Israeli commentators have worried about the "exodus" of companies from Israel (see, e.g., Cox 2001).[44] Part of this concern derives from confusion about the operational significance of the jurisdiction of incorporation. But part of the concern may also derive from a perhaps dimly perceived sense that a foreign incorporation makes it more likely that operations of the firm (and jobs and tax revenues) will tend to flow abroad as well.

Indeed, the Israeli experience is at least superficially consistent with this concern. Often, the choice to incorporate in the U.S. goes hand in hand with the executives spending more time in the U.S. Many of these executives end up concluding that living in the U.S. is preferable to living on an airplane. Although the best explanation is probably that all of these phenomena are driven by a common factor (namely, that the firm's principal customers and investors are in the U.S.), it does not always play that way in the public discussion (see Strasler 2000; Hermoni 2000).

Suppose, then, that countries object to the "emigration" of their most promising startups. Is there much that can be done about it? As I discuss below, the answer is basically negative. None of the standard regulatory devices is of much use.

The main legal barrier to corporate emigration—understood to be the incorporation of "local" enterprises in foreign jurisdictions—is the "real seat" doctrine. The use of this doctrine to prevent emigration of startups is only likely to make matters worse.

There are two main choice of law rules for corporations: the place of incorporation doctrine; and the real seat rule. Under the first, the law of the

place of incorporation governs both the question of the validity of incorporation as well as the internal affairs of the firm (See Drury 1998, 1999). This
doctrine—followed especially in the U.S., but also in the U.K. and Israel[45]—
grants entrepreneurs nearly unfettered freedom to choose corporate domicile.[46]

But the place of incorporation doctrine is what gives rise to the
"Delaware syndrome"—the practice of firms incorporating in Delaware out
of a preference for Delaware law, even when all their operations are elsewhere. Out of hostility to this phenomenon, many jurisdictions follow the
"real seat" rule (Drury 1998). For these jurisdictions, the applicable law is
the law prevailing in the jurisdiction in which the corporation has its "real
seat," defined by its "center of gravity," which is often defined as the place
"its head office or central management and control is actually located"
(Drury 1999).

The choice of law doctrine can have real consequences. Robert Drury
discusses two German judgments that refused to recognize companies
validly incorporated abroad, but whose businesses were managed in Germany. In these cases, Drury reports, the German court treated the firms as
private companies in the process of formation, which meant, inter alia, that
the directors or shareholders could be personally liable for the debts taken
on in the name of the company.[47]

Consider, for example, a high-tech startup in Frankfurt that wishes to target the U.S. capital markets by going public on NASDAQ. Under the cases
discussed earlier, incorporating in Delaware might not suffice under German law to ensure that the company would be treated like any other
Delaware corporation doing the same. If it is subsequently determined that
the real seat is Frankfurt, German law could be held to apply. The legal risk
created by this uncertainty can be viewed as tending to discourage corporate
emigration. For the already established company, these barriers—along with
a variety of others, including tax consequences of reincorporation—can make
it difficult for firms to move from country to country.[48]

But at the startup stage, the situation is quite different. The "center of
gravity" is entirely within the control of the founders. For the entrepreneur
starting a firm, any unfavorable legal rule can be avoided with relatively little difficulty by organizing operations to come within the real seat doctrine's definition of "center of gravity." If the legal rule depends on where
the corporate headquarters is located, the entrepreneur who wishes to

incorporate in Delaware can designate its U.S. branch office as its head-quarters.[49] Because of the importance of the U.S. product market, every technology firm that is aiming for NASDAQ will have a U.S. office of some sort. If, by contrast, the legal question is where board meetings are held—as a measure of where central management and control is actually located—they can be held in the U.S. In all of these companies, the key players are constantly in the U.S. on business, and board meetings can easily be scheduled to correspond. Directors located outside the U.S. can, as they often do, attend by telephone. If the question is where the executive officers are located, executives can spend more time in the U.S. If the question is where the largest number of employees is located, particular operations can be located in the U.S.

Here we see a perverse effect of the real seat doctrine: it is either irrelevant or, at the startup stage, counterproductive. It can have the undesirable effect of driving real economic activity out of the home jurisdiction as a means of avoiding the reach of local law. The risk of a real seat doctrine, for new firms, is that it can transform "formal" emigration (i.e., foreign incorporation) into the actual transfer of economic activity out of the home country.

A second way in which corporate emigration can be restricted is by limiting the ability of foreign firms to acquire domestic firms. Here, again, the ability to shape one's identity at the startup stage undermines such attempts and, indeed, can lead to earlier transfer of operations. It is not uncommon, for example, for countries to have limitations on the acquisition of sensitive industries (e.g., airlines, media companies, defense contractors). To take one example of this type of statute, the Investment Canada Act requires notice of any non-Canadian acquiring a Canadian business and, for larger transactions, prior approval.[50] For already existing companies, this can, in principle, limit emigration, although it has not often been used this way, except occasionally with regard to culturally sensitive situations.

But now consider startups. Along with IPOs, acquisition by a larger company is a key exit option for venture capitalists and entrepreneurs. If a jurisdiction restricts such acquisitions, it provides an incentive to avoid being categorized as a "Canadian business" from the outset.

Although the application of the Act is somewhat complex, consider just the definition of "Canadian Business." Under the Act, "Canadian business" "means a business carried on in Canada that has (a) a place of business in Canada, (b) an individual or individuals in Canada who are employed or self-employed in connection with the business, and (c) assets in Canada used in carrying on the business."[51]

As with the real seat doctrine, an entrepreneur who wishes to avoid the limitations of the Investment Canada Act can avoid it by "carrying on the business" outside of Canada. If this means spending more time at the Santa Clara office than at the Toronto research and development facility, that can be arranged. If it means holding board meetings south of the border, that too is easily accomplished.

Conclusion

At the birth of a company, everything is malleable. But choices must be made. For some venture capital sectors, the exit options are local: an IPO on the Taiwan Stock Exchange or acquisition by a large Taiwanese firm. In such circumstances, there is no need to look abroad for equity finance, and little reason to present the firm to the world as anything other than Taiwanese.

But for a variety of reasons, a venture capital sector may choose or be stuck with foreign exit options: an IPO on the NASDAQ; acquisition by a foreign firm. For these firms, it matters whether the foreign investors or acquirers view it as domestic or foreign, strange or familiar. Many of the target investors—large U.S. institutions—may invest in "technology companies" but not in "Israeli" companies. To attract these investors, it matters how one presents the firm.

The Israeli success on the NASDAQ shows that this strategy can succeed. It is a matter of mindset, investor relations, and U.S. securities law. Conveniently, by distinguishing between "issuers" and "foreign private issuers," U.S. securities law allows—indeed invites—foreign firms to present themselves as American, so long as they take on the same set of disclosure obligations as other American firms.

Endnotes

I am grateful to John Alton, Susannah Khavul, Henry Hansmann, Ed Iacobucci, Jeff Macintosh, Curtis Milhaupt, and Estee Solomon Gray for very helpful comments. I am also grateful to participants in the University of

Cambridge's Venture Capital Roundtable and participants in the Columbia conference. Data and analysis are as of April 2002.

1. The most current and comprehensive treatment is in the set of papers from the Stanford Institute for Economic Policy Research Conference, which is being published as Silicon Valley and Its Imitators (2002). For a more journalistic account, see Rosenberg (2002). Other important contributions include: Saxenian (1994, 1999); Saxenian and Li (2002).

2. On the venture capital process, see, generally, Gompers and Lerner (1999). On exits, see ibid.: Part III; Cumming and MacIntosh (2002); Black and Gilson (1998).

3. Geographically, one finds local clusters of venture capital firms. For a description of Taiwan VC, see Saxenian and Li (2002). At the same time, one also finds firms which operate more internationally but within a particular industry sector. For example, Jerusalem Venture Partners, a Jerusalem based venture capital firm, has a speciality in optical networking and has invested in optical networking startups in Israel, the U.S. and India. http://www.jvpvc.com /investments/optical_port.html (visited April 19, 2002). Similarly, one finds cross border venture capital flowing through ethnic networks, as described in Saxenian and Li (2002).

4. On the evolution of Israeli VC, see, also, de Fontenay and Carmel (2002); Rosenberg (2002: chapter 6).

5. The now prominent funds that trace their origins to the Yozma initiative include Gemini, Polaris, Walden, Star-Israel and Giza.

6. On the reciprocal relationship between Silicon Valley and Taiwan's Hsinchu science park, see Saxenian (1999: chapter 4).

7. http://www.nasdaq.com/reference/israel_companies.stm (visited April 19, 2002). Because of the ambiguity in defining an "Israeli" company, explored in more detail below and in Rock (2001), this number must be viewed as a lower limit.

8. http://deutsche-boerse.com/INTERNET/EXCHANGE/index_e.htm(visited January 31, 2002).

9. http://www.nyse.com/pdfs/forlist020124.pdf (visited January 31, 2002).

10. In the case of ASE Test, shares trade on the TSE through a Taiwan Depositary Share facility. ASE Test (2000). Form 20-F: 52.

11. When investors lose confidence in a market, it can take a long time to recover, which provides a strong incentive for companies to look for capital elsewhere. For an interesting discussion of the New Zealand experience, see Warbrick (1994).

12. SEC Release: Integrated Disclosure System for Foreign Private Issuers, Release Nos. 33-6360; 34-18274, 17 CFR Parts 210, 229, 230, 239, 240, 249, and 260 (November 20, 1981): 4–6.

13. See SEC Staff Guidance: International Financial Reporting and Disclosure Issues, 5 Fed. Sec. L. Rep. (CCH) ¶29,741, p. 21,813 (July 21, 2000).

14. SEC Form 20-F, item 6.B.1

15. SEC Form 20-F, item 17, instruction 3. See, also, Lane (1998: XI.B.3) (Disclosures about Segments (SFAS 131)).

16. Securities Exchange Act, rule 3b-4, 17 CFR 240.3b-4 (2000). The Securities Act definition in rule 405 is identical. 17 CFR 230.405. Rule 3b-4 was recently narrowed. Previously, the SEC had focused on record ownership. Now, it looks through intermediaries to determine beneficial ownership. Karmel (2000).

17. Delaware General Corporation Law §101(a).

18. http://www.state.de.us/corp/special.htm. Twenty-four hour service runs from $50 to $100 extra, while same day service is between $100 and $200 extra. (Ibid.) For more detail on Delaware fees, see http://www.state.de.us/corp/sch-fee.htm and also Kahan and Kamar (2001).

19. Delaware General Corporation Law §141(g); §211(a).

20. Ibid. §144(i).

21. Ibid. §§131, 132.

22. http://www.state.de.us/corp/agents/agt2.htm. For examples of the services provided, try clicking on one of the links. See, e.g., http://www.delawareinc.com/.

23. For example, Taiwan Semiconductor Manufacturing Company (NYSE ADR: TSM) and the Israel pharmaceutical firm Teva Pharmaceuticals (Nasdaq ADR: TEVA).

24. Mercury Interactive Corp., Form 10-K for the year ending Dec. 31, 2000, item 1. Available at SEC Edgar database.

25. http://quotes.nasdaq.com/ (symbol: MERQ) (visited February 12, 2002).

26. Ibid.

27. Mercury Interactive Corp., Form 10-K for the year ending Dec. 31, 2000: 6.

28. Ibid.: 9.

29. Klein, an American, was named to the board in 2000, when he was promoted to chief operating officer.

30. http://www-svca.mercuryinteractive.com/company/.

31. Multex.com, Inc., Mercury Interactive Corp., Stock Snapshot (May 20, 2000) (on file with author).

32. Multex.com, Inc., ACE Consensus Estimates, Mercury Interactive Corp. (May 20, 2000) (on file with author).

33. http://www.nasdaq.com (symbol CHKP) (visited February 13, 2002).

34. http://www.checkpoint.com/index.html.

35. See, e.g., the Multex Stock Snapshot for Check Point ("Check Point Software Technologies Ltd. is the worldwide leader in securing the Internet.") (June 18, 2000); Morgan Stanley Dean Witter Analyst Report ("Israeli-based Check Point") (Jan. 19, 2000 report).

36. http://quotes.nasdaq.com/quote.dll?page=full&mode=basics&symbol= ISSI%60&selected = ISSI%60 (visited January 30, 2002).
37. ISSI 10-K for the fiscal year ending September 30, 2001 available in the SEC Edgar database.
38. Ibid.: 11.
39. Ibid.
40. http://www.issiusa.com/ (visited January 30, 2002).
41. Ibid.
42. Ibid.
43. Ibid.
44. See also Strasler (2000) ("Another trend in Israel's high-tech field is even more worrisome: the brain drain to the United States. Between 70–90 percent of Israeli high-tech companies founded in the past two years are registered in the U.S."); Hermoni (2000) (Discussing Israeli alarm over the fleeing of high tech companies from Israel to the U.S. as indicated by incorporation in Delaware).
45. On U.S. choice of law, see, Pinto (1990); On Israeli choice of law, see c/a 5634/90, Pinto v. The Guardian of Absentees' Property 93 (3) Takdin, 5753–7754: 75; on UK choice of law, see Drury (1998).
46. Because California does not entirely adhere to the "internal affairs" doctrine, but, instead, includes a concept of "pseudo foreign corporation" in its law, there remains some question (not often discussed) of whether Silicon Valley startups really can choose Delaware incorporation as freely as they do. Surprisingly, whether California's pseudo-foreign corporation provisions violate the "full faith and credit" clause of the U.S. Constitution has never presented itself to the U.S. Supreme Court. If this lurking conflict ever causes real mischief (which so far it has not), the Supreme Court will have to address it.
47. (Drury 1998, citing O.L.G. Dusseldorf [1994] W.M. 808; L.G. Marburg [1994] R.I.W. 63.) Whether these judgments survive the *Centros* decision is an important question beyond the scope of this essay. See Xanthaki (2001).
48. For a thorough and probing discussion of these issues as they pertain to already established companies, see Drury (1999).
49. Comverse and Mercury Interactive, two major Israeli firms, have done just this.
50. R.S.C. 1985, c.28 (1st Supp.). See Finnerty (2000).
51. R.S.C. 1985, c. 28, s. 3

References

Ace Test. 2000. 20-F Form, available in the Securities and Exchange Commission's Edgar database.

Black, Bernard S. and Ronald Gilson. 1998. Venture Capital and the Structure of Capital Markets: Banks versus Stock Markets. *Journal of Finance Economics* 47: 243–77.

Cox, James. 2001. Israeli Tech Start-ups Cross over to Delaware. *U.S.A. Today*. January 23, 2001.

Cumming, Douglas J. and Jeffrey G. MacIntosh. 2002. Venture Capital Exits in the United States and Canada, U. Toronto Law School Working Paper.

Daniels, Cora. 1999. Fortune's One Hundred Fastest Growing Companies, *Fortune*, Sept. 6, 1999, at 90.

Decker, William E., Jr. 1994. The Attractions of the U.S. Securities Markets to Foreign Issuers and the Alternative Methods of Accessing the U.S. Markets: From the Issuer's Perspective. *Fordham International Law Journal* 17: 10–24.

de Fontenay, Catherine and Erran Carmel. 2002. Israel's Silicon Wadi: The Forces Behind Cluster Formation in Silicon Valley and Its Imitators.

Drury, Robert R. 1998. The Regulation and Recognition of Foreign Corporations: Responses to the 'Delaware Syndrome.' *Cambridge Law Journal* 57: 165–94.

———. 1999. Migrating Companies. *European Law Review* 24: 354–72.

Finnerty, Pat. 2000. Legal Aspects of Acquiring Canadian Energy Companies by Nonresidents. *Natural Resources and Environment*. 15-FALL: 92–136.

Fordham Symposium. 1994. Entering the U.S. Securities Markets: Opportunities and Risks for Foreign Companies. *Fordham International Law Journal* 17: S1–S164.

Goldman, Lea. 2002. A Fortune in Firewalls. *Forbes*. March 18, 2002, at 103–6 and cover.

Gompers, Paul and Josh Lerner. 1999. *The Venture Capital Cycle*. Cambridge: MIT Press.

Hermoni, Oded. 2000. The Estimate: 90% of Israeli High Tech Companies Are Registered in the U.S., *Ha'aretz*, Sept. 8, 2000 (North American Edition, p. 6).

Kahan, Marcel and Ehud Kamar. 2001. Price Discrimination in the Market for Corporate Law. *Cornell Law Review* 86: 1205–56.

Karmel, Roberta. 2000. Will Convergence of Financial Disclosure Standards Change SEC Regulation of Foreign Issuers?. *Brooklyn Journal of International Law* 26: 485–525.

Lane, Brian. 1998. Current Issues and Rulemaking Projects: Division of Corporation Finance. Compensation for Executives and Broad-Based Employee Groups: Strategy, Design, and Implementation (ALI-ABA June 1998).

Licht, Amir. 2001. David's Dilemma: A Case Study of Securities Regulation in a Small Open Market. *Theoretical Inquiries in Law* 2: 673–709.

Mercury Interactive Corp., Form 10-K for the year ending Dec. 31, 2000, at Item 1, available at SEC Edgar database.

Morgan Stanley Dean Witter Analyst Report, Check Point (Jan. 19, 2000 report) (on file with author).

Multex.com, Inc., Mercury Interactive Corp., Stock Snapshot (May 20, 2000) (on file with author).

Multex.com, Inc., Mercury Interactive Corp., ACE Consensus Estimates, (May 20, 2000) (on file with author).

Multex.com, Inc., Check Point, Stock Snapshot (June 18, 2000)(on file with author).

Pinto, Arthur R. 1990. The Internationalization of the Hostile Takeover Market: Its Implications for Choice of Law in Corporate and Securities Law. *Brooklyn Journal of International Law* 16: 55–88.

Rock, Edward B. 2001. Greenhorns, Yankees and Cosmopolitans: Venture Capital, IPOs, Foreign Firms and U.S. Markets. *Theoretical Inquiries in Law* 2: 711–44.

Rosenberg, David. 2002. *Cloning Silicon Valley*. London: Reuters.

Saxenian, AnnaLee. 1994. *Regional Advantage: Culture and Competition in Silicon Valley and Route 128*. Cambridge: Harvard University Press.

———. 1999. *Silicon Valley's New Immigrant Entrepreneurs*. San Francisco: Public Policy Institute of California.

——— and Wendy Li. 2002. Bay-to-Bay Strategic Alliances: Network Linkages Between Taiwan and U.S. Venture Capital Industries, *International Journal of Technology Management* (forthcoming).

SEC Release: Integrated Disclosure System for Foreign Private Issuers , Release Nos. 33-6360; 34-18274, 17 CFR Parts 210, 229, 230, 239, 240, 249, and 260 (November 20, 1981).

SEC Staff Guidance: International Financial Reporting and Disclosure Issues, 5 Fed. Sec. L. Rep. (CCH) ¶29,741, p. 21,813 (July 21, 2000).

Shilades, Christopher and Peter Goldmacher. 2000. Comment, Mercury Interactive Corp, Merrill Lynch (Mar. 1, 2000) (on file with author).

Silicon Valley and Its Imitators, forthcoming 2002, (Timothy Bresnahan, Alfonso Gambardella, AnnaLee Saxenian and Scott Wallsten, eds.). Palo Alto: Stanford Institute for Economic Policy Research.

Silicon Wannabes, Business 2.0, October 1999, available at: http://www.business2.com/articles/mag/0,1640,13166,FF.html.

Strasler, Nehemia. 2000. The Brain drain. *Ha'aretz* (English edition) September 8, 2000.

Velli, Joseph. 1994. American Depositary Receipts: An Overview. *Fordham International Law Journal* 17: S38-S57.

Warbrick, M. Shane. 1994. Practical Company Experience in Entering U.S. Markets: Significant Issues and Hurdles from the Issuer's Perspective. *Fordham International Law Journal* 17: S112-S119.

Xanthaki, Helen. 2001. Centros: Is this Really the End for the Theory of Siege Reel. *Company Lawyer* 22: 2–8.

Yen, Jody. 2001. Web Stock Scorecard, Forbes.com 12/26/01. Available at http://www.forbes.com/2001/12/26/1226sf.html.

15 Engineering a Venture Capital Market

Replicating the U.S. Template

Ronald J. Gilson

The venture capital market and firms whose creation and early stages were financed by venture capital are among the crown jewels of the American economy. It is hardly surprising, then, that other countries have sought to emulate American success in developing an effective venture capital market. In this essay I seek to identify the core of the U.S. venture capital contracting model, and then assess the extent to which this model provides guidance in fashioning such markets in other countries.

The analysis starts with what should be a noncontroversial premise—that the particular U.S. historical experience in developing a venture capital market is not duplicable elsewhere. But while the path along which the U.S. market developed was surely idiosyncratic, the outcome of the development was not. My second, and perhaps most important, point is to recognize that the keystone of the U.S. market is private ordering—the contracting structure that developed to manage the extreme uncertainty, information asymmetry, and agency costs that inevitably bedevil early-stage, high-technology financing. Startup and early stage companies are peculiarly suited to commercializing innovation, yet the character of their organization and the nature of the activity present inherent barriers to their finance. The U.S. venture capital contracting model manages these barriers and thereby makes early-stage financing feasible. The question, then, is whether other countries can replicate the U.S. contracting template: can we engineer a venture capital market?

The third step in the analysis takes up the engineering problem. Here the difficulty is that replicating the U.S. venture capital contracting structure

confronts a daunting problem of simultaneity. Three central inputs are necessary to the engineering process: capital, specialized financial intermediaries, and entrepreneurs.[1] The problem is that each of these inputs will
emerge if the other two are present, but none will emerge in isolation of the
others.

This brings us to the fourth step: who will be the engineer? The U.S. venture capital market developed organically, largely without government assistance and certainly without government direction. Countries now seeking
to develop a venture capital market must necessarily follow a different path
than did the U.S., and understandably look to government to provide direction when market forces are unlikely to solve the simultaneity problem. As a
result, government programs are commonplace in countries seeking to
develop a market. Most such programs, however, have been unsuccessful.
The reason, I will suggest, is that most government programs have tried to
substitute for the market by having the government both provide capital and
itself act as the financial intermediary. Programs structured in this fashion
fail because the government cannot respond to the trio of contracting problems inherent in early-stage, high-technology financing. The point is illustrated by discussion of three different government programs—a remarkably
unsuccessful early effort in Germany; a recent and more successful program
in Israel; and a newly launched program in Chile.

The final step in the analysis is to describe an approach by which the government can help engineer a venture capital market. The approach recognizes that the key to the engineering task is solving the simultaneity problem
without substituting the government (which cannot solve the contracting
problems of venture capital financing) for critical market participants.

I. An Overview of the Organizational and Contractual
Structure of U.S. Venture Capital

Institutional investors dominate U.S. venture capital. During the 1990s,
institutional investors—pension funds, banks, insurance companies, and
endowments and foundations—represented more than 75 percent of the
total capital raised by venture capital funds. These institutions typically
invest through intermediaries—venture capital limited partnerships, usually
called "venture capital funds," in which the investors are passive limited
partners. These funds are typically blind pools: the particular companies in

which the fund will invest are not yet known. Consistent with the legal rules governing limited partnerships, the limited partners may not participate in the day-to-day management of the fund's business, including especially the approval of particular portfolio company investments.[2] In this respect, the venture capital fund's governance structure formalizes the standard Berle-Means problem of the separation of ownership and control (Berle and Means 1932). The general partner (GP) puts up only one percent of the capital, but receives essentially complete control over all of it.[3]

The GP actually makes and monitors the venture capital fund's investments. The GP is typically itself a company that consists of investment professionals, which expects to continue in the venture capital market by raising successive funds after the capital in a particular fund has been invested in portfolio companies. This expectation, and the GP's investment in a business infrastructure, provides a powerful performance incentive. Commonly, the GP will begin seeking investors for a successor fund by the midpoint of the existing funds fixed, typically ten-year, term. At the close of the partnership's fixed term, liquidation is mandatory. The GP's principal contribution to the venture capital fund is expertise, not capital. This is reflected in the ratio of capital contributions. In most funds, the GP contributes one percent of the fund's capital, while the limited partner investors contribute the remaining 99 percent.

The GP's compensation is also skewed. The GP usually receives an annual management fee for its services, but the fee is relatively small, usually 2.5 percent of committed capital (Gompers and Lerner 1996: 491).[4] The primary return to the general partner is a carried interest—that is, a right to receive a specified percentage of profits realized by the partnership. Twenty percent is a common figure (Sahlman 1990: 491; Halloran et al. 1998: 46).

The venture capital fund's equity investments in portfolio companies typically take the form of convertible preferred stock (Sahlman 1990; Gompers 1997).[5] While not required by the formal legal documents, the fund is also expected to make important non-cash contributions to the portfolio company. These contributions consist of management assistance, corresponding to that provided by management consultants; intensive monitoring of the portfolio company's performance which provides an objective view to the entrepreneur; and the use of the fund's reputation to give the portfolio company credibility with potential customers, suppliers, and employees (Black and Gilson 1998: 243, 252–55; see also Bygrave and Timmons 1992; Barry

1994; Hellmann and Puri 2002). While each investment will have a "lead" investor who plays the primary role in monitoring and advising the portfolio company, commonly the overall investment is syndicated with other venture capital funds that invest in the portfolio company at the same time and on the same terms (Lerner 1994).

The initial venture capital investment usually will be insufficient to fund the portfolio company's entire business plan. Accordingly, investment will be "staged." A particular investment round will provide only the capital the business plan projects as necessary to achieve specified milestones set out in the business plan (see Gompers 1995). While first-round investors expect to participate in subsequent investment rounds,[6] they typically are not contractually obligated to do so even if the business plan's milestones are met; the terms of later rounds of investment are negotiated at the time the milestones are met and the prior investment exhausted. Like the provision of noncapital contributions, implicit, not explicit contract governs the venture capital fund's right and obligation to provide additional rounds of financing if the portfolio company performs as expected. The venture capital fund's implicit right to participate in subsequent rounds—by contrast to its implicit obligation to participate—is protected by an explicit right of first refusal.

A critical feature of the governance structure created by the venture capital fund's investment in the portfolio company is the disproportionate allocation of control to the fund. In direct contrast to the familiar Berle-Means governance structure of outside investors having disproportionately less control than equity, the governance structure of a venture-capital-backed early-stage, high-technology company allocates to the venture capital investors disproportionately greater control than equity. It is common for investors to have the right to name a majority of a portfolio company's directors even though their stock represents less than a majority of the portfolio company's voting power.[7] Additionally, the portfolio company will have the benefit of a series of contractual negative covenants that require the investors' approval before the portfolio company can take important business decisions, such as acquisition or disposition of significant amounts of assets, or a material deviation from the business plan. The extent of these negative covenants is related to whether the investors have control of the board of directors; board control acts as a partial substitute for covenant restrictions (Gompers 1997).[8]

These formal levers of control are complemented by the informal control elements that result from the staged financing structure. Because a financing round will not provide funds sufficient to complete the portfolio company's business plan, staged financing in effect delegates to the investors, in the form of the decision whether to provide additional financing, the decision whether to continue the company's project (Gompers 1997; Admati and Pfleiderer 1994).

Two final characteristics of investments in portfolio companies concern their terms and their expected performance. While these are not short-term investments, neither are they expected to be long-term. Because venture-capital limited partnerships have limited, usually ten-year terms (Halloran et al. 1998: 1–20), GPs have a strong incentive to cause the fund's portfolio company investments to become liquid as quickly as possible. Assuming that the GP has invested all of a fund's capital by the midpoint of the fund's life, the GP then must seek to raise additional capital for a new fund in order to remain in the venture capital business. Because the performance of a GP's prior funds will be an important determinant of its ability to raise capital for a new fund, early harvesting of a fund's investments will be beneficial (Black and Gilson 1998: 255–57).[9]

Venture capital funds exit successful investments by two general methods: taking the portfolio company public through an initial public offering of its stock (an "IPO"); or selling the portfolio company to another firm. The likelihood of exit by an IPO or a sale has differed over different periods. Between 1984 and 1990, 396 venture capital-backed firms went public, while 628 such firms were sold to other firms before going public. Between 1991 and 1996, the order reversed, with 1,059 firms going public and 524 being sold (ibid.: 248, table 1). It is also common for the terms of a venture capital preferred stock investment to give the venture capital fund the right to require the portfolio company to redeem its stock. However, redemption does not operate as a viable exit mechanism because portfolio companies lack the funds to affect the redemption (Black and Gilson 1998; Gompers 1997).[10] Such put rights are better understood as a control device that can force the portfolio company to accommodate the fund's desire to exit by way of IPO or sale.

The fact that portfolio company investments are of limited duration rather than long term is critical to the operation of the venture capital market. The non-cash contributions made by the venture capital fund to the portfolio company—management assistance, monitoring, and service as a reputational intermediary—share a significant economy of scope with its provision of capital. The portfolio company must evaluate the quality of the fund's proffered management assistance and monitoring, just as potential employees, suppliers, and customers must evaluate the fund's representations concerning the portfolio company's quality. Combining financial and nonfinancial contributions enhances the credibility of the information the venture capital fund proposes to provide the portfolio company and third parties. Put simply, the venture capital fund bonds the accuracy of its information with its investment.

The importance of the portfolio company investment's limited duration reflects the fact that the venture capital fund's non-cash contributions have special value to early-stage companies. As the portfolio company gains its own experience and develops its own reputation, the value of the fund's provision of those elements declines. By the time a portfolio company succeeds and the fund's exit from the investment is possible, its non-cash contributions can be more profitably invested in a new round of early-stage companies. But because of the economies of scope between cash and non-cash contributions, recycling the venture capital fund's non-cash contributions also requires recycling its cash contributions. Exit from a fund's investments in successful portfolio companies thus serves to recycle its cash and, therefore, its associated non-cash contributions from successful companies to early-stage companies.

II. The Economics of Venture Capital Contracting: the Special Problems of Uncertainty, Information Asymmetry, and Agency Costs

All financial contracts respond to three central problems: uncertainty, information asymmetry, and opportunism in the form of agency costs. The special character of venture capital contracting is shaped by the fact that investing in early-stage, high-technology companies presents these three problems in extreme form. Precisely because the portfolio company is at an early stage, uncertainty concerning future performance is magnified. Virtually all of the important decisions bearing on the company's success remain to be made, and most of the significant uncertainties concerning the outcome of the company's efforts remain unresolved. Additional uncertainty concerns the quality of the company's management, which takes on heightened importance because so large a portion of the portfolio company's value depends on management's future decisions. Finally, the technology base of the portfolio company's business exacerbates the general uncertainty by adding scientific uncertainty—the entrepreneur's beliefs about the underlying science sought to be commercialized may prove incorrect.

The same factors expand the information asymmetries between potential investors and entrepreneurs, as intentions and abilities are far less observable than actions already taken. Similarly, the fact that the portfolio company's technology involves cutting-edge science assures a substantial information asymmetry in favor of the entrepreneur, even if the venture capital fund employs individuals with advanced scientific training.

Finally, the importance of future managerial decisions in an early-stage company whose value depends almost entirely on future growth options creates the potential for very large agency costs. Because the entrepreneur's stake in a portfolio company with venture capital financing can be fairly characterized as an option, the entrepreneur's interests will sharply diverge from those of the venture capital investors, especially with respect to the risk level and duration of the investment (Black and Scholes 1973; Myers 1977).[11]

The organizational and contractual structure of the U.S. venture capital market responds to this trio of problems. The effectiveness of the response serves to make the market feasible. Absent a workable response, the extremity of uncertainty, information asymmetry, and agency problems likely would raise the cost of external capital to a point of market failure, leading to a similar collapse in the formation of early-stage, high-technology companies. Because of the link between firm size and innovation, vertical integration is not a functional substitute for contracting failure. Institutional and contractual techniques thus have an important influence on the successful commercialization of cutting-edge science. Research and development by large companies with access to the public capital markets simply is not a substitute for the activities of early-stage companies, financed through the private equity market, and dependent on contractual solutions to the problems of uncertainty, information asymmetry, and agency costs.

The organizational and contractual techniques observed in the venture capital market reflect three basic characteristics. First, very high power *incentives* for all participants—investors, GPs, and entrepreneurs—are coupled with very intense *monitoring*.[12] Second, the organizational and contractual structure reflects the use of both explicit and implicit contracts. Thus, the governance structure of both the portfolio company and the venture capital fund is composed of market as well as formal aspects. Third, a pivotal aspect of this mix of formal and market governance, especially repeat play and reputation mechanisms, is that the two contracting nodes which constitute the venture capital market—the venture capital fund limited partnership agreement and the portfolio company investment contract—are determined simultaneously. As we will see, this braiding of the two relationships facilitates the resolution of problems internal to each.

This part shows how multiple forms of incentive and monitoring techniques, including contractual, control, and market mechanisms, operate in connection with each contracting node to resolve the problems of uncertainty, information asymmetry, and agency associated with early-stage, high-technology financing.

A. *The Venture Capital Fund-Portfolio Company Contract*

Five organizational and contractual techniques discussed in part I—staged financing, allocation of elements of control, form of compensation, the role of exit, and reliance on implicit contracts—respond to the problems posed by financial contracting in the face of extreme forms of uncertainty, information asymmetry, and agency costs.

1. *Staged Financing.* By giving the investor a valuable option to abandon the enterprise, the staged-financing structure discussed in part I responds directly to the *uncertainty* associated with contracting for early-stage, high-technology investments. The milestones in the business plan are keyed to events that, when they occur, reveal important information and thereby reduce the uncertainty associated with the project's ultimate success. Thus, a first milestone may be the creation of an operating prototype, which eliminates uncertainty about the portfolio company's ability to reduce its science to a commercial product. The decision about additional investment is then made only after the passage of time and performance has replaced projection with fact. The result is to reduce the uncertainty associated with the funding of further rounds of investment.

Without more, however, staged financing does not increase the expected value of the portfolio company's project. To be sure, the investor receives an option to abandon, but the value of that option to the recipient is exactly balanced by the cost of the option to its writer, the entrepreneur.[13] Absent an unrealistic assumption about investor risk aversion, merely shifting exogenous uncertainty from the investor to the entrepreneur does not create value. For this to occur, staged financing must accomplish something more.

The first respect in which staged financing creates, rather than merely transfers, value is its reduction in *agency costs*. Staged financing aligns the interests of the venture capital fund and the entrepreneur by creating a substantial performance incentive. If the portfolio company does not meet the milestone funded in the initial financing round, the venture capital fund can shut the project down by declining to fund the project's next round. Even if the venture capital fund chooses to continue the portfolio company's project by providing another round of financing, it can still impose a performance penalty by assigning the portfolio company a lower value in the new round. To be sure, the portfolio company may seek financing from other sources if the existing investors decline to go forward, or are willing to go forward only at an unfavorable price, but the overall contractual structure significantly reduces the availability of a market alternative.

First, potential investors know they are being solicited only because investors in the prior round are dissatisfied with the portfolio company's performance. Second, the investors rights agreement gives the venture capital fund a right of first refusal with respect to future financing that serves as a substantial deterrent to potential alternative investors. Such an investor will be reluctant to make the outlay to acquire the information necessary to decide whether to make an investment knowing that that investment will be significantly reduced if the terms negotiated turn out to be attractive, since the existing investors will have the right to take part or all of the transaction for themselves. Thus, the potential investor knows that it will be allowed to make the investment only if the existing investors, who have better information about the project, believe that the investment is unattractive.

The incentive created by staged financing in turn operates to reduce uncertainty in a manner that creates value, rather than merely shifting it from the investor to the entrepreneur. While staged financing only shifts risk with respect to exogenous uncertainty—that is, uncertainty that is outside the parties' capacity to influence—it actually can serve to reduce endogenous uncertainty, the variance in the project's success that can be influenced by the entrepreneur's actions. By increasing the incentives to expend effort, staged financing reduces this element of uncertainty.

That brings us to the effect of staged financing on the *information asymmetry* between the venture capital fund and the entrepreneur. Staged financing serves to bridge the information gap in two important ways. First, every incentive has an information related flip side that responds to adverse selection problems. In deciding which portfolio companies to finance, the venture capital fund has to distinguish between good and bad entrepreneurs under circumstances in which an entrepreneur has better information about her own skills than does the investor. Because the incentive created by staged financing is more valuable to a good entrepreneur than a bad one, an entrepreneur's willingness to accept an intense incentive is a signal of the entrepreneur's difficult-to-observe skills. The signal is particularly important for early-stage and high-technology portfolio companies because the absence of a performance history and the technical nature of the projects makes the entrepreneur's skills particularly difficult to observe.[14]

Staged financing reduces information asymmetry in a second way by its impact on the credibility of the projections contained in the entrepreneur's business plan. These projections are critical to valuing the portfolio company and therefore pricing the venture capital fund's investment. Yet, the entrepreneur obviously has better information concerning the accuracy of the business plan's projections of timing, costs, and likelihood of success. Without more, the entrepreneur has an obvious incentive to overstate the project's prospects. By accepting a contractual structure that imposes significant penalties if the entrepreneur fails to meet specified milestones based on the business plan's projections—the venture capital fund's option to abandon then becomes exercisable—the entrepreneur makes those projections credible.

At this point, it is helpful to note a more general contracting problem associated with the allocation of discretion between parties to an agreement. Discretion creates the potential for the party possessing it to impose agency costs. Staged financing, like other organizational and contractual techniques we will consider, responds to agency problems that result from entrepreneur discretion by shifting that discretion to the venture capital fund. However, this technique has a built-in limitation, which we might call the principle of the conservation of discretion. Without more, shifting discretion from the entrepreneur to the fund does not eliminate the potential for agency costs; it merely shifts the chance to act opportunistically to the fund. For example, staged financing coupled with a right of first refusal made potent by high information costs allows the venture capital fund to behave opportunistically in negotiating the price of a second round of financing. The fund is then in a position to exploit its monopsony power by reducing the value assigned to the portfolio company even though it has met its projections. In such settings, the goal is to shift discretion to that party whose misuse of it can be most easily constrained. As will appear, misuse of the discretion shifted to the venture capital fund is policed by market forces in the venture capital market whose functioning is crucial to the feasibility of the entire organizational and contractual structure.

2. *Control*. The venture capital fund-portfolio company contract stands the Berle-Means problem on its head. Instead of investors having disproportionately less control than equity as in public corporations, the venture capital fund has disproportionately more control than equity. Like staged financing, this allocation of control responds to the problems of uncertainty, information asymmetry, and agency associated with early-stage, high-technology investments.

Extreme *uncertainty* concerning the course and outcome of the project stage being financed creates discretion. The presence of uncertainty means that an explicit stage-contingent contract that specifies the action to be taken in response to all possible events cannot be written. Thus, the contractual structure must deal with uncertainty through a governance structure: creating a process that will determine the response to an unexpected event. The particular allocation of discretion between the fund and the portfolio company reflects the influence of concerns over both *agency* and *information asymmetry*.

Two types of control are allocated to the venture capital fund as a response to agency and information asymmetry problems. First, as we have seen, staged financing allocates an important periodic lever of control to the venture capital fund. By reserving to itself the decision whether to fund the portfolio company's next milestone, the venture capital fund takes control over the continuation decision. This power, in turn, gives the venture capital fund the incentive to make the investment in monitoring necessary to evaluate the portfolio company's overall performance. Absent the power to act in response to what it discovers, the venture capital fund would have no reason to expend time and resources in the monitoring necessary to balance the intense incentives created to align the two parties' interests.

Second, giving the venture capital fund disproportionate representation or even control of the portfolio company's board of directors, and the restriction of the entrepreneur's discretion through the use of negative covenants, gives the fund interim control—the power to reduce agency costs in the period between financing rounds. In its most extreme form, this interim control carries with it the power to replace the entrepreneur as the portfolio company's chief executive officer. As with the allocation of periodic control, the allocation of interim control gives the venture capital fund the incentive to monitor the portfolio company's performance during the course of reaching a funding milestone. The discretion unavoidably given to the portfolio company's day-to-day managers by the occurrence of unexpected events is policed by the disproportionate control and resulting monitoring activity allocated to the venture capital fund.

The periodic and interim monitoring encouraged by the disproportionate allocation of control to the venture capital fund also serves to reduce the last of the contracting problems—information asymmetry between the venture capital fund and the entrepreneur. The balance of information between the parties is not static as the portfolio company moves forward on its business plan. Ongoing learning by the entrepreneur increases the information disparity and therefore the entrepreneur's discretion, which in turn increases agency costs. Ongoing monitoring by the venture capital fund, made possible by the disproportionate allocation of control, balances that influence.

Finally, as with staged financing, the allocation of control serves to reduce information asymmetry by providing the entrepreneur the opportunity to signal her type. Giving the venture capital fund the power to terminate the entrepreneur in the event of poor performance gives the entrepreneur a powerful incentive to perform. The flip side of this incentive is a signal. By her willingness to subject herself to this penalty for poor performance, the entrepreneur credibly provides information to the venture capital fund about her own skills (see Hellmann 1998).

3. *Compensation.* The structure of the entrepreneur's compensation responds primarily to agency costs and information asymmetry problems. Perhaps more starkly than with any other organizational or contractual technique, the portfolio company's compensation structure creates extremely high-powered performance incentives that serve to align the incentives of portfolio company management and the venture capital fund. In essence, the overwhelming percentage of management's compensation is dependent on the portfolio company's success. Low salaries are offset by the potential for a large increase in value of the entrepreneur's stock ownership, and by the award of stock options to other management members. The performance incentive is further heightened by the practice of requiring the entrepreneur and other members of management to accept the imposition of a staged vesting requirement on some or all of their stock or stock options. The vesting requirement gives the portfolio company the right to purchase a portion of the entrepreneur's or other management's stock, at a favorable price, if employment terminates prior to a series of specified dates. It also

restricts exercise of options until after the manager has completed a series of employment anniversaries, following each of which an additional number of options both are exercisable and no longer subject to forfeiture if employment terminates (Benton and Gunderson 1998; Sahlman 1990: 507).

While aligning the interests of the venture capital fund and entrepreneur in some circumstances, the intensity of these incentives can also lead to agency costs in others. In particular, the option-like characteristics of the portfolio company's compensation structure can lead the entrepreneur to increase the risk associated with the portfolio company's future returns, because the venture capital fund will bear a disproportionate share of the increased downside but share only proportionately in the upside. Thus, the intensity of the performance incentives created by the compensation structure gives rise to a corresponding incentive for the venture capital fund to monitor the portfolio company's performance. This monitoring, together with the signaling properties of the entrepreneur's willingness to accept such powerful incentives, also serve to reduce information asymmetries.

4. *Exit.* The terms of the disproportionate allocation of control to the venture capital fund create another powerful incentive for the entrepreneur. As developed by Black and Gilson (1998), the control structure created by the venture capital fund's investment gives the entrepreneur a valuable call option on control. In effect, the venture capital fund and the entrepreneur enter into a combination explicit and implicit contract that returns to the entrepreneur the disproportionate control transferred to the venture capital fund if the portfolio company is successful. The explicit portion of the contract is reflected in the terms of the convertible preferred stock that provide the venture capital fund its disproportionate board representation, and in those of the investors' rights agreement that contains the negative covenants requiring venture capital fund approval of important operating decisions. Both documents typically terminate these levers of control on the completion of an IPO of a specified size and price. The terms of the preferred stock almost universally require conversion into common stock, with the resulting disappearance of special board representation, on a public offering. The negative covenants also expire on an IPO.

The implicit portion of the contract operationalizes the definition of success that makes the entrepreneur's call option on control exercisable. By triggering automatic conversion on an IPO, the measure of success is delegated to independent investment bankers who are in the business of identifying venture-capital–backed companies successful enough to be taken public, and whose own incentives make their ex post determination of success credible ex ante. As we will see in the next section, it also allocates to the market enforcement of the venture capital fund's implicit promise to agree to an IPO when one is available to the portfolio company and the entrepreneur exercises her call option on control by requesting one.

5. *Reliance on Implicit Contract: The Role of the Reputation Market.* Crucial elements of the organizational and contractual techniques in the venture capital fund–portfolio company relationship have at their core the transfer of discretion from the entrepreneur to the venture capital fund. Staged financing, by giving the venture capital fund an option to abandon, transfers the continuation decision from the entrepreneur to the fund. Board control by the venture capital fund disproportionate to its equity, including the power to dismiss the entrepreneur herself, also transfers to the fund the capacity to interfere in the portfolio company's day-to-day business. As a result, the effectiveness of these techniques is subject to the conservation of discretion principle. Reducing the agency costs of the entrepreneur's discretion by transferring it to the venture capital fund also transfers to the venture capitalist the potential for agency costs—the opportunity to use that discretion opportunistically with respect to the entrepreneur.

For example, giving the venture capital fund an option to abandon gives the venture capital fund an incentive to monitor, gives the entrepreneur an incentive to perform, and reduces agency costs by shifting the continuation decision to the venture capitalist. But when coupled with the fund's right of first refusal, this transfer of discretion also creates agency costs on the part of the fund. What prevents the venture capital fund from opportunistically offering to provide the financing necessary for the portfolio company's next stage only at an unfairly low price, relying on a right of first refusal to prevent the entrepreneur from seeking financing from other sources? Similarly, the transfer of disproportionate control to the fund also creates the potential for opportunism by the fund. To align incentives, the entrepreneur's returns come from appreciation in the value of her portfolio company stock and stock options. However, the venture capital fund's power to terminate the entrepreneur, coupled with the vesting requirements covering the entrepreneur's stock and options, gives the fund the discretion to behave opportunistically. What prevents the fund from unfairly terminating the entrepreneur so as to secure for itself the returns that had been promised the entrepreneur?

The conservation of discretion principle counsels that discretion be vested in the party whose behavior is more easily policed. In the context of the venture capital fund–portfolio company relationship, the presence of an effective reputation market with respect to the GP's characteristics provides the policing that supports the transfer of discretion to the fund.

For a reputation market to operate, three attributes must be present. First, the party whose discretion will be policed by the market must anticipate repeated future transactions. Second, participants must have shared expectations of what constitutes appropriate behavior by the party to whom discretion has been transferred. Finally, those who will deal with the advantaged party in the future must be able to observe the party's past behavior.[15] All three of these attributes appear present in the venture capital market.

Although it is unlikely that a GP will have future dealings with the same entrepreneur,[16] the GP will anticipate raising successor venture capital funds, which in turn will require future dealings with different entrepreneurs in connection with investing the new funds' capital. The requirements of shared expectations of proper conduct, and the observability of a GP's satisfaction of those expectations, also appear to be met in the venture capital market. The community of venture capital funds is relatively concentrated (Ben Daniel et al. 1998),[17] and remarkably localized. For example, the offices of a significant percentage of U.S. venture capital funds are found along a short strip of Sand Hill Road in Silicon Valley (Saxenian 1994: 39–40). Moreover, venture capital funds typically concentrate their investments in portfolio companies geographically proximate to the fund's office.[18] This geographical concentration of providers and users of venture capital facilitates satisfaction of the informational element of a reputation model. Saxenian notes that geographical proximity has fostered in Silicon Valley extremely efficient informal transfers of information concerning the performance of GPs and entrepreneurs. Credible accounts of opportunistic behavior by particular GPs can be expected to circulate quickly among members of the entrepreneur community who must select a GP with whom to deal, and among members of the GP community, who must compete among themselves for the opportunity to invest in the most promising portfolio companies and therefore have an interest in noting and transmitting to the entrepreneur community instances of misbehavior by a rival.

B. *The Investor-Venture Capital Fund Contract*

In this part, we turn to the investor-venture capital fund contract. How do the organizational and contractual techniques discussed in part I—virtually complete control vested in the GP, highly incentivized compensation, mandatory distribution of realized investments, and mandatory liquidation after a fixed term—respond to the problems of financial contracting in the face of extreme forms of uncertainty, information asymmetry, and agency costs?[19]

1. *Control.* Organizing the venture capital fund as a limited partnership serves to vest virtually complete control in the GP. Short of participation in largely inconsequential advisory committees and the right, typically restricted by the limited partnership agreement, to replace the GP, the legal rules governing limited partnerships prevent investors from exercising control over the central elements of the venture capital fund's business. Most important, the investors are prohibited from insisting on an approval right of the GP's investment decisions. Thus, the venture capital fund's formal governance structure presents an extreme version of the Berle-Means problem of the separation of ownership and control: the GP receives control grossly disproportionate to either its one percent capital contribution or its 20 percent carried interest.

The efficiency explanation for the allocation of control to the GP reflects in the first instance the extreme uncertainty and information asymmetry associated with investing in early-stage, high-technology portfolio companies. By investing through a financial intermediary, investors secure the benefit of the GP's skill and experience, which help to reduce the level of uncertainty and information asymmetry that must be addressed in the contract governing a portfolio company's investment. However, securing the benefit of the GP's expertise comes at a cost: the GP must be given the discretion necessary to exercise its skills and experience on the investors' behalf. And consistent with the principle of the conservation of discretion, the allocation of control to the GP creates the potential for agency costs that must be addressed by other elements of the venture capital fund's organizational and contractual structure.

2. *Compensation.* The GP's compensation structure is the front line response to the potential for agency costs resulting from allocating to the GP the control necessary to apply its skill and expertise on behalf of the investors. The bulk of the GP's compensation comes in the form of 20 percent carried interest distributed to the general partner when realized profits are distributed to the investor limited partners. Thus, the compensation structure aligns the GP's interests in the fund's success with those of the investors: the GP earns returns that are proportional to those earned by the investors. However, other agency problems appear in the details of the car-

ried interest. For example, suppose that the first investment realized by the venture capital fund yields a $1 million profit after a return to the investors of their $1 million investment. The GP's share of the profit is $200,000. Now suppose that the next investment realized loses $500,000, leaving cumulative profits from the two investments of $500,000. If the GP keeps all of its first $200,000 distribution, then it ends up having received not 20 percent of the venture capital fund's profits from the two investments, but 40 percent ($200,000/$500,000). This would give the GP an incentive to realize profitable investments before unprofitable investments, even if that meant realizing the profitable investments prematurely. Various formulations of what are called "claw back" provisions respond to the potential agency cost growing out of this element of uncertainty in one fashion or another either by delaying the GP's distribution, or holding back some portion of it, so that the GP's carried interest can be finally calculated after performance is known (Halloran et al. 1998: 64–73).

3. *Mandatory Distributions and Fixed Term.* While aligning the interests of the GP and the investors, the intensity of the GP's compensation incentive in turn creates a different agency cost. The GP's carried interest has option-like characteristics, which may cause it to prefer investments of greater risk than the investors. This is especially true with respect to the fund's later investments if the early ones have done poorly. In that circumstance, the GP actually may be best served by making negative net present value investments if the investments are sufficiently risky. The same problem arises with respect to operating decisions that concern a portfolio company that is doing poorly. Then the option-like character of the GP's carried interest may align its interests more closely with those of the entrepreneur whose compensation under the venture capital fund-portfolio company also has option-like characteristics. In that circumstance, both the GP and the entrepreneur may prefer a riskier operating strategy than would best serve investors.

The venture capital fund's fixed term, together with the operation of the reputation market, responds to this agency cost problem. The fund's fixed term assures that at some point the market will measure the GP's performance, making readily observable the extent to which the GP's investment decisions favored increased risk over expected return. Thus, the limited partnership's fixed term assures that opportunistic behavior by the GP with respect to either venture capital fund investment decisions or portfolio company operating decisions will be punished through the reputation market when it seeks to raise the successor funds that justify the GP's investment in skill and experience in the first place. The expectation of such a settling up helps support the use of intense compensation incentives by constraining option-induced GP opportunism.

Mandatory distribution of the proceeds from realized investments and the venture capital fund's fixed term also respond to a different variety of agency costs resulting from the allocation of control to the GP. Because the GP receives a fixed fee, typically in the range of 2.5 percent, of committed capital, the GP would have an incentive to keep capital within the fund for as long as possible. If given the opportunity, the GP would simply reinvest the proceeds of realized investments. Moreover, that opportunity would make it unnecessary for GP's to raise successor funds, the anticipation of which allows the reputation market to police GP performance. Mandatory distribution of realized proceeds and a fixed term respond to this potential free cash flow problem. Both devices require that the GP allow the investors to measure its performance against alternatives available in the market before it can continue managing the investors' money.

C. Braiding of the Venture Capital Fund-Portfolio Company and the Investor-Venture Capital Fund Contracts

A final means by which the organizational and contractual structure of the venture capital–portfolio company and investor–venture-capital fund contracts responds to the contracting problems posed by extreme uncertainty, information asymmetry, and agency costs is through the braiding of the two contracts. By braiding I mean the fact that the structures of the two contracts are intertwined, each operating to provide an implicit term that supports the other, and thereby increasing the contractual efficiency of both. This characteristic is particularly apparent with respect to the role of exit and of the reputation market.

1. *The Braiding of Exit.* As we have seen, the obligation of exit from each of the two contracts comprising the venture capital market—the fixed term of the investor-venture capital fund contract, and the incentive to realize and then distribute the proceeds of the investment that is the subject of the venture capital fund–portfolio company contract—responds to contracting problems presented by each of the relationships. Here the focus is on how these two functions of exit complement each other. As we saw in part I, by

the time a portfolio company succeeds, the venture capital fund's non-cash contributions to a portfolio company can be more profitably invested in a new round of early-stage companies. But because economies of scope link the provision of cash and non-cash contributions, recycling the non-cash contributions requires the venture capital fund to exit: to recycle its cash contribution from successful portfolio companies to new early-stage companies. Moreover, the venture capital fund's exit provides the means to give the entrepreneur an important performance incentive: a call option on control, the exercise of which is implemented by the venture capital fund's realization of its investment in the portfolio company by means of an IPO.

In turn, the recycling of investments from successful portfolio companies to new early-stage companies supports the investor–venture capital fund contract. Realizing portfolio company investments provides a performance measure that lets investors evaluate the GP's skill and honesty, and to reallocate their funds to the GPs with the best performance. And by providing the GP's primary tool for persuading investors to provide capital for successor funds, exit supports the core of the incentive structure that aligns the interests of investors and the GP.

In sum, the braiding of the role of exit in the investor–venture capital fund contract and the venture capital fund–portfolio company contract increases the efficiency of both contracts.

2. *The Braiding of the Reputation Market*. The venture capital fund–portfolio company contract responds to a number of problems by shifting important elements of control to the fund. The fund's option to abandon resulting from staged financing, its board representation and even control, and its power to replace the entrepreneur, combine to reduce uncertainty and to reduce agency costs both by providing the entrepreneur powerful performance incentives and by providing the fund the means and therefore the incentive to monitor. In turn, the entrepreneur's willingness to transfer control, and to accept so heavily incentivized a contract structure, reduces information asymmetry by signaling the entrepreneur's type. However, each of these transfers of discretion from the entrepreneur to the fund carries with it the potential for opportunistic behavior by the fund. The entrepreneur is at risk in connection with negotiations over the terms of the next round financing, in connection with the fund's exercise of control through board influence and its power to replace the entrepreneur, and in connection with the fund's ability not to honor the implicit call option on control it has written. The efficiency of the venture capital fund–portfolio company contract

therefore requires a credible constraint on the fund's misusing its transferred discretion.

The braiding of the venture capital fund–portfolio company contract with the investor-venture-capital fund contract supports a reputation market that constrains opportunistic behavior by the fund. Because the fund is unlikely to engage in repeated deals with any particular entrepreneur, the reputation market constraint instead grows out of the investor–venture capital fund contract. Because the GP needs to raise successor funds, it will have to make investments in new portfolio companies run by other entrepreneurs. If a GP behaves opportunistically toward entrepreneurs in connection with previous portfolio company investments, it will lose access to the best new investments that, in turn, will make raising successor funds more difficult. The impact of the GP's behavior toward current portfolio companies on the success of its future fund raising efforts serves to police the fund's exercise of the discretion transferred to it in the venture capital fund–portfolio company contract. In turn, the contract's support of the transfer of discretion to the fund by the venture capital fund–portfolio company contract helps reduce uncertainty, information asymmetry, and agency costs in contracting with the portfolio company and therefore results in higher returns to investors. And this encourages investors to reinvest in the GP's successor funds. Again, the interaction between the two contracts supports the efficiency of each.

III. The Engineering Problem

The central lesson to be learned from the U.S. venture capital market is that it is overwhelmingly the product of private ordering—an extremely effective contracting structure that covers the entire venture capital cycle, from initial investment in the VC fund, to the VC fund's investment in a portfolio company, to the exit from the portfolio investment to allow the VC fund's cash and non-cash investment to be recycled.[20] Can this model be replicated elsewhere? Who will be the engineer? Can the government act as the engineer in creating a system that is driven by private ordering?

The discussion must begin with a caveat. I have in mind a relatively restricted engineering problem. To function effectively, any form of effective capital market requires a range of social, legal and economic institutions, such as honest courts, an effective auditing profession, and informational and reputational transparency, to function effectively (see Black 2001). Because of the braided aspect of venture capital contracting, the full spectrum of foundational institutions is important to the venture capital market. For present purposes, I will assume away the more difficult problem of how to engineer the foundational structure of capital markets, focusing instead on the more limited task (but nonetheless plainly interesting to many nations and multinational entities like the EU and OECD): How to engineer a venture capital market.

At this level, engineering a venture capital market confronts a difficult coordination problem that I will call simultaneity. A venture capital market requires the simultaneous availability of three factors, the provision of any one of which is contingent on the availability of the other two. A venture capital market requires entrepreneurs, investors with the funds and the taste for high-risk, high return investments and, as the discussion of U.S. venture capital contracting illustrates, a specialized financial intermediary to serve as the nexus of a sophisticated set of contracts.

The government is the natural engineer to confront the venture capital simultaneity problem. Since the government did not play an instrumental role in the development of the U.S. venture capital market, the idiosyncratic U.S. experience does not provide an example for other countries trying to establish a venture capital market other than through accretion. No institution other than the government has the right incentive to invest in the public good that results from establishing a venture capital market. The problem, however, is the mismatch of a government acting to create a market in which it has no long-term role. The response, I will argue, reflects the lesson of the U.S. experience and the character of the simultaneity problem. The government can act to induce the development of the necessary specialized financial intermediary, and also act to provide, in effect, seed capital to the new market. That leaves the third factor necessary to solve the simultaneity problem—entrepreneurs. Here the hypothesis is simply that the presence of a venture capital framework and funding will induce entrepreneurs to reveal themselves.

An understanding of the governmental role in engineering a venture capital market that I have in mind can be seen from examining governmental efforts in three different countries: one early German failure that got every element wrong and whose failure highlights the shape of what is necessary for a successful government effort; a more recent Israeli effort that got much of the structure right; and a current Chilean program that was structured with precisely this analysis in mind. These examples are not intended to be illustrative of the wide range of government efforts to create a venture capital market. Rather, the survey's goal is to highlight what is necessary for a successful government effort.

A. *The German WFG Experience*

The German WFG program[21] provides a fascinating example of an early effort to create a national venture capital market that failed miserably. The nature of its failings, and its mirror image of the core principles of U.S. venture capital contracting, provide important guidance on the limits of governmental engineering.

Formed in 1975 at the insistence of the German federal government and with the express goal of developing a German venture capital market, WFG began with 10 million DM in funding, ultimately increased to 50 million DM, that was provided by 29 German banks, including the largest banks and the leading savings and loan institutions. The banks' involvement was encouraged not just by governmental pressure, but also by a generous government guarantee: the government insured up to 75 percent of WFG's losses. As an inducement to entrepreneurs, WFG's return from a successful portfolio company investment was capped by the requirement that the entrepreneur be granted a call option to purchase WFG's position at cost plus a moderate interest rate. Thus, WFG had quite muted incentives to make successful investments. They were protected on the downside by the government guarantee, and limited on the upside to a moderate interest rate—a low risk (because of the guarantee) and a low return (because of the call option) investment, a strange vehicle indeed for investing in early-stage, technology companies whose essential characteristic is their high risk.

WFG's governance structure reflected the program's government origin—a stakeholders' dream of a compromise. WFG had a twelve-person board, comprised of two industry representatives, three bank members, three government members representing the ministries of commerce, finance, and research and development, two management consultants, and two scientists. A mixed board committee selected the projects to be funded, pursuant to quite general criteria that nonetheless pointed in the right direction. The focus was to be on the innovative character of the project's technology, the existence of attractive commercial applications, and the quality of the entrepreneur.

WFG's investments were structured to be passive, perhaps because the return character of its investment gave it no incentive to be active. Only minority investments were made, and WFG received no control rights at all, even over important decisions. Consistent with this passive structure, WFG personnel provided no technological or management assistance to their portfolio companies even though the board members appeared to have the credentials to be useful.

Comparing U.S. venture capital practices with those of WFG reveals a dramatic difference along every important dimension. Indeed, it would have been difficult for WFG to get the structure any more wrong.[22]

In the U.S., the venture capital contracting structure turns the Berle and Means problem on its head. Instead of less control than equity, venture capital investors in the U.S. take significant control positions, more than proportional to their equity. Not only do they obtain veto rights over major decisions, retain the continuation decision, and often control a majority of the board, but also retain the right to terminate the entrepreneur. In contrast, WFG took a minority position in portfolio companies and obtained no control rights

An example highlights the difference. A recent study of a sample of Silicon Valley portfolio companies shows that professional managers replace more than half of founding entrepreneurs (Hellmann and Puri 2002). WFG never replaced an entrepreneur.

Control and equity give U.S. venture capitalists the means and incentives to monitor highly incentivized managers. A 20 percent carried interest based on a one percent capital contribution gives them a huge stake in the upside. The impact of portfolio company failure on a venture capitalists' ability to raise subsequent funds and, hence, on the value of their human capital, assure that they also share the downside.

WFG lacked both the incentives to succeed and the means to monitor. Given the government guarantee and the enterpreneurs' call option, why should the banks bother to monitor? In all events, WFG lacked levers of control to act even if monitoring led to discovery of a problem. Control and equity also give U.S. venture investors the incentive to provide non-capital inputs to portfolio companies. WFG provided nothing but its initial capital investment.

In short, WFG was a government program that created a financial inter-mediary that had no incentives, did not monitor, involved the government (through board representation) in project selection and, not surprisingly, produced dismal results. Over its lifetime, WFG experienced an internal rate of return of negative 25.07 percent. In every year of its existence, pro-ceeds from the government guarantee exceeded revenue from investments. In terms of addressing the simultaneity problem, WFG generated funds for venture investing, but created a hollow financial intermediary that was inca-pable of playing the central role that the U.S. venture capital contracting system contemplates. Keep in mind that a significant negative return for WFG necessarily parallels significant failures for the entrepreneurs the WFG funded. A pattern of failure will not call forth entrepreneurs.

B. The Israeli Yozma Program

In contrast to the early WFG program, a more recent Israeli program came closer to getting the incentive structure right.[23] Plainly influenced by the U.S. experience, the Israeli government established Yozma Ltd. in 1993 with the intention of creating the infrastructure for an Israeli venture capital market. In particular, Yozma created nine venture capital funds, in which it invested along with private investors. The structure of Yozma's participation in these funds was quite different than both the German government's and the banks' participation in WFG.

First, Yozma provided no guarantee against loss. Rather, Yozma provided capital to the funds, matching up to 40 percent of the capital invested by pri-vate investors. Thus, unlike WFG, private investors and the funds' managers bore their share of the downside risk.

Second, the Yozma structure preserved intense performance incentives on the upside. Like WFG, Yozma's return on its investment was capped: the private investors had a call option on Yozma's investment at cost plus (i) a nominal interest rate and (ii) 7 percent of the future profits from portfolio company investments in which the fund was then invested. This cap, how-ever, had very different incentive properties than the cap on WFG's return. Because Yozma's investment was made in a venture capital fund, rather than directly in the portfolio company as with WFG, and because the call option was held by the other investors rather than by the entrepreneur as with WFG, the returns to the investing entity were not capped at all. Rather, the

cap served to leverage the returns, and therefore the incentives, of the investing entity instead of dampening them. WFG's subsidy to the banks and to
the entrepreneur eliminated any incentive for WFG or its constituent banks
to monitor the entrepreneur's conduct. In contrast, Yozma's subsidy to other
investors increased their incentive to assure that the portfolio companies
were carefully monitored.

Finally, Yozma did not make investment decisions.[24] The funds' managers selected the portfolio companies in which the fund would invest.
Thus, while Yozma's investments were passive like those of WFG, these passive investments were made through funds whose managers and other
investors were highly incentivized. In this critical respect, the Yozma structure tracked the U.S. pattern of interposing a highly incentivized intermediary between passive investors and the portfolio company.

Yozma's performance was consistent with this more highly incentivized
investment structure. Investment decisions were made by those who bore
the investment's risk and return. The Yozma funds ultimately increased in
size to more than $200 million and in 1997 were successfully privatized.

C. The Current Chilean CORFU Program

A Chilean program begun in 2001, "designed to provide an incentive for the
development of venture capital funding in Chile" (CORFU 2001: 1), takes
the Yozma concept a step further in the direction of the U.S. venture capital
contracting model. The program contemplates that a government agency,
the Corporation for the Incentive of Production (CORFU) will invest in privately managed venture capital funds structured roughly in accordance with
the U.S. model. The fund manager's compensation has the same structure
as developed in the U.S.—a 2.5 percent fixed annual fee on assets under
management and a carried interest based on fund performance. Perhaps
because of the early stage of the Chilean venture capital market, the program has a number of features that seem to be substitutes for the operation
of a reputation market among venture capitalists.

First, the CORFU program seeks to insure more direct investor monitoring of the fund manager's performance rather than relying only on the structure of the fund manager's incentives and its investment in reputation. Each
fund must have at least five unrelated investors holding at least 10 percent of
the fund's equity each, or at least one institutional investor holding at least

20 percent of the equity. By requiring the presence of large investors, the structure encourages internal monitoring of the fund manager.

Second, because the fund manager is likely to have a smaller investment in reputation at this stage of the development of a national venture capital market, the CORFU program requires a larger capital investment by the fund manager than the U.S. pattern of a one percent capital contribution by the general partner. The Chilean program requires the fund manager to invest at least 15 percent of the fund manager's total assets in the managed fund. Note that the requirement is keyed to a percentage of the fund manager's assets, not of the fund's assets, an effort plainly designed to ensure that even new fund managers—most local venture capitalists would necessarily be new—have a direct share of the downside.

CORFU investment in qualifying venture capital funds takes the form of "loans" that leverage the private investors' and the fund manager's equity stakes in the fund. While denominated loans, the CORFU contribution is functionally preferred equity with a cap on return. The loan accrues interest at 3 percent with a term equal to the shorter of the life of the fund or 15 years. No interest or principal payment is due until the fund makes a distribution to shareholders, and final payment occurs on liquidation. CORFU has a distribution preference, receiving on liquidation first its principal and interest, following which the private investors receive an amount equal to their original investment.[25] Then CORFU receives an amount equal to an annualized return of 9 percent on the principal of the loan, and the remaining funds are paid to the private investors and the fund manager.

Like the Yozma program, the Chilean program provides a subsidy to fund investors, including fund managers, through capping its return on its investment. Again, unlike the WFG program, the key feature of the CORFU program is its focus on the incentives of the financial intermediary. CORFU remains a passive investor in a fund whose investment structure, patterned after the U.S. model, is plainly intended to encourage the kind of active venture capital fund–portfolio company relationship found in the U.S.[26]

IV. A Template for Government Engineering of a Venture Capital Market

These three examples, together with the lessons of the U.S. venture capital contracting model, provide guidance in constructing a rough template for government efforts to engineer a venture capital market. The strategy reflects a central theme: the government should address the simultaneity problem by providing capital and helping to create the necessary financial intermediaries that together will encourage the supply of entrepreneurs, while at the same time maintaining the pattern of intense incentives coupled with intense monitoring that characterizes U.S. venture capital contracting.

Extending both the Yozma insight and the Chilean CORFU program, the government would issue a request for proposals for venture capital funds with the goal of selecting a number of funds run by competing professionals. The structure of these funds, and the structure of the fund–portfolio company contract, would generally track the U.S. pattern. A requirement of matching nongovernmental investors, as reflected in the CORFU program, provides interested monitors of the fund manager in the period prior to the operation of an effective reputation market.

Under this arrangement, the fund managers would have the incentive to seek out promising entrepreneurs, the experience to provide nonmonetary assistance in the development of the portfolio companies and, given the fixed term of the fund, the obligation to exit the investment when their noncapital inputs were no longer necessary. In turn, the government's participation as a passive investor in the fund allows the government to provide funds to the new market, but without itself participating in the capital allocation process.

This requirement of allocative passivity is central to carving out an effective role for the government in engineering a venture capital market. The most important flaw in the WFG model was the German government's creation of a financial intermediary with essentially no incentives to succeed. Direct funding by the government, the most common form of government assistance to creating an entrepreneurial sector, has the potential to make things even worse through a kind of Gresham's law. Like WFG, direct government programs typically will lack the incentives to carefully monitor portfolio company management and also will be subject to political pressure over issues like management replacement and job maintenance. Additionally, those running government programs are unlikely to have the experience and incentives to provide portfolio companies noncapital inputs.

To make matters worse, the flaws that arise from the government acting as the financial intermediary in the effort to engineer a venture capital market may well be attractive to entrepreneurs, who often view the monitoring and intervention of venture capitalists as unwanted intrusions. The best entrepreneurs may then prefer the government program to private venture capital funds, and more frequently fail because they will not receive the benefits associated with an experienced financial intermediary and a proper incentive and monitoring structure. This leaves the less talented entrepreneurs to the private sector, who also will fail more frequently, thereby discouraging development of private-sector financial intermediaries and decreasing the supply of entrepreneurs. In short, a misconceived government plan can operate perversely to actually discourage the development of a private venture capital market.

To be sure, even if the government invested in a private venture capital fund that formally allocated the government a passive role, a realist would fear that the government still would try to influence the selection of portfolio companies (and the interaction between the venture capital fund and the portfolio company) informally through the implicit promise of future government funding. Such an effort presents the fund manager with a tradeoff. Fund managers whose initial efforts are successful will have the capacity to attract private investors for future funds; in other words, the market makes an implicit promise of future investment conditioned only on performance and without the risk of breach. In contrast, making politically influenced portfolio decisions reduces the likelihood of the fund's success, thereby reducing the value of fund manager's carried interest. In turn, the reduced success of the fund makes it more difficult for the fund manager to secure private investors for future funds.

The result, then, of acceding to the government's effort at informal influence is to substitute the government's implicit promise of future funding for that of the market. A fund manager would have reason to question the credibility of the government's implicit promise — implicit promises typically require the support of reputational sanction for breach that is lacking in the government setting. Moreover, the reduced access to the market for future funding as a result of reduced success due to government meddling serves to render the fund manager's human capital investment specific to its relation with the government, thereby creating the potential for subsequent opportunistic conduct by the government. To be sure, a government retains the means to pressure fund managers if it loses sight of why it is engaged in the effort to engineer a venture capital market in the first place, but that is true of any government involvement, and the proposed structure both limits that effort to the informal, and creates important incentives for the fund manager to resist.

This model of channeling government efforts to assist in creating a market into passive investment through incentivized intermediaries has an interesting, if inadvertent, precedent in the United States. Early in the development of the leveraged buyout movement, state pension funds were among Kohlberg, Kravis, Roberts' earliest investors. These early passive investments in KKR had the unintended consequence of providing government support for the development of a private equity market, through an intensely incentivized financial intermediary, with precisely the results hoped for here: successful performance by early KKR funds both attracted much more private investment into the private equity market, led to the creation of many more funds, and generally fueled the private equity market's restructuring of U.S. industry.

V. Qualifications and Conclusion

Any effort at financial engineering should close with qualifications. However clever the blueprint, there will always be more moving parts than the engineers contemplate. In the case of a government effort to engineer a venture capital market through passive investment in a highly incentivized intermediary, the qualification concerns the premise that derives from how I framed the simultaneity problem. The supply of entrepreneurs was treated as solely a function of the availability of funds and specialized intermediaries—if we build it, the entrepreneurs will come. But what about an entrepreneurial culture as a precondition of a venture capital market? Why not a three factor simultaneity model, instead of only two?

Two recent papers assessing the slow development of a German venture capital market, even after funds and intermediaries were said to be available, argue that Germany lacked the appropriate entrepreneurial culture, with those having the skills necessary to form technology-based startups lacking the tolerance for uncertainty critical to leaving the nest of large-firm employment (Becker and Hellmann 2001; Fiedler and Hellmann forthcoming). In this view, the final elements necessary to launch a German early-stage venture capital market was the internet explosion and a large number of young Germans having been exposed to the United States business culture, especially through business school training.

To some extent the cultural criticism can be deflected. One characterization of the criticism is that the success of venture capital–backed internet startups changed the culture, thereby providing the final element necessary to engineering a venture capital market. But this is simply rephrasing the simultaneity analysis I have offered, albeit with an intermediate step in the process added: providing capital and incentivized financial intermediaries attracts some entrepreneurs whose success, in turn, attracts still more entrepreneurs. Stated more generally, a cultural change occurs between the government's engineering effort and the appearance of the market.

I readily confess to discomfort with too easy a recourse to culture as an explanation for when a high technology venture capital market develops (Black and Gilson 1998: 271–72). Too many degrees of freedom are left with respect to the direction of causation and with respect to defining the variables. Nonetheless, I cannot avoid a nagging doubt that my three-factor simultaneity model, like the two-factor asset pricing model, may turn out to be analytically lovely but empirically challenged. Different countries may respond quite differently to the same engineering efforts. As with the two-factor asset pricing model, other factors may explain the empirical results in ways that turn out to be difficult to explain analytically even though their presence is revealed empirically. Should that prove true, the consolation will be that the engineering effort still will have taught us something important by more clearly framing the phenomenon that then needs explanation, but now with a range of experience in different countries that will require more disciplined analysis than the cultural account has provided to date.

Endnotes

An earlier version of this paper was given as the 2001–2002 John R. Raben Fellowship Lecture at the Yale Law School, at the Atlanta Federal Reserve Bank conference on Venture Capital Markets: What's Next? and at the Columbia Law School conference on Global Markets, Domestic Institutions. I am grateful to the participants at these events for their helpful comments. A more comprehensive account of the subject matter of this chapter can be found in Ronald J. Gilson, Engineering a Venture Capital Market: Lessons from the American Experience, Stanford Law Review (2003).

1. Any financing market also requires a range of foundational attributes, like property rights, honest and effective courts, and the like. Detailing the general social and institutional infrastructure necessary to support a capital market of any sort is beyond my ambitions here. For an interesting assay of these issues with respect to the necessary preconditions for a stock market, see Black (2001).

2. Under Delaware law, the limited partners can make certain extraordinary decisions, such as replacing the general partner or terminating the partnership (See Del. Code Ann. tit. 6, § 17–303[b][8][e]). However, these rights are typically restricted by contract (See Halloran et al. 1998). Venture capital funds frequently do appoint advisory committees, usually made up of investor representatives, that monitor the fund's performance (Sahlman 1990: 493).

3. Even if one treated the venture capitalist's carried interest as a measure of the value of its human capital contribution, it is still putting up less than 20 percent of the capital but receiving complete control. The particular terms of the fund's governance are set out in the limited partnership agreement (See Halloran et al. 1998). Gompers and Lerner (1996) examine the terms of such agreements.

4. In most cases, the agreement provides for a breakpoint above which the management fee is reduced, either on funds under management or the number of years after the partnership's creation (Halloran et al. 1998).

5. Kaplan and Stromberg (2000) report that convertible preferred stock was used in 95 percent of a sample of 200 financing rounds in 118 portfolio companies made by 14 venture capital firms between 1996 and 1999. Gilson and Schizer (2003) argue that this consistency is driven by the tax efficiency of this capital structure in delivering high powered incentives to management.

6. Sahlman (1990: 475) reports that venture capital funds invest one-third of their capital in new investments and two-thirds in later round financing of companies already in their portfolios.

7. In Gompers' sample of portfolio company investments, venture capital investors on average controlled the portfolio company's board of directors, but held only 41 percent of the equity (Gompers 1997). The venture capital fund's right to select a specified number of directors is contained in the portion of the portfolio company's articles of incorporation that sets out the rights, preferences, and privileges of the convertible preferred stock the investors receive. This portion of the articles will typically be added by amendment simultaneously with the closing of the venture capital investment. Benton and Gunderson (1998) set out a standard form of restated articles of incorporation in connection with a convertible preferred stock venture capital financing.

8. The negative covenants are contained in a different closing document, the investors rights agreement. Benton and Gunderson (1998) set out a form of investors rights agreement with illustrative negative covenants.

9. This incentive may cause a GP without a performance record with prior funds to harvest investments earlier than would be optimal for the investors in order to establish a record sufficient to allow the raising of a new fund (see Gompers 1997).

10. Kaplan and Stromberg (2000) report redemption rights in 84 percent of the financing rounds in their sample.

11. The application of option pricing analysis to transactional and contractual structuring is developed in Gilson and Black (1995: Chapter 7).

12. This is consistent with the "monitoring intensity principle" of Milgrom and Roberts (1992: Chapter 7), which predicts that because intense incentives give rise not only to incentives to perform but also to incentives to cheat, intense incentives require a significant investment in monitoring.

13. Brealey and Myers (1996) contains an accessible discussion of how to value the option to abandon.

14. Conceptually, the signal will result in a separating equilibrium, in which only high-quality entrepreneurs will accept the incentive, when the low quality entrepreneurs' alternatives are more valuable to a low quality entrepreneur than the incentive contract (Gompers 1997).

15. Smith (1998) examines the information characteristics of the reputation market for venture capitalists.

16. It is not, however, impossible. Both successful and unsuccessful first round entrepreneurs may found a new start-up company in need of venture capital financing (see Saxenian 1994: 38).

17. In 1987, the top 5 percent of firms acting as venture capital fund GPs controlled 20 percent of venture capital raised. The figure rose to 37 percent in 1992, and to 44 percent in 1997.

18. Lerner (1994) reports that venture capital providers located within five miles of a portfolio company are twice as likely to have a board representative than providers located more than 500 miles from a portfolio company.

19. Empirical evidence of the value of the organizational and contractual structure is beginning to emerge. Barry and Turki (1998) report that development stage companies that use an IPO as a substitute for venture capital on average experience poor long-term performance. In contrast, the portfolios of venture capital funds on average earn favorable returns. Gilson (1998) suggests that the different post-transaction governance structures associated with the two forms of development stage financing could explain the different levels of performance.

20. The term "venture capital cycle" belongs to Gompers and Lerner (1999).

21. The abbreviation stands for "Deutsche Wagnisfinanzierungsgesellschaft," which translates roughly to "German Venture Financing Foundation" (see Becker and Hellmann 2001). I have relied heavily on Becker and Hellmann's careful account of this effort.

22. To some extent this comparison reflects a fair degree of hindsight bias: the U.S. venture capital contracting structure had not yet crystallized in 1975. However, Becker and Hellmann (2001) report that the deficiencies in the WFG structure were noted at the time.

23. This discussion draws on Goshen (2001).

24. Through another program, Yozma made direct investments in portfolio companies, much as investors in a U.S. venture capital fund sometimes also have the right to invest directly in portfolio companies in which the fund invests.

25. CORFU receives 50 percent of any preliquidation distribution to fund investors. While the program document does not specify in greater detail other features of the fund's governance, CORFU has discretion to choose only funds that have satisfactory governance structures, and any post investment changes in governance require CORFU consent.

26. The author is grateful to LatinValley.com, the first fund manager to participate in the CORFU program, for copies of the program documentation. Prior to the adoption of the CORFU program, the author and principals in LatinValley.com made a presentation to the Economics Minister of Chile suggesting a general approach toward encouraging a Chilean venture capital market similar to that reflected in the CORFU program and in this essay.

References

Admati, Anat and Paul Pfleiderer. 1994. Robust Financial Contracting and the Role of Venture Capitalists. *Journal of Finance*. 49: 371–402.

Barry, Christopher. 1994. New Directions in Venture Capital Research. *Journal of Financial Management*. 23: 3–15.

—— and L. Adel Turki. 1998. Initial Public Offerings by Development Stage Companies. *Journal of Small and Emerging Business Law* 2: 101–21.

Becker, Ralf and Thomas Hellmann. 2001. The Genesis of Venture Capital — Lessons from the German Experience, working paper.

Ben Daniel, David J., Jesse R. Reyes and Michael R. D'Angelo. 1998. Concentration and Conservatism in the Venture Capital Industry. Unpublished paper.

Benton, L. and Robert Gunderson, Jr. 1998. Portfolio Company Investments: High-Tech Corporation. In *Venture Capital and Public Offering Negotiation*. M. Halloran, L. Benton, R. Gunderson, Jr., and J. del Cavo eds. New York: Aspen Law & Business.

Berle, Adolph A. and Gardiner C. Means. 1932. *The Modern Corporation and Private Property*. New York: Commerce Clearing House.

Black, Bernard S. 2001. The Legal and Institutional Preconditions for Strong Securities Markets. *UCLA Law Review* 48: 781–855.

—— and Ronald Gilson. 1998. Venture Capital and the Structure of Capital Markets: Banks versus Stock Markets. *Journal of Financial Economics* 47: 243–77.

Black, Fischer and Myron Scholes. 1973. The Pricing of Options and Corporate Liabilities. *Journal of Political Economy* 81: 637–54.

Brealey, Richard and Stewart Myers. 1996. *Principles of Corporate Finance* (5th ed.). New York: McGraw Hill.

Bygrave, William D. and Jeffrey A. Timmons. 1992. *Venture Capital at the Crossroads*. Boston, Mass.: Harvard Business School Press.

Corporation for the Incentive of Production, Venture Capital Program (CORFU). 2001.

Fiedler, Marc-Oliver and Thomas Hellmann. Against All Odds: The Late But Rapid Development of the German Venture Capital Industry, *Journal of Private Equity* (forthcoming).

Gilson, Ronald J. 1998. Understanding the Choice Between Public and Private Equity Financing of Early Stage Companies: A Comment on Barry and Turki. *Journal of Small and Emerging Business Law* 2: 123–31.

——. 2003. Engineering a Venture Capital Market: Lessons from the American Experience. *Stanford Law Review* 55: forthcoming.

—— and Bernard S. Black. 1995. *The Law and Finance of Corporate Acquisitions* (2d ed.). Westbury, N.Y.: Foundation Press.

—— and David Schizer. 2003. Understanding Venture Capital Structure: A Tax Explanation for Convertible Preferred Stock. *Harvard Law Review* 116: 874–916.

Gompers, Paul A. 1995. Optimal Investment, Monitoring, and the Staging of Venture Capital. *Journal of Finance* 50: 1461–89.

——. 1997. Ownership and Control in Entrepreneurial Firms: An Examination of Convertible Securities in Venture Capital Investments, Harvard Business School Working Paper.

Gompers, Paul and Josh Lerner. 1996. The Use of Covenants: An Empirical Analysis of Venture Partnership Agreements. *Journal of Law and Economics* 39: 463–98.

——. 1999. *The Venture Capital Cycle*. Cambridge: MIT Press.

Goshen, Zohar. 2001. The Israeli Venture Capital Market, working paper.

Halloran, Michael C., Gregg Vignos and C. Brian Wainwright. 1998. Agreement of Limited Partnership. In *Venture Capital and Public Offering Negotiation*. M. Halloran, R. Gunderson, Jr., and J. del Cavo, eds. New York: Aspen Law & Business.

Hellmann, Thomas. 1998. The Allocation of Control Rights in Venture Capital Contracts. *Rand Journal of Economics* 29: 57–76.

—— and Manju Puri. 2002. Venture Capital and the Professionalization of Start-Up Firms: Empirical Evidence. *Journal of Finance* 57: 169–97 (forthcoming).

Kaplan, Steven and Pers Stromberg. 2000. Financial Contracting Theory Meets the Real World. NBER Working Paper 7660.

Lerner, Josh. 1994. The Syndication of Venture Capital. *Financial Management* 23: 16–27.

Milgrom, Paul and John Roberts. 1992. *Economics, Organization & Management.* Englewood Cliffs, N.J.: Prentice-Hall.

Myers, Stewart. 1977. Determinants of Corporate Borrowing. *Journal of Financial Economics* 5: 147–75.

Sahlman, William A. 1990. The Structure and Governance of Venture-Capital Organizations, *Journal of Financial Economics* 27: 473–521.

Saxenian, AnnaLee. 1994. *Regional Advantage: Culture and Competition in Silicon Valley and Route 128.* Cambridge: Harvard University Press.

Smith, D. Gordon. 1998. Venture Capital Contracting in the Information Age. *Journal of Small and Emerging Business Law* 2: 133–76.

Index